WRIGHTSCAPES

WRIGHTSCAPES

Frank Lloyd Wright's Landscape Designs

Charles E. Aguar and Berdeana Aguar

Research and travel funded in part
by
The National Endowment for the Arts
and
The Graham Foundation for Advanced Study for the Fine Arts

McGraw-Hill

New York   Chicago   San Francisco   Lisbon   London   Madrid   Mexico City
Milan   New Delhi   San Juan   Seoul   Singapore
Sydney   Toronto

Cataloging-in-Publication Data is on file with the Library of Congress

McGraw-Hill

A Division of The McGraw-Hill Companies

Copyright © 2002 by Berdeana Aguar. All rights reserved. Printed in the United States
of America. Except as permitted under the United States Copyright Act of 1976,
no part of this publication may be reproduced or distributed in any form or by any means,
or stored in a data base or retrieval system, without the prior written permission of the publisher.

1 2 3 4 5 6 7 8 9 0   DOC/DOC   0 7 6 5 4 3 2

ISBN 0-07-137768-9

The sponsoring editor for this book was Shelley Carr, the editing supervisor was Daina Penikas,
and the production supervisor was Pamela A. Pelton. It was set in Berling Roman
by North Market Street Graphics.

Printed and bound by R. R. Donnelley & Sons Company.

McGraw-Hill books are available at special quantity discounts to use as premiums and sales promotions,
or for use in corporate training programs. For more information, please write to the Director of Special Sales,
Professional Publishing, McGraw-Hill, Two Penn Plaza, New York, NY 10121-2298.
Or contact your local bookstore.

FOR CHARLIE

My beloved lifetime soul mate and coauthor

Deceased February 22, 2000

CONTENTS

"WRIGHTSCAPES" DEFINED

The eventual success of a cultivated environment is not merely the result of plants or structures upon the landscape, but rather the sum of both the tangible and the intangible—that is, the unification of the substantive elements upon the site *with* the personalities and experiences of those who visit or reside in the total environment that has been created. Thus, this environment ultimately becomes both a literal and a sensual experience of the pervading essence—or spirit—of the place. The amalgamation of criteria that creates this spirit-of-place should be, to a greater or lesser degree, inherent in each property designed by Frank Lloyd Wright.

1. The residence was designed to meet the needs of a specific client and site, or was designed as an affordable home, and Wright or his representative personally provided input as to siting.

2. The residence was oriented to take advantage of natural factors inherent to the site: optimum solar exposure, prevailing winds, views, natural terrain, existing trees, and other vegetation.

3. The architecture and landscape treatment are responsive to and "at one" with the site–that is, there is a perceived (if not actual) interrelationship with the Nature of the site.

4. The natural landscape has been preserved, or the structure and plantings present a total composition that follows the fundamental design elements of unity, harmony, scale, simplicity, color, form and texture.

5. The hardscape—outdoor furniture and construction, such as walls, paving material, water features, paths, parking areas—is in harmony with and suitable for the architecture.

6. The softscape—plant material—is appropriate to the site and has been retained in a natural form, even as plantings have been replaced and landscape design format has been changed to meet the life-style requirements of contemporary owners.

7. Extensions of architecture into the Nature of the site—balconies, verandas, open porches, and outdoor rooms—have been retained to respect, or adapted to complement, Wright's original design intent with respect to indoor-outdoor relationships.

8. The passage of entry from property line to front door provides an experience in itself—an entry experience—with exposure to unifying and/or contrasting textures of both built and natural materials.

9. There is a "sensed" experience of the total environment—a sense of place—that transcends building and plant materials, not only in what is seen, but in what is perceived: the feel of textures underfoot and of intermittent coolness and warmth to the skin; moving out from the shade and into the sun; the smell of flowers, grass, fruit, or any scents vivified by rain or air; the sounds of crunching gravel, singing and chirping birds, or splashing water; and other sensory qualities.

FOREWORD

Wrightscapes is a comprehensive and intriguing look at the work of Frank Lloyd Wright from the outside. It provides a view from the perspective of his designs in settings or landscapes. Unlike the many excellent examinations of Wright's work as an architect, Charles and Berdeana Aguar's approach is to view him as a planner and more commonly as a landscape architect. The point of view is to see how the designs of the outside flow into, out of, around, and in a few classic cases, under the architecture of the building.

This is not to say that the book attempts to lay claim to Wright as a landscape architect simply because of his success and legacy. In the context of history, it would be as if the designers of Roman aqueducts or Egyptian pyramids were engineers simply because the design work, if performed today, would require a licensed engineer. It would be as if military encampments protecting the frontiers of an ancient empire were laid out by certified planners, rather than the generalists who designed them. Instead, it has only been during the past few centuries with knowledge, technology, and the growing complexity of contemporary structures that the specializations of architecture and engineering became separate. A separation in the specialties of architecture and landscape architecture is an even more recent and subtle one, which is still evolving. Early structural and design knowledge was more limited and passed on through mentoring, guilds, and practical firsthand experience. Projects were designed by builders and artisans who are only labeled now by us, based on how we define their work. There were no national or international professional organizations or licensing exams to create practice boundaries. Educational background did not define what early practitioners designed. Otherwise, Frederick Law Olmsted would have been a fruit and vegetable farmer, a minister, and perhaps an arborist. By project definition, Babylon must have had a landscape architect. Certainly the great gardens and grounds of the palaces of renaissance Europe or the terraces of ancient Peru involved what we now call the talents of a landscape architect.

Planning and landscape architecture in the nineteenth and early twentieth centuries only began to develop as professions separate from general architecture or building and setting design with the urban and environmental problems associated with the industrial revolution. It would seem that the recognized need to consciously design the landscape in terms of new towns, parks, and restored sites came when mankind began to overrun a significant amount of the natural countryside. This generated a need to escape or to re-create a lost ideal.

There is no question that Wright was a building architect by the strictest contemporary definition. He was also a planner, ably critiquing the city designs of many such as Corbusier. He also designed a number of planned communities, some of which were partially implemented. He was a landscape architect as well; thus the Aguars' title *Wrightscapes*.

The book presents an almost humorous vision of Wright practicing landscape architecture. On one hand Wright succeeds as an astute and sophisticated designer whose sensitive blending of building and land is legendary. He also ventures with some of the early luminaries of the landscape architecture profession, such as his friend Jens Jensen. On the other hand, he begrudges the destructive landscape meddling of those such as Thomas Church, who would dare to step in for a Wright homeowner and help with an otherwise undesigned setting. Instances where neither Wright nor even the least capable of those in his tutelage show up to site a designed home or when a floor plan is flipped to avoid a tree not known to be on a site demonstrate Wright's penchant for electing to leave landscape design to chance in some cases.

The periods when Wright practices give form to his human nature as well. *Wrightscapes* gives a good sense of periods ranging from successful catering to the wealthy to periods of almost mass-producing designs for moderately priced housing in desperate times of economic downturn or postwar building booms. Wright designed in urban neighborhoods, commuter communities, the remote woodlands of Pennsylvania, and in the rural coastal hills of California.

Architecture, planning, and landscape architecture remained intertwined enough to be singularly practiced by talented generalists through Wright's life, and he availed himself of the opportunity. *Wrightscapes* includes his legendary successes and gives background to his lesser outcomes.

Ironically, Charlie Aguar's curiosity about Frank Lloyd Wright started with his own educational journey at the University of Illinois. He began in architecture, finished as a landscape architect, and went on to planning. It was an education that spanned the same areas as Wright's practice. He was privileged to have visited Wright's work in Chicago and Oak Park with Hideo Sasaki and began this research interest during the winter of 1947–1948. He and his wife, Berdeana, celebrated their first wedding anniversary at Taliesin in 1948. Decades later, after tens of thousands of miles driven to sites in the family camper, and hundreds of interviews with first and second owners and tenants of Wright's buildings, the writing began in 1994. Wright himself and his students were interviewed beginning in the early 1950s. Homesites under construction were observed. Correspondence, small archives, and personal collections were examined in an effort to get a comprehensive view of Wright's "landscape." Most of what Charlie saw, he recorded on 35-mm slides. His faculty colleagues at the University of Georgia, School of Environmental Design half-jokingly and half realistically feared that a small fire in his home where he kept this pictorial archive of thousands of slides could cause an explosion that would level most of his neighborhood.

Charlie had completed two comprehensive volumes of Frank Lloyd Wright's works by the time of his death in 2000. The publisher challenged that it be condensed to a single book. Berdeana, his wife, writer, editor, coinvestigator, and fellow traveler on the decades-long Wright journey finished this labor of love and curiosity in 2001.

Charlie was persistent in what he believed in, whether it was Wright, his love of teaching, or projects that added quality of life to his hometown. Athens, Georgia, dedicated the first leg of the Oconee River Greenway system only months before he passed away and 27 years after he and his design students of many studios began another long journey of vision and advocacy. *Wrightscapes* required that persistence and a love of the subject. It was one of Charlie's longest and most rewarding journeys.

JOHN F. (JACK) CROWLEY, DEAN
College of Environment and Design
The University of Georgia

PREFACE

The name of Frank Lloyd Wright is widely recognized throughout the world. The diversified body of work he conceived throughout the final decade of the nineteenth century and the first half of the twentieth century represents some of the most creative and universally admired architecture ever produced. He is perhaps the most influential designer of the second millennium. Literally hundreds of books have been published describing the transcendent beauty of his architecture and decorative arts, and most attest to the "organic character" of his architecture. Yet, little attempt has been made to focus upon the all-embracing comprehensiveness of his environmental vision that brought this organic character to fruition. *Wrightscapes* has been written to fill that void.

Our avocational interest in Frank Lloyd Wright evolved at a close-up and personal level. We grew up during the 1930s and early 1940s within 35 miles of what was then known, locally, as the "haunted" Dana House in Springfield, Illinois. And Charlie first heard about Wright's Imperial Hotel when it was set aside as a "cultural landmark" that B-29 bombardiers were to protect from direct hits during the waning months of World War II. As a member of a B-29 photo reconnaissance crew, he was not directly involved in accomplishing "hits," however, except in the form of parachutes carrying food and medical supplies to prisoners of war. Immediately following the war, Charlie enrolled in architecture at the University of Illinois, but switched over to landscape architecture after the second year in order to meet qualifications required to pursue a graduate degree in city planning. It was through this course of study that he was introduced to Wright's multifaceted talents—although not through any of his professors of architecture, because Wright was looked upon as a "has-been" within the profession during this time frame. It was within the Departments of Landscape Architecture and City Planning that Wright's works were used as exemplary models for study and his organic principles of design and theories on decentralization were elaborated upon.

Field trips were a significant part of the educational process during those years—for the ex-GIs in particular, after several years away from the classroom. Professor Stan White led a memorable trip to Wisconsin where many Frank Lloyd Wright sites were visited. An entire day was devoted to touring Taliesin—Wright's famous home and studio near Spring Green—where Charlie and his classmates met Wright and interacted with apprentices. Professor Karl Lohmann led another group to Chicago to study the postwar developments just then getting underway, as well as Riverside—the mother of all planned suburban garden communities, designed by Frederick Law Olmsted—where two of Wright's landmark residences were at that time in advanced stages of decay. But it was Hideo Sasaki, a young instructor fresh from Harvard School of Design, who provided Charlie's first real insight into the illusions Wright was able to create by unifying house and site. When the firm of Saarinen and Swanson hired Sasaki to prepare land use studies for the central area of Wilmette, a suburb of Chicago, he in turn hired Charlie to spend part of his 1947–1948 Christmas school break helping him in this endeavor. Sasaki had a way of starting early and completing the consulting tasks by late afternoon, so there was ample opportunity to tour the many Wright-designed residences in the Chicago suburbs of Oak Park and River Forest. To emphasize that Wright—unlike most architects during this postwar period—would go to great lengths to avoid destroying a single tree, Sasaki pointed out one house designed around a large tree (Isabel Roberts, 1908). He also pointed out the great contrast between the just-completed "floating" School of Architecture building on the campus of the Illinois Institute of Technology, designed by Mies van der Rohe, and the house Wright designed four decades earlier for Frederick C. Robie. At that time, the Robie House windows were covered with plywood and graffiti and there was a billboard touting the high-rise building slated to take its place.

Charlie introduced me to the transcendental environment of Taliesin on June 8, 1948—our first wedding anniversary, and Wright's 81st birthday—when we traveled there to explore the possibility of his applying for admission to the Taliesin Fellowship. After leaving the school facilities, we unabashedly visited the residence as well, where we were greeted by Mrs. Wright. Although she informed us that Mr. Wright was resting for his birthday party, she invited us into the living room and suggested that we tour the grounds. While we of course admired the architecture, we were *most* impressed with the way the natural light created a golden glow that reflected off the Oriental art, with the harmonious surroundings, the interior and exterior spaces, the stone-walled courtyard, the tea circle under a canopy of magnificent oak trees, the pools of moving water, the light-dappled hilltop garden, and the breathtaking panoramic views of the countryside. It was this overall sensory experience, this incredible sense-of-place, that we both found so intoxicating.

Inasmuch as the Fellowship did not fall within the government funding guidelines, we returned to Champaign-Urbana buoyed by our Wrightian experience, but committed to keeping our jobs and stretching the GI Bill to the limit. From that day forward, however, we were "hooked" on Wright and avid devotees of his well-publicized philosophical statements on organic architecture and the "nature" of the site. Over the next 40 years, we made a special point to drive past, walk around, and photograph Wright-designed residences—some while they still were under construction during the 1950s. Despite being diverted by other subjects and motivations, our special interest in Wright never waned, even becoming obsessive during the 1990s.

In 1970, following 20 years as a practicing professional—10 of which were spent as a principal in an interdisciplinary design group made up primarily of architects—Charlie joined the faculty of the School of Environmental Design at the University of Georgia, newly evolved from the Department of Landscape Architecture in response to the heightened environmental awareness of the late 1960s. During his 22-year tenure, the term "environmental design" was not used in the sense of an academic discipline, however, nor as a professional designation. Rather, it was used to define a design "philosophy" based upon interrelating the built environment—structuring of land, as well as buildings—by harmonizing everything that has a bearing upon the natural and cultural evolution of both the immediate and greater site environment: that is, the prehistoric, historic, and cultural heritage; the natural processes of geol-

ogy, topography, vegetation, climate, microclimate, and weathering by wind, sun, or water; the watershed and viewshed; utilities and infrastructure; circulation; light and shadow, and other phenomena of sensory perception. Therefore, the environmental designer designation generally is ascribed to any architect, landscape architect, or other designer who is highly responsive to and practices the philosophy just described—which Wright assuredly was and strove to do throughout his career. He in fact came close to defining his approach to architectural design as environmental design, when he wrote: "Architecture in all its aspects is to be studied as environment. . . . Nature is the great teacher—man can only receive and respond to her teaching."

Within the purview of Charlie's teaching responsibilities, he guided the development and presentation of fifth-year seniors' final projects and masters' theses. It was during one of our early explorations of the region searching for potentially appropriate subjects for these assignments that we discovered what remained of Wright's "Auldbrass" Plantation—then vacant, open to trespass, and in a serious state of neglect. It seemed an excellent subject to develop for restoration and adaptive use. It was not until spring quarter 1989, however, that Auldbrass finally was selected by a student as a senior project—coincidentally, just after it was purchased by motion picture producer Joel Silver to be restored and expanded under supervision of Eric Lloyd Wright, grandson of the architect. During the November 1989 open house celebrating the completion of the first phase of the Auldbrass restoration, Charlie was introduced to the Seamour Shavins—original owners of the only Wright-designed residence in Tennessee. They were kind enough to agree to an informal videotaped interview and the questions and answers came freely, after which they suggested that he conduct this sort of interview with other owners of Wright properties—nationwide. They believed this to be a project where time was of the essence, since the list of surviving original clients shortens with each passing year. Over the next few months, we reflected on the Shavins' suggestion and launched a serious review of the plethora of books on Wright that have surfaced over the last three decades. It soon became all too apparent that although more has been published about Wright's life and works, perhaps, than any other architect at any time in history, there has been no definitive analysis of those qualitative aspects of his holistic approach to design that combine with his architecture to bring about the sense-of-place that is the consequence of environmentally sensitive design as it was so artfully created by Wright. Nor has anyone interpreted the rationale behind his ecological sensibilities. These omissions were incentive enough to warrant probatory research.

During the decade-plus spent on this venture, we traveled across the length and breadth of America and personally visited and studied 157 sites in 22 states. Within this process, Charlie conducted videotaped interviews with 9 of Wright's former senior apprentices and 97 homeowners—37 of whom were original clients, or "first families," as we began to refer to them. Together, we studied the many books written on Wright's evolutionary development as an architect, as well as the sociological and interpersonal influences that molded his personal philosophy of environmental design. And we conducted a systematic, detailed analysis of the body of work Wright designed during his 70-year career to try to ascertain "What worked?" as well as "What didn't work, and why?" These are the basic questions that require a constant focus when conducting any postconstruction evaluation, because the answer directs and coalesces with many of the seemingly inconsequential factors determined through interviews and personal observation.

This investigation was not without disappointment. Working chronologically—based upon the premise that Wright's ecological sensibilities and environmental sensitivities didn't "just happen," but developed over a number of years within the social and historical context in which he lived and worked—we uncovered distressing truths. Wright was very much a human being, with professional failings along with the highly publicized personal faults. He designed some buildings before a site was selected. He was not above selling a plan designed for a client with an unusual site in a particular climatic zone to as many as three others in as many different zones, bringing about environmental consequences that were not properly addressed. And there were many instances where neither Wright nor any member of his staff visited the site before or after construction. So this research also involved separating Wright's rhetoric from reality. But it never was our intent to write another book deifying Wright. We merely tried to be as thorough and as objective as possible, as we tried to meet our goal of presenting a new view of Wright's body of work. In the end, the preponderance of exceptionally good examples of environmental design far outweigh the sometimes thoughtless incidences.

I hope that the insight developed herein will help readers better understand and appreciate those elusive qualities of Wright's designs—his environmental designs, or *Wrightscapes*—that weave together the essential character of that sense of mystery or "spell power" Wright considered to be the soul of his architecture.

BERDEANA (MRS. CHARLES E.) AGUAR

ACKNOWLEDGMENTS

The first comprehensive book addressing the landscapes and environments created by Frank Lloyd Wright could not have been undertaken without extensive research, financial support, and motivational encouragement from a variety of sources. The initial grant funding received from the National Endowment for the Arts (1989) and the Graham Foundation for Advanced Study for the Fine Arts (1992) facilitated travel to 157 sites and allowed the authors to personally experience, evaluate, and photograph the all-encompassing elements of environmental design that characterize a *Wrightscape*. Friends in high places wrote letters to support this funding: Bill Swain, FASLA, landscape architect for Fallingwater; Grady Clay, author-director of the Gazetteer Project; and Larry Sommer, director of the Montana Historical Society. Eric Lloyd Wright, architect—son of Lloyd and grandson of FLlW—also wrote letters of support and provided Charlie with encouragement and invaluable tips on the direction of this research. Former Dean Darrell Morrison of the University of Georgia School of Environmental Design generously allocated a travel allowance that allowed Charlie to attend the organizational meeting of the Frank Lloyd Wright Building Conservancy at Taliesin West in 1990, where initial contacts were established with homeowners and staff members of the Frank Lloyd Wright Foundation. Marsha Parks, the on-staff secretary, typed the many letters required to set up and confirm appointments for interviews, as well as follow-up letters of appreciation. And faculty colleague Catherine Howett provided constructive criticism of our objectives, procedures, and grant application drafts. She also offered encouragement as the original concept for scripting and developing a video documentary on Wright's developed landscapes changed direction and expanded in scope as we embarked on the in-depth research necessary to support this writing.

Special recognition must be given the fantastic resources of the University of Georgia Libraries, especially the Interlibrary Loan Service, which provided access to out-of-print books, theses, journals, and other periodicals from libraries throughout the country. The Library of SUNY in Buffalo, New York, provided the rare Darwin D. Martin plans and photographs. The Getty Research Institute for the History of Arts and the Humanities in Los Angeles, California, made it possible for a hands-on review of copies of unpublished plans, photographs, and correspondence of the excellently preserved but less accessible originals at the Frank Lloyd Wright Archives in Scottsdale, Arizona. Members of The Frank Lloyd Wright Building Conservancy welcomed Charlie to their organizational meeting in 1989 at Taliesin West and invited him to share his preliminary findings during their second conference held at Grand Rapids, Michigan, in 1991. Meeting and getting to know so many homeowners on a first-name basis greatly facilitated research and quickened the pace of this project, as did the magnificent compilation of materials made available through the efforts of Bruce Brooks Pfeiffer, director of the FLlW Archives. And Indira Berndtson, administrator of historic studies, was most helpful during our visits to the Archives and when answering our many inquiries over the years.

Seamour and Gerte Shavin—owners of the only Wright-designed home in Tennessee—deserve recognition for the suggestion made during an informal videotaping session at Auldbrass Plantation in 1989 that sparked Charlie's initial interest in this research. Recognition also must be given to other original homeowners and current owners who graciously agreed to oral history interviews and gave access to their homes and grounds—often on holidays and at inconvenient times of day and night—so Charlie or both of us could experience and interpret the indoor-outdoor aspects of Wright's brilliant use of space and light within a variety of situations. The list of homeowners is long: Dr. and Mrs. M. G. Ablin, Gloria Berger, Mr. and Mrs. Q. Blair, Drs. Harold and Doris Blumenthal, Karen Brammer, Ms. E. Brauner, Eric and Anne Brown, Mr. and Mrs. B. Buehler, John and Staci Cannon, John Christian, William and Jan Dring, Mr. and Mrs. R. Fawcett, Jeanette Fields, Mrs. C. E. Gordon,

James and Carolyn Howlett, Katherine Jacobs, Mr. and Mrs. Patrick Kinney, Sterling Kinney, Peter and Meg Klinkow, Russell Kraus, Kenneth Laurent, Mr. and Mrs. George Lewis, Edward and Ann Marcisz, Dr. Ward McCartney, Ruth Michael, Tom Miller, Ron Moline, Maya Moran, Gertrude Mossberg, Dr. and Mrs. Paul Olfelt, Mary Palmer, Mr. and Mrs. Ted Pappas, John and Ruth Pew, Dr. William Pollak, Loren Pope, Dr. Jack Prost, Mr. and Mrs. Roland Reisley, Milton and Sybie Robinson, Mildred Rosenbaum, Mary Sample, Mary Lou Schaberg, Nicketas Sohiar, Dale Smirl, Mrs. M. M. Smith, Dr. Ted Smith and Susan Skipper-Smith, Walter Sobel, Dr. Susan Solway, Mrs. Walter Swardenski, Richard and Laura Talaske, John and Betty Tilton, Mr. and Mrs. William Tracy, Mrs. E. Van Tamelon, Christine Weisblat, Elizabeth Wright. We also are deeply indebted to relatives of deceased homeowners, including Carolyn Brackett, Nathan Grier Hills, Sidney Oscar Hills, and Susan Winifred Penner, who graciously answered our questions and furnished historic photographs.

Senior fellows, present and former trustees, and staff members of the Frank Lloyd Wright Foundation Board have provided valuable leads and information through interviews. These include Cornelia Brierly, Penny Fowler, John de Koven Hill, John H. Howe, Dixie Legler, Oscar Munoz, Frances Nemtin, William Wesley Peters, Margo Stipe, and Edgar Tafel. Julie Aulik, Jill Dowling, and Peter Rathbun of the Taliesin Preservation Commission were equally generous with their time during the two days we spent at Taliesin in 1996 with guests, apprentices, and staff. House museum directors and staff, scholars, and other resource persons also provided invaluable assistance and mention of seemingly inconsequential information that provided insight when combined with our analyses: Howard Ellington, Dr. Donald Hallmark, W. R. Hasbrouck, Thomas A. Heinz, James Johnson, Meg Klinkow, Don Kolec, Jack Lesniak, Carla Lind, Joan Lupton, Fran Martune, David Nederwald, Martha Neri, Stephen Siek, William A. Storrer, Jack Quinan, and Christopher Vernon.

A heartfelt "thank-you" also must be given to our many long-time friends who provided us with news articles and up-to-date happenings regarding Wright-designed properties in or near the vicinity of their homes: David Bell, Miriam Campbell, Grady Clay, Glen and Phyllis Hawk, Bill and Ruth Knack, the late John Linley, Bill and Sue Majewski, Robert and Anna Lou Marvin, Byron and Nora Peters, Kenneth and Ellie Peters, Larry Sommer, Bill Swain, John and Merle Schwendimann and Warren and Jeanette Wofford.

Last, but certainly not least, it must be pointed out that this book could not have been published—following Charlie's sudden and unexpected departure from this world in February 2000—had it not been for the technical support and motivational encouragement provided by John F. "Jack" Crowley, Dean of the University of Georgia College of Environment and Design. Nor without the dedication of time and creativity provided by our son Richard Aguar, who reorganized his father's many illustrations, diligently tracked down illusive sources, and negotiated the complicated procedures involved with obtaining copyright clearances. Or without his able assistants: son Kenneth Aguar, grandson Forrest Aguar, Debra Roberts, and Adam Yost—as well as Julian Price and Meg McCloud, who opened their studio as work space. I also must acknowledge the loving support and motivational encouragement provided by the rest of our progeny: daughter Catherine Payne, sons David and Daniel Aguar, and grandchildren Matthew Brown, Kiley, Nathan, Sonia, and Tessa Aguar. I thank you all from the bottom of my heart.

BERDEANA AGUAR

WRIGHTSCAPES

Introduction: Forces That Shaped the Young Architect

Frank Lloyd Wright—christened Frank Lincoln Wright—was born to William and Anna Wright in Richland Center, Wisconsin, on June 8, 1867, just two years after the end of the Civil War. He was strongly influenced by the period of growing American self-awareness that evolved in the course of the next two decades. During these times, walking or horse and buggy were the dominant modes of transportation. Goods were processed and assembled by hand. Shops were modest, with many located in the home of the proprietor. And the number of employees was small. The social implications of this culture were that employers and employees lived and worked in close proximity to nature and to each other; the self-made man was much admired; and individualism was basic to the pursuit of personal goals. This credo for living became the "ideal" that guided Wright's lifetime pursuits and personal philosophy of design.

THE FORMATIVE YEARS

William Wright was an educated man with many aptitudes. He pursued such diverse career modes as music and law in college and earned his livelihood through each at the professional level; but he also served as a superintendent of schools for a period of time and was an ordained Baptist minister.[1] Perhaps because he vacillated between his talents and interests, rather than focusing on developing one as a lifework, the family had lived in six towns and four states by the time his son was a teenager. During Wright's senior year in high school, the parents' marriage disintegrated and William Wright left the family—never to be seen or heard from again. The most meaningful legacies the son inherited from his father were a gift for oratory and persuasion, a multifaceted individuality that caused him to approach each problem to be solved from a variety of perspectives, a great love for classical music, and an appreciation for the "structure" of music—which the adult Wright often likened to the structure of architecture.

Anna Lloyd Jones Wright and her relatives exerted the stronger influence upon Wright during his formative years. In 1845, she and her immediate family migrated from Wales to America and settled in southwestern Wisconsin near where other relatives already had established themselves—referred to by some as the "Valley of the God-Almighty Joneses."[2] Although members of this extended family capitalized on the lead mining that was central to the area's economy at this time, most family members carried on the farming traditions of their Welsh forebears: the once distinguished, if radical, Lloyd clan of Castell-hywel. All were intensely religious, free-thinking, and staunchly independent. Several were clergymen. And every family member felt a deep bond with nature, stemming from their Celtic ancestors who assigned special meanings to trees, stones, and flowing bodies of water. The dominance of this American contingent of the clan was so meaningful to Wright that he was motivated to change his middle name from Lincoln to Lloyd—in accordance with Celtic society, wherein a child belongs to the mother's family.[3] He seldom failed to use his adopted full name of Frank Lloyd Wright, even bringing the Welsh double "Ll" into play when initialing drawings or placing his stamp of approval on the work of his draftsmen.

In *An Autobiography*, Wright wrote that even before he was born his mother intended him to be an architect. He described the 10 full-page wood engravings of old English Cathedrals she framed "in flat oak and hung . . . upon the walls of the room that was to be her son's" to instill these images in his earliest memory.[4] He explained how the Froebel building blocks she purchased for him as a nine-year-old taught him the geometrical shapes and proportions of architecture. Even before he provided an insight into these motivating influences, however, he wrote about the heritage of the Lloyd Jones family and the land upon which they settled. And he reminisced at length about the summers he spent working on the farms of his uncles, where his appreciation of the natural landscape was nurtured. From the nostalgic perspective of a sexagenarian, he remembered the laborious farm chores as "adding tired to tired." But he also communicated a perceptive sensitivity for the geography and geology of the region: "The Valley they all lovingly called it in later years, and lovable it was, lying fertile between two ranges of diversified soft hills, with a third ridge intruding and dividing it in two smaller valleys at the upper end. A small stream coursing down each joined at the homestead and continued as a wider stream on its course toward the river. The lower or open end of The Valley was crossed and closed by the broad and sand-barred Wisconsin, and from the hills you could look out upon the great sandy and treeless plain that had once been the bed of the mighty Wisconsin of ancient times. . . . As a boy I learned to know the ground plan of the region in every line and feature."[5]

As Wright's uncles taught him how to work the farm and disciplined his work ethic, they also schooled him in the knowledge to be gained through observing nature. Farmers, of necessity, have always been weather-wise and nature-wise. They study the indigenous flora and fauna, the terrain, the cycles of life and weather. They observe that different species of vegetation grow in wet or dry areas, on cool or hot slopes. They note the arc of the sun and the direction of prevailing breezes. They appreciate the way tree canopies provide cooling comfort during the hot days of summer. They understand the value of wetlands that serve as nature's sponge and as a haven or habitat for wildlife. And they respect the power of natural forces: wind, rain, floods, drought, blights, tornadoes, et al.

By the 1880s when Wright was a teenager, the way his uncles and other Wisconsin farmers sited and oriented their structures relative to climatic conditions was considered the "natural" or "organic" way of things.[6] Homes, barns, and outbuildings were built in secure valleys or on south-facing slopes so both humans and animals were sheltered and/or benefited from the elements. Windows of the most lived-in spaces were faced toward the south to access the warmth of the winter sun. Doors and windows were placed to capture cross-ventilating summer breezes. The steepest sloping roofs were faced toward prevailing winter winds, for the same reason that ships at sea tack into the wind: to lessen the impact. Floor levels and doorways were adjusted as the contours of the land dictated, and sometimes houses and barns were molded into the hillside or man-made berms of earth were formed around structures to moderate temperatures during both summer and winter. Deciduous trees—White, Red, or Scarlet Oaks, Plane Tree, Hackberry, and Chestnut—were planted to control erosion and provide summer shade. Functional shelterbelts or windbreaks of evergreen trees—Red or White Cedar, Red or White Pine, and Hemlock—were planted to protect against prevailing winter winds. Even the locations of the well, outhouse, and fireplace were dictated by the mechanics of wind and the laws of gravity. It also was for more than convenience and ornament that herb gardens were situated near the kitchen and flower borders were near living areas; the same breezes that carried privy and barnyard odors away from the house carried the sweet scents of herbs and flowers into the house.[7]

The adult Wright would base the art and craft of his site planning and certain aspects of his architecture upon his innate understanding for this anatomy-of-place. Indeed, he recalled how many of these same considerations came into play when his Uncle Thomas, a self-taught country-architect, built his home: "By the eldest son, Thomas . . . a small house was built on a gently sloping hillside facing south. Balm-of-Gilead trees and Lombardy poplars were planted by the Mother and her brood around the little house and along the lanes; lanes worm-fenced with oak-rails split in the hillside forests which clung to the northern slopes and hill-crowns. The southern slopes were all too dry for wood, and were bare except where rock ledges came through. . . . The kitchen was a lean-to at the rear. An outside stairway led to a cool stone cellar beneath. A root-house was close behind, partially dug into the ground and roofed with a sloping mound of grass-covered earth."[8]

Wright's strong feeling for leaving wood unpainted also stemmed from his summers in The Valley. During the waning years of the nineteenth century, farmers were well aware that the oldest surviving wooden structures were those where the natural state of the wood has been retained. Timber was of better quality in those days, of course, but even city boys like Wright would have come to understand that paint actually has a decaying effect on *any* wood that has not been properly dried, that soft wood seasons better without paint, and that once painting is introduced the process must be repeated on a regular basis. Wright in fact first set forth the following proposition very early in his career: "Bring out the nature of the materials, let their nature intimately into your scheme. Strip the wood of varnish and let it alone—stain it. Reveal the nature of the wood, plaster, brick or stone in your designs; they are all by nature friendly and beautiful."[9]

A few months after his parents' divorce in 1885, Wright dropped out of high school and applied for admission to the University of Wisconsin, beginning winter quarter 1886. Lacking a high school diploma, he was admitted as a "special student," which generally indicates insufficient scholastic requirements for formal registration. Wright later claimed that he enrolled as a prospective civil engineer, since no courses in architecture were offered at that time. He described the "university training of one Frank Lloyd Wright, Freshman, Sophomore, Junior and part-time Senior" and maintained that he gave up "this miserable college education" near the time of his graduation: "only another winter and spring term."[10] According to research conducted by Thomas S. Hines, Jr., however, neither the duration nor civil engineering claim bore any relevance at all to Wright's actual courses of study. Although he worked for a time as a general student assistant to an engineering professor and joined the student association of engineers as a "member of the class of 1889," his college transcripts record liberal arts courses and only two quarters of study: a French language course from January to March 1886; geometry and drawing from September to December.[11] Wright then quit his formal education and in late spring 1887 boarded a train for Chicago to seek work as an apprentice in the office of a practicing architect. In so doing, he transported himself away from the basically placid and personal agrarian society he had experienced during the first 19 years of his life and literally thrust himself into the bustling impersonal society of a city very much in the throes of the Industrial Revolution—a city where the labor agitation that had been fomenting throughout the country over the past decade had been more violent than anywhere else, culminating in the infamous riot at Chicago's Haymarket Square the previous spring.

To better understand Wright's perspective of Chicago's urban landscape in 1887, it is necessary to appreciate the immediacy of this midwestern city's historical development. Consider that little more than five decades had passed since the initial town laid out on the southwest shore of Lake Michigan at the mouth of the "Chicagau" River appeared as described by historian Walter Havighurst: "In 1832, with a population of five hundred, the town established a ferry service across the river, enlarged the log jail and spent twelve dollars on an estray pen for lost animals. So began the city of Chicago!"[12] Consider also that railroad lines did not extend as far west as Chicago until the 1850s, and streetcars of the 1880s still were horse-drawn. Moreover, it had been only 16 years since the devastating Chicago fire of October 8, 1871. Because the central business district had been basically wooden—even the sidewalks were wood-planked, and wood blocks surfaced the downtown streets—nothing was left standing except the few, so-called "fireproof" buildings of brick and stone; and the interiors of many of these had been destroyed. Based upon this experience, fireproof construction was the dominant prerequisite force in the initial rebuilding of Chicago's downtown. Other than the fact that the primary building materials were stone or brick, however, the hastily rebuilt business core looked basically the same.

Wright would apprentice under the guidance of the new generation of architects who undertook the more demanding challenge of the 1880s: to rebuild a new central core that would both accommodate the prodigiously multiplying corporate facilities and contain them within the finite boundaries imposed by Lake Michigan and the maze of girding railroad lines that serviced the unprecedented industrial expansion of the age. It was because of these exigencies that architects looked to the form of the skyscraper, an option not conceivable prior to the enabling technological innovations that emerged in rapid succession between 1876 and 1890: the hydraulic elevator, steel-frame construction, plate glass, electric transformer, electric lights, electric elevator, and the telephone.[13] Chicago's first skyscraper was built in 1883. The new "Skyscraper Chicago," writes historian Donald L. Miller, "was constructed building by building, one taller and more innovative new building rising out of an older city that was itself new, in a process of ceaseless demolition and construction that made all of Chicago appear . . . like an enormous construction site."[14] At the time of Wright's arrival, this amazing reconstruction-rebirth process essentially had reached the midpoint. Thus, Chicago was still very much a work-in-progress as Wright began his years of apprenticeship.

THE YEARS OF APPRENTICESHIP

In making the decision to look for an apprenticing position in the office of a practicing architect, the 19-year-old Wright was not doing anything unusual for the times. The idea of a professional architect with formal training and academic qualifications would be a product of the waning years of the nineteenth century. The first architecture courses were not introduced into the curriculum of the famed "Ecole des Beaux Arts" in Paris until 1819. Five more decades would pass before the first architecture courses would be introduced into the curriculum of an American institution. And it would not be until just before the turn of the century, in 1897, that the State of Illinois would pass the first licensing law for architects, by which time Wright had been functioning as a practicing architect for four years.

In other words, Wright learned his craft by doing—that is, by observing, thinking through, and personally experiencing the rapidly evolving sociocultural changes of the times and incorporating all he learned during his apprenticeship years into his own individualistic mode of architectural design.

Joseph Lyman Silsbee

Wright's first months of apprenticeship were spent under the tutelage of prominent Chicago architect Joseph Lyman Silsbee. His tenure with Silsbee would be brief—less than a year—but it was during this time frame that he was introduced to Chicago's architectural community, crafted his technical skills of drafting, and began a serious study of architecture history through books made available to him from Silsbee's personal library. It assumedly was through this period of concentrated research that Wright first became aware of oriental influences upon the European arts, as he traced the evolution of architectural design and studied notable cultural movements—from the days of Roman intercourse with the Chinese during the Christian era through to British and American dealings with the Japanese during the early-to-mid nineteenth century. This would be consistent with Wright's interest in Oriental *objets d'art* and Japanese prints, which commenced while he was in Silsbee's employ, as well as the astuteness of observations he made during his 1908 lecture on Japanese prints at the Art Institute of Chicago, where he remarked on the significance of the oriental influence on the works of such renowned artists as "Whistler, Manet, Monet, the 'Plein-air' school of France—Puvic de Chavannes, M. Boutet de Monvel."[15] He went on to explain his belief that it was through the works of these renowned artists that the "simplifying, clarifying" aspects of the oriental aesthete were spread to the "arts and crafts of the occident on both sides of the Atlantic."

According to Kevin Nute, however, Silsbee was essentially an enthusiastic amateur with respect to Far Eastern art and probably did nothing more than expose Wright to his collection. It is Nute's contention that Silsbee's real significance turns out to have been not what, but "who" he knew in the field of Oriental art: his first cousin Ernest Fenollosa.[16] As a member of the Imperial Fine Arts Commission, Fenollosa participated in the inspection tour of America's leading art establishments that began in mid-October 1886 and ended at Chicago in April 1887. Nute theorizes that since Wright was firmly established in Silsbee's office by early 1887, it would have been strange if Silsbee had not drawn his attention to the presence of such an illustrious relative.[17] Although it is not known if Wright indeed did meet Fenollosa at that time, comments he made in 1917 clearly support that he was aware of and sympathetic to Fenollosa's interest in Japanese arts: "When I first saw a fine

print . . . it was an intoxicating thing. At that time Ernest Fenollosa was doing his best to persuade the Japanese people not to wantonly destroy their works of art. . . . Fenollosa, the American, did more than anyone else to stem the tide of this folly. On one of his journeys home he brought many beautiful prints; those I made *mine* were the narrow tall decorative form hashirakake. . . . These *first prints* had a large share I am sure in vulgarising the Renaissance for me."[18]

That Wright's introduction to Japanese prints instilled in him a passionate appreciation for their beauty and value as works of art—as it formed his aversion to the ornate, his appreciation for simplicity of line, and his perception of a fundamental interrelationship of the *landscape* to architecture—was confirmed by Wright in retrospect several decades later when he likened the Japanese print to Froebel's blocks, with respect to training the young mind to see: "It was the great gospel of simplification that came over, the elimination of all that was insignificant. . . . They were anti-realism, the Japanese print. . . . So here you have a new way of looking at the landscape. And the landscape has never seemed the same to me since I became familiar with the print."[19] Wright further mused: "Were the menage of the Japanese print deducted from my education, I don't know what direction the whole might have taken."

It seems reasonable to assume Wright also would have been interested in professional journals or books addressing Japanese architecture, such as the illustrated article on the art of Japanese buildings written by British architect Josiah Conder in the April 1887 edition of *American Architect and Building News* and a book by Edward Morse being highly touted at the time: *Japanese Homes and Their Surroundings*. Morse, unlike other writers on the subject of Japanese architecture who related to "monuments," presented a comprehensive analysis of the domestic architecture that is the substance of construction throughout the Japanese countryside. Published just one year prior to the onset of Wright's apprenticeship under Silsbee, *Japanese Homes* attracted much attention. There were four editions with eight or more printings during its first decade of issue. Nute contends that Wright would have been aware of this book from an early stage, and it would have given him access to an almost scientifically observed analysis of the Japanese dwelling.[20] It seems equally significant that Morse devoted an entire chapter to the subject of "Gardens," wherein he communicated the aesthete of the Japanese residential garden and its importance to the Japanese at the personal level: "The secret in a Japanese garden is that they do not attempt too much. That reserve and sense of propriety which characterize . . . all their decorative and other artistic work are here seen to perfection. . . . So much do the Japanese admire gardens, and garden effects, that their smallest strips of ground are utilized for this purpose."[21]

Drawings Wright drafted for Silsbee support that by as early as 1887 he had begun to include in his works oriental rendering techniques such as the giving way of symmetry to casual arrangements, foreshortening, representation by linear means (contours), and the introduction of landscape backgrounds.[22] Wright's introduction of landscape features and foliage into architectural delineations was unique for the times and set his drawing apart—so much so that some of those published in professional journals and trade magazines were identified by his name rather than Silsbee's.

Wright historian Grant Manson observed it was during this period also that Wright took a special interest in making tracings of famous buildings and the details of their ornament.[23] This activity, together with his interpretative drafting technique, prepared him to take samples of his work and apply for a position with Adler and Sullivan, the firm that had just won the coveted commission to design the Chicago Auditorium Building. Wright was one of several new draftsmen hired to work on this monumental project. It most probably was the much-heralded fact that the new Auditorium was the biggest architectural commission in the history of the city that caused Wright to seek this position, however, rather than the reputation of the firm. The two principals—engineer Dankmar Adler and architect Louis Sullivan—had formed their partnership just six years earlier. Although Adler already had developed a reputation by this point in time, Sullivan was relatively unknown until the Auditorium met with great acclaim. Nonetheless, a comparison of backgrounds makes it easy to understand why Wright looked upon Sullivan as his mentor, rather than Silsbee or Adler.

Louis Sullivan

Louis Sullivan was the son of artistically inclined immigrant parents. Like Wright, he had dreamed of being an architect since an early age, did not finish high school, and was nevertheless allowed to enroll in college. He grew up in the urban environment of Boston, however, and attended MIT—where the first architecture courses

in America had been introduced into the curriculum four years earlier. Even so, he too became discouraged with academia after completing his first year of coursework and decided he would rather apprentice in the office of an architect. He first worked for a Philadelphia architect, but then went to Chicago to apprentice in a firm headed by architect William Le Baron Jenney—the only classically trained architect-engineer in Chicago at that time. He then quit this position to study architecture at the *Ecole de Beaux Arts* in Paris. After less than a year at that facility, he again grew impatient with academic life and returned to Chicago. The year was 1875. Sullivan was 19, the same age Wright was when he arrived in the city 12 years hence.

Over the next four years, Sullivan supported himself by working on a freelance basis while continuing his studies on his own. Presumably, it was during this introspective period that Sullivan formed his personal philosophy of design based upon the transcendentalist writings of Emerson, Thoreau, and Whitman, which he so strongly impressed upon Wright as an ardent young apprentice—that is, that architecture should be designed on a regional basis, dependent upon local materials and local geographical and climatic conditions.

Sullivan began working with Adler in 1879. The merging of their talents was so successful that they formalized their partnership two years later. In so doing, they joined the ranks of those Chicago designers who were striving to develop a new kind of commercial building that could be identified as unique to the American Midwest. During the ensuing two decades, when Chicago would grow faster than any other city in the world, the firm of Adler and Sullivan designed and constructed many of the landmark buildings that shaped Chicago's emerging skyline. In each of these, the skeletal framework of construction was exposed. Sullivan has since been acknowledged as the progenitor of this simplified style of commercial design that has come to be known as the Chicago School of Architecture. Thus, Sullivan was reared and trained at a time when American schools had yet to perfect a professional curriculum for architecture. He lived and worked in dramatically evolving urban environments as a young adult. And his architectural destiny was formed as a consequence of Chicago's urbanization, a phenomenon of the 1880s and 1890s.

Wright, too, became actively involved in the Chicago School Movement during his tenure with Adler and Sullivan. At the same time, however, Wright was working on the firm's residential commissions after hours at his suburban home—was in fact encouraged by Sullivan to do so, assumedly because the firm's emphasis was toward commercial assignments and the design of their clients' personal homes was taken on as a favor. In this way, Wright began to earn a reputation as a domestic architect who designed homes for the rising stars of industry. When this happenstance is related to Wright's agrarian upbringing and the social geography of the times—when there was a heretofore unprecedented demand for single-family homes to meet the needs of Chicago's rising middle-class suburbanites—it becomes increasingly clear that his architectural destiny was formed less by the urbanization of Chicago than by the historical phenomena that were the sociocultural *consequence* of urbanization: decentralization and suburbanization.

To appreciate the impact decentralization and suburbanization had in shaping Wright's architecture and his holistic approach to environmental design, it is essential to have at least some sensibility for the significance of this critical period in American history. Consider that as recently as 1870 two-thirds of all Americans still lived on farms or in towns of fewer than 2500 persons. Chicago also was a pedestrian city prior to the fire. The summer before the incident, more than 25,000 people lived in or near the business core—representing all economic classes, ethnic backgrounds, and occupations. Less than a decade later, however, scarcely anyone of means lived in the heart of the city. This exodus came about in reaction to the masses of immigrants and migratory workers who centralized in the urban area to fulfill the manpower needs brought about by the Industrial Revolution. As the existence of mass transit made outlying areas more readily accessible, more and more Chicagoans began relocating to the outskirts of the city—including Wright, in the late 1880s—first, to communities that developed along the horse-drawn streetcar routes, and then to the more remote communities that literally cropped up along the interurban rail lines that radiated ever outward during the closing decades of the nineteenth century.

As developers bought land along the transportation routes, they perpetuated the gridiron pattern of settlement established in the inner city by platting streets to parallel the tracks to a depth of a few blocks on either side, planting whips of trees along their lengths, and subdividing properties into as many lots as possible. They lured potential buyers on Sunday outings by promoting

their subdivisions as being outside fire limits, where people could build "wooden" houses. Some described their property as being away from streets leading to the cemeteries. In so doing, they capitalized upon the trend that originated with the mass-transit horse-drawn streetcars, when Chicagoans began taking picnics to the "end of the line" to enjoy the parklike open spaces of the new cemeteries developed there. "These semi-rural cemeteries . . . had become so attractive for Sunday outings," Peter O. Muller points out, "that one of them began charging admission to families failing to produce a burial-lot certificate."[24] The popularity of these cemetery open spaces was the genesis of Chicago's magnificent chain of parks and tree-lined boulevards.

Chicago was but one of many American cities inspired to develop a parks system after New York's Central Park was opened to the public with great fanfare in 1856. Much of Central Park's success stemmed from its easy accessibility and its central urban location, but it also had to do with the rural picturesqueness of its design, founded on the naturalistic concepts of the English Landscape Gardening School that had become popular throughout Europe during the first quarter of the nineteenth century. This shifting of the ideal from the grandeur of Renaissance-Baroque formality to the naturalization of the garden landscape did not begin to have an impact in America before the 1840s to 1850s—when Andrew Jackson Downing and William Cullen Bryant raised public awareness of nature-inspired realism and initiated the push for the development of a public park in the heart of New York City. It was because of their persuasive writings that a design competition for a "central park" eventually was held and the British architect Calvert Vaux collaborated with American landscape designer Frederick Law Olmsted on the imaginative work selected as the winning design. A key element in their layout was the innovative method they devised for separating pedestrian and vehicular traffic on different levels—a planning treatment Wright would emulate in 1909 within his plan for the Bitter Root Town Project. Because of its scale and imaginative layout, this initial model of urban park systems is credited with ushering in a new movement of landscape design.

A by-product of Central Park's opening was the escalation of real estate property values immediately surrounding the developed open space. The monetary impact was so substantial that park development became big business in cities across America. Influential Chicago entrepreneurs proposed to convert the former

City Cemetery on the North Shore of Lake Michigan into a public park, to be known as Lincoln Park. The push then began to convert the vast marshy open space on the South Shore into a park, and the firm of Olmsted and Vaux was commissioned to begin the design process. Coincidentally, Olmsted was in the Chicago area supervising the implementation of a plan his firm had designed two years earlier for Riverside, Illinois—a suburban community nine miles southwest of the Chicago Loop. It was this chain of events that led to the development of three landscapes in the Chicago area that significantly impacted upon Wright as a designer. All were conceived by Olmsted and Vaux or the subsequent Frederick Law Olmsted and Company: the village of Riverside, Chicago's South Shore parks, and the grounds for the World's Columbian Exposition.

Riverside, Illinois (1868)

There can be little doubt Wright would have been aware of Riverside from the time of his earliest apprenticeship years. Except for its geographics—within a 10-mile radius of the city core and directly accessible by commuter rail—Riverside was unlike any other community laid out during Chicago's initial era of suburbanization. The 1600-acre property was situated along the banks of the Des Plaines River. Almost half this acreage (700 acres) was developed as public open space—complete with a self-contained village fronting onto a large village common, a forested greenway along the river, walkways, pavilions, rustic bridges, a dammed-up pond for skating and boating, and gently curving streets interconnected by parkway units designed to meander naturally throughout the village. Only the area nearest the station was subdivided into standardized lots. The balance of the acreage was arranged into generous, irregularly shaped lots to allow the building of gracious homes set well back from the curving streets (Figure 1-1). The prestigious homes built in Riverside were designed by Chicago's most prominent architects, and the uniqueness of the Olmsted and Vaux design was much

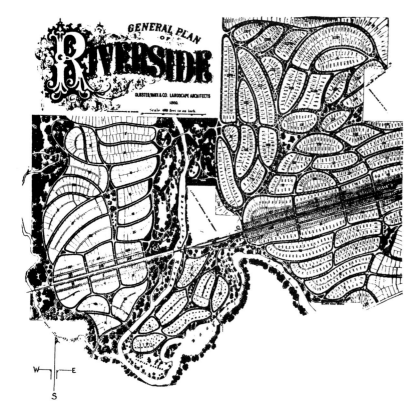

Figure 1-1 Riverside, Illinois—curvilinear road system laid out by Frederick Law Olmsted in 1868. (*Courtesy of the Newberry Library, Chicago, Illinois.*)

touted—both locally and through national publication. By the time the thousands of shrubs, deciduous trees, and evergreens Olmsted introduced into the featureless prairie landscape reached a degree of maturity in the mid-to-late 1880s, when Wright arrived on the scene, Riverside was seen as a popular destination for Sunday outings as a place to stroll or ride through on horseback or by carriage to admire the elegant homes and parklike environs.

Although Riverside never was used as a model for Chicago's pattern of settlement, as Olmsted had hoped, the curvilinear street system was seen as an ideal for suburban development—a means of ruralizing an urban space and setting it apart as a different sphere for living. It was at this point in time that many designers of note began using curves for the sake of curves—including designers who historically favored geometric formality, such as Sullivan and Wright. The curvilinear roadway system Sullivan and Wright designed in 1890 for Sullivan's 41.5-acre winter vacation colony in Ocean Springs, Mississippi, is an excellent example of this illogical design rationale. Even though the terrain was flat and featureless, they fashioned a very elaborate arrangement of winding carriage trails and riding paths to interconnect the complex of structures (Figure 1-2). Considering that Sullivan's personal cottage overlooked the Gulf of Mexico, this winter vacation retreat must have been situated at one of the southernmost distances from Chicago directly accessible by railroad—the ultimate perpetuation of the sociocultural pattern of settlement in this era of decentralization when first cemeteries, then suburban communities, public parks, and recreation retreats were situated near the "end of the line."

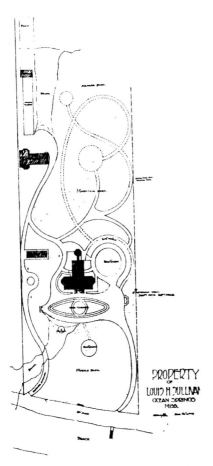

Figure 1-2 Curvilinear roadway system laid out by Frank Lloyd Wright in 1890 for Sullivan's winter vacation colony in Ocean Springs, Mississippi. (© 2002 by The Frank Lloyd Wright Foundation, Scottsdale, Arizona.)

South Shore Parks Development Plan—Chicago, Illinois (1870)

The land the South Parks commissioners acquired for park development was ideally situated alongside Lake Michigan and convenient to the central business district. This location also was readily accessible to mass transit; railroad and interurban lines already were in place, and access by lake transport was a foreseeable option. Fully two-thirds of the acreage was a water-soaked flatland, however, liable to frequent overflow and traversed by low ridges of sand. The entire landscape was barren except for a few scrubby trees stripped of foliage by the gale-force winds that blew in off Lake Michigan. Olmsted and Vaux proposed that there be two parks—Washington Park furthest inland, Jackson Park nearest the lake—interconnected by way of a mile-long, 650-foot-wide greensward median feature with picturesque water basins and pleasure walkways, bordered on both sides by broad boulevards (Figure 1-3). This grand "Midway Plaisance" was designed to serve as an aesthetic access-way between the parks, but its more important function was to integrate the waterway conduit system required to drain the entire acreage into Lake Michigan so it would sustain development over time.

South Shore park development was impeded after the Chicago fire because public spending was directed toward rebuilding the inner city. Although the Midway Plaisance and Washington Park were developed essentially as planned, the shoreline was improved only a limited extent. Even so, the monetary impact on the area surrounding the parklands was as substantial as anticipated. Fine stone townhouses were built along the nearby residential boulevards. The wide, tree-lined streets and the well-kept riding paths in the park attracted the wealthy horse crowd to such an extent that, in 1884, the Washington Park Race Club built a clubhouse and grandstand adjacent to the park. Although these forms of recreation passed into oblivion with the advent of electric streetcars and the automobile, the parks-midway environs would continue to attract crowds of sightseers well into the next century. Wright himself would capitalize upon the popularity of this public garden environment in 1913, when he designed the Midway Gardens.

In any event, considering that the offices of Adler and Sullivan were located in Chicago's downtown Loop—six miles to the north of the South Shore parks—it seems reasonable to assume that Wright and his asso-ciates already were familiar with the 633 acres of marsh-land awaiting development as Jackson Park when Olm-sted recommended this property as the site for the World's Columbian Exposition.

World's Columbian Exposition—Chicago, Illinois (1893)

Members of Chicago's architectural community would have been intensely aware of the advent of a nationally sponsored exposition to celebrate the quadricentennial of Christopher Columbus's discovery of America. The movers and shakers who lobbied so earnestly for the honor of being selected as the host city for the Exposition were the same men who had backed and built the Auditorium. Architects likewise would have kept themselves informed about the selection of the planning team. Chicagoans Daniel Hudson Burnham and John Wellborn Root served as supervising architects; Frederick Law Olmsted and Company as supervising landscape architects; A. Gottlieb as consulting engineer; and sculptor Augustus Saint-Gaudens as advisor on the execution of fountains and statues.

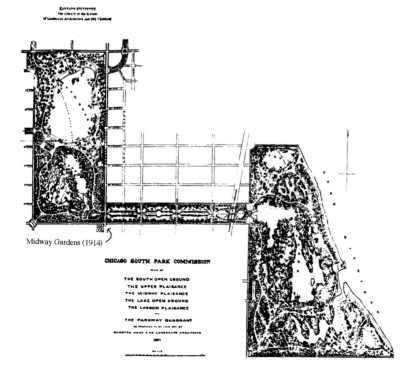

Figure 1-3 Olmsted's 1870 site plans, Chicago South Shore—Washington Park, Midway Plaisance, and Jackson Park. (*Courtesy of the Chicago South Park Commission.*)

Architects assuredly also would have followed with interest Olmsted's selection of the fair site, his proposed layout, and the manner in which the property was prepared for development—beginning in August 1890. Working closely with Burnham and Root, Olmsted put forth a coherent site plan for fitting the buildings to the configuration of the land he had previously laid out as Jackson Park. Building upon his prior proposal to the South Park Commission for stabilizing this marshland for development, he recommended that the low-lying parts of the property be deepened by dredging to effectively drain the area into Lake Michigan, and that the dredged-up material be used to form islands or to fill and contour the site. He configured one of the low-lying areas into a natural-appearing lagoon surrounding the "Wooded Isle," a land formation he envisioned as a naturalistic open space to be "held free from buildings . . . [to] serve as a foil to the artificial grandeur and sumptuousness of the other part of the scenery."[25] He set aside the Midway Plaisance as an area for entertainment—the first fair midway. And he configured the remaining low-lying areas into navigable, Venice like canals with vertical walled edges to interconnect with a formal water basin centered in the architectural Court of Honor, where he introduced extensive docks, piers, bridges, viaducts, and towers (Figure 1-4). That Wright was inspired by this form of land reformation is supported by the fact that just two years later, in 1895, he proposed the same process of development for a marshland area a few miles to the south of the fair site within his conceptual plans for Wolf Lake Amusement Park.

Much has been written about Wright's involvement with his firm's assignment to design the Transportation Building, the strong debate that developed with respect to the architectural theme for the Exposition (classicism versus functionalism), the perpetuation of this controversy between architects that would continue well into the next century, and the Ho-o-den—an archetypal Japanese structure replicated on Olmsted's naturalistically landscaped Wooded Isle. This building and Mayan architecture exhibited at the fair have been identified by historians as Wright's source of inspiration for a number of the "modern" design elements represented in his architecture. To this point, however, there has been no similar influential association made with respect to the physical layout of the Exposition itself. And yet, the microcosmic city was every bit as influential as the architecture, as it both spawned the City Beautiful Movement and provided a viable format for Wright and other designers to study the basic concepts of urban design and community planning. This reasoning is supported by John Coleman Adams, who in 1896 described the fair as a city that "had been carefully and studiously planned."[26] He elaborated: "The plotting of the grounds, the manner of their development, the placing of the buildings, the communicating avenues and canals and bridges, all exhibited a prevision, a plan, an arrangement of things with reference to each other. The problem of the architect, the landscape gardener and the engineer had been thoroughly thought out before the gates were opened. The result was preeminently satisfying." Walter Burley Griffin, who would work with Wright for some five years

Figure 1-4 Bird's-eye perspective of buildings and grounds, World's Columbian Exposition, Chicago, Illinois. (*Supplement to Harper's Weekly, December 19, 1891.*)

after the turn of the century, made a similar correlation. "The Chicago Exposition gave me my first lesson in town planning,"[27] he said; and he recalled it as "our great example of a scheme or system . . . it provided a place for everything and everything in its place."[28]

The Exposition also has been linked with the Garden City Movement and the Prairie School Movement, although more indirectly. As all three of these movements were developing essentially parallel to each other and to that period in Wright's life when he was himself trying to find his way as a practicing professional, he was actively involved with—and influenced by—each of them.

City Beautiful Movement

The City Beautiful Movement was a largely upper-class expression of civic consciousness that spread across the United States during the first quarter of the twentieth century. The wave of enthusiastic support for civic beautification generated by the Exposition and the much-publicized plans subsequently developed by Burnham for Chicago, Baltimore, Cleveland, San Francisco, Manila, and Washington, D.C., prompted many architects, landscape architects, and engineers to claim city planning and beautification as being within their professional province. The more prominent of these were actively sought as speakers by private business groups and civic or society-based volunteer organizations of smaller communities throughout the country. That Wright was one who participated in this promotional activity is verified by the caption "Architect Talks on City Beautiful" that headed an article in the April 25, 1906 edition of the *Illinois State Journal* covering Wright's lecture before the joint membership of the Springfield Women's Club and the Springfield Business Men's Association. Although the text of Wright's lecture was not published, it was reported: "he discussed the need of landscape gardening in civic beautification, declaring that a greater necessity existed for the landscape architect than for the building architect."[29] Wright here may not so much have been beating the drum for the role of the landscape architect, as he was informing his audience that civic beautification was a cause he was championing, that he realized the importance of landscape architecture to this process, and that citywide planning was a role he was more than capable of assuming. It would not be until 1909, however, that Wright would have opportunity to test his abilities—with his Bitter Root Town Plan.

The timing of Wright's 1906 Springfield talk and his development of the 1909 Bitter Root Town Plan are relevant because they demonstrate he was at the forefront of the civic-based sociocultural movement that transpired between 1906 and 1916, the decade identified by planner-historian John L. Hancock as the "progressive era [that] signaled the real beginning of responsible social changes in modern America."[30]

Garden City Movement

Inasmuch as support for the City Beautiful Movement was limited to the laity, who were not knowledgeable about the comprehensive sociological needs of the citizenry, limited pragmatistic city planning was implemented beyond physical planning and aesthetics. Reality-based sociologic and economic planning would emerge under the mantle of the Garden City Movement, a parallel movement linking development with social reform based upon theories first postulated in 1898 by Ebenezer Howard in his influential book *Tomorrow: A Peaceful Path to Social Reform*—perhaps better known by the title used when it was reissued in 1902: *Garden Cities of Tomorrow*. A Britisher by birth, Howard had migrated to America in the 1870s and worked for four years in Chicago, which was sometimes referred to as the "Garden City" during this period. City planning historian William H. Wilson explains Howard's thesis for development: "Howard envisioned compact residential settlements surrounded by a permanent buffer of unsettled land in orchards, farms, and parks. The garden cities included all the services, retail shops, and industry required to support their residents. . . . Their transportation arrangements would emphasize intercity rail transit and highways but allow few through streets for heavy traffic within the cities themselves."[31] British architect Raymond Unwin demonstrated the worth of Howard's principles with Hampstead Gardens, a suburb of London, and in 1902 joined with Barry Parker to design Letchworth, England—the first, and much heralded, Garden City.

The Garden City Movement directly links to the Exposition by way of the sizable three-dimensional model of the planned industrial village of Pullman, Illinois, that was on prominent display in Adler and Sullivan's Transportation Building. The model graphically showed fair visitors the self-contained and highly livable pedestrian community as it had been developed in the name of social reform by railroad industrialist George M. Pullman for employees of the Pullman Palace Car

Company. By that date, Pullman was a veritable land-scaped oasis amidst Chicago's grimy South Side, with 1750 custom-designed housing units, a school, industrial plant, and administration building—each equipped with running water, gas, and indoor bathrooms (all relatively novel concepts for the working class within this time frame)—as well as playgrounds, athletic fields, parks, churches, a library, marketplace, a hotel, and a shopping arcade (considered a forerunner to the enclosed mall)[32] (Figure 1-5). The community was made easily accessible to fair visitors by way of excursion cars added to trains commuting to this destination from the Exposition or Chicago's Loop and was lauded by observers from all over the world. "No place in the United States has attracted more attention or been more closely watched than Pullman," observed an 1893 article in the *London Times*.[33] It certainly is plausible to believe Wright would have been among the 2000 or more sightseers a day known to have visited Pullman, including architects from other parts of the United States and Europe. After all, he was closely involved with Adler and Sullivan's Transportation Building, where the model was housed. Moreover, the Garden City theories formed the basic premise of the layouts Wright prepared for the City Club Competition in 1913 and his famed Broadacre City models. And he is known to have visited communities founded upon these theories as they developed across America during the 1920s and 1930s.

That Wright in any event was intensely interested in and well-informed about the evolutionary development of the field of town planning, as well as design alternatives for residential development, is confirmed by his career-long fascination with community-scale planning. When Wright's chronicle of works is analyzed—even excluding the many individual commissions designed for nonresidential urban use such as theaters, country clubs, educational and religious buildings, bridges, medical clinics, shops, sports pavilions, airpark hangers, gas stations, and hotels—there were 41 commissions where a number of land uses were coordinated into the design whole and should be considered community or urban design in scale (see Appendix B). Although only 8 of these commissions were implemented (and 4 partially implemented, with 29 that never progressed past the phase of presentation drawings), the complete body of work represents 62 years of sustained interest—from 1895 to 1957—and so attests to Wright's dedication to the principles of community planning that first piqued his interest during the World's Columbian Exposition.

Prairie School Movement (1900–1915)

The Prairie School Movement was essentially a regional manifestation of the Arts and Crafts Movement, a reform effort originated in England in the 1860s, described by architecture historian H. Allen Brooks as "an approach to a problem . . . that advocated no spe-

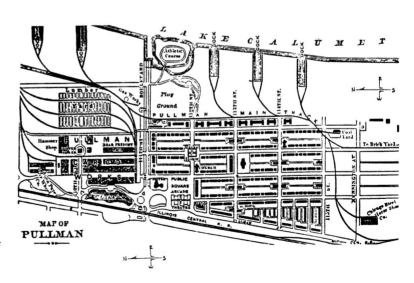

Figure 1-5 Pullman, Illinois—a model industrial town based on the Garden City philosophy (1880). (*Harper's Monthly Magazine.*)

cific vocabulary of forms. It pleaded for simplicity, elimination, and respect for materials. Its most salutary effect . . . was the purification of public taste."[34] That Wright was captivated with this reasoning is supported by the fact that he was among the founding architects of the Chicago Arts and Crafts Society, established in October 1897 at Jane Addams' Hull House.[35] Moreover, the first two articles ever published about Wright in the 1897 and 1899 issues of *House Beautiful*, the earliest influential homemaker magazine in America, praise him in the most glowing arts and crafts terminology as one of the finest and most understanding designers in America.

The term "Prairie School" initially related to a relatively unstructured splinter group of about two dozen design professionals who held similar objectives as to the evolution of an original design form that would most closely personify the spirit of the prairies of mid-America and distinguish the domestic architecture and developed landscape of the American Midwest from designs originated by eastern architects. It is only over time that the term has come to be used to describe the architectural form identified with their collective works and the emulative structures their work engendered. Most of these designers at one time or another maintained office space in Steinway Hall, a commodious loft on the top floor of the Steinway Piano Company headquarters building designed by Chicago School architect Dwight H. Perkins. Perkins rented the Steinway loft quarters shortly after construction was completed in 1896, and then offered space to other independent-thinking design professionals with persuasions similar to his own. The work environment Perkins arranged was unique, in that individuals or groups of individuals occupied separate offices but shared communal drafting rooms and support staff, informally consulted with each other, and sometimes formally collaborated on design projects.

Wright was among the first to move into Steinway Hall, where he shared space with Perkins, Myron Hunt, and Robert C. Spencer, Jr. Of this four-member core group, Wright was the only one who had not received at least some training at MIT. Three other architects occupying space early on were H. Webster Tomlinson, Walter Burley Griffin, and Marion Mahony. Tomlinson entered into a partnership with Wright for a short time. Griffin and Mahony would later join Wright's staff at his Oak Park Studio.

It was Mahony who subsequently told Grant Manson about the profound effect the Ho-o-den had upon

the evolving domestic architecture of "all the early members of the Chicago School."[36] She alleged it was because of their mutual fascination with this structure that they "all began to collect prints and noticed in the architectural ones the essential formula for a modern occidental architecture." She described "the sympathetic affinity of the Japanese house with immense quantities of light and air" and the way the eaves functioned "as awnings for the house rather than, as formerly, being merely boundary lines for abstract areas of design." Mahony also pointed out that Wright's close friend Robert Spencer was the first to react to the Japanese influence, that a rendered perspective of one house he designed in this manner was hanging on Wright's studio wall when she first came to Oak Park in the mid-1890s.

A primary distinction between the Arts and Crafts and Prairie School styles of architecture is the horizontal line. The more dedicated Prairie School designers visually extended the horizontal line beyond the architectural limits to include the surrounding landscape. There were strong differences of opinion, however, between those who advocated that the architect could conceive the "whole design" for the house and grounds and those who believed a landscape specialist should be involved. Landscape architecture historian Robert E. Grese references an article in a 1902 issue of *Architectural Record* wherein the author observed that "the bulk of influential landscape design work in the United States was going to architects who blurred the distinction between architecture and landscape architecture, designing both buildings and grounds."[37] He said the author went on to suggest this trend was preferable, that it was "desirable for 'the whole design' to be 'imagined and worked out by the same designer.' " That the latter approach was the reasoning championed by Wright is supported by the ground plans he prepared for publication in *Architectural Review* (Boston, June 1900) and *Ausgefüührte Bauten und entwürfe Von Frank Lloyd Wright* (Berlin, 1910), the historic volume of Wright's work most generally referred to as the "Wasmuth Portfolio."

Few Wright historians are aware that the movement to develop a prairie style of landscape design was at work on its quiet revolution even before the concept for a prairie style of architecture gained popularity. The first course in landscape gardening was introduced into the curriculum of the Department of Horticulture at the University of Illinois in 1868—five years prior to when the first course in architecture was introduced at this institution. By 1907, interest in landscape gardening had broadened to such an extent that the University of Illinois established a formal degree program in "landscape architecture" under the direction of Joseph Cullin Blair.[38]

An important first step toward popularizing a prairie style of landscape cultivation was taken by Blair in 1901 when he hired Wilhelm Miller to supervise the establishment of an outreach program of continuing education, so all citizens of Illinois would have access to the latest thinking on the subject. Miller was a landscape gardener influenced by the Arts and Crafts Movement who favored the use of vernacular plantings in the naturalistic form put forth by the English School and Olmsted. He also was a prolific writer and came to this position with four years' experience as associate editor of *Cyclopedia of American Horticulture*. In Miller's writings for this publication and articles appearing in *Architectural Record*, *Country Life in America*, *Garden Magazine*, and the circulars published by the university, he postulated the need to develop a new mode of landscape gardening to fit the peculiar scenery, climate, and soil inherent to the prairie—instead of copying the manners and materials of other regions. The wide distribution of Miller's writings contributed significantly to furthering the conservation of Illinois' native scenery and the restoration of its local vegetation before and after the turn of the century. Within this same time frame, however, the well-known landscape painter Charles A. Platt published articles in the then-new *Harper's Magazine*, published monthly. Platt's writings counteracted Miller's efforts by fueling a renewed interest in the use of formal geometry in landscape design, as explained by Grese: "Platt advocated the adaptation of organizational principles used in Renaissance Italian villas as a means of unifying house and garden. . . . Platt believed that the 'naturalized' approach to landscape design . . . neglected the architectural aspects of outdoor design."[39] Frederick Law Olmsted vehemently declaimed Platt's approach. "We have an organized enemy before us," he wrote, "strong in its conviction, able, proud even to superciliousness. . . . They are mostly cultivated gentlemen to be dealt with courteously, but they are doctrinaires and fanatics and essentially cockneys, with no more knowledge of nor interest in real rurality than most men of Parisian training and associations."[40]

Thus, there was the same ardent discourse and debate between those who defended the formal classical landscape and those who preferred the natural or organic landscape as there was with respect to classic architecture and the so-called "honest" architecture of Sullivan, Wright, and other architects of the Chicago

School. At the same time that Wright was developing his personal manner of architectural design, therefore, he also was caught up in this ongoing debate as to the design and articulation of the landscape.

The strongest argument to support the prairie style of landscape gardening was put forth by Miller in the November 1915 issue of *The Prairie Spirit in Landscape Gardening*. He traced the development of the "Illinois Way" of landscape design over the previous two decades and depicted exemplary private estates and public parks designed by Sullivan, Griffin, William Drummond, Ossian Cole Simonds, and Jens Jensen. He contended that the same principles and methods used by the designers of these selected examples could be developed by the farmer, city dweller, or humblest renter in proportion to their means on the average farmstead or city lot. He went on to spell out common problems associated with planting for the sunny and shady sides of a house and addressed such special challenges as arbors, pergolas, banks, soils, specialty gardens, and windbreaks. He explained the principles of conservation and restoration of the landscape. And he provided detailed lists broken down into stratified and nonstratified materials for specific groups of plantings. Most important, he saw to it that this writing was widely distributed throughout the American Midwest. Thus, Miller's document effectively served as the "how-to-do-it" guide to the prairie style of landscape gardening, for untold numbers, whether amateur or professional.

That Wright was contacted by Miller with respect to this significant writing is supported by Wright's letter to Miller, dated February 24, 1915—nine months prior to the publication of Miller's essay—wherein he responded to specific questions posed by Miller. Although he acknowledged "the influence of the prairie in developing the forms I have used and dedicated the types to the prairie," he took issue with the "prairie style of architecture" phraseology and clearly did not give Miller permission to include his designs within any "grouping" of architectural works. "I am sorry," he wrote, "that an American university should feel that the work of a man is only worthy of university recognition and support when it has got far enough along to be recognized as the work of many, loses its individual distinction and becomes a matter of 'the group.'"[41] Nevertheless, Wright commended the research effort being made by Miller: "You are doing good work, I think, in running these things down or setting them up in scholarly fashion."

Presumably, it was because of this rebuff—however slight it may have been—that Miller did not include any of Wright's works in this publication or in the article that appeared in the December 1916 issue of *Architectural Record*, wherein he singled out Simonds, Jensen, and Griffin as designers who used a high percentage of planting materials native to the Middle West and were most influenced by the characteristic features of the prairie.[42] The significance in all this lies in the fact that each of these three designers had by this date substantially influenced Wright's personal evolving landscape design philosophy, either by example or through personal and professional interaction.

Ossian Cole Simonds

Ossian Cole Simonds studied architecture under William Le Baron Jenney at the University of Michigan and in 1878 joined the staff of Jenney's Chicago office, where Sullivan also apprenticed. Like Jenney, Simonds practiced as a landscape gardener and in 1880 began to design a new section of Chicago's Graceland Cemetery, wherein he continued the curvilinear road system originated by

Jenney and landscape architect H. W. S. Cleveland when they laid out the initial cemetery in 1860—preceding the similarly meandering road system laid out by Olmsted in Riverside (Figure 1-6). Graceland is the site of Sullivan's famed Getty Tomb and has been linked with Olmsted's Central Park as one of the two best-known early examples of landscape design in America.

Simonds' most significant work occurred after he took over management of the grounds and undertook a studied effort to re-create the primal character of the native Illinois prairie by transplanting common tree species with strong horizontal branching and other stratified plant forms from the Illinois wilds. Many of these species were at that time looked upon as common weeds. In merging the forms of the landscaped lawn and the long prairie view, Simonds set a standard for landscape gardening that subsequently was emulated by many of the Prairie School architects—Wright among them. Throughout his career, Wright would advise clients to select plantings from the wilds and transplant these to their sites, rather than introducing exotics from plant nurseries.

Jens Jensen

Jens Jensen emigrated from Denmark and settled in Chicago in 1885—just two years prior to Wright's arrival on the scene. According to Jensen biographer Leonard K. Eaton, Jensen started out as a laborer for the West Chicago Park District and rose to superintendent of Humboldt Park, one of the largest parks on Chicago's West Side. In this capacity, Eaton states, he developed "a more extensive international reputation than any American artist of his period except Frank Lloyd Wright."[43]

Jensen opened his own office at about the same time as Wright and established stature as an independent landscape architect by building his reputation among Chicago's wealthy elite. Within this process, he involved himself in Chicago's social and environmental reform organizations—including the Chicago Arts and Crafts Society founded by Wright and his contemporaries and the Committee on the Universe, a group that met informally at Perkins' house for Sunday evening dinners. Through these associations, Jensen participated in various architectural competitions and sometimes exhibited his work alongside the work of Steinway Hall architects. Jensen also prepared the planting plan for a rare residential design by Sullivan—the Henry Babson estate in Riverside. And he collaborated with or prepared planting plans for projects of Wright's design, although the extent

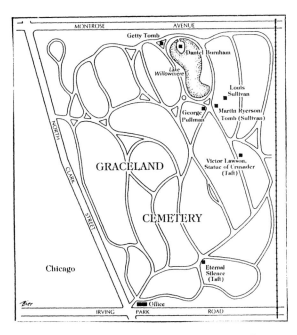

Figure 1-6 Curvilinear roadway system laid out in Chicago's Graceland Cemetery by Osian Cole Simonds in 1880. (*Courtesy of Walter L. Creese, author of The Crowning of the American Landscape, © 1985 Princeton University Press, Princeton, New Jersey.*)

of their professional association is subordinate to the circumstance of their decades-long friendship and the significant influence each had upon the other through discourse and debate. In a letter written to Jensen in 1930, Wright refers to their 27-year friendship at that point and his lack of same with fellow architects: "My work has suffered great hindrance in this country because of malicious propaganda by the 'brother'-architects themselves. God knows they should be my friends."[44]

The similarities in the personal and professional lives of Jensen and Wright are extraordinary. Like Wright, Jensen was strongly influenced by his childhood on the farm. His visionary talents were intuitive or self-taught; his conceptual sketches were crude; and he preferred to leave the construction detailing to others in his office. Moreover, he scorned the formal gardens designed by eastern landscape architects and looked to the prairie as a powerful political and aesthetic symbol. He, too, fathered six children, first used a room of his house as an office, occupied an office in Steinway Hall, eventually built a small studio near his home, and later moved to Wisconsin, where he lived, worked, and taught in an informal school he established on the premises: a school of the soil, known as "The Clearing." And as at Taliesin, there was a disastrous fire that forced Jensen to rebuild and start again.[45]

As Jensen—like Wright—was a strong-willed man with a powerful personality and a genius for publicity, he locked horns with the American Society of Landscape Architects, characterizing its membership as a group of politicians. Eaton asserts: "The Society, of course, reciprocated, and most of the time seems to have seen Jensen in the same light as the leadership of the American Institute of Architects saw Frank Lloyd Wright during the twenties and thirties: a dangerous genius who was forever making life difficult for them."[46]

Jensen remained professionally active throughout his lifetime. Relying on garden science skills and care in plant selection to create the illusion of naturalness, he originated a magnificent legacy of extraordinary parks and private estates where decorative man-made artifacts were avoided, plant materials were native to the prairies, savannas, and forests of the Midwest, and the reconstructed prairie landscape reigned supreme. Upon Jensen's death in 1951 at age 91—the same age as Wright at his demise eight years hence—*The New York Times* recognized him as "the dean of American landscape architects."[47]

Walter Burley Griffin

Walter Burley Griffin grew up in the north Chicago suburbs of Maywood and Elmhurst, attended high school in Oak Park, and was awarded a bachelor of science degree in architecture from the University of Illinois at age 22. In his insightful essay on Griffin, Paul Kruty wrote: "Walter was a precocious child. His mother recalled that . . . he was a voracious reader who spent his remaining free hours working in his garden [where he had almost everything in the way of perennials that would grow here]. By his senior year in high school, Griffin had resolved to become a landscape gardener. Seeking guidance, he paid a call on the famous Ossian C. Simonds, who cautioned him, surprisingly enough, to study architecture rather than to pursue landscape gardening."[48] At Illinois, Griffin was exposed to a rather progressive curriculum developed by noted architect Nathan C. Ricker, who stressed the "science" of building. Griffin also took elective courses relating to horticulture and forestry, as well as the only available class in landscape gardening. This training, together with his natural bent toward indigenous plant materials, was enough in those preprofessional days to add the title of landscape architect to his letterhead when he became a practicing architect in 1899. "After graduation," Griffin biographer James Birrell writes, "Griffin was admitted to the American Institute of Architects and commenced practice working with Dwight H. Perkins and Robert C. Spencer, Jr. in Room 1007, Steinway Hall."[49] He also worked with other Steinway Hall architects, depending upon work availability.

Griffin became an ardent professional activist within the Prairie School Movement. As a thwarted landscape gardener, he was particularly interested in the thesis of the "whole design" involving both architecture and site. Certainly, he was more qualified than most for this undertaking as few, if any, of the other prairie architects were knowledgeable about ecological relationships and botanical associations. Christopher Vernon advocates: "It was Griffin who perhaps most completely articulated the Prairie School of landscape design. . . . Not only did his architectonic residential landscape dissolve into more open naturalistic surroundings, but Griffin also harmoniously inserted these designed environments into the expansive landscape of the Midwest itself."[50]

It was through the connection at Steinway Hall that Wright and Griffin established a working relationship—most likely because of the innovative aspects of environmental design Griffin would have introduced into the critiques taking place in the communal drafting room. At some point after the turn of the century, he began working with Wright on a full-time basis at The Studio in Oak Park. Birrell assigns the beginning date for their professional association as 1900.[51] Johnson places him in The Studio between 1901 and 1905. The reality of the situation probably was that Griffin and Wright consulted on projects at Steinway Hall between 1899 and 1900 and Griffin moved to the Oak Park office once commissions warranted it. Regardless of Griffin's exact tenure with Wright, he brought to The Studio a degree of landscape professionalism not found in other architecture offices of the day.

In summation, Wright's "organic" design aesthete was inspired by much more than the primary motivating influences generally cited—that is, the Froebel building blocks he played with as a child, the teachings of Joseph Lyman Silsbee and Louis B. Sullivan, the Japanese exhibits associated with the World's Columbian Exposition in Chicago, and the substance of Japanese prints. Wright's sensitivity for the environment and his basic ecological sensibilities were acquired during his formative years as his farmer uncles taught him to respect the inevitability of climatic conditions and build in the nat-

ural way of things. His recognition of the need for urban planning derived from his personal experiences with Chicago's initial decentralization and suburbanization. There also were the philosophical writings brought to life for him by Ernest Fenolossa, the writings and lectures on Japanese architecture by Edward Morse, and the naturalistic urban landscapes designed and laid out by Ossian Cole Simonds, Frederick Law Olmsted, and Jens Jensen during the mid-to-late 1800s and the early 1900s. Most significantly, there were the City Beautiful and Garden City Movements, which directed views toward urban planning and residential development throughout America from the turn of the century to the mid-1900s, as well as the design concepts and personalities associated with the ascendancy and parallelism of the Prairie School Movement—which spawned both a prairie style of architecture and a prairie style of landscape architecture.

The coalescence of all these influences, or forces, affected everything Wright learned during his years of apprenticeship and formed the philosophical basis for his personal vision of merging his architecture with nature, the developed landscape, the visual and fine arts, and the larger environment of community as he conceived, defined, and constantly refined his principles for organic architecture during the 70-year span of his professional life.

Wright's personal involvement with the processes of decentralization and suburbanization began within months of his arrival in Chicago—as soon as he felt he could afford to ask his mother to make a home for the family in the big city. They settled on the "red brick house on Forest Avenue in the west-side village of Oak Park," Wright wrote, because the area "looked much like Madison to Mother."[52] Moreover, he was impressed with the generously shaded village streets that cloaked the ugliness of the "aggregation of uninspired carpenter work" representative of the majority of houses in the area.

In choosing to live on the outskirts of Chicago, the Wright family adopted the developing behavioral patterns of the new breed of suburbanites—that is, limiting interaction with the central city core to the daily commute to and from work, occasional nighttime entertainment, and periodic daytime shopping sprees in the department stores (another phenomenon of decentralization). Presumably, they also would have socialized with their neighbors during the early evening hours of the spring, summer, and fall—a "cherished town custom" of Chicagoans, according to Miller, that transmuted to Chicago's suburban communities.[53] Rather than sit on the front stoop of a townhouse like the urbanites, however, the suburbanites strolled through the neighborhood or sat upon the elevated front porches of their period houses (Figure 2-1). In his autobiography, Wright wrote a lengthy derogatory statement that clearly expresses his disdain for both the architecture and porches of this era:

> Houses senseless. Most looked equally comfortless . . . endless rows of drab or white painted wood porch houses set regularly apart, each on its little painted cardboard lawn. High front steps went straight up to jigger-porches wriggling with turned ballisters [sic], squirming with wanton scrollwork. This prevalent porch-luxury was seldom of use but still the roofs continued to shut out the sun from the parlors and sitting rooms. These . . . had all the murderous corner-towers serving as bay windows in the principal sitting room. Where did that soul-destroying ornament come from? Never from earth. This popular fetish—for it was more than a *feature*—was either rectangular across the corner,

round, or octagonal, eventuating above in candle-snuffer roofs, turnip domes, or corkscrew spires. The forms were utterly meaningless, though apparently much ingenious scheming and copying had gone into them.[54]

It was Wright's distaste for the meaningless way these porches were designed that inspired one of the more innovative design elements of his first personal residence, which he began building two and one-half years after he arrived in Chicago—shortly after marrying Catherine Lee Tobin. The outdoor living spaces Wright designed as porch alternatives are the most overlooked features of his Oak Park home.

Figure 2-1 A typical Victorian Gothic-style house (circa 1889) with porch and frontally direct approach. (*The American Home, by M. M. Foley.*)

ENVIRONMENTAL DESIGNS, 1889–1897

Frank Lloyd Wright Home—Oak Park, Illinois (1889)

Wright described his property of choice—an abandoned plant nursery purchased from landscape gardener John Blair—as a "tanglewood of all sorts of trees, shrubs, and vines."[55] It was situated at the southeast corner of the intersection of Forest Avenue and Chicago Avenue. Forest Avenue had been paved, but Chicago Avenue had not. There were existing houses on the lots to the south and east.

The modest two-story residence Wright designed for this site has been likened by architecture historians to other steep-roofed, shingle-style houses designed during the mid-to-late 1880s by Silsbee and east-coast architect Bruce Price (Figure 2-2). At the same time, it is *un*like these or any of the other homes being built in Oak Park during this turn-of-the-century period. There is no frontally direct approach. There is no steep flight of entry steps. And there is no front porch adornment. Nor does the house appear to float in a sea of evergreen shrubbery surrounding the foundation. It instead gives the appearance of nestling down among the trees. This appearance could be attributed in part to the sheltering imagery of its distinctive triangular gable, as has been suggested. But it has more to do with the combination and all-inclusiveness of Wright's environmental design approach—that is, the asymmetrical siting, the extended setback and increase in gradation, the horizontal treatment of the wraparound veranda, the redistribution of the entry steps, the width of the entry walkway, and the selection and use of perennials and deciduous varieties of plantings instead of exotics and evergreens.

In siting his home, Wright chose to disregard the centered placement established by existing houses in the area. He instead positioned the main structure so that the south facade was a minimal 10 feet from the boundary and arranged the carriageway/walkway so there was just enough width for a narrow planting bed along the outer edge. The west (front) facade, on the other hand, was 94 feet from the Forest Avenue right-of-way—a setback half again as deep as other houses on the street (Figure 2-3).

Wright's rationale for siting the house so close to the southernmost boundary is not clear. The view was not a consideration, because the living room is on the north side of the house and there originally were no windows on the north wall of that room. Perhaps he felt this siting gave him more control, since the location of an existing house to the south was a reality and the property to the north was still relatively undeveloped in 1889. It may have been that he wanted to distance his home from Chicago Avenue, from whenever in the future it would

Figure 2-2 West facade of Frank Lloyd Wright's original shingle-style Home (1889) in Oak Park, Illinois. (*Courtesy of The Frank Lloyd Wright Preservation Trust, Oak Park, Illinois.*)

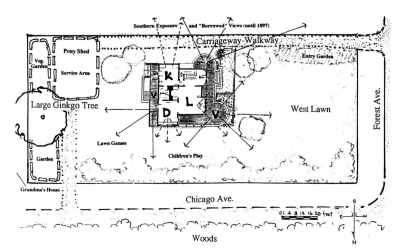

Figure 2-3 Conjectured site plan for Wright's Oak Park Home as sited in 1889. (*By Charles E. Aguar, based on historic photographs and on-site measurements. © 2002 by Berdeana Aguar.*)

be paved and the streetcar line extended—which did not occur until 1906. Or, perhaps he was from the beginning thinking ahead to a time when he could afford to build the expansions that in time extended to the north and east edges of the property.

There is no question as to Wright's rationale for the extended setback from Forest Avenue, however. This decision clearly was based upon perception and logic. The gain of some 34 feet of intervening space between the front facade of the structure and the public right-of-way lengthened the visual perspective, so the house appeared lower to the ground than it actually was. The increased setback also allowed Wright to adjust the gradation to accommodate two low steps between the carriageway and entry walkway, thus reducing the number of steps necessary to reach the level of the front threshold. And it assured the protection of as many existing trees as possible, a necessary consideration for the due-west orientation. Most important, the increased setback allowed Wright to develop the open space for outdoor living, in the forms of a large front yard and the verandas that wrap around three sides of the house.[56]

As Wright configured and arranged the wraparound verandas, he was both creating an alternative to porches in general and experimenting with the shape and utility of outdoor living space (Figure 2-4). The veranda that originally extended across the entire width of the rear facade was directly accessible to two glazed doors—one from the dining room, and one from the kitchen.[57] As the portion nearest the dining room was partially pro-

tected by the second floor overhang, it provided a sheltered sitting area overlooking the rear yard—a place to catch the benefit of the slightest breeze while preparing fruits or vegetables or watching the children at play during the late afternoons of summer. The veranda along the

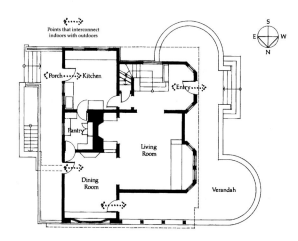

Figure 2-4 First-floor plan of Wright's Oak Park Home as originally built. Wright's use of glazed doors at four points of outdoor-indoor transition provided means to extend lines of sight that interconnect inside living areas with the site environment. (*By Charles E. Aguar, based on personal analysis and plans of record. © 2002 by the Frank Lloyd Wright Preservation Trust, Oak Park, Illinois. As delineated, © 2002 by Berdeana Aguar.*)

north facade of the living room was totally protected from the elements by the broad overhanging eave of the triangular gable, plus a roof extension, and was directly accessible to the dining room by way of a glazed door—thus providing a contained place for the children to play outdoors, even on a rainy day, and an alternate sheltered entry during downpours or blustering snowstorms. The veranda facing Forest Avenue originated with the half-round projection at the southwest corner of the house, extended across the front to envelop the half-round projection at the northwest corner, and was directly accessible to the entrance hall by way of the glazed front door. This streetside veranda served many purposes in addition to providing a means to reach the front entry—in the sense of the prevalent porch luxury of the neighboring period houses. It was a place for sipping coffee in the early morning. It was a place to greet arriving guests, linger with departing guests, or socialize with guests during their visit. And it was a place to unwind at the end of the day. The streetside veranda also served as a contained roofless playroom of ideal proportions with corners, curves, hiding places, and a seemingly endless track for tricycles and other wheeled toys. Moreover, it was visible from the living room windows and easily protected by way of a temporary gate at the top of the entry steps. Protected outdoor play space was a very important design consideration, as the Wrights would raise six children in Oak Park, and many more children would play on the premises—including those who attended the kindergarten Mrs. Wright at one time operated.

Wright's arrangement of the wraparound verandas stylistically allies to the design characteristics detailed by Morse in *Japanese Homes*—that is, the verandas generally are 3 to 10 feet wide, proportionate to the size of the house and in height from the ground, and sheltered under broad overhanging eaves.[58] Morse theorized: "Accustomed as we are . . . to a front door with steps and rail and a certain pretentious architectural display, it is difficult to conceive of a house without some such distinctive character to its portal. . . . In the common class of their [Japanese] houses, and even in those of more importance, the entrance is often vaguely defined; one may enter the house by way of the garden and make his salutations on the verandah. . . . In a better class of houses the entrance is in the form of a wide projecting porch, with special gable roof . . . [and] no special display is made beyond the porch-like projection and gable roof of the external boundaries of this entrance."[59]

Wright's use of glazed doors at the four points of outdoor-indoor transition provided the means to extend lines of sight into the site environment and should be seen as an effort by Wright to interconnect the inside and outside living areas with the nature of the site. He also developed a cohesive combination of hardscape and softscape treatments that worked together to more directly link with the out-of-doors and visually lower the structure to human scale. He began by circumscribing the streetside veranda with a battered brick parapet measuring seven feet in height, from ground level to coping. This treatment firmly connected the structure to the ground, masked the existence of the basement, and created the impression that the house was much larger than it actually was. He then used dressed limestone for the parapet coping to create a light color longitudinal band that contrasted with the darker buff color of the Chicago common brick used for the parapet, the dark brown stain of the shingles, and the forest green trim—a treatment that overscored the horizontal imagery created by the half-round projections at each corner. He also introduced two successively lower bands of dressed limestone to reemphasize this longitudinal line: the coping that crowned the slightly elevated brick edging that extended from the entry steps around the curve of the northwest projection and defined the planting bed at the base of the parapet, and the masonry base that supported the brick edging and followed along the entry walkway to terminate at the low masonry pedestal by the carriage entryway. Viewed from streetside, the only breaks in the trilayered longitudinal banding were the brick piers on either side of the four low-rise entry steps. Moreover, the two bottom steps spread out to wrap around the piers and visually anchor the structure to the ground. To emphasize this element of gravitational pull toward the ground, Wright introduced vines around the parapet base and allowed them to scale the outer wall of the parapet and cascade into the contained areas of the outdoor living space.[60] With this all-encompassing treatment, Wright established a sense of containment that was both defining and nonrestrictive for anyone using this thoughtfully considered outdoor living space.

Wright's developed landscape and entry experience were as dissimilar to his neighbors as his architecture was to their ornate homes. By the last quarter of the nineteenth century, there was a veritable potpourri of landscape "styles." Often, a heavy-membered cast iron fence surrounded the property. Eclectic plantings were placed around the entire house foundation to soften or mask the unsightly masonry foundation. Evergreens were intermixed with a multiplicity of deciduous plants and tiered down to an edging of flowers arranged in a carefully selected cacophony of clashing colors. Masses of shrubs were set out away from the house so as to be visible to those looking out from the elevated major rooms of the residence, as well as to passersby. The same treatment was used to draw attention to the front door, to accent the corners of the house, or to mark the property boundaries. Rarely was consideration given to the basic design principles for harmony, balance, and order. Topiary and other perverse manipulation of natural plant forms also was cultivated. The visually chaotic landscapes thus created not only detracted from the architecture but totally dominated any natural elements remaining on the site.

Historic photographs support that Wright, on the other hand, limited introduced plantings to deciduous shade trees and indigenous varieties of flowering shrubs or perennials. The front yard was maintained as a parklike greensward. The masonry edging for the crushed-rock entry walkway was established as close as possible to the base of the southwest projection—leaving just enough space to plant vines. The entry steps, the entry sidewalk, and the mounting blocks leading from the carriageway

Figure 2-5 Open, uncluttered, and receptive character of original entry approach for Wright's Oak Park Home. (*Courtesy of The Frank Lloyd Wright Preservation Trust, Oak Park, Illinois.*)

were arranged to accommodate a small existing pine tree, with the lower branches assiduously pruned so as to completely expose the texture of the brick parapet, the cascading plants, and the longitudinal band of coping (Figure 2-5). And the area around the unpaved entry walkway was left free of other plantings to preserve the base plane of the lawn, expose the longitudinal band of the masonry base, emphasize the expansive width of the walkway, and draw attention toward the perennial bed at the base of the parapet to the north of the entry steps. The overall effect of this treatment was open and receptive—in sharp contrast to the straight-line entry walkway, the imposing flight of stairs, the heavy foundation planting, and the exotically flamboyant landscapes of his neighbors.[61]

In choreographing an entry approach, Wright introduced three turns to be negotiated between the public right-of-way and the front threshold. The first turn off Forest Avenue directed movement onto the carriageway, lined with flowering plants along both sides. These plantings—together with the overhead canopy of existing trees and the perennial bed at the base of the parapet to the north of the entry steps—were intended to bring into play all the senses that are experienced when entering any garden: the scent of flowers; the sights and sounds of butterflies, bees, birds, or tree leaves rustling in the breeze; the feel of surfacings underfoot; the sensation of movement through light and shadow or warmth and coolness, et al. Of course, the conclusive aesthetic experience would be dependent upon the time of day and time of year. During the morning hours on the clear days of spring, summer, or fall—when the house is in shadow—the garden foliage and branching backlighted by the sun attracts the eye more than the house. From midafternoon on, the house is highlighted and the dark-brown textured surface of the shingles creates the illusion that the house is recessed more deeply among the trees. At the same time, the flowers and colorful leaves of the garden are in full sun, which accentuates the sense of approaching the house through a garden. Natural climatic events create alternative experiences, whether ice or snow or rain highlights the glistening surfaces. And approaches at night involve the size and angle of the moon as well as the clarity of the sky, with the warm welcoming glow of lights through the windows coming into play, silhouetting features of the garden.

The second turn occurred at the point where the carriageway intersects with the two steps that access the entry walkway. Here, the eye was drawn to the expansive width of the walkway, the sensuous curvature of the battered walls that provide a textured neutral background for the clinging vines cascading down the parapet, and the plantings contained in the perennial bed at ground level. (Originally, the overhead canopy of leaves and branches of trees extending into the then-existing oak forest would have imparted a sense of infinity). It was not until the third turn toward the house that attention was directed eastward and upward to access the wide, low entry steps that provided access to the level of the front veranda, the threshold, and the point of outdoor-indoor transition.[62]

There is some basis for conjecturing that the techniques of circuitry and sequentiality Wright introduced into his choreography of the entry experience were Japanese inspired. In Morse's chapter on Japanese gardens, there are illustrations of staggered pathways and bridges that are common features in both public and private gardens in Japan. Teiji Itoh maintains that the Japanese architect and garden designer chose to use the indirect approach as an aesthetic element within the total design process. Through the introduction of a "right or a left-hand turn between the gate to the building," Ito writes, "the revelation of the building is gradual rather than immediate. . . . Even though the building lot may be quite small, a long approach can be obtained, and thus the impression of a larger area is given."[63] Whatever the inspiration for Wright's entry choreography, his use of turns and steps as deliberate landscape experiences should be recognized as techniques to organize otherwise undifferentiated space. The turns signaled movement from one realm to another and gave momentary pause for reflection upon a new perspective, while the act of ascending first one grouping of steps and then another heightened the anticipation for arriving at the point of destination that ascension in and of itself creates. Wright would use all of these design techniques ever more adroitly and creatively throughout his career to develop the entry experience into an art form that extended beyond sight and movement through space to include a veritable palette of sensory perceptions.

The construction of his Oak Park home not only presented Wright with his first opportunity to live in a house designed to his specifications for his personal use, it also provided a means for him to experience and analyze the consequence of any errors in judgment he had made during his design process. For example, he did not realistically consider that the benefits of views, privacy, and solar exposure made possible through his placement of the house so close to the south boundary were "borrowed" and not under his control. This oversight would cause problems in 1897 when the neighboring house was replaced by two multistory houses, with one positioned so that its north facade almost abutted the Wright carriageway. This placed a bay window of the neighboring house barely 10 feet from Wright's southern facade, blocking out sunshine and views and seriously compromising the area of privacy for both the southwest corner of the verandah and the south-facing bay window in Wright's new dining room, added during an 1895 remodeling and expansion. Nor did he adequately gauge the architectural treatment necessary to counteract the negative impact of a westerly orientation. Although he created the illusion of a massive sheltering roof—by lowering the roofline to accentuate the triangular gable—no shelter was in fact provided to the west-facing windows of the second floor, nor to the window bay and entry bay extension of the living room, directly below. With the ridge of the roof aligned as it was on an east-west axis, the broad overhangs are to the north and south, so the only area on the west inset enough to benefit from the gable is the windowless wall space between the first floor bays. Therefore, during the winter months when Oak Park's prevailing winds originate from the west, all west-facing windows and the front door were totally exposed to sleet and snow, as they were exposed to rain and the harsh penetrating rays of the late-afternoon sun, year-round. Until existing and introduced shade trees matured sufficiently, Wright was forced to resort to artificial means of sun control. Historic photographs depict half-drawn blinds in living room windows and document that a canvas awning was installed to shade the west-facing windows on the second floor of the gable.

Laboratories, of course, are where mistakes can be made and corrected, or where valuable lessons are learned so the same mistakes will not be repeated in the future. That Wright experienced problems during the time he lived in his Oak Park home and recognized there were flaws with his siting, orientation, and outdoor-indoor transition treatment becomes apparent when it is realized that most of the changes he would make in 1911—when remodeling his residence for use by others as rental property—had to do with trying to correct or at least ameliorate these areas of his original design (see

"Oak Park Home and Studio Remodeling," Chapter 4). Moreover, the protection of west-facing windows and points of outdoor-indoor transition were requisite elements of every house with a similar westerly orientation that Wright subsequently designed and built in the Chicago area.[64] Furthermore, an assessment of Wright's domestic architecture from this point forward confirms that, with few exceptions, his structures were purposefully sited to abut existing public streets, secreted behind high privacy walls or in front of auxiliary buildings he installed alongside inward boundaries, or otherwise arranged to ensure he would have complete control of peripheral influences. And windows in primary living areas generally were oriented toward the south to southeast, when special vistas or other mitigating areas of compromise were not a primary consideration. Thus, the valuable acumen Wright gained from identifying and analyzing flaws in his Oak Park home benefited future clients as he continued to address the challenges and concerns of siting, orientation, and outdoor-indoor transition throughout his career.

The World's Columbian Exposition marked the end of Wright's approximate 6-year apprenticeship with Adler and Sullivan. He suddenly found himself without a job in late summer 1893 following an altercation that occurred after Sullivan found Wright in violation of his contract because of his design of a number of houses, apart from the firm. Among the last of these culprit commissions were the side-by-side residences for George Blossom and Warren McArthur. Located just a few blocks inland from Lake Michigan, both were designed in 1892 and rushed to completion to accommodate friends or relatives traveling to Chicago to attend the much-heralded Exposition. The classical countenance of these residential structures validates Wright's orthodox mind-set prior to that historic event.

George Blossom and Warren McArthur— Chicago, Illinois (1892)

The George Blossom House is very extroverted in appearance and expresses the fully academic phase of the revived New England Colonial style, complete with the unified classicism of a formal portico with Ionic columns. Historically painted in light hues, it stands fully exposed on a corner lot at the intersection of Kenwood Avenue and 49th Street in the Hyde Park neighborhood of Chicago. The next-door Warren McArthur House, on

Figure 2-6 Side-by-side houses designed by Wright in 1892 for Chicagoans George Blossom and Warren McArthur. (*Photograph by Charles E. Aguar. © 2002 by Berdeana Aguar.*)

the other hand, is very introverted in appearance and allies with the rusticated dwellings designed by Silsbee during the 1880s. Because of the somber tone of the Roman brick, the subdued tint of the stucco, and the dark hued shingles on its gambrel roof, it merges with the trees, shrubs, and vines on its site and appears appreciably smaller than the Blossom House—even though it actually is larger, with three full stories of living space[65] (Figure 2-6).

As Wright set about the business of designing these two houses at least somewhat in tandem, he sited both at the established setback from Kenwood Avenue, but slightly off center toward the intervening driveway that followed along the Blossom north boundary. This siting left a mere two-and-one-half feet between the south edge of the Blossom House terrace and the public sidewalk that followed along the southern boundary. And there was just enough width for a sidewalk and minimal entry landing between the south wall of the McArthur House and the driveway (Figure 2-7). The benefits of this siting were that it gave Wright complete control over the sight lines into and out from both houses and put as much distance as possible between the structures and those factors over which he had no control—49th Street to the south, Kenwood Avenue to the east, and

neighboring residences to the north and west. With this studied organization of the site, the juxtaposition of rooms and outdoor living space, and the considered arrangement of windows, Wright was able to assure that the issue of privacy was absolute.

It was on the basis of privacy that Wright aligned the first floor levels of both houses at the same elevation—contrary to appearances—and arranged the living rooms on opposing sides: Blossom to the south and McArthur to the north. It was on the basis of privacy also that Wright made the critical decision to limit glazed openings on the first floor level of the south side of the McArthur House to those that access natural light into the entrance stairwell—that is, one side window and the art glass panels in the entry door. Under ordinary circumstances, this decision might have meant that the rooms on the south side—the dining room and parlor, or reception room—would be somewhat dismal and stuffy. And this could have been the case, had Wright not conceived the innovative octagonal-shaped window bays that wrap around the southeast and southwest corners of the house. Because of their conformation, these windows not only provide for cross ventilation and admit considerable natural light year-round—as well as light reflecting off the Blossom House—they also allow sig-

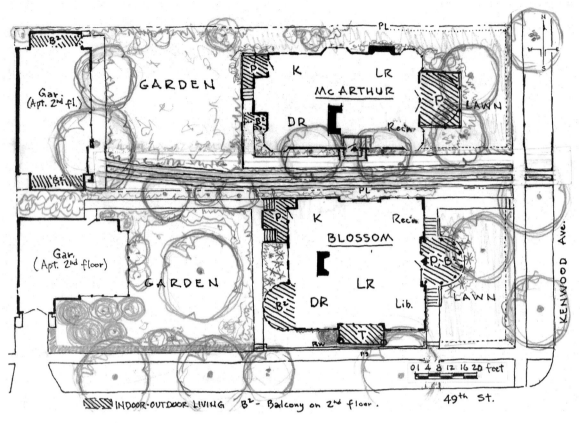

Figure 2-7 Conjectured site plans for George Blossom and Warren McArthur Houses. (*By Charles E. Aguar, based on historic photographs and on-site measurements.* © *2002 by Berdeana Aguar.*)

nificant solar penetration during the winter (Figure 2-8). These corner window bays should be recognized as forerunners to the corner windows Wright later would develop more fully as a means to "break the box."

Wright also developed a combination of illusionistic design treatments to minimize the vertical impact of the Blossom House, as viewed from either street. He introduced a conservatory at the west end of the dining room to replicate and balance the shape and radius of the front portico. He sculpted a two-foot-high earthen terrace around the two public sides of the house to raise the ground level above the plane of the public rights-of-way. And he bounded the length of the south elevation with a masonry retaining wall to emphasize the horizontal banding of the "water table" that girded the foundation[66] (Figure 2-9). He then introduced three steps between the public and entry sidewalks so fewer steps

were needed to access the level of the first floor living space by way of the entry stairs, which he placed on the opposing sides of the portico—thus, eliminating the traditional frontal approach.

Wright's inspiration for forming the earthen terrace in this manner most probably was derived from *The Art of Beautifying Suburban Home Grounds of Small Extent*, the book written by Frank J. Scott that served as the "landscape bible" for American homeowners during the early decades of suburbanization. The Blossom terracing exactly replicates a sketched example Scott described as one of the "less common, and perhaps more elegant forms for ground surfaces next to the street."[67] Moreover, the effect of the terracing adheres to all the central points put forth in the text. The earthen terracing causes the grounds to look much larger than "those which are on a plane, level with the street." The retaining wall falls

Figure 2-8 Natural daylight infiltrates through wraparound corner window bay of McArthur House. (*Courtesy of Ruth Michael. Photograph by Charles E. Aguar. © 2002 by Berdeana Aguar.*)

within the two to three feet above sidewalk level that is as high as Scott advises "on street lines from which it is intended that grounds shall show their beauty." And steps such as Wright installed to gain the rise from both rights-of-way were recommended for a circumstance when the distance from the street is as minimal as the Blossom site. Wright used the earthen terrace as a means to relate each house to the other, as well, by extending it across the front of the Blossom House and tapering it to the lower height necessary to coalesce with the ground surface of the McArthur site. At the same time, however, Wright retained the original ground level to the rear of

both houses and within the public medians along the streets so as to preserve existing trees. All these illusionary exterior treatments involving the manipulation of the antithetical spatial elements of verticality and horizontality would be developed more fully by Wright throughout his career.

Wright demonstrated a marked commitment to environmental concerns with respect to the Blossom House. The semicircular shape of the dining room conservatory allowed Wright to install a bank of windows that worked with the Palladian window on the south wall to bathe the dining room with natural light all day

Figure 2-9 Low retaining wall and masonry water table visually minimize vertical mass of Blossom House. (*Photograph by Charles E. Aguar. © 2002 by Berdeana Aguar.*)

long.[68] Along with the balcony above the portico, the conservatory balcony (since enclosed) provided outdoor living space accessible to the second floor—both of which would have served as sleeping porches in the days before air conditioning. He also inset sections—12.5 feet wide by 1.5 feet deep—at the midpoint of three of the exterior walls, from ground level to the roof. Assuredly, Wright intended that these insets introduce a three-dimensional quality and create shadow lines to visually break up the length and breadth of the structure. But he used them to accomplish a great deal more than that. The inset on the front (east) facade created what could be described as an entry wall of glass, in the form of wide sidelights on either side of an exceptionally broad (3 feet, 9 inches) glazed door. This treatment emphasized the main entry and admitted natural light more deeply into the entry hall. The inset on the north facade more effectively dispersed the natural light that issued through the bank of windows at the second-floor landing. And the inset across the south wall of the living room increased the depth of the side yard just enough to install a modest terrace. This inset also defined the width of the wide sidelights on either side of the French doors that open onto the terrace.

Consider all the environmental benefits Wright introduced by way of the south-facing terrace and French doors. The French doors admit natural light into the living room year-round, and maximize solar penetration during the winter months. They also admit cooling breezes blowing in from nearby Lake Michigan and provide controlled access to and from the terrace. The terrace, in turn, provides a prospect for outlooks and a controlled outdoor living space that is exceptionally private—even though it almost abuts the sidewalk—because the raised earthen terrace and the turned baluster railing physically buffer and visually screen this area from the near presence of the public. The indoor-outdoor relationship Wright here established should be seen as a precursor to the extended walls of glazed doors opening onto the more spatial outdoor living spaces he would later design for his Prairie and Usonian residences.

Wright's manner of unifying all these design considerations within his planning process for the Blossom and McArthur houses verifies that he was working within the more inclusive sphere of environmental design—even at this early stage. He was using natural "light itself in light, to diffuse or reflect, or refract light itself," as he would later describe it in *The Natural House*.[69] And he

was perceiving outdoor space as put forth by landscape designer Norman T. Newton: "Space must be appreciated as a material with which to work—as a vibrant, pliable fullness, not an emptiness. To speak of space as a void is to dismiss one of its chief potentials."[70] It is for these reasons that occupants of both residences continue to enjoy the privacy of their living spaces as Wright originally envisioned they would, even though all the surrounding properties have been fully developed during the century since they were constructed.

When the 26-year-old Wright went about launching his career as an independent architect, he set up an office in the Schiller Building. This was the first of several offices he would maintain at a downtown Chicago location, although he also would continue to work out of his Oak Park Home. Wright's first major commission within this arrangement was the William H. Winslow residence. As such, it is the earliest commission for which rendered presentation drawings were prepared and consequently the first to elucidate Wright's art of designing buildings free from the control or influence of others—a design process that went far beyond the architectural limits of the structure to include his intent with respect to the landscape and the entry approach.

William H. Winslow—River Forest, Illinois (1894)

The front facade and entrance approach for the Winslow House reflect the formal classicism of the Beaux Arts. And yet, the architecture represents the simplicity, elimination, and respect for materials put forth by the Arts and Crafts Movement—as does the landscape treatment. However, Wright's February 1915 letter to landscape designer Wilhelm Miller characterizes it as "the first important work which recognized artistically the influence of the prairie."[71] But it is within the introductory paragraph prepared for the Wasmuth Portfolio that Wright perhaps most clearly spelled out the significant features of the Winslow property: "The setting of the basement outside the main walls of the house to form a preparation for the projecting sill courses [water table]; the division of the exterior wall surfaces into body and frieze, changing the material above the second story sill line, the wide level eaves, with low sloping roofs; the one massive chimney; and the feeling for contrast between plain wall surface and richly decorated and concentrated masses; the use of the window as a decorative feature in itself; the lines of the building extending into the grounds, the low walls and parterre utilized to associate it with its site."[72] The text then states that a "beautiful elm standing near gave the suggestion for the mass of the building."

This is an especially telling introduction as it focuses on the design features and surfacing materials that layer together to create the streetside appearance Wright intended to convey through this residence and others in the portfolio. His mention of the beautiful elm as a relevant factor in his design consideration is particularly significant, since the preservation of existing trees would become synonymous with Wright from this point forward. This appears to be another instance where Wright may have been inspired by the text in Scott's book on the art of beautifying suburban home grounds, wherein he wrote: "Trees already grown are invaluable. To have them, or not to have them, is, to speak in business phrase, to begin with capital or without it."[73] Scott went on to point out that trees are magnets of home beauty, particularly those that have grown up singly, or in groups of a few only. He emphasized that trees such as this "are worth more than a whole catalogue of nursery stuff for immediate and permanent adornment," and concluded: "one fine spreading tree, of almost any native variety, is of inestimable value in home adornment." Certainly, the majestic presence of the mature American Elm (*Ulmus americana*) that originally graced the grounds of the Winslow House was the most character-defining feature of the site. And the approximate 100-foot spread of its canopy influenced virtually every aspect of Wright's design process—much more than the mere mass of the building that Wright implies, both aesthetically and fundamentally.

Aesthetically, the elm ameliorated the negative aspect of the building's westerly orientation and substantially contributed to the ambiance of the entry experience. Its widespread branching provided a foliate canopy of shade during summer as it also cast shadows upon and generally softened the extreme formalism of the facade and approach, year-round (Figure 2-10). That Wright was aware of the negative aspects of the westerly orientation—as well as the ineffectiveness of the roof overhang to provide protection to these areas because of the two-story height of the structure—is clearly represented by his inclusion of drawn shades for the west-facing windows in the perspective drawings, his provision of a protected entry on the north by way of the porte-cochere, and his orienting the broadside of the living room toward the south.

Fundamentally, the elm established the ground level, the situation of the building, and the location of the driveway. It also determined the positioning, depth, and structuring of the low walls that associated the house with the site, as well as the placement and elongated shape of the planting bed in the parterre median feature centered within the wide approach walkway (Figure 2-11). The parterre normally is thought of as an aesthetic feature; it is to be enjoyed as an entry garden while proceeding along either side. But in this instance, it also served the important utilitarian function of providing a means of accessing moisture to the fibrous root system of the elm to compensate for the expanse of impermeable concrete surfacing.[74] Care must be taken

Figure 2-10 An Ernst Wasmuth photograph depicts the "beautiful elm" that was the most character-defining aspect of the William H. Winslow House site (1894) in River Forest, Illinois. (*Out-of-copyright photograph of record from Wasmuth Portfolio, 1911.*)

to avoid grading too closely to any tree, since only a few inches of cut or fill can destroy the life-supplying root system, but the methodology of development is especially critical in the case of the elm species because the roots are so fibrous and shallow.

The precise detail of Wright's parterre design demonstrates his instinctive ability to articulate outdoor space in a manner that impels the observer to look in some direction or sequence of directions. The parterre was accessed by way of two exceptionally wide, low-rise steps leading from the public sidewalk. Three additional low-rise steps accessed the level of the entry terrace, where the front door flanked by two square windows was simplistically framed as a picture, proportionate to the height of the brick facade and the breadth of the terrace and entry approach. By choosing to install a terrace as an entry threshold, Wright effectively created a promontory from which to pause and view the entry garden. By then bounding the walkway on both sides with low masonry retaining walls and defining terminal points with vertical planes and low pedestals for planting urns, Wright explicated the form and size of the parterre and entry walkway so their positive spatial character is clearly revealed when viewed upon arrival or departure, from the terrace or from the street.

Wright's manner of sloping and beveling the earth away from the public sidewalk across the width of the property was important enough to his design process that he continued it alongside the driveway so as to create an earthen terrace, delineated it on both plan and perspective in the Wasmuth Portfolio, and labeled it in German as *abhang* (slope). His inclusion of this inscription provides the first indication that Wright perceived beveled earth sculpting as an architectural treatment to

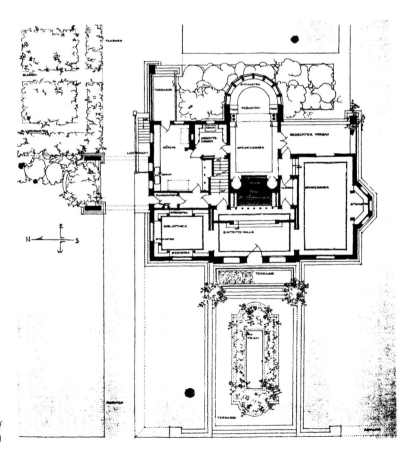

Figure 2-11 Ground-floor plan of the Winslow House delineates the entry parterre as Wright originally perceived it. (*Out-of-copyright plan of record from Wasmuth Portfolio, 1910.*)

relate the structure with the site. In this instance, he used the earth-sculpting technique to repeat and emphasize the sharp-edged alignment of the entry steps and the expansive width and horizontality of the approach walkway. With grass as the surfacing material and no foundation planting to obscure where the house made contact with the ground, the earthen terrace was meant to establish an underlying base plane of green from which the house would appear to rise as demarcated planes of surface materials, each carefully proportioned for horizontal effect: the masonry plane of the water table, splayed out at its base so as to firmly attach the structure to the ground; the dominant plane of Roman brick; the striation of the coping; the ancillary plane of ornamental terra-cotta tile; the shadow line created by the broad overhanging eaves; the facia of the eave itself; the low hip roof; and the all-encompassing tree canopy over all.

To visually extend this north-south horizontal imagery even more, Wright proposed to counterbalance the vertical mass of the structure by appending a porte-cochere off the library on the north and a roofed arcade and pavilion off the dining room porch on the south. He also emphasized the appendage of the window bay off the south side of the living room by making it appear to

extend all the way to the ground. The full extent of Wright's intent as to horizontal counterbalancing never was realized, however, as the proposed roofed arcade and pavilion were never executed.

With the rear elevation, Wright intended that the cultivated landscape appear more naturalistic, in keeping with the softened informality of the east facade. The terrace, the roofed porch, and the 200-degree semicircular conservatory extension off the dining room—complete with a continuous cushioned seat under the panoramic expanse of electroglazed windows—provide contained places to relax or dine overlooking the garden. Slit windows in the angled walls of the second- and third-story levels of the octagonal stairwell also provide fleeting views into the rear yard from first one angle and then another to reinforce an indoor-outdoor relationship as the stairs are ascended or descended. These treatments attest to Wright's experimental creativity in shaping outdoor living space and encouraging interaction with the out-of-doors at this nascent point in his career.

To enhance the outward views from the stairway, the dining room, and outdoor living spaces, Wright paid particular attention to the rear stable. With its courtyards, print shop, and apartment above, it is one of the most beautiful accessory buildings ever designed by

Figure 2-12 An Ernst Wasmuth perspective of the Winslow Stable depicts existing trees that framed architecture. (*Out-of-copyright drawing from Wasmuth Portfolio, 1910.*)

Wright. Its layered hip roofs and wide-spreading eaves closely identify with the Prairie Houses still to come. And Wright gave equal consideration to the environmental design aspects of the stable, as supported by the way he placed the Sullivanesque arched doorway on axis with the porte-cochere and sited the structure so that two large trees would frame his architecture. Another tree was allowed to grow through the overhanging eaves of the multilayered roof, to visually anchor the building to its forested site (Figure 2-12).

The significance of the precedent-setting exterior design treatments Wright introduced with the Winslow House should not be shrugged off or regarded indulgently. Within the ornate Victorian orthodoxy of the 1890s, Wright's considered sculpting of the earthen terrace, his elimination of foundation plantings, his provision of architectonic containment for introduced plantings, his delineation of these plantings as perennials, and his consideration and *inclusion* of existing trees within his design process for both house and stable showed remarkable originality, environmental awareness, and sensitivity for the times.

.   .   .

Historic photographs of the Winslow House dramatically support how changes made to Wright's carefully crafted site environment alter the streetside appearance of his architecture. The most conspicuous change occurred when the specimen tree that inspired so many aspects of Wright's environmental design fell victim to Dutch Elm Disease during the 1950s, and was never replaced. Evergreen plantings introduced over the years within the parterre and around the foundation also obscure the clean-cut imagery of Wright's design intent (Figure 2-13). There have been architectural alterations and intrusions, as well. During the building boom following World War II, a house was built in the area where the arcade would have stood. In 1962, the roofed porch south of the dining room was enlarged and enclosed with aluminum-framed sliding glass doors. And the beautiful lines of the stable were compromised when this structure was adapted to accommodate the automobile. Specifically, the graceful arched doorway was replaced with a square door; a second, semidetached

Figure 2-13 A 1992 photograph of the Winslow House reflects the negative effect of deviating from Wright's design intent. (*Photograph by Charles E. Aguar. © 2002 by Berdeana Aguar.*)

garage was added to the northwest corner; and the uncommon custom brickwork and ironwork of the carriage yard were removed and replaced by an assortment of shrubs common to the typical suburban accessory building.

The design approach Wright developed for the Winslow House formed the basis for his experimental expressions of environmental design well into the next decade. Nowhere is this more apparent than with his antithetical design for the Chauncey L. Williams House, which backs up to and rose simultaneously with the Winslow House, according to Manson, with Wright supervising their construction as one job.[75]

Chauncey L. Williams—River Forest, Illinois (1895)

Wright sited the Williams House in conformance with existing houses to face east toward Edgewood Place. As this is a relatively short loop street, rather than a through street, he had to envision the presence of the house as it would be viewed from the most likely approach route— by way of Lake Street, to the south. He also had to make allowances for the verticality of an existing three-story period house to the immediate north of the site. These considerations provided the rationale for Wright's individualistic manner of sculpting and arranging earthen terracing at dissimilar ground levels on either side of the entry walkway—at grade level to the north and some two feet higher to the east and south. The sides of the terracing were beveled inward and visibly mitered in accordance with Wright's delineation of the ground sec-

tion of the front elevation—the only original drawing existing in the archives—and the entry walkway essentially functioned as a demarcator to visually separate the disparate levels (Figures 2-14 a–b).

Had Wright not maintained the integrity of the grade level to the north, the house would have appeared subservient to the adjacent three-story structure when viewed from Edgewood Place. And had he not sculpted, arranged, and characterized the earthen terrace as he did, the house would not have appeared to "grow" from the site. Instead, it would have appeared "set up box-wise on edge to the utter humiliation of every natural thing in sight," as he described other houses of that era during a lecture he presented the very next year before the University Guild of Evanston, Illinois.[76] The shadows, depth, and sharp periphery edging created through Wright's incisive sculpturing brought the terrace into relief to dramatize its elevation over the natural grade. The mounds of boulders set into the brickwork around the visible baseline and on either side of the entry doorway intensified this treatment. And the painstakingly flared arrangement of the boulders visually affixed the house to the site, as did the boulders along the base of the north facade and those overscoring the earthen terracing. The pierced-brick privacy wall installed to the height of the brick dado and extending westward from the southwest corner of the house emphasized the horizontal line and provided strong counterbalance for the low brick wall that circumscribed the semicircular entry terrace on the east.

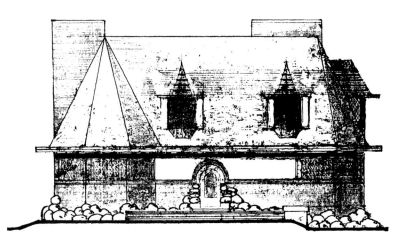

Figure 2-14 a Front elevation of the Chauncey L. Williams House in River Forest, Illinois, supports the importance that Wright gave to the beveled angle of the earthen terrace. (*By Charles E. Aguar, based on historic photographs and the only surviving original drawing of the house. © 2002 by The Frank Lloyd Wright Foundation, Scottsdale, Arizona. As delineated, © 2002 by Berdeana Aguar.*)

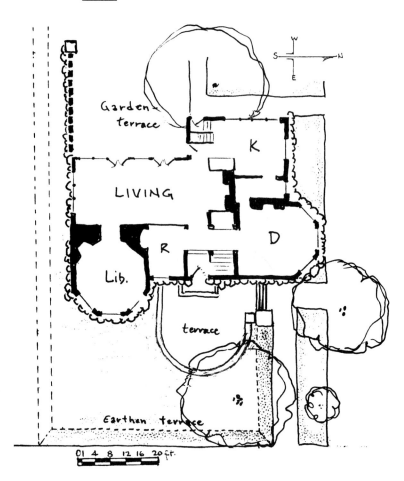

Figure 2-14 b Conjectured site layout of the Williams residence. (*By Charles E. Aguar. Based on historic photographs and floor plan S.O33 in The Frank Lloyd Wright Companion by W. A. Storrer, © 1993. Original drawing © 2002 by The Frank Lloyd Wright Foundation, Scottsdale, Arizona. As deliniated, © 2002 by Berdeana Aguar.*)

The installation of the earthen terrace also provided Wright with the means to create a much more meaningful entry experience than would have been possible without it. The approach involves three sets of steps and four turns to be negotiated from grade to first-floor level (some four feet above the public sidewalk) before passing though the reception hall doorway into the living room to face the expanse of glazed openings along the length of the west wall that frame the view onto the garden terrace at the rear of the house. There is direct access from the living room onto the terrace through two pairs of French doors to create a strong interrelationship between the indoor and outdoor living spaces. This arrangement of the rear living room opening onto a garden terrace was an extremely visionary concept that Wright *originated* with the Williams House. Not only was this indoor-outdoor

connectedness unique for the times; it should be seen as a precursor to Wright's Usonian house organization some four decades hence. Even more impressive is the fact that this arrangement antedates by more than a half-century the so-called "innovative" indoor-outdoor layouts generally credited to California architects and landscape architects of the 1950s.

Wright's overall environmental design for the Williams House should be recognized for the comprehensiveness of his thought processes with respect to streetside appearance, proportional relationship to extant structures, entry experience, horizontal illusionism, outdoor living accessibility, and privatization. As with the Winslow House, however, changes made to the Williams

Figure 2-15 Appearance of the Williams House after the earthen terrace was leveled and plantings were allowed to obscure Wright's design intent. (*1993 photograph by Charles E. Aguar. © 2002 by Berdeana Aguar.*)

House architecture and site environment have altered the streetside appearance and compromised the indoor-outdoor interrelationship of Wright's intent—through the addition of an enclosed sunporch across the west facade of the living room, the introduction of foundation plantings, a row of evergreens along the property line, and the grading away of the incisive earthen terrace (Figure 2-15).

Nathan G. Moore—Oak Park, Illinois (1895, rebuilt 1923); Pergola & Remodeling (1905–1906)

In 1894, Nathan G. Moore was residing in a frame house situated at the southwest corner of Forest Avenue and Superior Street (then called Wabun), across the street and some 300 feet to the south of the Wright family residence. At that time, Moore owned the original 50-foot lot upon which his house was built and one and one-half lots to the immediate south. This expanded property extended to within a few feet of the Victorian House (1883) occupied by Frank S. Gray, who owned half of the intervening lot and an additional lot.[77]

Moore originally asked Wright to prepare plans that would allow him to remodel and expand his existing home in the style of the Tudor English architecture then coming into vogue in suburban communities like Oak Park. Even after he decided to forgo the remodeling

option, move his existing home to an empty lot to the west, and proceed with plans for a new house, he cautioned Wright not to deviate from this form. Wright pointed out, however, that this was the first time "an English half-timbered house ever saw a porch. The porch was becoming to the house."[78] Although Wright did not define his use of the word "becoming," it would seem he was describing the appropriateness of the porch within the context of his overall site planning, rather than the appearance of the porch itself. Because it was the uniqueness of Wright's siting and environmental design—including the porch as outdoor living space overlooking the sunken garden—that set the Moore House apart from other period houses in the area (Figure 2-16).

Wright proposed to forgo siting Moore's new house conventionally, centered to face Forest Avenue. He instead situated it lengthwise on the original corner lot so that the north (rear) facade abutted the public right-of-way along the as-yet unpaved side street (Figure 2-17). The east (side) facade was set back from Forest Avenue compatibly with existing houses, and the south (front) facade faced the expanse of open space preserved by way of his unique zero-lot-line siting methodology. (It should be noted this was two decades before American zoning ordinances began to specify that domestic buildings had to have a minimum setback from the public street, and eight decades before zero-lot-line

Figure 2-16 South facade of the
Nathan G. Moore House in Oak
Park, Illinois, as designed by Wright
in 1895 with sunken gardens.
(*Courtesy of the Frank Lloyd Wright
Archives, Scottsdale, Arizona.*)

siting was encouraged as a means to obtain maximum useable space in an innovative way.)

Two benefits of this siting were that it left ample room to expand garden space to the west and allowed Wright to position the utility spaces, service-family entry, stairway circulation space, and living room fireplace wall nearest the most publicly compromised boundary, to the north. Other obvious benefits were that it maximized the distance between the south facade and the Gray House; created a streetside impression of spacious intervening grounds; and allowed Wright to orient the social living spaces toward the south—both inside and outside. But another important benefit has been overlooked to this point—this arrangement oriented the main entrance toward the open space and provided the means to develop an entry experience that would not have been possible, had the Moore House been sited conventionally.

Wright began by circumscribing the open space along the Forest Avenue right-of-way with an ornamental wall-fence designed to harmonize with the architecture and provide an elegant finish to the street in the manner suggested by Scott for an in-town property—that is, the protective enclosure was a "work of art," "comparatively transparent," and did not "unnecessarily conceal the beauty it encloses."[79] Here again, Wright fac-

tored the preservation of existing trees into his design consideration by curving an inset into the wall-fence to accommodate the trunk of a sizable tree (Figure 2-18). He then installed an "intersecting approach route" in the form of an entry sidewalk that extended from Forest Avenue to the alley, but was set apart from the house, and a crosswalk leading from this entry sidewalk to the broad steps that access the porch and the main entry threshold. Within the open spaces set apart and defined by these intersecting walkways, he sculpted out and embanked the earth to form sunken gardens. The crosswalk essentially functioned as a garden bridge from which all the outdoor living spaces were directly accessible, by way of the sets of steps leading up onto the porch and down into the sunken gardens. Thus, the overpowering event of the entry experience was the contemplation of the sunken gardens from the prospect of the walkways—whether people entered the property by way of the alleyway or the main gate opening off Forest Avenue. This combination of a spacious porch overlooking sunken gardens and expansive grounds under the canopy of several shade trees that graced the yard at this point in time provided exceptional outdoor living space that was easily accessible and remarkably private—considering the limited acreage, the mass of the structure, and the inherently exposed character of a corner lot.

Figure 2-17   The north facade of the Moore House encroaches on the public right-of-way along Superior Street. (*Photograph by Charles E. Aguar. © 2002 by Berdeana Aguar.*)

.   .   .

The Moore property's outdoor living space was substantially aggrandized a decade later, in 1905, when Moore acquired the Gray property and an additional lot to the immediate south—doubling his frontage on Forest Avenue—and commissioned Wright to design a pergola (Figure 2-19). This commission historically has been mentioned only in passing or in conjunction with the remodeling of the Gray House that got underway the following year—generally described as a wedding gift for the Moores' daughter Mary and son-in-law Edward R. Hills. However, Wright initially redesigned the Gray House at

the time the original agreement to purchase was made in 1900, some six years before the remodeling took place. Moreover, the wedding did not come about until two years after the land purchase, in 1908, and the couple did not occupy the house until 1911 or 1912.[80] This chronology of events suggests that Moore's acquisition and development of the Gray real estate may have had more to do with his long-range intent to eventually put together and control at least four lots. This reasoning is strengthened when combined with the fact that Moore's freestanding coach house with living quarters above was built across the alley from the fourth lot while still registered under Gray's name, many years prior to Moore's acquisition of the fifth lot and the 1906 remodeling.

Figure 2-18   The Moore House's ornamental wall-fence was arced to accommodate the trunk of an existing tree (since removed). (*Photograph by Charles E. Aguar. © 2002 by Berdeana Aguar.*)

Figure 2-19 The Frank S. Gray House in Oak Park, Illinois, as it appeared when Nathan G. Moore acquired it in 1906. (*Courtesy of Northwest Architect, Volume XVI, 1952.*)

Wright's remodeling plans proposed to rotate the Gray House ninety degrees so that the original south facade faced east toward Forest Avenue—shifting it to a new foundation that lay closer to the south boundary. The rationale behind this reorientation unquestionably was environmentally motivated. Not only did it extend the north-south length of the structure and allow Wright to develop a stronger horizontal line of the Prairie House imagery as viewed from Forest Avenue, it maximized the open space available for development as private outdoor living space between the west facade and the alleyway, enhanced the interrelationship between the two structures, and oriented the covered veranda additions to overlook the intervening space—as it had been developed and maintained since 1895 (Figure 2-20). These remodeling plans were based upon Moore's acquiring the property owned by Gray at that time, in 1900. It presumably was not until 1905, when the opportunity arose for Moore to acquire the additional lot to the south of

Gray, that the decision was made to move the main body of the remodeled structure onto that property. It was this chain of events that motivated the need to develop plans for the expanded intervening landscape and inspired the design of a landscape composition that was decidedly more comprehensive than the "pergola" designation in the job listings implies.

Included within the landscape composition was a sizable new conservatory appended to the west end of the Moore's first-floor living space, replacing the one or more greenhouses that had previously occupied this area. The conservatory is identified on the construction drawings as the north terminus for the lattice-roofed pergola that was to serve as the interrelating medium to reach an elaborate open-air pavilion to be built over a concrete base at the south terminus (Figure 2-21). The east side of the pergola opens onto the lawn, but the west side is latticed and covered with grape vines to screen from view the vegetable garden that was to fill

Figure 2-20   A 1992 photograph shows the relationship between the Edward R. Hills (formerly Frank S. Gray) and Nathan G. Moore houses, after the 1906 remodeling of the Gray House. (*Photograph by Charles E. Aguar. © 2002 by Berdeana Aguar.*)

the intervening space along the alleyway. The plans also depict a less elaborate 20-foot-long arbor with latticed roof and sides extending from the main pergola through the vegetable garden to the point of access at the alleyway, where two additional brick piers were to be erected on either side of a latticework gate. Thus, the pergola was specifically designed as an ambient shaded passageway through which to stroll from one house to the other, as background for the view from Forest Avenue, or as background for the view from the elevated prospect of the primary living spaces of the Huertley House, directly across the street—which Wright had mindfully sited to overlook the Moore open space three years earlier (see Arthur Huertly, 1902). The pergola also functioned as an elegant finish for the tree-shaded green plane of the naturalistically maintained open space, giving the entire composition the appearance of a spacious parklike grounds, with the three diverse Wright-designed structures—the Moore House, the Hills House, and the coach house—linked into an integrated whole.

. . .

Although the Moore pergola historically has been listed as an unbuilt project, photographs (c. 1906) within an article in a 1952 issue of *Northwest Architect* written by architect William G. Purcell—a former Oak Park resident and nephew of Frank S. Gray—clearly show that a latticework architectural garden feature was constructed (Figure 2-22).[81] These photographs do not support that the pavilion served as the southern terminus for the pergola, however. The pergola instead appears to continue on to the privatized outdoor living space at the rear of the rotated remodeled structure. The arbor leading to the alley also may not have been erected, according to the Moore grandsons: Nathan Grier Hills (born in 1915) and Sidney Oscar Hills (born in 1917).[82] Neither brother remembers a pavilion or a rear arbor, but both vividly recall picking grapes and using the pergola as the connecting link between their house and the home of their grandparents, which they entered by way of the conser-

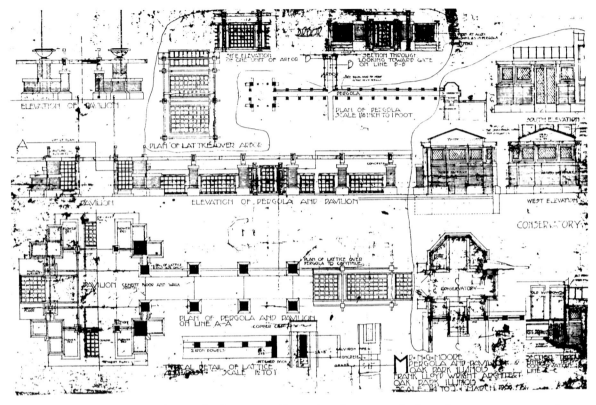

Figure 2-21   1904 construction drawings for the Moore-Hills pergola and intervening landscape between structures. (© 2002 by The Frank Lloyd Wright Foundation, Scottsdale, Arizona.)

vatory. They also recall this garden feature being in place for the party celebrating their grandparents' 50th wedding anniversary in 1931. Moreover, research conducted by Carla Lind confirms that a section of the pergola nearest the southwest corner of the grounds remained in place until the mid-1960s.[83]

Drastic changes were made to Wright's landscape composition following a disastrous fire in the Moore House during December 1922. Although Wright was called upon to redesign and remodel the structure at that time, he was preoccupied in California and undoubtedly was not closely involved with the supervisory aspects of the reconstruction. Historic photographs support that shade trees destroyed by the fire never were replaced; the sunken gardens were filled with earth; a circular concrete fish pond was installed in the open space between the crosswalk and the alley; and evergreen shrubbery was installed as a hedge along the inside of the concrete and iron fence-wall.[84] All of these landscape treatments were contrary to Wright's original design intent. The filling in of the sunken gardens eradicated the overpowering event of the entry experience. The circular pond was out of keeping with the modular geometry of the overall landscape composition. And the hedge compromised the carefully perceived lines of sight from the Forest Avenue right-of-way. Although the pond and hedge have since been removed and the wall-fence has been extended past the Hills House, no other effort has been made to interrelate the two disparate structures. Thus, the intervening landscape between the residences no longer represents Wright's inspired creative impulse of the early 1900s (Figure 2-23).

Figure 2-22 Southern extremity of pavilion at privacy wall for Hills' sequestered garden, circa 1906. (*Courtesy of Northwest Architect, Volume XVI, 1952.*)

Figure 2-23 South facade of the Moore House after the sunken gardens were filled in and a fire destroyed shade trees. (*Photograph by Charles E. Aguar. © 2002 by Berdeana Aguar.*)

Wolf Lake Amusement Park Project— Chicago, Illinois (1895)

The marshland character of the property Edward C. Waller proposed to develop as Wolf Lake Amusement Park was similar to the sites selected for the company town of Pullman and the World's Columbian Exposition. It was located 12 miles south of Chicago on the Illinois-Indiana state boundary line. The major thoroughfare of

Indiana Avenue provided a direct connection to downtown Chicago, and two existing rail lines bisected the site. Although the property did not front upon Lake Michigan, it was just a short distance inland. There were two lakes immediately adjacent: Hyde Lake to the west and Wolf Lake to the east (Figure 2-24).

In the preliminary scheme Wright drafted directly onto the original plot plan, he established his geometry

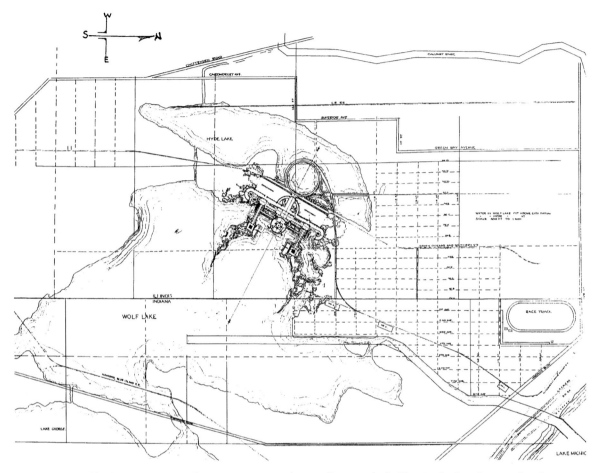

Figure 2-24 Wolf Lake Amusement Park Project (1895) in Chicago, Illinois, as drafted by Wright directly onto plot plan. (© 2002 by The Frank Lloyd Wright Foundation, Scottsdale, Arizona.)

on a 60-degree angle, with the main axis running northwest to southeast and the secondary axis running northeast to southwest. This layout oriented the main facade so that summer breezes from the southwest and prevailing breezes from the west would pass over the two water bodies and provide natural air conditioning to the complex. No further attempt was made to respond to the natural wetland surroundings, however. To the contrary, the scheme corroborates that Wright proceeded to dominate the landscape in much the same way Olmsted did for the grounds of the Exposition, as he molded and restructured the reclaimed land into artificial islands and beaches replete with any fabrications necessary to

accommodate the fanciful activities and water sports that he and Waller envisioned.

That the intent was to create a seasonal world's-fairlike environment—a "Disneyland" of its day with many of the popular amenities that visitors had enjoyed during the six months of the Chicago Exposition—is supported by Wright's text narrative in the 1910 Wasmuth portfolio: "Designed to utilize, by means of dredging, a tract of swamp land bordering on a shallow lake in the vicinity of Chicago, as an amusement resort. The concessions usual to such a project are here screened in a back field by means of uniform entrances constructed on a spacious circular mall. At the center of the arrangement is

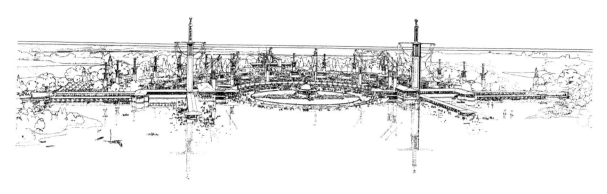

Figure 2-25   Perspective drawing of Wolf Lake Amusement Park Project. (*Out-of-copyright drawing from Wasmuth Portfolio, 1910.*)

the band stand, with a circular track and field for races and fetes. A covered pergola extends around one side, with seats for onlookers. Back of this a water-court connects the inner lagoon with the lake, so that boats from the cluster may find their way to the lake. Bridges, carrying sale booths, cross this water court, connecting the central field with the mall" (Figure 2-25).[85]

An important design element missing from this text—but certainly relevant and noteworthy to anyone analyzing Wright's drawings for Wolf Lake—is the consequence of the landscape treatment with respect to the overall ambiance of the final presentation scheme. Wright here attempted to balance the hardscape necessary to accommodate throngs of people with softscape, by creating a park-like atmosphere through the introduction of plantings.[86] While he did not propose anything as august as the grand scheme accomplished by Olmsted at the Exposition, he did depict an expanse of grass in the center island, planting beds as foreground to the domed music pavilion, formal gardens between the mall and the wide inland canal, and a semicircular garden on the lake side of the sports track encircling the island. He also suggested restoration of the adjoining wetlands as a forest preserve. These man-made but natural-appearing surroundings would have created a proportionate balance and contrast for the formal classicism of the layout and architecture.

The Wolf Lake Project also provided Wright with his first opportunity to expand his sphere of influence so as to encompass areas of environmental, public, and social concern. Although he did not go into detail, he did touch upon some of the planning elements that must be addressed in addition to recreation when designing a

project with public connotations—land use, transportation, and circulation. He proposed building an expansive circular causeway far out into Hyde Lake at the rear of the complex by tying onto one of the two existing rail lines and then routing the commuter trains over a spur line onto the causeway. The centerline of the circle was on axis with the grand promenade, and the entry experience he crafted directed patterns of movement through one or the other of the rather narrow parallel passageways so that, when the exposed area of the mall was reached, the entire palette of senses would be assaulted with colorful sights, the sound of music, and the upward and outward spatial experience of the out-of-doors. The ultimate consciousness would be the panoramic view of the broad expanse of water.

Wright further proposed that a canal be dug between Lake Michigan and Wolf Lake for routing excursion boats directly to the complex—a scheme that would have required dredging Wolf Lake (which he mentioned) and the building of several bridges to elevate the existing rail lines and roads to accommodate the big-lake form of transport (which he did *not* mention). Nor did he propose any bridges on his plan. As the lake steamers shown on the original presentation drawing were eliminated from the Wasmuth perspective—which limits water craft to sailboats, rowboats, and canoes—perhaps by this date, some 15 years later, Wright realized the impracticality of excursion boats on such a small inland lake.

Another circumstance not addressed by Wright in the dozens of conceptual sketches he prepared was that the development of this property that he described as "a tract of swamp land" (and that today would be classified as "wetlands") would have been first and foremost a project in land reclamation. Thus, had the Wolf Lake Project evolved past the preliminary presentation drawings, much more than design and layout would have been involved— not only to reclaim the land but to accommodate the density of population required to make the facility in any way profitable. As Wright's planning acumen was embryonic at this point in time, he did not begin to address the magnitude of public services and infrastructure that would

have been mandated. These mandates would equate with those needed for a medium-size city—including accessing sources for gas, water, electricity, telephones; the handling of fire and policing, security, first aid, sewage disposal, solid waste disposal; and the management of circulation for masses of people, and their transport to and from the site on a daily basis. In addition to all of these requisites, this "city" would have operated on a part-time and sea-

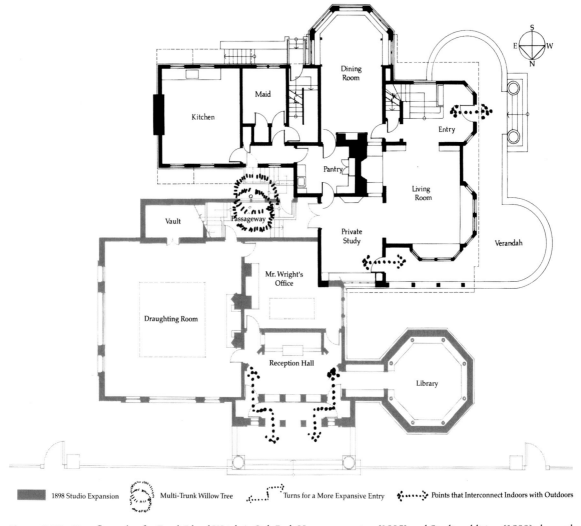

Figure 2-26 First-floor plan for Frank Lloyd Wright's Oak Park Home expansion (1895) and Studio addition (1899) shows the location of a multitrunk Willow tree in the passageway between the House and Studio, as well as turns that Wright purposely introduced to facilitate a more expansive entry experience. (*By Charles E. Aguar, based on personal analysis and ground-plan of record. © 2002 by The Frank Lloyd Wright Preservation Trust, Oak Park, Illinois. As delineated, © 2002 by Berdeana Aguar.*)

sonal basis, needing to be emptied at night and cleaned up for crowds arriving the next day; then closed down for many months, only to be revitalized for another season. To address these many technological details, Wright would have needed a large interdisciplinary staff, and he would have functioned more as master planner, much as Burnham did with the Exposition.

The site proposed for Wolf Lake Project remains undeveloped and much of the marginal land surrounding the property has been protected as parks, forest preserve, or conservation areas. Had 1895 been the age of feasibility studies and environmental impact statements, the concept of an amusement park of this magnitude to be developed on this particular piece of property never would have proceeded to even the preliminary design stage.

Oak Park Studio Opens

By 1897, Wright determined that his commissions had stabilized enough for him to afford to build a sizable, semidetached studio addition onto that portion of the site in Oak Park that extended north toward Chicago Avenue (Figure 2-26). Although The Studio architecture was basically classical in design, it was at the same time quite avant-garde, particularly in the conspicuousness of the apselike shape of the octagonal library and the churchlike entrance where the setback from the public sidewalk is virtually nonexistent. Even so, Wright managed to create a circuitous entry for his clientele by incorporating the public parkway into his design of an entry or doorway garden. A double-entry walk installed between the public sidewalk and roadway circumvented a large existing shade tree. Additional shade trees were planted in the same space. And two carriage mounting blocks were situated directly upon the curb. Since the entry experience originated at the mounting blocks, proceeded across the public sidewalk to access the three expansive steps that boldly encroached onto the sidewalk to provide access onto a five-foot-wide verandah and involved twists and turns to traverse the narrow sheltered loggia to the point of outdoor-indoor transition, the illusion was that The Studio boundary originated at the curb of Chicago Avenue.

In the process of fashioning an enclosed passageway between The Studio and the dining room, the verandah at the rear of the house was eliminated. However, Wright was able to save a multitrunk willow tree close to the north wall of the house by devising a flexible collar that allowed the tree to grow and sway in the wind without undue damage to the house struc-

ture. "The great, sprawling old tree gave us a grateful coolness in the studio in summer," Wright observed: "I liked the golden green drooping above."[87] From the street, the willow appeared to grow right out of the center of the house—an illusion that added to Wright's fame as an architect who would go to any lengths to save a tree.

By choosing to establish a primary work place very visibly in his home community, Wright was making himself highly accessible to the upper-scale clientele he hoped to attract from Oak Park, River Forest, and other nearby suburbs. This was another extremely avant-garde concept for the times, when the breadwinner normally commuted to the downtown Loop where all matters relating to business were conducted. In the 1898 brochure Wright prepared to announce the completion of The Studio, he stressed his willingness to accommodate clientele by arranging appointments in Oak Park appropriate for commuters (8:00 A.M. to 11:00 A.M. and 7:00 P.M. to 9:00 P.M.). He even offered to make himself or staff members available for consultation at a separate downtown location from 12:00 noon to 2:00 P.M., where "a record of work, together with plans and details in duplicate will be kept on file . . . accessible to clients and contractors."[88] In the text of the brochure, Wright reasoned as follows: "The practice of architecture . . . has fine art as well as commercial elements. These should be combined to their mutual betterment, not to their detriment. . . . To develop in better sense, this fine art side . . . the architect should place himself in an environment that conspires to develop the best there is in him. The first requisite is a place fitted and adapted to the work to be performed and set outside distractions of the busy city. The worker is enabled on this basis to secure the quiet concentration of effort essential to the full success of a building project—the intrinsic value of which is measured by the quality of that effort."[89] It was with this announcement, then, that Wright for the first time professionally alluded to his thinking with regard to urban decentralization—a rationale he would more fully develop during the 1930s within his conceptualization of Broadacre City.

As Wright went about the process of opening The Studio, he gathered around himself a special group of talented people to address all the technical and auxiliary aspects of his designs. The support Wright was provided through this capable staff over the next 11 years would give him the freedom to experiment with creative new ideas and to hone his concepts for an environmentally inspired organic architecture as he approached architectural maturity during the Oak Park Studio years.

3 | The Oak Park Studio Years: 1897–1909

Frank Lloyd Wright never maintained a one-man office, with the exception of the period when he worked at home under the name of Adler and Sullivan, or independently—designing what he always referred to as his "bootleg" houses. Particularly in his fledgling professional years, he like others before and since embraced societal interaction with respected colleagues and enjoyed the stimulation of their discourse on subjects of mutual interest as he continued to explore and absorb alternatives for developing environmentally sensitive architectural design. During the Oak Park studio years, Wright maintained a staff of six, on the average, to draft his designs. Twelve to 18 young Wright disciples came and went. Within this group, however, there were three degreed architects with professional experience in their own right: Walter Burley Griffin, Marion Mahony, and Harry Robinson. Wright also worked in consort with other design professionals and cultivated the expertise and talents of respected artists and artisans, such as interior designer George Neiddecken, glassmaker Orlando Giannini, and sculptors Richard Bock, Albert Louis Van den Berghen, and Alfonso Iannelli.

There is limited record of The Studio work ethic methodology except in the area of drafting presentation drawings, which other authors have addressed at some length. However, in an essay on his personal experience as a member of the staff, Barry Byrne noted: "There was stimulation, approval, and supplementing accord, but not what one could call close direction."[90] He also observed that within the hierarchy of The Studio during the early years, Griffin and Mahony were the two staff members closest to Wright: "Mahony seems to have been particularly close personally to Wright; Griffin appears to have been the man Wright discussed things with to get them clear in his own mind."[91]

Mahony was the only staff member to work with Wright throughout the entire period The Studio was in existence. According to Mahony biographer Janice Pregliasco, their association began in 1895 while both still were working out of the loft in Steinway Hall and she served "as 'superintendent' of a nonexistent drafting force."[92] Pregliasco also points out that Mahony was the second female to be awarded a bachelor of architecture degree from MIT and the first female architect to be licensed in Illinois. Nonetheless, she is rarely alluded to as a contemporary of Wright or other Prairie School architects. Her most recognized contribution to Wright's work habitually is limited to her distinctive presentation drawings.

Byrne referred to Griffin as "the office manager," but he also characterized Wright's relationship with him as unusual because he "allowed" Griffin to continue a separate private practice as an architect.[93] Brooks reaffirmed this professional recognition when he noted that Wright and Griffin actually were in competition with each other during the winter of 1901–1902 with respect to the architectural commission for William H. Emery in Elmhurst, Illinois—an assignment that ultimately was awarded to Griffin.[94] Kruty, on the other hand, described Griffin's responsibilities as going far beyond the mundane day-to-day operations of the office: "Griffin . . . wrote specifications, made regular checks on the progress of projects under construction, and attempted to mollify clients and contractors who had been slighted in some way or another by Mr. Wright. . . . Thoroughly trained, both academically and through practice, and with a personality that seemed to bring out the best in people, he lent stability to the boiling energy at the studio."[95] And Vernon reasoned: "Given Griffin's education in landscape design and his knowledge of horticulture, it is improbable that anyone else in Wright's employ at the time would have been given the responsibility for executing the highly detailed landscape designs associated with Wright's work of the period. Upon receipt of a new commission, it is most likely that Wright would have originated the design of the structure and site organization, and Griffin subsequently would have prepared any detailed landscape and planting designs."[96]

In actuality, detailed designs for landscape and plantings were an exception among the plans that issued from The Studio, and these few landscapes of substance are all the more noteworthy for their *un*commonness. A search of Wright's residential designs through 1899 elicits no site plans or "ground plans," as Wright subsequently labeled them. The familiar ground plans displayed in the Wasmuth Portfolio for William H. Winslow, Chauncey L. Williams, Nathan G. Moore, The Studio, and the Joseph Husser villa (demolished) were modified and embellished with cosmetic images of plantings and gardens in afterthought, for publication.[97] A chronicling of plans prepared after 1899, on the other hand, obviates a pattern that supports the reasoning that

Wright's site work of the period did not begin to present a plasticity of form comparable to his architecture before the turn of the century, which coincides with when he first established a working relationship with Griffin through their association at Steinway Hall. There is then a marked difference in the landscape character of Wright's site work after mid-to-late 1905, which coincides with when Griffin left The Studio. This is not to say the conceptual images for the Prairie House environments of 1900 to 1905 did not originate with Wright. The considerable reliance upon the architectonic subdivision of the landscapes and the strong geometrization of the indoor-outdoor relationships were unquestionably Wright-inspired. Griffin, left to his own initiative, would have relied more upon the natural dictates of the site. Further, as sculptor Richard W. Bock asserted, "Wright . . . was always the dominant character wherever [sic] he was. . . . Nothing could go on unless Frank had his finger in the pie."[98] Nevertheless, a tracing of the actual progression of events makes it reasonable to postulate that it was Griffin's support of Wright's rhetorical vision, together with his empathetic interpretation and execution of Wright's *intent* with respect to the site environment, that imparted the organic third dimension to Wright's Prairie House designs and set his built architecture apart as unique—not only from the ornate architecture of the era, but from those designed by his contemporaries.

ENVIRONMENTAL DESIGNS, 1900–1909

It was in 1900 during an address before The Fellowship Club, a ladies' civic organization in Oak Park, that Wright for the first time made public statements expressing his distaste for the visually chaotic environments associated with the Victorian Age:

> Now, English landscape architecture is saddled with the most glaring evidence of this degeneracy—for it is just that. Magnificent yew and splendid box trees trimmed into animal shapes, barrels with roosters crowing on their tops, a railroad train running along the top of a hedge, are some of the most absurd, and this element is manifest in instances less and less striking until we can scarcely say where the genuine artist leaves off and his decay begins. . . . Now what is this but the same decay of the normal sense, the breaking down of the normal appetite, which is inevitable it seems in long continued over-use of the

senses—whether a sense of form, color, taste, or touch? And much evidence of this tendency in human nature is beyond mention in polite society.[99]

Wright went on to express his advocacy for the naturalistic landscape. He advised his audience to "respect a tree for its inherent grace of character rejecting any treatment which does not preserve it and emphasize it." He said it was better to "mass and group foliage according to its true nature—that is, as it naturally grows best to show its full beauty as a lilac, a syringa, an elm, an oak, or a maple. And it would be a criminal offense to make a maple grow like an elm, or in any way to mar or disturb the natural tendency of these things."[100] He also suggested that everyone in the audience should read "a charming book by an English woman, Gertrude Jekyll, called *Home and Garden*, [which] shows very well this attitude toward our subject, and it should be in every library." The book recommended by Wright was based upon the theories and principles put forth by proponents of the English Landscape Gardening School and was illustrated with pictures of naturalistic gardens developed by British designers—including talented amateurs, like Jekyll.

The significance in the timing of Wright's 1900 lecture lies with the fact that the earliest site plan of record for a Wright-designed residential property also was drafted in 1900, for a two-acre site in Illinois on the gently sloping north bank of the Kankakee River. The site was subdivided into two lots for Mr. and Mrs. Harley Bradley and Mr. and Mrs. Warren Hickox; Warren Hickox and Mrs. Bradley were brother and sister. The architecture and landscape treatments Wright developed for these clients correspondingly identify with the plans Wright would "introduce" to a national audience the following year through two articles appearing in the February and July 1901 issues of the *Ladies Home Journal*, entitled "A Home In A Prairie Town" and "A Small House With 'Lots Of Room In It.' " Historians generally recognize these hypothetical plans as the prototypes for Wright's Prairie House architecture.

Harley Bradley and Warren Hickox— Kankakee, Illinois (1900)

The Bradley-Hickox commission provided Wright with his first occasion to design for anything other than the level subdivided lot that typified the urban prairie landscape and his earliest opportunity to exercise virtually total control over the architecture, interior design, and the landscape on a domestic level. In his effort to meet this challenge, Wright developed a cohesive design treatment that represented a radical departure from the ornateness of the Victorian age—both architecturally and environmentally.

The site was characterized by a woodland grove of mature trees. That Wright considered this grove relevant to his siting of the buildings is evidenced by the number and proximity of extant trees saved during construction, as documented by historic photographs of the Bradley House published in the *Chicago Architectural Annual* shortly after construction was completed in 1902. Moreover, Wright's text narrative noted that the house "stands in a small glen on the banks of the Kankakee River"[101] (Figure 3-1).

The Bradley-Hickox site plan was rudimentary, at best, and was probably inspired by site plans Wright examined on drafting boards in the community drafting room at Steinway Hall, but prior to Griffin joining his staff in Oak Park. Although key elevations were noted and all existing trees were located, none were categorized or labeled except for three large masses of what appear to be existing vegetation along the river edge, simply labeled "willows." Nonetheless, these were the elements Wright used to establish and maintain grade levels and adjust the structures to accommodate for the differential in the slope leading to the river bank and preserve as many trees as possible, in the process.

When the site plans for each house—historically reproduced as separate entities—are placed side by side so that the 25-foot grid lines of the land survey merge, an entirely new insight is presented (Figure 3-2). As the manner in which Wright interrelated the two houses becomes manifest, the Bradley-Hickox site plan becomes a means for studying Wright's nascent efforts in the structuring of outdoor space. The Bradley House was sited at the midpoint toward the northern extremity of the lot abutting the river, and oriented to face east toward the street. The Hickox House also was sited toward the northern extremity of its lot, but oriented to face south toward the river. Their studied placements were so precise as to form an axis between the centerline of the Hickox House and the centerline ridge of the Bradley porte-cochere. This positioning not only assured adequate buffer between the houses but also created privatized expanses of usable outdoor space to the east and south of each house. It was this open space that Wright developed for outdoor utility and outdoor living, principally in the form of the sizable verandas or terraces that in essence created roofless rooms of outdoor space. The Bradley House also had a capacious roofed porch that extended the interior space of the living room into the out-of-doors. The spaces thus created became important and dramatic aspects of the expanded footprint of the structures.

It was with these houses that Wright introduced a dark-stained wood trim baseline for horizontal emphasis and first used street-side planters, retaining walls, and privacy walls to create defining geometric sight lines and structure a visual continuum into the out-of-doors. The latter treatment is most evident with the Bradley House, where there were two parallel means of approach adapted to accommodate the change in grade to below street level: a ramped carriageway with concrete retaining walls, and a wide masonry walkway with steps leading from the right-of-way to the entry level. The walkway and carriageway were separated by a raised masonry planter that was design-inclusive with the architecture, in that it harmonized with the urns and planting boxes at terminal points of the structure. From

Figure 3-1 A 1992 photograph shows the relationship and environment of the Harley Bradley and Warren Hickox Houses (center and right, respectively) in Kankakee, Illinois. (*Photograph by Charles E. Aguar. © 2002 by Berdeana Aguar.*)

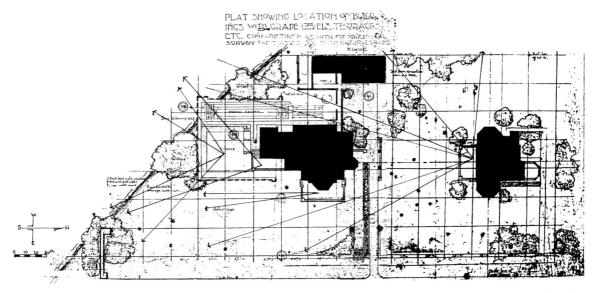

Figure 3-2 The site plans for the Bradley and Hickox Houses historically have been reproduced as separate entities. When the plans are placed side by side as cojoined here by the author, an entirely new insight is presented. (*By Charles E. Aguar, based on historic photographs, personal analysis, and original drawings of record. © 2002 by The Frank Lloyd Wright Foundation, Scottsdale, Arizona. As delineated, © 2002 by Berdeana Aguar.*)

either approach, a generous porte-cochere completely shelters the primary entrance, correcting the oversight Wright made with his own Oak Park residence. Wright in fact took special pains to protect *all* points of outdoor-indoor transition for the Bradley House, including the stable and chauffeur's quarters and the two doors on either side of the windowed bay that penetrates the open veranda east of the living room.

It was the imagery created by this combination of design treatments, together with the purposeful *exclusion* of foundation plantings, that caused landscape architect Christopher Vernon to observe that the Bradley House setting "most closely resembled what most likely was Wright's intended effect: the crisp foundation of the house clearly is visible; grass and trees predominate in the scene."[102]

"A Home in a Prairie Town," *The Ladies Home Journal* (February 1901)

Wright was one of several architects selected by the *Ladies Home Journal* to prepare designs for their "New Series of Model Suburban Houses Which Can Be Built at Moderate Cost" in the February and July 1901 issues.[103] His inclusion in these publications represented

his first nationwide consumer recognition as an architect. The Studio project list for the year 1900 includes three projects for this purpose: "Home in a Prairie Town" (#0007), "Small House with Lots of Room" (#0008), and "Quadruple Block Plan" (#0019). While it can be assumed from these identifying numbers that Wright prepared three separate designs, it is not clear if the *Journal* ever intended that Wright prepare more than the two published articles. Whatever the original intent, the Home in a Prairie Town article incorporated the Quadruple Block Plan as well.

Within the one-page article were a total of seven drawings, including the site plan for the Quadruple Block scheme and two presentation perspectives—one for the house and one for the Quadruple Block. The ground floor plan for the house depicts the living room, dining room, and library as an interconnected unit of unbroken space, even though each of these spaces interpenetrates the site environment in a different direction—as does the kitchen (Figure 3-3). This arrangement admits the greatest possible amount of natural light into the main living areas, maximizes the potential for cross-ventilation, and affords views into the gardens and open space of the rear yard. On the second level, two can-

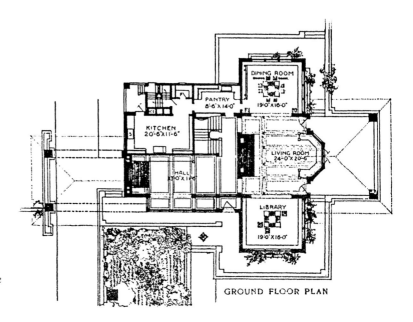

Figure 3-3 Ground-floor plan for Wright's concept of "A Home in a Prairie Town." (© *2002 by The Frank Lloyd Wright Foundation, Scottsdale, Arizona.*)

GROUND FLOOR PLAN

tilevered bedroom extensions with banks of windows similarly merge with the out-of-doors. But the most significant indoor-outdoor relationships were provided by the interconnecting terraces that originate at the porte-cochere and, together with the spacious roofed porch off the living room, surround approximately three-fourths of the house as integral elements.

To visually affix and in a sense "weave" the two-story structure firmly upon the earth, Wright introduced two low hip roofs with broad, overhanging eaves—one that extends over the spacious porch off the end of the living room and another that shelters the porte-cochere at the opposite extremity. He also projected the grid of the house onto the landscape in the form of privacy wall extensions to provide a geometric order to the site. To reinforce the ground-hugging illusion this treatment creates, he arranged bands of windows in horizontal groupings under the two levels of eaves; introduced dark-stained wood strips of banding to emphasize the clean horizontal lines of the eaves and parapets; left the water table completely exposed; and proposed the use of cascading varieties of plants to overflow the rims of the window boxes and terminal urns. All of these innovative treatments would become signature design elements identified with the physiognomy of a majority of Wright's Prairie House designs (Figure 3-4).

The landscape treatment was a very demonstrative aspect of the imagery put forth in the *Journal* article—principally because of the complete absence of Victorianism. There were no fountains, carpet bedding, parterres, or knot gardens. There were no evergreens. Foundation planting was omitted entirely. Instead, a broad rectangular entrance garden of herbaceous plantings contained within a masonry edging entirely filled the space between the house and the sidewalk right-of-way. Moreover, the forms of plantings suggest perennials selected for the utilitarian functions of screening, shading, and space separation—rather than as horticultural collections or exotic decoratives that would conceal, or draw the eye away from, the architecture.[104] This expansive entrance garden, together with the naturalistic planting to the rear of the house and the cascading varieties of plantings in the flower boxes and urns, suggest a house and garden merged as one—a treatment very much in keeping with the naturalistic tenets of the English Landscape Gardening School that Wright put forth during his address to the ladies' civic organization in Oak Park in 1900, the same year he was designing the Home in a Prairie Town.

The dual entry approaches were closely interwoven into the landscape treatment. The approach by way of the driveway led past the entry garden to the porte-

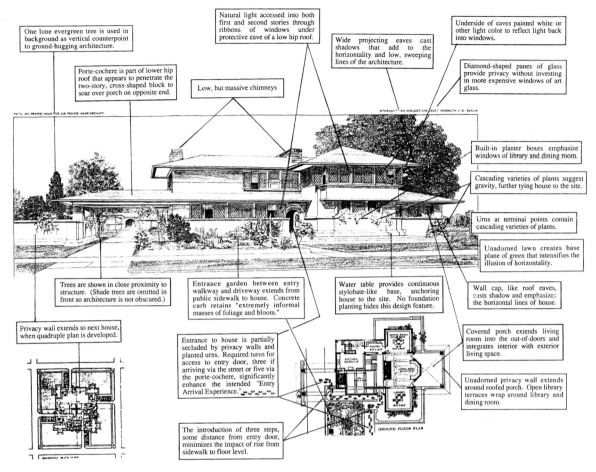

One lone evergreen tree is used in background as vertical counterpoint to ground-hugging architecture.

Porte-cochere is part of lower hip roof that appears to penetrate the two-story, cross-shaped block to soar over porch on opposite end.

Natural light accessed into both first and second stories through ribbons of windows under protective eave of a low hip roof.

Low, but massive chimneys

Wide projecting eaves cast shadows that add to the horizontality and low, sweeping lines of the architecture.

Underside of eaves painted white or other light color to reflect light back into windows.

Diamond-shaped panes of glass provide privacy without investing in more expensive windows of art glass.

Built-in planter boxes emphasize windows of library and dining room.

Cascading varieties of plants suggest gravity, further tying house to the site.

Urns at terminal points contain cascading varieties of plants.

Unadorned lawn creates base plane of green that intensifies the illusion of horizontality.

Trees are shown in close proximity to structure. (Shade trees are omitted in front so architecture is not obscured.)

Entrance garden between entry walkway and driveway extends from public sidewalk to house. Concrete curb retains "extremely informal masses of foliage and bloom."

Water table provides continuous stylobate-like base, anchoring house to the site. No foundation planting hides this design feature.

Wall cap, like roof eaves, casts shadow and emphasizes the horizontal lines of house.

Privacy wall extends to next house, when quadruple plan is developed.

Entrance to house is partially secluded by privacy walls and planted urns. Required turns for access to entry door, three if arriving via the street or five via the porte-cochere, significantly enhance the intended "Entry Arrival Experience."

Covered porch extends living room into the out-of-doors and integrates interior with exterior living space.

Unadorned privacy wall extends around roofed porch. Open library terraces wrap around library and dining room.

GROUND FLOOR PLAN

The introduction of three steps, some distance from entry door, minimizes the impact of rise from sidewalk to floor level.

Figure 3-4 Physiognomy of the Frank Lloyd Wright Prairie Houses. (*By Charles E. Aguar, based on personal analysis. Out-of-copyright drawings from Wasmuth Portfolio, 1910. As delineated,* © 2002 by Berdeana Aguar.)

cochere. From that point, there were two turns and two steps required to reach the entry veranda, which afforded views into the entry garden and the library terrace prior to making the final turn to the front door. The approach by way of the entry sidewalk was just as circuitous and interactive with the site environment, but followed along the opposite side of the garden. As with his Oak Park Home, Wright's use of turns and steps as deliberate landscape experiences presented dramatic contrast to the frontally direct entry experience for the period houses of the times.

Incorporated into the plan of this prototypical home, then, were many important considerations of environmental design: privacy, livability, and interpenetration of the site environment; maximum access to natural light and cross-ventilation; sight lines and views; outdoor living space; garden arrangements; and entry experience. Moreover, it was Wright's intent that all of these environmental considerations be incorporated into his Quadruple Block Plan, where he envisioned four of these houses being built as a unit.

Quadruple Block Plan, *The Ladies Home Journal* (February 1901)

The text of the February 1901 *Journal* article reveals that Wright's personal interest at this point lay at least as much with the subdivision of the land and the manner of unitizing the houses on the land as with the design of the house itself. This is not to say the design of the Home in a Prairie Town was less important to him as an architect, but his intent certainly seemed to be to promote the house and his Quadruple Block Plan as an entity. This reasoning is supported by the fact that he highlighted the Quadruple Block concept at the head of the article in both plan and perspective and devoted more than one quarter of the limited text to explain how the block plan would avoid "haphazard," "hit-or-miss" siting of the houses.

Although the perspective at the head of the article depicted the Quadruple Block concept as an oasis for relaxation and recreation, and the small-scale inset advocated the variety of orientations and spatial arrangements possible when four of the houses were sited and landscaped as a unit, this minimal exposure did not encourage interpretation and understanding. Even the Quadruple Block terminology was misleading as it suggested four houses per city block, which was not the case. Each Quadruple Block unit utilized but a fraction of the total acreage in a typical city block. There would be multiple units, each with four houses, but so arranged that the "community interests are of greatest value to the whole," and every home is afforded "perfect advantage of site, each to each."[105] The containment factor was a very important aspect of the plan. Low walls linked the clusters of houses in such a way that no matter how close the unit might have to be sited in relation to other houses or public thoroughfares, the living room, dining room, and library would serve as an insulated buffer.

The ingenuousness of Wright's Quadruple Block Plan can only begin to be appreciated through careful

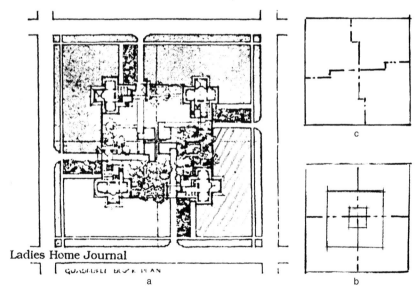

Figure 3-5 a–c   The ingeniousness of Wright's Quadruple Block Plan can only begin to be appreciated through careful study. Each unit should be envisioned as having been schematically divided into four equal lots (3-5 a). Each lot, in turn, should be visualized as having been arranged into three graduated squares: an axial square, a median square, and a perimeter square (3-5 b). Wright's methodology was to shift a segment of one property line from each lot counterclockwise into the driveway of the next house. Since a strip of land taken off of one parcel was added to the next, each dwelling retained the same acreage as if it were a square (3-5 c). (*By Charles E. Aguar, based on personal analysis.* © 2002 by The Frank Lloyd Wright Foundation, Scottsdale, Arizona. As delineated, © 2002 by Berdeana Aguar.)

Figure 3-6   Presentation perspective for Quadruple Block Plan. (© *2002 by The Frank Lloyd Wright Foundation, Scottsdale, Arizona.*)

study. Each unit should be envisioned as having been schematically divided into four equal lots (Figure 3-5a). Each lot, in turn, should be visualized as having been arranged into three graduated squares: an axial square, a median square, and a perimeter square (Figure 3-5b). Within this arrangement, the four stable-garage structures are grouped around the central axis and contained within the axial square, and the four houses are situated at the corner extremities of the median square. This siting positioned the outdoor living space of the roofed porch at maximum distance from any other house and each porte-cochere at the innermost location, where the distance between houses was most limited.

The methodology was to shift the four imperceptible straight property lines some 20 feet counterclockwise to the edge of the driveway for the adjoining house. Since the strip of land taken off one parcel was added to the next, however, each dwelling retained the same acreage as if it were a simple square (Figure 3-5c). The privacy wall installed along the median square boundary to link the houses "each to each" had the additional function of unifying and privatizing the open space between the garages and houses to develop for outdoor living and recreation: flower gardens, vegetable gardens, lawn games, paddock area, children's playground, et al. The unbounded open space outside the privacy wall was retained as a greensward to establish a base plane. This treatment had the effect of creating the pinwheel-like configuration that so contributed to the illusionistic imagery of broad sweeping lawns represented in the presentation perspective at the head of the February 1901 article (Figure 3-6).

Had Wright been successful in marketing this Quadruple Block Plan as an alternate format for land subdivision and development, the social and spatial definition he proposed would have created an organic har-

mony and order to suburban living that could have contained the unorganized "sprawl" aspects of development as it occurred throughout America during the twentieth century.

"A Small House With 'Lots of Room In It'," *The Ladies Home Journal* (April 1901)

The April 1901 issue of the *Journal* included plans for a modest livable home that could be constructed for $5835. This is a concept Wright obviously found to be highly motivating, as it represented his first of many attempts to design an affordable domestic architecture suitable for construction on a typical suburban site for families of moderate means. Yet, it is apparent from the 10 different drawings included within the one-page article that he invested no less creative thought in the design process than for the previous article. And his text elaborated on some of the considerations he gave to concerns of environmental design: "The plan disregards somewhat the economical limit in compact planning to take advantage of light, air and prospect, the enjoyable things one goes to the suburbs to secure. . . . The dining table commands the outdoor garden at the rear, and the low windows on the gallery to the street front. . . . The living room . . . has access to both gallery and terrace. . . . The range is set within a brick-lined, brick-floored alcove, formed by the two fireplaces, the space overhead ventilated into a chimney flue."[106]

As with the plans presented in the article published two months earlier, the demonstrative aspect of this house plan is the methodology used to access natural light, provide cross-ventilation, and interrelate the architecture with the site environment. There is a gallery outdoor living space sheltered under the deep overhanging eaves that is accessible to the living room and visible from the wall of low windows in the dining room. There is a living room terrace, a window bay that projects onto the terrace, a second window bay that extends outward from the entry foyer onto the porte-cochere, and a third window bay in the dining room—which Wright described as a " 'feature' with a little indoor garden closing the perspective at its farther end."[107] Windows on two sides of the kitchen afford views into the rear yard. There also is a fourth window bay that projects into the treetops at the spacious midpoint landing of the stairway to the second level, as well as a sizable balcony off the master "chamber."

Of the two site plans, Scheme "A" appears to have the most potential (Figure 3-7, a-b). In Scheme "B," the house is sited to create a large side yard that is penetrated by the

living room terrace. The area devoted to circulation is excessive, however, as there is a circular drive leading from the street right-of-way through the porte-cochere and out again, as well as another driveway along the property line that provides direct access to a garage-stable in the rear. The Scheme "A" site plan, on the other hand, presents the broad rectangular entry garden as filling the space between the entry sidewalk and driveway so that it becomes an integral element of the entry experience. There is a minimal raised earthen terrace and privacy walls of substantial height that circumscribe the streetside terrace and gallery—a treatment designed to work with the layering of the gable roofs and the roof extended over the porte-cochere to ameliorate the vertical impact of

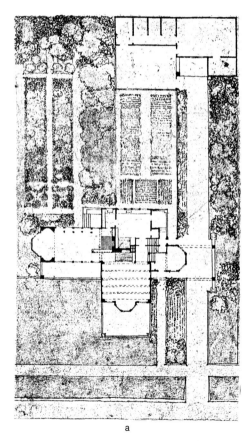

a

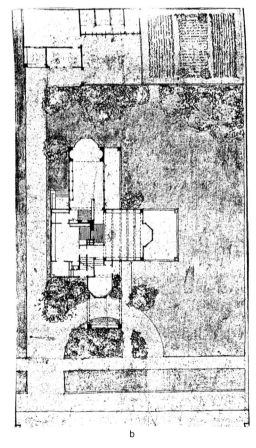

b

Figure 3-7 a–b   "A Small House with 'Lots of Room in It' "—two alternate site plans for Wright's concept of a modestly priced home. The arrangement at left (3-7 a) makes effective use of space and is the preferred layout, while that at right (3-7 b) reflects poor site planning and excessive circulation. (© *2002 by The Frank Lloyd Wright Foundation, Scottsdale, Arizona.*)

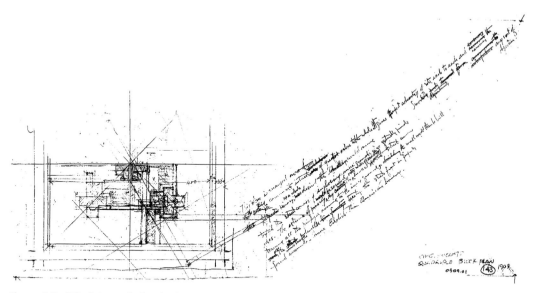

Figure 3-8 Wright's rough sketch plan for half of his Quadruple Block scheme, with a rare handwritten explanation, suggests that other possible applications were being explored from the outset. (© *2002 by The Frank Lloyd Wright Foundation, Scottsdale, Arizona.*)

what was essentially a three-story house (including the basement, which was partially above ground level).

An interesting aspect of the Scheme "A" layout is that the gallery privacy wall extends through the property boundary to include a neighboring structure. Moreover, the basement plan clearly delineates the footings for an extension of the gallery privacy wall. Therefore, it becomes suspect that A Small House initially might have been planned as another prospect for bolstering the Quadruple Block concept. The placement of the stable and paddock at what could be considered the axial portion of four contiguous sites lends support to this reasoning—as does the wordage in Wright's handwritten description upon what is believed to be his first sketch for one-half of the quadruple unit featured in the February article (Figure 3-8), which suggests that other possibilities in application were explored from the outset:

> This plan is arranged on the presumption that the common interests are of greatest value to the whole. It gives perfect advantage of site, each to each, and removes working departments from any objection. If greater privacy as a whole are desired, the dwelling would move toward the street corners, enclosing more ground for strictly private uses. The

extreme of privacy would be secured by butting the outer walls of houses (exactly) on the street corner, training all the principal rooms to the inner ground. A wall would then be built on the inner rim of the sidewalk, treating the street front in perfectly formal manner—more English then American, however.

The presentation drawings for both *Journal* articles clearly illustrate the aggrandizement of Wright's Prairie House architecture that occurred when the unifying dimension of landscape design became a fundamental substance of his architectural design. Although Brooks maintains that the drafting techniques within the articles identify with more than one delineator—suggesting perhaps a collaborative effort by Drummond, Mahony, Long, and Wright—it is improbable that anyone other than Griffin articulated the site plan and landscape design, even if he was not the delineator; they are too all-inclusive and dissimilar to any previously prepared for a Wright-designed property.[108] Regrettably, there is scant evidence that the landscape treatment—illustrated equally to the architecture in the *Journal* articles—ever was understood or even noticed. Prairie houses then and now often are "smothered" with exotic foundation plantings; urns and other container plantings are misplaced or misused; and planting beds are not established in the space-defining geometric forms detailed on the plans.

That the Quadruple Block Plan was an important concept to Wright is corroborated by his bulldoglike efforts to market its feasibility. He even announced in the July 18, 1901 issue of *The Reporter,* the local newspaper, that he himself would build eight houses in Oak Park to demonstrate the benefits of the grouping approach to development described in his article, captioned "New Idea for Suburbs."[109] When he was unable to secure adequate financial backing to implement the project, he evidently continued to recycle and recirculate the plans until the right client came along. This opportunity occurred just two years later, when Charles E. Roberts commissioned Wright to prepare plans for a community of 24 homes he proposed to build in Oak Park.

Charles E. Roberts Project—Oak Park, Illinois (1903)

The idea for developing Roberts' 24 homes as Quadruple Block units most probably was instigated by Wright. The Quadruple Block layout used in the comparative presentation drawing prepared to demonstrate the contrast between conventional subdividing and the platting of four houses grouped as a unit is a mirror image of the layout featured in the February 1901 *Journal* article. However, the footprint of the house—which differs substantially from the Home in a Prairie Town, including the omission of a porte-cochere—identifies this layout as having been customized to meet Roberts' program. Assumedly these layouts were prepared to convince Roberts of the feasibility of the concept and/or as a mechanism to use in marketing the concept to investors (Figure 3-9 a-b).[110]

The layout at the top of the comparative drawing represents a typical arrangement of conventional platting in the Chicago area, with the lots aligned along parallel streets and an alley centered midway in the block. In this hypothetical scheme, there are a total of 30 lots, each measuring 50 by 175 feet. The 15 lots above the alley are platted as identical semidetached Prairie Houses sited to conform to minimal setback with stables or garages to the rear by the alleyway, leaving approximately half of each lot to develop as usable open space. The 15 lots below the alley are laid out conventionally with the somewhat typically cluttered Victorian landscape—including wasted side yards, space-consuming driveways and turnarounds, and minimal usable open space. But the layout at the bottom half of the compar-

ative drawing demonstrates that by replatting a typical city block so that groupings of four houses are treated as one unit—with common front yards, private walled rear yards, and the alley converted into a pedestrian parkway with a garden median feature—there is no compromise as to livability or open space, and the number of salable houses would be increased to 32. Additional tracings of the Quadruple Block layout define the unusual offset platting that establishes a defined system of both public and private space, while providing equal-size lots for each house (Figure 3-10 a-c).

When the alternative Quadruple Block layouts are placed side by side, the variety that could be achieved becomes obvious (Figure 3-11 a-c). Alternative "A" is the same as the layout presented in the comparative drawing, but without driveways or garage. Layout "B" clusters the four houses in a zero-lot-line conformation so that the kitchen turns inward toward the kitchen of the nearest house, 30 feet distant. The living room is turned toward either the public sidewalk, 32 feet distant, or toward another house in the unit, 64 feet distant and separated by the parkway. The veranda overlooks the open space to the rear, where privacy is assured by the veranda parapet, the privacy-wall extension, and dense plantings of trees or shrubbery. A large rectangular entry garden extends across the front of each house, and the walkway approach has a median garden feature that extends from the street right-of-way to an exterior wall of the living room. For layout "C," each of the four houses is situated near a corner extremity of the unit. When the outer corner is the intersection of the public sidewalk, this siting establishes a very minimal setback of 4 or 5 feet between the living room window wall and the reception room. When the corner extremity is adjacent to the pedestrian parkway, however, the reception room is some 25 feet removed from the same space of another house in the unit. The parkway has been introduced as with layout "A" to establish continuity to the neighborhood, but here the feature is bounded at the outer edge by the walled perimeter of the four-house unit. At the axial intersection of the four lots, there is a fourplex garage-stable. Although the driveways end at the privacy walls, open space is provided to extend these to the rear service structure, if desired.

Roberts in the end also was unsuccessful in securing financing to proceed with development of the project. Nevertheless, the presentation drawings prepared for this client reveal the depth of innovative thinking invested into the grouped housing concept developed by Wright and members of The Studio staff.

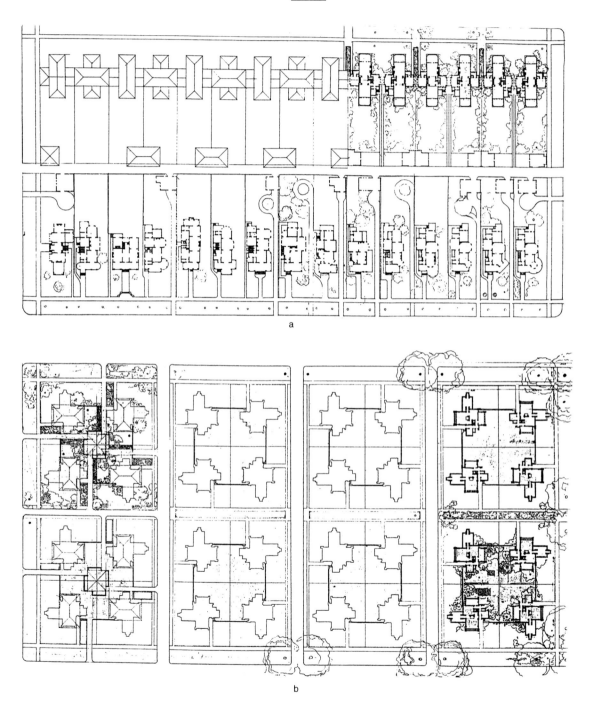

a

b

Figure 3-9 a–b Comparative presentation drawings for the 1903 Charles R. Roberts Project illustrate contrasts between a typical existing 30-lot city block in Oak Park (3-9 a) and Wright's envisioned 32-lot Quadruple Block Plan (3-9 b) that covers the same area but provides privacy and open-space benefits. (© *2002 by The Frank Lloyd Wright Foundation, Scottsdale, Arizona.*)

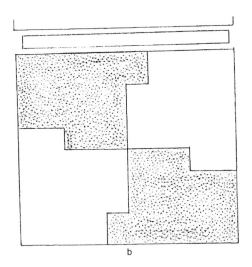

Figure 3-10 a Perspective sketch of 1903 Quadruple Block Project shows houses connected by privacy walls and illustrates how they would interrelate. (*Out-of-copyright drawing from Wasmuth Portfolio, 1910.*)

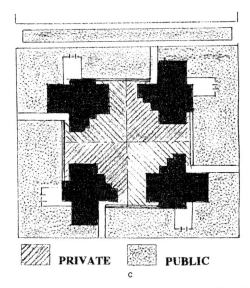

b

PRIVATE   PUBLIC

c

Figure 3-10 b–c Tracings of Roberts Quadruple Block layout show unusual offset platting for equal-size lots (3-10 b) and defined system of public and private spaces (3-10 c). (*By Charles E. Aguar, based on personal analysis and out-of-copyright plans of record in Wasmuth Portfolio, 1910. As delineated, © 2002 by Berdeana Aguar.*)

· · ·

It seems relevant that the Roberts' layouts identified as "B" and "C" replicate patterns sketched out by Marion Mahony during a 1940 interview with Grant Manson (by which time she was Griffin's widow) to support her voluntary critique of Wright's *Journal* plan. She alleged it was because "Griffin at once showed a flair for town planning which incited Wright's jealous emulation" that Wright's "so-called quadruple block plan" came about.[111] Mahony's opinion could be discredited as her bias

toward Griffin, as Manson suggests in a parenthetical aside. However, Donald Leslie Johnson also identified Griffin's involvement when he noted that "the initial developmental work on the Quadruple Block Plans of Wright was given to Griffin" and "the idea of pairing houses in a more pragmatic situation was Griffin's."[112] Johnson goes on to maintain that "land planning" was probably more important to Griffin than architecture: "He saw architecture as one aspect of a land planning scheme and subservient to the whole."[113] Based upon this insight, it seems reasonable to postulate that with

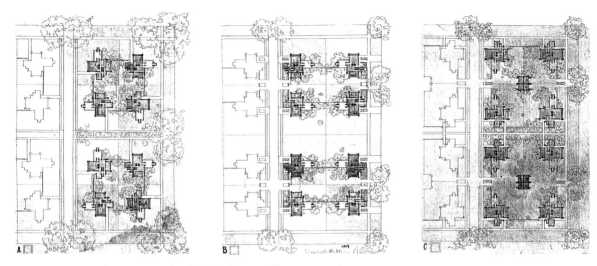

Figure 3-11 a–c   Alternative Quadruple Block layouts offer a variety of ways to eliminate mundane subdivision of land. (© 2002 by The Frank Lloyd Wright Foundation, Scottsdale, Arizona.)

the Roberts commission Wright may have embraced Griffin's concepts as to these variations on land subdivision.

The significance in all this lies with the coincidence of the February 1901 publication date of the *Journal* article and the series of lectures presented the previous year by Scotsman Patrick Geddes at Jane Addams' Hull House in Chicago, where he spoke on his comprehensive study of the sociological aspects of living in the city and its region. It was this study that led to Geddes' subsequent involvement with, and influence upon, Britain's early twentieth-century town planning and the Garden City Movement. Johnson observed that Oak Park staffer Barry Byrne "remembers that Griffin was deeply impressed with Geddes' speeches to that [Hull House] group."[114] As Geddes' remarks impacted upon Griffin to such an extent that he was still talking about them two years or more after the fact, when Byrne joined the staff in 1902, it is presumable that Wright also attended these lectures and that he and Griffin discussed their subject matter.

This reasoning would explain Wright's years-long preoccupation with promoting the Quadruple Block scheme and with community planning in general. In addition to the *Journal* article and the Roberts project, he incorporated the Quadruple Block concept into his

Bitter Root Town Plan of 1909, the Wasmuth Portfolio of 1910, the City Club Land Development Competition of 1913, the Suntop Homes in 1938, the Cloverleaf Housing Project in 1942, and the Jesse Fisher Housing Project in 1957. The Price Tower (1952) represents another very sophisticated, and much expanded, version of this same arrangement. Thus, irrespective of how the Quadruple Block concept of land subdivision was developed, or by whom, the sociological implications inherent to the thought process behind it should be seen as a noteworthy link to Wright's sociocultural development as an architect, landscape architect, and urban planner.

Frank Thomas—Oak Park, Illinois (1901)

The Frank Thomas property faced onto Forest Avenue and was situated down the street from Wright's Home in a highly visible and accessible location near the Oak Park business district. There were challenges, however, in the limiting width of the property and the dominating presence of row-house apartments to the immediate south, which had the potential to overpower any less imposing, or nonvertical, structure (Figure 3-12). Moreover, the property faced onto Forest Avenue, so the climatic problems associated with a westerly orientation were identical to those that Wright had been experiencing with his own home for some 12 years by this point.

Figure 3-12 Frank Thomas House (1901), adjacent row house, and site environment in Oak Park, Illinois. (*1992 photograph by Charles E. Aguar. © 2002 by Berdeana Aguar.*)

Wright at this time shared office space with Webster Tomlinson, whereunder the Thomas House is listed.[115] According to Mahony, Wright had completed plans to the point of working drawings when he invited others in Steinway Hall to critique his work.[116] It appears that with this commission Wright once again respected Griffin's opinions enough to accept criticism and indeed rearrange his entire layout if he was convinced a superior design would result, because changes were made to conform with recommendations Griffin made during this critique. Mahony elaborated upon her observations in a revealing article written for an Australian publication:

The lot was one next to a two-storey flat building [row house] built right out to the sidewalk line. Across the street from the flat was a beautiful open estate. The house was being set back on the lot as if shrinking from an ugly thing of which it was afraid, leaving the greater part of the ground to the front, allowing the other building to shut off the delightful view opposite. This was criticized as not a proper plan for the location and that the main rooms should be elevated above the eyes of the passersby, and that the house should have the form of the letter "L," one arm lying across the lot parallel with the street, the other projecting toward it alongside the flat building, acting as a screen to the ugly mass and benefiting the whole avenue. Lifting the basement out of the ground would enable the projecting room to overlook the charming woods across the street as well as the front garden, whilst

the verandah and living room would gain privacy, command the entire rear gardens, and look upon the graceful lines of the home itself instead of the ugly bulk of the adjacent building.[117]

Mahony concluded: "I saw the revolution in methods and results that took place when landscape architecture was made a part of architecture."

It again could be argued that Mahony's description of what occurred may have been colored by her personal bias toward Griffin—particularly since she neglected to mention that Wright already had employed the technique of a raised basement for Joseph Husser two years earlier, for a site on the North Shore of Lake Michigan. This was something of which she was well aware, since it was she who prepared the presentation drawings delineated in the meticulous Beaux Arts format. In that situation, however, the raised basement may have been seen as a measure of protection from the possibility of flooding, which would have been quite probable before the land was artificially built up and extended to support the subsequent construction of North Shore Drive. If so, Wright may have been thinking of the Husser's elevated main floor more as a "piano nobile," in the manner of the palazzos lining the Canal Grande in Venice; this would be in keeping with the Italian overtones represented in the Husser architecture. Even so, this rationale alone would not discount the possibility that Wright might have been inspired by Griffin's critique of the Thomas House. Since it was in 1899 that Griffin began participating in the group discussions and critiques that took place in the communal drafting room at Steinway Hall, there is a strong probability that he also contributed to Wright's design of the Husser House. The significance here, however, is not "who," but "what" inspired Wright's raised basement design approach. With the Husser House, this approach provided a superior prospect of the panorama of Lake Michigan. With the Thomas House, it gave better prospect to the woods directly across Forest Avenue. And the same rationale holds true for the five additional Prairie Houses where Wright used the raised basement approach: Arthur Huertly (1902), Ferdinand Tomek (1904–1905), Avery Coonley (1907), Eugene Gilmore (1908), and Frederick Robie (1908).[118] Whether the sites were level or uneven, the prospect of a peripheral view was the primary consideration.

The Thomas House was sited so the main body of the L was set back approximately 40 feet from the Forest Avenue right-of-way and some 20 feet from the north boundary. The three-story mass of the structure and the two-story dining room wing that formed the base of the L almost abutted the south boundary. This siting and arrangement left just enough width between the south facade and the dominating row house to give access to

the coal chute, but retained a sizable expanse of open space to the rear of the house, and enough open space to the west and north to allow Wright to install an interlocking reverse "L" terrace-porch that wraps around the west and north facades of the living room (Figure 3-13).

To visually merge the terrace-porch addition with the structural mass of the house, Wright extended the roof to overhang the greater expanse of the porch to the north of the living room. He then installed another overhanging eave to align with, and connect to, the roof over the dining room projection—a treatment that had the additional functions of shielding the living room windows from the late afternoon sun and sheltering the point of outdoor-indoor transition from the elements. By then raising the porch parapet to the height of the window grouping on the second level and using the same plaster surfacing to hide the understructure for this privacy wall as had been used to circumscribe the dining room projection, Wright crafted a means to create the illusion that the house spread out to fill the entire width of the lot and was much bigger than it really was. At the same time, the 580 square feet of outdoor living space

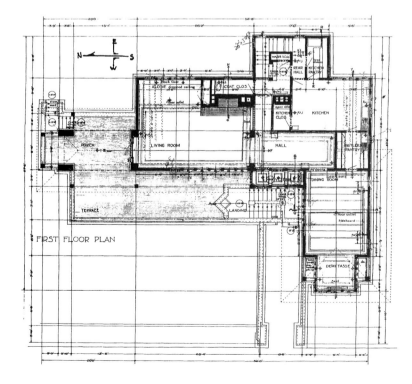

Figure 3-13 First-floor plan of the Thomas House. (© 2002 by The Frank Lloyd Wright Foundation, Scottsdale, Arizona.)

made available by way of the porch addition expanded by half the usable living space on the raised living level of the house. Wright's liberal attention to the detailing of this aspect of his architectural design attests to the importance he fixed upon private space for outdoor living at this point in time.

Wright resorted to further optical illusionism as he addressed the dual challenges of emphasizing both the verticality of the dining room projection and the horizontal countenance of the prairie house. To accomplish this, he used the same technique that he had introduced with the Williams House seven years earlier and formulated dissimilar landscape treatments on either side of the entry walkway (Figure 3-14). Here, he widened the walkway and essentially created a roofless entry corridor by bounding both sides with walls that were low enough to see over, but high enough to camouflage the disparities in grade. On the south side of this entry corridor, Wright preserved the integrity of the ground level and purposefully emphasized the water table surrounding the dining room with a broad contrasting band that also extended around the base of the walls on either side of the entry corridor. This treatment both related the structure to the ground and perceptively maximized the verticality of the plastered facade of the dining room projection so it would not appear subservient to the imposing tower of the row house immediately adjacent. On the north side of the corridor, he used the lower portion of the wall to retain a three-foot-high, beveled earthen terrace that extended across the baseline of the

porch privacy wall. He then overscored the flattened terrace crown with a false stylobate in the form of another broad contrasting band. This treatment visually maximized the intended horizontality of the porch addition as it also minimized the actual height of the plain plastered façade. All of these design treatments coalesce so the streetside impress of the Thomas House is commanding enough to hold its own and is completely unified in its horizontality.

The labyrinth-like entry experience Wright choreographed for the Thomas House begins at the curb and proceeds across the public sidewalk to the terminal pedestals for each wall. These pedestals were designed to be adorned by urns with cascading plantings to mark the threshold of the entry corridor. The combination of the planted urns together with the plantings in the sizable raised entry garden to the north were intended to create a feeling of entering and walking through a garden as the approach progressed along the corridor toward the Sullivanesque arch above an opening in the west facade. Upon passing through the arch to access the entry loggia, there are two choices: to turn right toward the recessed service doorway leading to the servant and utility rooms of the above-ground "basement," or left to continue the entry experience by ascending a stairway open to the sky. On the broad landing at the apex of this stairway, there is a wall with an inverted prow that serves as a planter for a minigarden. After making a second right turn and ascending a reverse parallel stairway leading to the top of the stairs, there is a 4

Figure 3-14   A presentation perspective of the Thomas House clearly shows dissimilarity of ground levels on either side of the entry walkway. (© 2002 by The Frank Lloyd Wright Foundation, Scottsdale, Arizona.)

by 6-foot entry landing formed by the L-shaped intersection of the two wings. It is from this vantage point that a sense-of-place is realized, as a visitor becomes aware of the peripheral wooded environment, the sequestered terrace, and the roofed porch some 40 feet to the north.

Through the retrospective analysis of the entry experience to this point and beyond, the reasoning behind Wright's design approach becomes clear. After passing through the arched portal, changing direction four times, and ascending a total of 18 steps, a visitor still has not yet entered the house. The beautiful art glass entry doorway is to the left of the entry landing, screened from view of the row house by the south wall of the dining wing and screened from view of the public rights-of-way by the veranda parapet, 6 feet to the west. Because of Wright's very specific arrangement of the parapet and the broad overhang of the intersecting eaves, the primary entrance is well-protected from all elements, as well as from Chicago's prevailing winter winds—even though the doorway faces due west. Thus, Wright's design of the Thomas House entry experience clearly went far beyond aesthetics to include consideration of the negative climatic conditions imposed by the westerly orientation, the intrusive negative aspects of the site environment, and the positive visual benefit of the peripheral environment.

William G. Fricke—Oak Park, Illinois (1901)

The lot upon which the William G. Fricke house was built is situated on the southeast corner of the intersection of Iowa Street and Fair Oaks Avenue. To compact this expansive, three-story structure onto an exposed suburban corner lot and still provide privacy and a generous amount of secluded outdoor living space required all the inventiveness Wright and his young staff members could muster.

To begin with, the house is sited so the mass of the structure abuts the public right-of-way along Iowa Street. The entry steps actually encroach upon the sidewalk, as does the ground-to-window-level planter feature that circumscribes the prow-like projection of the reception room (Figure 3-15). The west facade, on the other hand, is set back 40 feet from the public sidewalk to appear in conformance with existing houses facing Fair Oaks Avenue. Around this limited portion of the property, Wright installed an earthen terrace sculpted to a pronounced angle and beveled inward in the same manner, and for the same reasons, as the terraces for Winslow and Williams (Figure 3-16). Here, however, although the corner at the street intersection is visibly mitered, the terracing is tapered to ground level at the south boundary. This very subtle tapering assuredly was done to conform with the ground level of existing

Figure 3-15 A photograph of the 1901 William G. Fricke House in Oak Park, Illinois, depicts the effect of zero-lot-line siting. (*1992 photograph by Charles E. Aguar. © 2002 by Berdeana Aguar.*)

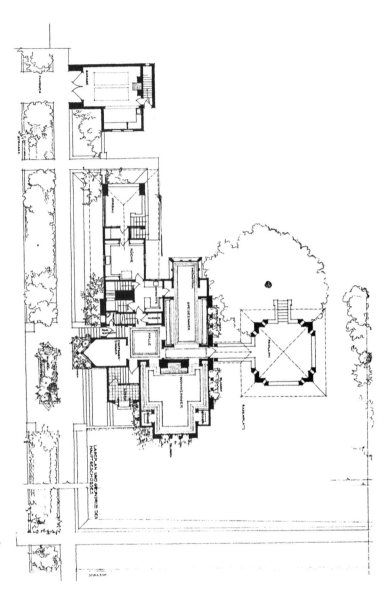

Figure 3-16 The ground plan for the
Fricke House delineates earthen terrace
and proposed parterre in sidewalk.
(*Out-of-copyright plan of record from
Wasmuth Portfolio, 1910.*)

houses to the south, but its more important function was
to assure the preservation of the root system of the specimen oak that so clearly influenced Wright's zero-lot-
line siting, as well as his site planning for the rear yard.

The entry approach was designed to begin at curbside on Iowa Street, progress across a sidewalk landing
and past either side of a formal garden parterre median
feature proposed for installation within the public sidewalk right-of-way. The 30-foot-wide, low-rise entry

steps installed at the inner edge of the sidewalk provide
horizontal emphasis to the architectural line of the
structure and essentially create a terrace feature of the
first landing. There then are two low-rise steps to a second landing, a left turn, two steps to the threshold of a
modest enclosed entry loggia, a left turn and then an
immediate right turn to the door that opens into the
vestibule. From the vestibule, there is another right turn
and three more steps to reach the interior entry landing

Figure 3-17   Historic photograph shows the Fricke garden pavilion and specimen Oak that inspired zero-lot-line siting. (*Out-of-copyright photograph of record from Wasmuth Portfolio, 1911.*)

that overlooks the loggia through an art-glass window and provides access to the front door. Through this carefully orchestrated sinuous pattern of movement, Wright accomplished two very important goals: he de-emphasized the spatial constraint imposed by the zero-lot-line siting, and he completely obliterated the boundary between outdoors and indoors.

Wright also was able to provide a surprising amount of privatized outdoor living space for the occupants. There is a sizable porch to the east of the kitchen, which is screened from view by a wall of louvers so that cross-ventilation is not compromised. There is a roofed loggia off the master bedroom, a balcony off the north bedroom, and a smaller balcony off the bedroom on the

Figure 3-18   West facade of the Fricke House after the adjacent pavilion and Oak tree were replaced by a post–World War II infill house. (*1992 photograph by Charles E. Aguar. © 2002 by Berdeana Aguar.*)

southeast corner. All are secreted behind parapet walls defined by dark-hued horizontal banding that emphasizes the prominent horizontal lines created by the multiple levels of broad overhanging eaves. But the most environmentally significant outdoor living space was the semidetached garden pavilion in the south yard, accessed by way of a roofed arcade leading from the central hallway.

The exact placement of the garden pavilion was determined by the location of the specimen oak tree. This arrangement is significant, as the pavilion—together with the presence and canopy of the oak tree—appropriated the entire open space to the south of the house as a garden, but did not in any way compromise access to the low angle of the winter sun (Figure 3-17). That this southerly orientation was an important consideration in Wright's siting and arrangement of the pavilion is confirmed in his text for the Wasmuth portfolio, where he characterized it as "a practical solution of the porch problem" and went on to describe the way porches generally "shut out the sun from the parlors and sitting rooms."[119] It was precisely because of these concerns also that the broad overhang only extends across the second story level in these areas.[120]

Unfortunately, both the pavilion and the tree were destroyed after World War II to make way for an infill house, and the open space that Wright had so artfully manipulated through his zero-lot-line siting methodology was lost in the process (Figure 3-18).

Ward W. Willits—Highland Park, Illinois (1901)

The Ward W. Willits House was carefully sited upon an estate-size forested site to preserve as many of the towering trees as possible so as to provide vertical and artistic counterbalance to the horizontality of the architecture. It is interesting to note, however, that Wright chose to face the front facade toward Sheridan Road in a traditional siting. This siting oriented the major windows somewhat disadvantageously, at 45 degrees east of south. The fact that Wright did not take advantage of being released from the circumspect limitations of an average urban lot—gridlocked by streets, alleys, and neighboring houses—would seem to suggest that he perhaps was more concerned with conforming to societally accepted normality at this point in his career, than his rhetoric would suggest.

The site circulation was designed so that anyone exiting heavily traveled Sheridan Road—by foot, horseback, carriage, or automobile—would immediately begin

to interact with the site environment by traversing through a proposed garden toward the entry steps, situated under protection of the generous porte-cochere. From the porte-cochere, the entry experience was choreographed to proceed up a short entry stairway and through a covered veranda to the main door, which opens into a vestibule and an elegant reception room. After then passing through a dramatic ceremonial chamber, ascending five steps, and changing direction three more times, the main living area is "discovered." This raising of the main living area some four feet above ground level provides uninterrupted views outward from the wall of glazed, floor-to-ceiling Dutch doors in the living room and the wall of French doors in the dining room, from the large sequestered outdoor living spaces onto which these doors open, from the second floor bedrooms and surrounding veranda. The Willits House marked Wright's first use of walls of floor-to-ceiling glazed doors as a design feature and the only time he would use Dutch doors in this manner. Together with the introduced garden elements of urns and built-in planters on both levels, this treatment interjected a meaningful element of sensory perception into the indoor-outdoor relationship and created the illusion that the house was subservient to the natural site environment.

The preliminary planting plan Griffin prepared for the Willits House clearly corroborates his influence upon designs originating from The Studio at this date (Figure 3-19). Griffin's plan proposed to develop the landscape so it related to and was in harmony with Wright's developing Prairie Style of architecture. No foundation planting is indicated in order to preserve the integrity of the prominent line of the water table, and no plantings are indicated near the large stable. However, plant groupings of native shrubs and small trees are shown arranged along the northern boundary and at the northwest and northeast corners of the property. All of the rather dense plantings within the center of the turnaround and bordering the outward side of the driveway appear as loose groupings of flowering shrubs and perennials. Similar plantings are suggested as fill-in between the walkway and driveway, along the property boundaries; and in the area southeast of the driveway; one mass of plantings actually extends into the neighboring property. The plantings selected for the semicircular arrangement surrounding the roofed porch, veranda, and dining room appear as native accent trees, for the most part. As the plantings are only partially contained within the semicircle, however, the division between lawn and planting bed would not be

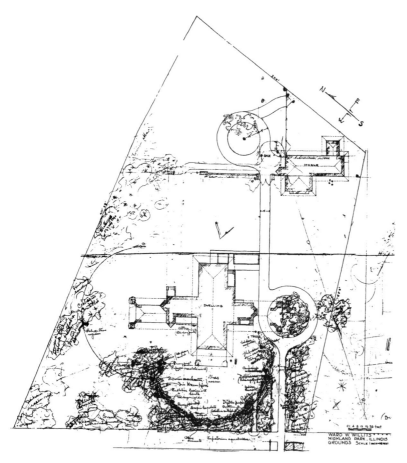

Figure 3-19 Preliminary planting plan prepared by Walter Burley Griffin for the 1901 Ward W. Willits House in Highland Park, Illinois, identifies some 150 plants by their botanical names. (© 2002 by The Frank Lloyd Wright Foundation, Scottsdale, Arizona.)

discernible on the ground. On the other hand, few native plantings are proposed for the more studied semicircular softscape set back from the terrace extension off the living room; these plantings are articulated as ornamental or exotic varieties of shrubs and perennials.

The above described treatments support Vernon's observations regarding Griffin's work—that is, that plantings at the perimeters generally are highly naturalistic in form and character but are ornamental, exotic, and more architectural ornamentation in the immediate vicinity of the residence.[121] On this basis, it can be presumed that the semicircular arrangement off the living room was designed to enhance views outward, rather than to screen the house from view as a design such as this might suggest. Nonetheless, both semicircular plant layouts should be seen as precursors to plant containment arrangements such as Wright would continue to

use throughout his career, the most detailed of which was the "floricycle" for the D.D. Martin House—also laid out by Griffin.

No final planting plan for the Willits House exists in the archives, making it impossible to determine if these planting arrangements met sound standards of landscape design by addressing the design principles of proportion, scale, balance, dominance, rhythm, and contrast—or by considering the elements of line, form, pattern, texture, and color. Although Griffin's longhand notes identify more than 150 plants by botanical name, there are no broadleaf evergreens such as holly or laurel to assure winter interest and provide screening; nor are there any juniper, pine, or other conifers (see Appendix C). This noninclusion of evergreens and conifers was in all probability intentional, however, in counteraction to the excessive use of these plantings within the Victorian landscape.

Historical photographs-of-record and careful on-site inspection of the property by the author do not support that the semicircular arrangement or other plantings ever were implemented as proposed on the preliminary plan or presentation drawing. Nonetheless, Wright on more than one occasion referred to the Willits House as "the first statement in modern architecture from grade to coping."

The Willits House still functions as a single-family residence. Although both the living room porch and the dining room veranda have been glazed and no longer provide the maximum indoor-outdoor interaction of Wright's intent, their enclosure is not as obtrusive as it would have been had this reconstruction been done absent Wright's careful detailing. Moreover, the wood deck added to the rear of the dining room—to provide new outdoor dining space—is tastefully done and the most convenient private space available, away from Sherman Road. This deck addition, together with the conversion of the Willits Stable into a residence made accessible by way of a separate driveway that originates from a side street, are the types of changes Wright might have made to adapt a century-old house to the lifestyle of current owners. Moreover, during the past decade all the over-

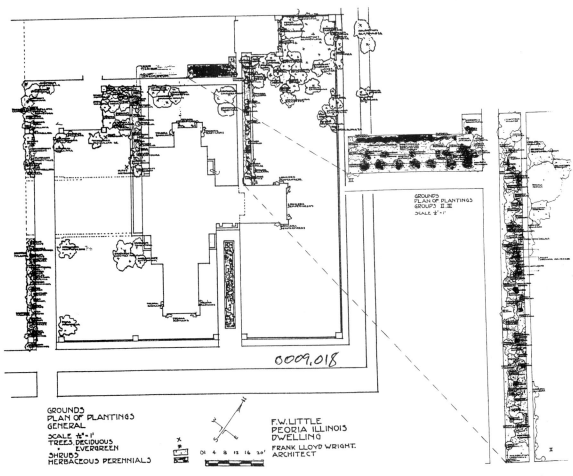

Figure 3-20   Walter B. Griffin's planting plan for the Francis W. Little House (1902) in Peoria, Illinois, is the most complete plan of record for any of Wright's prairie houses. (© *2002 by The Frank Lloyd Wright Foundation, Scottsdale, Arizona.*)

grown junipers and other evergreen foundation plantings—that had for so many years hidden the water table, the terrace parapet, and other architectural features—have been removed. Thus, the integrity of Wright's original design intent remains basically intact, but absent the landscape treatment envisioned by Griffin.

Francis W. Little—Peoria, Illinois (1902)

An analysis of the Francis W. Little House provides insight into the interactive-inspirational design methodology of The Studio by this date. As Johnson points out, there is a decided stylistic similarity in the massive corner piers used here, at Hillside Home School II, and the Dana House, as well as the house designed independently by Griffin for William H. Emery.[122] This structural detail was not used by Wright prior to 1902, when the design process began for all these structures. In addition to functionality, these piers defined the sizable raised planting boxes under the bands of windows in the living room and children's bedroom and served as pedestals for the large flattened planting urns that marked the corners of the parapet walls for the master-bedroom balcony. Since these planters had the effect of interposing a more immediate garden background into the living environment than any of the houses previously designed by Wright, it would seem this previously untried treatment initially may have been explored or suggested by Griffin—particularly since he served as the on-site construction supervisor, as well as landscape architect. This same collaborative analogy applies to the expansive privacy wall that envelops the sequestered garden space between the roofed porch and the stable-garage to visually expand the parameters of the architecture.[123] Again, sequestered gardens historically are associated with Griffin as a design specialty, whereas this design treatment was not used by Wright prior to 1902.

The Little House site plans are among the most particularized of any extant planting plans in the Frank Lloyd Wright Archives[124] (Figure 3-20). The "Grounds Plan of Plantings" is the most detailed, with multiple sheets enlarged to more clearly label each plant and perennial bed by both common and botanical names (see Appendix D.) Deciduous shrubs and trees predominate, except at the rear of the property where conifers, small accent trees, and shrubs were thickly planted to partially screen the garage, stable, and courtyard. Again, the influence of Griffin is evident. Not only are plant identifications in his hand, but the flower borders within the sequestered garden and elsewhere on the site are not contained within the precise architectonic raised beds generally associated with Wright's prairie house landscapes.

Arthur Heurtley—Oak Park, Illinois (1902)

The Arthur Heurtley site involved three 50-foot lots facing Forest Avenue and was located down the street from Wright's personal residence, one block north of the Thomas House, and directly across from the Moore House open space. It was this relationship to the Moore House open space that motivated Wright to employ the same raised basement approach he had used the previous year with the Thomas House. This reasoning is supported by the arrangement of the primary indoor and outdoor living spaces and the cause and effect of Wright's exacting siting methodology.

Wright sited the structure so the two-story mass of the west (front) façade was set back from the public sidewalk slightly more than existing houses, so as to accommodate a large entry terrace and still appear in conformance with neighboring structures. The north façade, on the other hand, was set back just enough to accommodate the prowlike offset of the breakfast-room window bay and provide a narrow strip of ground for plantings between the property line and driveway (Figure 3-21). This siting retained virtually the entire south half of the property as open space, as well as a sizable area to the rear of the house. It also preserved existing shade trees in several critical locations—including one directly across the driveway from the breakfast-room window-bay and two in the front yard to the west and south of the living room veranda. These were among a number of other shade trees Wright again carefully designed around and preserved, including the rare specimen oak tree in the rear garden that was "believed to be more than a thousand years old and the oldest living thing in Oak Park" at the time an article was published in the local newspaper 18 years later.[125] But the most significant consequence of this siting and arrangement was that the northernmost edge of the driveway precisely aligned with the south façade of the Moore front porch. Moreover, the north-south dimension of the structure generally paralleled the dimension of the sunken gardens to the south of the Moore House—as they existed in 1902 (Figure 3-22). Thus, the banks of windows along the second-floor living room and the first-floor playroom directly overlooked this peripheral open space, as did the living room veranda.

Another circumstance of this off-centered siting—and one that seems too coincidental to be a chance

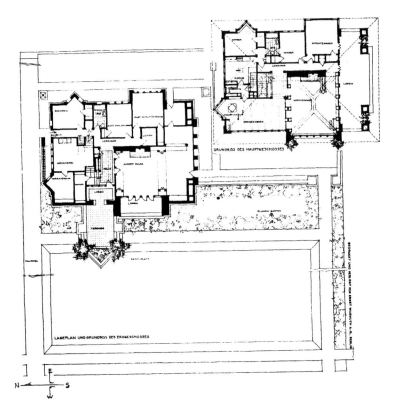

Figure 3-21 Floor plans and partial ground plan for the Arthur Heurtley House (1902) in Oak Park, Illinois. (*Out-of-copyright plans of record in Wasmuth Portfolio, 1910.*)

occurrence—is that the Heurtley House open space would have similarly correlated with the primary living space of the Gray House, if and when it was repositioned as Wright had proposed it should be when he drafted the plans for its remodeling two years earlier[126] (Figure 3-23). This is no less relevant because of the subsequent repositioning of that living space in 1905, when the remodeling actually took place and the entire structure was shifted onto the additional lot that was acquired at that time.

The environmental disadvantages Wright had to address with the Heurtley House once again related to the westerly orientation of the front entrance and the primary living spaces. Wright's initial thinking must have been that by increasing the depth of the eave by 1 foot, the 5-foot overhang would completely shelter the openings along the west wall—at least in this instance, where the primary living spaces and the veranda are on the second level. This theory was correct with respect to the dining room and upstairs entry hall. But the living room portion of the overhang was reduced by half when

Wright extended the west wall of the living room and correspondingly inset the west wall of the ground floor playroom, directly below, in order to create a 5-foot-deep overhead plane to protect the band of French doors that open onto the playroom loggia. Because neither the eave overhang nor the overhead plane proportionately relate to the correspondent openings, however, neither living space is adequately sheltered by the architecture.[127]

Wright's methodology for sheltering the main point of outdoor-indoor transition, however, represented an all-inclusive design approach that interrelated his architecture with the entry experience, streetside appearance, and environmental design solutions at a level of sophistication not exhibited prior to this date. The entry door itself is not visible from the street because it is inset 8 feet at the southeast corner of the entry loggia and diagonally removed from the arched opening in the west façade to deflect the brunt of the prevailing winter winds. To deflect the winds even more, Wright installed a 5-foot parapet around the entry terrace (Figure 3-24). That he also gave consideration to the need for adequate ventila-

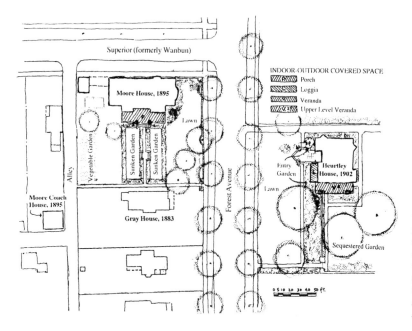

Figure 3-22 The Heurtley House was specifically sited so that its primary living spaces overlooked the scenic sunken gardens of the adjacent Nathan G. Moore House. (*By Charles E. Aguar, based on personal analysis and out-of-copyright plans of record in Wasmuth Portfolio, 1910. As delineated, © 2002 by Berdeana Aguar.*)

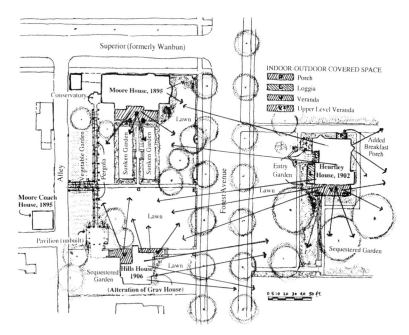

Figure 3-23 Relationships between the Heurtley, Moore, and Gray-Hills Houses after 1906 development of intervening open space. (*By Charles E. Aguar, based on personal analysis and out-of-copyright plans of record in Wasmuth Portfolio, 1910. As delineated, © 2002 by Berdeana Aguar.*)

Figure 3-24 The prow of the Heurtley terrace provides privacy and shields the main entry from prevailing winter winds. (*Photograph by Charles E. Aguar. © 2002 by Berdeana Aguar.*)

tion at other times of the year, as well, is evidenced by the arrangement of open spaces between bricks in some of the courses above the level of the triangular planting bed that filled the terrace prow.[128] This "pierced-brick" technique also introduced an ambient play of late-afternoon sunlight onto the terrace floor that relates to the sunburst pattern of the bricks over the vestibule arch. Other aesthetic functions of the terrace wall were to project the architecture into the public portion of the landscape and provide a backdrop for the entry garden in the triangle of the prow, as viewed from the bands of windows along the west wall of the dining room.

The Heurtley House represents Wright's first and only use of stacked, alternating courses of two colors of textured Roman brick, with every fifth course stepped back to form a double horizontal shadow line. The resulting rhythm and texture of this distinctive brick-work introduced a strongly repetitive metaphor of horizontality into the streetside appearance. In addition, Wright battered the Roman-brick walls at an eight-degree angle to suggest a strong connection to the earth. And he visually extended the parameters of the architecture even more expansively than was done with the Little House by using the same brickwork to enclose all the prominent outdoor open spaces—including the entry terrace, the adjacent ground-floor playroom loggia, the second-floor veranda, and the privacy wall that defined the L-shaped sequestered garden as well as all of the open spaces to the rear and south of the house. Even the informal planting beds that bordered the outermost

edges of all the approach routes were laid out to visually expand the parameters of the architecture by way of their boxlike, parallel arrangement alongside the south and north boundaries and across virtually the entire breadth of the property. It is this clearly articulated, outward progression of the architecture at ground level, together with the banding of the windows in the second-floor living spaces, that creates the streetside appearance described by Jack H. Prost, a one-time owner of the residence: "From the northwest the house appears low and shallow. . . . From the southwest, the house looks low, deep, and square. From the south the upstairs is a hole, an open porch, while from the north the upstairs is all windows, reflecting light, creating a screen. . . . The perceptual play between squares and rectangles, shallowness and depth, is achieved by hiding surfaces and angles in one scene and then revealing them as one moves, thus changing one's interpretation of the shape."[129]

The patterns of movement described by Prost directly relate to Wright's choreography of the entry experience, which was designed to direct movement as the property would be approached by foot or by some other form of transport, and according to the social function or mode of entertainment. From the south—the direction of the business district and train station—movement is directed from the public right-of-way onto the entry sidewalk to the point of intersection, where there is the option of going directly through the opening in the privacy wall and into the sequestered garden, or turning towards the entry terrace. From the north, movement is directed from the public right-of-way onto the entry driveway to the entry sidewalk leading to the entry terrace, where there is the option of going directly into the residence or moving across the terrace and proceeding on to the garden entrance. Each approach required changing direction two times and ascending three steps to reach the shelter of the entry terrace.

The situation of the terrace planting bed in the triangle of the prow immediately next to the pier-pedestals is another key element of the entry experience. In addition to adornment and the basic climatic functions of plantings—that is, to temper the heat of the sun, help channel any breeze that passed through the pierced brick, and otherwise improve the microclimate of the entry terrace—the planting bed identified the terrace as the destination of the entry experience. The backdrop of the brick parapet brought the plantings into relief and focused attention inward; and the finite shape of the prow created a sense of closure and security. This all-inclusive treatment coalesced with the subliminal function of the informal plantings alongside the entry sidewalks, which was to associate perennial garden plantings with the pattern of movement toward the entry terrace. Moreover, the elevation of the plantings in the distinctive shallow urns on either side of the front terrace focused attention upon the terrace pier and identified the steps as the point of entry.

As the entry terrace is crossed, the brickwork in the monumental arch directs attention toward the protective enclosure of the entry loggia and the ground floor entry hall. From this point, there is the option of going directly into the ground-floor playroom or proceeding up the complex entry stairwell, which involves five changes of direction before "arriving" at the upstairs reception hall that opens onto both the dining room and the living room—where the spatiality expands in all directions to invite movement toward the panorama of the greater site environment and the peripheral environment of the Moore House sunken gardens directly across the street. It was the ultimate resolution of all these carefully considered elements of environmental design—together with the quality and distinction of the architecture—that inspired Grant Manson to observe that the Heurtley House "has an almost classic unity and directness. . . . It is often considered the gem of the early Prairie Houses."[130]

The Heurtleys occupied their home for 18 years. During this time, they enclosed the south veranda by glazing the openings and also reduced its size by closing off the area next to the master bedroom to accommodate an additional bathroom. In 1920, the house was purchased by Mr. and Mrs. Andrew J. Porter (Mrs. Porter was Wright's sister), who subsequently converted the house into a two-level duplex. To gain additional living space, the loggia off the playroom was enclosed and a makeshift overhang was appended across the west facade in an effort to shield the glazed openings from the late-afternoon sun—a climatic condition that had become a problem after existing trees died over time and were never replaced. When Edward and Diane Baehrend purchased the house in 1997, they hired architect John G. Thorpe to restore it as a single-family residence. The guiding principle throughout this painstaking process was to restore the structure as closely as possible to reflect Wright's original design intent—including the restoration of the playroom loggia and living room veranda as outdoor living spaces—except for the area housing the bathroom addition on the east. In addition, the non-Wrightian garage and apartment were removed from the premises; and replicated massive urns, which had deteriorated or were lost over time, once again adorn the piers at the head of the steps leading onto the entry terrace.

Inasmuch as there is no landscape plan-of-record for the Heurtley House, the new owners intend to recreate the site environment based upon historic photographs and written descriptions. With the empathetic restoration of the landscape and the introduction of replacement shade trees on the west lawn, the Heurtley House eventually could represent one of the most complete restorations of any privately owned, Wright-designed Prairie House.

William Everett Martin—Oak Park, Illinois (1902–1903)

When siting the William Everett Martin residence upon two 50-foot lots, Wright complied with the established setback lines along East Avenue but left just enough room for a service walkway and entry veranda off the north side of the kitchen. This off-centered siting left ample space to accommodate a spacious roofed porch to the south of the dining room and allowed generous groupings of windows or glazed French doors along the south walls of the primary living areas. To assure privacy, no windows were placed along the north wall of the living room.

That both William and Winifred Martin actively interacted with Wright during the planning process is confirmed by correspondence preserved by members of the W.E. Martin family.[131] Even while Winifred and the Martin children were visiting relatives in Alabama during February 1903, William sent Wright's preliminary plans to her, together with sketches showing changes he would like to make. Interestingly, her response expressed concerns as to the orientation: "What I did not like about upstairs—you have all our bedrooms on the coldest sides of the house. A south bedroom for us would have a nicer outlook. South and east sides are warmest." She also sent sketches for his review, with the following explanation: "I have tried to arrange bedrooms giving S. wing for ours. I took off 4 feet clear across room for two closets—leaves room 16 × 19 with south and west front—west looking into the flower garden."[132] Granddaughter Carolyn Mann Brackett attempted to clarify any confusion as to the subsequent placement of the master bedroom and its relationship with the planned flower garden: "The original garden was planned for the back yard if the master bedroom was to be placed where the Martins wanted it. However, the master bedroom with a fireplace and additional door to the only bathroom on the 2nd floor was finally placed on the southwest side of the house, leaving the front yard the only place for a garden."[133]

Brackett went on to remember how the grounds appeared during the Depression years of the 1930s, when she and her sisters spent considerable time in the home of their grandparents: "The entire front yard with mature trees and bushes . . . provided a completely private enclosure . . . there were trees and high bushes along the sidewalk. Elms planted on the parkway for many blocks formed a canopy across North East Avenue. It was quite beautiful until they were destroyed by Elm Disease. The pathway leading to the entrance porch paralleling the street was so thick with trees and bushes . . .

one could not see the street."[134] She also remembers the meadowlike open space to the rear of the house with informally planted border and island gardens as "very private and a wonderful place to play."

Brackett advises that a third 50-foot lot, to the south of the original property, was acquired specifically for the purpose of developing it as a formal garden with a pergola. This did not occur until some six years after the house was built, however. Records verify September 24, 1908 as the land purchase date. Photographs-of-record confirm construction was complete with plantings in place before Winter 1910.[135] As with the landscape composition designed for the Moore House in 1905, the W. E. Martin plans of 1908 were much more comprehensive than the "pergola" designation in the job listings would imply. The pergola itself extended across the entire width of the additional lot and cantilevered over the relocated driveway to ensure that ingress and egress to and from vehicles would be sheltered—a precurser to the carport that Wright would "invent" some 30 years hence (Figure 3-25). Moreover, the entire garden environment was designed to conform with, and extend the lines of the house into, the out-of-doors—as delineated in a conjectured site plan prepared by Oak Park architectural historian Jack Lesniak (Figure 3-26).

The Lesniak site plan verifies that problems can be created when the Wasmuth portfolio drawings are accepted at face value and perpetuated from one publication to another. It seems the site plan in the 1910 Wasmuth portfolio expands the scale and proportion so the property appeared to be 200 feet wide, rather than 150 feet, and the pathways were drawn to appear much wider than they actually were. Moreover, the Wasmuth plans and perspective depict elements that do not appear on construction drawings and never were built.

Figure 3-25 East elevation of the pergola of the William E. Martin House (1902–1903) in Oak Park, Illinois, shows Wright's first use of the carport concept. (*By Charles E. Aguar, based on historic photographs, personal analysis, and original drawings of record. © 2002 by The Frank Lloyd Wright Foundation, Scottsdale, Arizona. As delineated, © 2002 by Berdeana Aguar.*)

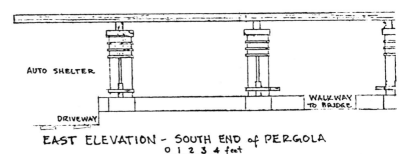

EAST ELEVATION - SOUTH END of PERGOLA

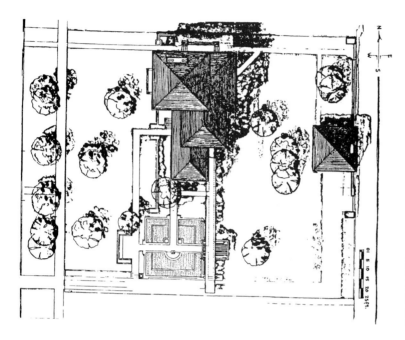

Figure 3-26 Plot plan of the W. E. Martin property following 1909 garden addition, as prepared by Oak Park historian Jack Lesniak. (*Courtesy of Jack Lesniak and relatives of the W. E. Martin family.*)

According to Bracket, the scaled plan prepared by Lesniak most closely represents the garden as built, because it is based upon her recollection and photographs.

The central focus of the garden addition was the distinctive square-within-a-square, two-depth lily pool with a half-round island planting bed centered around the intersection of a T-shaped bridge that spanned the pool. The cross sections for the pool detail that the innermost square was 6 feet deep with a water-line depth of 5 feet, whereas the moatlike border was 3 feet deep with a water-line depth of 2 feet. Because construction drawings were at some point damaged by fire, the labeling and design components are not always clear, but it appears that the railings for the island and bridge were made of steel, as were those portions shown extending down into the water as a safety measure to disunite the depths of the two pools[136] (Figure 3-27). That the pool originally was constructed as designed is confirmed by the detailing visible in a photograph taken in the winter of 1910. But the summer photograph included in the 1911 Wasmuth portfolio confirms that the moatlike border portion of the pool had by that date already been boxed in with concrete and converted to a planting bed.

It is known that Griffin was in charge of the house construction in 1902 but it is not known how much, if any, involvement he had with the original gardens. Brackett believes Griffin may have been involved with both landscape arrangements inasmuch as her mother (Lois M. Martin), born in 1905, "remembered Mr. Griffin being at the house quite often." Moreover, January 1914 correspondence between Griffin and Wilhelm Miller confirms that Griffin was at least in part "responsible for the landscape design of Wright's William E. Martin residence in Oak Park" in 1910.[137] Considering

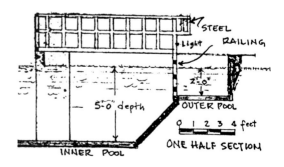

Figure 3-27 One-half section of the W. E. Martin garden pool. (*Deteriorated print retouched and relabeled by the author. © 2002 by The Frank Lloyd Wright Foundation, Scottsdale, Arizona. As delineated, © 2002 by Berdeana Aguar.*)

that Griffin disassociated himself from Wright in mid-to-late 1905, it may be that he was brought onto the scene by the Martins or by Marion Mahony—who along with Herman von Holst was responsible for completing all works-in-process when Wright closed The Studio and sailed for Europe in Fall 1909.

Whether Griffin was involved with this garden environment because of Mahony or the clients, however, it most probably was Griffin's empathetic interpretation and execution of Wright's design intent that inspired Wilhelm Miller to identify the William E. Martin garden addition as a "chief American work in landscape architecture."[138] And it was this garden—perhaps the most significant of any of the prairie houses in the Midwest developed to full potential—that set the William Martin residence apart. It truly became a house within a garden, endowed with all the ambiance of light and shadow, color, texture, and harmony found in Wright's architecture, but seldom in his landscapes (Figure 3-28). The geometric pathway system was choreographed as an entry experience that directed movement past or through the garden, whether arrival was by foot or by vehicle, as it also interrelated several custom-designed benches and bridges as vantage points from which to pause and reflect upon the garden. To traverse through this environment to reach the main point of outdoor-indoor transition would have been the quintessential entry experience.

Children who grew up in this especial garden environment have many happy memories and are able to describe their unique experiences a half-century or more later.[139] Carolyn Brackett reminisced: "The house was indeed a play area, inside and out. . . . We and our neighborhood friends acted out scenes from the Shirley Temple movies under the pergola and in the gardens." She also recalled that a water faucet was built into the planting box below the living room windows and that the box was filled with water in later years, rather than plants and soil: "William [her grandfather] enjoyed the late sun reflecting off the water and onto the ceiling. If the wind blows, lovely patterns are projected onto the ceiling. . . . In the 30's during the summer, my sister, Donna Mann Duncan, and I were allowed to go out the small window of the living room and plunge back and forth in the window box pool. It was quite deep to 4 and 5 year olds."

By the end of World War II, the W. E. Martin garden addition was in a state of disrepair, and the property was

Figure 3-28 Historic photograph of W. E. Martin garden expansion. (*Courtesy of relatives of the W. E. Martin family.*)

Figure 3-29 A 1989 photograph of W. E. Martin House, with post–World War II infill house and curving entry walkway. (*Photograph by Charles E. Aguar. © 2002 by Berdeana Aguar.*)

subdivided to accommodate an infill bungalow (Figure 3-29). When Laura and Richard Talaske purchased the property in 1993, they conducted considerable historical research before entering into the process of remodeling and restoration. Based upon their findings and a desire to accurately reflect Wright's original design intent, they invested extraordinary effort into restoring the landscape along with the structure. They began by removing the inappropriate evergreen foundation plantings that had been sheared into unnatural forms and allowed to completely obliterate the crisp, clean lines of Wright's architecture. They then removed an incongruous curving sidewalk from the front yard and reinstalled an entry walkway to the original configuration (Figure 3-30). And they relandscaped this area using indigenous varieties of prairie plants such as Wright and Griffin might have selected near the turn of the century. Most important, they undertook the Herculean task of trying to re-create or adapt to the imagery that once existed in the open space to the south—with technical assistance provided

Figure 3-30 The W. E. Martin House, after a garden wall was added and the walkway was restored to its original form. (*1996 photograph by Charles E. Aguar. © 2002 by Berdeana Aguar.*)

Figure 3-31 W. E. Martin garden renovation undertaken by the Richard Talaskes. (*John Thorpe, AIA. Courtesy of Laura and Richard Talaske.*)

by John Thorpe, A.I.A. Laura Talaske explains: "Our goal was to incorporate as much as possible of the original concepts, especially, of course, the pond, pergola and benches, and keep each in the same relationship to the other in the process, given the lack of the extra 50-foot lot. The new wall now incorporates a smaller bench (the wall is exactly on the same footing placement as the original) overlooking the pond, which is bisected by the path leading to the pergola and benches. Our new plan also includes a prow-shaped patio around the benches as a modern addition."[140] That the Talaskes' approach was eminently successful is supported by photographs taken even before the adaptive re-creation was entirely complete (Figure 3-31).

It is important to note that an approach such as described by the Talaskes could not have been considered, had it not been for Wright's foresighted concerns with privacy, southern exposure, and outdoor living space—all of which motivated the original off-centered siting that made it feasible to undertake a renovation process of this magnitude.

Edward H. Cheney—Oak Park, Illinois (1903)

Wright maintained that the design for the Edward H. Cheney House was conceived a full decade earlier, in 1893, while he still was in the employ of Adler and Sullivan.[141] Certainly, the generic concept of a house contained behind privacy walls would function very well if the structure was situated on almost any level prairie lot. On this particular Oak Park property, however, the term "privacy wall" really is a misnomer since the windows of the multistoried neighboring structures would overlook walls of any height.

Wright's intent was that the defining exterior privacy walls stretch across the entire width of the property, run along the property lines on both sides to a midway point, and then turn inward to enclose the dual entry landings–the main entry to the south and the service entry to the north. This treatment was to create the illusion that the structure behind the walls was a modest, ground-hugging bungalow nestled among the many

Figure 3-32 Wright's preliminary thumbnail sketch of the Edward H. Cheney House (1903) in Oak Park, Illinois, shows his intent to preserve existing trees. (© *2002 by The Frank Lloyd Wright Foundation, Scottsdale, Arizona.*)

mature, extant trees Wright intended to save during construction. Wright's preliminary thumbnail sketch clearly delineates the existing trees that he factored into his customization of the design for the Cheney site, including the tree on the south property line that caused Wright to build an inset into the privacy wall to accommodate its trunk (Figure 3-32). These trees determined the situation and mass of the building and also established the ground level both inside and outside the all-encompassing walls. It was on this basis that Wright proposed to fashion a two-tiered earthen terrace—the first tier outside the privacy wall 1 foot above grade of the public sidewalk, and the second tier inside the privacy wall at 4 feet above grade (Figure 3-33).

The first tier extends from the public sidewalk to the streetside privacy wall and around both sides to the midpoints where the rear walls enclose the entry landings. The terrace rim is beveled inward to emphasize the sharp-edged alignment of the entry steps on either side. The 9-foot-high privacy wall is situated atop this terrace to make it appear to be of-a-level with the 10-foot-high sections of the wall at the rear of the house, where the natural grade was 1 foot lower than the front. The sections flanking the terrace were to unify the brick foundation piers, masonry base, and parapet walls on the north and south sides of the terrace, which Wright conceived as a bridged deck to allow the introduction of natural light into the basement windows.

The lower portion of the flanking sections are shown as levee-like embankments bermed to the height of the masonry base–a treatment that would conceal the foundation piers and preserve the integrity of the all-of-

a-level height of the wall, as it perceptively increased the depth of setback. The earthen terrace inside the wall is shown dimensioned just wide enough to provide a foundation for the dual walkway approaches that follow along the privacy wall on both sides. Levee-like bermed embankments were to bound the entire walkway system to essentially "frame" the proposed, U-shaped sunken garden shown passing under the bridged terrace and wrapping around the east and west ends of the main living space, and the north side of the kitchen[142] (Figure 3-34 a-b).

In execution, only the walls along the north and south property lines and the section of the wall surrounding a portion of the front terrace were installed to the nine foot height. Although construction rubble was distributed as a base for the earthen embankment, the unifying wall sections on either side of the terrace were never completed as detailed, nor were the brick foundation piers and masonry base installed (Figure 3-35). The berm inside the wall also was never formed as proposed. Instead, the second-tier addition fills the entire space and the potential of the entry experience was never achieved. Nonetheless, the ingenuousness of the site manipulation and precision grading Wright envisioned for the Cheney property should be recognized as among the most creative of his career.

Susan Lawrence Dana—Springfield, Illinois (1902–1904)

The Susan Lawrence Dana House marked a turning point in Wright's career, as it represents the highest level of sophistication in Wright's design interrelationships to this point. It is not known who on his staff worked on this commission, other than Mahony, who was closely involved with detailing the art glass and other artistic aspects of design. Additional staff members were less involved, if at all, since there were a number of equally significant commissions being processed through The Studio during 1903 and 1904. For this reason, Wright made the rare decision to engage S.J. Haines, a noted Springfield architect, as on-site construction supervisor.[143]

Wright originally was retained to remodel the existing Lawrence family home, situated at the northwest corner intersection of Fourth Street and Lawrence Avenue on a natural rise some three feet higher than the street. When the client's intent shifted toward the design of a new house, Wright was asked to incorporate the existing house into his design. Within this redesign process, Wright maintained the same elevated ground

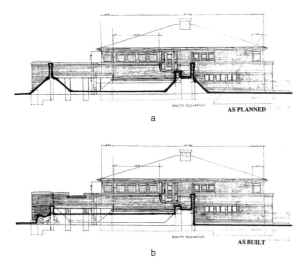

Figure 3-34 a–b Sections of the Cheney House show south elevation with proposed grading for bermlike embankments (3-34 a), and south elevation as actually built, without berms or privacy walls across front (3-34 b). (*By Charles E. Aguar, based on personal analysis and plans of record. © 2002 by The Frank Lloyd Wright Foundation, Scottsdale, Arizona. As delineated, © 2002 by Berdeana Aguar*)

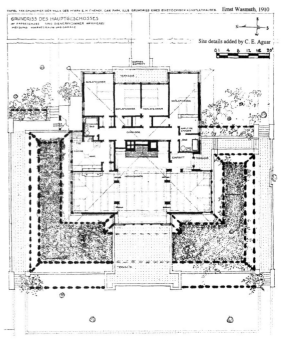

Figure 3-33 Ernst Wasmuth site plan of the Cheney House emphasizes levee-like earthen embankments. (*By Charles E. Aguar, based on personal analysis and out-of-copyright plans of record in Wasmuth Portfolio, 1910. As delineated, © 2002 by Berdeana Aguar.*)

Figure 3-35 A 1996 photograph at the Cheney residence shows exposed brick piers and masonry base, prepared for privacy walls that were never completed. (*Photograph by Charles E. Aguar. © 2002 by Berdeana Aguar.*)

level and meandered the new house around extant vegetation so as to preserve as many of the 15 shade trees as possible. These mature trees not only formed the basis for the mass of the house and expanded auxiliary structures—the Lawrence family barn and carriage house at the northwest corner of the property—they also deter-

mined the arrangement of the sidewalks and all points of access. Most important, they helped preserve the character and identity of the neighborhood as they provided shade, filtered sun and dust, and created silhouettes and shadows that heightened the three-dimensional impact of Wright's architecture. Only two trees were lost—one during the relocation of an accessory building, the other during construction of the porch adjoining the south-facing terrace. As the latter tree still was depicted as growing through the roof in construction drawings, Wright apparently gave serious consideration to leaving it in place as a source of shade. Since photographs taken while the house was under construction verify that the tree had by that time been removed, however, it must be assumed that either Wright's thinking changed as to the feasibility of the operation or he was at that point unable to resolve how it would be accomplished.

The remodeled main house was arranged so that its greater length paralleled Lawrence Avenue to the south, and the base paralleled Fourth Street to the east (Figure 3-36). There was just enough setback from both rights-of-way to accommodate the leveled crown of the three-foot rise, which Wright again sculpted as an earthen terrace. The plane of green grass stabilizing the sharply beveled embankment established the foundation for the streetside impression as it combined with the amber planes created by the copings and prominent baseline, the bronzed plane of the gypsum plaster frieze, the eave facades of oxidized molded copper, and the red-clay tiles of the hip roof to visually extend and emphasize the hor-izontality of the residence. The dark gold coping of the privacy walls that sequester the rear yard extended this visual line an additional 50 feet westward to Third Street. As viewed from either of the intersecting streets, there-fore, the Dana House appears as a palatial edifice that fills the entire site. Since the structure actually occupies but 26 percent of the site, however, this imagery is an illusionistic reflection of Wright's precise siting, his sculpting of the defining earthen terrace and his pavilion-like arrangement of the building units and the connecting privacy wall extensions (Figure 3-37).

Figure 3-36　Presentation perspective shows south elevation of the Susan Lawrence Dana House (1902–1904) in Springfield, Illinois. (*Out-of-copyright drawing from Wasmuth Portfolio, 1910.*)

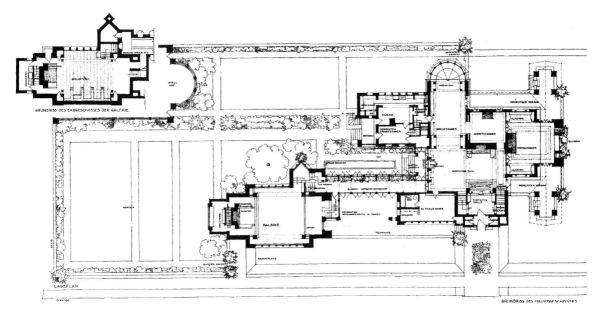

Figure 3-37　Site plan and main-floor plan for the Dana House. (*Out-of-copyright plan of record from Wasmuth Portfolio, 1910.*)

Wright choreographed the entry experience to begin on Lawrence Avenue at curbside, where the wide entry landing is one step above street level and immediately adjacent to the public sidewalk. From the sidewalk, movement proceeds up three broad low-rise steps to reach the level of a spacious entrance court defined on either side by the low walls that retain the earthen terrace. As the entrance court is crossed, the brickwork represented in the monumental arch over the entry provides a strong artistic accent that causes the eye to be drawn inward through the multifarious display of autumnal colored art glass that make up the magnificent fanlights overscoring the arch, both outside and inside. Because the doorway is overt and the entry walkway is straightforward, the initial impression is that the approach is frontally direct and relatively unimaginative. As with Thomas, Fricke, and Heurtley, however, the totality of the entry "experience" is both indirect and imaginative, as it continues on the inside and does not culminate until the first-story (second level) reception hall is reached.

Immediately upon passing through the doorway and the barrel vault entry, the spatiality expands dramatically (Figure 3-38). Directly ahead in the entrance hall stands Richard Bock's sculpture *The Flower In the Crannied Wall*, which draws the eye forward and upward to its commanding height and beyond–to the ceiling of the reception hall two stories above. To "arrive" at this destination, however, it is necessary to search out and negotiate a series of twists and turns and changes in level–first through the narrow hallway to the right leading to a large coatroom in the basement (a half-level below) and then through the enclosed stairwell to the left, which ascends to the reception hall landing where the spatiality expands even more dramatically in all directions: downward into the entrance hall, upward to the cantilevered third-floor balcony circumscribing three sides of the far-reaching space, and outward to the commanding axial, lineal, and vertical amplitude of the dining room–terminating some 55 feet ahead in the low-ceilinged breakfast alcove with the half-circle bay of art-glass windows depicting the stylized motif of native sumac. But the ultimate consciousness of the entry experience is the water feature centered upon the reception hall wall to the left of the entry stairway, accentuating *The Moon Children* fountain sculpted by Bock. This setting, as described by Donald P. Hallmark, provides "a stunning interior use of running water, a small reflecting pool, planters filled with flowers, and cascading foliage surrounded by several bays of art glass."[144]

It is only by actually walking through Wright's carefully choreographed progression-of-entry that his developing art of daylighting can be understood and appreciated. By illuminating the entrance hall with refracted daylight transmitted through the barrel vault artglass and the two-story-high windows across the

Figure 3-38   Historic photograph of the Dana House's barrel vault entry with Richard Bock's sculpture in the entrance hall. (*Out-of-copyright photograph of record from Wasmuth Portfolio, 1911.*)

south wall of the reception hall, Wright compensated for any visual discordance that might occur during the abrupt transference from the harsh sunlight reflected off the concrete of the entrance court. By then enclosing the interior entrance stairwell and temporarily lessening the perception of luminance, Wright allowed the pupil of the eye to adjust to the level of light in the reception hall so that attention focuses upon the interior open spaces washed with refracted light, the half-circle bay of art-glass windows in the breakfast alcove, the backlighted bays of art glass surrounding the fountain feature, and the fountain feature itself. Thus, the sense of arrival is subtly intensified. This astute control of luminance gradation should be seen as an evolving integral design element in Wright's choreography of the entry experience.

From the central location of the reception hall, movement is directed according to the social function or mode of entertainment: straight ahead toward the dining room for a formal dinner; to the immediate left through the conservatory toward the gallery for a performance or concert; through one of the double art-glass doorways toward the walled garden for a lawn party; or through any of the primary living spaces to one of the adjoining roofed porches—the combined square footage of which increased by more than 50 percent the usable living/entertaining space on the first floor. The floor plans clearly support that Wright strategically sited and arranged the architecture to allow the introduction of these outdoor living spaces, with each carefully designed to enhance and be in consort with the specific societal use of the adjacent interior space.

The most significant outdoor living space is the roofed porch in the wing housing the magnificent studio-gallery. This porch functions as a unit with the glassed-in hallway-conservatory on the north and the walled, veranda-like terrace on the south to accommodate a large number of guests attending performances. Since this spatial combination functioned much as mezzanines and lobbies do for theaters and opera houses, Wright went to great effort to enhance the sense-of-place in this area by installing an extensive planter alongside the base windows of the north wall of the conservatory—complete with concealed radiators to maintain the proper temperature, a watering system, and a continuous skylight to bathe this space with natural light. Then, across the south wall of the gallery porch, he installed a wall of screened doors that open onto the terrace to interrelate the indoor-outdoor spaces in this area and provide direct access to the south terrace and gallery by way of the stair-

way leading off the entrance court.[145] Wright also gave special consideration to the terrace lighting by installing glass prisms (glass blocks) as flooring for a portion of the terrace. This treatment provided a source of subtle, indirect illumination for guests arriving after dark when the scones lining the walls of the basement space were left lighted. At the same time, the glass prisms admitted natural daylight into the billiards space in the basement below to supplement the natural light admitted through a grouping of small grilles Wright installed in the walls in this area.[146] This inventive manner of introducing natural light into the partially submerged basement without installing windows, in the normal sense, underscores Wright's developing skill as an environmental designer. Had he installed windows, instead of omitting every other brick to form a window-like grouping of small grilles, he would have introduced a jarring vertical element and compromised the illusion of horizontality he had gone to so much effort to create.

The entry experience into the sequestered garden environment simulates the approach from the entrance hall to the reception hall, in that there are optional points of access on either side of the Bock sculpture and there is a sense of discovery in the twists and turns required to move through the service hallway to reach the double art-glass doors and access the stairs leading to the courtyard. At the base of the stairs, a narrow elongated reflecting pool draws the eye downward and outward toward the prowlike projection off the gallery landing, with art-glass windows above and a planter feature below. This projection, together with the paralleling walls of the kitchen wing to the right, the conservatory wing to the left, and the spreading overhead branching of one of the carefully preserved shade trees create a certain sense of enclosure as movement progresses into the open space of the sequestered garden.

The ultimate consciousness of the sequestered garden is one of far-reaching uncluttered space, instead of the profusely planted stroll garden generally found behind other homes of stature at the turn of the century. There never were such elements as garden furniture, fountains, sculptures, pergola, or other garden shelter, and no changes in grade, created vistas, or any event or landmark to give pause to the flow of movement or evoke thought in the viewer. The single such element, the narrow reflecting pool, suggests by its shape and placement in the transitional corner of the courtyard that it was intended to be viewed while strolling from the house to the rear garden or from the vantage point of the conservatory. It had the additional function of reflecting light into the windowed wall of the bowling alley. Although the Dana House would not necessarily be expected to have a "garden" in the formal sense of the domestic architecture of its time, it seems highly unusual that the outdoor space is not visible from any of the interior spaces normally associated with gardens. Nevertheless, Wright and his client certainly knew how they wanted this outdoor space to function. Indeed, the Dana House walled garden was very specifically designed to accommodate elaborate lawn parties or to encourage the movement of groups of people strolling and intermingling. It is for this reason that all spaces between the walkways were maintained as lawn, so as not to constrain spillover onto these areas or in any way limit the servicing of guests.

The landscape analysis in the *Historic Structures Report* prepared during the process of restoring the Dana House as a house museum lists two dozen species of mainly herbaceous plantings—flowers, ferns, and ground covers—that were known to have grown on the property in 1905.[147] Ornamental understory trees were used selectively. Only three had been planted by 1905, and these were situated *inside* the privacy wall—two near the horse paddock and one just inside the wall as accent to the gateway access from Lawrence Avenue. Nor were any shrubbery or perennials arrayed outside the Dana House

privacy wall, either as foundation planting or as an entry garden. Flowering shrubs were planted at the inside corner of the gallery, at the base of the bowlike projection of the gallery stairway landing, along the south wall of the kitchen wing (in full sun), and along the north side of the gallery (in dense shade). There also were border plantings along the wall and the carriage house yard to associate perennial garden plantings with the pattern of movement, as at the Heurtley House. It is this very thoughtfully considered *exclusion* of planting ornamentation that so underscores the "hanging garden" imagery put forth by the plantings to be displayed in the many built-in planters and urns that dramatize the public impress of the Dana House architecture (Figure 3-39).

Through this analysis, Wright's intent with the Dana House site environment becomes clear. He wanted to create only a visual "impression" of a garden. By providing mere glimpses of trees, grass, and flowers so they would not be consciously noticed, Wright evoked a subliminal response that complements, rather than competes with, the conception of the interior as an awe-inspiring work of art. Certainly, the summer garden display could never match the brilliant, year-round displays so artfully depicted in the richly organic geometric abstractions of the art glass, the varying planes and wide-ranging openness of the interior spaces, the many built-in containers provided for arrangements of fernery and

Figure 3-39 Historic photograph depicts "hanging garden" imagery of the Dana House. (*Out-of-copyright photograph of record from Wasmuth Portfolio, 1911.*)

dried plants, or the setting for the fountain feature. All of these enhancements can be seen as cultivated garden elements in accord with the Japanese connotation of "garden in building" as put forth by Heinrich Engel: "Garden in building manifests man's aesthetic awareness of his environment. Complying with man's psychological wants and stimulating man's aesthetic senses, it performs the role of art . . . [it] is architecture that employs forms and products of nature. In the residence, it is the mediating space that brings together the contrasts of technical and organic substance, of geometric and natural form, and of human and infinite scale."[148]

The Dana House was procured by the State of Illinois during the early 1980s for the purpose of restoring it to its former elegance and maintaining it as a museum.[149] Since that date, it has been known as the "Dana-Thomas State Historic Site," in commemoration of the two dominant owners: Susan Lawrence Dana and Charles C. Thomas, publisher. Each held title to the property for more than 30 years. The $5 million restoration completed under auspices of the Historic Sites Division of the Illinois Historic Preservation Agency, with additional financial support provided by the Dana-Thomas House Foundation, represents the state's first historic site acquisition purchased solely on the basis of architectural merit.[150]

It seems significant that Bock could not commit to design the sculptures for the Dana House until at some point during 1903, when work was well under way, because of a prior obligation to complete his statuary for the Louisiana Purchase Exposition in St. Louis, Missouri.[151] It perhaps was because of Bock's personal recounting of exhibits he saw at the Exposition that Wright decided to himself attend the event and suggested that others on his staff also take advantage of the experience, as supported by historian Meryle Secrest when she observed: "Wright went and was fascinated. He must go to the fair, Wright told his new draftsman, Charles White, in May 1904; 'it is a liberal education.' "[152]

Louisiana Purchase Exposition—St. Louis, Missouri (1904)

The centennial anniversary of the Louisiana Purchase of 1903 was the first historical event of sufficient consequence to merit a national celebration comparable to the Chicago Exposition of 1893. This celebratory vehicle represented the work of the world's most noted

artists and classical architects and was the largest and most spectacular World Fair held in America up to that time, as well as the first of the twentieth century. Even so, historians generally have given scant attention to Wright's attendance and impressions of this event. Those that do suggest Wright's primary interest would have been the German installation, although mention has been made of the Japanese prints he is known to have purchased at the event. It would seem more logical to assume Wright would have made it a point to thoroughly explore both the German and the Japanese installations, considering that he linked and identified with both in his autobiography: "The lands of my dreams—old Japan and old Germany."[153] And it certainly would seem more than happenstance that less than a year after attending this event, Wright's country of choice for his first trip abroad would be Japan.

The reality is that the Japanese persona and particularly the "Imperial Japanese Garden," as the official Japanese exhibit was known, could hardly have been ignored by any fair visitor—least of all by Wright. The sizable site allotted to Japan was near the geometric center of the Exposition layout and accommodated not one but six pavilions within a hill and water garden setting, all contained inside the limits of a privacy wall.[154] Thus, Wright at the St. Louis Exposition was afforded an exceptional opportunity to obtain a very comprehensive, if encapsulated, view of Japanese culture, architecture, and landscape cultivation and articulation. Consequently, there is ample reason to believe he would have been every bit as influenced by what he saw there as at the Chicago event, if not more so.

Consider the layout of the Imperial Japanese Garden. At the highest point of the walled compound was the Main Pavilion, an abridged adaptation of the eighth-century Reception Hall of the Imperial Palace at Heian-kyo, Kyoto. There also was the very elaborate Formosa Pavilion near the main entrance, a large Bazaar, the Commissioner's Office, and Bellevue (an L-shaped cluster of three small buildings). Nearest to the water garden was a reproduction of the Golden Pavilion (1395), also from the vicinity of Kyoto. It was this three-story square structure built of wood, supported by slender posts, encircled by open verandas, and sheltered under dipping hip roofs with deep overhanging eaves that would have been of critical interest to Wright. The entire first floor was without permanent partition and precisely sized to a unit system based on the three-foot width of the "tatami" straw mats, used as floor covering. There were no solid bearing walls; interior space was divided into rooms by sliding screens into place as needed. This would have been Wright's first meaningful exposure to the *shinden-zukuri* style of architecture, later known simply as the "shinden system." This construction methodology typified an important milestone in the evolution of architecture as it allowed the development of open flexible planning, both internally and externally.[155] Where there was a complex of these halls in Japan, all would be linked by roofed bridges. Wright's "zoned plan layout" and his subsequent use of roofed bridging suggest an inspirational relationship with this architecture.

The most significant demonstrative aspect of the Japanese compound, however, was the manner in which the replicated buildings interpenetrated the hill-and-water garden (Figure 3-40a). All six structures were arranged within a system of pathways laid out diagonally among picturesque plantings—including accent and shade trees, shrubs, and Japanese artifacts—and all related to the informal water body that wound through the center of the garden, as well as to a central island. Participatory interaction with this landscape was encouraged by way of an arched bridge leading from one shore to the island, a plank bridge from the opposite shore to the island, and stepping stones across the water amenity at strategic points of access. While the garden

was decidedly contrived and, like the buildings, merely presented a semblance of the articulated built environment of the Japanese homeland, it did present an "image" of Japanese architecture in relation to features of the landscape. Moreover, since the Observation Wheel was situated near the northwest corner of the compound, fair visitors were afforded a sweeping aerial view of the replicated Japanese cultivated environment (Figure 3-40b).

As Wright by this date had been working closely with Griffin on landscape designs for some four years, both at Steinway Hall and The Studio, he would have perceived the garden layout and the indoor-outdoor relationship inherent to Japanese architecture differently than he had nine years earlier at the Chicago Exposition. As viewed in birds-eye perspective from the Observation Wheel, he would have noted that the wall surrounding the exhibit appropriated the entire acreage as a garden, with the buildings thus becoming harmonious components of the whole. He also would have taken note of the pathway system that brought about a diagonal-line approach to-and-between the structures so there never was a head-on view of any structure, with the lines of sight constantly changing from one end of the garden to the other. Upon then walking through, studying, and experiencing the pavilion interiors, Wright

a

b

Figure 3-40 a–b Views of the Imperial Japanese Garden exhibit at the 1904 Louisiana Purchase Exhibition in St. Louis, facing toward the fair's Observation Wheel (3-40 a) and as seen from it (3-40 b). It was here that Wright presumably first experienced and began to fully comprehend Far Eastern aesthetics. (*Courtesy of the Missouri Historical Society, St. Louis, Missouri.*)

would have become sensitive to views outward onto a landscape cultivated in the Japanese tradition, where each garden element is treated as a featured part of the room so the interior living space unites with the garden and the greater environment.

It seems credible to assume, then, that it was at the Louisiana Purchase Exposition where Wright first personally experienced and began to more fully comprehend Far Eastern aesthetics and Lao-tse's spatial concept of architecture within the context of the cultivated site environment. This reasoning is supported by an analysis of extant plans of record. Those plans prepared prior to 1904 suggest that Wright visualized the cultivated landscapes of his domestic architecture in the societally accepted occidental tradition—in afterthought. His exterior architectonic elements were designed as extensions of the architecture, and little, if any, consideration was given to plantings as anything other than adornment. Plans of record prepared during 1904, however, support that Wright at this point in time began to visualize his cultivated landscapes in the oriental manner, where the landscape is an integral element of the whole design. For example, it appears the St. Louis Exposition revivified Wright's interest in the pergola, which originated at the Chicago Exposition. While it could be argued that Wright used arcades and pergolas over a 26-year period both before and after the St. Louis event, from 1894 to 1923, most can be traced to a source of Japanese influence by way of the coincidence of time—such as the Darwin D. Martin pergola-conservatory and the Nathan G. Moore pergola-conservatory addition, both of which were designed shortly after Wright attended the St. Louis Exposition.

It was the layout of the Exposition grounds, however, that appears to have impressed Wright's environmental sensitivity to a greater extent than any other aspect of the event. The classical garden treatment represented throughout most of the grounds appealed to Wright's lingering proclivity for the Beaux Arts formality of the West, as described by Messervy: "Western gardens have traditionally been based upon the compositional technique called perspective: a set of axial lines, such as paths, pools, planting beds, or hedges, which recede into the distance and end in a 'vanishing point' . . . these orthogonal lines have tremendous dynamism, and bring a strong sense of depth to a garden space."[156] The Imperial Japanese Garden, though, appears to have stimulated Wright's ever-growing fascination with the spatial inclusivity of the East, as described by Heinrich Engel: "Con-

trary to Western concept the [oriental] residential garden is architectural space, i.e., three-dimensionally controlled space, in extent and proportion related to the interior rooms. It enriches interior space and is no more independent from the entire organism of the dwelling than is the individual room."[157]

It is Wright's synthenization of these two garden design philosophies that is reflected in the layout and working drawings prepared during 1904–1905 for Darwin D. Martin and H. J. Ullman, as well as the site expansion plans for Nathan G. Moore. With these plans, there is a discernible difference in Wright's *approach* to his design process. The garden layout and hardscape elements are for the first time seen planned with and integral to the architecture—clearly demonstrating a degree of finesse previously missing from Wright's work—as he began to think of the arrangement of the landscape as the *first* step of his design process, rather than the last. Thus, it seems plausible to argue that, just as the Ho-o-den at the World's Columbian Exposition of 1893 inspired foundational design elements that have come to be identified with the domestic architecture designed by Wright and other architects of the Prairie School, the Japanese Imperial Garden at the Louisiana Purchase Exposition of 1904 was the source of inspiration for certain foundational design elements that have come to be identified with Wright's Prairie House landscapes.

Darwin D. Martin—Buffalo, New York (1904)

The Darwin D. Martin property was situated on the northwest corner of the intersection of Summit Avenue and Jewett Parkway (formerly Jewett Avenue) in a suburban residential area designed by the Olmsted Brothers—relatives of Frederick Law Olmsted. The terrain had no natural characteristics save for a slight downslope to the northwest in the direction of the Niagara River and the Canadian border, three miles distant (Figure 3-41).

The dominant motivational design force for the Martins was the development of, and relationship with, the site environment—that is, the layout of the grounds (1.6 acres), the cultivation of plantings, the maintenance of the gardens, and vistas onto the grounds. This observation is supported by the catalog of structures, which included a personal conservatory, a sizable functional greenhouse, a substantial two-story "cottage" for a full-time gardener, and an expansive pergola-arcade that interconnected the house and conservatory.[158] These were in addition to the principal residence; a two-story

Figure 3-41 Historic photograph of the Darwin D. Martin House (1904) in Buffalo, New York. (*Out-of-copyright photograph of record from Wasmuth Portfolio, 1911.*)

garage-stable with apartment above, and a residence for Mr. and Mrs. George Barton (Mrs. Barton was a sister of Darwin and William Martin). Support for Wright's early awareness of the Martins' motivational interests is provided by his letter to them, dated January 2, 1904: "I sympathize with your desire for a larger garden—we will get it together with all of Mrs. Martin's practical requirements, but don't freeze your architect down to certain areas for various parts of the plan; 'proportion' must determine these things within reasonable limits; and give him a free hand within that limit; stretch the limit until your discretion deflects to the breaking point, let her break, even, for once and you will be pleasantly shocked by the result."[159] It may have been this early awareness of the Martins' propensity for gardening that caused Wright to take particular note of the garden layouts at the St. Louis Exposition, some four months later. Nonetheless, Wright sometimes lost patience with his important clients if they broached garden concerns important to them before he was prepared to furnish graphic evidence that the grounds were of as much consequence to him as the architecture. "For Heaven's sake don't speak of shrubbery yet—all things in good time," he wrote on July 25, 1904.[160]

Wright's siting of a number of structures on this particular corner lot was complicated by the fact that the north property line was the only boundary aligned to a compass bearing. The street intersection (south and east boundaries) splayed out to form an approximate 118-degree obtuse angle. Presumably, this irregular con-

figuration influenced Wright's decision to situate the Barton House—as the first structure within the complex of buildings to be sited and built—at the far northeast corner of the property. That Wright was aware of the difficulties he would experience siting the remaining structures is substantiated by a letter to Martin, wherein he seems to be attempting to preclude any possible objections to his proposed solution to the problem: "I have begun work on the Jewett Avenue property and I write to ask if you find an objection to squaring your building with the Barton's, disregarding the Jewett Avenue frontage as far as a parallel is concerned. . . . No two of the lot lines are parallel and the front of the house might break away gently in several offsets to coincide approximately with the slope of the street. I think it important that the Barton house and your own stand square with regard to each other, leaving square angles in the court between, barn and all. I know the buildings along that street (except the church?) are set parallel with it but it is in a corner anyway which makes a positive lining up impossible. What do you say?"[161] Martin evidently concurred with Wright, as the principal residence was in fact squared with the Barton House, and all other structures in the complex were laid out in accordance with good principles of site planning, including the gardener's cottage and greenhouse that were sited on a spur of land appended to the original acreage (Figure 3-42). The church to which Wright referred is situated diagonally across the street intersection from the southeast corner of the Darwin Martin property, making this corner a

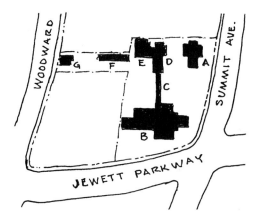

Figure 3-42 Location and identification of major units on Martin estate: A—Barton House; B—Main House; C—Pergola-Arcade; D—Conservatory; E—Garage and Stable; F—Greenhouse; G—Gardener's Cottage. (*By Charles E. Aguar, based on personal analysis and out-of-copyright plans of record from Wasmuth Portfolio, 1910.*)

very public space—a fact that would significantly affect Wright's design treatment in this area.

For reasons unknown, when Wright prepared the D. D. Martin plan for inclusion in the Wasmuth Portfolio—five years or more after the fact—he chose to misrepresent the outward splay of the intersection and the layout of the gardens as proposed and surveyed. This drafting instead depicts the site configuration as squared and the landscape treatment as beautification, rather than functionalism, which does not correctly represent the grounds as developed. Because these inaccuracies pertain to several important areas, no true understanding of Wright's comprehensive vision for the D. D. Martin complex can be acquired when using the most frequently republished Wasmuth plan as a source of reference. For interpretation of Wright's site planning as he intended it to interrelate with his architecture, it is necessary to compare the first floor plan and elevations with the preliminary site plan Wright and/or Griffin drafted in 1904 (Figure 3-43).[162] With the insight of this analysis, the consciously considered relationship Wright intended between the floor plan and site plan becomes apparent, as does the dissimilarity of Wright's design approach when compared to his earlier cruciform-shaped Prairie houses—irrespective of any architectural similarities there may be.

It was with the D. D. Martin property that Wright first demonstrated a concern for how best to relate and design structures and their adjacent exterior spaces to meet the needs of the client and "fit" within the cultural landscape and its public context, while at the same time considering the psychological intimacy of interior and exterior space and the strategic placement of plantings between public and private zones. It was within this context that Wright sited the primary residence to face upon Jewett Parkway so the northwest corner of the porte-cochere roof extended to the west property line. This siting maximized the distance of the roofed porch off the living room from the publicly compromised southeast corner of the property. It also helped Wright establish the five axes, labeled "A" through "E." And it gave him greater plasticity in the extendibility of the grid structuring into the site environment, in that it allowed him to juxtapose the two dwellings and auxiliary structures in a manner that configured them into a balanced and interconnected—albeit asymmetrical—grouping upon the site.

Axis "A" established the east-west baseline for the entire property by beginning at the stable-garage, passing through the immediately adjacent conservatory, and aligning with the south wall of the living-dining wing of the Barton House. Axis "B" established the north-south baseline in like manner by dividing the stable-garage and formal garden into equal parts. Additionally, it set up a line of sight leading from the center of the rear porch off the kitchen through a wide grass panel pathway with flowerbeds on either side to terminate at the midpoint of a diamond-shaped, pool-and-fountain feature centered upon a brick privacy wall. The front facade of the stable provided an architectural backdrop. Thus, the fountain focal point was intended to tie the residence to the garden environment and serve as an "event" that created a sense of discovery for persons strolling through the garden.

Axis "C" (north-south) established the siting of the conservatory in relation to the stable and the principal residence, as it determined the scale and proportion of the conservatory and the distance from the pergola-arcade to the front door. There is a direct correlation between the approximate 90-foot length of the pergola-arcade-porch and the combined lengths of the conservatory at one end and the hallway space at the other end that establishes a psychological intimacy between the interior and transitional spaces. There is a further correlation between the pergola-arcade and the basement

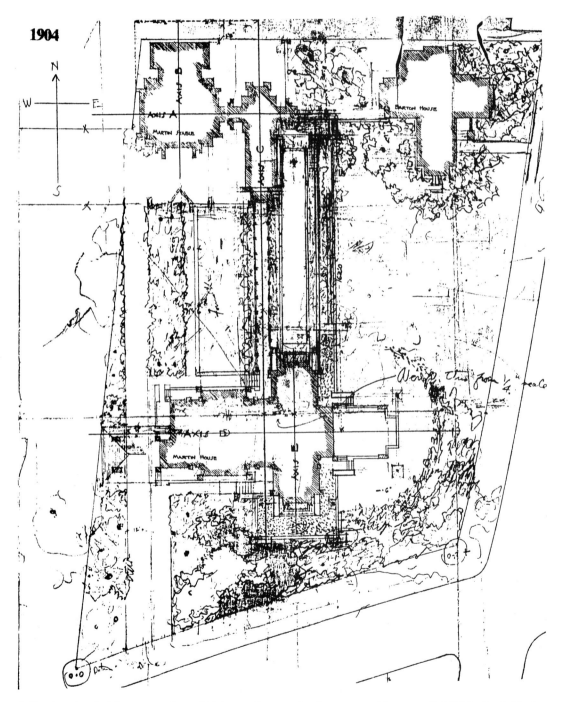

Figure 3-43 Site plan for Martin estate shows 118-degree obtuse angle of property and five axes. (© *2002 by Frank Lloyd Wright Foundation, Scottsdale, Arizona.*)

passage directly beneath. Wright used the basement passage as a source of subtle indirect illumination by installing glass prisms in the flooring of the upper passageway and setting in place a course of small window-like grilles on both sides of the lower passageway by omitting every other brick—as he had used both methods in a more limited manner to admit natural light into selected aboveground basement areas at the Dana House. These design details were subservient to the function of the basement passage as a conduit for the steam pipes coming from the furnace in the garage, but significant nonetheless.

While working drawings depict the pergola-arcade as open along its entire length—as a "pergola" in the more literal sense of the word—historic photographs show clear glass installed within the openings between a range of pillars punctuated with bolection-type molding of finely crafted oak. Nearest the conservatory, these openings appear as a series of art-glass windows, so as to establish both a visual and psychological threshold that would differentiate this realm of space from the pergola-arcade. Since the entire length of the glazed-in space essentially would function as a solar collector during sunny days, and a certain amount of heat may have been radiated from the steam pipe conduit directly below, it is probable that the connecting doors could have been left open for the greater part of the year.[163]

Functionally, the pergola-arcade provided protected passage between the conservatory and the residence, as well as the stable-garage. Aesthetically, it interlinked the

transition space with the gardens on each side so that, irrespective of weather, the approach to and from the conservatory was analogous to a stroll through the garden. It also linked with the ultimate consciousness of the entry experience, which Wright intended to be a visual projection into infinity. The sight line likened to a one-point perspective, in that it originated at the front door and continued through the entrance hall, through the hallway alongside the fireplace wall, and through the entire length of the pergola-arcade and conservatory before focusing upon the large plaster cast of the *Winged Victory of Samothrace* situated amidst tropical plants some 200 feet distant (Figure 3-44). As Wright specified that all doors connecting with the pergola-arcade be of glass, this focused perspective would have raised consciousness even when doors were closed—particularly as the entire length and width of the cruciform shape of the conservatory was illuminated with natural light by way of the two-level, sky-lighted roof of translucent glass. At night, the perspective down the combined length of the pergola-arcade-conservatory would have been even more focused and dramatic as the backlighted, diamondlike prisms in the floor of the pergola-arcade visually directed movement through the passageway, the incandescent bulbs at the junctures of each of the bolection-type moldings sparkled like 28 giant fireflies, and the sky-lighted conservatory destination glowed with moonlight.

The third north-south axis, Axis "E," divided the library, living room, dining room, and the terraces at each extremity to establish a line of sight into a cleared

Figure 3-44 One-point perspective from D. D. Martin House main point of entry through pergola-arcade and conservatory. (*Out-of-copyright photograph-of-record from Wasmuth Portfolio, 1911.*)

area to the east of the pergola-arcade, following along its entire length and beyond. It is apparent from Wright's preliminary site plan that he originally proposed that a 12- by 100-foot reflecting pool occupy this space, with a fountain at the end of the impressive vista.[164]

Axis "D" (east-west) was the main axis for the principal residence. It divided the essentially symmetrical living quarters as well as the living room porch (which Wright labeled "veranda" on some plans). However, it did not pass through the west extremity of the porte-cochere (or "carriage porch") that was shifted off-axis to the south—much as the kitchen and porch off the Barton House entry were shifted off-axis to the west. Wright's asymmetrical arrangement of these architectural spaces on the diagonal corner extremities of the property helped establish a balance to the composition of the entire site. It is significant that Axis "D" also was used to establish the point of radius for the semicircular arrangement of plantings (generally referred to as the "Darwin Martin floricycle") proposed to interpose within the space surrounding the living room porch and the obtuse angle of the public southeast corner of the street intersection. This arrangement was treated as architectural space on the working drawings. A section of the ground level on the east elevation is shown stepped down one foot, and the stairs on either side have two steps more than shown for the stairs leading to the main entry porch.

The functionality of Wright's treatment in this area ties directly to his concern for the public exposure inherent to the southeast corner of the property. It also allies with the great pains he took architecturally to create a sphere of privacy for this area by installing massive brick piers at either corner of the space, and then interspersing two partial brick piers alongside the south wall of the dining room. These four vertical piers function much like vertical louvered blinds, in that they admit natural light and permit unrestricted views outward but significantly compromise passersby viewpoints.

To create a similar sphere of privacy for the living room porch, Wright circumscribed the entire space with a 9-foot-high brick parapet and topped the corner extremities to both physically and psychologically separate this open space from the public. Since the floor level of the porch was established at 5 feet above grade to merge with the level of the first floor, the public character of the intersection was completely screened from the range of vision of anyone seated on the porch. At the same time, there were sweeping views of the horizon on all sides.

Consider what Wright's innovative environmental design approach for the southeast corner of the property accomplished. It created a private though shallow, bowl-like arena from which to view the floricycle. It tilted the seasonal array of flowering shrubs, bulbs, and perennials to provide a broader perspective. It raised the flowering trees and treelike shrubs nearest the rights-of-way to place them within the horizon-like range-of-vision of anyone seated behind the brick privacy parapet. And it effectively obscured the public viewpoint during seasons of foliage. This analysis puts forth a basis of reasoning for Wright's intent with respect to the floricycle: (1) it was to draw attention from, or mask, the incongruity of the house alignment with the obtuse angle of the street intersection; (2) it was to provide a visually aesthetic sphere of privacy for the living room porch; and (3) it was to display the flowers and perennials so as to be viewed from a sitting position from the dining room and library and from a standing position on the porch, the stairway landing, or the stairway on either side of the porch, from within the bowl or the pergola-arcade, and from the public rights-of-way.

Wright also gave attention to creating a strong psychological intimacy between the living room and porch, as described by historian Martha Neri: "The interior and exterior spaces flow mellifluously. . . . Flowing continuously from the outside to the inside are the ceramic tile floor, brick walls and wood molding. . . . The only division between the two areas the row of doors that opened onto the porch."[165] That Neri should remark on this impression through her independent observation is revealing, as this continuation of sight lines from the indoors into the out-of-doors would appear to relate to the sight line extensions created by the tatami mats Wright would have seen at the St. Louis Exposition. This treatment, together with his use of the term "veranda" to label the porch, could be seen as Wright's adaptation to the Japanese concept of the veranda as the "mediating agent from the interior . . . clearly conceived as interior space."[166] In the literal sense, this concept attaches to the area sheltered under the broad eaves as a space that belongs to both the interior and the exterior, a "pivoting space" that historically has been given great emphasis by the Japanese. Wright even went so far as to emplace glass prisms (glass blocks) in the floor of the bedroom porch immediately above that area of the living room where the doors opened onto the porch—essentially creating a form of skylight to illuminate this interior-exterior transitional space with diffused light.

An October 6, 1904 letter from Wright to Darwin Martin suggests that Griffin did not begin the process of detailing the "Plan of Plantings" until that date and that Griffin too may have been influenced by the Japanese Imperial Garden and other aspects of the St. Louis Exposition: "Concerning the planning of the grounds— the general scheme has been determined upon and the Barton premises worked out more in detail. All that remains to be done for that particular portion of the work is for Mr. Griffin to complete the diagram in detail. He was engaged upon it when I left yesterday but went to the Exposition last night taking it with him to finish up on the way."[167] While it can be assumed that various sketches and details changed hands after October 1904, Griffin's Plan of Plantings bears the completion date of February 15, 1905–one day after Wright departed Oak Park for Vancouver to embark on his first trip to Japan (Figure 3-45). He would be absent from The Studio for three months. The coincidence of the completion date would suggest that Wright approved the plan just prior to his departure.

According to Neri, who laid out a chronology of events based upon correspondence and entries in Darwin Martin's diary, the detailing of the floricycle caused the Martins some consternation. In a letter written to Griffin after reviewing the initial Plan of Plantings, Martin observed that the landscape feature, which they then were calling a hemicycle, "is horribly big and deep."[168] Griffin apparently then prepared a simplified planting plan sometime prior to May 1905, the date when Neri notes, "Martin's diary states perennials, shrubs and trees were planted. Semicircular garden shape appears in photos." She goes on: "Summer 1905, Martin hires Pittsburgh landscape architect to do work, plans are drawn. // November 1905, Wright makes reference in letter to new garden plan. // February 1906, Martin discusses new floricycle plan he has received. // March 1906, last reference to floricycle plan."

The hiring of landscape architect Johnson Elliott from Pittsburgh in Summer 1905 would coincide with the timing of the disagreement between Griffin and Wright that led to their disassociation at some point after Wright's return from Japan (May 14, 1905). Perhaps Elliott was brought in because Wright was disappointed with the floricycle when he first viewed it. Wright may not yet have perceived the fact that landscape architecture is an art subject to the dimension of time wherein the consideration of natural progression, the whims of climate, and appropriate maintenance must also be fac-

tored into the design process. Historic photographs verify that the new plantings did not appear plenteous, as Griffin had arranged the flowering trees and shrubs to allow for their predictable size at maturity—at which time they would, and indeed did, fulfill Wright's original vision. The planting plan suggested by Elliott assuredly did not articulate Wright's intent. Moreover, the foundation plantings he indicated directly contradicted Wright's design criteria in this area. Nonetheless, Wright's persistence in the matter of the floricycle arrangement is indicative of the importance he placed on this landscape feature relative to his overall plan.

It is not known who detailed the "Floricycle Plan of Arrangement," the only extant plan labeled as such. Even though this work is attributed to Wright and The Studio, there is nothing about it that relates to Wright's preliminary plan or to the floricycle, as planted. Indeed, it appears to have been conceived as a mathematical equation—that is, all the plantings were delineated with a compass and arrayed in rigid order as one planting unit, duplicated 14 times (Figure 3-46 a-b). As specifications list 6 species of flowering shrubs, 31 perennials, and selections from 5 types of bulbs for each of the 14 units, the total plantings would have included an implausible 140 flowering shrubs, 3630 perennials, and hundreds of thousands of bulbs. Even the "Directions for Laying Out and Planting" appear to relate more closely to the assembly of elements of engineering than to elements of nature: "Establish the concentric lines 1′0″ apart. Commencing at the center, mark off on either side the radial subdivisions 1′0″ apart on the inner line. Drive stakes well into the ground at each intersection. The stakes occuring [sic] at the apex of the diagonals may remain 1′0″ above the ground to mark plainly the group divisions. When these points are fixed, the plantings are intended to proceed by taking each separate variety in turn and planting it exclusively until the spaces allotted to it in the semicircle are filled. It was intended to proceed with the plants specified for the other divisions in the same manner."[169] It seems reasonable to presume that a contrived layout such as this would not have appealed to, nor been given serious consideration by, anyone knowledgeable about horticulture and gardening such as Darwin and Isabelle Martin were.

In the final analysis, historic photographs support that the Plan of Plantings was executed basically as Griffin detailed it, as was the floricycle. Perennials, bulbs, and flowering varieties of shrubs and trees predominated— selected for seasonal variety of flowerage and fruit.

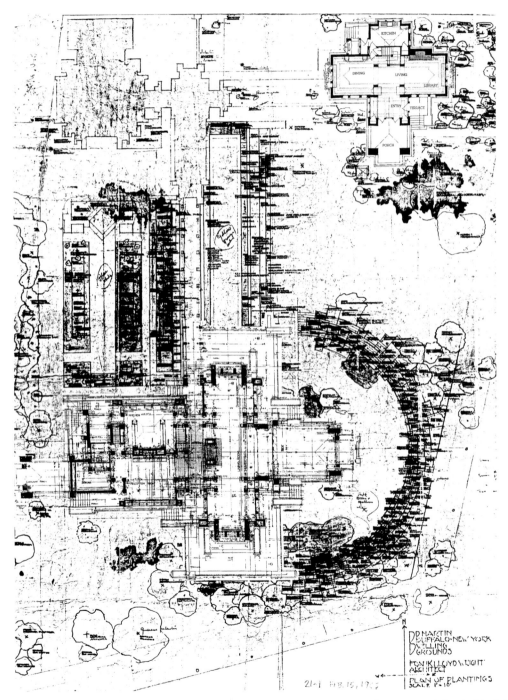

Figure 3-45 Walter Burley Griffin's 1905 plan of plantings for the D. D. Martin property fine-tunes and details Wright's 1904 site plan. (*Courtesy of the University of Buffalo, State University of New York.*)

There was stringent use of evergreens and conifers, probably still in counteraction to their association with the Victorian landscape. It is for this reason, however, that historic winter photographs of the Darwin Martin grounds do not necessarily depict planting interest and may even appear devoid of plantings. Nevertheless, it was Griffin's landscape design that clearly tied Wright's architectural composition into a unified whole, as it was Wright's mindful perception of the entire site as architectural space that set the property apart as a Wrightscape that provides many opportunities for study by environmental designers of any persuasion. And it

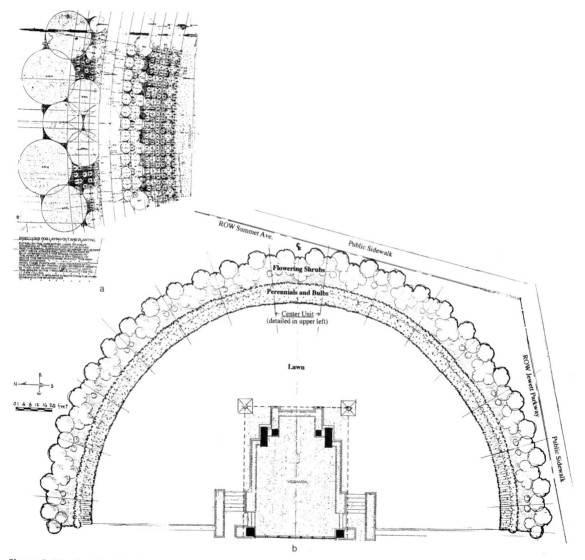

Figure 3-46 a–b Plans for the D. D. Martin "Floricycle"—including one unit of the planting design that was duplicated 14 times to form the half-circle garden element (3-46 a), and a depiction of how the complete layout would have appeared if developed (3-46 b). (*By Charles E. Aguar, based on plans of record. Courtesy of the University of Buffalo, State University of New York. As delineated,* © *2002 by Berdeana Aguar.*)

was Wright's awareness of the manifestation of both his and Griffin's visionary efforts that caused him to observe that the Darwin Martin estate was "a well nigh perfect composition."[170]

Before Darwin Martin's death in 1935, he attempted to donate the entire complex to the City of Buffalo or the University of Buffalo, but with no success; a property such as this was considered to be something of a liability during the period of the Great Depression. After his death, his son and heir stripped the house of the custom-designed furniture, rugs, doors, lighting fixtures, and white oak trim, and even much of its wiring and heating equipment, for use in hotel and apartment properties he owned. The house then remained empty for 17 years. At some point, the greenhouse was razed; the site was sub-divided; and the Barton House and Gardener's Cottage were sold as separate realty. When a local architect bought the main house and what was left of the complex in 1954, the main structure was weatherized and pro-tected from trespass and vandalism, but the insensitivity of the remodeling corrupted the purity of the architec-ture and landscape even further. The unique garage with apartment above, the pergola, and the conservatory were demolished. A new entrance was cut into the basement to access the office and drafting room—involving new steps, walks, and paved parking areas—and the main house was sectioned off into three living units. Within this process, doorways were sealed and sheltered outdoor spaces were enclosed. The final insult was the erection of several nondescript, multistory apartment buildings—complete with paved parking lots, trash storage, and related uses—in the area of the former garden-pergola-conservatory environment. In other words, Wright's "well nigh perfect composition" sustained the greatest damage possible, short of total demolition.

In 1967, the property was purchased as the presi-dent's residence by the State University of New York (SUNY) at Buffalo. At the turn of the twenty-first cen-tury, the house and grounds are being restored in an ambitious joint project involving SUNY, the State Office of Historic Preservation, and the Martin House Restora-tion Corporation. The ultimate goal is to rebuild the entire complex.

H. J. Ullman Project—Oak Park, Illinois (1904)

The site layout for the H. J. Ullman Project is in the sin-gular genre of the Darwin D. Martin estate, although much smaller in scale and never developed past the project stage. The proposed site was located at the northeast corner intersection of Euclid Avenue and Erie Street, four blocks east of The Studio. A comparison of an early study of the house and grounds and the most fully developed ground plan is particularly telling, how-ever, as the early study appears to be in Wright's hand—which suggests the concept as it originally may have been conceived prior to his attending the St. Louis Fair (Figure 3-47). The finalized ground plan, on the other hand, represents the garden layout and hardscape ele-ments as having been planned with, and integral to, the architecture in the manner of the Japanese. Every aspect of the outdoor space is organized in tandem with the interior space (Figure 3-48). It is this level of carefully conceived orderliness and harmony between interior and exterior space that sets the Ullman plan apart from other extant Prairie House plans in the Frank Lloyd Wright Archives. Only the much-better-endowed Dar-win Martin commission comes close to such skillful inte-gration.

The footprint of the house and privacy walls is the same in both the early study and final plan. That is, the mass of the structure fronts onto Erie Street; the west facade of the living and dining rooms is set back from Euclid Avenue; and a large portion of the side and rear yard space is enclosed by privacy walls. From this point, however, the differences outweigh the similarities. The early study places the main entry to encroach upon the public sidewalk in the same manner as The Studio and the residences for Moore and Fricke. The final plan, on the other hand, has a wide "welcome mat" in the form of a gridded hardscape extending across the right-of-way almost to the curb of the street. This treatment helps de-emphasize the spatial constraint imposed by the zero lot-line siting and creates the sense of an entry experience that begins at curbside, rather than the sidewalk. More-over, the house has been redesigned into an intricate interwoven connection of four split-level planes of space. The living room is situated some 3 to 4 feet below ground level; the entry hall, kitchen, and dining room are at ground level; the study, a roofed porch equal in size to the dining room, two maids' rooms, and a bathroom are on the mezzanine level; and family bedrooms and bath-rooms are on the upper level. Each level is defined by massive piers placed directly opposite on either extrem-ity of a wing extension, with the levels reached by way of half-flights of stairs arranged in stairwells on either side of the living room fireplace. This spatially manageable layout appears to be Wright's interpretation of Griffin's

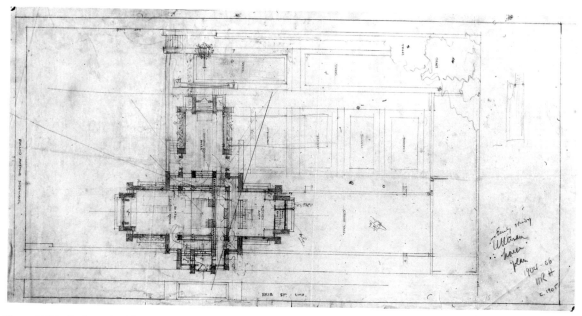

Figure 3-47 Early study of house and site for H. J. Ullman, Oak Park, Illinois, as prepared by Wright prior to the 1904 St. Louis Exposition. (© *2002 by The Frank Lloyd Wright Foundation, Scottsdale, Arizona.*)

Emery House concept. Or, as Brooks postulates: "The theme is sufficiently similar to suggest that Wright may have been conscious of the Emery interior (unless Griffin himself prepared the Ullman design for Wright)."[171]

The new window arrangements also are highly original and well-conceived. The ceilings of the living room, stairwells, and entry hall are raised to the level of the mezzanine, so these spaces would be flooded with natural light all day long by way of the window groupings on the south and north walls of the stairwells and the banks of tall windows on the south and north walls of the living room.[172] During winter months, when the low angle of the sun affords deeper penetration, the open stairwells would have functioned as solar collectors, as would the large light well heat-traps proposed to be installed between the piers to reflect light into the west window of the sunken living room and the windows on the south and east sides of the kitchen. The kitchen light well on the east would reflect light into the partial basement under the kitchen, as well. Thus, the Ullman Project represents a major breakthrough in using sunlight for passive solar warming, as well as natural lighting.

The intent with regard to the site environment in both plans appears to have been to create viable yardspace that would accommodate multiple activities. Yet,

in the early study, there is no obvious relationship to the grid over which the house was designed, nor was any consideration given toward establishing a psychological intimacy between the indoor and outdoor spaces. There is the same disregard for views looking out onto the site environment, and the only informal or natural-appearing element in the entire landscape is a grass panel in the northeast corner leading to several existing trees.

The outdoor space put forth on the final plan, however, has been completely reorganized and precisely arranged with garden features and planting beds configured to the same grid as the house, in proportion to adjacent interior spaces, and on axes with sight lines for viewing from every room. Just as Wright's house interiors were consistently organized to create a sense of space much larger than fact by eliminating the clutter of furniture, reducing the number of walls, and massing window openings to maximize the indoor-outdoor relationship, the outside space here has been organized into a series of roofless rooms with low walls that would not restrict the range of peripheral vision, and open to the sky to heighten an illusion of space without measure. Because the sky serves as a filter of natural light—adding dimension to color definition in hue, tone, and intensity—both interior and exterior surfaces might at different times

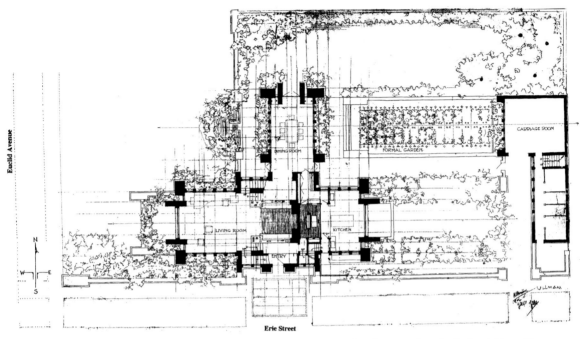

Figure 3-48 Final garden layout for H. J. Ullman House, as prepared by Griffin after attending the St. Louis Exposition. (© 2002 by The Frank Lloyd Wright Foundation, Scottsdale, Arizona.)

appear flat and/or detailed with texture, which would intensify the correlation of the indoor and outdoor spaces. The northern third of the walled area is shown as a free-form oval of lawn bordered by informal plantings that blend into the natural garden environment surrounding the four existing trees in the far northeast corner, providing soft contrast to the adjoining formal sunken garden and the predominately architectonic treatment elsewhere. A six-sided privacy wall has been designed as a garden feature to the west of the north wing in the same manner and for similar reasons as the entry terrace at the Heurtley House: (1) as a focal point of the house if viewed from the public right-of-way and (2) as a plant-draped visual background for the pool and fountain if viewed from the interior—in this case, from the dining room or the roofed porch above the dining room. Had the architecture not been so tastefully extended into the public portion of the landscape, it would have appeared as an intrusive barren wall.

Whereas it is not possible to determine how much, if any, credit can go to Griffin for the rearrangement of the architecture in the final plan—other than any simi-

larity there may be to his Emery House, or because of the circumstance that the Ullman commission is known to have been placed under Griffin's supervision during Wright's extended trip to Japan—it is not illogical to postulate that the much-improved site planning, at least, was most likely developed by Griffin.[173]

WRIGHT'S FIRST TRIP TO JAPAN

When Wright and his wife Kitty arrived in Japan with former clients and traveling companions Mr. and Mrs. Ward W. Willits in early March 1905, he already was astutely aware of the simplicity of line, the minimum of detail, and the organic quality of Japanese prints—which he had been collecting for a number of years by this point. He also had had opportunity to study the clean-cut structuring of indigenous Japanese architecture, as well as its interrelationship with the cultivated landscapes replicated for the expositions in Chicago and St. Louis. And yet, in An Autobiography Wright glossed over the 1905 trip to Japan and stated he did not become intrigued with Japanese prints until "my later years at the Oak Park workshop."[174] He went on to imply it was not until a second trip to Japan in 1913 that he would have opportunity to become "more closely acquainted with things Japanese." He even went so far as to intimate he found the Japanese dwelling to be "a perfect example of the modern standardizing I had myself been working out." This revealing statement makes it suspect that Wright's misleading inferences were made to counter any suggestion that his early design process had in any way been influenced by the domestic architecture and landscapes of the Japanese.

The reality is that Wright's enlightened perspective allowed him to reinforce and capitalize upon what he already knew so he could direct his attention more precisely to the "cause and effect" of the Japanese design approach. The cultural heritage represented by the temples, shrines, and gardens in and around the ancient capital and pilgrimage city of Kyoto gave Wright opportunity to explore the evolutionary art of Japanese buildings—from the shinden-zukuri style of the Heian period, to the shoin-zukuri style of the Maramocha period, to the free-form sukiya style of the Mayamocha period. Through this process, he would have been made more fully aware of the elementary complementary and opposition characteristics of "Yin and Yang" that are the philosophical foundation of oriental design. He also would have perceived the full import of the geomantic manner in which the Japanese interrelate their architecture and cultivated landscapes within Japan's larger natural environment and scenic beauty: mountains, waterfalls, torrential streams, et al. Horiguchi Sutami explains: "One cannot separate Japanese architecture and gardens from their natural surroundings . . . They transcend the distinction between nature and artificiality and are supplementing each other . . . To attempt to divide it into nature, architecture, and gardens, as it is done in the West, will cause nothing but confusion."[175] Wright's first realization of this reasoning is supported by his description of the arrival experience, which suggests that he was as unprepared for his initial introduction to the resplendency of the Japanese landscape as anyone else who visits Japan for the first time: "Imagine, if you have not seen it, a mountainous, abrupt land. . . . All shore lines abrupt . . . sloping foothills and mountain sides all antique sculpture, carved, century after century, with curving terraces. The cultivated fields rising tier on tier to still higher terraced vegetable fields, green-dotted. And extending far above the topmost dotted fields, see the very mountain tops themselves. . . . For pleasure in all

this human affair you couldn't tell where the architecture leaves off and the garden begins. I soon ceased to try, too delighted with the problem to attempt to solve it. There are some things so perfect that nothing justifies such curiosity"[176]

The Japanese landscape Wright contemplated in 1905 was the appreciable result of a centuries old, and solicitously cultivated, empathetic relationship with the land. It expressed a culture and philosophical beliefs that had evolved since 100 B.C. but did not begin to develop into artful management until the middle of the sixth century, when Buddhism first was introduced to Japan through missionizing Chinese scholars and monks. It was within the framework of Shinto that the attitudes of today were formed with respect to the use of natural materials for construction, the harmonious siting of buildings with the land, and the naturalistic development of the landscape.

The concept of the *shakkei* garden is an important aspect in the development of the organic character of the Japanese countryside, as well as the Japanese prints so admired by Wright. According to Teiji Ito, this interrelation of painting with landscape design occurred when the fundamental style of the traditional Japanese garden was established in the Heian period: "The yamato-e painters played an important role in garden making. . . . This relationship between landscape gardening and landscape painting was, indeed, so close that the same characters were used for both. . . . Pronounced *senzui* it meant garden; *sansui*, landscape painting."[177] Itoh also devoted a great deal of text to explaining first the complexities of interpretation associated with the word itself and then the nuances of implementation:

> The literal meaning of the Japanese word *shakkei* is "borrowed scenery" or "borrowed landscape"—that is, distant views incorporated into garden settings as part of the design. In its original sense, however, shakkei means neither a borrowed landscape nor a landscape that has been bought. It means a landscape captured alive. The distinction here is peculiarly Japanese, and it reflects the psychology of the garden designers. Its implications run more or less like this: when something is borrowed, it does not matter whether it is living or not, but when something is captured alive, it must invariably remain alive, just as it was before it was captured. . . . [From the point of view of] gardeners and nurserymen of former times . . . every element of the

design was a living thing: water, distant mountains, trees, and stones. Without a realization like this, it is impossible to perceive the essence of a borrowed-landscape garden.[178]

Itoh went on to explain that there must be an inter-mediary object—a tree trunk or branch, a window sill, the edge of a terrace, a well-placed art object—between the foreground and the background in order to "capture" the more distant scenery and bring it to the forefront so there is one integrated vista. That Wright personally iden-tified with the concept of the borrowed landscape is evi-denced through his increasingly significant use of this technique—in presentation drawings, in establishing indoor-outdoor relationships, and in creating both interior and exterior spatial illusions. Thus, when Wright boarded the ship in Yokohama Bay in late April 1905 for the weeks-long voyage back to Chicago, he brought with him a greatly enhanced perception of Japanese architecture and its responsive relationship with the land.

It was this impress that would evidence itself upon Wright's return through both subtle and distinct changes in his personal developing manner of environ-mental design, as represented by the two residences Wright designed for William A. Glasner and Thomas P. Hardy. While it could be argued that Wright's design approach for these commissions was inspired by the rugged terrain of the sites—both of which are the antithesis of the level prairie landscape for which Wright generally designed—the manner in which the architec-ture relates to the natural site environment is so directly opposed to the site treatments and manipulation Wright historically practiced that this aspect of their design must be attributed to observations he made during his trip to Japan.

ENVIRONMENTAL DESIGNS, 1905–1909

William A. Glasner—Glencoe, Illinois (1905)

Wright sited the Glasner House to face northeast along the edge of a natural ravine on a wooded suburban site, adapting his architecture as much as possible to the nature of the environment so the ravine feature, extant undergrowth, and trees were retained as an indigenous "garden" (Figure 3-49). He then carefully planned a pro-gression of arrival that follows the Zen principle of hide-and-reveal, in that the house can be contemplated as it unfolds sequentially but is never fully revealed from any single viewpoint. Much of his design technique in this instance had to do with his extensive use of the diagonal line, including for orientation (Figure 3-50).

Beginning with the first view from the broad walk-way connection leading from the driveway, the house appears as a low one-story structure. As one proceeds down the walkway, the house is screened from view by the angled wall of the octagonal library off the living room. This wall parallels the diagonal line of the entry terrace retaining wall, which was aligned on a southeast-northwest compass bearing to establish the dominant sight line for views throughout the entry experience. As the walkway angles along the retaining wall and narrows

Figure 3-49 Presentation perspec-tive drawing for the William A. Glas-ner House (1905) in Glencoe, Illinois, reflects the Japanese influence on Wright. (*Out-of-copyright drawing from Wasmuth Portfolio, 1910.*)

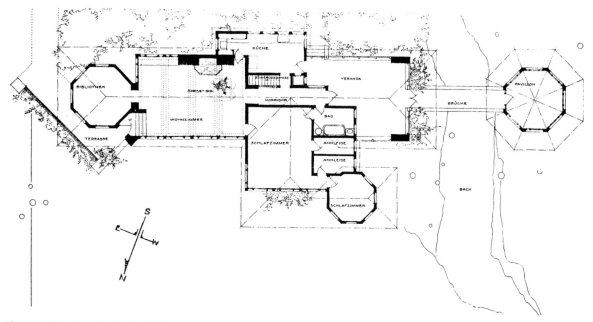

Figure 3-50 Site plan for the William A. Glasner House. (*Out-of-copyright plan of record from Wasmuth Portfolio, 1910.*)

to veer off along another wall of the octagon, the house emerges but becomes secondary as glimpses of the ravine take precedence. As the walkway again widens—both inward to follow a diagonal wall of the octagon and outward into the ninety-degree angle of the entry terrace—the point of outdoor-indoor transition is offset into a corner so that it is almost hidden, but the solid wall at the apex of the terrace serves as both a trimming line and a midway focal point to capture the view of the unexpected two-story height of the north facade of the house, which appears to drop into and merge with the natural terrain. When standing close to the terrace wall, however, the projecting nature of the facade itself becomes a capturing device for the view into the greater ravine environment. This treatment created both a static and active visual impression of a firmly rooted building reaching out into nature in a most dramatic fashion.

Both the entry terrace off the living room and the large porch off the kitchen relate closely to the concept and function of the Japanese balcony, which is "basically different from the stone verandah or terrace facing the geometrical composition of a European garden," Horiguchi Sutami explains, in that "the Japanese let them-

selves be immersed into the flow of nature by going out on their balconies."[179] The proposed, but unbuilt, semi-detached octagonal pavilion—sometimes labeled "tea room" on plans—would have more deeply penetrated the nature of the site. Moreover, the arched bridge by which this pavilion was to be reached would have been strongly reminiscent of a Japanese tea house garden bridge which invites the user to pause, reflect, and interact with nature before participating in the tea-making ceremony.

Wright's choice of rough-sawn, dark-stained horizontal board-and-batten as the primary building material for all surfaces below the first-floor window level replicates hewn timber such as is traditionally used by the Japanese in a forest setting.[180] This treatment expresses a strong horizontal pattern and establishes an equilibrium with gravity while providing an interesting rhythm of design and harmonizing with the wooded nature of the site so that, from the opposite side of the ravine or from the bridge on busy Sheridan Road, it is difficult to determine "where the architecture leaves off and the garden begins," as Wright himself described the cultivated environments of the Japanese.[181]

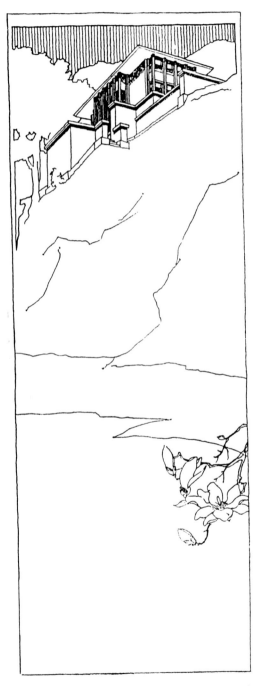

Figure 3-51 Marian Mahony's presentation perspective for the Thomas P. Hardy House (1905) in Racine, Wisconsin. (© *2002 by The Frank Lloyd Wright Foundation, Scottsdale, Arizona.*)

Thomas P. Hardy—Racine, Wisconsin (1905)

The site for the Hardy House is urban in location, but on a steep embankment overlooking Lake Michigan, affording spectacular panoramic views of the lake amenity. It is perhaps best known as depicted by Marion Mahony's artistry in the style of a Japanese print (Figure 3-51), as described by Pregliasco: "It is little more than three inches wide and is composed mainly of empty space. . . . A delicate, flowering branch is introduced midway up the page. Less than a half dozen lines describe the lakeshore, and cliff. At the uppermost edge of the paper is a house of planes and tall windows perched dramatically atop the bluff. . . . The eye is first captured by the beauty of the flowers, then moves upward to the majesty of the house. All is done with supreme simplicity and delicacy of line. The asymmetrical placement of the house on the page, the emphasis on the primacy of the flowers, and the striated rendering of the sky are all attributes of Japanese prints."[182]

Pregliasco's description presents an artistic interpretation of the borrowed view. The blank space in the foreground at the bottom of the page represents the great lake; the flower serves as the device to capture the precipitous terrain leading up from the lake, the stacked masses of the architecture, and the artistic groupings of windows. Few people have opportunity to experience the sense-of-place established from this point of view, however, since the Hardy House can only be approached from Racine's busy Main Street. Viewed from streetside, the house by itself is rather modest appearing (Figure 3-52). The primary building materials of white plaster with dark stained wood accent make a forthright statement to literally command the attention of passersby but, because there is only a narrow space between the walls of the house, the public sidewalk, and the busy highway, the structure gives the impression of being impounded upon a limited site. Wright's design emphasis here was inward—away from the street, but expanding downward into the nature of the site and reaching out toward the lake amenity. This treatment is a textbook example of the Japanese approach to urban housing and site treatment such as Wright would have seen in Tokyo and other Japanese cities, as described in *Japanese Homes* by Morse: "The houses that abut directly on the street have a close and prison-like aspect. . . . With a plastered outside wall the surface is often left white, while the frame-work of the building is painted

Figure 3-52 A 1992 photograph shows the proximity of the Hardy House to Racine's Main Street, just to left of sidewalk. (*Photograph by Charles E. Aguar. © 2002 by Berdeana Aguar.*)

black. . . . Whatever is commonplace in the appearance of the house is towards the street. . . . There is here no display of an architectural front. . . . The largest and best rooms are in the back of the house. . . . the artistic and picturesque face is turned towards the garden, which may be at one side or in the rear of the house [where] all the rooms open directly on the garden"[183] (Figure 3-53).

It is only in retrospectively thinking through Wright's planned progression-of-entry that his original intent for extending the high garden containment walls on both sides of the house can be understood. They were to screen off any streetside views of the lake amenity so the interior experience of coming upon the panoramic view of the feature to be captured—the vast expanse of lake and sky—would be heightened to the utmost. The bisymmetrical garden-entryway treatment also is in harmony with Wright's vision of the entry experience. These garden spaces were intended to serve as respites in the progression, more of a prologue to the ultimate experience of the sense-of-place. Upon then entering through either of the unassuming doorways into what Nute likened to the "corridor-like *irikawa* surrounding the main living space,"[184] a ninety-degree left or right turn is required to access one of the stairways that lead down into the living area from either side of the fireplace. It is only at this point that the two-story height and openness of the living room is revealed, which

makes the upward and outward expanse of space all the more dramatic. Then, the living room becomes the foreground; the frames of the wall of glass doors trim the view to the outside; the rear terrace becomes the middle scenery; and the parapet wall "captures alive" the spectacular views over Lake Michigan so that the great lake and sky above are brought into the living environment.

Within a month or two after Wright's return from Japan, he and Griffin came to a parting of ways. Kruty offers this explanation: "Apparently only a substantial loan to Wright from Griffin and cash advances from Ward Willits made the trip possible. . . . Wright, returning in May laden with Japanese art and artifacts (but also short of money), offered Griffin a cache of prints in lieu of payment. Although Griffin protested, Wright eventually forced the prints on the unwilling creditor and announced the debt paid. . . . By spring 1906, he [Griffin] had returned to the Steinway Hall building as an independent architect."[185] Brooks concludes: "The rupture was complete; the two men apparently never spoke to each other again."[186]

Coincident with Griffin's departure and the necessary restructuring of personnel relative to office management and supervision of construction, there is a marked difference in designs originating from The Studio. Over

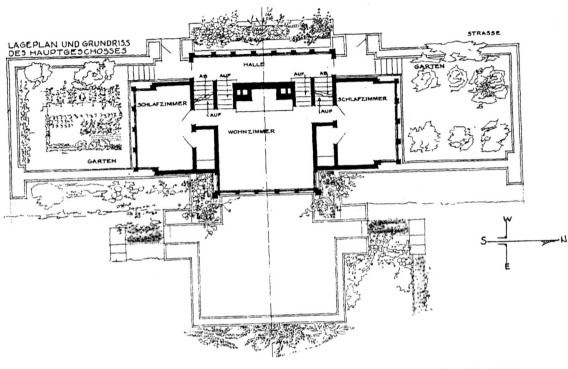

Figure 3-53   Ground-floor plan for the Hardy House. (*Out-of-copyright plan of record from Wasmuth Portfolio, 1910.*)

the next three years, only a limited number of plans address landscape treatment except in extremely general terms. This is not to say that the brilliance of the architecture was in any way diminished; it was not. It was only the "whole design" that fell short.

After all, Wright had been relinquishing his personal oversight control of The Studio for a period of years by this point. In essence, he had been functioning as he described the role of artists in his famed paper, *The Art and Craft of the Machine:* "The artist today is the leader of an orchestra, where he once was a star performer."[187] This arrangement worked very well when someone with Griffin's personality, academic background, and technical expertise was involved with the design and construction supervision processes, because he could function as the orchestra's "virtuoso," playing all the incidental solos in the interpretation and implementation of Wright's architectural designs. To this performance, Griffin had been contributing his talents as a landscape architect. When the amalgamation of these

contributions was removed from The Studio, it was comparable to an orchestra performing absent an entire section of instruments. In substance, Griffin did for Wright's whole design and site environments what Marion Mahony did for his renderings and art-glass designs, what George Neiddecken did for his interior designs, and what Orlando Giannini did for his glass works.

There really was no other staff member qualified to step in and fill the void Griffin's leaving precipitated. According to Brooks, "Mahony was a gifted designer, but perhaps more an artist than an architect," and Drummond was "respected by Wright for his skill, but did not have prior training."[188] Nor did Byrne have training or prior experience when he first arrived in 1902 at the age of 19. Nonetheless, Byrne maintains he and Drummond "were handed rough preliminary designs of buildings to develop into working drawings" and they also "wrote specifications, supervised construction, and dealt directly with the clients during construction." The first indication that such precipitous role upgrading might bring about a diminution of quality with respect to the whole design came to surface with the houses for Frederick R. Tomek and A.W. Gridley, where the ground plans never were developed to full potential.

Ferdinand F. Tomek—Riverside, Illinois (1904–1905)

The Tomek House represents Wright's first use of the raised basement approach since the Heurtley House. In this case, the site is a large corner lot where there is an expansive naturalistic open space within the median at an intersection of the gently curving streets of Riverside. It was Wright's manner of orienting the primary living spaces to overlook this peripheral environment that inspired subsequent homeowner Maya Moran—who with her family restored the house and grounds during their two decades of occupancy—to remark on the "unendingly fascinating" illumination and the "everchanging views from the continuous wall of windows . . . down into the garden . . . over the expanse of Olmsted's parkway and the wide-angled vista."[189]

Architecturally, the Tomek House is one of the most visionary residences to issue from The Studio during this period (Figure 3-54). It was in fact the prototype for the landmark Prairie house Wright would later design for Frederick C. Robie in Hyde Park. One of the most remarkable structural achievements represented in the architecture of these two residences was the exuberant extension of the eaves. In the case of the Tomek House,

they cantilever over the living room porch that looks out upon the parklike median and over the breakfast room that looks upon a proposed sequestered garden space. They extend some 16 feet from the outer wall of the offset spaces and more than 20 feet from the fulcrum points on either side, to create the illusion that the entire eave is cantilevered to this extraordinary depth. With these dramatic, gravity-defying eaves Wright was following in principle a notable characteristic of the sukiya-style architecture. While Wright's treatment might be seen as exaggerated (as the depth of such eaves in Japan generally varies from about 3.5 feet to somewhat over 7 feet, but has been known to reach as much as 11 feet), his intent for the exterior open spaces over which the eaves project clearly was in keeping with the sukiya tradition, as explained by Itoh: "Functionally, these broad eaves serve the purpose of protecting the building from destructive weathering and of helping to adjust the atmospheric conditions inside. . . . At the same time, in a perhaps more psychological than physical sense, the broad eaves and the area under them serve to unite the interior and exterior space—in a word, to unite architecture with nature . . . the area under the eaves plays a dual role, belonging to both interior and exterior."[190] It was the psychological sense of this unification that caused Moran to observe that the living room porch is "integral to the house . . . an extension of the living room."[191]

The site plan for the Tomek grounds does not exhibit a comparable Japanese influence and environmen-

Figure 3-54 A photograph of the Ferdinand F. Tomek House (1904–1905) in Riverside, Illinois, shows cantilevered extension of roofline. (*Courtesy of Maya Moran Manny.*)

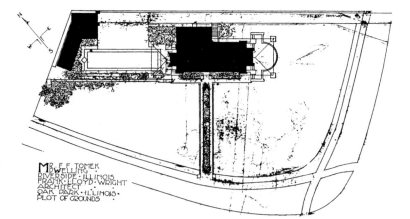

Figure 3-55 The 1905 site plan for the Tomek House was divided geometrically into quadrants. (© 2002 by The Frank Lloyd Wright Foundation, Scottsdale, Arizona.)

tal sensitivity, however (Figure 3-55). The geometric layout instead appears to have been guided by the land-locked arbitrary boundaries defined on the "Plot of Grounds." The site was essentially divided into quadrants, and the proposed garage-workshop was precisely fitted into the platted point of intersection for the northwest corner of the property. The house was set back the maximum distance from the street rights-of-way to parallel the north boundary and centered upon the long axis aligned on a northwest-southeast compass bearing. This siting oriented the house beneficially, but left just enough space for a minimal-width driveway to abut against a proposed privacy wall that was to extend along its length to the midpoint of the intersecting property line. The intervening space between the two structures was left as open space to be developed as a modest garden with a large reflecting pool that was to be sequestered behind a privacy wall extending from the house to the west boundary. The balance of the site was to be left basically undisturbed, other than the frontally direct, double-entry walkway on either side of a flower bed median feature that leads from the public sidewalk to the centered front door.

It is not known why development was limited to the northwest quadrant of the site. One consideration may have been to protect as many existing trees as possible; historic photographs show a number of mature trees. Or Wright may have believed the undeveloped portion of the site would better relate with the naturalistic environment of the median. There also is the fact

that Tomek was an avid gardener who would in all likelihood develop the property himself. And this could have worked out very well, had Griffin still been on staff to interpret and articulate Wright's intent with respect to enhancing the natural attributes of the site. As the plans, construction, and grounds were developed and executed under the direction of Barry Byrne, however, Wright's likely site development intent does not appear to have been fully understood or expressed. For example, the hardscape elements of the ground plan were based almost exclusively on the unifying grid. Both the entry walkway and the formal reflecting pool were precisely scaled to the same 85-foot length as the house, assumedly in an attempt to harmonize with the architecture. The minimally delineated softscape was nonspecific with respect to planting material, however, and did little to interrelate the architecture with the landscape. Nor was space provided for plantings between the driveway and the privacy wall. Moreover, existing trees were not located on the Plot of Grounds.

As it happened, the walkway-median and the driveway were the only site development elements actually executed as proposed. The garage-workshop was never built, nor was the privacy wall alongside the driveway, the reflecting pool, or the privacy wall that was to sequester the garden. Since an additional purpose of the garden privacy wall had been to extend the horizontal line of the architecture onto the landscape and provide a counterbalance for the cantilevered eave, the northwest end of the house appears disproportionate without it.[192] This condition was not mitigated when Emily Tomek sold the house in 1924, subdivided the property, and allowed another house to encroach upon the northwest portion of the site that was to have accommodated the garage-workshop and the larger portion of the sequestered garden.

By 1947, when the author first visited the community of Riverside as a student, the Tomek House was almost completely obscured from view by evergreen trees that had been allowed to grow up around the foundation. When the property was again searched out 40 years later, the transformation in the grounds was remarkable. It was obvious that a chain saw had been prudently put to work, as well as the skills of someone with an artistic bent and an avocation for gardening: Maya Moran. In her book *Down to Earth: An Insider's View of Frank Lloyd Wright's Tomek House,* she explains the rationale employed throughout her family's decades-long restoration of the property:

> For most people the word *restoration* conjures up a structure; they seldom consider the immediate physical surroundings. In 1974 I felt the house deserved a better setting: evergreens obscured the house, flowers were absent, and grass omnipresent, even in the middle of the walk leading up to the house. . . . The first improvement on the exterior was similar to the one we made on the interior—removal. . . . Tall evergreens were replaced by deciduous trees and prairie plants, and the clean lines of the Tomek House could be seen once again. . . . Furthermore, through the years an appropriate, well-balanced, long blooming display has been created. All is in proportion and all together it provides the right setting for a Wright house—the Wright garden—architecture, landscape, and nature blended into a harmonious whole.[193]

In restoring the Tomek grounds, Ms. Moran exhibited extraordinary originality in conceptualizing Wright's architecture and the surrounding space as a composite entity (Figure 3-56). And because she had the foresight to grant the very first conservation easement to the Frank Lloyd Wright Building Conservancy, the integrity of the Tomek House and grounds will be preserved in perpetuity for future generations.

Figure 3-56 Naturalistically recreated landscape treatment introduced to the Tomek site by Maya Moran. (*Courtesy of Maya Moran Manny.*)

A. W. Gridley—Batavia, Illinois (1906)

The A. W. Gridley House, like the Willits House, was one of several Prairie houses based upon the basic cruciform plan Wright originally designed for *The Ladies Home Journal* article, "A Small House 'With Lots of Room in It.'" Moreover, the 2.3-acre site was every bit as spacious and wooded as the Willits' estate. Thus, all the natural elements were in place to develop and merge the organic qualities of house and site. Yet, when the Gridley grounds plan is compared to the siting, site circulation, and landscape planting plan designed five years earlier for the Willits House through the com-

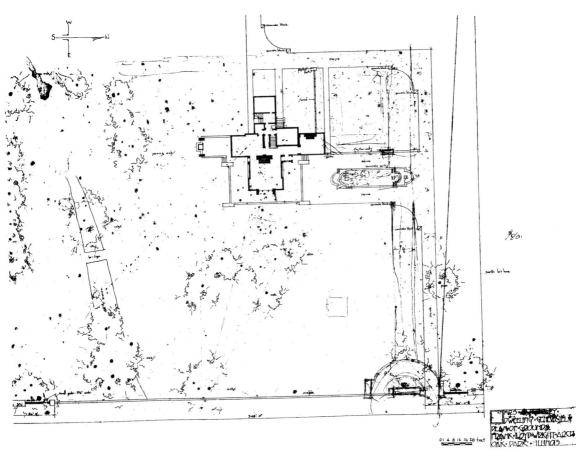

Figure 3-57 Site plan for the A. W. Gridley House (1906) in Batavia, Illinois. (© *2002 by The Frank Lloyd Wright Foundation, Scottsdale, Arizona.*)

bined efforts of Wright and Griffin, it can be seen that where every nuance of detail for the development of the Willits site was orchestrated to establish a sense-of-place, little comparable effort went into enhancing, or building upon, the natural attributes of the Gridley site.

Whoever undertook the Gridley assignment was perfunctorial with respect to the site environment. Existing trees and a natural drainage swale formed by an intermittent stream in the southeast quadrant were notated on the site plan (Figure 3-57). There also is the suggestion of a footbridge over the swale and an exterior gate to access the southeast quadrant. But the house was situated far back in the northwest corner of the property without consideration for advantageous

orientation, and no means were suggested to encourage interaction with, or enjoyment of, the natural site amenity. Moreover, the sketchy circulation system was not carefully thought out with respect to turning radius or circumnavigation of the formal flowerbed proposed to be centered in the auto-courtyard; and the proposed half-circle entrance feature was not a practical form of ingress or egress for the property.

Had such a simple act as aligning the Gridley House 90 degrees clockwise been considered, sight lines could have been established toward the amenity from the living room and wraparound terrace; the servant and kitchen portions of the house would have been convenient to the service area access to the north; and the main living area would have oriented more beneficially toward the south.

. . .

Wright would not have been unmindful of the marked disparity in the articulation of his whole designs following Griffin's departure. Nor would he have been unconcerned about the limitations of his staff with respect to technical background. It undoubtedly was because of concerns such as these that he hired Harry Robinson to work at The Studio in July 1906, soon after Robinson graduated with a bachelor of science degree in architectural engineering from the University of Illinois.[194] There followed what appears to be a second evolutionary period in Wright's development of ground plans, as he explored how he himself could best advance and control the site environment with or without the augmentative talents of a landscape architect.

"A Fireproof House for $5,000," *The Ladies Home Journal*—April 1907

When the *Ladies Home Journal* asked Wright to design a house plan for a third article, he continued his effort to create an affordable residence for families of modest income—this time in the form of a "fireproof" house. The fireproof concept may have come about because of the Iroquois Theater fire of December 1903 that involved two of the Wright children and his mother-in-law, as suggested by Walter Creese.[195] An event such as this certainly could have awakened the sociological preoccupation with fireproof construction that was drummed into Wright's consciousness during his apprenticeship with Sullivan, when he was involved with the rebuilding of Chicago's central core. On the other hand, the cubistic configuration and poured concrete construction methodology replicated what Wright already had demonstrated on a grand scale with the design of Unity Temple (Oak Park, Illinois—1904). And within the text of the *Journal* article Wright described this manner of construction as a "cost-saving" process. He also elaborated on certain aspects of the consideration he gave to environmental design: "The roof slab overhangs to protect the walls from sun and the top is waterproofed with a tar and gravel roofing pitched to drain to a downspout located in the chimney flue, where it is not likely to freeze. To afford further protection to the second-story rooms from the heat of the sun a false ceiling is provided of plastered metal lath hanging eight inches below the bottom of the roof slab, leaving a circulating air space above, exhausted to the large open space in the centre of the chimney. In summer this air space is fed by openings beneath the

eaves, which may be closed in winter by a simple device reached from the second story windows."[196]

The plan featured in the article, which has come to be known as the "Prairie Square," differed from the typical American "Four-Square" in that the fireplace was shifted from an outside wall to a central location and the stairwell abutted an outside wall (Figure 3-58). There also is an appendage on the outside of the square that accommodates both a service entry and the main entry through a compartmented foyer arrangement. In all these respects, the Fireproof House identifies with the Frederick D. Nichols residence (1906), which itself

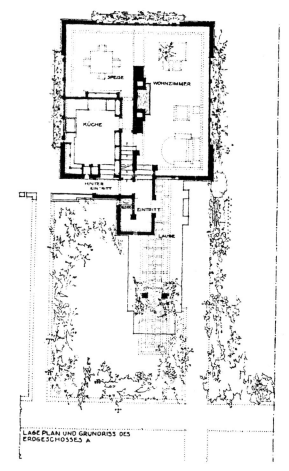

Figure 3-58   Ground-floor plan for Wright's "Fireproof House for $5,000." (*Out-of-copyright plan of record from Wasmuth Portfolio, 1910.*)

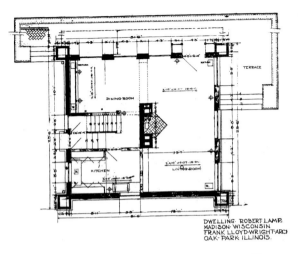

Figure 3-59 First-floor plan for the Robert M. Lamp House (1904). (© *2002 by The Frank Lloyd Wright Foundation, Scottsdale, Arizona.*)

appears to be a reworking of the layout for the Robert M. Lamp residence (1904).[197] Through the process of interpreting the plans for these three houses, together with the ground plans and perspectives that Wright included in his presentation of the Fireproof House in

the Wasmuth Portfolio, it is possible to trace the influence of Wright's trip to Japan—particularly with respect to the marked differences in the entry experience and indoor-outdoor connectedness.

The first-floor plan for the Lamp House places the service entry at ground level, with the stairs on the inside of the house and the main entry by way of a wraparound terrace on level with the first floor. The front door is situated around the corner of the terrace and opens directly into the living room (Figure 3-59).

The first-floor plan for the Nichols House is less cubistic in form as it has a short appendage that accommodates the dual entryways so there is direct access to the inside stairwell (Figure 3-60). The service door and stairwell are on the side closest to the kitchen. The main door is closest to the living room and opens onto a small vestibule with an entry closet on the outside wall directly opposite the entry stairs. There are two sizable built-in planters under banks of windows of the primary living areas and a limited terrace extending off the appendage with an overhanging arbor that is wide enough to serve as a space-defining element for the terrace, as well as the main entry. There is no further elaboration of an indoor-outdoor relationship.

The Fireproof House environmentally improves upon the Nichols plan in several significant ways. The

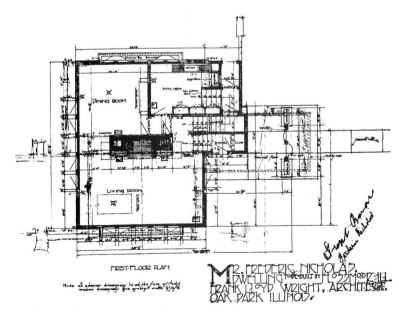

Figure 3-60 First-floor plan for the Frederick Nichols House (1906). (© *2002 by The Frank Lloyd Wright Foundation, Scottsdale, Arizona.*)

concrete terrace has been shifted off-center toward the living room side of the house and raised one step above ground level, commensurate with the top edge of the water table. The appendage, in turn, has been turned from a parallel position to be perpendicular to the house and extended outward to accommodate an enlarged closet. This considered rearrangement centers the main entry door in the wall, allows a more spacious vestibule, reduces the number of steps needed to reach the first-floor living area, and shifts the entry vestibule to the side in an asymmetrical position. By then adding a window to the end of the vestibule to overlook the terrace and entry walkway and a third planter under the bank of living room windows directly opposite the stairwell, sight lines were directed toward the gardenlike environments in all directions—whether ascending the stairs to reach the level of the living room, descending the stairs to reach the level of the vestibule, or using the principal interior living spaces.

Wright's preliminary sketches suggest the arrangement of plantings on the grounds and propose French doors to open onto an as-yet-undeveloped terrace. These changes represent the plan as it would be articulated in the 1910 version of the Wasmuth Portfolio, where the ground plans and perspective depict the house with the living room to the front and a narrow lawn between the house and a parallel sidewalk. The walkway to the front door is shown turning off the pedestrian parkway and passing between a narrow entry

garden contained within a masonry border on one side and a trellis with cascading vines on the other side. This manner of arranging plantings around the periphery, together with the masonry-edged delineation, appropriates the entire open space as a garden. The trellis planted with vines establishes a sense of the dwelling as part of the landscape and creates interesting shade and shadow patterns as counterpoint to the severe simplicity of a poured concrete structure.

The Wasmuth perspective and ground plan also suggest that in advocating there were alternate ways to arrange the house on the lot, Wright—in *his* mind, at least—may have been continuing to promote the Quadruple Block scheme. This postulation is supported by the fact that privacy walls extending from the sides of both houses correspond to those shown with the houses designed for the previous *Journal* articles. Moreover, there is a similar flat-roofed house visible above the privacy wall extension, and there is garden foliage behind the grove of trees to the right of the perspective (Figure 3-61). This arrangement suggests Wright was thinking of the lower sidewalk as public space and the perpendicular sidewalk as incorporated within one of the pedestrian parkways running alongside a garden median feature, such as was proposed for Roberts' Quadruple Block plan in Layouts "B" and "C." This might explain the absence of site boundaries, the inward manner of planting arrangement, and the fact that there is no provision for off-street parking, a driveway, garage, or stable.

Figure 3-61 Perspective drawing suggests that Wright was thinking of his "Fireproof House" within the context of a Quadruple Block Plan layout. (*Out-of-copyright drawing from Wasmuth Portfolio, 1910.*)

Mrs. Thomas R. Gale—Oak Park, Illinois (1907–1908)

The Thomas R. Gale commission doubly challenged Wright's ingenuity because of the program requirements of a young widow with small children and the limitations prescribed by a suburban infill lot.[198] Wright nonetheless was able to build into his design a composite of functional and aesthetically controlled outdoor living space, based upon environmentally inspired considerations. It was in fact Wright's manner of introducing enclosed out-door living space on two levels at streetside, the illusionary aspects of his site treatment, and the ecological basis for the 5-foot 6-inch depth of the cantilevered overhangs of the flat roof that most contributed to Wright's avant-gardism in this instance.

Wright addressed the constraint of the minimal site by crafting a sequential entry experience that capitalized upon the larger streetscape and its situation within the bend of Elizabeth Court. From Forest Avenue, the house is completely hidden from view and just begins to emerge when the side yard of the neighboring Queen Anne

Figure 3-62 a–c Sequential views of entry approach to the Oak Park, Illinois, home of Mrs. Thomas R. Gale (1907–1908). (*Photographs by Charles E. Aguar. © 2002 by Berdeana Aguar.*)

house is reached. It is only from the curve in the public street and sidewalk that the entire streetside facade of the house comes into full view (Figure 3-62 a-c).

The immediate first impression from the public rights-of-way is of the parapets that circumscribe and seclude the outdoor living spaces: the cantilevered balcony off the two north-facing second-floor bedrooms, the sizable walk-out terrace off the north end of the living room that has been raised to the first-floor level, and the terrace over the first-floor reception space. The parapet copings for all these spaces have been emphasized as contrasting horizontal banding in conformance with the banding created by the broad overhanging eaves, the cap of the massive chimney of the fireplace, and the deep wood facing that trims the baseline of the entire structure.[199] Not visible from streetside are the second-floor balcony stretching from the terrace to the southeast corner of the house; the rear eave overhang that protects the south-facing second-floor bedrooms from overheating in summer and admits solar penetration in winter; and the cantilevered extensions of the bedrooms themselves—all of which serve the same purpose for the south-facing windows of the kitchen and dining room at the first-floor level. It was the combination of all these elements of environmental design, together with the installation of an earthen terrace at 1.5 feet above ground level, that most contributed to the horizontal modernity of the Gale House. At the same time, the house holds its own with the three-story period houses immediately adjacent.

J. Kibben Ingalls—River Forest, Illinois (1909)

The J. Kibben Ingalls commission presented Wright with basically the same challenges that he had faced with the Gale House. In this case, two of the young couple's children had tuberculosis, so the sleeping porches and adequate ventilation were in keeping with the therapeutic treatment of a time when there were no medicinal means to combat this illness. Moreover, the infill property was equally constrictive as it was only 55 feet wide. Yet, Wright designed a house where there is remarkable interaction with the out-of-doors and absolute privacy, as explained by present-day owners John and Betty Tilton:

Wright did a remarkable job of siting this house, considering the proximity of the classic Queen Anne house across the driveway to the south and the infill limitations of this 55-foot lot, which was

once the side yard of the Tudor-style house on the north. The lot was platted exceptionally deep—some 330 feet—which is at least double many lots, both here and in Oak Park.

Although Wright lined up the front-facing living room wall to match the setbacks of other houses, he projected the large porch or covered terrace so that it juts out in front. This means we can have our morning coffee or read the paper in complete privacy, as though we were in our own private shelter in a large public park. Due to a double row of old elm trees, we barely can see houses across the street. Despite the fact that adjoining neighboring houses have very narrow side yards, we have to look back over our shoulder to see them from this vantage point. And the shadows caused by the cantilevered roofs and balconies add privacy, as occupants in the shade cannot be seen from outside.

The orientation is excellent, as our bedroom window wall faces east, so we receive early morning sun into our bedroom. Wright introduced wrap-around windows for all the major living spaces within the structure. . . . When you are outside looking into the house, the interior appears dark. But, from inside looking out, all the outside is bright and open. . . . This was part of Wright's way of relating inside to outside. Despite all the glass, this house is very private, quiet, and comfortable due to the long setback from the street and the arrangement of the rooms to accommodate the limitations of the narrow lot and the older houses on each side. The large number of windows provide adequate cross-ventilation, and we only this year succumbed to installing air conditioning. However, we did not seal the windows and take advantage of days like today, when we can let nature's cooling breezes keep us comfortable.[200]

The Tiltons then explained how the flexibility inherent to the basic cruciform layout of the prairie style of architecture allowed them to modernize and increase their interior living space by some 30 percent and the outdoor living space by an implausible 400 percent, all without changing the streetside appearance or compromising the integrity of Wright's architecture (Figures 3-63 a-b, 3-64 a-b, 3-65). Although John Tilton is an architectural designer who has restored other Wright-designed homes and has visionary qualifications beyond the ken of most homeowners, some of his comments bear repeating—if only because he points out illusory "tricks" Wright used to

Figure 3-63 a–b South elevations of the J. Kibben Ingalls House (1909) in River Forest, Illinois, before and after its extensive 1981 remodeling. (*Courtesy of John Tilton.*)

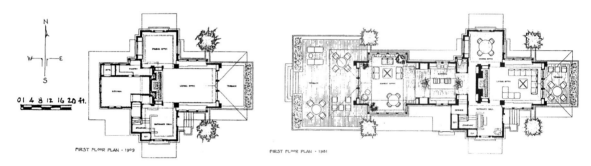

Figure 3-64 a–b First-floor plan of the J. Kibben Ingalls House before and after its 1981 remodeling. (*Courtesy of John Tilton.*)

Figure 3-65 Expansive outdoor living space added to the rear of the Ingalls House preserves the integrity of the original design. (*Courtesy of John Tilton.*)

lower construction costs for clients of modest means and explains the potential for expanding the livability of these individualistic residences within the process of restoration, remodeling, and modernization:

> Wright's houses make such rational design statements that anyone with a reasonable amount of intelligence can extend them in a very plausible way. We installed a new kitchen and added the family room in 1981, and also reconditioned all the original art-glass windows and added 21 new, matching ones. We have maintained a respectful attitude to retain the spirit of the original design in our major remodeling and expansion. . . . Instead of concrete urns, we have cantilevered pedestal wooden boxes that seem contemporary but are built from original plans drawn by Wright's office; the original ones had rotted long ago. . . . We replaced the water table around the foundation with redwood boards, for maximum life expectancy. Contrary to appearances, it was not a concrete slab, but was built of 2″ × 12″ boards that also had rotted out. . . . We painted the privacy banding and other wood trim in two shades of green and the stucco a light cream. We did not try to match original paint chips, because we felt we had artistic license to use colors of this time period.[201]

The Tiltons also understood the importance Wright placed in the balcony planters and massive urns, particularly with respect to the plantings that should be selected, as supported by comments made during their 1990 interview: "After two mature trees on the north side recently died and were cut down, we were able to develop a shade garden around the birdfeeder—with rhododendron, redbud, dogwood, and pachysandra ground cover, and add 500 daffodil bulbs for spring color. This year we tore out the overgrown junipers that had woven together into a mass four feet tall, covering the entire water table and most of the parapet of the front terrace."[202]

This final consideration—the area of landscape adornment and whether it is to be or not to be—is always an area of concern for owners or restorationists of a Wright-designed property, the prairie style in particular. In the area of an entry garden, which Wright intended to begin at the public right-of-way, the plantings should be low, ground-hugging, and deciduous. And careful consideration must be given to the predictable size of plantings at maturity. The same criteria hold true

in the area of the foundation because *any* variety of evergreens ultimately will hide the water table and violate Wright's strong commitment to exposing the juncture point of structure to ground. Wright also intended there would be a base plane of green—either lawn or ground cover—from which the house would appear to rise as demarcated planes of surface materials, such as he first proposed with the Winslow House.

Another consideration within the parameters of restoration—perhaps the most vital of all—is the importance of initiating a program of replacement planting so that well-established trees such as those along the right-of-way will be in place whenever existing mature trees inevitably succumb to disease, natural disasters, or age.

At the same time that Wright was working within the context of designing homes for clients of moderate means, he also would demonstrate his new command over the site environment through his method of thinking through and detailing the manner in which domestic commissions for three well-to-do clients would be aggrandized by the landscape: for Avery Coonley, Burton J. Westcott, and Frederick C. Robie. Wright's design approach for each of these commissions again can best be represented as Japanese-inspired although, rather than adapting his architecture to the nature of the site in the manner of the Japanese, he expressly manipulated the landscape to unite with the architecture.

Avery Coonley—Riverside, Illinois (1907)

The Coonley site originally encompassed an entire block at the far south end of Olmsted's planned community of Riverside. Formed in the shape of a teardrop by the gentle curvature of Bloomingbank and Scottswood Roads, it was situated directly across from a parklike greenway known as Indian Gardens. By 1907, the entire acreage was graced with stately shade trees, and this open space along the edge of the Des Plaines River created a sense of spaciousness and near-rural tranquillity. It was because of the proximity of this peripheral environment that Wright once again chose to use the same raised basement design approach he had used under similar circumstances for Husser, Thomas, Huertley, and Tomek.

An analysis of the evolutionary site plans reveals that Wright had but one land-planning layout in mind and never considered alternative approaches (Figure 3-66 a-c). Version "A," the earliest conceptual plan, was drafted directly onto the topographical map and appears to be in Wright's hand.[203] No contours are indicated for the northwest portion of the site. But the 1-foot contours delineating the original terrain for the balance of the site represent that the center of the block was basically level; the southwest portion was gently sloping; and the widest eastern portion had a slope ranging from an elevation of approximately 3 feet above the southern perimeter of Scottswood to some 10 feet at the intersection of Scottswood and Coonley Roads. Although Wright logically chose to site the complex of buildings within this widest portion of the property, he did so with little consideration for the natural terrain. He literally reversed his process of purposefully creating changes in grade with earthen terraces as he had for clients whose sites were basically level; in a sense, he drafted the layout as if the map before him was a blank sheet of paper.

The planned land uses for the Coonley complex included the house with living quarters and guest quarters, a servants' wing, a stable and carriage house, carriage yards, horse-grooming areas, a large sunken garden, and a raised garden. In "A," the main axis is centered through the dining room and a large formal reflecting pool; the servants' wing is aligned along the northwest side. The northwest-southeast axis centers on the stable, located some 125 feet east of the main structure, and the gardeners' quarters are aligned along the southwest side. A straight-line driveway paralleling this axis is the principal means for ingress and egress for the site. This driveway crosses the entire width of the acreage to provide relatively direct routes to and from Riverside's commuter railway station by way of Coonley Road to the north or Scottswood Road to the south. The stable and garage are served by way of an interior lane and service entry. A pergola designed to bisect two tennis courts is shown extending some 400 feet, from the south end of the gardener's house to a half-circle garden feature at the far-west end of the property.

The contour lines on version "B" have been omitted, although black dots representing the location of tree trunks suggest that a tree inventory had been made by this time. These existing trees directly relate to Wright's structuring of his architecture and outdoor living spaces. Whoever drafted this and the subsequent "C" version, however, incorrectly centered the main axis so as to pass *through* the servants' wing, rather than aligning it along the northwest side—as Wright delineated it on the topographical map and, more important, as it was aligned when built. Each of these plans support Wright's precise, architectonic restructuring of the site to create the level space necessary to accommodate the planned land uses, including the infrastructure required for implementation (grading, sewer pipes, power lines, pavement, curbing, foundations, steps, fences, bridges, arbors, trel-

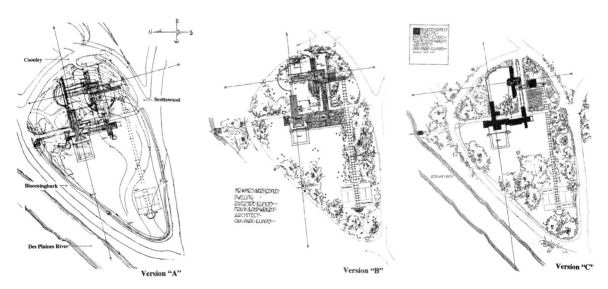

Figure 3-66 a–c Evolutionary versions of site plans for the Avery Coonley House (1907) in Riverside, Illinois. (*By Charles E. Aguar, based on historic photographs, personal analysis, and original drawings of record. © 2002 by The Frank Lloyd Wright Foundation, Scottsdale, Arizona. As delineated, © 2002 by Berdeana Aguar*)

lises, et al.). Terraces were cut into the ground, and all were circumscribed by an extensive system of retaining walls.

The Coonley House represents Wright's first use of his "zoned plan," a layout that typifies the Japanese *sukiya* style of building structuring—where separate units of space interrelate as clearly defined functions for living, dining, sleeping, playing, and working. This interpretation is reinforced by the manner in which the balanced asymmetrical form of the architecture interlocks with the gardens, as well as by the strategical arrangement of the indirect path systems in the gardens. And yet, the nucleus of the layout is the very *un*naturally formed reflecting pool. It is the view of this pool that is "captured alive" and brought into the living room environment through the wall of doors, with the living room balcony serving as the middle scenery and the ornate iron railing as the capturing device. At the same time, views are carefully controlled so the pool can be seen only partially from the living room or even from the principal balcony viewpoint. Wright then introduced symbolistic patterns of nature-inspired ornamentation—such as ferns, the common locust tree, tulips, and other motifs—within the inanimate mediums of electroplated art glass, glazed ceramic tile, molded bronze, concrete, and wrought iron. All of these man-made elements were interwoven with the natural vegetation, color, and textures so that every detail viewed from the second-story living quarters shares a rhythm and harmony with the whole, beginning with the interior ceiling, rugs, and murals and extending through the art-glass windows to the outer surfaces—from the garden furniture, to the wall tile, to the trellis, to each hardscape garden structure, and even to reflections in the pool and shadows cast by pergolas and balcony railings (Figure 3-67).

Even though Wright used inanimate mediums to establish this interrelationship, rather than the animate medium of plantings in the manner of the Japanese, his layout follows the Japanese system of planning, defining, and articulating space, as described by Messervy: "Japanese architecture . . . is an architecture of vistas, of continuity, of perspective. There is a constant movement of space, a gentle shifting from place to place; but no matter how far one pursues the movement one never arrives at a conception of a plastic whole. The tension, the immobility necessary to produce plastic unity are lacking; everything changes with one's movements, and with time. Its unity . . . is created by a consistency of approach which makes the sequence of spaces part of a

single mood."[204] It was to this end result of Wright's design that Elizabeth Faulkner, the Coonley daughter, was responding when she remarked: "It was a large house, but it seemed intimate and homey . . . it had all sorts of angles, so that you never saw more than a small part of the house at any one time—which gave it that feeling of intimacy."[205]

It fell to landscape architect Jens Jensen to detail the complex planting plans required to successfully articulate the defining vision of Wright's layout and design (Figure 3-68). Sources compiled by Grese confirm that Jensen worked on the Coonley landscape plans between 1908 and 1917, but it is not known when or how Jensen became involved.[206] Presumably, he was retained by Queene Coonley, who most probably would

Figure 3-67   Shadows create a symbolistic pattern of nature-inspired ornamentation on the walls of the Avery Coonley House. (*Photograph by Gilman Lane. Courtesy of the Gilmore Collection, Oak Park Public Library, Oak Park, Illinois.*)

have known of Jensen by his reputation—either through social circles or through his work with Chicago's Humboldt Park (1906–1907). The Coonley sunken garden is analogous to the large sunken garden Jensen designed for Humboldt, and the smaller raised garden is not uncommon to formal flower gardens in circles or squares he designed for several parks and residences. There also was the more immediate association of Jensen's involvement with the landscape design of Sullivan's Henry Babson estate, another Riverside property under construction in 1907.[207] Or Jensen could have been recommended by Wright, although in Wright's 1930 letter to Jensen, he alluded to their never having provided work for the other: "During 27 years for instance never has any work on your account come to me or any on my account gone to you. . . . It would be quite natural that you should want to work with me, whenever you could? Yes? But is it that a Star is seldom willing to share with a Star. The Star will seek lesser men to accomplish his purpose, as a matter, he mistakenly thinks, of self-

preservation."[208] Whatever the motivation for the initial contact with Jensen, it most likely did not occur until after the Coonley House was built—an assumption supported by Eaton's observation that Jensen did not become involved with the Babson House until after construction was complete, as was "usually" the case "in the early years of his practice."[209]

It is significant that the Coonley commission represents the first instance where Wright allowed massed plantings proximate to his architecture in the Jensen manner—an allowance that would seem to demonstrate a certain new level of maturity on Wright's part, as well as the respect he must have held for Jensen's talent and reputation as a designer of the landscape. While Wright and Jensen did not actually collaborate on the Avery Coonley commission in the true sense of the term—in that they only considered the aesthetics of planting enhancement and did not work together in developing a site analysis, determining optimum locations for principal and secondary structures and outdoor elements, or in

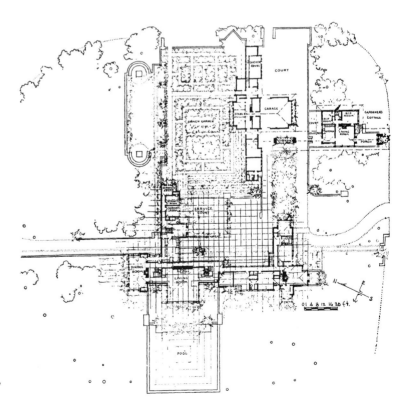

Figure 3-68 Site plan for the Avery Coonley House, as laid out by landscape architect Jens Jensen. (© *2002 by the Frank Lloyd Wright Foundation, Scottsdale, Arizona.*)

laying out elements of site circulation—their mutual involvement undoubtedly contributed to their long-standing friendship.

Wright's overall environmental design methodology for siting and developing the Coonley complex was visionary, even if it was basically in conflict with natural conditions inherent to the site. It was here that he first adjusted the use of long axes and sight lines by shifting the mass of two structural elements to the edge of each axis. By arranging the three separate buildings in asymmetrical juxtaposition in a manner less formal than Italian villas, Wright avoided any manifestation of bilateral symmetry and created an innovative balance seldom, if ever, attained by his contemporaries. His treatment of the grounds around the buildings, on the other hand, was geometrically organized in the Italianate mode, but formal only to the extent of carrying the lines of the structure into the out-of-doors. At the same time, he

represented the prairie style through the horizontality of his architecture, his placement of urns at terminal positions, and his use of cascading plantings. When Wright's architectural composition was then unified and enhanced by Jensen's individualistic manner of landscape design, where the formal sunken garden of squares-within-squares provided counterpoint balance to the otherwise informal plantings that he selected to command visually from the surrounding streets, there developed an intimate inter-relationship between the architecture and the nature of the site that was, and still is, extraordinary. Thus, the Coonley complex clearly represents Wright's mind-set for developing an American architecture that would corporeally and psychologically unite with its site without fully embracing either the purest form of the primarily indigenous prairie landscape treatment then being promoted by Wilhelm Miller, the heavy hand of classicism formalized during the Renaissance and championed by

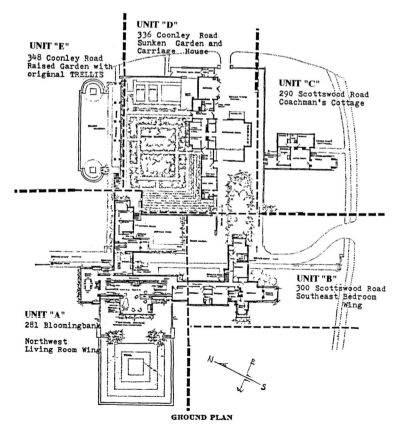

Figure 3-69 Ground plan showing division of the Avery Coonley estate into five separate living units in 1952–1957. (*Courtesy of James and Carolyn Howlett.*)

those trained in the Beaux Arts, or the subtleties in the manipulation of the landscape that had evolved over centuries in the Orient. This hyperbole blend of American, Italian, and Japanese space-making went far beyond anything Wright had done prior to this time, heralding the embryonics of an entirely new form of environmental design based upon a domestic architecture that would not begin to emerge into full flower until four years hence—with his own "Taliesin."

The west end of the Coonley block was never developed as planned. This area was subdivided in 1952 and sold off as four individual lots. None of the houses built there were designed by Wright, however. The original Wright structures and developed acreage also were subdivided in the 1950s and converted into four separate living units: the north wing of the main house, the south wing, the former gardener's cottage, and the carriage house (Figure 3-69). At some point, another house was built within the northeast quadrant of the property; although not designed by Wright, it is compatible with his architecture and is not obtrusive. Even so, the charismatic nature of Wright's extraordinary site environment remains intact, as attested to through the author's 1990 interview with Carolyn and James Howlett, who had lived in the carriage house as a residence since 1953:

> The stable, like other parts of the Coonley complex, is not an isolated unit behind the main house, but is itself a series of structures integrated with the house and gardens—an essential part of the total design. . . . We especially enjoy the easy access to the gardens, courtyards, and outdoor work areas from every room in the house. We live and work

outdoors to a greater extent than is normal in the Chicago area because of the warmer climate in winter due to the sun-drenched "sunken garden," our largest outdoor space, plus the easy flow of movement from inside to outside.

> Varying degrees of warmth, exposure, shelter, and air flow are always available to us from the four gardens that open out from the four wings (Figure 3-70). One of our gardens is on a terrace higher than our house level and, on hot summer nights, we sometimes hang our hammocks there for sleeping. Another, just outside the kitchen, serves for outdoor dining. In this climate, we are able to enjoy outdoor living earlier in the spring than our friends, and longer in the fall—thanks to control of sun and wind, deep overhanging eaves, breezeways, and vine-covered arbors.

> We feel like we are revisiting Japan when we return from a vacation, and many of our artist friends have said we live within a Piet Mondrian painting. We prefer to think of living with a piece of beautifully proportioned sculpture—a sculpture with Mr. Wright's square motif constantly recurring in both structure and surface ornamentation, in both positive and negative form. . . . Frank Lloyd Wright was a genius to be able to design something like this that is so adaptable to the lifestyles of five families eighty-five years later.[210]

Burton J. Westcott—Springfield, Ohio (1907)

The Westcott House is situated at the intersection of East High Street and Greenmount Avenue. The topography of the property to the immediate west and the park across the street to the east supports that the natural ter-

Figure 3-70   Photograph of Carriage House garden, owned by Carolyn and James Howett since 1953, in the former Coonley estate. (*Photograph by Charles E. Aguar. © 2002 by Berdeana Aguar.*)

rain was in the form of a hill—sloping up from East High Street and then down toward the alley that originally delineated the north boundary. When Greenmount Avenue was cut through, however, its surface was established some 7 feet below the surrounding terrain—leaving sharp escarpments along either side of the street. Assumedly, it was for this reason that Wright was inspired to once again use sculptured earthen terracing as his medium of design unification. At the same time, Wright essentially followed the dictates of the site when he manipulated the crown of the hill into a mesalike earthen platform, established the front elevation at the crest of the hill so the broadside of the living quarters faced south toward East High Street, and arranged the three-story mass of the house, the interconnecting portion of the pergola, and the garage-stable in an unbroken stretch along the Greenmount Avenue escarpment. The length of continuous structuring extends more than 160 feet, from north to south. Stephen Siek, who has conducted extensive research on the Westcott property, aptly describes the effect created: "The house seems not to terminate at its rear elevation, but rather continues outward in a horizontal embrace."[211]

The front elevation of the Westcott House closely allies with the central portion of the front elevation of the Coonley House, as corroborated by Wright in the March 1908 issue of *Architectural Record*. When Wright noted that it essentially is the same disposition of ele-

ments as in the Coonley House, however, he most likely was making reference to the similar use of a metal grid of cantilevered beams and the two levels of casement windows overlooking a pool. The metal grid at the Coonley House faces southwest and supports an arbor of vines that deflect the penetrating rays of the late afternoon sun, whereas the metal overhanging grid at the Westcott House faces due south and does not impede solar penetration during the winter, but supports a custom-designed awning that creates a treelike canopy to shelter the garden terrace during summer. And the water feature for the Coonley House was designed to function as a formal reflecting pool, whereas the Westcott water feature was designed to function as a lily pool. Moreover, the base for the Westcott pool is shown as gravel over a clay lining, rather than concrete, and the two underwater concrete bases for the lily tubs have the purpose of elevating the bright bloom of the water lilies and the deep green of the lily pads so they merge with other plantings to become integral elements of the garden imagery. This organic structuring belies the geometricity of its shape and the 19-foot-long concrete flower box installed at the edge of the garden terrace as foreground to the pool.

An historic photograph verifies that Wright used three existing trees, ranging from 6 to 16 inches in caliper, to establish the finished grade of the lower and upper earthen terraces (Figure 3-71). Both terraces were precisely graded into pronounced rampartlike embank-

Figure 3-71 The earliest known photograph (circa 1909) of the Burton J. Westcott House in Springfield, Ohio, shows the trees that dictated the form of the earthen terracing. (*Courtesy of the Clark County Historical Society, Springfield, Ohio.*)

ments to project a compelling countenance that is at once bold and incisive. The upper terrace establishes the grade for both the main floor living area and the garden terrace between the living area and the lily pool. The lily pool is level with the garden terrace and breaches the upper terrace, as do the steps on either side leading down onto the greensward lawn of the lower terrace. Two massive concrete urns—possibly the tallest and largest ever designed by Wright—were positioned on pedestals at the base of the steps on either side (Figure 3-72). As these urns were raised above the level of the pool to be in line with the concrete flower box, they establish the terminal points of the garden and thereby extend the garden imagery onto the site environment. They also emphasize the elevated height of the upper earthen terrace and visually separate the house and garden from the public realm. This all-inclusive treatment accentuates the natural impact of gravity, expresses the weight of the building mass, and provides a means to create a secluded garden environment with controlled view-shed from the bedroom balconies and the bands of casement windows on both levels. The overall effect of this "highly unusual" treatment, observed Siek, is "a strong persistent garden theme [that] dominates the front yard."[212]

As Wright went about the business of designing an entry approach for the Westcott House, he was faced with the challenge of considering two main points of entry: a direct entry off Greenmount Avenue and an entry from the garage-stable or garage apartment, by way of the pergola. The streetside approach breaches the earthen terracing, with abutments installed on either side of the wide sidewalk offset, and then proceeds

through the doorway into the low-ceilinged entry hall under the pergola before ascending the steps leading to the expansive space of the reception hall. Siek describes Wright's attention to environmentally articulated detail in this area: "In summer, the ribbon of clerestory casements . . . open to admit air, well over the heads of visitors and host. . . . Directly above the staircase looms a spacious skylight of leaded glass, tinged with gold and issuing a brilliant flood of illumination, the light in turn being refracted from a similar skylight cut directly into the tiled roof. In the evenings lights placed a few inches above the steps themselves, in glass cases built directly into the plastered walls provide the necessary guidance."[213] Siek also notes that "the large enclosed radiators in the hall . . . have slats which permit the warm air to rise and escape . . . there are intake vents . . . to trap the colder air admitted by the front door [which is] heated by the hot pipes."

Wright appears to have invested much more creative thought into the approach through the pergola, most probably because of the functional circumstance of its structure, which was in addition to its aesthetic contribution to the entry experience. The section of the south elevation for the garage-stable—incorrectly labeled "north" elevation by the delineator—clearly shows the bulwarklike structuring Wright specified for the plastered concrete retaining wall of the pergola (Figure 3-73 a-c). While the parapet wall is only 8 inches thick above the walkway, where it is topped by oriental-appearing windowlike openings, the density spreads out to a substantial 4 feet 8 inches at the base of the underground buttress. Wright used this structuring to hold back the many hundreds of tons of earth-fill needed to form a base

Figure 3-72 A 1992 photograph of the Westcott House shows the two massive concrete urns that separate the house and garden from the public realm. (*Photograph by Charles E. Aguar. © 2002 by Berdeana Aguar.*)

for the pergola walkway and to level a portion of the rear yard so as to extend the platform base for the house and accommodate the extensive sequestered garden space.[214] He also installed concrete window wells to hold back earth from the 10 windows on the south and west sides of the garage. Thus, the rear yard was every bit as manipulated as the front yard, and every vestige of the natural slope of the site was eliminated.

The pergola walkway was connected to the garage at street level and to the apartment above by two sets of stairs. The entry experience by way of the pergola therefore involved ascending or descending one of these accesses to reach the level of the walkway and stroll along its length under arborlike rafters draped with cascading vines. The particularized detail of the pergola suggests a rather grand garden arrangement and the 8-foot width of the walkway indicates that it served as outdoor living space—in essence, a covered terrace—from which to interact with the garden from any of the open gateway points along its length. Near the rear facade of the house, the pergola walkway converts into a bridged deck structuring to allow the introduction of a service entry, together with a stairway to facilitate coal delivery into the basement. The decking then continues over the

breached point of entry from Greenmount Avenue, where the pergola was roofed over and the square patterning of the art-glass clerestory windows over the entry hall to the west mirror the square patterning of the pergola windows to the east. This amalgamated treatment created a threshold that differentiated this realm of space from the realm of the garden, allowed the pupils of the eyes to adjust to the gradated luminance, and significantly enhanced the pergola entry experience.

Upon entering the reception hall by way of either entry, the first impression was intended to be the unbroken plane of space comprising the reception hall, living room, and dining room—which measured 62 feet from end to end. Wright's uncluttering treatment in this area

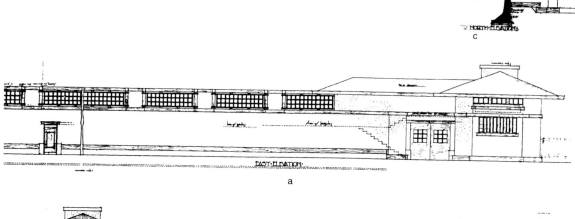

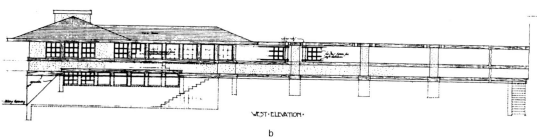

Figure 3-73 a–c   South elevation of the Westcott garage and stable (3-73 a), and west and east elevations of pergola and garage-stable (3-73 b–c). (© 2002 by The Frank Lloyd Wright Foundation, Scottsdale, Arizona.)

had the effect of emphasizing the garden imagery that seemingly surrounded the entire length and breadth of the space. That this was Wright's design intent is supported by his provision for plantings in 17-foot-long, zinc-lined flower boxes beneath the bands of casement windows at either end. These were in addition to the plantings on the terrace, in the lily pool, and in the massive urns—as all would be viewed from this primary living space through the ribbon of casement windows and the glazed doors that opened out upon the garden terrace, as well as from the balconies and bedrooms above.

With the Burton J. Westcott House, then, Wright exhibited his full and complete understanding of the use of natural and man-made environmental elements to enhance the cultural landscape and its public context. This, even though he architectonically manipulated the site to facilitate his architecture—from beginning to end. He preserved existing trees and incorporated them into the cultivated environment. He oriented the house for ideal solar penetration into the primary living areas. He used both overhanging eaves and a custom-designed awning to control summer sun. He used continuous bands of windows wrapping around corners of the house to facilitate an indoor-outdoor relationship and maximize air cooling by cross-ventilation. He used natural convection to draw air through the chimney vents. And he provided large skylights to introduce natural lighting over the stairwell and entryway. He also respected the psychological intimacy of interior and exterior space and the strategic placements of the pool, terrace, pergola, built-in planters, and urns between public and private zones. It was Wright's studied consideration of all of these critical environmental concerns that allowed him to create this masterfully executed "whole design," which prompted Wright historian Grant Manson to observe that the Westcott House "always seemed to me one of the warmest and most ingratiating of the Prairie Houses."[215]

For the better part of a century, the Burton J. Westcott House was allowed to progressively deteriorate. This process began during the 1940s when the house was converted to apartments and the side terraces and balconies were stuccoed over so the structure appeared as one solid mass, from foundation to roof. It is a process that continued through the 1990s—in spite of the fact the property was listed on the National Register of Historic Places, and in spite of the efforts of owner Sherri

Snyder to independently restore the house. In September 2000, Snyder sold the property to the Frank Lloyd Wright Building Conservancy. According to an article in the December 3, 2000 issue of *Montana Standard*, Snyder took this action to make sure "everything stays intact."[216] The article concludes: "The conservancy plans to resell the house to a locally formed foundation that intends to raise the estimated $2.7 million it will take to restore the home so the public can tour it as a museum."

Frederick C. Robie—Chicago, Illinois (1908)

The Frederick C. Robie property is situated at the northeast corner of the intersection of Woodlawn Avenue and East 58th Street on the outer edges of Hyde Park, one of Chicago's original suburban communities. Robie had definite ideas as to the type of home he wanted and prepared many preliminary sketches to help make clear to an architect what he envisioned for this particular site. At the time Wright entered the picture as Robie's architect-of-choice, then, he was challenged to bring to life certain preconceived preferences of his client. Moreover, everything had to fit within the confines of an urban site of moderate size (60 by 180 feet) that was the same width as, and only one-third longer than, a tennis court built to standard specification. Considering that there also were deed restrictions dictating a 35-foot setback from Woodlawn Avenue, the extent of usable space was compromised even more. Even so, the articulation of open space and the consequence of outdoor living were so important to Wright that he allocated more than half the limited area of the site (56.5 percent) to these features.

Wright was challenged by environmental considerations from the onset of the design process. The site was directly across from the marshy area reclaimed as an open-space park during Olmsted's development of the properties for the South Park District and the Columbian Exposition (see Chapter 1). The soils of the neighborhood had the problem of poor drainage inherent to any low-lying topography. It was for this reason that surrounding houses were elevated on an earthen terrace 2 feet higher than ground level—rather than for the purpose of visual perspective that generally inspired Wright's installation of earthen terracing. It was for this reason also that Wright limited excavation under the house and based his construction upon the Chicago Foundation System for isolating piers to provide adequate bearing capacity on spongy soils.[217] It might seem paradoxical, then, that Wright literally flaunted the nature of the site soils by choosing to build the Robie House at ground level, but analysis establishes that this seeming incongruity was in fact based upon logic and perception.

Wright's primary consideration for building at ground level was the preservation of existing trees. This reasoning is supported by historic photographs documenting the immediate proximity of mature trees on both sides of the auto-court privacy wall and within the covenant-specified setback area. Had Wright followed the standard established by existing houses and built upon an earthen terrace, he would have lost the benefit of these trees. The shape of the lot—with the narrow width fronting upon Woodlawn Avenue (west boundary) and the length running parallel to East 58th Street (south boundary)—dictated the horizontal emphasis, and the southerly orientation dictated the placement of the primary living spaces on all three levels (Figure 3-74). The parklike peripheral environment to the south was an additional benefit and once again motivated Wright's use of the raised basement approach. The vertical height and proximity of existing and/or potential

houses on the land-bound sides of the property dictated the massing and arrangement of areas not intrinsic to primary living.

Using these exigencies as his basis, Wright divided the house into two principal units: a primary living unit and a service unit. The three-story mass of the service unit abutted the north boundary and was set back to the depth of the entrance court, while the three-story living unit was sited forward but set back from the south boundary. This siting and arrangement retained a sizable expanse of open space to the rear of the house for the courtyard and enough room to the south to allow Wright to install a walled garden court directly accessible from the ground-floor billiards room and playroom, by way of 12 French doors. This garden court and the parapet of its privacy wall established the baseline for the stepped-back balcony terracing that causes the house to appear as a series of horizontal planes—an effect made more manifest when cascading varieties of plantings are cultivated within the built-in planters that circumscribe and define the lengths of the three balcony parapets (Figure 3-75). The overall illusion was of a

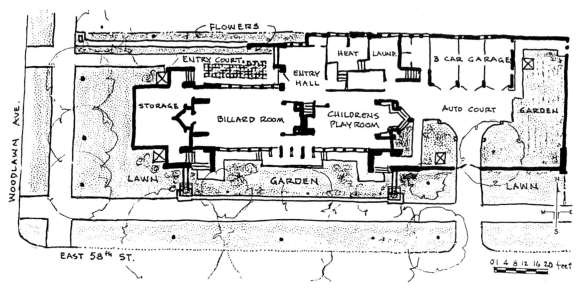

Figure 3-74 Conjectured site plan shows allocation of open space for Frederick Robie House (1908) in Chicago, Illinois. (*By Charles E. Aguar, based on historic photographs, personal analysis, and original drawings of record. © 2002 by the Frank Lloyd Wright Foundation, Scottsdale, Arizona. As delineated, © 2002 by Berdeana Aguar.*)

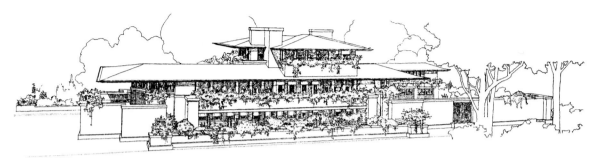

Figure 3-75   Cascading varieties of plantings emphasize the horizontal planes of the Robie House architecture. (*Out-of-copyright drawing from Wasmuth Portfolio, 1910.*)

structure much more firmly entrenched than other houses on the block. It was this imagery that caused both Manson and Hitchcock to liken the Robie House to a ship deeply afloat on the water.

Coincident with the organization of the architecture on the site, Wright built into his design a composite of functional outdoor living elements and aesthetic open space. The consequence he placed on outdoor living is supported by the demonstrable ratio of outdoor-to-indoor space on the two levels allocated to primary living. At ground level, this ratio is more than doubled: 1680 square feet for the billiards room and playroom, compared to 3440 square feet for the combined open spaces of the south garden and auto-garden courtyard. On the second level, the ratio is reversed. The combined spaces of living-dining room and guest bedroom compute to 1936 square feet, compared to 838 square feet for the living room porch, balcony, and guest room balcony. Moreover, the 720-square-foot swath of open space paralleling the privacy wall on the southeast corner of the lot—together with the 1690 square feet set aside for the entrance court on the northwest corner—established an asymmetrical balance to the composition of the entire site.

Wright's attention to proportion of the architectural spaces within the northwest quadrant was especially important to his all-inclusive approach. Where the setback covenant prescribed the placement of the west wall of the house proper, Wright arranged that only the center of the salient post in the living-room prow comply with the 35-foot setback requirement. He then slyly followed "the letter while violating its spirit," as Donald Hoffman so aptly describes it, by projecting the porch into the prescribed setback area so that "the west wall of

the porch is only 18 feet four inches from the lot line."[218] This placement brought the living room porch proportionately closer to the row of existing trees within the setback space, so their canopy shaded the porch from the penetrating rays of the late afternoon sun. The tree canopy also appropriated the porch, united it with the site, and helped ameliorate its upright presence. As the porch constituted 414 square feet of open space, had a full level of storage beneath, and was bounded by a story-and-a-half brick wall, it could have been visually overpowering had it not been for the trees and Wright's studied consideration of these antithetical spatial elements of verticality and horizontality.

The vertical massing of the service unit lessened the visual impact of the porch as viewed from the west, as did the lowering of the level of the porch floor to 18 inches below the level of the living room, the correspondent lowering of the brick parapet wall, the stone coping across the top of the parapet, the wide masonry water table at its base, and the introduction of built-in planters along the width of the porch and at the tops of the stairways on either side. The verticality of the trees similarly lessened the visual impact of the porch, as viewed from the intersection at the southwest corner of the site—as did the tree canopy, the lowering of the porch level, the planters, the 1845 square feet of open space that wrapped around the porch as a lawn to establish a horizontal baseline plane of green, and the exuberant Japanese-inspired cantilevered eaves (such as Wright first used for the Tomek House).

In this case, the eaves cantilevered over the living room porch and also provided sheltered access to and from the ground-floor playroom and auto-garden courtyard to the east. It was Hoffman's sense of the psychological unification created by these sheltering eaves that caused him to observe: "the porch would be in fact an integral part of the house."[219] It was this same perception of the spatial combinability of the playroom and court-yard that evoked a long-felt memory for Robie's son, who recalled "the fun I had riding my tricycle out from the ground-floor playroom into the rear courtyard and back."[220] He explained: "Father gave me a little auto-mobile with a real brass-trimmed radiator. Many times, in my play, I would take him from the house to work, a long and fascinating trip from the playroom to the far-thest of the three garages. . . . To me, this last garage was his office. . . . And then, later, I would pick him up and bring him home. . . . Father intended for the playroom and the courtyard area to be my world, and it was."

However much thought Wright gave to these and other of the Robie House exterior spaces, it was in the area of his entry approach that he appears to have placed the most significance—even treating it as architectural space on his working drawings. Where Wright inset the north wall of all three levels some 5 feet—a design fea-ture meant to create a shadow line that could either lessen or increase the visual impact of the service unit, depending upon the time of day—he bordered the entire 70-foot length of the entrance court with a retain-ing wall installed to the same inset as the north wall of the house and at the same 2-foot height as the neigh-boring earthen terrace (Figure 3-76). He retained more than half the depth of this inset as an earthen terrace and the balance as a ground-level earthen strip to fashion a continuous two-tiered entry garden that originated at streetside with a 5-foot-wide masonry planter and ter-minated at the brick support pier for the guest room bal-cony. The mass of the stone coping along the top of the retaining wall introduced an additional horizontal ele-ment into Wright's overall scheme of things, as it also provided seating and a means to interact more closely with the garden environment.

Through this manner of terracing the entry garden and leaving the open space surrounding the porch devoid of plantings, Wright established a line of sight that directed movement past the entry garden toward the main point of outdoor-indoor transition. At the point where the adjunct stairway to the living room porch terminates and the walkway widens to signify a threshold, he installed an expansive welcome mat of tile to identify this space as the entrance court. This detail has the additional purpose of visually directing move-ment toward the 5-foot-wide art-glass entry door, which is completely secreted from the street or public sidewalk by its discreet placement diagonally removed from the entry sidewalk. This places the entry in the southeast corner of the entry loggia under the deep overhang of the guest room balcony and behind the parapet wall for the porch stairway—a location and arrangement that exactly corresponds to the main entry for the Heurtley House, as does Wright's motivation: to protect the main entry from the elements and the prevailing winter winds, in particular. Because of the depth of the balcony overhang, however, the entry loggia always is in shadow, making it appear as a cavelike opening rather than a des-tination. Anyone not specifically looking for a point of entry might easily pass it by.[221]

Throughout this carefully planned progression of arrival, Wright artfully followed the Zen principle of hide-and-reveal; and he continued on the inside. From the art-glass door, there is a short diagonal walk across

Figure 3-76   Entrance court and entry garden approach to Robie House. (*Photograph by Gilman Lane. Courtesy of Gilmore Collection, Oak Park Public Library, Oak Park, Illinois.*)

the spacious entry hall to the entry stairwell, which is integrated into the central fireplace mass. Upon ascending the stairway and negotiating a sequence of turns, there is a strong sense of containment until the midpoint of the central landing, where the confinement of the ceiling is eliminated and the space above expands beyond the staircase balustrade to the height of the vaulted living-dining room ceiling. Upon reaching the destination of the primary living space, therefore, the eye is immediately drawn toward the remarkable prospect of the out-of-doors. Through this process of manipulating the complementary Yin and Yang attitudes of space and form, horizontal and vertical, light and dark, and the sequence of drawing attention to outdoors, indoors, and outdoors again, Wright both controlled the gradations of luminance and created a sense of anticipation that heightened the impact of reaching the main destination.

It is significant that the main destination in this case is the living-dining room, south balcony, and north porch, rather than the hearth. Not only did Wright place more emphasis upon sight lines into the out-of-doors and less on the hearth as refuge; he went so far as to limit the familiar inglenook seating by half so as to encourage views outward through the wall of glazed doors and across the middle scenery of the south balcony—where the parapet wall captures the borrowed view of the trees and the open space of the peripheral environment and brings it into the primary living space. Wright was so concerned with the visual benefit of the borrowed scenery to the south that he built a small balcony into the southeast corner of the dining room to provide an additional viewing platform for this purpose.

The functionality Wright built into his environmental design of outdoor living spaces for the Robie House was crucial to the comfort level of living in a house so close to two public rights-of-way and so open to the out-of-doors. Certainly, his enclosure of outdoor living spaces had to do with privacy, as described by Grant Hildebrand: "The parapet wall of the south terrace . . . is disposed to intercept exactly a sight line from the center of the near sidewalk; a view from that position reveals only the wood trim of the tops of the French doors, and no glass at all of the main floor spaces. This can hardly be accidental, as the planter forward of the upstairs bedroom does exactly the same thing, to the inch."[222] But the enclosure of outdoor living spaces had to do with noise abatement, as well, as did the density of the brick

walls. Because street noise is directed outward and upward on a diagonal line, the height and stepped-back aspect of the balcony parapet walls had the effect of blocking the direct path of sound transmission and lessening the level of impact at the various points of reception—from ground level to belvedere. The exaggerated height of the walls around the auto-garden courtyard also had to do with both privacy and noise abatement, as did the purposeful lowering of the south garden to some 18 inches below street level. Landscape architect John Simonds explains: "Areas susceptible to noise impact may be lowered and dug into the sheltering earth. . . . Spaces can turn their backs to the sources of annoyance and focus away, or inward. . . . With sound, as with light, the angle of incidence is equal to the angle of reflection. In spaces where people are exposed to noise, this fact is a consideration in the shaping of walls, slopes, and building profiles."[223]

Wright's manner of installing the five piers along the wall of French doors leading from the billiards room into the south garden supports his concern for both the public viewpoint and living comfort at ground level. The interspersion of the three partial piers had the same purpose as the staggered full and partial piers Wright installed in the south wall of the dining room at the Darwin Martin House—that is, the piers function much like vertical louvered blinds in that they admit natural light and permit unrestricted views outward, but passersby viewpoints are significantly compromised. The piers also fit into Wright's strategy to build into his design of the south garden the means to ameliorate conditions of weather during the range of seasons. By lowering the garden elevation and installing a masonry terrace in the section immediately in front of the doors, Wright created an elongated sun trap that would collect solar heat during the fall and winter months as the low-angled sun moved from east to west throughout the day. The further massing of the five piers collected and retained solar heat, as well. Conversely, the depth of the overhanging balcony directly above was more narrow and the eave was significantly deeper, so as to prevent direct exposure to the elevated angle of the sun during spring and summer. And when all the doors were left open, they would work with the intricate system of ventilation channels Wright built into his design throughout the house.[224]

The prows in the living room, dining room, and playroom also should be seen as having been inspired by environmental considerations. By extending the prow out from the exterior walls so that the four art-glass casement windows and side panels angle in four directions, Wright created a means to "capture" natural daylight from dawn to dusk that was infinitely more effective than the conventional flat-surfaced glazed opening, or even a window bay.

With the sophistication of Wright's approach to his whole design of the Robie House, he developed the science of building on the level urban lot into an art form. In so doing, he fulfilled every nuance of the Japanese Zen philosophy of residential design as described by Heinrich Engel: "the functional organization interlocks environment with house, [but] it is the scale, or rather the extent, of the garden space that brings about the psychological intimacy of interior and exterior space. . . . The resulting space is not only three dimensionally controlled, i.e., architectural, but its extent is of the same value as the spaces of the interior house organism. . . . The residential garden becomes but another additive space in the succession of spatial cells that constitute the constructed house and is thus incorporated into the dwelling organism."[225] At the same time, however, there is little about the Robie House that would appear to directly relate to the Japanese, as Wright by this point had assimilated and completely transformed the essence of the Oriental design philosophy within his personal palette of environmental design. As the Robie House is seen as the terminal masterpiece of Wright's prairie house architecture, therefore, it also should be recognized as his terminal masterpiece of environmental design for his executed Prairie Houses.

The Robie House was used as a single-family residence until 1926, at which time the building and its furnishings were sold to the Chicago Theological Seminary for use as a dormitory. In 1948, when the author was taken to the site by landscape architect Hideo Sasaki—then his instructor at the University of Illinois—the property was in a serious state of disrepair; the art-glass windows were boarded up with graffiti-painted plywood; and the house was projected for demolition to accommodate a new structure. In 1957, the architectural firm of Webb and Knapp purchased the property, undertook emergency restorations, and used it as their headquarters while developing and supervising the urban renewal of the Hyde Park neighborhood. Webb and Knapp donated the house to the University of Chicago in 1963, the same year it was designated a National Historic Landmark. In 1992, the University approached the Frank Lloyd Wright Home and Studio Foundation and suggested the two groups work together to restore the structure for use as a house museum. The Foundation agreed; a restoration master plan was developed; the three-car garage was converted into a bookstore; and an expanded public tour schedule was set up to continue while refurbishing was underway. The estimated $3 to $4 million restoration, complete with an archival repository available to the public, is projected for completion by the year 2007.[226]

Coincident with the inspired environmental design efforts put forth for Coonley, Westcott, Robie, and others, Wright seemingly ignored or compromised environmental design considerations for some of the less consequential domestic architecture emanating from The Studio during 1908–1909. The most extreme support for this inference are the four variations of a plan turned out by The Studio for Reverend William Norman Guthrie, Frank Baker, Walter V. Davidson, and staff member Isabel Roberts. The only difference in the plans for Guthrie and Baker was the name of the client, and the plans prepared for Roberts and Davidson exhibit only slight variations. The standard for siting each house appears to have been to face the two-story glazed facade toward the street—a treatment that happened to orient each house toward a different major point on the compass (Figure 3-77 a-d). Within this process, the wide divergence in latitudinal locations was ignored, as were the climatic factors inherent to each site. Thus, it appears that it was with these four residences that Wright first countermanded his own rhetoric with respect to every structure being designed from the ground up "integral to site, to purpose, to environment, and to the life of the inhabitants."[227] Inasmuch as the Guthrie plan was the only one designed to meet this standard, it is the author's belief that Guthrie was the original client. This reasoning is supported through analysis of the cause and effect in the siting and orientation of each structure.

Reverend William Norman Guthrie—Sewanee, Tennessee (1908)

The site on which the Guthrie House was to be built was located 40 miles northwest of Chattanooga at a lat-

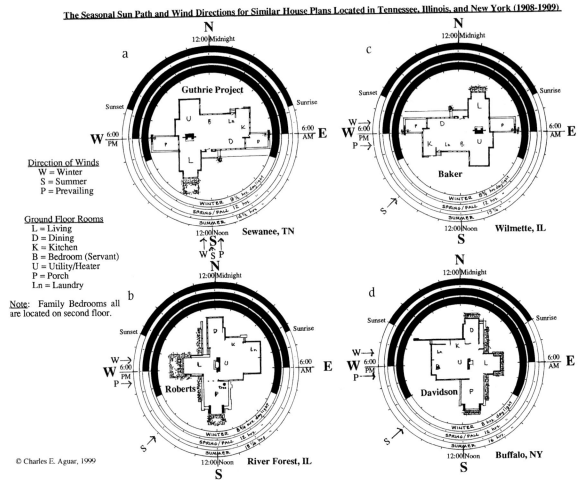

Figure 3-77 a–d Effect of seasonal sun path and wind directions on four houses with different orientations and latitudes. (*By Charles E. Aguar, based on personal analysis and plans of record. © 2002 by The Frank Lloyd Wright Foundation, Scottsdale, Arizona. As delineated, © 2002 by Berdeana Aguar.*)

itude of 35° 12′ N. Wright proposed to site the structure so that the two-story glazed facade of the living room faced due south, toward the street. Early sketches of what the author believes is the Guthrie layout demonstrate how Wright could visualize the entire plan, two floor levels, and roof structure as he quickly transferred concept to paper—in this case to a small sheet of stationary. A thumbnail sketch of the front elevation clearly illustrates the consideration he gave to the location of existing trees on the site—for their protective

canopy, as well as vertical contrast (Figure 3-78). Had this house been built as sited and oriented according to these plans, the living and dining rooms would have had complete access to the prevailing southerly breezes during summer, and the primary living areas would have been light and airy year-round. Moreover, the roof overhangs together with the canopy of the deciduous trees would have excluded excessive light and heat during the summer and maximized solar penetration during the winter.

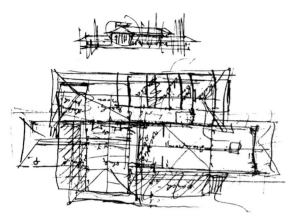

Figure 3-78 Wright's earliest sketch for the Reverend William Norman Guthrie House (1908) in Sewanee, Tennessee, arranges both levels with roof lines overlaid for solar benefit and protection. Thumbnail sketch of front elevation shows consideration of existing trees. (© *2002 by The Frank Lloyd Wright Foundation, Scottsdale, Arizona.*)

Frank Baker—Wilmette, Illinois (1909)

The site for the Baker House was located 4 miles north of Chicago and some 500 miles north of the Guthrie site. This location computes to a latitude of 42° 05′ N, where the mean minimum January temperature is 19° Fahrenheit (more than 14 degrees colder than in Tennessee) and the snow-sleet total is 10 times that for the Guthrie location (38.6 inches). And yet, when the Baker House was rotated 180 degrees to face the public street, the two-story glazed facade of the living room was faced due north so it was completely exposed to the penetrating "nor'easters" that blow in off nearby Lake Michigan. At the same time, there was no benefit from the prevailing southwesterly summer breezes.[228] There also was minimal access to solar gain in any of the primary living spaces, except through the west-facing window wall of the kitchen, where sun penetration is so excessive that awnings had to be installed. Conversely, the functionality of the roof overhangs—designed for a southerly orientation—was completely discounted.

Walter V. Davidson—Buffalo, New York (1908)

The Davidson House was rotated 90 degrees from the Guthrie orientation so the two-story glazed facade faces due east. Therefore, the living room receives no solar benefit when needed during the winter months, except through the offset corner portion of the south wall at sunrise, but is fully exposed during the summer months—from sunrise to late morning. There also is no benefit from summer breezes, which originate from the southwest.

Isabel Roberts—River Forest, Illinois (1908)

The Isabel Roberts House is a mirror image of the Davidson plan, so the two-story glazed facade of the living room faces due west and is completely exposed to prevailing winter winds. The westerly orientation also poses a problem during the longer days of summer. At the same time, the dining room and kitchen receive reflected light only, and the prevailing southwesterly summer breezes do not directly benefit this area of the house, so the summer comfort level in the living room would have been severely compromised in the days before air conditioning. Although Wright went to great effort to preserve existing shade trees so their canopy might eventually help ameliorate the environmental consequence of the situation—even going so far as to construct the south-facing living room porch and roof around a specimen English Elm (*Ulmus procera*)—historical photographs support that window shades were installed across the exposed expanse of living room windows at an early date.[229]

Of the three built structures, the Roberts House is the only one where the two-level flower boxes across the front facade were built to unify with the low-pitched roof and create the horizontal layering imagery of Wright's intent. But the streetside appearance of the 1990s also represents many alterations. In the mid-1920s, Harry Robinson was engaged to cover the cracked plaster and wood trim with a light tan brick veneer. Then, in 1955—46 years after construction—Wright was called upon by then-owner Warren Scott to undertake a major remodeling. The changes Wright at this time made to the original design illustrate that he was not averse to change, if it would benefit the client and a new age. In addition to architectural updating, he installed air conditioning and copper roofing, strengthened the sagging roof cantilevers with steel, and expanded the interior living space by enclosing the living-room porch with glazing. Within this process, he gave careful consideration to protecting the elm tree by replacing and expanding the rubber gasket of the roof opening, enlarging the floor opening to accom-

Figure 3-79 A view of the Isabel Roberts House (1908) in River Forest, Illinois, shows a specimen English Elm tree still growing through the roof of the porch almost a century after construction. (*Photograph by Charles E. Aguar. © 2002 by Berneana Aguar.*)

modate the trunk, and installing a watering pipe for the covered portion of the root system (Figure 3-79). That this elm survives in the late 1990s gives unmistakable testimony to Wright's commitment to the aesthetic and environmental benefit of even one shade tree.

A possible explanation for Wright's abrupt reversal in his attention to design specificities relating to client and site might be that he was of a mind-set for finding a way to make a change in his life. According to Oak Park staffer John S. Van Bergen, Wright at this point in time was "too distracted" to perform much of the work of The Studio—assumedly because of his involvement with Mamah Borthwick Cheney, the wife of former client Edwin H. Cheney (1903).[230] Van Bergen also maintained that most design work was handled by Mahony and Drummond, citing in particular Mahony's "wonderful perspectives" for a proposed planned community in the Bitterroot Valley of Montana. While Van Bergan most probably was correct in crediting Mahony and Drummond for design details and rendering, there is little evidence to support that Wright was anything other than personally very much caught up in the conceptual and planning processes for the Bitterroot Valley projects. The development of city planning procedures was still evolving at this point, and Wright presumably would have been highly

motivated to want to continue on in his effort to make his mark in this promising new profession. To understand why Wright himself would have been spearheading the design of the Bitterroot Valley projects, however, it is necessary to establish the historical context for all that had occurred before Wright was brought into the picture.

According to historian Donald Leslie Johnson, the remote Bitterroot Valley of Montana was not opened to settlement until the 1850s. And agricultural development did not become a significant factor prior to the 1880s, when a spur of the Northern Pacific Railroad was extended into the area.[231] By 1900, apples had become a primary crop of the region; the "Big Red Macintosh" apples were known throughout the world. Because newly planted orchards require seven years for trees to mature and bear fruit sufficient for production, however, orcharders devised a real estate development scheme promoting apple production as a money-making venture for investors. Chicago financier W. I. Moody hired fellow Chicagoan Frederick D. Nichols to superintend the works of the Bitter Root Valley Irrigation Company, or BRVICo. This is the same Frederick D. Nichols for whom Wright designed a prairie house in 1906—the same year BRVICo began construction on a dam to raise the level of Lake Como and excavation of the Big Ditch for irrigation to the region. By November 1908, when Wright was commissioned to design the project, at least 18 midwestern academics had invested in the project, as well as Frank I. Bennett, a Chicago alderman. Moody and Nichols must have believed that an announcement to the effect that the design aspects of their project had been placed in the hands of a renowned architect would provide assurance to the investment world that University Heights was legitimate and worthy of consideration.[232]

Como Orchard–University Heights Community—Bitterroot Valley, Montana (1909)

Wright is reported by newspaper account to have visited the Como Orchard–University Heights site with BRVICo officials in February 1909. While it must have been difficult to conduct a site investigation in the foothills of the Sapphire Mountains at that time of year, Wright would have developed some sense of the rugged terrain–including the visual backdrop of the crest of the Bitterroot Mountains that form the Great Continental Divide. He also would have learned that the billed attraction of Lake Como was in fact located two miles to the southwest, hidden behind a mountain ridge rising 1800 feet above the lake level.

Wright chose to site the central University Heights Clubhouse on a relatively level natural bench of the downward slope, with the steep mountains rising behind

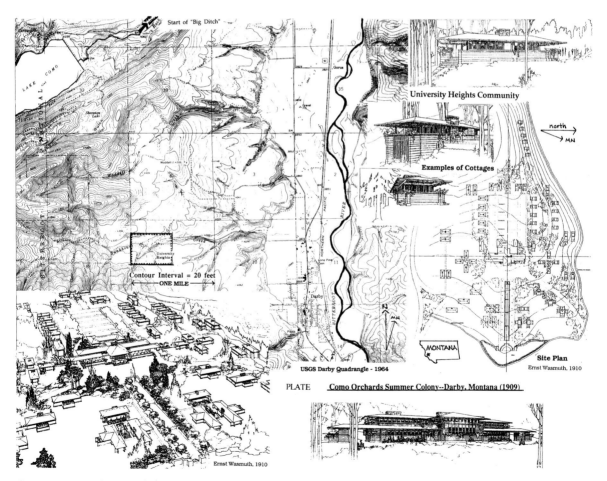

Figure 3-80 Wright's site plan and perspective for the Como Orchards summer colony community in Darby, Montana. (*By Charles E. Aguar, based on personal analysis and out-of-copyright plans of record from Wasmuth Portfolio, 1910.*)

and the most pronounced grade leading down to Bunkhouse Creek (Figure 3-80). The Clubhouse entry was situated on a right-angle axis with a geyserlike fountain at the source of an elongated water feature that emptied into a pond at its base. Lined by trees and sidewalks on either side, the water feature was depicted as a formal focal-point promenade with groupings of steps spaced along its length to distribute the approximate 15-foot differential in elevation. This siting and arrangement oriented the extensive windows across the front of the building to provide a commanding outlook across the proposed water feature and the Bitterroot River Valley. The back of the building faced toward the graded recreation area with tennis courts, which utilized approximately 75 percent of the bench. This would be a logical siting had this property had a more moderate slope. Here, however, Wright's placement of the sizable service building with vehicle parking some 10 feet up the slope would seriously compromise views of the mountain backdrop from the use areas of the clubhouse.

Sixty-one cabins also were proposed, with the larger cabins placed in clusters and a majority of the smaller cabins sited against the grain of the natural contours in soldierlike rows. In the perspective, the roofs of all cabins appear to be level in elevation. The near-impossibility of maintaining roof lines at the same elevation becomes evident when one considers there is a differential of 45 feet between the lowest-to-highest contour lines in the area where the structures were proposed. This meant the terrain could vary as much as 10 feet from one end of a 30-foot cabin to the other. The several "Examples of Cottages" clearly illustrate the excessive underpinning and "filler" construction that would have been required to create this illusion of levelness.

Whether by intention or coincidence, Wright's plans bear enough resemblance to Burnham's 1905 City Beautiful planned layout for Baguio, Luzon, Philippine Islands, to suggest an inspirational relationship—particularly with respect to the rusticity of the architecture, the planned informal use of the development, and the osten-

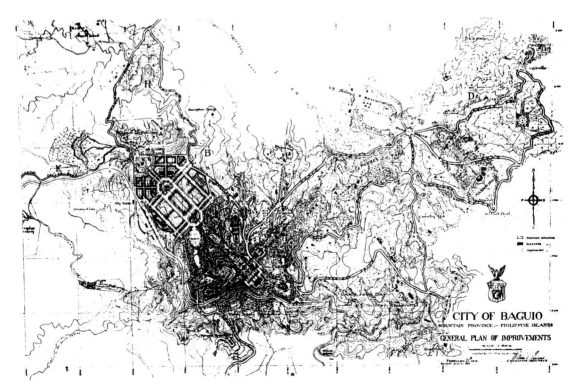

Figure 3-81   Daniel H. Burnham's plan for the City of Baguio in the Philippines may have inspired Wright's layouts for his Bitter Root, Montana projects. (*Courtesy of Robinson Fisher.*)

tatious formal water feature[233] (Figure 3-81). It is presumable there would have been newspaper publicity and likely some form of public display of Burnham's work in this area, since even a noted Chicagoan did not normally prepare plans for new towns in remote locations. Wright may even have had some personal discussions with Burnham, whom he called "Uncle Dan," between 1905 and 1909.[234] After all, this summer colony provided Wright with his first opportunity to experiment with community planning. However, it was his design for the Bitter Root Town Project, incorporating the full range of components inherent to a city, where it appears Burnham's Baguio report had considerable relevance.

Bitter Root Town Project—Bitterroot Valley, Montana (1909)

It is believed that, upon returning to Chicago from the reconnoiter of the summer colony site, BRVICo officials decided to expand Wright's commission to include a plan for the proposed new town of Bitter Root, with a vision that it would become the fourth-largest town in the state. The site was approximately 35 miles northeast of the colony site and on the opposite side of the Bitterroot River.[235] It is not known if the intended town site was identified to Wright during his brief visit to Montana or whether the possibility of this phase of development was ever discussed with him at that time, as BRVICo did not begin to promote a new town until much later in 1909.[236]

Primary considerations for selection of the site were proximity to Three Mile Creek and the existence of a north-south state road known as Eastside Highway, which bisected the site. Wright treated this highway as his secondary axis and established the town center at the intersection of his east-west axis, which he treated as a heavily planted boulevard with low walls, sculpture, and environmental terminal point features that appear to symbolize large fountains (Figure 3-82). He situated the railroad station at this town center and at a low elevation. He then arranged landscaped blocks to the east and west so that outward views would be across gardens. He also invested much thought into the separation of surface vehicles and pedestrians for that section of the road that passed through the commercial district—such as Olmsted and Vaux designed for New York's Central Park—even introducing an electrified rail line as an open "subway" under the road. It might seem irrational that Wright detailed such an elaborate transportation scheme for this remote area, until the thinking of the times is taken into consideration. Johnson maintains: "During the early months of 1909 there were a variety of proposals for rail lines down

the eastern side of the valley. There was talk of connecting eastern Idaho with the Bitterroot Valley, of additional spurs to serve rural industry, and of a Northern Pacific loop on the east side of the valley. Moreover, it was suggested that an electric rail line be extended from Missoula south, perhaps to Hamilton and even over the Sapphire Mountains to Anaconda. It was this electrified line that Wright proposed should bisect the town."[237]

The 13 compact blocks for the proposed commercial district were laid out with geometric formality into four grid segments, and all community service buildings were set within the continuity of formal axes along sight lines facing other monumental structures. The formality of this geometric layout has been criticized by some historians as being totally inappropriate for the irregular terrain of the region. As Wright himself never provided any explanation for the geometricity of his design, it seems appropriate to use a portion of Burnham's supporting text for "Plan of Baguio, Luzon, Phillipine Island." The logic in Burnham's defensive argument is in context with the City Beautiful idiom of the time and equally applicable to Wright's plan:

> Accepting the principle that a regular geometric street system is the most convenient for the closely built sections of the city, the aim of the plan has been to lay down a geometrical scheme which will adapt itself as closely as possible to the ungeometrical contours. . . . This street system may seem at first sight to be somewhat arbitrary, failing as it sometimes does to conform strictly to the lay of the ground. Such partial failure is, however, inevitable in any orderly arrangement. While maintaining a street system convenient for traffic, the intention is to carry through the lines of the streets to commanding points on the hillsides and thus permit the location of monumental buildings where they command a view down neighboring streets. . . . To pursue the opposite course and destroy vistas by clinging closely to the contours, thus avoiding difficulties in grading and filling, would throw away the unique monumental possibilities of the proposed city. The hill towns of Italy and France, not to mention those of Japan, abound in instances of the charm and convenience of a plan in which the lines of the level streets are carried steeply up the hillsides to terminate the vista at points of especial interest.[238]

Wright's methodology of creating a boulevard as the principal axis also allies with Burnham's explana-

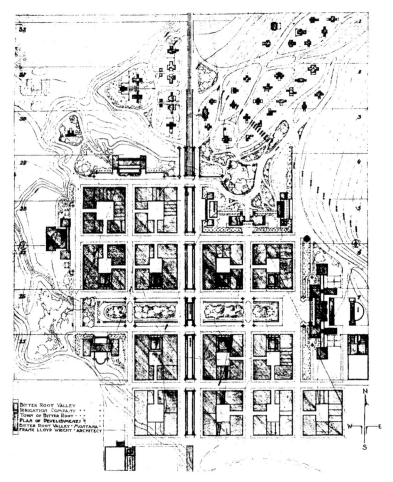

Figure 3-82   Wright's planned layout for the Bitter Root New Town Project in Montana. (© 2002 by The Frank Lloyd Wright Foundation, Scottsdale, Arizona.)

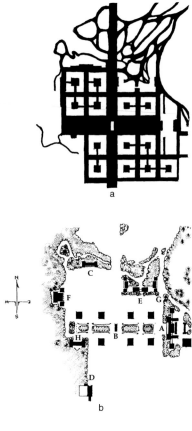

Figure 3-83 a–b   Land allocated for Bitter Root Town Project streets and transportation (3-83 a), and distribution of public buildings and open space (3-83 b). (*By Charles E. Aguar, based on personal analysis and out-of-copyright plans of record from Wasmuth Portfolio, 1910. As delineated, © 2002 by Berdeana Aguar.*)

tion of his treatment for Baguio: "The axis has been treated as an open esplanade with a central *tapis vert* of greensward. . . . The possible railway approach to the town . . . [has been] treated as a formal gateway to the city, and facing the . . . axis toward the business center, such a terminal would make an imposing and fitting entrance to the city. . . . The Government buildings, while reasonably accessible from the business quarter, should be so located and so treated in their approaches and surroundings as to make clear their preeminence over all other buildings of the city."[239]

There are similarities between the areas surrounding the commercial districts of both planned communities, as well. All public or semipublic buildings and recreation areas at the edges of the Bitter Root commercial district were situated along curvilinear streets that followed the dictates of meandering creeks, arroyos, and steeply contoured topography—in the manner of Olmsted's Riverside, and in the manner prescribed for Baguio by Burnham. He wrote: "In order to provide ample area for recreation . . . the valley [is] shown provided with side stretches of greensward forming a continuous parkway. A large area suitable for play fields is also located at the west of the town where the enclosing hills form a natural hollow."[240] This arrangement of public and semipublic land uses was by far the best feature of Wright's plan, as the larger natural environment was efficiently interwoven with the city center—going from the wild landscape to the formality of apple orchards and neatly arranged gardens, to rows of trees and shrubs punctuated with flower beds, public sculpture, and other features of the townscape.

The streets for the suburban large-house development to the northeast of the Bitter Root commercial district were aligned on the diagonal some 45 degrees from the highway-rail axis, just as Burnham deviated from the diagonal grid with the Baguio residential streets. However, while Burnham aligned the streets diagonal to the four points of the compass to allow "each of the four sides of the houses to profit by direct sunlight at some time during each day,"[241] Wright inexplicably faced the individual houses in a precise north-south or east-west orientation, and few were sited to follow the natural terrain. Some slopes interpolate into gradients greater than 25 percent, and many houses were established against the grain, so there could have been an elevational differential of as much as 15 feet from one end of a structure to the other. Additionally, the smallness of the blocks resulted in a street system so excessive that certain lots had streets on two, sometimes three, sides with only 20 to 30 feet between structures, creating an immoderate density for a large house in 1909 Montana.

The truth is that Wright was far from ready to proceed with the Bitterroot assignment. He had no technical background for developing a sensitive, mountainous site where thin soils, rock outcroppings, and extreme weather fluctuations required special consideration. Neither his limited engineering background nor his apprenticeship training had prepared him for this eventuality, and he had no reasonable geological background of local conditions. Even though he had developed plans for more than 160 commissions by this time, all but 3 were designed for level sites—the exceptions being the houses for Hardy, Glasner, and Westcott. So he was very much experimenting with how best to compensate for marked differentiations in site terrain.

In the end, the smaller-than-normal subdivision blocks, the multimodal highway-subway, and the wide parkway-boulevard dictated that more than 60 percent of the land be dedicated to circulation, street rights-of-way, and other means of transportation (Figures 3-83 a-b). It probably was because of the inordinate costs that

would have been involved for infrastructure that Wright's grandiose plan was spurned by BRVICo officials. They instead had a local surveyor prepare a scaled-down, nondescript plat that included unbuildable lots over the arroyo; it was this version that was recorded as the official town plan. Despite BRVICo's outright rejection of the Bitter Root Town Plan, which must have been construed as a personal affront, an apparently undaunted Wright invested time and money far beyond the architectural mandate in order to detail the one Bitter Root design that has never been assigned an identifying file number—the notable "Plan for Village of Bitter Root."

Village of Bitter Root Development— Bitterroot, Montana (1909)

The Plan for the Village of Bitter Root evidently was done entirely on speculation. This was a calculated decision that would not have been made lightly, nor by anyone other than Wright. It would seem he felt he had to prove to himself, at least, that he was fully capable of originating an urban-scale plan independent of other influences. Whatever the reason, the "village" concept presents a feeling of informality and pedestrian scale much more appropriate for Bitterroot Valley than the pretentiousness put forth by the Town Plan—a circumstance that attests to Wright's maturation as an environmental designer *when* and *if* his personal introspection was brought to bear upon the design process.

Wright's suggested plan for development of the Village represented flowing space in the free-form style of Jensen, but with edges and plantings in the manner of Griffin (Figure 3-84). A great deal of attention was given to the design details of the streetscape furnishings, including a watering trough near the market, small bridges, planting boxes, stairways showing level changes, and naturalistic water features. The Eastside Highway bridge was redesigned with pedestrian walks on each side of a carriageway separated by open space looking onto a pond and a greenway along the valleylike arroyo. Each important building became a node of interest with an especial environmental setting—such as the inn set off by a pond and park and the village library immediately across the highway situated within an area labeled as Harriet Park. Architectural design elements were presented with remarkable clarity—so expressly particularized that the first floor plan is detailed for most buildings. If there is a town center, it is the Open Air Market, a rectangular business block where the windows of all buildings overlook a landscaped central court in the manner of a shopping center with an enclosed mall.

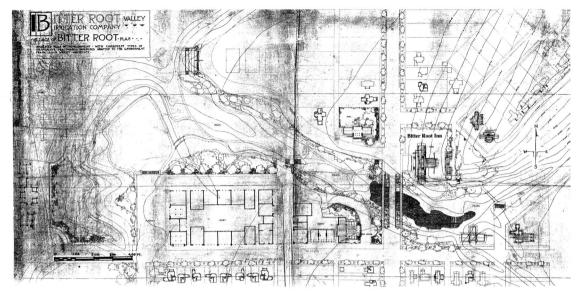

Figure 3-84   In contrast to Wright's grandiose and pretentious Bitter Root Town Plan, his design for the Village of Bitter Root presents a mature, informal, pedestrian scale that is more appropriate to the region. (© *2002 by The Frank Lloyd Wright Foundation, Scottsdale, Arizona.*)

The Village Plan also shows houses in relation to subdivision lot lines and structures sited more in relation to contours. A full block of houses opposite the shopping center uses one plan arranged in a way to provide variety in setback, side yard, and main entryway. One double lot on a corner is shown with a suggested garden layout. It is believed this was Wright's way of encouraging a streetscape more interesting than the normal uniform front yard setback for his house plans, which could be purchased from BRVICo but would not have supervision in siting or construction by Wright's office.

Only one building of Wright's design was ever constructed within the area: the two-story, frame board-and-batten Bitter Root Inn. Although the gardenlike setting for the Inn never was developed as proposed, photographs retained in the archives of the Montana Historical Society appear amazingly close to the plan and perspective in the Taliesin archives.

Oak Park Studio Closes

In October 1909, prior to departing for Europe, Wright closed The Studio as his base of operations. The professed purpose for Wright's first trip to Europe was to solidify contractual negotiations with Ernst Wasmuth for

a portfolio devoted to his works and to attend to finalizing drawings for publication. Although all publication drawings would in fact eventually be finalized, as Wright set sail for Europe accompanied by Mamah Borthwick Cheney—not to return until October 1910—the European experience could be looked upon as a year-long exile from reality. According to Van Bergen, Wright had been "making secret plans for flight" for a period of time; he alleged that Wright "simply closed up when the outstanding jobs were finished [after he] collected in full on these jobs before they were done."[242]

Wright in the end turned over all his commissions to Herman von Holst, who had maintained an office at Steinway Hall for several years. He, in turn, made arrangements with Mahony to fulfill all obligations of these final commissions credited to The Studio. Most of the former Oak Park Studio staff in their independent careers began to design in the traditional manner, after a short period of copying or adapting Wright's personal style. In his book *My Father Who Is On Earth*, John Lloyd Wright recognized The Studio staff as a group who made "positive contributions to the pioneering of the modern American architecture for which my father gets the full glory, headaches and recognition today."[243]

The Pivotal Years: 1909–1915

Wright did not speak or write extensively about his European experience, but his most telling observations relate to the organic integrity of the architecture built during the evolutionary process of adapting to the land and terrain. Of England: "the old English architecture . . . not only belonged there, it belonged to the people who lived in it."[244] Of Italy: "No really Italian building seems ill at ease in Italy. All are happily content with what ornament and color they carry, as naturally as the rocks and trees and garden slopes which are one with them. . . . It lies close to the earth . . . it is an organic thing."[245] But he seems to have most personally related to the clarity, simplicity, and unique secular Gothic style of the rusticated masonry seen throughout the central and northern area of Tuscany. "Go to Umbria, go to Assisi," he wrote, "that's the part of Italy, if you ever get a chance to go, that I advise you to see."[246]

Much of Wright's attraction to the Tuscany region of Italy had to do with his affinity for the vista of wide green valleys and rough ranges, the rivers, tributaries, and lakes—so similar to the landscape of Wisconsin—referred to in Italian travel literature as a "painting-landscape." He first set up operations in the Renaissance town of Florence, but in late spring moved his entire operation to the picturesque medieval town of Fiesole—just up the hillside, overlooking the Arno River valley. Wright's selection of this locale placed his improvised studio near the Villa Medici, one of several country estates built by members of the Medici family as rural retreats for pleasure and show—as was the custom of those of means during the fifteenth to seventeenth centuries. "It should be noted," writes landscape architect Norman T. Newton, "that in Italy the term *villa* refers to the place as a whole—not to either house or grounds alone, but to the total complex seen as a unit."[247] Wright would have found this concept entirely compatible with the similar Japanese philosophy. This was the philosophy upon which he based the design of his own villa: Taliesin.

Wright assuredly also would have taken excursions to explore other landscapes, both natural and cultural, and he would have observed the individualistic medieval townscapes. In so doing, he would have experienced their pedestrian scale and the humane quality of the spaces between the buildings—the plazas, town squares, small parks, sidewalk cafes, and other intimate spaces

structured for public use within the protective town walls of the Middle Ages. When Wright discoursed upon his impressions of any foreign landscape, however, it was not to Renaissance towns and gardens that he referred—nor to the gardens of comparable environs in China and Japan, for that matter—but to the tillage of the land. This observation was perhaps an anachronism stemming from when the boy Wright added "tired to tired" as he labored in the fields of his uncles' farms. Everywhere, the adult Wright—the environmental designer—saw purpose, beauty, and art in the cultivation of the land. In Japan: "The cultivated fields rising tier on tier to still higher terraced vegetable fields, green-dotted."[248] In England: "these beautifully managed landscapes—there are no fences, hedges everywhere, beautifully tilled fields."[249] And in Italy: "When you see Italy, when you see the fields . . . you see how cultivation, tillage, is architecture. How it makes a pattern, and how carefully, how imaginatively they treat everything they do. Then you look at the buildings and they belong to the tillage, and the tillage and the buildings are of course part of the ground. It is all one beautiful harmony with a synthesis, I think, that exists nowhere in the world except in China and Japan."[250]

Wright returned to the United States in October 1910, professedly to spend the holiday season with his family while completing the introductory text for the Wasmuth Portfolio—but antithetically, it seems, to initiate the process of intellectually, emotionally, and physically separating himself from his former life. This reasoning is based upon the celerity and sequencing of the course of events that took place as the ensuing year progressed. In January 1911, Wright made another brief voyage to Europe for a face-to-face meeting with Wasmuth. He returned to Oak Park in March. On April 22, he recorded detailed construction drawings labeled "Cottage for Anna Lloyd Wright" for two structures arranged in an "L" to be built on a specific tract of land in the Lloyd Jones Clan homestead valley of Wisconsin. However, the much-enlarged versions of the same plans were recorded in June under the name of "Taliesin."

Construction of Taliesin reportedly was under way by May. In August, Edward Cheney divorced Mamah and was awarded custody of their children. Mamah, on the other hand, moved to Taliesin even though construction was incomplete. At the same time, the original Studio space was being converted into housing for Kitty Wright and the four children still living at home, and the original family residence was being converted into a sizable rental unit that would provide them with a source of income upon Wright's departure. It is not known when work was finalized at either location, but newspapers report that by December Wright had placed his former home in Oak Park up for rent and moved to Taliesin.[251]

It is this chain of events that set in motion a metamorphic process of design for three undertakings that would cause 1911–1912 to come to be the most pivotal years of Wright's prolific 70-year career: the Home and Studio Remodeling in Oak Park, Illinois; the Sherman M. Booth Project in Glencoe, Illinois; and the development and construction of Taliesin—Wright's new home and studio near Spring Green, Wisconsin.

ENVIRONMENTAL DESIGNS, 1911–1916

Home and Studio Remodeling—Oak Park, Illinois (1911)

Remodeling the Oak Park Home and Studio to accommodate the altered needs of his family was not a responsibility Wright took lightly. He took great pains to

existentially separate the semidetached structures by sealing off all interconnecting doors and installing a double wythe brick firewall around the north and east sides of the residence. He also thought through details of minutest concern as he continued to explore new ways to expand his family's living space into the out-of-doors and control outdoor space to both enhance and augment their indoor living space (Figure 4-1).

All decisions Wright made during the conversion of his home into rental income property appear to have been motivated by his desire to forestall criticism from future occupants by at least trying to rectify some of the problems that he and his family had experienced during their years of occupancy with respect to the disadvantageous westerly orientation and the subsequent construction of the neighboring house to the south. Thus, all elements of his remodeling worked together to protect or direct attention away from the west-facing front veranda as a point of outdoor-indoor transition, to shelter the outdoor living spaces, or to screen these spaces from public view. Within this process, Wright totally redefined the purpose and function of the wraparound veranda and front lawn as usable spaces for outdoor living.

To redress the loss of privacy enjoyed prior to the neighboring house being built so close to his driveway,

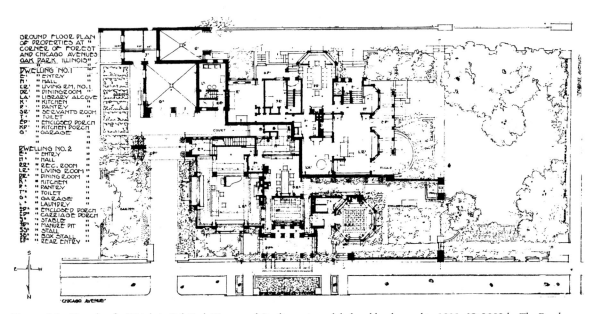

Figure 4-1   Site plan for Wright's Oak Park Home and Studio, as remodeled and landscaped in 1911. (© *2002 by The Frank Lloyd Wright Foundation, Scottsdale, Arizona.*)

Wright removed the exposed projection from the south-west corner of the veranda. As its removal significantly altered the horizontal proportions of the entire structure, he filled in the void with an offset garden (11 by 30 feet) circumscribed by high brick privacy walls.

To protect the principal point of outdoor-indoor transition from the elements at all times, he installed a new main entry on the south side of the entry hall that could be accessed directly off the driveway. Coincidentally, he moved the original front door to the area between the two window bays on the west wall of the living room—the only position where it would be at least partially protected by the gable overhang. To further shelter this door, as well as shade the west-facing living room windows and a substantial portion of the veranda, Wright designed a roof with a trellis extension cantilevered outward to the depth of the new entry stairway—installed parallel to the veranda so it faced away from both the driveway and the west lawn. He then introduced masses of deciduous plantings and trees along the inward side of the driveway and out onto the lawn across from the southwest terminus of the garden privacy wall. This combination of treatments ameliorated the dominating presence of the garden privacy wall, screened the entry from the family unit, secreted the ground-level terrace from street view, and de-accentuated the former entry by representing it as a private place to move *from*, rather than as a focal point of entry—all without detracting from the entry experience.

In converting The Studio to housing for his family, Wright was equally creative. He installed a new family driveway between Chicago Avenue and a new point of outdoor-indoor transition under a porte-cochere to the east of the structure. An existing mature ginkgo tree accentuated this entrance and shaded much of the driveway and the usable outdoor space to the eastern extremity of the lot—where Wright installed a compost area, a kitchen garden, and a landscaped lawn or play yard. He also added a new family stable and two-car garage; a sizable laundry room filled the space between this garage and the kitchen of the former residence.[252] The new main entry opened directly into a vestibule that was accessible to the family living room (former drafting room), a stairway leading to the second-floor bedroom addition, and a new kitchen tucked into the former passageway between the residence and studio. The multiple-trunk willow tree continued to grow along one wall. This thoughtful remodeling fashioned the former studio space into more than adequate living

quarters and basically equated with the living space in the former family residence, as expanded in 1895.

At the same time, Wright increased outdoor living space by some 40 percent, to in excess of 1250 square feet. He began by sealing off the east and west sides of the former entry veranda facing Chicago Avenue and covering the entire space with a canopy to create a private, totally enclosed, and sheltered terrace or play area with easy access to and from the living area. To de-emphasize this space as a focal entry point, he installed a decorative 2-foot-high, cast-concrete wall between the two mounting blocks at streetside and completely circumscribed the north and west boundaries of the property with brick walls, enclosed by a broad masonry cap of the same square-within-a-square design. At the juncture of the walls on the northwest corner of the site, Wright created a gateway of space and identified this juncture as a threshold of entry from Forest Avenue by installing two brick piers on either side of the entry walkway that paralleled the defining wall. He then introduced masses of deciduous plantings and shade trees along both sides of the entire length of the entry walkway so the palette of sensory experiences was comparable to, but more focused than, that which he arranged for the original family unit some 20 years earlier. Wright also introduced an alternate entry from Chicago Avenue, recessed into the small passageway between the former reception hall and library and offset from the entry gateway so it would not be readily visible from the public right-of-way. And he installed French doors on the west side of the dining room (Figure 4-2). All of these points of outdoor-indoor transition provided alternate means for accessing the new family quarters by way of the sequestered outdoor living space that Wright created to the west of the octagonal library, labeled "Library Garden."

Wright's design for the Library Garden was inspired by the domestic gardens such as he had experienced in Italy. Copy excerpted from a 1925 sales brochure alludes to the Italian connection: "The masonry walled courts between the buildings are treated as enclosed gardens—the one opening from the dining room being fitted as are many Florentine gardens." Moreover, the square-within-a-square design of the privacy-wall balustrade is analogous to an art form found at the Baptistery of San Giovanni and other Florentine architecture of note. This balustrade introduced ambient patterns of light and shadow into the outside living environment similar to those patterns introduced into the inside living environment through Wright's use and placement of art-glass

Figure 4-2 French doors open onto Wright's Home and Studio library garden. (*Photograph by Charles E. Aguar. © 2002 by Berdeana Aguar.*)

between ground level and the base threshold by distributing five steps throughout the garden, and introducing directional changes within the entry walkway and the garden path. And he used the brick and stone from the demolished southwest veranda to form a wall that would bound the west side of the garden open space and define the parameters as a roofless room. This wall was customized to create specific effects. The portion of the wall that wrapped around the southwest corner of the garden conformed in height and design to the high privacy walls and accommodated a windowlike feature at eye level above a reflecting pool. This feature was on axis with the pathway leading from the French doors off the dining room so it would function as a visual focal point to direct the line of sight through the opening and create an ancillary relationship with the greater site environment. The remaining 14-foot expanse of the west wall was installed at ground level, rather than at the raised level of the inner garden, to replicate the 7-foot height and arc of the half-round projection at the northwest corner of the main house (Figure 4-3).

The lowering of the west boundary essentially created an arced interspace of that portion of the wall. This treatment served several functions. It served as a containment element that identified where the garden ended and the west lawn began. It provided space and background for an ornamental hawthorn and other plantings, without compromising usable outdoor living space. It served as a midlevel frame for the "borrowed" view, bringing the expanse of the outer landscape environment into the smaller space of the roofless room, creating the illusion that the garden was larger than it actually was. And it encouraged views outward into the larger environment—while looking through the new library window and over the sequestered garden; while seated at the table placed on a paved surface in the garden for dining *al fresco;* or while strolling along the garden pathway. Moreover, it architecturally allied with the veranda parapet of the former residence and brought the semidetached structures into harmony by visually anchoring the former studio to the ground, thus lessening its appearance of appendance.

The substance of the exterior amenities Wright designed during the Oak Park Home and Studio remodeling represented some of his more noteworthy expressions of environmental design and were superior, overall, to anything he had fashioned originally. Together, they visually unified and tangibly extended Wright's architecture onto the site and appropriated the entire open

windows in his Prairie Houses and the fretted wood panels he would subsequently use in his Usonian houses. Wright then proceeded to soften the Italian formality by forming the ground level of the Library Garden as an earthen terrace, de-accentuating the change in elevation

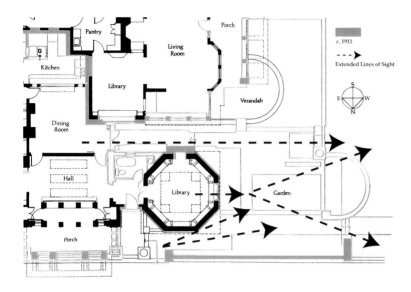

Figure 4-3 The west walls of the Oak Park Home and Studio Library Garden were customized to work together and extend lines of sight that would create an ancillary relationship with the greater site environment. (*By Charles E. Aguar, based on personal analysis and ground plan. © 2002 by The Frank Lloyd Wright Preservation Trust, Oak Park, Illinois. As delineated, © 2002 by Berdeana Aguar.*)

space of the west lawn as a garden environment so it served as the unifying medium between the separate, but equally important, entry gardens of both units.

The Frank Lloyd Wright Home and Studio was identified as a National Historic Landmark in late 1975 under the auspices of The Frank Lloyd Wright Home and Studio Foundation, a nonprofit corporation established in Oak Park the previous year; the property has been maintained as a museum since that time.[253] Within this process, it was determined to restore the property as it was in 1909 when Wright last occupied the premises, rather than as he redesigned the spaces in 1911. Based upon this reasoning, the decision was made to raze the Library Garden. At the same time, however, neither the width of the entry sidewalk for the house nor the containment for the foundation planting beds at the base of the parapet were restored to their original conformation. More significantly, the landscape was preserved as it had evolved between 1911 and 1925—*not* as it was maintained prior to the redesign. Thus, the re-created site environment hides the purity of Wright's innovative front porch alternative and directs attention away from—rather than toward—the visual perspective of Wright's original intent: that is, the base plane of an unadorned front lawn shaded by deciduous trees, the horizontal planes of the wraparound veranda, and the open receptivity of a wide entry threshold.

Sherman M. Booth, Jr., Project—Glencoe, Illinois (1911–1912)

Sherman M. Booth, Jr., commissioned Wright to design a mansion-scaled residence to be built upon a 15-acre site endowed with a sylvan environment amidst rugged ravines carved out during the glacial melting of the Ice Age (Figure 4-4). The site was basically triangular in shape. The eastern boundary was only four-tenths of a mile inland from Lake Michigan and the north boundary followed along a primary stream that flowed directly into this water body through one of the more predominant ravines in the area. The west boundary followed the diagonal line of the Chicago North Shore and Milwaukee interurban rail line and intersected with the east boundary at the vortex of the triangle.

The level area on which the original farmhouse had been built was selected as the optimum building site, as identified on the conjectured inventory and analysis of site conditions (Figure 4-5).[254] This site was adjacent to the north bluff escarpment and was girded by three ravines. Much about the originality and dramatic character of Wright's architecture had to do with his careful juxtapositioning of the house in relation to these topographic features, as well as his conscientious consideration of viewpoints to access the scenic beauty their presence engendered.

Booth saw this project as much more than an isolated domestic dwelling, however. It appears he was

Figure 4-4   Presentation perspective of Sherman Booth Project, Glencoe, Illinois, 1911 (unbuilt). (© *2002 by The Frank Lloyd Wright Foundation, Scottsdale, Arizona.*)

thinking of developing this property as a demonstration for a new type of nature preserve, where his home would involve only a few acres of the site and the major portion would function as a public or semipublic park. This assumption is supported by the catalog of additional structures within Wright's job listings—a Summer Cottage, Stable, Park Features, Railway Station #1, Station #2—and by the extensive layout put forth on the "Planting Plan, Grounds of Mr. Sherman M. Booth." Perhaps Booth saw the park as something that might become a catalyst for encouraging neighborhood development in the manner of the picturesque model community of Highland Park, a geologically similar suburb to the immediate north. Both communities had incorporated the same year, in 1869. Highland Park had been redesigned and expanded in 1872 by landscape architect H. W. S. Cleveland with partner W. M. R. French, providing the city fathers with a very responsive manner of planned development.[255] It would not be until 1910–1912 that the Glencoe government would commission

landscape architect Jens Jensen to similarly develop Glencoe Streets and Parks.

As a founding member of the Glencoe Park District and chairman of the Park Board, Booth would have been particularly sensitive to the quality of development demonstrated in Highland Park. He would have known that Jensen had surveyed potential parklands and natural areas for preservation on a regional scale between 1899 and 1904 and had become a leading spokesperson for park reform.[256] He also would have known that Jensen wrote the "Report of the Landscape Architect" that constituted more than one-fourth of the 149-page bound book and the series of fold-out maps in the *Report of the Special Park Commission* compiled by Dwight Perkins in 1904 (see Appendix E). Within this significant text, Jensen had recommended the creation of forest parks "to preserve for present and future generations lands of natural scenic beauty situated within easy reach of multitudes that have access to no other grounds for recreation or summer outings."[257] It would have been within this

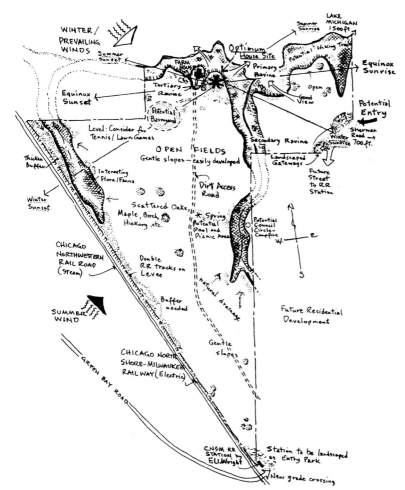

Figure 4-5 Conjectured inventory and analysis of site conditions for Sherman M. Booth Project. (*By Charles E. Aguar.* © 2002 by *Berdeana Aguar*)

context that members of the Glencoe Board of Commissioners originally approached Jensen. Considering this background, it seems credible to presume that Booth initially consulted with Jensen and depended upon his direction for the developmental planning and siting *prior* to bringing Wright into the picture.

There are several arguments to justify this reasoning. First, it seems remarkably coincidental that Booth's tract abuts a particular half-mile section of property that was among those identified as "Proposed Park/Preserve Land" within Jenson's 1904 Report[258] (Figure 4-6). Then, there is the fact that Wright returned to Oak Park on October 8, 1910, after a year abroad, was in New York between November 15 and 20, set sail for Europe on January 16,

and returned to Oak Park in late March.[259] This agenda left little time, logistically, to develop a site-specific design by April 1911, if Wright also had to concern himself with the complicated site analyses necessary for the custom design of a large, rugged property such as this.[260] Moreover, Wright's site development experience at this point had been limited almost exclusively to the relatively flat prairie landscape. He had not yet designed a road system, other than for the Bitterroot Valley projects in Montana (where he showed little understanding of how to design for an irregular terrain). Nor had he used any form other than straight-line geometrics to lay out an access road or driveway, even for larger sites such as Willits, D. D. Martin, and Coonley. It therefore seems illogical to theorize that Wright suddenly acquired the expertise to lay out the type of circulation and underlying comprehensiveness represented within this plan. Then, there is the wordage in Jensen's October 18, 1912 letter to Wright which seems to support an ongoing affiliation with the Glencoe Board of Commissioners and suggests a certain dominance in his working relationship with Wright at this point: "I am wondering how you are getting along with those fountains, etc. for Glencoe. The Board of Commissioners are [sic] very anxious to get my layout so as to be able to lay this matter before the public and use it as campaign material for funds. I know you are very busy but wont [sic] you please give me those sketches in a very crude way, so I can put them on the plans, you understand what I mean just the outline so I can name on the plan what it is going to be, fountain, vase or whatever."[261] Lastly, there is the matter of Jensen's distinctive signature authenticating the document and identifying his status as the primary designer, rather than that of "delineator" or "draftsman"—to which his association with this project historically has been relegated.[262]

The "Planting Plan" represents much more than the name implies (Figure 4-7). A plan of this complexity required having the experience and ability to interpolate all the information that would have been anticipated by the initial site analysis—that is, the configuration of the primary and secondary ravine escarpments; spot elevations to profile the ravines and gauge the slope of the entire acreage; the location, caliber, and species of significant existing trees identified by survey; the conformation and arrangement of site circulation (including pedestrian pathways, roadway, approach bridge, and parking courtyard}; and the location, size, form, and proposed usage of the existing farmhouse, the gardens, and open space for activities. Moreover, since a large portion of these 15 acres had been cleared for farming, a fundamental consideration would have been the reforestation and redefinition of the land. To address these matters required having the knowledgeability to select hardy native trees and understory plantings; arrange them in a manner that would re-create the spatial qualities, natural light, and shade contrasts of the prairie landscape and its forested borders; give careful consideration to the transitional zones between plant communities; and have the foresight to envision the effect the introduced plantings would create at maturity, years into the future.[263] The very *last* consideration would have been the conformation and siting of Wright's structures: the residence, stable, garage with chauffeur's quarters, retaining walls, and three park gateway features.[264]

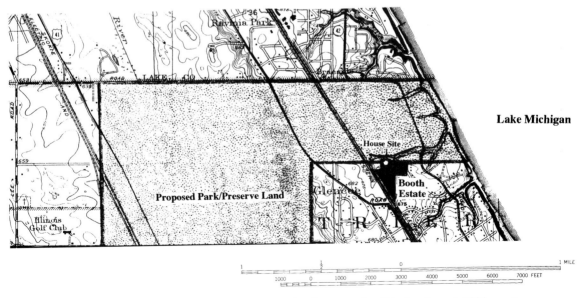

Figure 4-6   Location of Booth property in relation to "Proposed Park/Preserve Land" in Jens Jensen's 1904 report. (*By Charles E. Aguar, based on USGS map, Highland Park Quadrangle, 1926 edition. As delineated, © 2002 by Berdeana Aguar.*)

The most indisputable support for Jensen's authorial status with respect to the Booth-proposed park, however, are the five Jensen signature design features represented in the plan. (1) There is the ready accessibility to vehicular and pedestrian traffic. According to Leonard K. Eaton, access to public transportation was an important consideration to Jensen as a designer: "Jensen's parks were designed for a population which got about . . . by streetcar. He believed that no home should be located more than two miles from a park and that a station within walking distance was ideal."[265] (2) There is the placement and function of the gateway features designed by Wright. This introduction of statuary at "the places where park and city meet" is in keeping with Jensen's personal philosophy, as explained by Robert E. Grese: "Jensen believed that pictorial or allegorical sculpture . . . has a 'decorative beauty appropriate to its site and surroundings and a meaning in itself that the person of average intelligence can read without the aid of a guide book.' "[266] (3) There is the stone council ring beside the trail overlooking The Clearing (Figure 4-8), again explained by Grese: "These were low, circular, stone seats set around a council fire which could be used for storytelling, drama, music, dance, or conversation. Jensen believed that a democratic spirit was created when people came together, all seated on the same level around a central fire

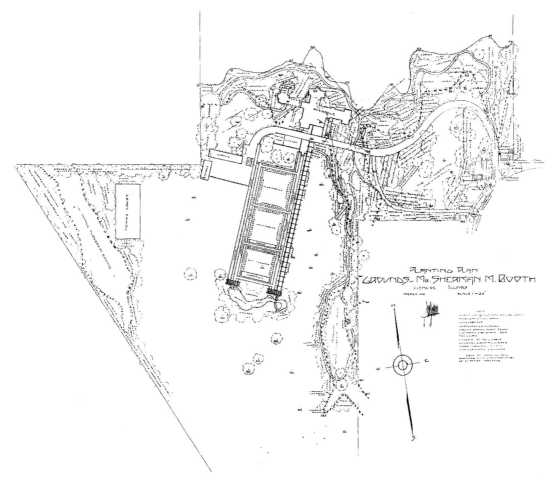

Figure 4-7 Planting plan for Sherman M. Booth property, as proposed by landscape architect Jens Jensen. (© 2002 by The Frank Lloyd Wright Foundation, Scottsdale, Arizona.)

pit. For him, this seating arrangement suggested ties with the early pioneers on the wilderness frontiers and with our Amerindian forebears at a council gathering."[267] (4) There is the spring-fed swimming pool shaped as a natural lagoon and hidden in a thick grove of cedars to the southwest of the cultivated gardens. "Jensen's swimming pools were unique," writes Eaton, "in reality swimming holes shut in by natural rock walls and surrounded by carefully chosen planting"[268] (Figure 4-9). And (5) there is the contour-hugging layout of the roads and trails. Wright relied on the T-square and triangles, whereas Jensen favored freehand drawing of the curved line. Jensen wrote: "Landscaping must follow the lines of the tree with its thousands of curves. . . . A curved line is poetic—it is romantic—it is mysterious and it is a part of life. A straight line is forced and dominating, but whether it is curved or a straight line, it must be fitting."[269]

Based upon all the foregoing considerations, it seems reasonable to presume that Wright's involvement with this project did not begin until after he returned from Europe in October 1910—at which time he met with the client to develop a program and then took the already prepared topographic map of the house site aboard ship on his return to Europe to develop the preliminary design concepts and complicated structuring. This reasoning is supported by Anthony Alofsin's notation within his chronology of significant events for this period: "21 January 1911. Wright on board H.M.S. *Lusitania;* site of Sherman Booth House, Glencoe, Illinois, under consideration; Wright takes plot plan to Germany."[270] Thus, there is a strong basis for reasoning that the Sherman Booth Project represents the only "collaboration" between Wright and Jensen in the true definition of the word—that is, the only commission where Wright and Jensen deliberated together during the entire process of working out the difficult problems of siting, access routes, and general land use.

In the end, Wright's excellent site-specific house plan for Sherman Booth never was executed, nor were the site and park ever developed as so artfully envisioned by Jensen. Only the stable and garage with chauffeur's quarters were sited as indicated on the grounds plan and executed as detailed in working drawings. Nevertheless, the Sherman Booth Project together with the Wright-

Figure 4-8 Example of Jens Jensen signature Council Ring in park bordering Lake Springfield, Illinois. (*Courtesy of Charles Kirchner.*)

Figure 4-9 Example of Jens Jensen signature Swimming Pool in Chicago's Columbus Park. (*Courtesy of Robert P. Pleva.*)

Jensen collaboration should be recognized as pivotal to Wright's evolution as an environmental designer. It was at this point in Wright's career—with his simultaneous design of the Taliesin Home and Studio—that he began to move away from the symbolistic architecture of the Prairie House and toward the more substantive organic architecture his rhetoric had always proclaimed, but he had not yet fully realized.

Taliesin Home and Studio—Spring Green, Wisconsin (1911–1912)

The 31.6-acre property recorded in Anna Wright's name on April 22, 1911, was within the intricate hilly landscape of the Driftless Area of southwestern Wisconsin formed over millions of years by the once-turbulent Wisconsin River. At this locality the river had effused to some 4 miles in width, as evidenced by the escarpments

that line the river's floodplain—including the steep slope that constitutes the northeast boundary of the bench upon which Taliesin would be built. Situated just south of a bend in the Wisconsin River and 1 mile north of Hillside Home School, which was owned and operated by Wright's two maiden aunts, this acreage had at one time been incorporated within the land holdings of the Lloyd Jones family but had been sold off during the depression of the 1880s. By purchasing this property, therefore, Wright and his mother were bringing it back into the bosom of the homestead valley.

In looking to reestablish himself so far removed from the urban-suburban environment of Chicago–Oak Park, it would seem that Wright was exhibiting feelings comparable to those held by the Japanese, as described by landscape architect Brooks Wigginton: "These people have long believed that they can overcome evil within themselves if they will go back to the natural wilderness to find the 'way of the gods,' away from the distractions of everyday life."[271] At the same time, however, Wright was following the ancient Chinese art of *feng-shui*, which professes that "the ideal site for a house and garden is halfway up a mountain with a commanding view and with water nearby."[272]

In his autobiography, Wright confirmed that the acreage purchased in his mother's name had not been selected randomly: "This hill . . . was one of my favorite places when as a boy looking for pasque flowers I went there in March sun while snow still streaked the hillsides. When you are on the low hill-crown you are out in mid-air as though swinging in a plane, the Valley and two others dropping away from you leaving the treetops standing below all about you. And 'Romeo and Juliet' still stood in plain view over to the Southeast. The Hillside Home School was just over the ridge."[273]

Within these four sentences Wright alludes to all the fundamentals upon which he based his environmental design of Taliesin (Figure 4-10). The combination of "pasque flowers," "March sun," and "snow" in the first sentence attests to his awareness of the length and intensity of Wisconsin winters, the natural solar benefits to be derived from a southeasterly orientation, and the fact that spring always comes much earlier on the sunny side of the hill. The second sentence confirms his familiarity with the lay of the land paralleling Lowery Creek in the floodplain below, the presence of the hill in relation to the floodplain, and the best prospects for realizing a wide unbroken view of the surrounding region. The reference in the third sentence to the landmark "Romeo and Juliet" windmill that Wright designed in 1896 corroborates his studied knowledge of the prevailing wind patterns for the area at all seasons of the year. He knew the harsher winds generated from November through March tracked from west to northwest and the gentler breezes of May through October tracked from southwest to due south. Thus, he was well aware that if he built on the north-to-southeast slopes, in the natural way of things, the "storms of the north" would break "over the low-sweeping roofs" while the summer breezes would flow unimpeded across the leeward side of the valley.[274] The reference to "Hillside Home School" in the

fourth sentence serves as a reminder that Wright had studied the surface structure and composition of the geological formations of the immediate area during the time he spent designing and supervising the construction of Hillside Home School II, from 1900 to 1903. It may have been during this time frame, in fact, that he first made note of the elongated natural bench formation atop the northeast-facing escarpment and thought of it as a potential homesite. A paper wallet in possession of the State Historical Society of Wisconsin contains more than two dozen photographs Wright made of these environs at that time.[275]

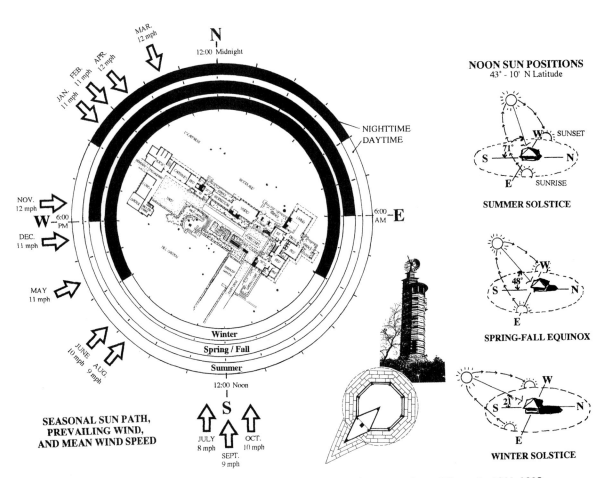

Figure 4-10 a–e Seasonal sun and wind analysis for Taliesin Home and Studio, Spring Green, Wisconsin, 1911–1912. (*By Charles E. Aguar, based on Climatic Atlas of the United States, U.S. Department of Commerce. As delineated,* © 2002 *by Berdeana Aguar.*)

Figure 4-11 a–b   Pattern of contoured tillage on Japan's steep hillsides (4-11a) that inspired contour tillage at Taliesin (4-11b). Contoured tillage at Taliesin was unique to this area, where lined tillage was "the norm." (*"Rice Terrace" photograph © by Yoichi Midonkawa, from "The Ocean and the Sand" by Mark Holborn, courtesy of Shambhala Publications, Inc., Boston. Taliesin photograph courtesy of The Frank Lloyd Wright Archives, Scottsdale, Arizona.*)

In purchasing such a large parcel of land, it is apparent that Wright was from the beginning thinking of Taliesin within the context of the Japanese and/or Italian "villa," where the total complex of house and grounds is conceived as a unit. Indeed, he first characterized his vision for the landscape—the gardens, the crops, the livestock—before he described the architecture he intended to build there: "Yes, Taliesin should be a garden and a farm behind a real workshop and a good home. . . . I saw it all; planted it all; laid the foundation of the herd, flocks, stable and fowl as I laid the foundation of the house. . . . Taliesin was to be a complete living unit genuine in point of comfort and beauty, yes, from pig to proprietor."[276] And as he proceeded to lay out the grounds

for his personal villa, it was the contoured tillage of Japan, the orderly horizontal manner of tillage distinctive to the peninsular region of Italy, and the controlled order of Italian orchards, olive groves, and vineyards that Wright strived to emulate (Figures 4-11 a-b, 4-12 a-b). Within this process, he fully developed the hyperbole blend of American, Italian, and Japanese space-making he originally explored with the Coonley House and site five years before.

It is not known what mapping Wright used during his design process with Taliesin. Although the 1902 USGS quadrangle map would have been available to him, it would seem he would have found the 20-foot contour intervals and scale (1 inch = 1 mile) to be of lim-

Figure 4-12 a–b   Pattern of Italian grid tillage as viewed from Fiesole on the hillside looking toward Florence, Italy (4-12 a). The southeast slope of Taliesin (4-12 b) originally emulated grid tillage of Italy. (*Mid-eighteenth-century drawing by Guiseppe Zocchi, courtesy of the Pierpont Morgan Library, New York. Taliesin photograph courtesy of the Frank Lloyd Wright Archives, Scottsdale, Arizona.*)

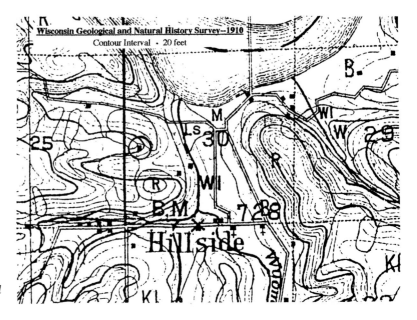

Figure 4-13 1910 Soils Map overprinted onto earliest known topographic survey for area surrounding Talieson. (*Courtesy Wisconsin Geological and Natural History Survey.*)

ited value for establishing grades at the various levels needed for structures of the complexity of Taliesin, for which 2-foot contour intervals generally would be used. It seems more likely he would have used the 1910 Soils Map with soils identification overprinted onto the topographic survey—despite the generalization of contour lines (Figure 4-13). Certainly, his manner of developing the land suggests a familiarity with the identifications keyed onto this map. Crops and pasturage were planted on the most productive soil (identified as "Wl" or Wabash Loam), and groves of trees were allowed to evolve naturally on Midway Hill or other rough stony areas unsuitable for anything other than forestry (identified as "R"). Regardless of what mapping was in fact used, Wright let the natural dictates of the site define the composition and configuration of the structures.

Wright's siting of his new home and studio followed the Italian concept of terracing such as he would have seen at the Villa Medici (Figure 4-14 a-b). Essentially segmenting the hillside into a giant L-shaped staircase, with two steps cut down from the rim of the bench, he lodged the living and guest quarters along the farthest promontory to the southeast and the studio workspace along the sheer escarpment to the northeast, then interconnected the two units through roofed bridging over a spacious entry loggia and terrace. Within the "L" thus formed, he carved out an expansive exterior

foyer at ground level to accommodate future land uses. This arrangement placed the primary structural mass of the living quarters at 56 degrees east-of-south and the studio at 34 degrees west-of-south, a layout and orientation which—though uncommon—maximized the number of rooms into which solar gain could be accessed during winter and early spring, eschewed exposure to the heat of summer inherent to a due south elevation, admitted northeast light into both structures year-round through the bands of windows along the escarpment side, and allowed for Wright's strategic directional control of sight lines from the majority of indoor and outdoor living spaces.[277]

Wright's touchstone for his architecture, he wrote in *An Autobiography*, was the "countenance" of the Driftless Area landscape. He described the organic integrity he intended to build into his design and the presence he wanted the structuring to represent as "an abstract combination of stone and wood as they naturally met in the aspect of the hills around about. . . . The lines of the hills were the lines of the roofs, the slopes of the hills their slopes, the plastered surfaces of light wood-walls, set back into shade beneath broad eaves, were like the flat stretches of sand in the river below and the same in color, for that is where the material that covered them came from."[278] In fulfilling this mental image, Wright discernibly embraced the straight-line construction and rus-

Section: Taliesin I--Spring Green, Wisconsin

b

Section: Villa Medici--Fiesole, Italy

a

Figure 4-14 a–b Section of Villa Medici (4-14 a) near Fiesole, Italy, site that probably inspired Wright's terracing of Taliesin as shown in the other illustration (4-14 b). (*Villa Medici section courtesy of Professor William A. Mann, University of Georgia School of Environmental Design. Taliesin section* © *2002 by The Frank Lloyd Wright Foundation, Scottsdale, Arizona.*)

tic beauty of the Japanese sukiya architecture. Unlike his limited symbolistic experimentation with this architecture at the Coonley estate—where he defied the site environment and attempted to fuse the sukiya and prairie school styles—at Taliesin, he so faithfully represented the foundational philosophy of sukiya architecture that Teiji Ito's wordage describing it could be used to describe Taliesin: "The surrounding terrain was of course taken into the design, and natural forms of land and water—hills, ravines, rivers, and ponds—all played a part in the planning . . . emphasis is on the natural beauty of its materials . . . colors are those of nature in its more subdued mood . . . rooms do not stand in predictable sequence or foursquare order . . . there is no clean-cut separation of indoor and outdoor space . . . [and] nature is invited in . . . or viewed as an extension of the room itself."[279] Wright's purposeful use of the diagonal line in his arrangement of doorways and windows also is analogous to sukiya architecture: "The diagonal line arrangement of component structures—that is, rooms which are actually separate entities but are linked together only at

one corner—offer the major advantages of views from all sides and maximum ventilation in summer. At the same time it allows for more light from outdoors . . . the outdoor scenery is also a part of the atmosphere of the room, and not merely in the picture-window sense of Western architecture. . . . And as the scenery changes from hour to hour with the changing light, and from season to season, the atmosphere of the room changes with it."[280]

It is important to note, however, that Wright did not limit his concerns for views and cross-ventilation to structural orientation and window placement and arrangement. Through the judicious protection of existing shade trees, the careful juxtapositioning of planned outdoor living spaces to align with trees and indoor living spaces, and at least partial sheltering under broad eave extensions over those outdoor living spaces not shaded naturally, Wright assured that air passing through these spaces would become cooler than ambient temperatures before being channeled into the living spaces: from the terrace to the northwest of the studio and the terraces to the northwest and southeast of the living room; from the kitchen court to the kitchen and sitting room; and from the garden court to the southwest wall of the same sitting room. Even the loggia-terrace was placed so the prevailing breezes from May through October, which regularly track from due south to west-southwest at greater than 5 miles per hour, channel air movement through the porte-cochere and the forecourt so the entry portico functions as a true breezeway, benefiting both structures.[281] Wright also placed sizable contained pools of water in exposed locations of the forecourt—to the left of the porte-cochere and to the immediate right of the loggia step—to utilize these same prevailing breezes for evaporative cooling. This was in addition to the functional purpose of the pools as sources of water for fire control and their aesthetic benefit as features to mark the thresholds to the courtyard garden and the loggia.[282] In his use of all these techniques of environmental design, Wright was not introducing anything new, however. He was following centuries-old methods for designing with respect for the forces of nature, such as he would have read about and personally observed during his summers in The Valley and his trips to Japan and Europe.[283]

Both the April and June 1911 plans-of-record demonstrate the extent to which Wright considered the Taliesin architecture and surrounding space compositionally (Figure 4-15 a-b). It is significant, for instance, that the April plan—upon which the original grading was based—arranged the buildings to integrate with the landscape, but also spaced them to allow for their expansion and the introduction of additional structures. The June plan introduced a porte-cochere gateway off the southeast tail of the living quarters. The studio wing was more than doubled in length—to incorporate a workroom, an apartment, storage space for carriages, and a stable for horses. And a third structure was added to the initial blueprint to accommodate requisites of agriculture husbandry. As the barn was seated in the service court and essentially stepped up to fit into a saddle between the Taliesin hill and another hill in the secondary ridge, situated some 75 feet to the northwest, the natural site topography that formed the crown of the hill was not significantly compromised through additional grading. Again, this ability to expand, extend, or remodel "a complex of rooms . . . without destroying the beauty of the overall appearance . . . [is an] amenability of the sukiya structure," Itoh explains. "[The] floor plan . . . represents an assemblage of single rooms, each of which is a unit in itself. How these units are grouped together does not matter at all . . . as long as the additional con-

struction preserves the harmony of proportion, texture, and technique."[284]

Of even more significance—aesthetically and environmentally—was the fact that Wright left enough room on the April plan to accommodate his anticipated arrangement of *exterior* functions: that is, approach and circulation, courts, terraces and gardens. As he then went on to detail and develop this extensional landscape, he retained a midlevel open space that has come to be known as the "Tea Circle" to physically separate and screen the service yard from the courtyard garden; and he oriented every aspect of this new and controlled landscape inward. In so doing, he correspondingly dramatized the enclosing structures, as well as the enclosed space and all the features within that space, so as to transmute the total volumetric space into an architectural entity. This all-inclusive spatial arrangement represented the fullest expression of the harmony and balanced composition that should be brought about between structures and surrounding space to develop a full and meaningful integration with the natural landscape.[285]

The section-elevation drawings further reveal that Wright designed the exterior hardscape elements—retaining walls, water features, terraces, and stairways—simultaneously with the structures (Figure 4-16 a-d). He used their verticality together with the verticality of the architecture to bound and unify the exterior foyer and median-level open space so that all elements within the extensional environment appear and function integrally. Moreover, he purposefully considered existing trees, their canopies, *and their root systems* in the arrangement of rooms and verandas, in the placement and height of retaining walls, in the situation and arrangement of the midlevel terrace and the "wild" garden, and in establishing the elevation of the first floor level for the living quarters, studio, and loggia-terrace. For example, the height of the retaining wall bounding the southwest extremity of the courtyard garden was determined by the base of the trunk of the lowest tree within the grouping of trees that appropriated the crown of the hill—as was the placement of the wall, which was slightly forward of the trunk so as not to disturb the core of the tree root system. And the natural situation of the landmark oak trees on the northeast slope of the hill, with one slightly lower than the other, determined the grade levels of the terrace landing and the terrace, as well as the number of steps leading to them. Moreover, the canopies and root systems of these trees shaped the

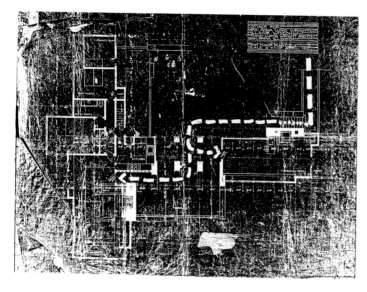

Figure 4-15 a Earliest known site plan for Taliesin (April 1911). Entry carriageway by way of cut through highest part of hill required massive retaining walls and nine steps to reach level of entry loggia. (© *2002 by the Frank Lloyd Wright Foundation, Scottsdale, Arizona. As delineated, © 2002 by Berdeana Aguar.*)

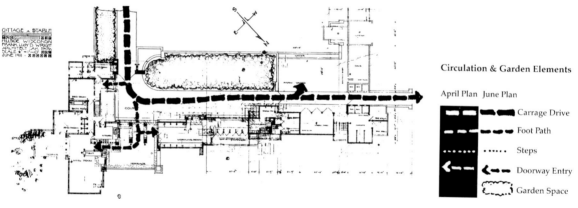

Figure 4-15 b Expanded site plan for Taliesin (1911) details one-way carriageway from southwest through porte-cochere at ground level of entry courtyard. Entry loggia easily accessible by foot. (*By Charles E. Aguar, based on historic photographs, personal analysis, and plans of record. © 2002 by The Frank Lloyd Wright Foundation, Scottsdale, Arizona. As delineated, © 2002 by Berdeana Aguar.*)

boundaries of the terrace space and the open space labeled "wild garden." Indeed, had Wright not left the space surrounding the terrace "wild," in the undisturbed sense of the word, the oak tree roots would have been violated to such an extent the tree would have died within a very short time. Most significantly, the trunk of the lower oak tree that established the level of the terrace landing also established the floor level of the living quarters, studio, and loggia-terrace, as well as the number of entry steps. This observation is supported by the exact correspondence of both the number of steps and the level of the final destination established for these diagonally opposite features of the inner compound.

As Wright initially explored the rudiments of circuitry and sequentiality with his Oak Park Home to create an entry experience for guests arriving by foot or by carriage, he utilized the greater site environment of Taliesin to create an entry experience for guests arriving by carriage or other conveyance. It is with the original approach route sketched onto the earliest known plat showing the Taliesin property in its entirety, as published in the February 1913 issue of *Western Architect*, that the significance of Wright's collaboration with Jensen on the Sherman Booth Project contemporaneous with his design of Taliesin becomes evident (Figure 4-17). Because it was here that Wright for the first time in his career designed an entry feature to visually separate public and private spaces, analogous to Jensen's practice of using allegorical sculpture to identify "the places where park and city meet." And it was here that Wright for the very first time forewent a straight-line approach in favor of a curving approach, such as Jensen had proposed for the Booth Project—including the reverse curve that led to an elevated vantage point. As Wright conceived this original entry approach at Taliesin, he represented a masterpiece of environmentally sensitive

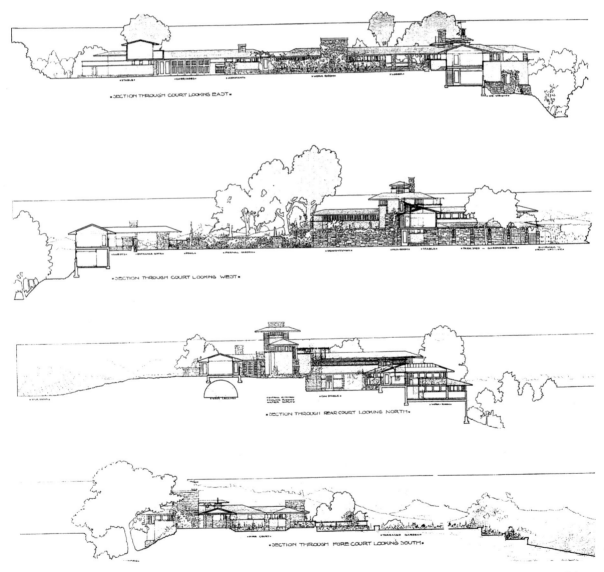

Figure 4-16 a–d   Taliesin sections through Courtyard, 1911–1914. (© *2002 by The Frank Lloyd Wright Foundation, Scottsdale, Arizona.*)

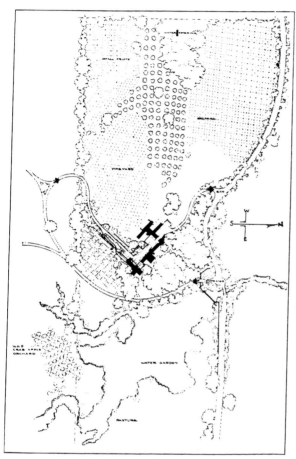

Figure 4-17 Sketch of Taliesin grounds by C. H. Ashbee. (*Western Architect, February 1913 issue*)

of the entry experience was the spillway with rocks on the far side arranged to create the effect of a waterfall. The act of moving toward the gateway intensified the kinetic quality of the water falling toward the roadway—especially when the water spray was backlighted by the sun, as it was for many hours of the day because of the spillway's northerly orientation. The flowing water commanded the senses both audibly and visually to direct attention toward the water feature and thence toward the narrow, undulating water form behind the dam and the expansive marshlike area beyond, which at that time was allowed to naturally accumulate water in the hollows and low places to form what Wright descriptively referred to as the "Water Garden."[286] By their placement at the beginning and to one side of the approach, the spillway and naturalistic water form of the pond established an oblique line of sight that followed the path of the creek across The Valley toward the borrowed view of The Welsh Hills on the horizon. The effect of this treatment was that the presence of the water was known, but not its form; the form could not be realized until viewed from elevated vantage points from within and around the structures near the crown of the hill.

As the creek meandered through The Valley, so the entry approach followed along the natural contours. Under a canopy of trees, the roadway passed the Water Garden to the left and the lower edge of the vegetable and flower gardens to the right, which emulated the Italian grid tillage Wright had admired in Umbria. Curving westward up the gentle slope of the hill, the roadway then looped through a meadow and reversed direction so the upper edge of the gardens was to the right and vineyards briefly came into view on the left[287] (Figure 4-18 a). From this position, the stone retaining wall lining the cut surface of the hillside to the left—that appeared as a natural outcropping—hid the mass of the studio and barn from the range of vision so attention was directed toward the roofed bridging of the porte-cochere and loggia, creating a sense of anticipation for what lay ahead (Figure 4-18 b). As horses strained up the steepened grade of the straightaway, the carriage would have slowed and the dioramic treetop view of the landscape passed through a short time before would have reinforced the beauty and spatiality of the Taliesin setting.

To this point, Wright's meticulously choreographed entry experience was expansive and apart from the viewer. Titillating glimpses of the Taliesin structure, from first one angle and then another, were interspersed with a sensory kaleidoscope of natural and manmade land-

site planning that anticipated every turn of the head and controlled what was seen, when it was seen, and from which perspective, as well as what was heard and sensed—from the moment the access road turned south off County Road "C" and passed through the gateway, to the moment of arrival at the broad stone steps leading to the roofed loggia-terrace between the home and studio.

Wright's gateway feature was framed on either side by pillars of striated stone and designed as a unit with the thick stone dam that impounded the creek to form the pond and spillway. While the gateway feature was the obvious physical manifestation of the point of entry, or threshold to the property, the more responsive aspect

Figure 4-18 a   Main entrance to Taliesin as viewed from the south meadow. Vineyards to left, entry valley to right and below. (*Courtesy of The Frank Lloyd Wright Archives, Scottsdale, Arizona.*)

scape features, including the imagery and scents of the bounty of the earth and the sight and sound of cattle in the pasture. As the roadway crested to the level of the forecourt, however, a line of sight similar to a one-point perspective was brought about to direct attention through the frame of the porte-cochere, across the spacious width of the forecourt and the breadth of the loggia-terrace to focus upon the protective canopy of trees on the escarpment beyond. This treatment imparted a sense of arrival, a sense of shelter, and a sense of welcome into the inner compound.

As Wright positioned the porte-cochere to equate with the archaic definition—that is, as an entrance for carriages leading into a courtyard—the forecourt served as a human-scale community crossroad from which all inner compound movement originated to reach the barn, stable, service yard, courtyard garden, Tea Circle, the loggia-terrace, and points of outdoor-indoor transition for either the studio or living quarters. Thus, it was at the point the carriage or other conveyance halted to discharge passengers within the forecourt or slowed to negotiate the sharp left turn to reach the sizable service

Figure 4-18 b   Approach to porte-cochere. Stone retaining wall for hill garden at left, family quarters to right. (*Courtesy of The Frank Lloyd Wright Archives, Scottsdale, Arizona.*)

yard that visitors, family members, and staff would begin to actively participate in the entry experience at a subjective level of intimacy. Whether arrivals exited their vehicle in the forecourt or in the service yard, and then strolled back toward the forecourt upon the stone-lined walkways on either side of the earthen median strip, they would have become aware of the courtyard garden as they approached and mounted the low stone steps to reach the capacious space of the loggia, the vantage viewpoint of the open terrace extension overlooking the Wisconsin River valley, or one of the two main points of outdoor-indoor transition. Either way, a sensory interaction with Wright's carefully crafted environment of the sequestered inner compound subtly invaded the senses—through the melodic tones of trickling water, the sounds of buzzing insects, singing birds, or the sharp clip-clop of horses' hooves striking earth or stone; the lowing of cows in the distance; the heady aroma of apples, grapes, and flowering plants of many varieties; the sensations of the warmth of the sun, the coolness of shade, breezes wafting up the hill or through the breezeway; or the feel of textures underfoot—grass, soft dirt, or stone.

There is a marked difference in Wright's landscape treatment at Taliesin, compared to his Prairie Houses. Most changed was his manner of planting containment and arrangement. There were no elongated flower boxes. There were no planting urns at terminal points. There was no architectural emphasis of the water table because the foundation of the structure and its connection with the ground were completely obscured by the massing and height of plantings in the geometric planting beds on either side of the entry steps. One planting bed extended across the length of the studio wing and the other across the length of the kitchen terrace privacy wall. Perennials and herbaceous plantings were arranged with the tall varieties against the walls and borders of lower varieties and ground covers in the foreground to display a range of plant architecture and color (see Appendix E).

The coincidence of Wright's turnabout with respect to foundation planting supports another Jensen influence—despite the dissimilarity of Wright's geometric formality and Jensen's characteristic naturalism. The only two houses where Wright had accepted plantings proximate to his architecture before this date had been for Coonley and Booth, where Jensen designed the planting plans. Jensen's letter to Wright dated October 18, 1912, alludes to his awareness of the Taliesin site: "I hope you are enjoying these beautiful fall days and I

really envie [sic] you your beautiful home site."[288] Further, it is known that both Wright and Jensen corresponded with a nursery during 1912 concerning planting stock for use at Taliesin, which establishes that Wright and Jensen discussed the Taliesin landscape at least to some degree.[289] Wright may have been consulting with Jensen about the type and hardiness of plant stock that would create the overall effect he envisioned, because most of the plantings Jensen ordered for Wright relate most closely with the orchards and gardens outside the parameters of the inner compound: gooseberries, grapes, blackberries, raspberries, plums, pears, rhubarb, asparagus, and 285 apple trees. Or perhaps Jensen placed the order using his letterhead as a friendly courtesy, for the benefit of a professional discount. This might explain why Phlox, Rugosa Rose (*Rosa rugosa*), and Mock Orange (*Philadelphus*) were included in the list of plantings. The generic "Phlox" designation is not specific enough to determine its intended use, since there are more than 50 species comprising the Phlox Family and there is a wide range in size and form. Moreover, the ornamental qualities of Mock Orange and Rugosa Rose (the latter being an oriental rose common to China, Korea, and Japan, also known as the "Sea Tomato" of Japan) are so contrary to the native prairie plantings Jensen favored that their inclusion suggests they were selected by Wright. There is little other indication, and no documentation, that Jensen was involved with the design or planting of the Taliesin courtyard garden, although the form, substance, and intended use of the stone seating arrangement in the Tea Circle closely identify with his signature council ring, such as he had proposed that same year for the Booth Project.

The Tea Circle was the focal point of Wright's design and layout for the new and controlled landscape of courtyards-terraces-gardens. Considered together as a unit, these open spaces represent an uncommon blend of geometricism, biomorphism, and symbolism (Figures 4-19, 4-20). Clearly, the oak trees were the landmarks for every aspect of Wright's environmental design. Their elevated position and expansive canopies announced a destination for anyone crossing the threshold into the courtyard garden. The interconnecting forecourt and service yard were laid out to direct movement functionally across the landscape and separate the spaces of human and animal habitation. But these open spaces also were designed so as not to impinge upon the cultivated landscape or detract from the ambiance of the natural site environment. The courtyard garden, on the

Figure 4-19   View looking northwest toward rear courtyard over pool and fountain in entry garden. (*Courtesy of The Frank Lloyd Wright Archives, Scottsdale, Arizona.*)

ness, rusticity, natural textures, while *wabi* describes the sense of quietness, astringency, good taste, and tranquility produced in the precincts."[290] Teiji Ito notes that the tea garden "is usually spoken of as the 'dewy ground,' or 'dewy path,' that is, the *roji* . . . The word had several connotations, among them: 'on the way' or 'while walking.' "[291] And Lorraine E. Kuck alludes to this space as "an escape from the world, a transition area between the solitude of the tea room and the distractions of the workaday world."[292]

There also is the water basin inset in the stone terrace of the Tea Circle, which emulates the imagery and situation of the ritual tea garden water basin: "near the waiting bench."[293] There is Wright's manner of placing artwork—early on, the plaster cast of *A Flower in the Crannied Wall* and, later, the more typical Japanese lantern—at the terminal point of the Tea Circle stairs closest to the entry roadway in the requisite position for a Japanese tea garden, and for the requisite reason: "near the interior gate, near the waiting bench, near the ritual water basin . . . [to enhance] the aesthetic quality of the garden."[294] And there is the Tea Circle itself, which functions as the tea serving areas in Japan did before the establishment of a teahouse structure—that is, the tea serving area was open on one side and guests looked out over the terrace or veranda at a small garden. Indeed, the tradition of everyone on the premises at Taliesin coming together in the late afternoon to take refreshment and commune within the space of the Tea Circle has been followed, weather permitting, ever since Taliesin has been in existence. In the mid-1990s, an ancient Korean bell hanging from the remaining oak tree replaced the school bell once attached to the tower to signal tea time, the end of the workday, or an emergency call for help (Figure 4-21).

Based upon the logic of these insights, Wright's intent for the Tea Circle becomes evident: that it simultaneously engage the site, separate the workday environment from the living environment, serve as a destination for the courtyard garden, and assume spiritual control of the inner compound of Taliesin.

other hand, was laid out in the regularized order of the secular gardens of Italy as a place to be slowly walked through and/or contemplated from the extremity vantage points and from the forecourt. Its intimate dimension was determined by the rectangular stone water feature at the garden threshold off the forecourt; the stone retaining wall along the base of the hill; the observation terrace, seating, and retaining wall designed as a unit with the massive stone pier for the porte-cochere on one end; and the stone mass of the Tea Circle, landing, and terrace on the other end.

At the same time, the quiet rustic simplicity and composition of the naturalistic plantings and stonework, the setting apart of the Tea Circle, and even the name itself suggest that Wright's inspiration for this space was the Japanese tea garden—as its essential attributes are elaborated upon by authorities. David H. Engel writes: "The tea garden should contain those ineffable qualities of *sabi* and *wabi*, sought after and prized by Japanese tea masters and all those who take part in the tea ceremony. By *sabi* they mean the appearance of antiquity, age, hoari-

With Taliesin, Wright artfully and successfully merged the conflicting attributes of American, Italian, and Japanese space making. It is this very friction that gives Taliesin its creative tension—because it is the dissonance between formality and tastefulness, tension and repose, and the dialectical synthesis between tradition and anti-

Figure 4-20   View from rear
courtyard looking east toward
forecourt. Tea Circle on right.
(*Courtesy of The Frank Lloyd Wright
Archives, Scottsdale, Arizona.*)

Figure 4-21   June 1996 photograph
of character-defining White Oak and
Korean bell in Taliesin Tea Circle.
(*Photograph by Berdeana Aguar;
© 2002 by Berdeana Aguar.*)

tradition that provides the newness and unmistakable creativity that *is* Taliesin.

Regrettably, neither of the specimen oak trees that were the character-defining landscape features of the Tea Circle and inner courtyard survived the twentieth century. The one on the inside of the semicircular seating arrangement died at some point after 50 years and was not replaced. With its loss, there no longer was enough canopy to shield the seating area from the more penetrating rays of the late afternoon sun, nor enough root system to reinforce the root system of the magnificent landmark White Oak in the Wild Garden. Even so, this specimen oak survived until it was uprooted during a severe wind storm in June 1998; its age was estimated to be 225 years. The structural and material impairment caused by the uprooting and felling of this tree was substantial, involving the upheaval of the Tea Circle masonry and damage to the studio wing—precipitated by a mud slide that involved a 300-square-yard section of the escarpment slope northeast of the studio wing and endangered a structural pier supporting the studio balcony.

The Taliesin Preservation Commission—created in 1990 to ensure the preservation of Taliesin and to provide for public access to the site—estimated reconstruction costs in the range of $250,000, over and above the budget already in place. But there can be no quick fix or financial cost to rectify the priceless loss of the aesthetic of the tree itself—or of the tree lost in the 1950s, for that matter. It will be a half-century or more before the ambiance of the landscape will again even begin to reflect Wright's vision for the Tea Circle and the entire inner courtyard. These nature-induced occurrences demonstrate, unequivocably, that the preservation and/or restoration of the structures alone only partially meet Wright's holistic vision for his architecture. Indeed, the loss of these trees clearly establishes the need to understand and respect the importance of farsighted replacement planting with respect to Wright's carefully considered site environments. Had replacement oak trees been introduced into the Taliesin Tea Circle landscape decades ago—based upon the full knowledge that the original specimen trees have a reasonably predictable life span and by nature will become vulnerable to disease and environmental forces—the loss of their character-defining presence could have been more readily ameliorated.

With Taliesin an actuality, but his practice essentially nonlucrative, Wright in January 1913 traveled to Japan

to personally follow up on some six months of contact concerning the possibility of his being commissioned to design the Imperial Hotel in Tokyo. But he also reestablished contact with former and potential clients so as to have work ready when he returned in May, and he consciously arranged to direct both public and professional attention toward the multiplicity of his architectural talents in his absence—through respected publications, exhibitions, and competitions. The American version of *Sonderheft* and monograph were put into distribution in America during January. Taliesin was featured in the January issue of *Architectural Record* as well as in the February issue of *Western Architect*. Wright's nonjuried entry for the City Club of Chicago Land Development Competition was selected for inclusion in the City Club Housing Exhibition on March 7. He advertised in a special issue of *Arts and Decoration* prepared for the International Exhibition of Modern Art (New York Armory Show), on view at the Art Institute of Chicago from March 19 to June. And his work was on display at the Art Institute of Chicago during the 26th annual exhibition of the Chicago Architectural Club from May 11 to June. The most significant of these farsighted promotional efforts was his entry for the Chicago Land Development Competition.

City Club of Chicago Land Development Competition (1913)

It is indicative of Wright's fascination with community planning and his dedication to the promotion of his Quadruple Block plan that he entered the City Club of Chicago Land Development Competition at all. He normally refused to enter these events because he felt a jury tended to select a mediocre entry as a means of averaging the very best and very worst, or to eliminate the most controversial. It must be assumed that Wright considered this competition to be above the norm, since the competition program was drawn up by the Illinois chapter of the American Institute of Architects. Moreover, two reviewers on the five-member panel of jurors were Jensen and George Maher, with whom he had worked during his tenure in Silsbee's office. Even so, Wright chose to submit his entry "hors concours" so it would not be subjected to critical competitive evaluation. This was an unfortunate decision, since his presentation held its own very well in relation to other entries, including works by Drummond and Griffin.[295] His presentation was one of 26 featured in the book *City Residential Land Development—Studies in Planning*, published three years after the event. He was in fact allocated more space than any other entrant—a generous 7 pages, with 4 in color.[296]

Wright was one of five competition entrants who chose to work within the established gridiron of Chicago's street system (Figure 4-22). To control the speed of traffic moving through the development, he limited the number of through streets to three (with one running north-south and two running east-west). He also confined faster through-traffic to boundary thoroughfares, and introduced speed-impeding "jogs" into all remaining interior street alignments (Figure 4-23). This treatment divided in half some of the standard Chicago city blocks, with the larger blocks retained for business and civic facilities, parks, recreation, and two lagoons. Although reviewers criticized Wright's plan for the "inconvenient arrangement of its arterial system, which is distinctly bad," they appreciated that Wright was trying to eliminate "unsightly alleys."[297] The reviewers here were referring to Wright's resurrection of the Quadruple Block concepts detailed for the article in the February 1901 issue of the *Ladies Home Journal*, as well as the

optional layouts previously prepared for investment purposes. For the purpose of this competition, he adapted the plans to be in conformance with the hypothetical site set forth in the program through his detailing of the requisite drawings. Basically, he expanded his land development scheme to include sociocultural elements by introducing shops, schools, apartments, single-family homes, community facilities, and other public buildings. All were interspersed within a strong pattern of parks, playgrounds, and water features linked by landscaped streets to form a greenway system (Figure 4-24). Street trees were delineated in special patterns, with trees evenly spaced only on streets leading to parks, schools, and other public open spaces where more organic forms appeared naturally in clumps of woodland drifts as counterpoint to those planted architectonically.

The facade of trees Wright established for the commercial-apartment strip on the north edge and the symmetrical canopies of trees used as basques alongside the lagoons and adjoining public spaces most likely were inspired by landscapes he had seen in Europe, since

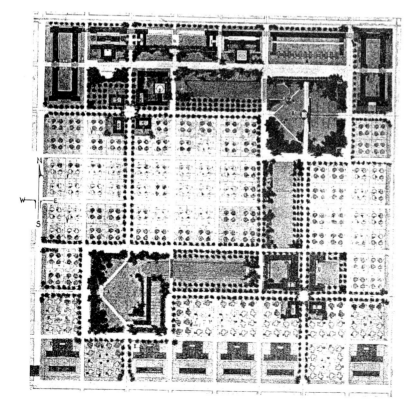

Figure 4-22 Wright's plan for City Club of Chicago land development competition (1913) shows strong pattern of open space. (© 2002 by The Frank Lloyd Wright Foundation, Scottsdale, Arizona.)

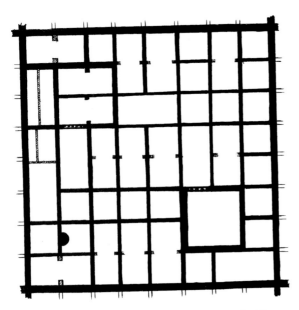

Figure 4-23 Delineation of street system pattern for City Club of Chicago land development competition. (*By Charles E. Aguar, based on personal analysis and original drawings of record. © 2002 by The Frank Lloyd Wright Foundation, Scottsdale, Arizona. As delineated, © 2002 by Berdeana Aguar.*)

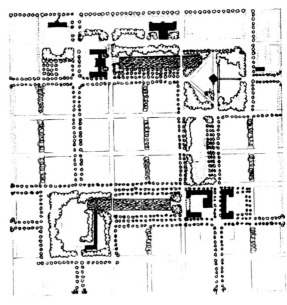

Figure 4-24 Pattern of parks, playgrounds, street trees, landscaped greenways, schools, and public buildings for City Club of Chicago land development competition. (*By Charles E. Aguar, based on personal analysis and original drawings of record. © 2002 by The Frank Lloyd Wright Foundation, Scottsdale, Arizona. As delineated, © 2002 by Berdeana Aguar.*)

these treatments were not then in vogue in the Midwest. Therefore, Wright's more immediate inspiration may have been the livable, parklike neighborhoods he so admired four years earlier in London: "The whole aspect of London is so much richer and pleasanter and human-like and strongly built, firmly established. . . . Green breaking through it everywhere—parks, yards overflowing with green. Flowers everywhere, and nothing straight and dull, nothing rectangular in the place. It was a great and pleasant surprise to see this great city in the world so habitable. Somehow they had succeeded in making London habitable to an extreme . . . every man was so close to his borough. And it seems practically so. Within a block or two or three you can find everything you could ever want. There will be a theater, a cinema, a dry goods store, a barber, a turkish bath—you couldn't think of anything that wouldn't be within reach almost anywhere in London."[298] Regardless of Wright's source of inspiration, the end result puts forth a feasible methodology for developing a parklike environment comparable to Olmsted's Riverside, but within the context of Chicago's urban gridiron framework.[299]

The insightful practicality of Wright's City Club plan reflects his thorough familiarity with how to design for the level prairie urban community. After all, he had personally followed the selfsame sociological patterns of those who assumedly would live on this land, and he had for years observed their patterns of commuting by public or private transport, their manner of schooling, worshipping, shopping, and pursuing leisure activities. Moreover, his text as published in *City Residential Land Development—Studies in Planning* provides a thoughtful and logical explanation for his manner of land use distribution within the proposed quarter-section of land. This writing represents one of very few instances where Wright both clearly expressed and defended his design rationale for a specific project or commission. The unfortunateness is that here, once again, he selected a publicity medium where his explanation of the benefits of the Quadruple Block land subdivision scheme reached a limited American audience. Further, the official archival listing of Wright's works never has assigned a number for this competition presentation and it has been largely ignored or given only slight reference in contemporary publications. It is for these reasons that Wright's text has been printed herein in completely unabridged form (see Appendix H).

Almost immediately upon returning to Chicago in May 1913, Wright received a letter informing him that he had been selected to design the Imperial Hotel. This would be one of the most challenging commissions of Wright's career, requiring many three-week-long trips by steamship to and from Japan and some six to eight years of concentrated effort. By August 1913, the Imperial Hotel plan was in process. Within this same time frame, Wright was approached by a group of investors about the possibility of his designing "Midway Gardens." One of the principal investors for this proposed garden resort and restaurant complex was Edward C. Waller, Jr., the son of the patron who 18 years earlier had sponsored Wright's Wolf Lake Amusement Park project.

Midway Gardens—Chicago, Illinois (1913)

The site on which the investors proposed to develop this urban garden resort was a little over 2 acres in size and was situated at the southwest corner of the intersection of Cottage Grove Avenue and 60th Street. This placed it directly across 60th from Washington Park and diagonally across from the west terminus of the Midway Plaisance (Figure 4-25). The site also was immediately accessible by streetcar and one mile west of an urban train station connecting the downtown Loop with Jackson Park, the former site of the World's Columbian Exposition—where the Palace of Fine Arts, the Ho-o-den on The Wooded Isle, and the beaches fronting on Lake Michigan were still popular excursion destinations. Lastly, the site was within a short walking distance for collegians, as the University of Chicago campus occupied the intervening space between the two parks and its main quadrangle faced south onto the plaisance greensward. Thus, this property benefited from the same attributes of convenient location and easy public accessibility that had made this area a good choice for the Exposition and the civic and cultural improvements that had occurred during the subsequent 20 years.

Wright apparently saw this commission as an opportunity to experiment with some of the basic design concepts he had begun to develop for the Imperial Hotel, since the time frame for completion of the Gardens was compressed into less than a year, with 90 days of actual construction. The architecture for both

developments exhibit similar complex ornament representing primary geometric forms and the European idealizations of form with archaeological material, oriental lineage, and Wright's personal expressions of abstract artistry. It is the artistry of this architectural detail that has been largely addressed in contemporary literature. The notable exception to this scrutiny has been the ornament of plantings—their placement, containment, arrangement, and contribution to the overall effect. This, even though the hardscape and cultivated landscape were integral to the "gardens" environment in the defining connotation of the word, as confirmed by Wright: "The Midway Gardens were planned as a 'summer garden,' a system of low masonry terraces enclosed by promenades, loggias, and galleries at the sides, these flanked by a Winter Garden."[300] Moreover, the significance of Wright's landscape treatment and open-space planning in context with the architecture has been left uninterpreted to this point. Again, even though these were the critical foundational influences that formed the basis of his design layout and effected the volumetric exterior space of the summer garden that was the "essence" of the entire complex—as such open spaces are construed by Simonds: "Open spaces assume an architectural character when they are enclosed in full or in part by structural elements. . . . Each such defined open space is an entity, complete within itself. But more, it is an inseparable part of each adjacent space or structure. . . . A defined outdoor volume is a well of space. Its very hollowness is its essential quality. . . . Such spaces, be they patios, courts, or public squares, become so dominant and focal in most architectural groupings that the very essence of the adjacent structures is distilled and captured there."[301]

The greater site environment influenced Wright's architectural design and open-space planning in a number of ways. For example, the socially confluent makeup of the Cottage Grove Avenue–60th Street intersection and easy accessibility to public transit determined the situation of the main points of access and the architectural mass of the complex that housed the winter garden restaurant, private clubroom, and tavern. This reasoning is supported within Wright's autobiographical text: "The Winter Garden stood forward on the main street. . . . The Bar, 'supporting economic feature,' was put on the principal street corner. . . . At each extreme outer corner of the lot toward the main street were set the two tall welcoming features . . . to advertise the entrances to both summer and winter gardens."[302]

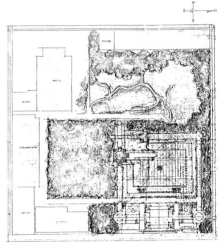

Figure 4-26 "Preliminary plan, first scheme" for Midway Gardens, Chicago, Illinois, 1913, (© 2002 by The Frank Lloyd Wright Foundation, Scottsdale, Arizona.)

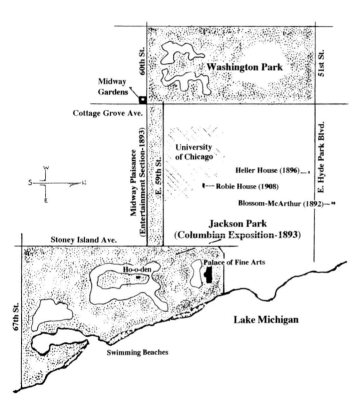

Figure 4-25 Diagram of relationships between Midway Gardens and Jackson Park, Washington Park, and Midway Plaisance in Chicago. (*By Charles E. Aguar, based on personal analysis and plan of record, Chicago South Park Commission. As delineated, © 2002 by Berdeana Aguar.*)

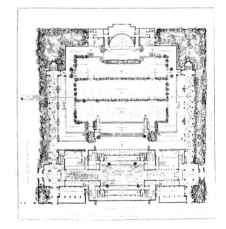

Figure 4-27 Plan and layout for Midway Gardens as built. (© 2002 by The Frank Lloyd Wright Foundation, Scottsdale, Arizona.)

Whereas this text was describing the development as built, the same basic reasoning was in place for Wright's earlier asymmetrical "Preliminary Plan, Second Scheme" where the structural mass within the northeast quadrant was part of a scheme encompassing the entire block (Figure 4-26). In this preliminary plan, related or competing recreational land uses—dance hall, saloon, skating rink, restaurant, casino, theater—were arranged in strip fashion along the boundary streets; and the major portion of the southwest quadrant and inner grounds were intended to function as a public, or semi-public, parklike garden.[303] This arrangement would have made the recreational facilities easily accessible from without and within the complex, and the open space would have appeared as an extension of the greater site environment of Washington Park. The obvious drawbacks of this scheme were the separation and ranging distribution of the recreational facilities, which would have made them difficult to monitor and service.

Wright's final plans for Midway Gardens provide a textbook demonstration of his extraordinary ability to design in three-dimensions—that is, as the spaces were to be "experienced" (Figure 4-27). The winter garden structure occupied approximately one-third of the acreage and was designed to accommodate both the activities within the enclosed spaces and the functional changes in elevation necessary for movement between the five levels of space. The stairways and ramps served the additional function of providing constantly changing lines of sight for viewing the many forms of art and architecture, as well as the landscape architecture, activities, and performances that took place within the open space of the summer garden that occupied the remaining two-thirds of the block (Figure 4-28).

The summer garden open space was designed to function as an amphitheater defined by the enclosing structures. The bandstand stage and acoustical shell feature were aligned on the principal axis and midpoint of the winter garden, but offset from the central amphitheater on an elevated island of space between two proposed open spaces on either side of the privacy walls. The acoustical shell itself was designed to be open on both sides so that performances could be heard and viewed equally well from a selection of vantage points within a 180-degree radius. Therefore, this stage-and-shell feature was for the most part viewed asymmetri-

cally. Indeed, the controlling factor of every aspect of Wright's layout appears to have been to provide unobstructed views of this feature: from the arcades and terraces on either side; from the three, tiered-down terrace levels within the space of the amphitheater; from the winter garden restaurant, where there were walls of windows and doors opening off the dining levels terraced downward toward the amphitheater; from the stairways, arcaded balconies, roof gardens, and balconies cantilevering off the four towers and two belvederes.[304] Thus, the distinctive quality of the complex reflected the basic syntax of the pre-Renaissance public spaces such as Wright had experienced in medieval towns throughout Europe, where the structures that enclose the central public open space relate functionally to adjoining structures but aesthetically and environmentally to the central space and greater environment.

Wright's decision to forego a grand formal entryway in favor of the two points of entry situated at each extreme outer corner of the lot also was in keeping with this concept, as was his manner of routing the clientele circuitously through narrow hallways toward the amphitheater. By approaching the amphitheater from the corners in the same way the narrow, winding pedestrian streets of European townscapes approach public squares and piazzas, the sense of enclosure was not compromised. And the diagonal sight lines magnified the psychological impact of the initial view of the transcendental open space, which must have seemed to reach outward and upward into infinity from either angle. The

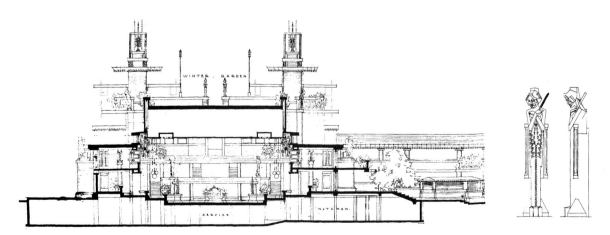

Figure 4-28 Partial longitudinal section of Midway Gardens multilevel winter garden. (© *2002 by The Frank Lloyd Wright Foundation, Scottsdale, Arizona.*)

end result of this imaginative layout was that Midway Gardens became an extraordinary exploration of planes of three-dimensional space from which to see and be seen, participate in spontaneous events (discussions, speech-making, romancing, and the like), and view the kaleidoscope of people in motion, the overlapping colors, textures, lights, and bandstand performances within the amphitheater—an experience not unlike exploring, viewing, and participating in all the excitement and vitality of the grand open space of the "Piazza San Marco" in Venice, albeit on a more intimate scale.

Much about the hardscape for Midway Gardens was functional. The hundreds of linear feet of built-in planters that defined the conformation of the terrace levels within and surrounding the amphitheater served as physical barriers, as did the planters built into the walls of the arcades, balconies, stairways, and roof gardens (Figure 4-29). The heights of the planters were carefully scaled to include plantings-in-place so as not to impede views outward into the amphitheater, but to sheath views inward from the lower terrace levels. The heights of the privacy walls along the arcades were scaled to include the dozens of masonry urns in rows atop the parapets, again with plantings-in-place. But the hardscape and cultivated landscape also were integral to the composition of the complex as a whole. The urns on the privacy walls—which were additional to those situated at terminal points throughout the complex—served as intermediary capturing devices to integrate foreground and background, whether that background was the amphitheater or the peripheral environment of Washington Park. The suspended built-in planters over arbored portals and on pedestals functioned in like manner, but assumed more important spatial and psychological significance as sheltering overhead planes that integrated with the all-encompassing layered effect created by the roofs of the arcades, the overhanging terraces, and the cantilevered balconies—all the while creating moving shadows and sun patterns. The inanimate elements of architectural ornament—including the spires, statues, and textures—also contributed to Wright's purposeful dramatization of the experience of being in an outdoor environment. Without the animate ornament of plantings, however—the cascading varieties, in particular—the hardscape and architectural ornament alone would not have articulated the contrasting textures or the full sense of rhythm of Wright's intent. It assumedly was for this reason that Wright expressed regret when there was not enough money to

complete the finishing touches, such as "the sky-frames on the four towers of the Winter Garden intended to be garlanded with vines and flowers like the tops of the welcoming features. Nor any to plant the big trees at the corners of the Gardens."[306] Nonetheless, with the addition of the kinesthetic vitality of masses of people—the most essential and animate ornament of all—Wright's creation of Midway Gardens purportedly was successful beyond belief, if only for a brief two years.

According to Twombly, when World War I erupted in Europe a few months after the June 1914 grand opening of the Gardens, the sentiments of Chicagoans began to turn against those of German extraction, who comprised a large percentage of Chicago's population that attended the Gardens. While America did not officially join with the Allies until 1917, attendance at the Gardens so diminished that it became economically unfeasi-

Figure 4-29 Balcony viewpoint of Midway Gardens multilevel entertainment complex reveals integrated design, open to sky. (© *2002 by The Frank Lloyd Wright Foundation, Scottsdale, Arizona.*)

ble to maintain operations.[306] Kruty, on the other hand, presents a valid argument that financial problems resulted from the underfunding of the construction itself, the exorbitant overhead of servicing subsequent loans, and a combination of other factors.[307] For whatever reason, the facility went into receivership in 1916, at which time it was taken over by Eidelweiss Brewery and the facility was renamed Eidelweiss Gardens, the name formerly used by a smaller beer garden near the north end of Washington Park. This beer and dance hall operation attracted a less affluent clientele and also became financially unviable with the onset of the era of prohibition: 1920–1933. Unfortunately for posterity, after having stood vacant for a number of years, the entire Midway Gardens complex was razed in 1929— just four years shy of the revocation of prohibition.

In August 1914, Wright received word of a disastrous fire at his Taliesin home and studio. He did not learn the full extent of his personal deprivation until he was en route by train to Spring Green, however. He wrote: "In less time than it takes to write it, a thin-lipped Barbados Negro . . . had turned madman, taken the lives of seven and set the house in flames. In thirty minutes the house and all in it had burned to the stone work or to the ground. The living half of Taliesin violently swept down and away in a madman's nightmare of flame and murder. The working half only remained."[308] Those killed included two workers, the young son of the gardener, Mamah, and her two children—who were visiting at the time.

Even as Wright experienced the despair of bereavement, he busied himself with the restoration of the Taliesin living quarters as family and friends rallied around in his support—including Harry Robinson, who chose to stand by Wright rather than join Walter and Marion Mahony Griffin in Australia.[309] Since a majority of the design work for the larger commissions—Midway Gardens, A.D. German Warehouse, Imperial Hotel, Little Chicago Theater—was carried out by Wright and his revolving staff at Taliesin, Robinson was mainly responsible for supervising the construction of residences in the Chicago area. During 1915, this responsibility would have involved the Ravine Bluffs Housing Development.

Sherman M. Booth, Jr., Ravine Bluffs Development—Glencoe, Illinois (1915)

The Ravine Bluffs Housing Development represents a redesign of the property originally set aside for the Sher-

man Booth Project of 1911–1912. Whether due to an overextended budget or other factors, Booth was unable to construct the mansion Wright designed for him or to proceed with the grounds development as laid out and designed by Jensen. In 1915, therefore, Booth contracted to have the property subdivided so as to accommodate a number of homes, in addition to his own residence.

The circulation layout for this subdivision exhibits none of the free-form creativity of the original park layout, where the sensory perception of the entry experience took precedence over all else. Here, the emphasis was upon fiscally feasible development. There are two relatively straight-line roads that bisect the property: Meadow Road (north-south) and Sylvan Road (east-west) (Figure 4-30). Meadow Road most probably fol-

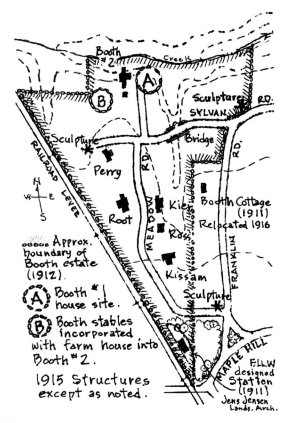

Figure 4-30 Conjectured map of Sherman M. Booth Ravine Bluffs Development in Glencoe, Illinois, 1915. (*By Charles E. Aguar, based on USGS Map, Hlighland Park, Illinois Quadrangle, 1926 edition. As delineated, © 2002 by Berdeana Aguar.*)

lows the access route as it originally was cut through for the existing farmhouse, an assumption based upon the way it generally traverses across the most level and easily negotiated portion of the property. Sylvan Road enters the property at the same point Jensen had placed the vehicular gateway into the original park but was laid out straightforwardly, rather than curving up the slope to overlook the primary ravine. Thus, the cost for bridge structuring was substantially lowered. One of the two railway waiting stations designed by Wright was erected at the intersection of the east and west boundaries of the property within a triangular railway park designed by Jensen, and Wright's three distinctive concrete sculpture gateway features also were constructed.[310]

The plans for Booth's personal residence were laid out with an eye toward cost management, as well. The stable and chauffeur's quarters with garage were moved to the area of the existing farmhouse near the edge of the escarpment, and these disparate structures were merged into one large residence. Booth also built four rental homes within the subdivision, assumedly to generate income to offset the costs of development. These were situated in the area set aside on Jensen's Planting Plan as the large formal garden for vegetables and cutting flowers. Purportedly, Wright's office did not supervise the construction of these houses, but their interesting siting, spacing, and variety in orientation suggest that someone—probably Robinson—may have been involved to some degree. In the end, although Ravine Bluffs Development does not literally

"preserve" the sensitive sylvan environment of the 15-acre site as open space, all of the ravines have been retained in a natural, parklike state and the neighborhood environment generally is much more amenable than most urban subdivisions.

Henry J. Allen—Wichita, Kansas (1915)

The single-family residence commissioned by Henry J. Allen of Wichita, Kansas, is generally characterized as Wright's last Prairie House (Figure 4-31). This connotation is based upon such physiognomic features as the porte-cochere extension, pronounced water table, expansive hip roof, chimney mass, and broad overhanging eaves—with the underside surfaced in an integrally colored ocher plaster to reflect light into the windows. There also are several built-in, zinc-lined planter boxes under the expansions of windows on both levels. Then, there are the raked horizontal brick joints, piers, and brick masses—here interspersed between every grouping of two windows and/or French doors that privatize the living areas.[311] Although this treatment completely changed the banding imagery of windows under the eaves within the context of Wright's other Prairie House layouts, the element of horizontality was not significantly compromised because of the narrowness and uniform placement of the brick masses.[312] At the same time, there are decided stylistic differences that reflect the transitional status of Wright's design process and most heedfully ally with his Japanese mind-set at this juncture in his life.

Figure 4-31 View near entry at southeast corner of Henry J. Allen House (1915) in Wichita, Kansas. (*Photograph courtesy of Wichita Eagle/Wichita Beacon, Wichita, Kansas.*)

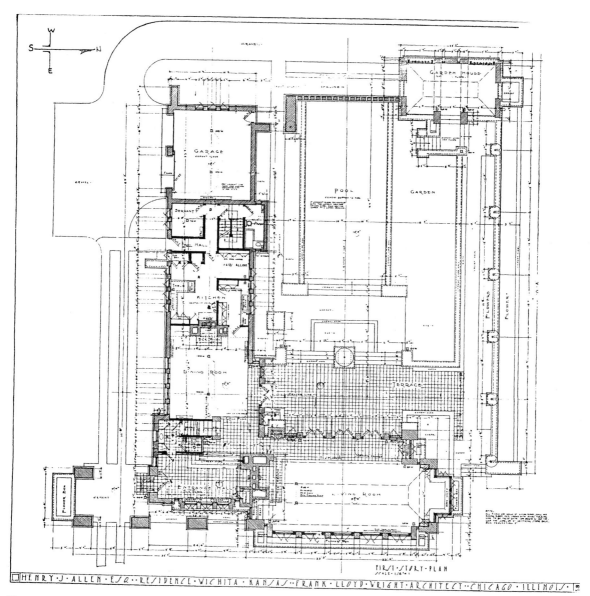

Figure 4-32 Ground plan for the Allen House. (© *by The Frank Lloyd Wright Foundation, Scottsdale, Arizona.*)

To begin with, the Allen House layout is very atypical for a Prairie House. The two wings of the living quarters are arranged in an "L" around an inner courtyard-garden, with the two-story wing over a basement defining the south boundary and the single-story living room wing defining the east boundary (Figure 4-32). A walled promenade defines the north boundary and a garden house plus privacy wall the west boundary. All of the enclosing elements are of the same brick material and are scaled proportionately so as to not completely cut off the outside world. All structural and spatial elements are laid out in a sukiya-like organization on a 3-foot grid, the same grid as the Kyoto tatami mats (roughly 3 feet by 6 feet).[313] And there is no obvious central axis. Indeed, all structures and garden elements are balanced asymmetrically—even the large sunken reflecting pool that is the dominant landscape element of the courtyard-garden. Moreover, the concrete urns are not placed at terminal points as with other of Wright's Prairie Houses, but are used to emphasize specific points of concentration in the courtyard or are placed in a row atop the promenade privacy walls, which are scaled to include the urns with plantings in place, as was done at Midway Gardens.

Another important consideration in Wright's Allen House design was the physical and functional interdependency between the interior and exterior spaces, as well as the psychological intimacy brought about by the spatial ratio between the building coverage (22 percent) and the enclosed area of the courtyard-garden (44 percent). Here, there was no separation in the design of house and garden, no adaptation of garden to house after construction was complete—in the occidental tradition. Nor was the garden laid out in the manner of the classical European gardens, where geometric patterns are best recognized and appreciated from a bird's eye perspective. Rather, the whole composition was laid out and designed in the Oriental tradition as one indivisible space, and as it was to be viewed through the sequentiality of movement through space, whether that movement took place within the shelter of the house or within the realm of the courtyard. Indeed, the lines of interior and exterior circulation *controlled* the three-dimensional visual unfolding of Wright's plan—beginning with the entry experience, which originated outside the front door under protection of the porte-cochere, whether arrival was by foot or vehicle.

The front door opens into an exceptionally spacious entrance hall. The quarry tile floor surfacing that starts at the entrance visually directs movement from ground level to the elevated level of the first floor where there is a central lobby at the vortex of the intersection of the wings. There is no pronounced sense of enclosure, because there are no walls or doors separating the lobby from the living areas. There is only a bookcase built into the corner of the vortex to obscure immediate views into the out-of-doors. But the visual consistency of the floor surfacing invites movement into either the living room or the dining room. It is not until movement proceeds past this point of intersection and into one of these primary living areas that the full impact of Wright's design intent is experienced, by way of the dramatic upward and outward expansion of space created by the vaulted ceilings and the banks of French doors that open onto the commodious terrace rectangle—which completely fills in the right angle of exterior space formed by the juncture of the two wings and is surfaced the same as the interior spaces. Upon entering either the living room or dining room, therefore, the primal focus is visual interaction with the out-of-doors.

By purposefully elevating the first floor level a minimal 2 feet above grade, as he did, Wright created the means to introduce a sense of anticipation into the entry experience through the act of ascending steps to reach the central lobby. This treatment also created the means to introduce controlled dimensional interest and depth into the inherent levelness of the bounded inner space of the courtyard by way of the Japanese-inspired process of horizontal "layering," as explained by Messervy: "Eastern tradition uses horizontal lines to 'layer' space: to create a sense of foreground, middleground, and background that is useful in making a small space seem much larger."[314] There is the elevated level of the terrace that facilitates movement from the terrace at the northeast corner of the courtyard, through the contained garden beds on either side of the walls, to the garden house destination point at the northwest corner of the courtyard.

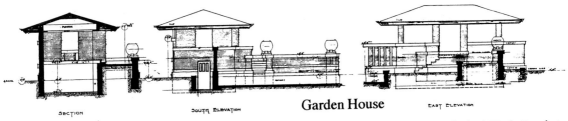

Figure 4-33   Sections through centerlines of garden and garden house at Allen estate. (© *by The Frank Lloyd Wright Foundation, Scottsdale, Arizona.*)

This level is directly accessible to both the first floor and the paved promenade. There is the sheltering overhead plane of the hip roof on the garden house that is elevated above the promenade level so as to provide a better prospect from a sitting position for looking out over the courtyard-garden.[315] (Figure 4-33). There also are the incidental levels of the masonry slabs and brick piers with built-in planters, the large masonry urns, and the masonry edging for the areas of planting containment on the terrace and at ground level—where there is the subliminal level of the sunken reflective pool (Figure 4-34). This lowering of the pool allows a more perceptive observation of the water lilies and koi fish—as well as the myriad of reflections generated by clouds, sunlight, textures, and shadows—when moving along the paved walkway at ground level. Thus, the entire open space "garden" represents an artful juxtapositioning of horizontal planes of hardscape construction, with the shape and placement of planting containment detailed throughout and patterns of movement carefully choreographed for effect.

There is no record that a planting plan or planting list ever was prepared for the Allen House, although Wright apparently had at some time agreed to do so. This is supported by Allen's observation in his January 1918 letter to Wright: "I would like to have the planting list for the garden; but I do not see any hope of getting it in time for spring as you have promised."[316] Howard W.

Ellington, executive director and restoration architect for the Allen House, believes that plantings in the end were selected by the Allens' gardener.[317] The lack of a planting list would seem to be a minor consideration, however, compared to Wright's continuous inattention to construction details for the Allen House because of his preoccupation with the Imperial Hotel. The first indication that Allen was apprehensive about the limited amount of attention Wright was giving the house was raised in his letter of November 13, 1916: "I enclose herewith the check desired by you. This, as I understand it, is a portion of the fee covering compensation for supervision of the work. I know, of course, that advance payment will not in any sense reduce your interest in the work. I am obliged to be away a good deal and I am going to add a word urging you to answer Shuler's [sic] letters on all subjects as promptly as possible."[318] Allen's concerns were well-founded, because Wright set sail for Japan the very next month—on December 28, 1916— and did not return to the United States until five months later—on May 17, 1917.[319]

Assumedly, Wright made arrangements for the working drawings and specifications to be completed during his absence, since these were provided to the Allens almost immediately upon his return. It is not known who was assigned this responsibility, but whomever it was failed to notate north point indicators on any of the plans. This grievous error caused problems when the plans were

Figure 4-34 Photograph shows horizontal "layering" that introduces controlled dimensional depth to Allen House courtyard. (*Archival photograph courtesy of Cooper-Hewitt National Design Museum, Smithsonian Institution / Art Resources, New York.*)

presented to contractors and subcontractors for the purpose of procuring bids. As they were prepared in standard plan layout format, the contractors must have presumed—logically—that north was at the top of the page and south at the bottom of the page. Not only is this orientation "standard," it is the orientation that was reflected in the labeling on the Allen House elevations. In point of fact, however, these plans misrepresent the true orientational alignment by exactly ninety degrees. The environmental consequence of the misorientation is that the terrace and the wall of French doors in the living room face due west rather than south, while the beneficial southern exposure is lavished upon the bedrooms, dining room, kitchen and maid quarters, the porte-cochere, garage, and basement. Furthermore, the two-story mass of the bedroom wing impedes the prevailing south-southwest breezes during the months of summer, so they only indirectly benefit the living room and terrace.

Ellington suggests that some of the confusion during the drafting process may have occurred because the William *Allen* White remodeling project for Emporia, Kansas, and the Henry J. *Allen* project for Wichita, Kansas, were evolving roughly at the same time.[320] Moreover, he does not believe the misorientation compromised the architecture: "Despite the mislabeling of the orientation, the house is placed on the site as Wright had intended for cross ventilation and automobile access. The two-story wing is correctly placed to provide cross-ventilation to the bedrooms . . . and provide visual privacy to the garden courtyard . . . from the neighboring 2-story house on the south."[321] Ellington also does not believe the misorientation minimized the effectiveness of Wright's unique convection ventilating towers, a refashioned version of a thermal chimney that tied into the stairwell and bathroom: "Operable interior clerestory windows above the bedroom wardrobe units allowed the air to flow from the south, across the bedroom, and exit above the closet through the interior windows; and they flow out through the hallway windows on the north."

Nevertheless, Allen's January 2, 1918 letter to Wright leaves little doubt that in his mind, at least, any errors that occurred related directly to Wright's continued inattentiveness: "I never met a fellow that I like any better than I do you. I have never enjoyed a day of companionship with any man as much as I enjoyed the day I spent with you in Chicago. I have never seen anybody in whose good intentions I had any more faith; and I have never met a man concerning whose probability to do the things he says he is going to do I have so little faith. . . . I desire to say entirely without rancor, that you are the most inveterate and scientific neglector [sic] of your clients that I have ever known. I haven't a very wide acquaintance with architects, but from what I know of you I would be willing to put you up as the champion neglector of the world."[322]

In spite of the problems with the plans and the client's frustrations, the Allen House upon its completion in 1918 manifested one of Wright's most artfully balanced gardens and harmoniously choreographed transitions between his architecture and the cultivated landscape. Indeed, the Allen House more than any other house built in the intervening years was as much a step toward the more modest Usonian layouts of the mid-1900s as it was a step away from the Prairie house. It is easy to understand why Wright referred to it as "among my best."[323]

The Allen House has been maintained as a single-family residence and retains the basic character of Wright's original design intent, with the exception of the garden house, which was enclosed by adding casement windows and glass doors approximately 12 years after the house was built, according to Ellington. In the late 1980s, subsequent owner A. W. Kincade bequeathed the house and grounds to Wichita State University, from whom The Allen-Lambe House Foundation purchased the property in 1990.[324] Since that time, the property has been maintained by the Foundation as "The Allen-Lambe House Museum and Study Center." Restoration of the house, gardens, and its interior is an ongoing process.

Wright's appointment as architect of the Imperial Hotel was not officially confirmed until Aisaku Hayashi, the hotel manager, arrived at Taliesin in February 1916 and the final details of Wright's contract were negotiated. Remarkably, Wright had been working on the design of this edifice for some three years merely on the basis of the original notification of his appointment. There were, in fact, well-advanced drawings in process by the time Antonin Raymond arrived at Taliesin in early spring 1916.[325]

Wright first experienced the subtropical climate of southern California during the winter of 1914–1915 when he traveled to San Diego to attend the Panama California International Exhibition and to visit son Lloyd, a landscape architect, who had been living in California since Fall 1911 when Olmsted and Olmsted sent him to work in the nursery they established to provide plant material for the Exhibition.[326] In *An Autobiography*, Wright noted the effect of bright sunshine on the "Yankeefied houses . . . defiant as ever they were in the mud and snows back there midwest at zero . . . [that] looked even more hard in perpetual sunshine where all need of their practical offensive defenses had disappeared entirely."[327] And he described the sun-baked countryside as it must have appeared before the onset of development: "What a poetic thing this land was. . . . Curious tan-gold foothills rise from tattooed sand-stretches to join slopes spotted as the leopard-skin with grease-bush. This foreground spreads to distances so vast—human scale is utterly lost."[328] He observed that "water comes . . . as a deluge once a year to surprise the roofs, sweep the sands into ripples and roll boulders along in the gashes, washes combed by sudden streams in the desert. Then—all sun-baked as before." And he was aware that the "neatly shaved lawns of their little town lots" were "kept green by great mountain reservoirs." Thus, when Aline Barnsdall—the oil heiress and patroness of the arts for whom Wright already was developing preliminary drawings for a theater in Chicago—decided to move her project to California, Wright had at least some perception of climatic conditions upon which to base the changes this move might have upon his design process. Barnsdall's decision had even more relevance when she expanded Wright's commission to include her personal residence.

ENVIRONMENTAL DESIGNS, 1916–1923

Aline Barnsdall's Hollyhock House— Los Angeles, California (1916–1921)

It appears Wright began developing the plans for Barnsdall's "Hollyhock House," as it came to be known, some three years prior to the June 23, 1919, date when she acquired the East Hollywood property upon which the residence would be built. This origination date is corrob-

orated by Antonin Raymond, who included Barnsdall's plans among those he saw on the drafting boards at Taliesin in Spring 1916.[329]

When the bird's-eye perspective of Hollyhock House represented as having been rendered in 1916–1918 is compared with the perspective prepared after construction was well underway in 1921, the details of conformance are striking—as to the proportion and situation of outdoor living spaces; the number of steps on terraces; the incidence of openings on exterior walls; the placement, height, length, and curvature of privacy walls; and the arrangement of plantings. Thus, it seems credible to conclude that what differences there were had more to do with detail and refinement than the sum and substance of a design rationale—which Wright himself never described except as he idealistically, if inaccurately, represented it in his autobiography: "As I have said of Taliesin, Hollyhock House was to be a natural house in the changed circumstances and naturally built; native to the region of California."[330]

Wright did indeed design an architecture "responsive" to the climatic conditions of southern California[331] (Figure 5-1). However, because he was urged by his client to undertake a basically conceptual design approach for a house that could be built on any site she might select at some future date, he did so with no knowledge of the phenomena of the landscape—land form, elevational changes, geological patterns, soils, vegetation, microclimate, or existing natural features—on which it eventually would be built. He also had no way of knowing if there would be a need for privacy screening or any potential for scenic views. Therefore, his end product had to be specific to the client but adaptable to any given site in the Los Angeles area, whether that site was in a developed urban area or on rural acreage, and whether the site had level or sloping terrain. Thus, the architecture that evolved could not "appear to grow easily from its site to sympathize with the surroundings," as advocated by Wright during his notable speeches of 1894 and 1901. But it could appear as "a work of Art," such as he described during a speech he delivered in 1900 to the Architectural League of the Art Institute of Chicago: "A work of Architecture is a great coordination with a distinct and vital organism, but it is in no sense naturalistic—it is the highest, most subjective conventionalization of Nature known to man, and at the same time it must be organically true to Nature when it is really a work of Art."[332]

As has been pointed out by many authors, the architectural grammar of Hollyhock House exhibits design characteristics associated with indigenous construction found in the American Southwest and the ancient Mayan culture—including his layout for wings of rooms to be arranged around an interior quadrangle of open space, the small windows, flat roof, and his proposed use of concrete as the primary building material. But these features also are in keeping with kindred architecture found in North Africa, Central Asia, China, Italy, Greece, and southern Spain. Architecture historian Calvin Straub provides a rationale for why climatic conditions inspired so many similar and/or identical characteristics in the architecture for these widely distributed geographical areas: "Flat roofs (no rain); thick mud and stone walls and domed roofs (heat insulation and little structural timber); small windows and openings (glare and heat control); shaded porches and walled 'oasis' gardens (protection from hot, dry winds); and, in general, introverted, protective environments. . . . This concept of creating an internalized, protected, and humanly enjoyable shelter by designing their structures around these 'oasis' open spaces and courts is their major response to the need for shelter."[333]

Wright's demonstrative use of the cast concrete "hollyhock" ornamentation allies with another design characteristic of Mediterranean architecture. It is well known

that the inspirational form of the hollyhock ornamentation rooted from Barnsdall's fondness for the flower. However, the repetitious manner in which Wright used it—as abstract capitals on the courtyard columns and planters, as finials projecting from the roof, and as ornamental bands applied on otherwise plain exterior walls—undoubtedly was motivated for the reasoning put forth by Straub for Mediterranean architecture: "The brilliant sunlight stimulated the development of ornamentation of the buildings that responded to the strong play of shade and shadow on their sculptural forms."[334] And Wright's manner of sloping the roof parapets inward to prevent visual distortion is a refinement representative of Greek vernacular architecture. Other characteristics of kindred vernacular architecture are his manner of insetting windows and doors to lessen the penetrating impact of the brilliant sun, his introduction of prominent stairway accesses to the roof, and his proposed development of roof gardens as places to stroll and enjoy the cool evening breezes. Even the inordinate depth of the many sizable built-in planters presumably was based upon the need to provide for more copious water retention in California than required in the Midwest, where the planters Wright designed were decidedly more shallow. Lastly, his introduction of a fountain-pool, stream-and-water garden within the realm of the garden court is a design enhancement indigenous to Morocco and Spain. "Water is one of the main features of these gardens," explains Straub. "Used carefully and sparingly because of its scarcity, it is both

Figure 5-1 Bird's-eye perspective of Aline Barnsdall's Hollyhock House (1916–1921) in Los Angeles, California. (© 2002 by The Frank Lloyd Wright Foundation, Scottsdale, Arizona.)

visually delightful and functional in helping to cool the air by sprays and channels of water that flow through . . . the courts, sometimes into the interior of the houses as well."[335] This latter concept allies with Wright's introduction of a reflecting pool around the hearth of the living room fireplace at Hollyhock House.

Because Wright was required to interweave Hollyhock House onto a man-made landscape of his own visualization, the issues of "privacy" and "control" were his primary concerns. Therefore, access to sweeping prospects were limited to the various terraces and rooftop overlooks; the banks of floor-to-ceiling windows or French doors only overlooked or accessed the courtyard and the outdoor living spaces under his architectural control; and all outdoor living spaces were circumscribed with privacy walls or parapets topped by planters, so as to be physically separated and visually screened from ostensible exterior intrusion (Figure 5-2). For all other exterior walls, Wright limited the use of windows except as a means to introduce natural light: by tucking bands of narrow windows under the eaves; by introducing skylights (not all of which would be installed); and by using art-glass windows with frosted glass, except for the most elevated panes. For example, Wright proposed no windows at all along the length of the living room on either side. And the living room focal point was not the view through the only glazed wall in the room; it was the bas-relief of art-stone that sets off the massive fireplace. That this was Wright's intent is supported by the situation of the fireplace on an exterior wall, by the end-to-end arrangement of the room, by the strong illuminating emphasis of the large skylight directly above the hearth, by the reflecting pool encircling the hearth, and by the grand assemblage of custom-designed furniture—angled and arranged as an intimate space to direct attention toward the fireplace as a feature.

As with the Allen House, the whole composition of Hollyhock House was laid out as it was to be viewed through the sequentiality of movement through space. Unlike the Allen House, however—where the raised

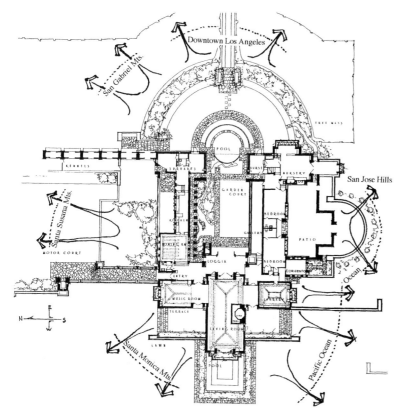

Figure 5-2 The floor plan for Hollyhock House was designed for privacy control, with prospects limited to terraces. (*By Charles E. Aguar, based on historic photographs, personal analysis, and original drawings of record. © 2002 by The Frank Lloyd Wright Foundation, Scottsdale, Arizona. As delineated, © 2002 by Berdeana Aguar.*)

living room wing and the horizontal layering of the court-yard levels had to do with enhancing the visual prospect—the raised levels at Hollyhock House had more to do with the physical and psychological interrelationship between the primary living spaces and the garden court. Wright not only raised the levels of all the living wings, he staggered their degree of above-grade elevation and proportionately raised the levels of all the contiguous outdoor living spaces as well—including the level of the garden court itself and the level of the exedra gathering space outside its realm. Each of the living wings, in turn, has a transition space designed to facilitate this interrelationship with the garden court—either by way of a colonnade, pergola, loggia, or bridged open space.

The colonnade serves as the transition space for the dining-service wing and functions as an open hallway leading from the living wing to the servants' quarters, or as a pathway to the performance area. Because all of the service rooms are physically separated from the colonnade by solid walls, only the dining room allies with the colonnade and the garden court. This alliance was vivified by Wright's manner of lowering the colonnade to the level of the garden court, his use of clear glazing in the four pairs of French doors that line the colonnade side of the dining room, his alignment of the door openings to correspond with openings between the columns of the colonnade, and his situation of the proposed water garden alongside the colonnade to encourage views outward into the garden court.

The pergola serves as the transition space for the bedroom wing and functions as a gallery and hallway leading from the living wing to the suite of rooms that comprise the nursery, the stairway leading to Barnsdall's quarters directly above, or the pathway to the performance area. However, its atypical width, its walled separation from the guest bedrooms and nursery suite, its glazed ceiling and wall enclosure, its design as a trellised garden feature with beams spaced to conform to every other pillar in the colonnade, and indeed its "pergola" designation—all support that Wright intended it to be viewed and experienced as an integral element of the garden court.

The loggia that parallels the primary living wing was planned to function in a combination of ways. Because of its placement in the center of the living wing hall, it functions as a crossroads of sorts for the entire structure. Because it was configured under roof and is considerably wider than the hall at either end, it functions as living-entertainment space, as well. At the same time, however, it psychologically allies with the garden court because Wright enclosed it in a manner suggestive of the out-of-doors. Specifically, he replicated the arrangement of French doors and fixed art-glass side panels on the opposing exterior wall of the living room at the point where the interior wall separates the loggia from the living room. He also introduced wall-to-wall folding glass doors across the exterior facade of the loggia. And he installed a large exterior-style planter on the inside of the loggia to interrelate with the stairs leading to the pergola. Even the "loggia" designation affiliates with the out-of-doors. Thus, the loggia functions as the intervening space where the atmosphere of the living wing merges with the atmosphere of the garden court—even when the folding doors are closed. When the doors are open, it serves as a transition space between the living wing and the widely extended steps that ascend into the openness of the garden court.

The bridged open space at the far end of the garden court functions as a stage, but it also serves as the transition space between the garden court and the exedra gathering space immediately outside the performance area. That this exedra gathering space, in turn, was seen by Wright as the destination focal point of the garden experience is supported by his manner of treatment—that is, the prominence of the fountain-pool feature, the tiered encircling arrangement of the exedra, the elevation and depth of the surrounding grassed strolling area, and the denseness of the forestlike backdrop (pine grove) that circumscribes the entire open space to both visually and representationally assimilate it into the realm of the garden court.

The result of Wright's emphasis on outdoor living space at Hollyhock House is worthy of note. The space allocated to terraces, patios, and garden court computes to 2.5 times that allocated to usable indoor living space. If the open space for the exedra gathering space arrangement is factored in, this ratio increases to 3.5 times. And, if the proposed roof garden also is included, the space allocated to outdoor living equates to approximately five times the usable indoor living space. It was through this all-inclusive, indoor-outdoor design approach that Wright created the "half house and half garden" structure that Barnsdall maintained was what "Mr. Wright believes that a California house should be," when she unveiled Wright's visionary drawings to the press in July 1919 and announced her acquisition of the Olive Hill property on which she intended to build her home and theater.[336]

Aline Barnsdall's Olive Hill Development— Los Angeles, California (1919–1924)

Olive Hill is a conspicuous mesa-like plateau that stands out from the levelness of the surrounding terrain because of its approximate one-hundred-foot elevation. Its name derives from the groves of olive trees planted on its slopes some 30 years earlier during the agricultural development boom that succeeded the proliferative building of irrigation projects in the western states during the late 1800s. When the Hollywood District was subdivided into the rectangular system established for the western United States, the hill was nearly centered in a quarter-quarter section of land. By the time Barnsdall acquired the tract, the usable land was slightly more than 35 acres. Since East Hollywood was not highly developed in 1919, there were unimpeded panoramic views from Olive Hill toward the Santa Susana Mountains to the north, the San Gabriel Mountains to the

northeast, the Santa Monica Mountains to the northwest, the San Jose Hills to the south, the city of Los Angeles to the southeast, and the Pacific Ocean 11 miles to the southwest. There also was a dirt road system already in place for servicing the olive groves, which might only need to be widened and paved to access Hollyhock House, the theater, and any other structures Barnsdall might decide to add in the future (Figure 5-3).

Because of its aesthetic singularity and easy accessibility, Olive Hill had been used as a site for Easter sunrise services for a number of years and was looked upon in somewhat of a public-private connotation. Perhaps it was for this reason that Barnsdall proposed a similar public-private usage as she promulgated her plans to develop the property. She also informed the press that the theater would be built on the east slope facing Vermont Avenue and her house would occupy the plateau, an area of approximately two acres where there was less than a 5-foot differential in elevation

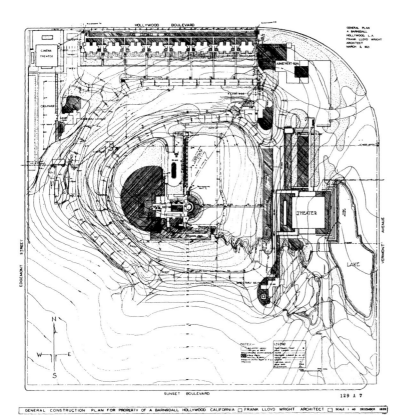

Figure 5-3 General construction plan for Aline Barnsdall's Olive Hill Development (1919–1924) in Los Angeles, California. (© 2002 by The Frank Lloyd Wright Foundation, Scottsdale, Arizona.)

over the entire surface.[337] Thus, when Wright met with Barnsdall in Los Angeles after returning to the United States in early September 1919, his client already had made unilateral decisions that would direct his development of the built landscape, as she had effected his method of designing her residence prior to site selection. She also may have made the decision to work with the existing service road system, although the ground-hugging circuitry and six reverse curves would not have been incompatible with Wright's design philosophy as to the choreography of entry experiences—which, in this case, he would have conceptualized as originating at the base of the hill at the point of entry onto the property.

It is significant that the entire top surface of the plateau was spread with the low, brushlike chaparral overgrowth characteristic to southern California. Indeed, the nonpresence of olive trees in this area substantiates that local orcharders were well aware that hill crowns are much hotter and dryer than the slopes because of consistent exposure to the combined effects of sun and air circulation and that these conditions were exacerbated where there are broad areas of levelness. They also would have known that anything planted on the plateau would be more vulnerable to the desiccating effect of the Santa Ana winds, a local annual phenomenon caused by hot, dry winds that blow from the east or northeast between October and February. Climatologist Gayther Plummer summarizes the conditions that precipitate this natural event:

> "There is a constant high pressure system that sits over the ocean off the coast of Los Angeles. The winds generated by this high pressure system move in a clockwise circulation pattern that draws the winds from the Mohave Desert to southern California. Santa Ana winds develop when a region of high pressure builds over the Great Basin—a high plateau east of the Sierra mountains and west of the Rocky mountains—and forces the winds downslope. These winds start out warm and dry, but they become even warmer and dryer due to compressional heating as they blow through the canyons of the mountains and descend into the Los Angeles Basin, where they end up with relative humidity in the single digits. This causes the brush-like vegetation to dry out even more so that even tiny fires can be whipped up into roaring conflagrations.[338]

Since Wright first visited the Los Angeles area during the winter months, it must be assumed he was at least somewhat aware of this climatic condition and that he and/or his client gave consideration to the disadvantages of siting the house on top of the plateau, as well as the advantage of panoramic views. On the other hand, since the ocean breeze typically blows onshore from the west-southwest during the late morning and afternoon hours and the inland breeze from the north-northeast predominates during the night and morning hours, the more-or-less constant air circulation may have been thought of as advantageous to natural ventilation—*if* the inherent drying effect of the Santa Ana winds could be adequately tempered.

Wright would have a brief two-and-one-half months to adapt the existing plans to the Olive Hill site prior to his scheduled departure for his fourth trip to Japan in mid-December. He asked Vienna-trained architect Rudolph M. Schindler to work with him and also prevailed upon his son Lloyd to return to California and devote full time to developing planting plans for the entire property. Lloyd's responsibilities also included supervising grading and construction, and serving as Wright's liaison with the client as he traveled back and forth between Japan and the United States at roughly six-month intervals.[339] Bringing the expertise of a landscape designer into this process would be one of the most important decisions Wright would make during this time frame. Lloyd at this time was working in his father's Chicago office but, because of his years of experience of having worked in the Los Angeles area, he already had developed a working relationship with local contractors and sources for building materials.[340] More important, he was abreast of which drought-resistant plant materials would best acclimate to local conditions, and he was knowledgeable about landscape design specificities, water hydrology, and the complexities of working under jurisdiction of a water irrigation district (see Appendix J.).

It does not appear that Wright made site-specific alterations to the existing plans before turning them over to Schindler and Lloyd. The only obvious adjustments have to do with the area of the motor court—where there was a ninety-degree rotation of the three-car garage from the side to the end of the motor court and a shifting of the driveway connection. Wright established his major axis by aligning the living room, garden court, terminal pools, and exedra arrangement with the east-west centerline of the block (Figure 5-4). This organization aligned the pathway leading from the exedra through the pine grove, with the grid opening between two rows of olive trees where Wright proposed to position the steps that were to stretch all the way downslope to the service road upon which the theater was to be built.[341] Curiously, these steps do not correspond with the axis for the theater—which aligns with an opening 20 feet to the south. Even more curious is the fact that this siting placed the entire length and width of the motor court, garage, and animal pen arrangement within the parameters of the plateau, but *not* the terminal areas at either end of the main axis. Had Wright proportionately decreased the length of the motor court and animal pens or adapted the southern-most indoor and outdoor living spaces to step down the slope in conformance with the natural contours, this problem would have ended at the drawing board. The environmental consequence of not making appropriate site-specific adjustments was that 31 olive trees nearest the parameters of the plateau had to be removed—increasing by 10 percent the number of trees (approximately 300) lost to construction during development of the property. Moreover, a 60-foot retaining wall had to be constructed across the south slope to retain the thousands of cubic yards of fill brought in to artificially raise this area to the elevation of the plateau and modulate a natural-appearing slope leading down to the wall. This retaining wall is at least 12 feet high at the southwest-ernmost corner where it angles back into the slope.[342]

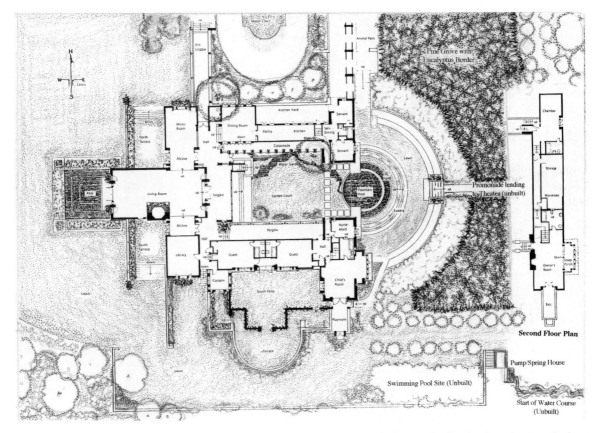

Figure 5-4 Floor plan for Aline Barnsdall's Olive Hill residence, based on general planting plan by Lloyd Wright. (*By Charles E. Aguar, based on historic photographs, personal analysis, and original drawings of record. © 2002 by Frank Lloyd Wright Foundation, Scottsdale, Arizona. As delineated, © 2002 by Berdeana Aguar.*)

It is not known to what extent Lloyd influenced his father with respect to any of these design modifications or those subsequently made relative to local climatic conditions, but it certainly appears that Wright relied upon Lloyd's environmental professionalism in some of these areas. For example, on the early 1919 detail layout of Hollyhock House, the pine grove encircling the performance area is depicted merely as aesthetic background screening; its proposed form even echoes the curvature of the fountain-pool. However, the pine grove depicted on the 1920 General Construction Plan, as well as the General Planting Plan developed under Lloyd's direction, extends northward to essentially bound the entire east perimeter of the plateau and is completely circumscribed by a double row of eucalyptus trees, planted 10-feet-on-center.[343] All of these changes—the tree selection, density of planting, and east-to-north directional bounding aspects of the expanded grove—were based on function rather than, or in addition to, aesthetics.

The Italian Stone Pine (*Pinus pinea*), a native Mediterranean conifer that constituted the greater mass of the grove, was reportedly selected by Barnsdall because she admired its uniqueness; it has an asymmetrical, umbrella-like head. The Blue Gum Eucalyptus (*Eucalyptus globulus*), a broadleaf evergreen imported from Australia, presumably was selected by Wright; he described eucalyptus trees as "adding beauty to the olive-green and ivory white of an exotic symphony in silvered gold and rose-purple."[344] Even so, both most probably were among tree species recommended by Lloyd for specific functional requirements. This reasoning is supported by the fact that both of these trees are naturally drought-resistant and hardy enough to withstand the arid conditions of southern California. Moreover, neither tree discards leaves and/or needles from the past season until new growth is formed so the moisture they release into the air is consistent year-round. And since their lower trunks are devoid of branches, their introduction into the landscape would not impede air circulation. It was precisely because of air circulation that the pine-eucalyptus grove, like the olive grove, was planted in orderly rows rather than massed. This arrangement facilitates the "channeling" of air movement, as opposed to impeding air circulation in the function of a windbreak in the Midwest. Thus, the functional purpose of the pine-eucalyptus grove meets the criteria dictated by climatic conditions relevant to this specific site: (1) to add consequential moisture to the air, (2) to temper the combined desiccating effects of the sun and the Santa Ana winds, and (3) to "sustain" the cooling benefit of air circulation. Moreover, the importance placed upon the implementation of this landscape feature is supported by the fact that this was one of the first areas detailed by Lloyd, three months prior to the ground breaking for the residence.[345]

The cumulative evaporative effect of the combined surfaces of the stream proposed for the courtyard, the ornamental pools off the living room and in the performance area, and the two swimming pools for the screened areas on either side of the exedra gathering space—as well as the spray emitted by the fountain—are all significant to moderating the plateau microclimate. And there was the noteworthy choice of grass as the surfacing material for all of the terraces and patios and for most of the surface area on the tiers of the exedra, as well as the proposed use of gravel, crushed rock, plantings, or other permeable surfacing in the area of the motor court. Permeable surfacing allows ground water recharge and avoids heat concentration associated with hard-surface pavement. Had impermeable surfacing been used to a significant degree in any of these areas, the inherent conditions of heat and aridity would have been worsened.

None of the site improvements proposed for Hollyhock House would have been supportable, of course, without adequate irrigation. Thus, a well-thought-out irrigation system was a requisite feature in Lloyd's design of the site infrastructure. It also was essential to further property development, particularly as hydrology—water and water play—was the dominant mediating element in Wright's design for the intervening landscape between the house and theater (Figure 5-5). This watercourse was intended to create an omnipresent ambiance such as Wright would have experienced in Italy at the Villa d'Este, except he proposed that it be laid out in a naturally evolving manner. Originating at the pump house, the water course is shown wending its way down the slope in a meandering, episodic mode so the progression of special and spatial experiences would elicit anticipation, suspense, and surprise. Walkways, steps, and bridges leading from level to level interweave with an alternately widening and narrowing waterway that was to intermittently riffle, surge, drip, gush, spray, and splash in the form of a water garden, fountain, another swimming pool, waterfalls, and cascades until it reached the base of the hill and formed the tranquil man-made lake in the open space separating the theater and Vermont Avenue.[346] This imaginative water landscape was one of the most auspiciously articulated such features ever designed for a Wright site—both as to sensitivity and functionality. Had it been implemented as proposed, it would have become the character-defining feature of the hillside. It also would have nurtured an extraordinary amount of plantings and introduced such copious amounts of moisture into the air across such a broad expanse of space that the microclimate of the plateau and the entire southeastern slope would have become eminently more environmentally satisfying. However, the impracticality of the proposed treatment becomes obvious when climatic conditions inherent to the area are reasonably considered—that is, there is a high propensity for earthquakes and the annual precipitation is minimal, so there is insufficient "natural" water source to actualize the process.

Any hopes Wright had of directing and controlling the site development became increasingly more difficult

following his mid-August 1920 meeting with Barnsdall in Los Angeles. The capricious client at that point decided she wanted to add additional structures, including commercial shops to be constructed along the main thoroughfares of Hollywood and Sunset Boulevards. Moreover, she had preestablished a budget and completion dates for each project. As Wright's December departure for Japan became imminent, Schindler was reassigned to California to continue detailing construction drawings, rather than from Taliesin, and take over supervision of the on-site construction of Hollyhock House and subsequent structures. This arrangement allowed Lloyd to concentrate on designing the expanded site infrastructure and planting plans, supervise their implementation, and continue on in his capacity as liaison during the critical next two years. Even so, with Wright in Japan—or en route to and from Los Angeles, Taliesin, or Chicago—and Barnsdall traveling hither-and-yon around the globe, the potential for communications

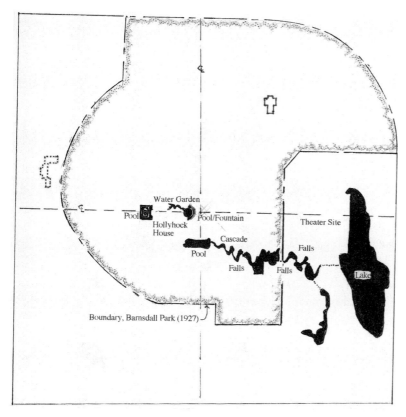

Figure 5-5 Diagram of water features proposed to circulate through southeast quadrant of Olive Hill site. (*By Charles E. Aguar, based on historic photographs, personal analysis, and original drawings of record. © 2002 by The Frank Lloyd Wright Archives, Scottsdale, Arizona. As delineated, © 2002 by Berdeana Aguar.*)

breakdown, confusion, and cost overruns was too great to be overcome. In the end, only Hollyhock House and Residences A and B were completed. Neither of the swimming pools on the plateau was installed. The hillside water landscape was not implemented. And the Hollyhock House rooftop was never developed as Wright envisioned the expansive open space in his early perspective—as a lush roof garden environment from which to view the scenic vistas. In fact, the leakage problems experienced with the flat rooftops at Hollyhock House foreshadowed the leaking flat roofs of Wright's subsequent textile block houses, for it was here that Wright first encountered the consequence of long periods of drought—during which every crack, crevice, and surface material contracts—succeeded by the sudden deluge of one of California's winter rainstorms.

The 1920 Block Plan served as a "master plan" of sorts for developing the entire acreage of the Olive Hill Development. Since it continued to be revised at the whim of Barnsdall, however, there is little to qualify Wright's Olive Hill as a planned community that integrated land and buildings, as some writers have suggested. By definition, "planned" communities are consciously created in response to clearly stated objectives. They are established by an organization with authority and sufficient funding to evaluate alternative sites; select and secure a site; assemble a planning team; prepare a long-range plan for infrastructure, roads, walkways, and structures for staged development; supervise incremental development; and exercise continued control until the community is "built out" to the planned viable size.[347] Although Barnsdall had ample funding to support elements of community development, there is no evidence that she and Wright ever discussed a set of objectives. There is more evidence to support that just the opposite occurred.

Aline Barnsdall deeded Hollyhock House and the upper slopes of Olive Hill to the City of Los Angeles in 1926; the property has since been known as Barnsdall Park. Over time, additional acreage has been made accessible to the public, but the inevitable encroachment of urbanized development has taken its toll with respect to the site environment. Since 1974, when Lloyd Wright was commissioned to direct a restoration of the house, attention has been directed toward ameliorating the deteriorated condition of the landscape—brought about by years of neglect. A comprehensive master plan

prepared by Peter Walker William Johnson and Partners in 1995 recognizes changing circumstances in social, economic, and environmental conditions and proposes specific strategies for restoring and refining the landscape. This outstanding effort awaits critical evaluation and analysis.

Wright returned to the United States on August 1, 1922 and to Taliesin shortly thereafter. His concern for the state of his affairs because of the extended time spent in Japan is reflected in his November 2, 1922 letter to Sullivan: "I am going to tell you a secret which I hope you will keep. I am extremely hard up—and not a job in sight in the world."[348]

In an effort to find some way to make a strong trend-setting statement that would attract nationwide attention, Wright resurrected the concept of creating an affordable architecture by developing a system of construction using concrete block as the primary building material. His thinking was that concrete block was the "cheapest (ugliest) thing in the building world" and "lived mostly in the architectural gutter. . . . Why not see what could be done with that gutter rat?"[349] Wright visualized the "textile block" concept as a means to introduce an esoteric and artistic quality of three dimensions in high contrast to the nondescript and utilitarian qualities of commercial concrete block. It should be noted, however, that Griffin introduced an interlocking construction system he called "Knitlock" that was patented in 1917, six years prior to the 1923 date on drawings Wright signed as "inventor" of his reinforced textile block design, even though he actually never did obtain a patent.[350] Moreover, Gebhard and Von Breton contend that Lloyd exerted considerable influence on his father's use of concrete block as a construction material. They contend it was Lloyd's use of steel in the block system used in the Henry Bollman house (Hollywood, 1922) that inspired his father to develop the knit block system used for the Storer house (Los Angeles, 1923).[351] Suffice it to say, there was overlapping experimental use of concrete and/or textile block as a primary building material at this point in time. And regardless of when or by whom the concept originated, it was Wright's ultimate decision to establish his personal testing ground for textile block construction in southern California that is of consequence to this writing.[352]

On the face of things, Wright's thinking along these lines could not be thought of as illogical. The population of Los Angeles had tripled between 1900 and 1910 and, with the opening of the Panama Canal in 1914 and the end of World War I, there was every indication the boom would continue well into the future. This reasoning is supported by statistics put forth in the 1923 end-of-the-year report of the Los Angeles City Planning Commission: "Twenty subdivisions are added on an average each week to the municipal mosaic; where during 1922 a new residence was completed every 26 minutes of the working day."[353] Moreover, Wright could identify with the cause of the small but influential minority of designers in the area who were striving to make the area visually different from the rest of the country. The sociological conditions of southern California and the mind-set of the California architects in the early 1920s were not unlike those experienced by the Chicago Prairie School architects at the turn of the century. Even bringing Lloyd into his California office on a collaborative basis follows the same pattern Wright originated when he tapped into the talents of Walter Burley Griffin. And, just as Griffin's landscape design skills helped set apart Wright's designs during the years he was formulating his Prairie House architecture, Lloyd's landscape design sensibilities augmented Wright's seminal designs for his built and proposed textile-concrete-block structures of the 1920s. It is not surprising, then, that in a letter to Sullivan dated February 5, 1923, Wright advised his mentor that he had "pitched in here to locate."[354]

Another significant influence upon Wright's thinking of these times has not been addressed to this point—that being the evolution of Wright's proclivity for the developing profession of city planning. Near the time Wright returned from Europe and began designing Taliesin, the National Housing Association was founded. By 1913, there were official planning boards in 18 cities, and Massachusetts enacted the first state legislation making city planning a mandatory responsibility of local governments. The first comprehensive zoning ordinance was enacted by New York City in 1916, the same year Wright began designing Hollyhock House. And it was during this same time frame that planned communities formulated on the reality-based sociologic and economic planning concepts first introduced by Ebenezer Howard were being developed, expanded upon, and highly publicized—including Kohler, Wisconsin (1916), Kingsport, Tennessee (1917), and Palos Verdes Estates, California (1923).[355] This influence is reflected in Wright's California job listings through his hypothetical designs for the Doheny Ranch Resort and Lake Tahoe Summer Colony,

both of which originated the same year Palos Verdes Estates was under development.

Doheny Ranch Resort Project—Beverly Hills, California (1923)

The presentation renderings of the Doheny Ranch Resort Project were developed to target the financial backing of Edward Laurence Doheny, who owned this acreage, and to give substance to Wright's vision of the design approach he would take—if and when he might be given opportunity to develop a plan for the subdivision of land within the ridge-ravine topography surrounding the Los Angeles Basin. The vision put forth in these drawings is of a terraced megastructure land development with resort facilities and housing, walled gardens, and lushly landscaped roof terraces (Figure 5-6). The whole was to be linked together through a stabilizing system of bridged roadways laid out to conform to the natural contours of the existing topography. Wright even went so far as to work up preliminary generic plans for a choice of three highly individualistic houses, using textile concrete block as the primary building material. Because there is no site plan in existence and the house plans were not developed in sufficient detail, there is no evidence to support that the perspective drawings were prepared for any reason other than to make a graphic, but theoretical, statement.

Had the plans for Doheny Ranch been fully developed and implemented, Wright might have established a design standard that could have impacted and meaningfully improved upon the appearance of the entire Los Angeles region, as it subsequently has been subdivided. Even more important, the land stabilization that would have been effected by his proposed concept of site-specific contour development could have substantially minimized the potential for the massive mud slides in California that have resulted in environmental disasters of increasingly epic proportion.

Wright's Lake Tahoe Project appears to have been prepared for reasons similar to the Doheny Project—to target financial backing—except that this was a resort for the mountainous region of central California. Inasmuch as none of the drawings suggest anything other than a piecemeal arrangement of architectural alternatives and there is none of the cohesiveness depicted for the Doheny Project, it is doubtful that Wright ever gave much thought to the type of infrastructure or integrated

Figure 5-6 Presentation drawing for the Doheny Ranch Resort Project (1923) in Beverly Hills, California, proposes concept for development of foothills (© *2002 by The Frank Lloyd Wright Foundation, Scottsdale, Arizona.*)

planning approach that would be required to protect the natural resources or environmental sensitivity of the Lake Tahoe region.

Wright's job listings in the Los Angeles area include one unexecuted residence—the Aline Barnsdall House Project—and four constructed residences: for Alice Millard, John D. Storer, Samuel Freeman, and Charles Ennis. An analysis of these plans supports that the genesis design was prepared for Aline Barnsdall. Not only do the Barnsdall drawings most appear to have been delineated by Wright's own hand, they are the only plans developed in sufficient detail to evidence both site specificity and underlying reasoning for design elements that may or may not reoccur in the other plans, whether they developed simultaneously or subsequently.

Aline Barnsdall House Project— Beverly Hills, California (1923)

The proposed site for the Aline Barnsdall House Project was situated on a south-facing slope of a land formation within the rugged ridge-ravine topography of Peavine Canyon in the Santa Monica Mountains. Pickfair Estate, the much publicized home of famed silent motion picture stars Mary Pickford and Douglas Fairbanks, was to the immediate north. From the upper reaches of the slope, there were unimpeded panoramic views toward the Los Angeles Basin and the Pacific Ocean. Wright

must have seen this setting as ideal for showcasing one of his first textile block houses.

Not since the Sherman Booth Project of 1912 had Wright had time, opportunity, or personal motivation to custom-design a substantial residence for a site of such magnificence (Figure 5-7). Perhaps it is because of the correlative environmental character of the sites that the parallels between the two projects are so striking. Consider that both sets of plans depict an approach by way of a bridge across a ravine. Both have a driveway paralleling the service wing. Both have a separate three-car garage with chauffeur's quarters and a parking-circulation court. Both feature a second-story dining room spanning the entrance court. And both have terraces and balconies all around, outstretching into a site environment girded by three ravines. The Barnsdall Project also relates to Hollyhock House in that there are three wings arranged around an interior quadrangle of open space in a zoned plan layout. Because the proposed property is isolated and protected by ridge formations to the east and north, however, there was no critical need to consider privacy or the effect of the Santa Ana winds within the design process. Wright's siting and design approach therefore represents the antithesis of the conceptual-adaptational approach taken with Hollyhock House. All of Wright's organizational diagrams support that the site and structure were dealt with as one entity and the parameters of the archi-

Figure 5-7   Presentation perspective for Aline Barnsdall House Project (1923) in Beverly Hills, California. (*Courtesy of Prints and Photographs Division, Library of Congress.*)

tecture were determined by, rather than adapted to, the natural topographic features of the site (Figure 5-8).

Access to the property was from the south by way of Summitridge Drive, a serpentine roadway configured to the natural contour of the ravine that formed the east boundary. Wright selected a natural bench down-slope from a reverse curve of this road as the most buildable site. He aligned the two-story primary living wing to stretch across the entire width of the bench, but set back from the rim to accommodate planned outdoor uses that fringe the land formation on all sides: the driveway approach and entrance court to the east; the living room terrace, pool-terrace, and enclosed garden to the south; a private garden-terrace and a separate garden-terrace to the west (Figure 5-9 a-b). He then arranged the central open space of the courtyard to parallel the axial line of the primary living wing and extend under the bridged second levels of the service and bedroom wings so as to interconnect the courtyard with the outdoor use areas on the west and east. Thus, the courtyard, per se, occupied only half the central open space. The remaining space was allocated to a sloping earthen bank flanked by dual stairways leading up to the level of a terrace that stretched across the base of the natural wooded slope to abut the wing extensions on either side, both of which extended northward into the slope.

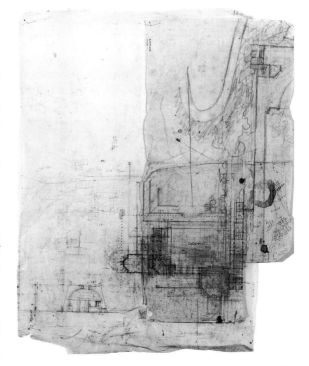

Figure 5-8   Early organizational diagram for Aline Barnsdall House Project. (© *2002 by the Frank Lloyd Wright Foundation, Scottsdale, Arizona.*)

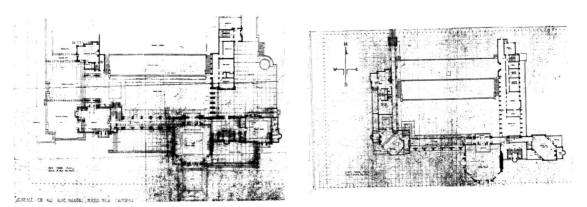

Figure 5-9 a-b Main and upper floor plans for Aline Barnsdall House Project. (*Courtesy of Department of Parks, Recreation, and Cultural Affairs, City of Los Angeles.*)

The only transition space designed to facilitate a direct interrelationship with the central open space was the loggia (with gallery above) that functioned as a two-level passageway between the use areas concentrated in the east and west extremities of the primary living wing. Even this was designed to facilitate a like interrelationship with the living room and living room terrace that paralleled the opposing side of the loggia-gallery, as supported by Wright's synchronic alignment of the two-story-high piers of textile block and glazed openings interspersed along both sides. All other interrelationship to inside use areas or the courtyard was by way of outdoor use areas on the exposed sides of the site. Wright further proposed that the garage-chauffeur's quarters be built into the slope at the circulation-court intersection for the approach bridge and that the foundations of all

Figure 5-10 South elevation, Aline Barnsdall House Project, showing proposed residence and approach bridge. (*Courtesy of Prints and Photographs Division, Library of Congress.*)

the outdoor use areas descend below the level of the bench to appear to penetrate and merge with the natural slope (Figure 5-10). This amalgamated treatment had the effect of anchoring the architecture to the site and visually unifying the built environment with the greater environment of the slope, the ridge, and the enframing ravines so that the architecture would appear to rise up from the canyon wall. It was toward this imagery that Wright choreographed his entry experience.

The entry experience was planned to begin as glimpses of the architecture came intermittently into the range of vision of anyone progressing up Summitridge Drive. Along this portion of the approach route, there could be no *direction* to the viewability of the architecture as all was totally dependent upon the topography, the curvature of the road, and the height and density of existing and future vegetation. From the juncture where the approach route turned west onto the point-of-access to the property, however, Wright was in complete control of what was to be seen, when it was to be seen, and from which perspective. The first evidence that it was Wright's conscious intent to control the unfolding of the panorama of the view is the uncommon arced approach bridge suggested by his earliest organizational diagram[356] (Figure 5-11). The introduction of a curve arcing away from the architecture almost immediately after turning onto the property allowed Wright to impede movement almost to a standstill at the right angle of the bridge parapet to signal entry into the realm of the property and give pause for reflection upon a more focused perspective—much as he had done with his original entrance into the Taliesin entrance court. The angular form of the parapet had the effect of concealing the immediacy of the ravine and at the same time capturing the peripheral vista through the ravine toward the Los Angeles Basin, as well as the resplendence of the architecture and the traversing foundations for the structure and driveway—all of which were to literally wrap around the hillslope to connect with the understructure of the bridge.

As the approach turned north into the arc of the bridge, attention was to focus upon the near presence of the enveloping wooded slope. This created a momentary sense of arrival at the circulation court. As the approach turned south onto the driveway and the slope disappeared from view, there would be peripheral awareness of the ravine to the east, but attention was to focus upon the 240-foot length of the driveway and the destination viewpoint: the two-story mass of the textile-block facade

of the dining-room/guest-room extension that stretched across the south terminus of the entrance court. That this was Wright's vision is confirmed by the manner in which he physically and visually separated the service wing from the range of vision of the driveway: by omitting glazed openings on the driveway side of the ground level of the service wing and screening the openings on the second level with the parapet of the terrace-balcony; by omitting openings on the north wall of the second-floor dining room; and by screening the openings on the north wall of the first-floor guest room with a separate parapet extension.[357] At the point where the service wing recessed to accommodate the balcony, Wright modulated the driveway outward to conform to the east rim of

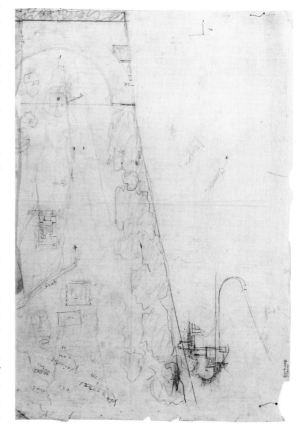

Figure 5-11 Wright's earliest organizational diagram of Barnsdall Project delineates uncommon arced approach bridge. (© *2002 by The Frank Lloyd Wright Foundation, Scottsdale, Arizona.*)

the bench. He also introduced a tile surfacing that extended under the overhang of the terrace-balcony and the bridged interspace of the service wing to the depth of inner courtyard, where he installed a row of textile block piers. This treatment identified the realm of the entrance court, formed space for vehicular maneuvering, separated the entrance court from the realm of the courtyard, segmented views into the courtyard without detracting attention from the entry experience, and injected oblique streaks of light into the cavelike recess to visually direct movement toward the point of outdoor-indoor transition. It also controlled the luminance gradation to intensify the sense of arrival upon entering the foyer.

The entry door opened into a modest foyer and faced upon a staircase leading to the second level. The foyer was to be illuminated by natural light introduced through an expansive art-glass window bay on the landing and the glazed doors flanking the staircase leading to the garden terrace to the east of the living room. Upon turning west toward the living room, the line of sight was to extend through the entire length of the loggia passageway—an entry treatment reminiscent of the D. D. Martin House. Within the narrowed space of the loggia, Wright propelled movement and the range of vision by way of his design. Movement was to accelerate where there were solid walls, slow where there were segmented views on the broadside, or pause and turn into either the courtyard or living room at the point where there were portals directly opposite on either side. In this manner, Wright made certain that the drama of the living room would not be revealed until *after* making the ninety-degree turn through the living-room portal.

As at Hollyhock House, the living room fireplace was situated along an exterior wall and there was to be a clerestory-like skylight. Here, however, neither design element was intended to relate to the focus of the space. By its placement at the salient point of the ceiling, Wright intended that this skylight draw attention to the majestic two-and-one-half-story height of the dome configuration. And the fireplace was intended to fade into the background, as supported by its placement along the only solid wall in the room. All other walls in the room were more visually magnetic by reason of their design as glazed single or double French doors interspersed between textile block piers. Even so, the focus of the living room was *not* the view, but *awareness* of the view—either through the portals of access leading toward the view by way of intervening outdoor use areas, or through Wright's manner of focusing attention

upon the *suggestion* of the view. By slanting the southwest and southeast corners of the living room to a 45-degree angle, Wright focused the line of sight upon the magnificent art-glass vertical element that dominated the entire height and breadth of the narrowed aperture of the south wall (Figure 5-12). Thus, it was Wright's intent that the view literally function as a backdrop to the art-glass feature and the full impact of the view remain elusive from within the realm of the living room. By then developing the intervening outdoor use areas in opposition around the living room—in the form of a large rectangular terrace on the west, a garden terrace on the east, the triangular terraces that filled in the open spaces at the southwest and southeast corners, and the terrace and pool on the south—Wright enticed and/or propelled movement toward the portals of access leading to the outdoor use areas at the same time that he sustained interest in the panorama of the view that would unfold in infinite variety from their vantage points—dependent upon the foreground, climatic conditions, the time of day or night, and the angle of the line of sight.

The approach to the second level would be less dramatic than the entry experience, but it was based upon the same design treatment. And, again, the focus was intended to be an *awareness* of the view that could only be experienced from the triangulated terraces at the southwest and northeast corners of the second-floor use areas. Because it is not happenstance that the walls in these use areas were angled to the identical 45-degree angle as the southwest corner of the living room. This angling generally paralleled the northwest-southeast diagonal line of the Pacific coastline. Thus, it was from the southwesternmost prows of the terraces adjoining the living room, dining room, and owner's bedroom that the full exuberant sweep of the view was meant to be experienced.

In the end, the capricious Barnsdall once again reversed her thinking and decided not to proceed to the stage of working drawings and execution. Although a May 18, 1923 article reported that Barnsdall had purchased "24 acres . . . at a cost of about $60,000 and will erect a residence to cost $150,000," the transaction never closed.[358] Had the Barnsdall House project been built—on this property in Beverly Hills, and in conformance with the incredible environmental integration of Wright's site-specific design—it would have joined the ranks of such exemplar domestic architecture as Dana, D. D. Martin, Robie, and his own Taliesin. Instead, it remained a child of Wright's imagination and assuredly

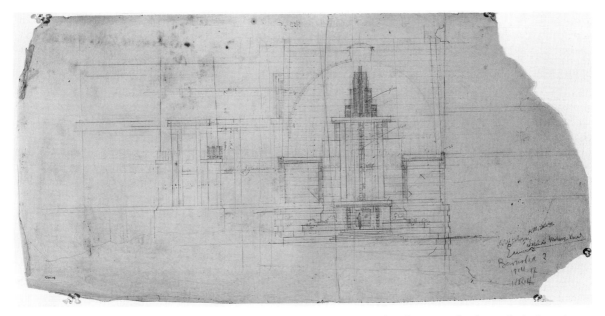

Figure 5-12 Art-glass feature in narrowed aperture of Barnsdall living room south wall. (© *2002 by The Frank Lloyd Wright Foundation, Scottsdale, Arizona.*)

Alice Millard's "La Miniatura"—Pasadena, California (1923–1924)

Alice Millard was the widow of George Madison Millard, for whom Wright had designed a house in Highland Park, Illinois (1906). Historic correspondence supports that it was Wright who initiated the concept of designing this house. Millard in fact reminded him he had been so eager to test his new construction approach, he offered to do so without charging the standard architect's fee (although he did retain an interest in the building in the form of a lien). This would suggest Wright could have used a similar approach with the Barnsdall Beverly Hills Project. Although there is no evidence to support this correlation, the chronology of design development for both former clients followed the same general time frame (early February through May). Moreover, La Miniatura—as Millard's new home came to be known—is no less site-specific in design than Barnsdall's, and Wright proposed the same form of block construc-tion for both, a methodology he did not use for any of his subsequent textile block houses. Unlike the Barnsdall House project, however, the basic plans for La Miniatura were approved in mid-March and construction was underway shortly thereafter, with plan development and detailing apparently proceeding in process.

It seems significant that La Miniatura was among the more than 60,000 houses for which the City of Los Angeles issued building permits in 1923, and that Wright described it as "the first-born Californiain [sic] in architecture."[360] In making such a declaration after hav-ing spent the better part of a decade developing plans for Hollyhock House and the Olive Hill Development, Wright tellingly reveals the inner rebellion he must have felt while following the precedents set forth by his client and other developers. He wrote: "Here I was in Los Angeles looking around me disgusted. There the Ange-lenos were many and busy as could be with steam-shovels tearing down the hills to get to the top in order to blot out the top with a house in some queasy fashion-able 'style,' some esthetic inanity or other. . . . What was missing? Nothing less than a distinctly genuine expres-sion of California life in terms of modern industry and American opportunity. That was all."[361] Clearly, with La

was among the 70 unbuilt projects to which Wright was referring when he observed that, of the 179 designs he had originated to this date, "the best ones had life only on paper."[359]

Miniatura as his first *executed* textile block house, Wright hoped to influence both the architecture and the character of development in California in much the same way he had influenced architectural development in the prairies of the Midwest. This reasoning is supported by his rejection of the property Millard originally purchased. He likened the design process for building upon her "treeless lot" to the "idiot-syncrasy" of the region.[362] The property he chose, on the other hand, was described as "a ravishing ravine near by, in which stood two beautiful eucalyptus trees."[363]

Wright's choice of wordage to describe this landform can only be thought of as romanticism. A more realistic word choice would have been "arroyo," which by definition is "a water-course in a dry region" or "an often dry gully or channel carved by water."[364] It was because of the geographical character of *this* arroyo that an underground street conduit had been installed by the Pasadena authorities. And it was because of Wright's disregard of this circumstance that mud inundated the ground floor use areas when the culvert overflowed during a heavy rain shortly after construction was complete. Wright unabashedly characterized this "unusual cloudburst concentrating on that ravine" as something of a phenomenon: "In every fair-weather region like this is always the unexpected that happens. No one in fifty years ever saw the culvert that now took the street water away below the basement of the house overflow. But the heavens opened wide, poured water down until it got to the level of the pretty concrete dining-room floor, determined to float the house if the thing could be done. The flood must have mistaken the house for another Ark, but this time, failing utterly to move it, left a contemptuous trace of mud on the lower terraces, put out the fires in the sub-basement, burying the gas heaters beneath solid mud. And went away. . . . But soon we got this little matter fixed up by aid of the city of Pasadena."[365] Nonetheless, Wright's decision to site the structure at the base of the arroyo resulted in architectural and environmental benefits that in the end far outweighed the frustration and inconvenience of this singular occurrence.

To begin with, the level floor of the arroyo provided a stable, load-bearing foundation requiring minimal excavation or grading—an arrangement that allowed Wright to preserve the existing trees and much of the natural vegetation, including shrubs, vines, and ground cover. This attribute is important because it was the situation and careful preservation of existing vegetation that most effectively determined Wright's siting and conformance of the entire structure (Figure 5-13 a-c). The two eucalyptus trees determined the setback from Lester Avenue (now, Rosemont), the proportional height and width of the structure, and the depth and breadth of the garden terrace to the southwest of the dining room. Together with the land form and other existing trees on the site, they also determined the situation of the main point-of-entry from Circle Drive (now, Prospect Crescent); the situation and arrangement of the garden pathway and the Jensenlike reflecting pool; the orientation of the expansive glazed walls of the living quarters toward the southwest to overlook the garden environment; and the manner in which Wright interwove the indoor and outdoor living spaces (Figure 5-14). But, perhaps the most consequential aspect of Wright's decision to site La Miniatura at the base of the arroyo was that he would have complete control over a very small-scale climatic area that was almost ideally formed for this particular region.

Consider that the southwest boundary provides unimpeded access to the prevailing southwesterly breezes that blow in from the ocean from late morning to late afternoon. And the slope to the northeast provides natural protection from the Santa Ana winds that blow in from the desert from late afternoon to early morning. This layout assured that the comfort level within the arroyo would remain relatively constant, because the recessive character of the land form retains moisture released by the profuse vegetation and the sizable water body of the reflecting pool to create what Simonds refers to as a "pool of cool."[366] Consider also that warm air rises as temperatures increase during the day, and daytime ocean breezes blowing across the pool and garden environment become cooler as they move inland to fill the void. And the air circulation pattern is reversed during the night when the prevailing east-northeast inland breezes flow downhill into the arroyo. Moreover, the shape of the arroyo cultivated a "venturi effect," described as follows: "A house in the bottom of a canyon [or arroyo] is subject to stronger diurnal winds than one on flat ground. A breeze can be speeded up by the 'venturi' effect of narrow canyon walls, particularly at night."[367] Thus, the land conformation, soil, vegetation, moisture content, wind direction, and natural circulation patterns were such that Wright was able to cultivate a microclimate for La Miniatura uniquely appropriate to climatic conditions of southern California.

In addition, the deep setback from Lester Avenue and the year-round shading provided by the eucalyptus

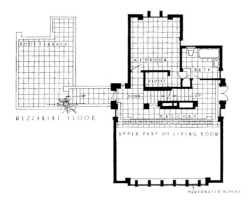

MEZZANINE FLOOR

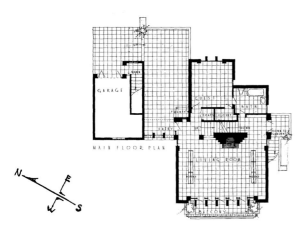

MAIN FLOOR PLAN

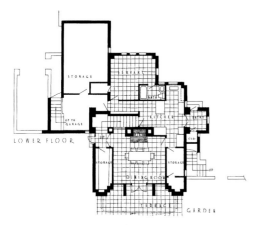

LOWER FLOOR

trees completely discounted negative aspects generally associated with a southwesterly orientation. This is because the natural slope of the ravine blocked the low-angled rays of the late afternoon sun, while the height and breadth of the eucalyptus tree branching effectively filtered the overhead rays of the midday sun. Therefore, there was no need for deep overhanging eaves such as Wright had designed for his Prairie Houses. By insetting the glazed portions of the walls and by interspersing piers to create a louvered blind effect, Wright was able to completely control the sunlight as it moved across the sky. It is this introduction of shafts of shaded and reflected light that combine with the diffused light introduced through the vertical columns of perforated textile blocks emplaced selectively throughout the house that soften the hard surface of the concrete block

Figure 5-14   Character-defining eucalyptus trees and other native flora determined the siting and layout of La Miniatura. (*Courtesy of The Frank Lloyd Wright Archives, Scottsdale, Arizona.*)

Figure 5-13 a–c   Floor plans for La Miniatura in Pasadena, California, designed by Wright for Alice Millard. (© *2002 by The Frank Lloyd Wright Foundation, Scottsdale, Arizona.*)

so the interior use areas of La Miniatura are illuminated with the glow of natural light from dawn to dusk.

Ultimately, then, it was Wright's "idea," that is, his carefully articulated environmental design approach, that established the unmistakable identifiable character of La Miniatura. And it was his complete satisfaction with the manifestation of this idea that caused him to expound upon it so enthusiastically in his autobiography: "La Miniatura stands in Pasadena against the blue sky between loving eucalyptus companions in spite of all friction, waste and slip, triumphant as Idea. . . . Seeking simplicity as sought in La Miniatura, you will never fail to find beauty. . . . As for me—probably living too long as a hermit—reading mostly in the book of Nature's creation—I may have these things out of drawing—because I would rather have built this little house than St. Peter's in Rome."[368]

It is not known how much, if any, influence Lloyd brought to bear upon Wright's design process with Barnsdall's Beverly Hills Project and La Miniatura. Neither project is listed in Lloyd's catalog of works—as are Olive Hill, Doheny Ranch, Storer, Freeman, Ennis, and the Millard studio addition. Moreover, the only site plan for La Miniatura bears the name of Heila Deusner, a landscape architect who practiced in Pasadena during the 1920s.[369] Inasmuch as Wright was much more personally involved with La Miniatura—from concept to

execution—than any of the other California houses, he most probably incorporated all he had observed and learned about California through working with Lloyd on Hollyhock House and Olive Hill with the anatomy-of-place he had evolved throughout his personal life and career experiences, and only began to rely on Lloyd's talents and involvement with some consistency as he found it necessary to devote more time trying to cultivate a clientele.[370] It was in all likelihood because of a lack of success in this area that Wright became disenchanted with California, reestablished permanent residency at Taliesin, and essentially turned over the operation of his limited California practice to Lloyd.

John D. Storer—Hollywood, California (1923–1924)

The John D. Storer House represents a reworking of plans Wright originated a year or so earlier for a specific site in Eagle Rock, California, owned by G. P. Lowes. This seems a highly unorthodox approach for Wright to have undertaken at a time when he was so assiduously promoting himself, particularly in light of the precipitous grade and irregular conformation of the subject property—conditions that normally mandate custom-designed plans (Figure 5-15). And in light of Wright's thinking along these lines, as he so forthrightly stated it in his March 1908 article for *Architectural Record:* "No man ever built a building worthy the name of architecture who fashioned it in perspective sketch to his taste

Figure 5-15 A 1992 photograph shows the irregular conformation of the John Storer House site (1923–1924) in Hollywood, California. (*Photograph by Charles E. Aguar. © 2002 by Berdeana Aguar.*)

and then fudged the plan to suit. Such methods produce mere scene painting. A perspective may be a proof but it is no nurture."[371]

According to architecture historian Robert L. Sweeney, the reworked plans for the Storer site initially may have been prepared on speculation for the Superior Building Company, for which Storer presumably was the principal[372] (Figure 5-16). This hypothesis might explain why Wright leveled off the slope in terraces to accommodate the existing plan and angled the far corner of the garage—that is, "fudged the plan to suit" the new site—so much so that a full-size car cannot be parked next to the outside garage wall. And it might explain why one of the bedrooms is partially buried in the hillside. But it does not explain why Wright rotated the plan 180 degrees and disregarded the consequence of ignoring environmental conditions intrinsic to the new site.

The difficulty with this reorientation lies in the fact that all the bedrooms and a large portion of the primary outdoor living space face due west. Moreover, the entry planter and largest terrace with a pool and gardens face due south, where they were exposed to the sun from morning to night, and the large sunken garden on the terrace of the lower-level dining room faces north, where sunlight is less beneficial.[373] Because there originally were no trees on the site, the penetrating rays of the late afternoon sun were a contention until years later, when the introduced grove of eucalyptus trees matured. It was for this reason that Lloyd suggested, designed, and installed decorative awnings to overhang the glazed openings and terrace at the west end of the living room as the house neared completion in October 1924.[374]

Nonetheless, the situation of the house midway down the south-facing slope and the stepped-back

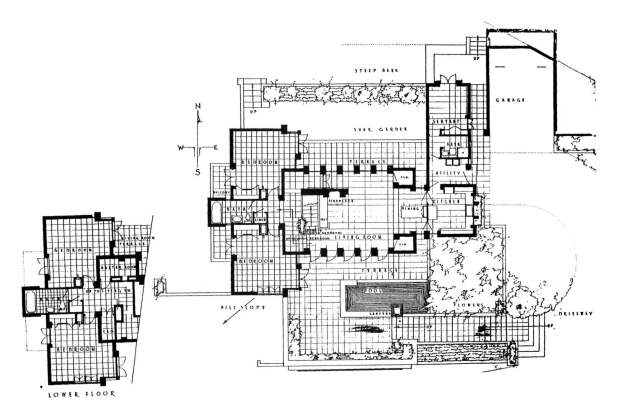

Figure 5-16 The ground-floor plan of the Storer House shows how Wright angled the garage and "fudged the plan to suit." (© 2002 by The Frank Lloyd Wright Foundation, Scottsdale, Arizona.)

arrangement of the service wing and living wing worked together to temper the effects of the Santa Ana winds, while providing unimpeded access to the prevailing ocean breezes—benefits equally, or even more, important than the aesthetically pleasing ocean-skyline views generally mentioned. Moreover, the introduction of terraces on all four sides of the structure encouraged maximum air circulation, and the piers interspersed along the walls of French doors had the effect of channeling breezes into the living spaces of the house, controlling the infiltration of sunlight, and interlocking the interior and exterior living spaces. Lloyd also introduced techniques used for Olive Hill to modify the microclimate of the terraces so that, in time, the air passing through the interior-exterior living spaces would be much cooler than the ambient temperature of the surrounding urban environment. Specifically, he introduced masses of drought-resistant plantings and substantial areas of permeable surfacing to nullify the heat-generating effects of the concrete block; he added copious amounts of moisture to the air through the evaporation of the water in the pool and the spray emitted by the fountain; and he introduced well-placed deciduous trees and the eucalyptus grove to shade the terraces and expansive glazed facades. Even so, the ponderous walls required to support the terraced hillside design caused the structuring to be visually formidable and environmentally intrusive for a number of years. It was only with the maturation of the lush, informally-planted vegetation that the climatic conditions exacerbated by the reorientation were ameliorated and the architecture took on the appearance of embracing the site—as it has appeared for the past half-century, and as it originally was envisioned by father and son.[375]

Samuel Freeman—Hollywood, California (1923–1925)

The Freeman site faces advantageously toward the south, the view, and ocean breezes. However, it is very minimal in size, basically 70 feet by 75 feet, with a small additional wedge formed by a curvature of road frontage. And there was virtually no buildable space, since the terrain sloped away from the road at a gradient of between 25 and 30 percent (Figure 5-17).

Wright met this challenge by laying out three two-story cubes on a 4-foot grid: (1) the primary living cube that houses the main-floor living room, bedrooms, and lounge; (2) the adjoining service cube that accommodates the main-floor kitchen, stairwell, ground-floor

bathroom and utilities; and (3) the garage cube with storage underneath that interconnects with the living-service cubes by way of roofed bridging over a modest loggia-entryway. The situation, size, and setback of the living cubes were dictated by the width of the property and the slope, which is so immediate that both levels are above grade on the east and west, as are the storage areas under the garage and the interconnecting passageway for the loggia. The northwest corner of the primary living cube almost touches the right-of-way and the storage space is built so as to precisely fit into the platted point of intersection for the north and west property lines.[376] The situation and size of the garage cube and the depth of the interconnecting loggia were prescribed by the proportions of the wedge formed by the road curvature, the northwest corner that extends to within inches of the right-of-way, and the east wall following along the east property line.

That Wright also gave substantial weight to the directional path of the Santa Ana winds is supported by the situation of the stairwell on the east end of the service cube and the basically solid character of all north and east walls (although the need for privacy also would have influenced Wright's treatment of the north wall on the main floor). Even the balcony extension on the northeast corner of the service cube would appear to relate to this climatic condition, because the minimal dimension (approximately 4-feet by 4-feet) makes questionable using the balcony as outdoor living space. Although it could be argued that the balcony and parapet provide both a prospect vantage point and the element of safety necessary to allow installation of the French doors—as has been suggested—it is equally as logical to reason that the function of the French doors was to encourage air circulation, admit significant natural light into the entry hall and stairwell, and protect these areas from the impact of the Santa Ana winds. This analogy is supported by the stepped-back arrangement of the cubes—a treatment that also deflects the winds and lessens their level of impact at the various points of reception, including the loggia entryway.

The attention Wright gave to natural light illumination in the living spaces of the Freeman House is worthy of note—particularly with respect to his artistry with glazed perforated blocks. To begin with, he introduced a row of the perforated blocks at or near eye level along the north wall of the entry hall. Inasmuch as these are the only openings on the north wall, other than the entry door, their fourfold purpose is evident. They were to (1)

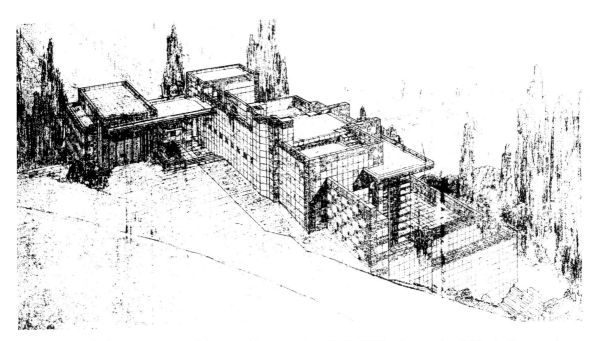

Figure 5-17   A bird's-eye perspective of the Samuel Freeman House (1923–1925) in Los Angeles, California, illustrates the precipitous nature of the site. (© *2002 by The Frank Lloyd Wright Foundation, Scottsdale, Arizona.*)

screen the entry hall from public view, (2) minimize the impact of the Santa Ana winds, (3) supplement the natural light provided by the glazed openings in the entry door and the French doors at the east terminus of the entry hall, and (4) adjust the gradated luminance so the sense of arrival upon entering the living room was intensified. There also is the clerestory of perforated blocks that Wright introduced along three sides of the raised section of the roof between the pair of reinforced-concrete beams that span the north-south alignment of the living room. This treatment accentuates the structural functionality of the beams, so this space visually expands upward, as well as outward—through the expanses of glazed openings in the south, east, and west walls. Of equal importance is the aesthetic benefit of introducing natural light into the walled-in, northernmost portion of the room—balancing the luminance gradation and infusing this space with a myriad of reflections, as the sun moves from east to west across the sky.

The double-wide column of perforated blocks Wright interspersed between the columns of solid blocks within the floor-to-ceiling sections of the south wall visually complements the expansive glazed open-

ings, but their more important function in this circumstance was to countermand the glare of sunlight. Assumedly, this treatment was introduced because the grade of the slope essentially negated the effectiveness of introduced eucalyptus groves or other drought-resistant trees, and budgetary constraints disallowed the extravagant terraced construction necessary to introduce consequential raised planting areas. Wright also buffered the penetrating rays of the late-afternoon sun by increasing the depth of the eave that overhangs the glazed openings on the west side of the living room, including over the mitered corner window.[377] He facilitated cross-ventilation by introducing windows on the east and west sides of the living room and a band of casement windows on the south end of the kitchen. And he installed an elongated "flower box" beneath the casement windows of the kitchen as a means to introduce drought-resistant plantings that would work with the plantings in the "flower boxes" on the living room and bedroom terraces and the "pool" at the northwest corner of the loggia to introduce moisture into the air.

Consider the consequence of Wright's careful deliberations in his design of the Freeman House. Had he not stepped back the service cube from the garage cube, the entry loggia would have been exposed to the elements at all times. Had the primary living cube not been stepped back to the west of the service cube, it would have been environmentally unfeasible to moderate the outdoor living spaces toward the view. It also would not have been advisable to install the transcendent floor-to-ceiling mitered windows at the southeast corners of the indoor living spaces that, together with the correspondent windows on the southwest corners, are the most notable aesthetic feature of Wright's design. These mitered windows are a more sophisticated use of corner windows than Wright had previously designed; they extend past a very thin floor plane to create the illusion of two-story windows, with no break at the intervening level of the floor.

Figure 5-18   Basic mound formation of the site for the Charles W. Ennis House (1923–1926) in Hollywood, California. (*Courtesy of Eric Lloyd Wright.*)

The Freemans occupied this home throughout their lifetimes. During the 1930s, they commissioned Schindler to custom-design furniture for the house, including bookcases and a built-in dining table along the east wall of the living room. Although this modification screened the kitchen from view, in accordance with the wishes of the clients, it significantly compromised the natural light and ventilation that Wright had so assiduously incorporated into his environmental planning.

The Freeman property ultimately was bequeathed to the University of Southern California, and the School of Architecture was assigned responsibility for maintaining and restoring the house and grounds. Saturday tours were offered for a fee until the property was declared unsafe because of earthquake damage sustained during the 1990s. The props and plastic "tent" of tarps put in place as a temporary expedient at that time did not adequately protect the structure from exposure to the elements. The extent of material damage effected was so extensive that the University found it necessary to refuse federal grant funding proffered in 1998, because it was felt that the $850,000 amount of the grant would be inadequate to bring the house up to seismic codes.[378]

Charles W. Ennis—Hollywood, California (1923–1926)

The size of the Ennis site was minimal, approximately one-half acre, and the basic formation was of a mound that sloped in all four directions (Figure 5-18). Both the natural and platted conformation suggested a site-specific design that would wrap around and/or step down in accord with the foothill topography. Thus, it is

difficult to comprehend why Wright would lay out a plan that required a level surface area of more than 15,000 square feet to accommodate the indoor and outdoor living-service spaces of his design (Figure 5-19). This treatment necessitated leveling the mound and building "in the middle of the top," the very technique he had so vehemently characterized as an "idiot-syncrasy of the region." It also required importing many hundreds of tons of earth-fill, erecting a massive underground bulwark of concrete footings, and enclosing the entire affair with extensive textile-block retaining walls (Figure 5-20 a-b). The negative consequence of this Herculean form of construction became evident seven months into the building process, when the monumental retaining wall on the south side of the house first began to bulge and crack (Figure 5-21). However, when Lloyd advised his father that some of the lower blocks were "popping," Wright maintained that the bulge and cracks were "of no great significance." But he then alluded to the additional wall courses that had to be laid to compensate for an inaccurate survey. This does not minimize Wright's disregard of the existing topography that caused the need for such expansive retaining walls in the first place. Nor does it alter the fact that Wright did not consider the undomestic scale of the living spaces—indoors or outdoors. Perhaps it was to the belated recognition of these errors in judgment that Wright was referring when he

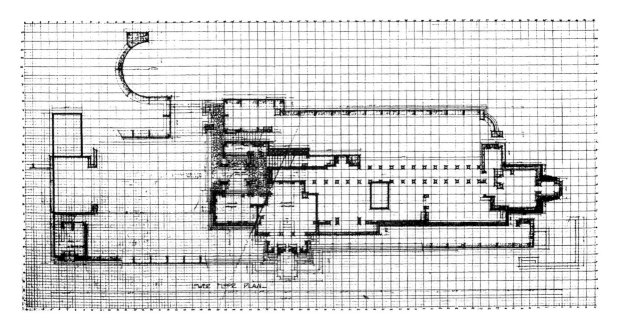

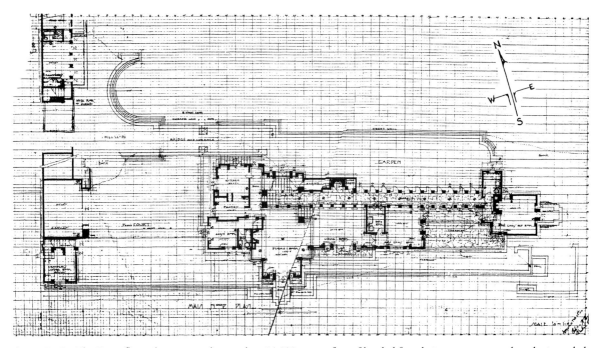

Figure 5-19 The Ennis floor plans required more than 14,000 square feet of leveled foundations to accommodate the intended land uses. (© 2002 by The Frank Lloyd Wright Foundation, Scottsdale, Arizona.)

a

Figure 5-20 a-b A massive retaining wall of concrete blocks was required to support the Ennis structuring. (*Figure 5-20 a courtesy of Eric Lloyd Wright; Figure 5-20 b courtesy of The Frank Lloyd Wright Archives, Scottsdale, Arizona.*)

b

subsequently observed that the Ennis House was "way out of concrete block size . . . out of bounds."[379]

Wright continued to experiment with and modify his concrete block construction methodology throughout the 1920s. However, the only "client" Wright was to write about when he prepared his memoirs a decade later was

A. M. Johnson, president of the National Life Insurance Company of Chicago. Wright claimed that Johnson "offered to grubstake me with $20,000 to prospect in his behalf with the structural idea for a skyscraper as I had already laid it before him the year before."[380] He then devoted several pages to the cantilevered glass office building he erected in model format—in front of which he often posed for photographs. But he made no mention

Figure 5-21 A photograph from the Frank Lloyd Wright files showing the Ennis retaining wall before the project was completed was marked with the notations "cracked blocks" and "bulged." (*Courtesy of The Frank Lloyd Wright Archives, Scottsdale, Arizona.*)

of the concrete block building he conceptualized for the same client to be built on the rim of a canyon in Death Valley, California, that is generally recognized as his initial introduction to the desert environment. Nor did he mention any of the several concrete block structures he designed for properties in Wisconsin and Texas—perhaps because none of these commissions ever reached the stage of execution. The high point of the year, it seems,

was Wright's introduction to Olga Ivanovna Lazovich Milanoff Hinzenburg, a Yugoslavian-born ballerina who would come to be known as Olgivanna (a derivative of her first two names). Within a year of this meeting, she and her young daughter Svetlana took up residence with Wright at Taliesin, where their daughter Iovanna was born.

6 | The Closing Years of an Era: 1923–1929

In the spring of 1925, a fire sparked by lightning and fueled by defective telephone wiring destroyed the living wing at Taliesin yet a second time. Moreover, the archival job listings indicate only one commission for the entire year. Matters were not much better in 1926, when there were only five job listings and none that progressed past the project stage. When burning leaves caused a third, but lesser, fire at Taliesin in February 1927, Wright found himself unable to make payments due and was forced to dispose of all his personal belongings at public auction. When even these monies were not sufficient to cover his delinquencies, the Bank of Wisconsin took title to Taliesin. This action prompted Wright to solicit well-to-do friends, faithful clients, Jensen, and family members to intervene and organize a corporation—the purpose of which was to assume control of Wright's estate and finances. This endeavor eventually was successful. "Wright, Incorporated" was formed; his debts were paid in full; and he was issued stock based upon his future earnings to create an alternative means of support. Thus, Wright did not join the ever-increasing ranks of those who lost their homes or farms as the Great Depression gained momentum.[381] Because the corporation retained title to Taliesin, however, Wright essentially became an employee of the corporation with rights of tenancy. Nonetheless, it was during this extended period of professional and emotional unrest that Wright began laying the groundwork for two of the more notable accomplishments of his life: the all-inclusive, character-defining garden environment of Taliesin III and the founding of The Taliesin Fellowship, which was first contemplated as the Hillside Home School for the Allied Arts.

ENVIRONMENTAL DESIGNS, 1924–1929

Taliesin III—Spring Green, Wisconsin: A Work In Progress (1924—)

In the process of rebuilding the Taliesin living quarters after the second and third fires, most of the architectural expansions Wright had envisioned in 1924 came to fruition or were expanded upon. Within this process, a great deal of attention was given toward fostering a more interactive relationship with Jones Valley—including the installation of a balcony or veranda that stretches across virtually the entire southeast facade and is directly accessible to the living room, the guest room, Mrs. Wright's bedroom, and an intermediary living space between the bedrooms known as the "Blue Loggia." This intermediary space merges with two architectural additions: the "Garden Room," formed by enclosing the former porte-cochere with glazing, and Wright's personal bedroom-office. The bedroom-office addition faces south and has a sizable semicantilevered terrace that affords additional prospects of Jones Valley, as well as Midway Hill and the Romeo and Juliet windmill to the southwest.

Wright took great latitude when it came to developing the cultivated landscape, however—as do many homeowners—by essentially directing projects on site as he matched his vision with existing circumstance. Inasmuch as the execution of these envisioned approaches sometimes evolved over a period of years and seldom were transposed to paper for posterity, it is difficult to trace the sequence or extent of development at a given time with any certainty. The chronology put forth herein is based upon syllogistic reasoning supported by a thoughtful assessment of historical photographs, the two projected plans prepared in 1912 and 1924, a November 1920 map prepared by Schindler that provides the most complete snapshot-in-time for this period, and a retrospective plan that records the landscape as it was developed under Wright's direction over time (Figure 6-1 a–c).

Plan "a" clearly delineates the location of the two landmark oak trees in the Tea Circle and the grove of trees that originally appropriated the hill.[382] Plans "b" and "c" obviate that some of the trees in the grove were casualties of the 1914 fire and the remaining trees were lost during the second fire, in 1925, or were sufficiently damaged to warrant their removal. Thus, it seems logical to first interpret Wright's thinking prior to the third fire, explain how this event affected the execution over time, and relate everything back to his original inspiration of 1911–1912.

An obvious difference between plan "c" and the earlier plans is that the carriageway leading from the entry approach into the forecourt has been eliminated—a decision assumedly motivated by the problems of parking, trafficability, noise, and fumes associated with the automobile. The new approach afforded two vastly different entry experiences: (1) the scenic route by way of the original entry gateway and approach, but bypassing the former access through the porte-cochere and proceeding on around the hill past the west wing to the garage or

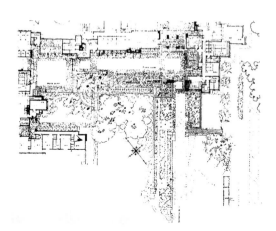

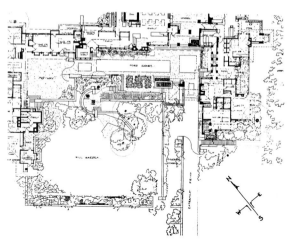

Figure 6-1 a Taliesin I projected plan (1912) shows hillside before 1914 fire that destroyed the living quarters. (*Western Architect, February 1913 issue.*)

Figure 6-1 b Taliesin II projected plan (1924) shows loss of trees on hillside before 1925 fire and rebuilding of east wing. (© *2002 by The Frank Lloyd Wright Foundation, Scottsdale, Arizona.*)

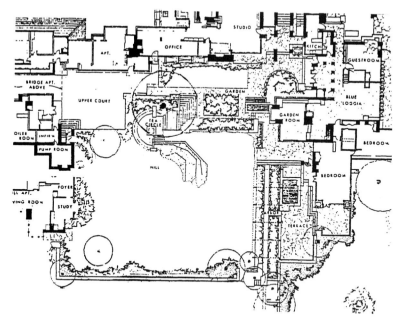

Figure 6-1 c Taliesin III (1925—) shows loss of trees on hillside after 1925 fire, and as modified over three decades. (*Courtesy of the Taliesin Preservation Commission.*)

Figure 6-1 a–c Evolution of the Taliesin gardens, Spring Green, Wisconsin.

under the bridging to the upper court; or (2) the most direct route along the ridge of the escarpment to the same destination. Either way, the entry experience then proceeds as a stroll journey through the transitional open space, with the flower garden border alongside the studio wing on one side and the Courtyard Garden on the other.

The enveloping corporeality Wright developed for the immediately surrounding environment of Taliesin III is exceptional. Plan "c" verifies that the former driveway open space set apart and defined by the two new additions has been developed into a "Terrace Garden" to merge with the Courtyard Garden. The Garden Room addition has been assimilated into the realm of the expanded garden space by way of an offset that combines with a rectangular stone pool-and-fountain feature at the garden threshold and a large contained planting bed formed in a semicircle around the northeast side of the addition—a treatment that both visually and materially integrates the water feature with the terminus of the former forecourt. This arrangement had the effect of transforming the forecourt open space into an entrance garden and assimilating all of Taliesin's architectural spaces into the greater site environment—both natural and man-made. Wright also has begun the process of developing the hillside open space into a "Hill Garden" and weaving it into the fabric of the earlier developed landscape of the Courtyard Garden and Tea Circle, as well as the Terrace Garden. Although the open space of the Hill Garden merges with the other garden spaces, it was designed as an elusive destination—in the sense that it is not visible from any of the primary indoor or outdoor living spaces and is only accessible by way of steps leading up from the Tea Circle or the Terrace Garden.

The plans for the Hill Garden itself are virtually the same in "b" and "c," except for the delineation of trees. Both plans set aside the crown of the hill by enclosing the approximate one-third-acre of open space with 560 linear feet of stone retaining walls. These retaining walls have the symbolic purpose of defining the limits of the built environment of Taliesin and serving as the capturing device to focus attention on the vista in all directions. Their functional purpose, however, was to provide containment for the many cubic yards of earthen fill Wright introduced to elevate and expand the parameters of the crown of the hill to make it appear as a low wall rising from a natural hillslope. Wright's retrospective wordage in *An Autobiography* reinforces this circumstance: "Stone was sent along the slopes into great walls. Stone stepped up like ledges on the hill and flung long arms in any direc-

tion that brought the house to the ground. . . . Finally it was not so easy to tell where pavements and walls left off and ground began. Especially on the hill-crown, which became a low-walled garden above the surrounding courts, reached by stone steps walled into the slopes. A clump of fine oaks that grew on the hilltop stood untouched on one side above the court. A great curved stone-walled seat enclosed the space just beneath them. . . . The hill-crown was thus saved and the buildings became a brow for the hill itself."[383] Wright was of course remembering the hill as it was when he envisioned the design, not when the work was actually executed. The information of what actually occurred was volunteered by former Senior Fellow William Wesley "Wes" Peters during an interview conducted by the author on August 10, 1989—at which time Peters was chairman of the board of the Frank Lloyd Wright Foundation. He explained that the natural appearance of the hill was a carefully crafted illusion, that the entire open space had in fact been reconformed and elevated by several feet over a period of time during the 1920s and 1930s—first by laborers, and later by apprentices working under his personal supervision and Mr. Wright's direction.

A study of Plan "b" supports that the limestone outcropping described by Wright was introduced into the area where the loss of trees from the first fire was most consequential, and the natural grade was retained where existing trees survived. This treatment allowed Wright to build up and round the crown to appear as a natural outcropping. It also brought about the means for Wright to capture the borrowed view of the sky and the distant Welsh Hills when looking toward the east. This, because the elevation and angle of the introduced outcropping screened the courtyard garden and forecourt from view, and the rooflines of the living quarters and loggia were subordinated enough to serve as the intermediary capturing device that framed the view and integrated the foreground and background. The canopies of the landmark oak trees in the Tea Circle to the left and the still-existing trees on the right were intended to direct and focus attention toward this borrowed view.

With the loss of the remaining trees in the grove, the means to focus attention toward the view to the east also was lost. One of the approaches Wright took to compensate for this circumstance in the mid-1950s was to position a large Chinese artifact at the eastern extremity of the outcropping as an alternate means to counterbalance the oak tree canopy in the Tea Circle and visually "trim" away extraneous elements that might draw attention away from the view[384] (Figure 6-2 a). He must have found this treatment to be inadequate, however, because shortly before his demise in 1959, he designed the elaborate arbor that today serves as a privacy wall for the Terrace Garden and creates a subliminal horizontal line extending from the underside of the studio-terrace eave to the limits of the peripheral vision of anyone standing on the hill and looking toward the east. Although Wright did not live to see it constructed, it was this horizontal extension, together with the urn on the outcropping and the canopy of the trees farther down the hill, that ultimately coalesced to create a true visual union between his architecture, his man-made landscape, and the greater environment (Figure 6-2 b-c).

Figure 6-2 a   Close-up view of Hillside Garden after addition of turquoise Ming vessel in 1955 and trellis that Wright designed before his death in 1959. (*Courtesy of James S. Ackerman.*)

Figure 6-2 b   Without the Ming vessel in place, the visual union between architecture and landscape is diminished.

Figure 6-2 c   Combination of Ming vessel and trellis "captures alive" the borrowed view—a textbook example of Wright's use of the Shakkei garden concept. (*Courtesy of James S. Ackerman.*)

Wright's purpose in expanding and elevating the level of the Hill Garden was the same as raising the first-floor living levels of his Prairie Houses: that is, to enrich the prospect value by intensifying the depth of the view. The act of ascending the stairway was intended to create a sense of anticipation for entering the realm of the Hill Garden and intensify the experience of the vista of seemingly illimitable open space, as it comes into perspective upon reaching the crown of the hill. By also treating the entire surface of the Hill Garden as a greensward, where the grass was to be maintained essen-

tially as a wall-to-wall carpet, Wright dramatized and focused attention upon the "range of vision" for anyone moving across the greensward toward the stone-walled boundary of the built environment. For a few brief seconds, there is a feeling of confusion, due to a paralax caused by the upward slant of the ground and the merging of several natural landscape features. Then, things fall into a logical perspective within this sensitively planned, well organized environmental design. When facing southeast, there are peripheral views through the tree foliage of the Welsh Hills in the distance and the Water

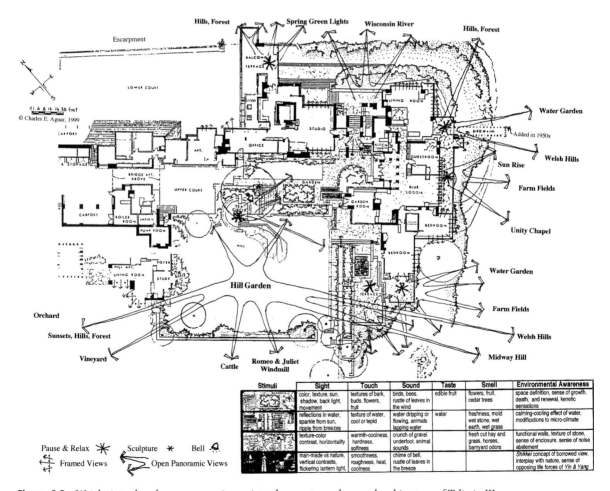

Figure 6-3 Wright introduced sensory experiences into the courts, gardens, and architecture of Taliesin III. (*By Charles E. Aguar, based on historic photographs, personal analysis, and original drawings of record. © 2002 by The Frank Lloyd Wright Foundation, Scottsdale, Arizona. As delineated, © 2002 by Berdeana Aguar.*)

Garden in the intervening valley, where the early morning fog shrouds the valley floor to create a sense of otherworldliness. Pivoting southward, there is Midway Hill, and the Romeo and Juliet windmill punctuates the treetops to claim the source of water for Hillside Home School. There also are the fields of crops, cattle grazing in the pasture, and the tracery of the vineyard. The culminating views are toward the southwest—where there are backlighted plantings, the apple orchard, and dramatic displays of the sky and clouds painted by the setting sun. But these experiences all have to do with sight. The accompanying chart of sensory experiences supports the many ways Wright also gave consideration to the senses of sound, smell, taste, touch, and overall environmental awareness, as well (Figure 6-3).

To visit Taliesin after the gardens were fully developed by June 1948—when the authors made their first pilgrimage to the site—was to engage in the ultimate sensory experience of a "Wrightscape." Taliesin seems to grow out of its site, as though it has been there forever. And yet, with the exception of the Wisconsin River, Jones Creek, the Welsh Hills, and the ledge of the escarpment upon which Taliesin stands, everything seen or experienced there was assiduously planned for or purposefully modified by Wright to fulfill his original vision. This is most evident in the gardens that completely envelop the Tea Circle, each founded on the same rationale as his original design to merely expand the parameters of the carefully cultivated "dewy ground" (in the vernacular of the Japanese garden), as places to be slowly walked through to reach the solitude of the Tea Circle destination sheltered under the broad canopy of the landmark oak trees. But this magnificent man-made landscape would not have the same effect had Wright's architecture not been sited and oriented as it was. It is because of his original vision that the colors, hues, highlights, backlighting, reflected light, and textures change every few minutes—as the sun charts its course, and as the observer moves from vantage point to vantage point. The preservation of this ensemble of cultivated-natural landscape was so important to Wright, that he made it his personal mission to purchase an extensive buffer—whenever financially possible—to minimize any obtrusive environmental impact, including the intrusion of man's carelessly placed structures, utility poles, and elements of outdoor advertising. This process involved decades, but his visual domain eventually computed to 20 times larger than the original acreage.[385]

In the final analysis, it must be determined that the charm of Taliesin is not in its individual parts, but in the organic integration of so many parts within such a limited-size ecosystem, and in the rhythm and harmony of the farm complex landscape as seen from the vantage points of the cultivated environment that Wright crafted to surround his home and studio. If Wright had built—and rebuilt—nothing else in his lifetime, his design and ultimate articulation of Taliesin near Spring Green, Wisconsin, would entitle him to be known as a landscape architect, as well as an architect—in a phrase, as an "environmental designer."

Hillside Home School for the Allied Arts— Spring Green, Wisconsin (1926–1928)

Wright's original thinking was to found a boarding school grounded in the Arts and Crafts concept of workshops that had flourished during the 1890s. Wright's December 7, 1926 letter to landscape architect Franz Aust follows up on what appears to be a previous discussion they had had on a matter he obviously already had given much deliberation. An enlightening aspect of his proposal—in addition to the concept itself—is the makeup of Wright's original list of endorsers for the venture: "I am suggesting as signers, myself, Jens Jensen, Dr. Ferdinand Schevill, yourself, Richard Lloyd Jones, Thomas H. Lloyd Jones. Then it would be easy to get such men as Frank Kimball, author and curator of Pennsylvania Museum of Fine Arts. In fact the thing might go from hand to hand, from man to man for signatures until we had a fairly representative group of one hundred or more of the most outstanding men in the United States who should be good judges of a matter of this kind."[386]

Thomas and Richard Lloyd Jones were first cousins of Wright. Thomas was a prominent professor at the University of Wisconsin (1915–1931). Richard was owner and editor of Madison's *Wisconsin State Journal* (1912–1919) until he left the area to establish another equally prestigious newspaper in Tulsa, Oklahoma. Ferdinand Schevill was a noted professor of history at the University of Chicago. Jensen was of course a long-time personal friend of Wright, but his greater significance lies in the fact that he was a landscape architect, well-known and respected throughout the Midwest. Aust likewise was a landscape architect—having worked with Wilhelm Miller at the University of Illinois until 1915, when he joined the faculty of the University of Wisconsin Department of Horticulture as a professor of landscape design. Wright's friendship with Aust had evolved through their shared affection for Jensen and their professional respect for each other. Wright consulted with Aust about the Taliesin landscape and plant selection. Aust, in turn, admired the manner in which Wright looked to the environment for inspiration. He called upon Wright to lecture to his students on this and other subjects, both at the University and on field trips to Taliesin. Aust also served as an active intermediary during Wright's subsequent efforts to arrange for the University of Wisconsin to formally sponsor his school under the umbrella of its mantle as an "Experimental College." The latter would take place a year or so hence, however, since Wright's attention was diverted to more immediate concerns as one personal problem after another besieged him.

It undoubtedly was this state of his affairs that caused Wright to accept the invitation of architect Albert C. McArthur to serve as a technical consultant for the Biltmore Hotel-Resort in Phoenix, Arizona. Since McArthur paid a substantial fee to obtain the "patent rights" for Wright's textile block system, it must be assumed Wright conveniently failed to mention that patent rights had never been granted. However, the consequence of the Biltmore alliance lies with the fact that it introduced Wright to the lucrative benefit to be derived from the emerging recreation of desert tourism and retirement. More significantly, it brought him into contact with Dr. Alexander Chandler—an important new client who owned a 1400-acre tract of land on which he planned to build a resort hotel to be known as "San Marcos in the Desert."

San Marcos in the Desert—Chandler, Arizona (1928–1929)

The commission for San Marcos in the Desert could not have come about at a more propitious time for Wright. In addition to providing the prospect of an income of $40,000 or more, it presented him with his first opportunity to demonstrate how his textile block system of construction could be applied to a large-scale project. He approached the assignment with much anticipation, and an April 19 letter to Lloyd—wherein Wright asks him to develop the presentation perspectives as soon as the topographic survey is available—suggests that he intended to draw his eldest son into the project almost immediately.[387] In Wright's enthusiasm, however, he evidently forged ahead absent the benefit of the land survey. This assumption is bolstered by Wright's April 30 letter to Chandler, in which he states he is "anxiously awaiting the plat and aeroplane [sic] views," but then goes on to explain he has cut and put together his "'stills' . . . as they belong, making a good panorama," that he was "all ready now to make drawings," and that "the scheme has taken shape definitely."[388] In other words, Wright apparently sketched directly upon a composite montage of photographs. Then, when the site topography turned out to be steeper than he had antici-

Figure 6-4 Presentation perspective of the never-realized San Marcos in the Desert Project, Chandler, Arizona. (© 2002 by Frank Lloyd Wright Foundation, Scottsdale, Arizona.)

pated based upon the photographs, perhaps he simply "fudged the plan to suit" as he did with the G. P. Lowes plan when he adapted it to the Storer site. This might explain why the presentation and working drawings propose a retaining wall of such monumental proportion under that section of the west wing that roughly parallels the main entrance road Wright placed within the deep, canyonlike arroyo that separated the natural land elevations on either side (Figure 6-4).

Wright's May 1927 letter to Lloyd that accompanied his conceptional layout describes "an architectural theme based on the triangle . . . the mountains . . . rising behind, triangles. The cross sections of the Suhuaro [sic] and all other desert plants,—triangles."[389] He also noted the degree to which his perspectives "show the character of the site with desert-growth and the rock-masses as they are, the building horizontally drifted between the rock ledges that terminate it,—belonging to all *naturally*." His wordage in *An Autobiography* further supports the degree to which he looked to the nature of the site for his inspiration: "I meant to embody in this desert resort all I had learned worthwhile about a natural architecture. . . . Arizona character seems to cry out for a space-loving architecture of its own. The straight line and flat plane, sun-lit, must come here—of all places."[390]

The structural form that Wright envisioned for San Marcos in the Desert generally followed the orthogonalized wingspread horizontality he had used to approximate the natural topography for the Johnson compound, except it was based upon the 30-degree angle rather than 60. All the public use areas were oriented toward the south—assumedly for the reasons of views and solar benefit. The guest quarters also were faced due south, or south-southwest, and arranged on three levels to encourage maximum air circulation, but stair-stepped back into the twin hills in such a fashion that the horizontal roof over the upper guest quarters served as a private terrace for the quarters below (Figure 6-5). All the guest rooms and public spaces were artfully interwoven with terraces and courts, and most featured plunge pools and/or fountain-pools to introduce moisture into the dry air of the desert and create a psychological cooling affect through the sound of running water. There also were to be swimming pools at the rear of the resort, in both formal and informal settings, and there were numerous planting beds throughout the complex.

The just-described siting and arrangement of a winter resort would seem logical to someone unversed in the climatic conditions of a desert environment. And it

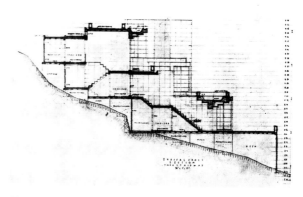

Figure 6-5 Cross section of San Marcos in the Desert guest rooms and private terraces on three levels, stair-stepped back into the twin hills. (© *2002 by Frank Lloyd Wright Foundation, Scottsdale, Arizona.*)

obviously seemed logical to Wright. After all, he grew up, apprenticed, and resided for the greater part of his life in the central United States, between 35° and 45° latitude. In that locale, the angle of the sun and prevailing winds merit equal consideration for all seasons of the year, and the most favorable orientation is for the long axis or principal façade (living-room windows) to face south to southeast, depending on the exact latitude. This orientation accesses optimum solar penetration during the winter, and controlling measures can be introduced and combined to effectively block penetration of the hot summer sun at the maximum aspects of midday and late afternoon: roof overhangs, deciduous trees, arbors, or other shading devices.

Below 35° latitude, however, the principal environmental considerations are capturing summer breezes and protection from the intense heat of the sun. Consider these facts: (1) sunshine in the Arizona desert averages 86 percent, year-round; (2) the days are exceedingly hot; and (3) the nights are exceptionally cool. These conditions do not support the expansive use of glazed openings oriented to the south-southwest.[391] The native population use adobe walls to slow the conduction of heat from the outside during the day and gradually release the stored heat to the interior during the cooler night. The only feature of Wright's design that in any way related to these characteristics was the massed verticality of the textured concrete block and copper "singing tower" that was to rise above the centrally bridged public use area like a giant saguaro cactus. This tower had a more important function than to emphasize the location of the lobby-entry court and provide counterbalance for the extended level plane of the 9000-foot-long structuring, as has been suggested. The tower and stairwells, together with the operable windows in the skylights and clerestories, were to function as a thermal chimney. During cool weather, the windows would remain closed to retain all solar heat that was absorbed. During hot weather, all operable windows and doors would be opened to create a ventilating convection that would draw the cooler air in through the lower openings, exhaust the heat built up in the skylight and clerestory spaces, and cool the public and private use areas.

Another important climatic consideration Wright did not address had to do with prevailing wind flow. For this locale, the prevailing breezes emanate from the east throughout the year—except during the month of July when they originate in the west, as they also do from November to March whenever winter storms blow in from the Pacific Ocean. Therefore, although the east wing of San Marcos in the Desert would be protected at all times as Wright designed it, the exposed living spaces in the guest rooms and terraces of the west wing would be subjected to every aspect of negative winter weather conditions. Granted, severe winter storms are less a contention in Arizona than some areas, but this does not neutralize their forcefulness or potentially debilitating impact. Then, there is the matter of Wright's placement of the only entrance roadway within the canyon-like arroyo. Again, Wright apparently did not give adequate thought to the flooding conditions generated by the occasional, but torrential, winter rainstorms that carved out this natural feature over millenia. It also is highly suspect whether he or consulting engineers would have been able to divert these waters into the aesthetic water feature he articulated onto the intervening landscape between the resort and the desert to the east of the arroyo.

The reality is that Wright would not develop a definitive faculty of how best to design for climatic conditions specific to Arizona until he lived in the area through a second winter, beginning in January 1929.

Correspondence of record confirms that preliminary studies were delivered to Chandler in September, that he approved the studies "in general" and instructed Wright to "go forward with the completion of these plans at once, in order that you can have prepared and submitted to me by January 1st, 1929, a set of plans and specifications complete in every detail."[392] Inasmuch as Chandler's deadline was not met and working drawings were not completed until well after Wright returned to Arizona, it seems reasonable to assume Wright devoted the last two or three months of the year toward refurbishing Taliesin, drafting conceptual house plans for his cousin's house in Tulsa, Oklahoma, and refocusing his direction on setting up some sort of professional money-generating operation on the premises—either in the form of a consortium of architects, or the School of the Allied Arts. This postulation is supported by a chronology of five sources: (1) an article in a July issue of *Capital Times* reporting that "dust, the mice and the moss are claiming empire over their invaded dominions" at Taliesin while the "romantic architect" is in exile;[393] (2) an article in the October 25, 1928 issue of *Wisconsin State Journal* reporting Wright's intention to employ "a large number of architects to live at Taliesin and work under his direction;"[394] (3) another article in the November 8, 1928 issue of the same newspaper captioned "Wright to Reopen Hillside School;"[395] (4) Wright's December 14, 1928 letter to his cousin stating he had "already spent some days making drawings;"[396] and (5) back-and-forth correspondence between Wright, Jensen, Aust, and Schevill relating to updating plans and developing a prospectus for sponsorship by the University of Wisconsin.[397]

As it happened, however, the school was again put on hold for the better part of another year after Chandler and Wright agreed that it might facilitate matters if Wright returned to Arizona.

On this first of many treks between Wisconsin and Arizona, a caravan of automobiles transported an entourage of 15, including 6 draftsmen, Will Weston—a long-time carpenter and handyman at Taliesin—and his wife Anna, who was a cook.[398] Upon their arrival, Chandler and Wright discussed thoughts Wright had previously expressed and had reiterated in his December correspondence: that is, that it would be more feasible for a group of this size to build a "sightly camp of wood and canvas . . . down near the building site," rather than spend several thousand dollars for suitable quarters elsewhere. Wright's reasoning was that this arrangement would give him opportunity to experiment with the formation of the concrete blocks and be on-site during the initial stages of the construction process. When Chandler agreed to this approach, he set in motion the means for Wright to begin experimenting with an architectural form that would be as responsive to climatic conditions specific to the desert southwest as San Marcos in the Desert was to its aesthetic character.

Ocatilla Desert Compound—near Chandler, Arizona (1929)

The site provided by Chandler for the Ocatilla Desert Compound was described by Wright as "a low, spreading, rocky mound rising from the great desert floor."[399] It was framed by mountain backdrop and defined by arroyos on the north and west—the same geologic features that characterized the proposed resort site, approximately one mile distant. Immediately after visiting the site for the first time, Wright set about designing the camp. He wrote: "It was cold. They said in Chandler 'unusual' weather, but whenever I had been there it was always 'unusual' weather: 'the coldest or warmest or wettest or dryest in thirty or fifty years.' The scheme was soon ready. Next morning we started in to build the first camp . . . by next night we had set up the first 'box-bottom' of the tent tops and put cots in it. . . . Next day there was room for all to sleep except my little family of three and myself. . . . But we came back for early breakfast to that wonderful dining-room sixty miles wide, as long and tall as the universe. We were shivering, oh, yes. But we were all singing happy in that clear cold sunrise. A great prospect! We had a sweeping view all around us of this vast battleground of titanic natural forces, called Arizona."[400] Wright also pointed out: "my draughtsmen . . . and I—we all made the camp between ourselves: put it together with nails, screws, rubber belting for hinges; rigged up the flaps with ship cord, all designed as carefully, probably more carefully than any permanent building."[401]

These commentaries are perhaps more telling than any of the architect's prior observations about Arizona—the first because it expresses his early experiencing of the fluctuations in climatic conditions, the second because it supports that he was personally involved with the actual construction process, at least at the on-site supervisory level. It is because of these associations that Ocatilla, though temporary and unrefined, is more relevant to Wright's development of a true organic character for the architecture he would subsequently design for this locale than the eminently more luxurious San Marcos in the Desert.

To begin with, Wright sketched his layout directly onto the topographic survey—an instrument so precise as to pinpoint the location and size of every saguaro cactus, in the same way trees are identified in most areas of the country (Figure 6-6). Armed with this most critical requisite for site-specific design, Wright was able to so adroitly conform the asymmetrical arrangement of wood-framed, tentlike structures to the irregular perimeter of the surface area of the mesa that the topography of the central knoll was left relatively undisturbed, every saguaro or scrubby tree was preserved, and limited grade change or supporting reinforcement was required. The latter was controlled even more by Wright's presence, because he was able to subjectively judge whether the leveling of a given structure was better accomplished by burying it into the ground or by raising and extending it on platforms supported by posts. Because of his involvement, grade changes were slight enough to be shoveled out by hand.

The encircling "wagon train" form of the camp layout suggests that Wright perhaps thought of his entourage as pioneers of the westerly winter resort movement. Clearly, however, it was the land form, "the great nature-masonry rising from the great mesa," that determined the predominantly horizontal dimension of the camp—an imagery Wright reinforced by circumscribing the lower portions of the tent structures with horizontally aligned board-and-batten walls, connecting "all the cabins about the mound" with a "low staggered box-board wall," and painting their surfaces with a cold-water paint that was "dry rose as the color to match the light on the desert floor."[402] And it was the land form of the central knoll that determined the placement of the symbolic "camp fire," although this feature again could ally with the wagon train campsite analogy.[403] Moreover, it was the land form together with the mature saguaros and existing trees that formed the basis for the asymmetrical arrangement and shape of the tent structures, determined the placement of the main point of access, established visual character and identity, and created silhouettes that heightened the three-dimensional impact of the camp (Figure 6-7). Lastly, it was the land form and location of the arroyo along the north boundary of the mesa that determined the situation of the automobile terminal point (carport) and other noise-generating interferences (experimental work yard, gas-generated light plant).[404] Thus, even though Wright characterized this layout as something of a quick study, and even though the layout was methodically angular-

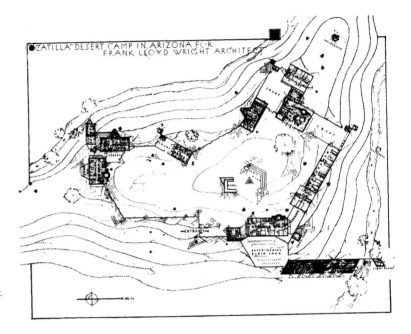

Figure 6-6 Plot plan for Ocatilla
Camp near Chandler, Arizona,
sketched onto a topographic survey.
(© *2002 by Frank Lloyd Wright*
Foundation, Scottsdale, Arizona.)

ized by his trusty 30–60° triangle, it is clear he under-took an intrinsic design response based upon his full knowledge of the phenomena of the landscape.

Wright also gave consideration to the entry experi-ence, site circulation, prospect vantage points, and indoor-outdoor use areas in the form of decked terraces and walled courts. He even adopted a red triangular form that he had painted on the gables of the camp structures and other accent points to underscore his tri-angular architectural theme. Fireplaces were built into exterior walls of the living room, dining room, and stu-dio. And historic photographs document a decor that included bright Navajo blankets used as throw rugs and couch covers, built-in shelves, custom-designed plywood tables, a grand piano and telephone, and an abundance of growing plants and dried arrangements. All in all, Wright wrote in a letter to his friend, landscape architect Franz Aust, it was a "very picturesque camp" of structures that appeared as "desert ships . . . in the midst of what is probably the most beautiful desert in all Arizona."[405]

It has been suggested by some that Wright's "desert ships" may have been inspired by the camps of tent-cabins that dotted the region to house migrant work-ers.[406] Considering the marked difference in the level of sophistication between these crude structures and those

of Wright's design, however, it seems more likely that Wright's creative impulse would have been Lloyd's use of canvas for his desert projects during the 1920s—most particularly the rookery tents Lloyd designed for Ellen True in Palm Springs in 1924, the same year father and son used canvas to create outdoor terrace rooms for the Storer House. The triangular form was a repetitive design feature in the rookery tents; each unit was graced with a fireplace; and framed canvas flaps were struc-tured to facilitate ventilation. Moreover, Gebhard and Von Breton cite them as Lloyd's "most way-out use of canvas . . . for partially or entirely covering whole build-ings" and allude to a father-son inspirational relationship in this medium: "Either tule mat or canvas was projected for roofs and walls on all of his [Lloyd's] desert projects of the 1920s. Canvas awnings originally formed an important visual and spatial element in the designs for Oasis Hotel, the Sowden house, the Samuel-Navarro house, and the Derby house. The rookery tents with their wood frames and canvas roof walls antidate by three years Frank Lloyd Wright's Ocatillo [sic] Desert Camp of 1927."[407]

This insight brings into question the extent of Lloyd's involvement with the Ocatilla layout. Gener-ally, he has been credited as the delineator of the per-

Figure 6-7 Wright, Olgivanna, and daughters Svetlana and Iovanna pose in Wright's Packard at Ocatilla, circa 1929. (*Courtesy of the Frank Lloyd Wright Archives, Scottsdale, Arizona.*)

spective renderings. However, Lloyd's resume lists "studies and working drawings" for Ocatilla Desert Camp together with "studies and perspective renderings" for San Marcos-in-the-Desert and "a number of individual houses planned for the project." Gebhard and Von Breton recount other of Lloyd's possible inspirational sources that would apply to Wright, as well. (1) Canvas awnings, exterior curtains, and canvas covers for courtyards were used extensively in the Spanish Colonial Revival houses of California and Florida. (2) Canvas awnings and coverings were used even earlier in the Mission Revival buildings. And (3) Schindler experimented with canvas during the early 1920s, including his personal residence—built while he was still working with Wright.

The ultimate consequence of the Ocatilla Desert Compound does not relate to Wright's initial design, however, but to his firsthand experience of living and working in the desert environment and the influence this brought to bear on his own Taliesin West (1937) and other domestic architecture designed for this locale. For example, when Wright arranged the structures to accommodate the natural topography and flora of the region, he coincidentally diversified their orientation so that, as the campers lived and worked in the various structures and adjusted the canvas-flap windows and

doors "like ship-sails when open . . . [to] shut against dust or open part way to deflect desert breezes into the interiors,"[408] he learned to objectively judge the orientation relative to climatic conditions and make adjustments as necessary. This reasoning is supported in his autobiographical retrospective on Ocatilla: "Screened openings for cross ventilation are everywhere at the floor levels, a discovery I made in seeking coolness, to be used during the heat of the day, closed at night."[409] It is in this same retrospective that he expresses his understanding of the natural forces that carved out the arroyos and formed the mesa topography: "What of the subsidence we see now changing the streamlines of these endless ranges of mountains coming by erosion gently down to the mesa. . . . In this geologic era, catastrophic upheaval has found comparative repose by way of these sculptors, Wind and Water. To these vast, quiet, ponderable masses made by fire and laid by Water—both are architects—now comes the sculptor—Wind. Wind and Water ceaselessly eroding, endlessly working to quiet and harmonize all traces of violence until a glorious unison is again bathed in the atmosphere of a light that is eternal." But it was in a letter to Aust that Wright perhaps best communicated the essence of this hands-on process of learning how to best design for the exposed climatic conditions of the desert southwest: "No man is really qualified as a director of landscape until he has soaked this desert into his system along with Arizona sunshine at least a number of times."[410]

By late May 1929, when the camp broke up for the summer, a mock-up structure of experimental concrete block molds had been completed and working drawings had been finalized. Within days of Wright's departure, however, at least half the camp that he and his entourage planned to reoccupy in August was destroyed by fire. August came and went with a date for the groundbreaking still unresolved, since Chandler did not have the necessary financial backing to begin. The fate of the winter resort was essentially sealed with the stock market crash of October 29, 1929 and the onset of the Great Depression.

Upon returning to Taliesin, Wright reasserted himself into the University of Wisconsin sponsorship debate regarding a School for the Allied Arts. Despite his efforts and apparent enthusiastic support for the "concept," he and the committee members came to an impasse during a meeting in early December, at which point Wright issued an on-the-spot ultimatum that gave the powers that be at the University until April 30 to accept his proposal.[411] He then turned his attention to plans he had been in the process of developing for five wealthy clients not too adversely affected by the stock market crash—including his first cousin, Richard Lloyd Jones. The distinctive, one-of-a-kind structure he designed for this cousin represents the culmination of his decade-long experimentation with textile block construction.

Richard Lloyd Jones' "Westhope"—Tulsa, Oklahoma (1928–1931)

"Westhope," the name by which the Jones home would come to be known, was derived from a nomenclature the Reverend Jenken Lloyd Jones (Richard's father) conceived for his family's summer cottage, built upon the south bank of the Wisconsin River overlooking the Lloyd Jones Valley. In a master's thesis analyzing the structure, Raymond Jontowne Wahl stated that Georgia Jones (Richard's widow) informed him during a November 1966 interview that "Westhope" was "a contraction designating not only a point on the compass, but the ancient Anglo-Saxon word 'hope' which means valley of a hill."[412]

The record of communication between the cousins concerning this structure reflects their childhood rancors and a jostling for superiority, tempered by their mutual bond of family and Wright's financial dependence on this contract. All of this acrimony is represented in Jones' November 26, 1928 letter to Wright wherein he scrupulously details the program of requisites his family of five will need. He dictated that the first floor contain a living room, a dining room that would "accommodate a party of twenty," a study "which shall be sizeable [sic] not less than 16 × 24," a pool room "which shall not be less than 22 × 16," a kitchen, pantries, and "something in the way of a vestibule or a receiving hall."[413] On the second floor, he prescribed five bedrooms and three bathrooms—two with a "combination tub and shower" and one with a shower only. He also provided Wright with pertinent climatic information: "The best exposure for bedrooms is south, so get as many bedrooms for the south bedrooms as can work in for our cool breeze in the warm weather is always from the south. . . . If it is possible I would like to have a roof of part of the first floor flat so that it could be used as a summer terrace and this should be a roof that would give us a view to the south, west and north. The least desirable outlook is toward the east. . . . Over the garage we should have about three servants rooms and they could have a balcony which would face the east, therefore giving us the protection of facing the street."

The direction of Jones' thinking demonstrates the like-mindedness of cousins similarly raised and influenced by Welsh relatives with a strong affinity for adapting to the processes of nature. Few clients would exhibit a cognitive depth of concern for orientation and prevailing breezes at this early stage of interaction. There also was Jones' regard for views, although this concern most likely bore upon the fact that the prospects of the Arkansas River Valley to the north and Turkey Mountain to the southwest were the *only* amenities that could be ascribed to the basically level and otherwise featureless four-acre tract of cleared farmland upon which he planned to build.

It appears that Wright did not visit the site until a year or more after he started working on the plans. This observation is supported by comments he made in his November 18, 1929 letter to Jones:

As to the drop in the lot, I understood from you . . . and the photographs themselves would seem to indicate, that the ten foot drop went from one corner of the lot to the other the long way of the lot, which wouldn't hurt our scheme in the least, the grade being changed somewhat to make a slight thickening of the base of the house take care of the matter. . . . What you now say about the slope of the ground would modify the arrangement of the house somewhat by varying the floor levels of the different portions of the group, which would improve it rather than hurt it from my standpoint. . . . However, I cannot visualize this as involving a ten foot decline or incline unless the photographs you gave me of your lot are deceptive. Will you kindly take time to go out to the lot or send some one out there to locate this ten foot drop precisely in relation to the various lot lines? . . . This sudden ten foot drop . . . is a surprise. Let us find out just what has happened and then I will see what we ought to do.[414]

Wright's closing remarks in the same letter suggest that Jones also took it upon himself to make a unilateral decision as to how the structure was to be sited: "I do not fancy very much your jamming your house up in one end of your lot as you indicated on the sketch, but if you will send me a little more concerning its typography [sic] we can study that out when you come."

The conceptual plans Wright originally sketched that first winter (at Taliesin) and detailed the following spring (at Ocatilla) were a variation of the zoned plan layout he had used with his California textile block

houses, but they also reflected his mind-set at that point in time through his incorporation of the triangularity of his designs for the Arizona desert. Jones objected to the angular approach, however, because he did not think it would live well: "It limits your view just exactly as blinders on a horse's bridle will limit the view of a horse. . . . I will sacrifice art gladly for the joy of seeing out of doors . . . give us a layout that would take the square block."[415] The plans that subsequently evolved most closely ally to the textile block houses of California. But the layout allies with the Allen House, in that the primary living wings stretch across the east side of an inner garden-court and wrap around the southwest corner; the servants' quarters and five-car garage wrap around the northeast corner, diagonally across; the privacy wall that bounds the inner garden court replicates the form of the exterior walls of the house; and steps were introduced to interject dimensional interest and depth (horizontal layering) into the inherent levelness of the bounded open space (Figure 6-8 a–b).

The unique rhythmic detail Wright devised for the exterior walls of Westhope alternated floor-to-ceiling columns of concrete blocks and glazed windows, with the vertically stacked components for each column measuring 15 inches in height and 20 inches in width (Figure 6-9). The garden court privacy wall differed only with respect to the components; the concrete-block columns were freestanding, and the alternating component was open space. Even when Jones argued he

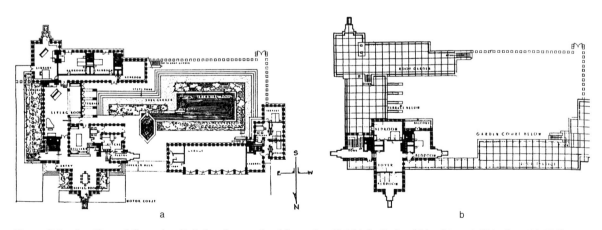

a   b

Figure 6-8 a–b   Ground-floor plan (6-8 a) and upper-level floor plan (6-8 b) for Richard Lloyd Jones's "Westhope" (1929) in Tulsa, Oklahoma. (© 2002 by The Frank Lloyd Wright Foundation, Scottsdale, Arizona.)

would "infinitely rather have your old style of architectural exterior, with the long horizontal windows," Wright staunchly defended his reasoning for this design methodology: "Now regarding this question of vertical articulation: the alternation of pillar and glass. Of course if you take the proper viewpoint your whole living room wall becomes a window with vertical mullions. All the walls become such. And you have outlook in every direction more than you could possibly have by building a wall and cutting a hole to look out of. . . . In this case the whole wall becomes a long horizontal window with vertical mullions dividing the glass in it. Now this gives you a distinctly dignified simple effect."[416] Wright did not go on to explain the enormous environmental benefit to be derived from the vertical articulation, or that this design form was integral to the very substance of his architecture.

It is important to note that Wright's construction methodology for Westhope incorporated everything he had learned over the past decade relative to designing responsively for climatic conditions in California and Arizona, and it was equally applicable to climatic conditions in the searing plains of Okalohoma. The massed stacks of concrete block used for the exterior walls provided the means to slow the conduction of heat from the outside during the day and gradually release the stored heat to the interior during the cooler night. The alternating columns of glass visually interlocked the interior and exterior living spaces, but the more important function had to do with their arrangement and operability. The operable windows within the columns were de-signed to channel breezes into the living spaces of the house and encourage maximum air circulation by working with the operable windows in the selectively placed raised clerestories, together with operable windows at the top of the stairwell—which functioned as a thermal chimney. The solid columns that formed the privacy wall of the garden court helped control the comfort level of the outdoor living spaces by impeding the impact of winds blowing in from the southwest. And they worked with the alternating columns of open-space to channel breezes across the sizable water body of the swimming pool and the profuse herbaceous vegetation to be introduced into the garden environment to moderate the temperature in the courtyard[417] (Figure 6-10).

The vertical articulation also was essential to the issue of privacy, a concern brought about by Jones' decision to "jam" his house into one end of the lot. The public presence of a structure the size of Westhope (8443 square feet) also had a great deal to do with the totality of Wright's art of day-lighting, which can only be understood and appreciated in context with the all-inclusiveness of Wright's design—particularly with respect to the finesse he exhibited in developing the interaction of opposing principles (Yin and Yang). Consider that the antithesis of the "outlook in every direction" is that the vertical mullions substantially constrain the range of vision from the outside looking in, as attested to by Wahl: "That 'Westhope' never lacks privacy inside despite the large number of windows is testimony of the screen's unusual composition. Because each pane is set toward the interior of a thick brace of

Figure 6-9 A unique rhythmic detail of Westhope's exterior walls featured alternating floor-to-ceiling columns of concrete blocks and windows. (*Photograph by Charles E. Aguar. © 2002 by Berdeana Aguar.*)

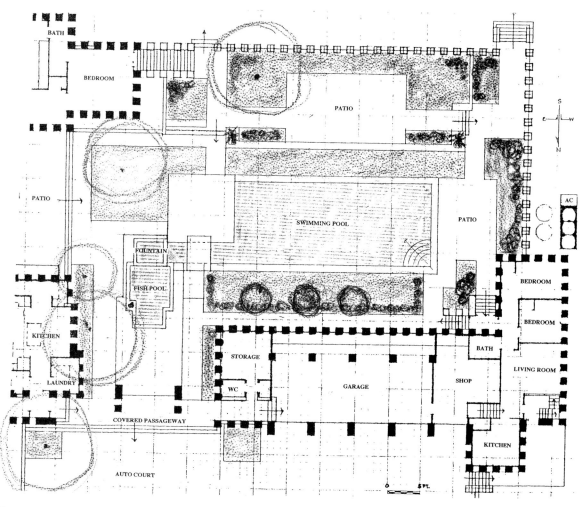

Figure 6-10 Westhope garden courtyard layout. (*By Charles E. Aguar, based on Raymond J. Wahl thesis and historical photographs. As delineated, © 2002 by Berdeana Aguar.*)

piers with only a narrow opening between for glass, little of the living room can be viewed from any single vantage point outside."[418]

The same interaction of opposing principles applies to the reverse telescopic form Wright conceived for the floor-to-ceiling window bays that project into the site environment (Figure 6-11). This distinctive detailing can perhaps best be described as a sophisticated interpretation of the *shakkei* concept of the borrowed view. From the inside looking out, the natural light dispensed through the expansive width of the innermost opening (the foreground) directionally attracts the eye. Then, the combination of the overhead plane of the ceiling and the progressively narrowing medium of enframement directs the eye toward the specimen plant or art object placed at the terminus (the intermediary object), which "captures" the proposed informally planted yard (the background) and brings it to the forefront as one integrated vista. In other words, the mind—rather than the eye—expands the scope of the perceived view. From the outside looking in, on the other hand, the backlighted projecting form of the bays directionally attracts the eye, rather than the darker recessed inner spaces, because the transparent glazed panes give a clear view of objects on the other side, reflect light, or allow light to pass through—whether the light is natural daylight or incandescent night lighting. This effect would not have been the case, however, had Wright not been selective about his "placement" of the bays. He planned for four only, to extend toward the four major points on the compass. But each was appended in a relatively obscure location, as opposed to high-use living spaces: one on the south wall of the library in a manner incidental to the living space; one (unbuilt) on the west end of the pantry; and two on the east and north walls of the entrance hall.[419] The significance here lies with the fact that these were areas of transition—that is, areas where there were no clerestories—so backlighting and daylighting were controlled.

When this complex combination of treatments is considered along with the location and expanse of the raised clerestories that infuse selected interior living spaces with natural light, it becomes apparent that Wright's foremost design intent was to heighten consciousness of the indoor-outdoor relationship and to essentially bring the out-of-doors inside, rather than to actually expand the range of vision from the inside looking out, as his cousin had requested. This reasoning is supported by an analysis of the plans, which substantiates that vistas were not of as much concern to Wright—from the standpoint of designing the primary outdoor and indoor living spaces—as the issues of privacy, control of the view, and the entry experience. Consider that Wright limited the principal prospect vantage points to the expansive terraces on the roofs of the bedroom and living-room wings, the roof terrace atop the servants' quarters, and the second-floor balcony that fills in the right angle of exterior space formed by the juncture of the two bedrooms on the southwest corner of the kitchen-bedroom wing. Although these outdoor living spaces originally afforded sweeping outlooks over the garden court toward Turkey Mountain, Wright assuredly would have been cognizant of the high probability that these views would be compromised as introduced trees matured and future development intervened. Moreover, none of the primary-use areas—living room, dining room, library—overlook or directly relate to the inner court. To visually or physically interact with the courtyard from any of these use areas, it is necessary to first proceed through an intervening transitional space. Thus, Wright used these transitional spaces to appropriately adjust the perception of luminance for anyone entering or leaving the primary indoor and outdoor living spaces so the eye would be immediately drawn to the open space environment and the sense of arrival would be intensified—whether that open space was the living room or the garden court.

Just as the Robie House is seen as Wright's terminal masterpiece of environmental design for his executed Prairie House architecture, Westhope should be recognized as the terminal masterpiece of environmental design for his executed concrete block architecture of the 1920s. Not only because it represents all of the design methodology described herein, but because of Wright's tenacity in defending his original vision. When the pencil rendering depicting Westhope as Wright envisioned it *could* be in 1928–1929 (Figure 6-12) is compared to the aerial photograph of the house taken while

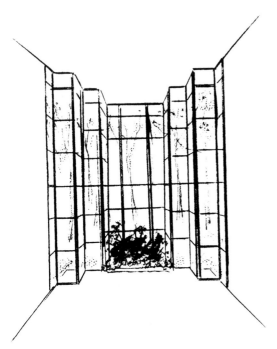

Figure 6-11 Reverse telescopic form of Westhope's floor-to-ceiling window bays. (*By Charles E. Aguar. © 2002 by Berdeana Aguar.*)

Figure 6-12 Wright's pencil rendering of Westhope, sketched in 1929. (© *2002 by The Frank Lloyd Wright Foundation, Scottsdale, Arizona.*)

Figure 6-13 1920 aerial photograph of Westhope, when still under construction. (*Courtesy of The Frank Lloyd Wright Archives, Scottsdale, Arizona.*)

the structure was under construction in 1930 when the site was barren and nondescript (Figure 6-13) and the materialized photograph taken by the author in 1992 (Figure 6-9), the merit of Wright's extraordinary visionary abilities becomes patently clear.

With the onset of the Great Depression, the careers of most non-government-sponsored designers came to a complete standstill, as did the careers of anyone involved with anything other than the indispensable basics for living. Frank Lloyd Wright was no exception. This placed him in a perilous position, professionally and personally. Although he had experienced extraordinary success as an architect early on, he had seemingly peaked before his time. And he had suffered through the personal anguish of two difficult divorces, negative press and notoriety, legal actions, arrest, the homicides, and the devastating fires at Taliesin—all of which threatened the loss of everything near and dear to his heart. Moreover, he was 62 years of age; he had a new wife; and two young children still lived at home. He had to find a way to once again reinvent himself—and he did. In fact, many have written that the most "productive" period of Wright's life occurred during his 70th to 90th years: 1937 to 1957.

Certainly, Wright's best known—that is, his most publicized—domestic architecture was yet to be conceived. But it cannot be denied that the prolificacy of these later years could not have become reality, and would not have flourished, had Wright not experienced the first 40 years of his career: 1889 to 1929. Because it was during the first 40 years of his career that Wright crafted and finessed the creative genius that would distinguish his work as "organic" throughout the next 30 years. It was during the first 40 years that Wright most consistently personally and professionally interacted with, and was significantly influenced by, landscape architects: Walter Burley Griffin (1899–1905), Jens Jensen (1907–1940s), Lloyd Wright (1912–1950s), and Franz Aust (1915–1930s). Most significantly, it was during the first 40 years that Wright was most closely involved with his clients and personally familiar with the sites and environments where their homes would be built.

Throughout the first three years of Wright's enforced professional indigence, he was for the first time in his life afforded the luxury to reflect on the abstract. And reflect he did. But he consciously did so in ways to direct attention toward himself and his work by participating in major exhibitions, writing for respected publications, and delivering a series of lectures at prestigious locations across the nation—including the Kahn Lectures on Art, Archaeology, and Architecture at Princeton University. In 1931, the Kahn lectures were published in book form and a traveling exhibition of his works was displayed in cities around the country. The ensuing positive reviews in major publications set the stage for the end products of Wright's endeavors during this time frame—the publication of two major books: his very insightful *An Autobiography* and *The Disappearing City.*

To a great extent, Wright's text for *Disappearing City* presented a negative "review" on how bad existing cities had become. His theoretical proposition for change was rather limited. Nonetheless, it attracted enough attention—together with the promotion of his exhibits and the publication of his lectures—that Wright was asked by the editors of *The New York Times Magazine* to respond to the January 1932 article written by the renowned Swiss painter-architect Charles-Edouard Jeannert, better known by his pseudonym: "Le Corbusier." Le Corbusier was one of the leaders of the International Style of architecture, which Wright strongly and vocally opposed. Within the January article, Le Corbusier put forth planning concepts he had introduced 10 years earlier, in 1922, to fuse architecture and modern transportation technology into a hypothetical city form he called "LaVille Radieuse." These plans focused on the use of high-rise apartment towers and rectilinear buildings designed for high density. He envisioned these structural forms grouped into central areas, but utilizing only 12 percent of the ground surface and meandering in a zigzag pattern within a parklike setting. He further suggested that vehicular traffic be confined to elevated roads connected directly to the buildings, so the ground level would be left free for pedestrian use.[420]

Wright's dual responses—in the March 20, 1932 *Times* article and another article published two months later in *American Architect*—literally attacked Le Corbusier's concepts of centralized urbanization and included him among those he labeled "skyscraperites." He

maintained that this type of development would become a means of "wiping out the city as it now stands only to reconstruct the towers for the lords a little further apart." This, even though he had himself designed three skyscraper projects within the same time frame—National Life Insurance Skyscraper (Chicago, 1924), Skyscraper Regulation Project (Chicago, 1926), and St. Mark's Tower in the Bauwerie (New York, 1929).[421] Wright had incorporated the model of St. Mark's Tower into the New York exhibition of his works in 1931. And within his apparently voluntary Skyscraper Regulation Project for nine city blocks in Chicago's downtown "Loop," he explored many alternative urbanization concepts similar to those put forth by Le Corbusier. These included varying the heights of skyscrapers to avoid dark shadows; providing better access to sunlight and air; and establishing a more humane scale for living in urban areas; developing roof gardens to create inner-city green spaces for outdoor living; introducing median-level or mezzanine walkways or "skyways" for pedestrian use above the street-level vehicular traffic; routing trucks below street level; and placing parking in underground garages. He even proposed replacing excessive tack-on signage typical to city streets with flaglike graphics that appear as part of the building. The logic of these plans demonstrate that Wright had a very clear understanding of the dynamics of modern city life.

At the same time, however, Wright had consistently directed his creative efforts toward responsive civic development at the more personal level, beginning with his plans for "A Home in a Prairie Town" and the Quadruple Block development published in the *Ladies Home Journal* (1901). Consider the record. There were the Quadruple Block plans developed for Charles E. Roberts (1903), his speech to civic-minded citizens of Springfield, Illinois (1906), the *Journal* plans for "A Fireproof House for $5,000" (1907), the plans for the Bitter Root Town Project and the Village of Bitter Root (1909), and his plans for alternative urban development prepared for the City Club Competition (1913); the American Ready Cut System Homes (1911–1916), Monolith Workers' Homes (1919), Wenatchee Town Plan (1919), and Concrete Commercial Building (1923); the conceptual suburban development plans for Lake Tahoe and Doheney Ranch (1923); the plans for Pre-Fab Sheet Metal Farm Units and a Roadside Market

(1932); and an Automobile-Airplane Service Station (1932).[422] Thus, when Wright went on to champion the single-family home as the dominant dwelling and asserted "the more sensible proceeding is to *let the automobile* take the city into the country," he was not stating anything other than what he firmly believed.[423]

As abridged and generalized as the articles responding to Le Corbusier were, they reflected the introspection Wright had invested in the talk he had earlier prepared for the City Club of Chicago—upon which both articles were based—and his theories were much better stated, overall, than in his book. But it was within the text of the book that he first used the two terms with which his name would come to be most closely associated throughout the final decades of his life and career: "Usonia" and "Broadacre City."

Wright used the term "Usonia" (said to have been novelist Samuel Butler's name for the United States) to describe a lifestyle and an architecture designed "for simple living, in harmony with nature, at a cost people of average means can afford."[424] Within this architectural objective, he established the site and environment as components basic to his design: "The Usonian house, then, aims to be a *natural* performance, one that is integral to site; integral to environment; integral to the life of the inhabitants. A house integral with the nature of materials—wherein glass is used as glass, stone as stone, wood as wood—and all the elements of environment go into and throughout the house."[425]

The term "Broadacre City" is said to have derived from Broad-acres ranch near the site of the Ocatilla Desert Compound outside Chandler, Arizona. Wright used the term, however, to personify his design approach for urban decentralization, which essentially restored rural primacy by distributing high-rise office buildings, industry, schools, civic and cultural facilities throughout the countryside amid farmland and neighborhoods of single-family and multifamily structures—all made easily accessible to a highway. Wright even recommended that airports or "plane stations" be located at 20-mile intervals near automobile service stops, and he suggested that highways could be used for "take off" by the "flying machine" (although he made no mention of landings). This was a very visionary concept only five years after Lindburgh's historic flight across the Atlantic and two years before the first aircraft with a passenger cabin was designed (even though the pilot was still in an open cockpit). It would be the second half of the 1930s before the DC-3 would revolutionize civil air transport.

Wright's thesis for Broadacre City appears to reflect his personal interpretation and synthesization of three notable philosophical reasonings put forth before and after the turn of the twentieth century: (1) the English Garden City concepts originated by Ebenezer Howard in the late 1800s; (2) the regional planning theory of "highwayless towns" and "townless highways" advocated by regionalist-naturalist Benton MacKaye in 1928; and (3) the utopianistic plea for a rebirth of true regionalism built up from neighborhood units, as espoused by social critic Lewis Mumford in several books he authored during the late 1920s and early 1930s.[426] In *Frank Lloyd Wright Remembered*, former apprentice Aaron Green states that Wright developed a "very warm friendship" with Lewis Mumford and respected his critical opinions above all others.[427] Thus, he assuredly was familiar with Mumford's insightful writings, as are all students of architecture and planning—then, and now. And he would have known of Mumford's formation of the loosely knit Regional Planning Association of America (RPAA) that originated the movement to develop "greenbelt decentralization" and inspired the Greenbelt Towns planned and developed under jurisdiction of Franklin Delano Roosevelt's "New Deal" Resettlement Administration in 1937 and 1938.[428]

To negatively critique Broadacre City in the context that it was Wright's one and only planning theory, or that it was *only* a planning theory—as has been done—is to do so without understanding the broader implications of his proposals for planning and social reform. Wright viewed urbanization as a threat to the quality of life for Americans of average means. Visionary that he was, he foresaw the impact the automobile would have on any form of decentralization and suburbanization that was not organized, or planned. In taking this approach, Wright was not alone. He was echoing the concerns of many professional-designers-turned-planners of this era, as supported within proceedings for national city planning conferences published annually since the first session was held in 1909. Broadacre City represented Wright's conceptual strategy for addressing these issues by becoming personally involved with planned development that would feasibly and sensitively integrate the man-made and natural environments. It was with this mind-set that he formulated his plans to develop an affordable Usonian architecture. It was with this mind-set that he conceptualized his Usonian communities. And it was with this mind-set that he resurrected his effort to found a school for architects: The Taliesin Fellowship.

Founding of the Taliesin Fellowship

The format devised for the Fellowship was rather loosely based upon the progressive education precepts originated at the Institute for the Harmonious Development of Man founded by Georgi Gurdjieff at Fountainbleau, where Olgivanna had been both pupil and instructor. Within the organizational process, Wright asked individuals with "name" recognition to assume the position of headmaster. He felt the headmaster designation would be necessary if he was to be at all successful in attracting a critical mass of students to such a remote location as Spring Green, Wisconsin. Among the many prominent figures courted were Dutch architect H. Th. Wijdeveld, artist Georgia O'Keefe, author-critics Lewis Mumford and Alexander Woolcott, and landscape architect Jens Jensen. Archival correspondence suggests that the establishment of such an ambitious school by a virtually penniless Wright was not taken seriously by most, although Jensen did offer his friend constructive criticism: "Now about that school . . . I shall both agree and disagree, as it is my privelege [sic]. . . . You will have to make some changes if I am to have anything to do with the school. The general principles are all right, but there are a lot of nasty rules and regulations and uniforms and labels; and why you want to submit intelligent minds, or whatever you call it, to the ordinary management demanded by the mediocre, I do not understand."[429]

In the end, the circular sent out in 1932 stated the Fellowship was to operate as an apprenticeship served under Wright and three as-yet unnamed resident associates. In lieu of a diploma, a personal testimonial written by Wright would be provided at the end of the apprenticeship, but there was no definitive time frame in which this could expect to be accomplished. Even so, 40 applicants were successfully registered by Fall 1932, originating from across the United States and from as far away as France, Switzerland, Russia, Denmark, Germany, Nicaragua, China, and Japan.[430] Nine already had been awarded degrees in architecture, 12 had studied architecture for from one to four years, and 4 held other professional degrees—including one in landscape architecture.

Wright's stated theorem for education within this format was: "Art in any creative sense may be inculcated or cultured in work but cannot be taught by a book."[431] Therefore, there was no formal curriculum in the traditional mode, and Wright did not "teach" in the academic sense of the word. His lectures or talks, while informative and consistent, were more intuitive than explicit. For drafting and design, he arranged that apprentices would learn through the observation of, and physical participation in, the design and construction of works-in-progress. However, former apprentice Edgar Tofel stated that drafting was for the most part limited to tracing and redrawing Wright's preexisting design schemes during the first years of the Depression. And drafting class schedules did not stand for long, as Mr. Wright would call everyone outside to work on the dam, haul something somewhere, or do anything else deemed necessary.[432] In many ways, the Fellowship of the early years could be likened to a "boot camp" for organic architectural training, albeit a camp that included other aspects of the fine arts and interaction with international celebrities which combined to facilitate a finer total environment.

The first "real" work-in-progress the apprentices would follow through all phases of design and construction was a modest house for Malcolm and Nancy Willey in Minneapolis, Minnesota.

ENVIRONMENTAL DESIGNS, 1932–1937

Malcolm E. Willey—Minneapolis, Minnesota (1932–1934)

The introductory letter Wright received from Nancy Willey listed all the qualities his clients wanted their new home to provide: "seclusion, retreat, freedom and breadth of outlook, privacy, expanse and beauty of a country home."[433] They also wanted a house that was "a creation of art," reflected "modern principles of architecture," and could be built at a cost "not to exceed $8,000." She then stated they had "little hope you would take on anything so trivial and that was also not near you." Wright's response reinforces the dire straits of architects in 1932: "Nothing is trivial because it is not big, and if I can be of any service to you, neither the distance nor the smallness of the proposed home would prevent me from giving you what help an architect could give you."

The site on which the Willeys proposed to build their home was a very modest corner lot that sloped gently toward the streets bounding the west and south sides of the property. But the minimal size was more than compensated for by the benefit of its situation on a bluff overlooking the Mississippi River, which had by this point widened a significant degree from its inception as a stream in Minnesota's upstate Itasca State Park. It undoubtedly was because of this peripheral environment that Wright's first inclination was to revert to the raised-

224 WRIGHTSCAPES

basement approach he had used with Prairie Houses under similar circumstances, as represented by his first design proposal in 1932.[434] By the time the plans were finalized in 1934, however, both the exterior appearance and the compact L-shaped layout forecast the basic one-story grammar of Wright's earliest Usonians—including the concepts of the combined living-dining room, a central utilities core "workspace" coordinated with the fireplace to facilitate an effective ventilating system, and a "gallery" hallway leading to the bedroom wing (Figure 7-1). But it was the break-through, zero-lot-line siting in tandem with the articulating brick privacy wall and other aspects of Wright's environmental design that set the Willey House apart from the norm.

Wright sited the Willey House so that the basically solid brick north and east walls of the primary living areas tucked into the northeast corner of the landlocked property lines. He then introduced a brick "Garden Wall" and extended it downslope the entire length of the east property line (Figure 7-2). As with the Heurtley

House, this very substantial brick wall repeated the rhythm and texture of the alternating bands of brick used for the house and introduced a strong repetitive metaphor of horizontality into the streetside appearance. It also visually defined the property and created the illusion that house and landscape were much more expansive than they really were. Most important, it screened the primary indoor and outdoor living spaces from the immediately adjacent neighbors and protected these living spaces from the prevailing northeasterly winter winds—an extremely relevant design consideration for Minnesota. The same design rationale applies to the basically solid character of the north and east walls of the primary living areas (Figure 7-3).

It is significant that Wright introduced no windows along the north wall of the gallery hallway in the normal sense, but he did introduce a grill-like pattern of openings in the brick that aligned with the band of small operable windows installed under the eaves behind the basically solid wall. And although he also introduced no

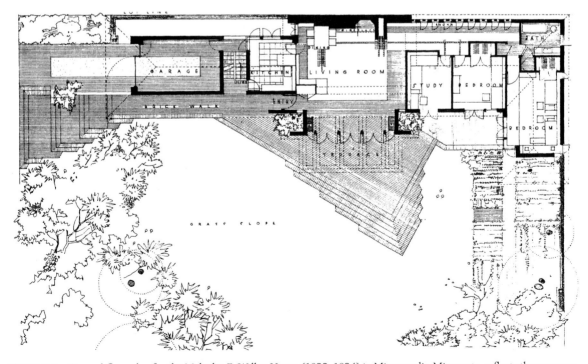

Figure 7-1 Ground-floor plan for the Malcolm E. Willey House (1932–1934) in Minneapolis, Minnesota, reflects the grammar of early Usonians. (© 2002 by The Frank Lloyd Wright Foundation, Scottsdale, Arizona.)

Figure 7-2 Garden wall for the Willey House extends along entire east boundary to visually define and visually maximize size of property. (*Photograph by Charles E. Aguar. © 2002 by Berdeana Aguar.*)

windows along the north wall of the living-dining room, he did install both fixed and operable windows on the three sides of the north-facing raised clerestory—but behind a separate, solid brick barrier wall that rose to the height of the clerestory roof. He then installed glazed

French doors along the entire south wall of the living-dining room to provide maximum access to the solar benefit of the low angle of the winter sun, and he introduced an expansive cantilevered-and-pierced overhang across the same space to shade the living-dining room

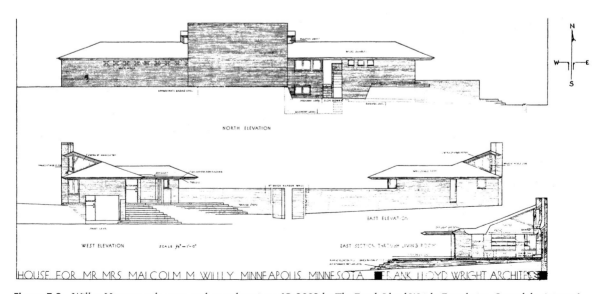

Figure 7-3 Willey House north, west, and east elevations. (*© 2002 by The Frank Lloyd Wright Foundation, Scottsdale, Arizona.*)

from the elevated angle of the summer sun. He also installed French doors at the southwest corner of the master bedroom. All the French doors, in turn, opened onto the south-facing brick terrace that echoed the triangularity of Wright's desert creations, with angularized wraparound steps leading down the slope.

Wright's motivation for each of these seemingly disparate aspects of his design clearly relate to his environmental vision. The pierced brick openings and the glazed openings in the upper reaches of the clerestory introduce daylight into the northernmost areas of the living room and along the entire length of the gallery hallway, year-round. During the summer months, when breezes inherently drift upland from the Mississippi River, the combination of the expanse of opened French doors and the opened windows near the ceilings of the raised clerestory and the gallery hallway work together to air-condition the house naturally, by creating a convectional current that forces the hot air out and simultaneously channels fresh air into and through the primary living areas.

Guest parking and the garage were accessible from the west right-of-way, where Wright retained enough open space along the north property line to allow the indroduction of a free-flowing entry garden that was to merge with the adjoining landscape so the structure would not appear constricted upon the site. This treatment complemented the entry approach that parallels the ground-level parking and then modulates up the natural slope by way of broad, low steps interspersed with three terraces that synchronically merge into the width of the entry walkway leading to the main entry and the living-room terrace, which overlooks the spacious park-like front lawn.

In all the foregoing respects, Wright both minimized the disadvantages and maximized the advantages of living in a small house on an average-size corner lot in a typical urban subdivision. Unfortunately, this carefully orchestrated spirit-of-place was severely compromised when Interstate Highway 94 and an intrusively massive barrier wall were constructed to parallel the south property line. When the authors revisited the Willey site during the 1990s, three sides of the grounds had been walled. Nonetheless, highway noise and exhaust pollution assaulted the senses.

By 1934, some members of the apprentice pool were becoming bored with tracing old file drawings and per-

haps with the servitude system, in general. Paying commissions continued to elude Wright and it became obvious that a substantive project was needed that would involve and challenge the apprentices until the depressive economy improved and commissions again materialized.[435] It was on this basis that Wright had the apprentices fabricate models to illustrate the Broadacre City he envisioned.

Broadacre City, in Three Dimensions (1934)

The model format was seen by Wright as a three-dimensional teaching tool that could then be used to "spread the word" of his concepts for decentralization more graphically and effectively than he had been able to do thus far, through exhibition in major cities. The basic conceptual elements of the models were patterned on topographic maps of the region in and around Taliesin. As Wright's thought processes moved from the abstract to the literal, he became caught up in a myriad of specific, if hypothetical, construction details (Figure 7-4a). The project list for 1934 includes 15 separate projects for Broadacre City, starting with the Master Plan and encompassing details such as highway overpasses and lighting, hospital groups, and arenas. By the time exhibition materials were complete, there were several individual architectural models and a series of enlarged drawings in addition to the 12-foot-square base model, with every detail color coded and keyed to numbers that explained transportation proposals and detailed specific architectural proposals (Figure 7-4b).

The first exhibition of the Broadacre City Models opened at the National Alliance of Arts and Industry at Rockefeller Center on April 14, 1935. Some 50,000 people attended. Other scheduled exhibitions also were well attended. During a March 1990 interview with the author, former apprentice Cornelia Brierly described the impact the models had upon those who attended these initial showings.

> I had the task of explaining the model and answering questions. . . . In Pittsburgh, anybody could come in to see it, and the crowds mostly passed through in lines. But at the Corcoran Gallery in Washington, D.C., it was by invitation only and the department heads, congressmen, and other governmental officials took lots of time and asked many questions. Engineers and transportation people—some were from Europe—seemed especially interested in Mr. Wright's highway proposals. This was a

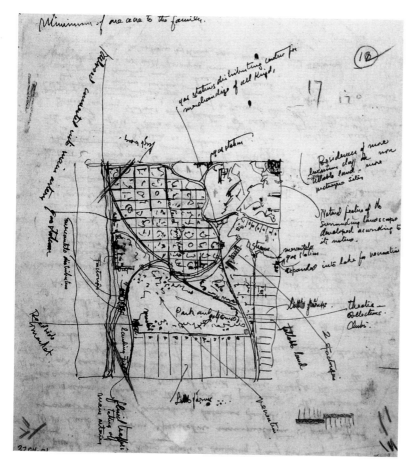

Figure 7-4 a Typical notes on sketch for the Broadacre City model (1934) read: "Residences of more luxurious class on non tillable land—more picturesque sites. . . . Natural feature of surrounding landscape developed according to its nature." (© 2002 by The Frank Lloyd Wright Foundation, Scottsdale, Arizona.)

very advanced form of transportation for 1935, when most roads were unpaved. The only cross-country route we had was the Lincoln Highway, and it was only a narrow paved ribbon interrupted by many small towns and intersected by narrow local roads. . . . Mr. Wright also developed the efficient and well-designed motel convenient to the highway system, but set back from the noise and well landscaped.[436] In 1935, the travelers stayed in hotels within the cities and close to the railroad stations, in tourist homes in small towns, or in rustic cabins of tourist camps on the outskirts. From the interest shown by highway people and the notes they took, I believe it [the model] had a tremendous effect on the development of the later inter-state highway system—even if what was built was not as far-reaching as Mr. Wright's ideas of separate lanes for cars and trucks, with a monorail in the center (Figure 7-5).

The interstate highway system was inspired by, and based upon, the regional planning philosophy introduced by Benton MacKaye seven years earlier. However, Brierly was correct in crediting these exhibitions as having influenced the direction of development far into the future. Indeed, no planning proposal ever has had as much exposure or influence as Wright's Broadacre City, due in large measure to the articulation crafted into the models and the quantity and quality of publicity generated through their exhibition.

Figure 7-4 b   Wright with completed Broadacre City model.
(© *The Bettmann Archive/Corbis.*)

The model construction costs were financed by Edgar J. Kaufmann, father of one of the apprentices and president of the Kaufmann Department Stores, Inc., in Pittsburgh. But Kaufmann's greater notoriety has to do with his status as the client who hired Wright to design a weekend retreat for his family on acreage located some 60-to-70 miles southeast of Pittsburgh. The architecture that originated out of this unlikely relationship has come to be adjudged by many as the most famous domestic architecture of the twentieth century, designed by Wright or any other architect: "Fallingwater."

Edgar J. Kaufmann, Sr., "Fallingwater"—Mill Run, Pennsylvania (1935)

The magnificent multiacred, wooded property on which Edgar J. Kaufmann, Sr., proposed to build a second home for his family is, without question, the most environmentally significant landscape of any of Wright's executed works. And the architectural statement articulated by the three-level structure of stone, glass, and concrete Wright designed to dramatically cantilever over the waterfall is recognizable to legions of people—from around the world, from all walks of life (Figure 7-6). At the same time, however, this structure cannot be viewed

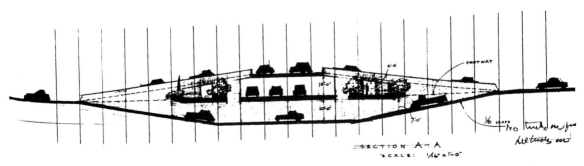

Figure 7-5   Sketch of Broadacre City highway intersection providing separate lanes for cars and trucks, with monorail in center.
(© *2002 by The Frank Lloyd Wright Foundation, Scottsdale, Arizona.*)

realistically without recognizing it as less a "union with nature" than a beautiful work of art that imperiously proclaims "dominion over nature." Fallingwater in fact belies every aspect of Wright's "prescription for a modern use," as put forth in the November 1955 issue of *House Beautiful* magazine. "First, a good site," he wrote, "then, standing on the site, look about you so that you see what has charm. What is the reason you want to build there? Find out! Then build your house so that you may still look from where you stand upon all that

Figure 7-6 Fallingwater—the most famous domestic architecture of the twentieth century—cantilevered over a waterfall near Mill Run, Pennsylvania. (*Photograph by Charles E. Aguar. © 2002 by Berdeana Aguar.*)

charmed you, and lose nothing of what you saw before the house was built, but see more."[437]

Ironically, the Kaufmann family's idealization for the siting of their new second home followed these very guidelines. They had been using this property as a retreat for a period of time and had told Wright their site-of-choice was at the base of the ravine to the south of Bear Run Creek, where the head-on view of the beautiful waterfall was directly opposite. Why, then, would Wright choose to ignore his own prescription and design the architecture to command visually and physically over the environment his clients saw before the house was built? He even incorporated the rock ledge upon which family members used to sunbathe into the living room floor—this, in deference to his client, who did not want to "shave" it, as Wright originally proposed to do.

Some historians have suggested that Wright intended Fallingwater to make a melodramatic statement that would warrant public attention, emphasize his unique talents as an architect, and revitalize his lagging career. Certainly, this is what occurred. Untold articles about the Fallingwater architecture have been written for newspapers and magazines. Chapters and even entire books also have been published about this work. But there is a substantive variance of opinions about the end result. Vincent Scully compared the dominating character of Fallingwater to the architecture of the International Style.[438] Meryle Secrest likened it "in feeling" to Taliesin.[439] It is true, as Secrest goes on to say, that the natural environment has been preserved and garden paths hug the steep hillsides or disappear into thickets of trees (Figure 7-7). Wright also oriented the primary living spaces for environmental benefit and expressly articulated a strong indoor-outdoor interrelationship, as he did with Taliesin. And the choreography of the Fallingwater entrance experience is every bit as sensuously meaningful as at Taliesin, if not more so—particularly as the structure begins to emerge through the woods when the entrance approach crosses the bridge over Bear Run Creek, at which point the sight and sound of water rushing over the boulders and plunging down the waterfall commands attention, stimulates the imagination, and raises the level of anticipation for whatever lies ahead. But it is at this point that the similarities between Fallingwater and Taliesin end.

At Taliesin, a definitive sense-of-place is visually established as the panorama of the natural attraction—the greater site environment—unfolds from multiple viewpoints, indoors and outdoors. At Fallingwater, this is

Figure 7-7 Naturalistic landscape surrounding Fallingwater, as approached through woods. (*Photograph by Charles E. Aguar.* © 2002 by Berdeana Aguar.)

not the case. Although Wright enticed and propelled movement toward the windows and toward the portals leading to the outdoor terraces on all three levels, there is no view of the natural attraction from any vantage point designed as part of the structure—unless looking straight down over the parapet of one balcony would qualify. Just as the most publicized artistic perspective of the Hardy House as viewed from Lake Michigan is not accessible to anyone approaching the structure from the access road or from the house and terraces, the head-on view of the singular entity of house and waterfall that is the most recognizable perspective of Fallingwater is only accessible from the site across the ravine, where the Kaufmanns envisioned their retreat would be built.

To the author of this writing, Fallingwater is the antithesis of Taliesin. It was perhaps Wright's greatest illusion, because it breathtakingly articulates his architectural artistry but contradicts every dictum he ever expressed with respect to site integrity or harmony with nature. Indeed, Fallingwater *overwhelms* nature, and at great cost, as the natural cycle of freeze-and-thaw conditions continually battles its architectural intrusion. This dilemma is attested to by Edgar J. Kaufmann, Jr., in the book he wrote 50 years after construction was completed: "the cantilevers fell and rose in response to temperature changes affecting the material . . . the constant movement reopened cracks and strained flashings . . . water penetrated . . . as distressing leaks. There were

seventeen such areas when we first moved in. . . . Some leakage still occurs."[440] These conditions make Fallingwater very expensive to maintain as a work of art. Periodic published accounts in magazines and newspapers confirm that the costs of repairing cracks in the concrete and Fallingwater's structural supports are significant. And in recent years, the problem of acid rain dissolving the mortar bonding has added to the high cost of annual maintenance.

Had Wright tried to obtain a building permit for Fallingwater under the more stringent environmental protection standards in place today, it never would have been constructed. Nonetheless, all designers—student designers, in particular—should "experience" this legendary structure at least once in their lifetime and arrive at their own opinions as to the complicated issues involved. Because, in spite of every logical argument faulting Wright's design methodology, Fallingwater evokes a responsive sense-of-place absolutely in keeping with the rugged character of the massive rocks, the turbulence of the waterfall, and the natural persona of the forested site. Indeed, it is the amalgamation of the disharmonious attributes of Wright's design that creates the incredible awareness so empathetically characterized by landscape architect John Simonds: "The precision and whiteness of the concrete forms contrast boldly with the natural forms, colors, and textures of the site. Yet the structure seems at home here. Why?

Perhaps because the massive cantilevered decks recall the massive cantilevered ledge rock. Perhaps because the masonry walls that spring from the rock are the same rock tooled to a higher degree of refinement. Perhaps because the dynamic spirit of the building is in keeping with the spirit of the wild and rugged woodland. And perhaps because each contrasting element was consciously planned to evoke, through its precise kind and degree of contrast, the highest qualities of the natural landscape."[441]

Herbert Jacobs I—Madison, Wisconsin (1936)

The first of two residences Wright would design for Katherine and Herbert Jacobs is recognized by most historians as the first "built" prototype of the affordable Usonian residence.[442] It evolved from the "City Subsistence Homestead" affordable housing scheme Wright first prepared for the Broadacre City Models in 1934 and plans proposed for C. H. Hoult in Wichita, Kansas, and Robert Lusk in Huron, South Dakota—both unbuilt. Perhaps that is why Wright so readily agreed to build the Jacobs House within their circumspect budget. In a book written about their experience of building with Wright, Katherine Jacobs described their first meeting:

> We were living in Milwaukee when we first came in contact with Mr. Wright. We had thought he was a rich man's architect but through my cousin, Harold Westcott—who had spent a summer with the Taliesin Fellowship—we were convinced to go see him about a house we hoped to build some day. Although we really didn't expect Mr. Wright to have interest in designing a small house such as we might afford, Harold knew that Mr. Wright needed work so we drove over to Spring Green. . . . In order to break the ice, Herbert said: "What this country needs is a decent $5,000 house. Can you build one?" Mr. Wright answered: "Do you really want a $5,000 house or do you want a $10,000 house for $5,000?" When we said we couldn't afford any more than that, he replied: "Well, come into my office, said the spider to the fly." It was a strong and beautiful web he wove, because we were captivated and encouraged. He told us we were the first to ask him for a $5,000 house. This wasn't quite true, but we were the first who were ready to build it.[443]

During an interview conducted by the author on August 22, 1992, Jacobs said they left the meeting forewarned that Wright would not begin planning their house until they settled on a property and location where they wanted to build. This did not occur until the following year, when her husband accepted a position with a newspaper in Madison, Wisconsin—less than an hour's drive from Spring Green and Taliesin. She explained the search and design process: "The lot we found was sixty feet wide in a new subdivision called Westmoreland that was then just outside Madison. . . . When we received the plans from Mr. Wright and studied them carefully, it suddenly dawned on us that he had designed it exactly sixty feet wide. Of course, we knew it could not be placed on a sixty-foot lot. We found a property across the street, a doublewide corner lot, and Mr. Wright just flopped the plan. And we got better exposure than we would have otherwise. Our bedrooms still faced south, but instead of the glassed living room facing west, it now faced east—but I never worried about it, or thought much about the important change this was." So, here again, Wright clearly countermanded his own rhetoric and "just flopped the plan." It appears to have been pure happenstance that the orientation was somewhat improved in the process.

There are no grading plans or planting plans of record for Jacobs I. However, Wright did draft a layout that suggests his recommendations as to the articulation of the landscape (Figure 7-8). He proposed developing a minimal entry garden of flowers between the north property line and the short driveway leading to the carport. He also proposed that the gently sloping lot be graded to form a tapered bank in the form of a hemicycle to be planted with groundcover—a treatment intended to create a sense of enclosure and to visually expand the narrow concrete terrace onto which the French doors open from both wings. And he proposed that two sets of bricked steps be installed to lead down to a sunken open space bounded by a privacy hedge, so this area could be used for an informal perennial garden and/or outdoor pursuits. This landscape never was fully developed, however. Jacobs explained: "We had no detailed planting plan but carried out Mr. Wright's landscape plan to a certain extent. Most ornamental shrubs were those we dug out of the woods, as Mr. Wright suggested. But the trees planted at the street corner were planted too close and got too big, so we had to take out some of them. We did have some dirt brought in to fill in some of the low spots. And we started a hedge along the side street, but it never grew enough to provide any privacy. When we could afford it, we added a low fence for more privacy from the front."

Jacobs went on to explain some of the innovations Wright used to trim construction costs: "He made it so all materials served more than one function so the workmanship was not duplicated. The brick wall sections and the wood is the same inside and out. The door frames are just 2 × 4s. . . . Simplicity such as this was true all through the house. And we were his guinea pigs for floor or radiant heating, which had never been used in an American house, ever. He asked if we were willing, and we said 'yes.' That was the kind of relationship we had with him. We had the courage and faith in him to let him have the freedom to try new things in order to get the most out of a creative person."

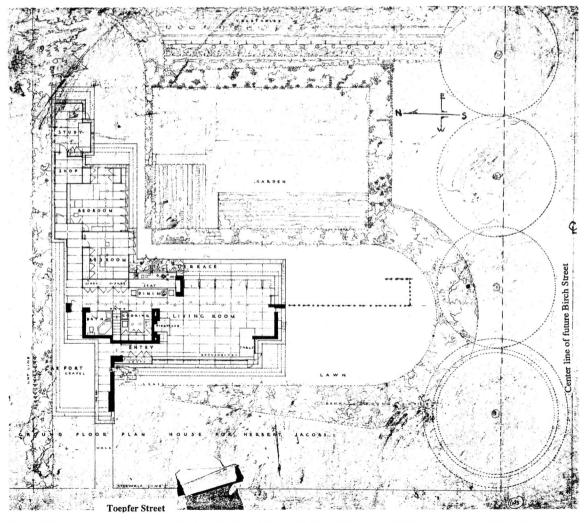

Figure 7-8   Ground plan for the first Herbert Jacobs residence (Madison, Wisconsin, 1936) proposes methodology for articulating landscape but offers no planting plan. (© *2002 by The Frank Lloyd Wright Foundation, Scottsdale, Arizona.*)

. . .

The physiognomy of Wright's affordable Usonian architecture evolved logically from the design and construction grammar of his Prairie Houses (Figure 7-9). The porte-cochere became a cantilevered carport. The covered porch off the living room became an open paved terrace. Urns at exterior terminal points became built-in planting boxes. The expansive banks of art-glass windows that provided natural light and privacy were replaced by bands of windows arranged behind grill-like openings in brick walls, or behind fretted plywood inserts inspired by the "ramma" ornamental fretwork of the Japanese. And the ambiance of patterned filigrees of natural light changing hourly, daily, and with each season of the year was equally palpable. The mitered corner windows introduced in 1892 as corbeled corner windows for the McArthur House, modernized and expanded for the Ennis House, and aggrandized for Fallingwater reappeared in the Usonians. By eliminating the corner support to both expand and angularize the perspective, Wright was able to create the illusion that outward views onto modest subdivision sites were of more panoramic proportion. The detailed floricycle conceived for Willits

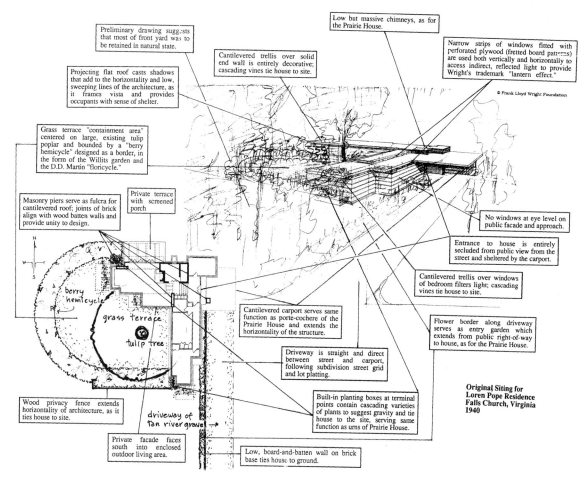

Figure 7-9   Physiognomy of Wright's Usonian domestic architecture. (*By Charles E. Aguar, based on personal analysis and drawings of record. © 2002 by The Frank Lloyd Wright Foundation, Scottsdale, Arizona. As delineated, © 2002 by Berdeana Aguar.*)

and D. D. Martin reappeared as a simple hemicircular formation of flowers or shrubs to contain and privatize the primary outdoor living spaces. And the formal contained perennial gardens that required constant attention were replaced by native plants dug from nearby woods. The coalescence of all these techniques afforded occupants of the most modest Usonians the same aesthetic benefits experienced by occupants of the most expensive residences of Wright's design.

It was during this same time frame, however, that Wright also began to introduce generic or preconceived plans to his clients on a fairly regular basis—basically following the precept: "Do as I say, not as I do." Former apprentice Frederick Gutheim described one such occasion: "I remember coming into Wright's studio office early one morning when he was opening his mail. Throwing one of the arriving letters across the table, he remarked, 'That's the kind of letter I like to get.' It was from a faculty wife in an Illinois college asking if Wright would design a house for her and describing in detail the proposed site. As I returned the letter, Wright called to his secretary, 'Gene! Send this woman the plans for the museum house.' It was a building designed for the garden of the Museum of Modern Art. I began to laugh. 'You're a fine one,' I said, 'preaching about building from the ground up and now you are going to build a house on a site you have never seen.' 'So what,' he grumbled, 'It ought to be built.' "[444] Assumedly, this was what occurred after Paul and Jean Hanna contacted Wright about designing a home to be built on an as-yet undetermined site in Stanford, California.

Paul Hanna—Stanford, California (1936)

Paul and Jean Hanna first contacted Wright in 1930 after having read, and been inspired by, newspaper accounts of his Kahn lectures. They visited him at Taliesin shortly thereafter and left with the understanding that he would someday design a house for them. That day arrived in 1935, when Paul Hanna joined the faculty at Stanford University. The Hannas had been inspired by their visit to Taliesin, and their list of requisites included "land on the brow of a hill, with view and drainage, large enough for gardening, playing, and privacy," "a house nestling into the contours of the hill," "walls of glass so that we could always be visually conscious of sunrise or sunset, the fog banks rolling over the hills, or trees and grass in the fields," and "a house with terraces and gardens that would accommodate up to two hundred guests for informal functions, sunning or relaxing in sunshine or shade, and children's activities."[445] (Figure 7-10).

The Hannas were very surprised, they said, to receive a set of plans for a two-story house before Wright had visited the area and before they had selected a site. It was only after they returned the plans, together with their request for a one-story structure, that Wright traveled to northern California and helped them select from three properties under consideration. The site of choice faced southwest on a gently sloping hillside and was within the expansive boundaries of the Stanford campus, originally laid out by Olmsted.[446] Once this selection was determined, the Hannas—like the Jacobs

Figure 7-10 Setting for the Paul Hanna "Honeycomb House" (1936) on the Stanford University campus, Palo Alto, California. (*1992 photograph by Charles E. Aguar. © 2002 by Berdeana Aguar.*)

before them—were willing to give Wright the freedom to exercise his creativity. The result is the remarkable Usonian that has come to be known as "Honeycomb House," due to the hexagonal unit system Wright used for its design, which was based upon the 120-degree angle rather than the conventional 90 degrees because, Wright explained, he believed obtuse angularity was more harmonious to human movement (Figure 7-11).

Wright's earliest rough sketches for the Hanna House support that he considered existing trees, outdoor terraces, contained garden areas, circulation, and site definition as integral elements of his design. The L-shaped layout differed substantially from Jacobs I, however, in that the gallery hallway and family bedrooms paralleled the primary living space, and the service units were housed along with quarters for servants and guests in the other wing. This arrangement allowed Wright to orient the walls of glass in all the primary living spaces for environmental benefit. Glazed openings along the walls facing due west were limited to the area immediately below the eaves. Of particular interest is the marked contrast between the contour-defining brick walls that extend the hexagonal unit system of the architecture into the out-of-doors and the free-flowing form of the driveway that introduces a Jensen-like—but very tight—reverse curve, in the manner of Taliesin (Figure 7-12).

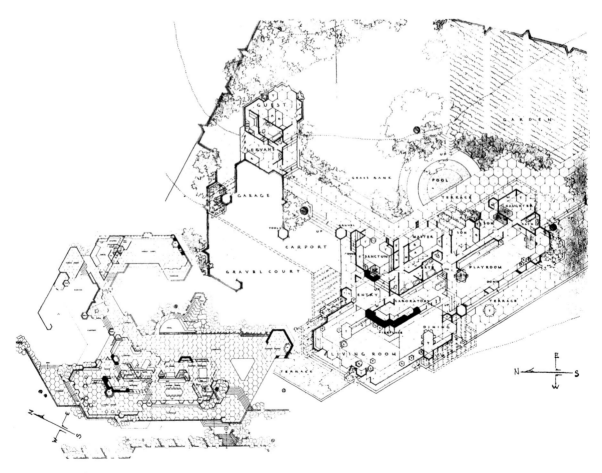

Figure 7-11 The site plan for Honeycomb House saved existing trees. Low brick walls delineate contours. (© 2002 by The Frank Lloyd Wright Foundation, Scottsdale, Arizona.)

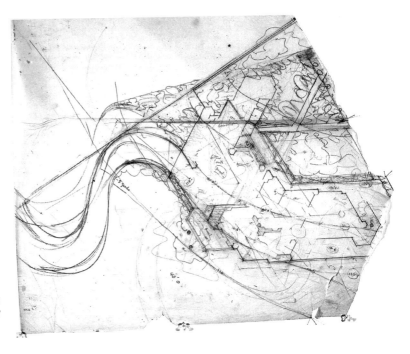

Figure 7-12 Wright's rough sketch for the Honeycomb House introduces Jensen-like reverse curves. (© 2002 by *The Frank Lloyd Wright Foundation, Scottsdale, Arizona.*)

In a book the Hannas eventually wrote about the home they occupied for 39 years—from 1936 to 1975—they verify the effort Wright encouraged them to make to accommodate and preserve existing trees. "Mr. Wright had sited the buildings to preserve the oaks, and we gave them special care—pruning, feeding, and watering. The lone cypress, allowed to project through the roof of the carport, had a problem—bark beetles had worked on it for years. Mr. Wright encouraged us to nurse it along. We kept it alive and growing slowly by annually cutting the dead branches and spraying."[447] The Hannas said Wright also suggested they "establish a line of tall conifers" along the rear of the property, for privacy. This advice and the placement of the defining, low-wall brick terracing of the contours—fashioned from the same brick used for the house—seems to be the extent of his direction with respect to cultivation of the landscape, however. Apprentice Kenaji Domoto told the author that he was later called in to install new plantings, but he only recalls designing a doghouse for them; he said all terraces and walls already were in place, and Mrs. Hanna "knew her plants quite well."[448] Indeed, the Hannas' book provides an account of their very personal process of developing their landscape over time, as they could afford it—a process similar to that described by most Usonian home-owners interviewed by the author while conducting research for this writing.

Another very significant detail came to light in the Hanna's book—that is, Honeycomb House was built over a branch of the San Andreas earthquake fault. Moreover, both they and Wright were informed of this problem prior to construction getting underway. It seems that at the time the Hannas were in the process of staking out their site, a Stanford University colleague and world-famous geologist interrupted them and gave them the shocking news. Wright's response to their frantic telegram was very simply put: "I built the Imperial Hotel." Apparently, this reference was meant to remind the Hannas of the widely published myth that this famous building was the only structure to withstand Japan's great earthquake of September 1, 1923. In reality, historic records verify that the area surrounding the Hotel complex was not near the center of the shock on that day; many other buildings performed far better; and the seven-story portion of the Hotel settled 2 feet during the event—a total of 3 feet, 8 inches in all.[449] It was precisely because of problems created by the Hotel settling into the mud that it was demolished in 1968.

It does not appear that the geologist's warning prompted Wright to add anything in the way of special construction to support the Hanna House in the event that seismic activity occurred. And no earthquake-related damage did occur for a period of 50 years—until the earthquake of October 17, 1989, which apparently for the first time involved the particular branch of the earthquake fault over which the house was built. An estimate prepared by the Frank Lloyd Wright Foundation placed the cost for installing seismic bracing and an overall restoration in the neighborhood of $1.8 million.[450]

Although less famous than Fallingwater, the Hanna Honeycomb House is one of 17 designs (9 of which are residences) that the American Institute of Architects has adjudged to be "the best examples of Frank Lloyd Wright's architectural contribution to American Culture." It also is listed on the National Register of Historic Places.

Abby Beecher Roberts—Marquette, Michigan (1936)

That a pattern of procedures was developing within the Fellowship format is revealed with the design and siting of the Abby Beecher Roberts House. As with Willey and Jacobs I, the Roberts plan was adapted from one that Wright had originated for the Broadacre City Models. As with Fallingwater, supervision of the construction process was entrusted to apprentices. And Wright again did not make adjustments specific to the site environment or climatic conditions of the area. When this client voiced her dissatisfaction with the relationship of house to site, however, Wright suggested she contact his friend Jens Jensen. Jensen biographer Leonard Eaton explains what occurred:

Jensen came over from Ellison Bay and worked out a planting plan. One of its major features was a row of sugar maples, which Jensen planted across the front of the house. In addition, he changed the entrance road to make the house more accessible, laid out a charming flower garden for Mrs. Roberts, and planted pine trees around an existing pool to make it more mysterious. None of these measures bore any direct relation to the house, and their location is indicative of Jensen's feelings about this type of landscape element. . . . Much the same theory

applied to water features; they were usually placed to one side. Wright, in contrast, had wanted to place a pool directly in the center of the meadow. Jensen took the meadow as it already existed (it was the kind of terrain which he might have created if it had not already been there) and emphasized its edges by planting evergreens along the sides. He also put in massed sumac for color in the fall. The effect of all these innovations was to infuriate Wright. He particularly demanded to know why Jensen had spoiled the elevation of his house with "those spindly trees." Jensen, with the long perspective of the landscape architect, replied that the trees would not always be spindly.[451]

According to apprentices of this era, Wright's concerns related to what he felt was a conflict with the architectural lines of the house. From his perspective, there were too many trees, too evenly spaced. For that reason, he had his apprentices remove several of the trees. This action defeated Jensen's purpose for planting them in the first place, because he clearly did not introduce the row of maple trees for aesthetic purposes, but to compensate for the original improper siting and orientation of the generic architecture Wright had selected to be built on this site (Figure 7-13). Consider that three sides of the living room were predominately glass and each was oriented in a different direction: southeast, north, and northeast—the direction of prevailing winter winds, the worst possible alignment for a northern Michigan locale. Therefore, Jensen's rationale for planting the row of maple trees around the living room was threefold: (1) to create a natural windbreak of trees that would deflect the force of winter winds; (2) to access solar heat during late fall, winter, and early spring; and (3) to eventually provide a sheltering canopy of shade during the summer.

Eaton concluded: "A tremendous altercation developed during which Jensen insisted that the importance of his art was at least equal to that of Wright. Since Wright always held out for architecture as 'the mother art,' it is easy to see that the struggle must have been hard. . . . While Jensen was a modest man personally, he was not at all modest in his claims for his art."

One circumstance that may have caused Wright to spend so little time on the Roberts House was his involvement

Figure 7-13 Historic photograph of
Abby Beecher Roberts Residence
(1936) in Marquette, Michigan,
shows "spindly" trees. (*Courtesy of
W. A. Storrer, S.236 in The Frank
Lloyd Wright Companion,* © 1993.)

with the very substantial commission to design and
supervise the construction of the Johnson Wax Administration Building in Racine, Wisconsin (1936).[452] Another
was health-related, as the aging Wright suffered through
two separate bouts of pneumonia during the winters of
1935 and 1936. The following year, 1937, would evolve
into a busy time frame also, as Wright and the apprentices were completing Fallingwater at the same time they
were beginning the design and construction process for
"Wingspread," an elaborate personal residence for the
Herbert F. Johnson family, the Johnson Wax chief executive officer. Therefore, when Wright's doctor recommended that he spend ensuing winters in Arizona, rather
than Wisconsin, he had the wherewithal to purchase land
and begin developing plans for what would come to be
known as "Taliesin West." The marked difference in the
overall environmental articulation of Wingspread and
Taliesin West warrants exploration.

Herbert F. Johnson's "Wingspread"—
Wind Point, Wisconsin (1937)

Wright maintained that the notable structure of Wingspread was the best-built, as well as the most expensive,
domestic architecture of his design. Named for the way

the four wings of living space were zoned around a free-
flowing arrangement of the primary living spaces in the
"great hall" under a triplicated raised clerestory, Wingspread was described by Wright as "resembling the Coonley house at Riverside, Illinois" but "better executed, in
more permanent materials."[453] Wright's correlation of the
Coonley House and Wingspread undoubtedly had more
to do with the zoning aspects of the architecture than
with the overall property development, as there is little
comparison between the basic environmental character
of the two sites or the cultivated landscapes as they were
developed and maintained over time. Although Wright
may have been trying to describe what he envisioned
Wingspread could become, as he was able to do so successfully with Westhope eight years earlier, his vision for
Wingspread would never be completely fulfilled.

The Wingspread architecture displays the excellence in design and craftsmanship possible when Wright
was afforded a sensitive client, an ample budget, and
a master builder—in this instance, Ben Wiltscheck.
Anchoring the pinwheel-like arrangement of the wings
is a magnificent, three-story-high compartmentalized
fireplace that opens onto each of the five areas for primary living—with spaces for socializing, dining, reading,

and listening to music on the ground floor, the mezzanine living space on the second level (Figure 7-14). But the aura of the architecture would have been markedly changed, had Wright not aligned the main axis as he did on a northwest-southeast compass bearing. This arrangement allowed him to orient the expanses of glass in the primary living spaces of the great hall to access full benefit from the arc of the sun throughout the day. The overall effect of these orientations, when combined with the natural light infiltrating from all sides through the bands of windows in the triplicated clerestory that surrounds the central open space of the great hall, clearly demonstrates Wright's unmatched ability to use natural light almost as a building material (Figure 7-15 a-c).

Wright's earliest sketch of the site depicted the basic arrangement of the wings, laid out the reverse curve approach route as it would be developed, and revealed his intent to relate the structure to the shallow ravine and integrate it into a naturally cultivated land-scape (Figure 7-16). Both the site plan and ground plan support that existing trees were located and taken into consideration when Wingspread was designed. And the site plan is one of the most detailed for this period (Figure 7-17). None of these layouts reference the natural contours of the topography, however, and there is no identification of existing plants or a proposed planting plan. Even so, the plans clearly suggest the naturalistic environment Wright wanted to develop, as did his technique for encouraging the naturalistic placement of trees. It seems he asked for a bushel of potatoes and then proceeded to demonstrate how to scatter them about, with the instruction: "Where a potato lands, plant a tree."[454]

Unfortunately, there does not appear to have been any follow-up or future involvement with respect to developing the site environment at Wingspread. As a result, the cultivated landscape of this expensive home in no way fulfills the vision of a house integrated into a

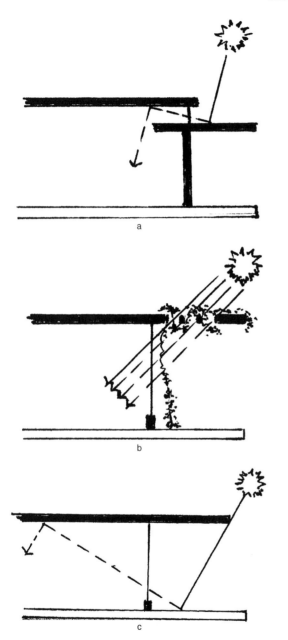

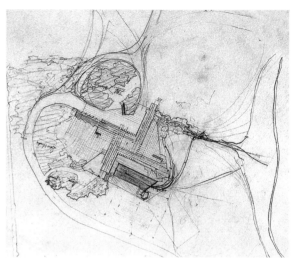

Figure 7-16   Wright's preliminary sketch shows Wingspread traffic circulation and relationship to ravine. (© *2002 by The Frank Lloyd Wright Foundation, Scottsdale, Arizona.*)

Figure 7-15 a–c   Wright used natural light almost like a building material. Clerestory window and light shelf (7-15 a) bounced sunlight to create a "glow" rather than strong shadows. Sunlight through trellis (7-15 b) was filtered through vines. Reflected light (7-15 c) bounced off paving under cantilevered roof overhang. (*By Charles E. Aguar, based on personal observation and analysis. As delineated, © 2002 by Berdeana Aguar.*)

natural forest environment—as Wright depicted it on the plans—or of a house rising up from a forest—as it appears in the most publicized perspective of Wingspread, wherein the master bedroom balcony artistically cantilevers over a grove of cedars (Figure 7-18 a). Instead, a virtual army of gardeners is required to maintain beautifully cultivated but care-intensive planting arrangements and greenswards as they have been developed over time. Therefore, the first-time visitor to Wingspread might be disappointed, if expecting a bird-walk-type cantilevered balcony with a panoramic view as sensuously meaningful as the one that overlooks the Wisconsin River Valley at Taliesin. The author's personal reaction was one of shock—after touring the house, being impressed with the excellent workmanship, and becoming immersed in the ambience of it all—to step out from the master bedroom onto the cantilevered balcony just as a maintenance man driving a noisy riding lawnmower passed underneath and the expansive lawn came into view, completely devoid of trees (Figure 7-18 b). What a way to shatter an illusion!

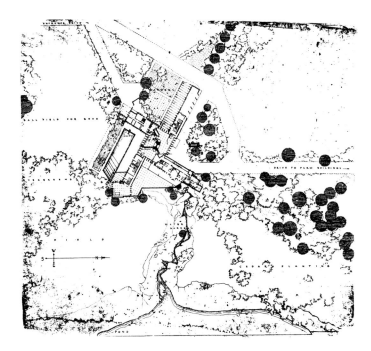

Figure 7-18 a–b A widely published drawing of Wingspread shows the master bedroom balcony cantilevering over a cedar forest (7-18 a). A photograph of the same location shows the landscape developed as an expansive lawn, completely devoid of trees. (7-18 b). (*Drawing © 2002 by The Frank Lloyd Wright Foundation, Scottsdale, Arizona. Photograph by Charles E. Aguar. © 2002 by Berdeana Aguar.*)

Taliesin West—Scottsdale, Arizona (1937–1950s)

At the turn of the twenty-first century, Taliesin West sensitively blends into the landscape of Maricopa Mesa as Wright envisioned it would more than 60 years earlier—as a dramatic abstraction of the McDowell mountain range backdrop (Figure 7-19). The marked contrast between the uninspired interpretation of Wright's environmental vision for Wingspread and the carefully orchestrated articulation of his vision for Taliesin West lies with his personal interest and involvement, beginning with his site selection and his knowledgeable response to the regional environment.

Wright did not select the acreage upon which Taliesin West would be built from among properties that were on the market, but by first touring the countryside and then searching out the owner of this particular mesa. His attraction to this property stemmed from its location—26 miles northeast of Phoenix in the desert environment that he had grown to love during the late 1920s—and the potential to develop the sense of the panomara: toward the McDowell mountain range to the north, Black Mountain and Granite Reef Mountain to the east, and the vast open space of Paradise Valley to the southwest—framed by the Camelback Mountains.

The original tent structures at Taliesin West were constructed of horizontally aligned board-and-batten walls and framed canvas roofs similar to those constructed for the Ocatilla Desert Compound 10 years earlier. And the facility was for many years referred to as a "camp," as supported by Wright's retrospective in the 1943 reprinting of his autobiography: "We devised a light canvas-covered redwood framework resting upon this massive stone masonry belonging to the mountain slopes all around. On a fair day when these white tops and side flaps were flying open, the desert air and the birds flew clear through. . . . Our new desert camp belonged to the Arizona desert as though it had stood there during creation. . . . The Arizona camp is something one can't describe, just doesn't care to talk much about. Something sacred in respect to excellence."[455]

All of the temporary construction at Taliesin West and most of the permanent construction was executed by the apprentices over a period of years, between the months of November and April. Wes Peters elaborated upon the design process: "Mr. Wright used to say that Taliesin West was his 'great architectural sketch.' Well,

Figure 7-19   A panoramic view of Taliesin West presents a dramatic abstraction with mountain backdrop. (*Courtesy of The Frank Lloyd Wright Archives, Scottsdale, Arizona.*)

the sketch plan had been drawn out on a piece of brown wrapping paper, but the larger master plan really was always in his mind. So, whenever the sketch needed an improvement or revision, he would call the gang together and we would all jump in to do it under the pressure of time and exingencies."[456]

Although Wright's decision to also use canvas, the cheapest redwood, and desert rubble masonry to construct the permanent structures was necessitated by economic feasibility, as was the years-long construction process and the free labor provided by apprentices, there is no question that the touchstone for his architecture was the "countenance" of the desert landscape—every bit as much as the countenance of the Driftless Area of Wisconsin was his touchstone for the original Taliesin. Moreover, his alignment of the terrace prow at precisely 45 degrees from the major east-west axis, as well as the south-by-southwest orientation of his layout, were determined by the prevailing breezes that originate from the east, year-round, and the storms that blow in from the Pacific Ocean, November through March (Figure 7-20). The directional wind patterns and the trajectory of the sun also dictated the arrangement and orientation of the primary living areas, the slope of the rooflines, the

arrangement and height of the battered desert rubble masonry structuring. And, of course, the play of sunlight and shadow were important to Wright's overall design considerations; it is for this reason that all sides of the structures are exposed, even where the areas of glazed surfacing are limited. As the sun moves across the sky, shadows of structural members constantly change, creating first straight lines on smooth concrete surfaces and then rugged textures when reflected on rock or moving water. And the deep horizontal strips within the desert stone masonry walls create shadow lines that emphasize the horizontality of the structure, serving the same purpose as the raked brick courses that Wright used for his Prairie House architecture.

Like Taliesin, Taliesin West is made up of the primary structure and other separate structures, but all are linked together by courtyards, terraces, walkways, and trellised pergolas to dramatize the enclosing structures, the enclosed spaces, and all the features within the spaces to transmute the total volumetric space into an architectural entity. A low desert stone wall establishes the architectural limits and serves the dual purpose of visually separating the cultivated landscape and hardscape areas from the natural forms of the desert while

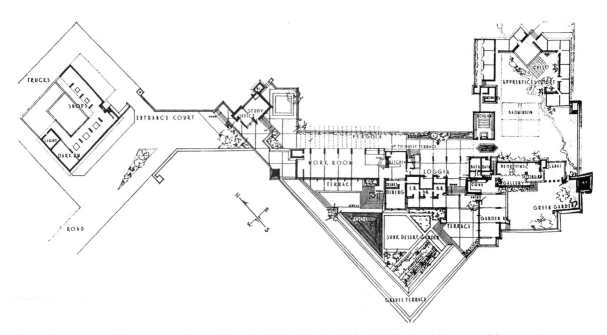

Figure 7-20   Ground floor plan for Taliesin West. (© *2002 by The Frank Lloyd Wright Foundation, Scottsdale, Arizona.*)

Figure 7-21　Looking across the desert floor toward Taliesin West. (*Photograph by Charles E. Aguar.* © *2002 by Berdeana Aguar.*)

also preventing snakes, desert creatures, and wind-blown cacti from encroaching upon the man-made open spaces—including the grass panel upon which Wright used to enjoy walking barefoot before the early morning dew evaporated. The manner in which Wright exercised diligence to maintain, develop, and enhance this site environment and articulate his vision is supported by comments made by Cornelia Brierly:

> In the beginning, we used a lot more prickly pear, creosote bush, and other cacti close to the building, but people were constantly being impaled in the needles. Subsequently, Mr. Wright was able to buy out a plant nursery and we added more colorful flowering plants, such as Bougainvillea and Lantena, which soften straight lines near the building, leaving the natural desert plants beyond undisturbed. We have stuck to native desert plants beyond the footprint of the building, its triangular beds, and rectangular courtyards [Figure 7-21]. Integrated grass panels, smooth steps and terrace surfaces, pools of water, and the kinetic effect of fountains also are part of the contrasts to the rugged textures of the desert. Mr. Wright was always placing vertical elements as sculptural units in locations where they would provide contrast for emphasizing the horizontal architecture. In the desert, he used the giant saguaro cactus, upright evergreens, and even narrow stones on end. Mr. Wright was constantly integrating

his buildings with the natural landscape. Here at Taliesin West, this integration begins at ground level, with the broad gravel paths and courtyards matching the desert floor and the roof angles echoing in an abstract way the background mountains. Both muted and brightly colored desert rock in what we call "battered rubble walls" or merely "desert stone masonry" reappear in painted surfaces, sculptures, oriental pottery, and American Indian art.[457]

The temperate Arizona climate permits year-round use of the several gardens and pools. Wright used these waters for psychological effect so occult senses are over and over again piqued by the sound of splashing water—contrasting with the noisy crunching sound of someone walking over broad gravel paths and birds singing in cacti, near and far. Taliesin West's colorful sunlit surfaces, splashing water features, breezy passageways, and indoor-outdoor relationships all commingle to create a spirit and exuberance eminently unlike the peace of the Wisconsin countryside.

Wright ultimately seemed to favor the compactness, the ease of circulation, and the desert setting he created in Arizona to his home overlooking the Wisconsin River Valley. From the time construction began in 1937 until his death at age 91 in 1959, he and his family more and more lengthened their periods of tenure surrounded by the extraordinary environment of Taliesin West.

As Roosevelt's "New Deal" programs became operational during the mid-to-late 1930s, the United States Government undertook the design and development of a series of new towns. The first was Norris, Tennessee— a model demonstration village designed in 1934 by the Land Planning and Housing Division of the Tennessee Valley Authority (TVA) to house construction workers while building Norris Dam.[458] Then came the three "greenbelt" towns developed as satellite communities at the edge of the then-urban fringe of prominent cities: Greenbelt, Maryland, north of Washington, D.C. (1937); Greendale, Wisconsin, southwest of Milwaukee (1938); and Greenhills, Ohio, north of Cincinnati (1938).[459] The nation's very best planners, architects, landscape architects, engineers, geographers, economists, and artists were called in on these town projects, and excellent community planning concepts were infused into their design and layout. Although the architecture was not award-winning, the houses were sound and inexpensive—utilizing painted concrete block, frame construction, and/or asbestos shingle siding.[460] The expectation was that this approach would alleviate unemployment and overcrowding, provide carefully designed neighborhoods and decent homes for families of modest incomes, and encourage home ownership.

That Wright was aware of and impressed by the ruralized context of these communities is supported within the text of *Architecture and Modern Life*, a compilation of chapters coauthored by Wright and Baker Brownell in 1937, wherein they discuss and analyze the pros and cons of this form of regional development. They describe how the streets of Norris "wind around the hills" and the "houses scatter through the woods" to create an effect "more pleasant than most summer resorts."[461] Brownell observed: "it is clear . . . that T.V.A. all in all is building more than a dam. It is building a civilization. The visitor there is looking into the next century." Wright concluded: "From within outward is no longer [a] remote ideal. It is everywhere becoming action. With new integrity action insists upon indigenous culture. The new reality."

ENVIRONMENTAL DESIGNS, 1937–1959

It assumedly was because of the public awareness engendered through these government undertakings that Wright was motivated to become more assertively involved in the design of alternative property development. This reasoning is supported by the wordage in his correspondence with the Federal Works Agency Division of Defense Housing, in connection with the Cloverleaf Housing Project of 1942 (see Cloverleaf Housing Project) and by his efforts to be appointed architect-in-chief for the State Department's building program after World War II.[462] Moreover, he personally designed nine planned communities between 1938 and 1957. Although only four were implemented, and then only partially, it is clear that he viewed each as a means to bring to fruition the image and social structure of community that he had been upholding as the foundation upon which future development should be based. Sometimes utopian, but also very practical, each of these Usonian communities proposed affordable homes carefully sited within a nature-responsive environment imbued with planned amenities such as community parks, community gardens, and separation of through traffic from local traffic.

THE USONIAN COMMUNITY

Otto Todd Mallery "Suntop Homes"— Ardmore, Pennsylvania (1938)

For the complex of "Suntop Homes" designed as a low-cost housing alternative for suburban development, Wright once again resurrected concepts he had originally developed for his Broadacre City models. This inventive spiral design wove multilevel apartments into a compact, four-unit module that perhaps can best be described as a sophisticated articulation of the Quadruple Block Plan (Figure 8-1). Each family unit consisted of four levels and was bounded on all sides by privacy walls built of the same material as the structure. There was a private garden terrace off the two-story living area, a mezzanine with kitchen-dining that was afforded the same ambiance, a balcony off the master bedroom secreted behind a privacy wall, and a sequestered roof garden on the fourth level. Thus, no unit intruded upon any other— tangibly or visually—and the interrelationship between indoor and outdoor living space was exceptional.

Only one four-family module was constructed. Property owners in the conservative Philadelphia suburban area objected to the introduction of any multifamily housing

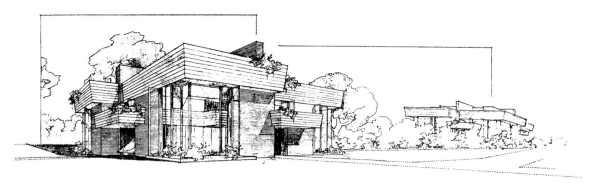

Figure 8-1   Presentation perspective shows Wright's unique concept for the Suntop Homes four-family-module (1938) in Ardmore, Pennsylvania. (© *2002 by The Frank Lloyd Wright Foundation, Scottsdale, Arizona.*)

on the basis that the population density conceivably could increase from 8-to-10 persons per acre to 30 persons per acre. This, even though when driving or walking past Wright's structure, it has the appearance of a single-family home, and even though each of the four units provided indoor and outdoor space and privacy that far exceeded that found in the single-family homes representative of the area.

The only flaw in Wright's original site layout for Suntop Homes was the intrusive character of the abnormally large area he dedicated to accommodating the automobile (Figure 8-2). Had this problem been addressed—as it easily could have been—and had these multifamily units ultimately met with the acclaim they justly deserved, the urban sprawl that today plagues every city in America could have been appreciably moderated.

Usonia I—East Lansing, Michigan (Unbuilt, 1939)

The Usonia I commission provided Wright with his first opportunity to custom-design both a new community and the individual homes to be built in that community. There were seven clients and all were faculty members at Michigan State College (now Michigan State University). The rural 17-acre site was located a short distance outside East Lansing on the east side of Herron Creek and was considered part of the 40-acre cooperative community known as "Herron Acres," a settlement of conventional homes on the west side of the creek.

Archival correspondence suggests that Wright had dreams substantially bigger than the reality of seven households. He proposed an eighth generic dwelling to

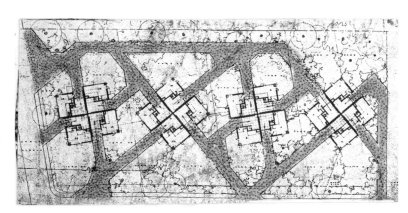

Figure 8-2   The site plan for Suntop Homes dedicates an abnormally large area to accommodating the automobile. (© *2002 by The Frank Lloyd Wright Foundation, Scottsdale, Arizona.*)

house a caretaker, as well as a Broadacres-type "little farm" co-op unit for the central section of the tract—complete with gardens, orchards, a central well, and a pond for raising fish. He mentioned the possibility of introducing a dog kennel, a horse stable, and bridle paths; he even made reference to a zoo. But his layout was of arguable practicality (Figure 8-3). The rectilinear loop road that was to provide access to each of the units was without curves or turning radii. The land on the outside of the loop was divided into seven lots ranging in size from 2 to 4 acres, but the pattern of garden plots and orchards was bounded by walls that ignored property lines, so the settlement was viewed as part-commune and part conventional land subdivision. There also were problems with the design of the structures themselves, including the floor heating. The plans in fact violated seven specifications listed within the Property

Standards and Minimum Construction Requirements mandated by the Federal Housing Administration (FHA), including a minimum ceiling height of eight feet, physical separation of the kitchen, and structurally sound walls and roof framing. When FHA refused to subsidize the venture, the project was aborted.[463]

Wright's use of the "Usonia" terminology to identify this particular undertaking postulates the thesis that his mind-set was to ultimately amalgamate and market his architecture and his communities as a singular entity. This reasoning bears credence in spite of, or perhaps because of, the confusion that exists between Wright's identification of the East Lansing project as "Usonia I" in his "List of Projects" for 1939 and comments he made during a lecture in London that same year, wherein he

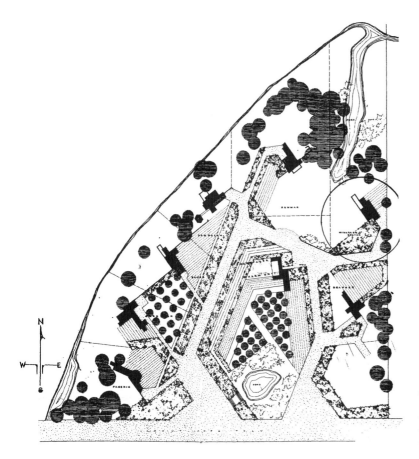

Figure 8-3 Wright's site plan for the never-realized Usonia I (1939) in East Lansing, Michigan, was artistic but of arguable practicality. (© 2002 by The Frank Lloyd Wright Foundation, Scottsdale, Arizona.)

referred to Taliesin as Usonia I, this project as Usonia II, and a community to be built in Wheeling, West Virginia, as Usonia III.[464]

Cloverleaf Housing Project—Pittsfield, Massachusetts (1941–1942)

For this commission, contracted by the Federal Works Agency Division of Defense Housing during the early months of World War II, Wright substantially refined the Suntop Homes architecture by improving the sound insulation between units and creating the means to introduce additional sources of light on all three levels. The site plan subdivided the property into a unique pin-wheel arrangement of lots to accommodate 25 four-family units and an office (Figure 8-4). Although the street layout once again dedicated an inordinant amount

of circulation space (47 percent) to accomodating the automobile, 2 percent of the site was set aside for street trees and greenway medians.

The initial reaction to Wright's proposal was very positive, as explained by architect Talbot Wegg, chief of the planning section for the Agency: "One look at these drawings was enough to affirm that FLlW was ever young, fresh, inventive, and skillful enough to design buildings which resembled no housing project of record. Here would be a project to honor Pittsfield and the USA."[465]

Nonetheless, the Cloverleaf Housing Project also was never carried through to completion. It has been said that politics interfered with the implementation process, that the majority leader of the House (a native of Massachusetts) did not like the idea of an architect from Wisconsin interfering with local architects' ability to "make a living." In reality, a procedure already had been set in motion to commission the nation's leading architects—regardless of their home base—in an effort to redress the mediocrity of most public housing. The rationale was that improved design might remove the stigma generally associated with government projects. Wegg stated that Wright's "attitude" had a lot to do with the rejection of his plan, that he seemed to be more concerned with bringing pleasure and honor to himself and a need to "discharge disturbing fiscal obligations" than anything else. Excerpts from Wright's November 1941 letter corroborate this interpretation: "It is high time I took a hand in governmental building in my own country and cooperation (with your agency) will be only the beginning, I foresee, of a real pleasure to me. . . . I should be a great strength to you in your endeavor, and the liberality and intelligence of that endeavor I respect. So don't worry about results. You will be gratified. . . . The personal idiosyncrasy (whatever it may be) shall not get in the way, too much, and only serve to make work a little livelier and more interesting."

Wegg went on to describe "an unusual departure from normal procedure," when Wright participated in the site selection and toured potential sites with an entourage of government officials:

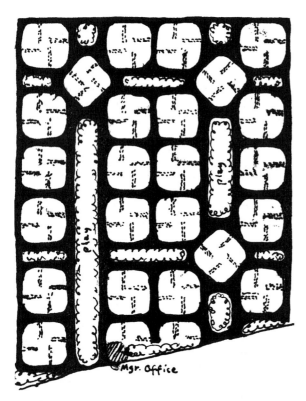

Figure 8-4 Site plan for the unbuilt Cloverleaf Housing Project (1941) in East Lansing, Michigan, shows multifamily layout. (© 2002 by The Frank Lloyd Wright Foundation, Scottsdale, Arizona.)

Preliminary reconnaissance had been made and four potential sites had been lined up. . . . The first, generally level and verdant, had been farmed and the open fields would insure a pleasant environment as well as reasonable development costs. FLlW was not impressed. While the troupe examined it on foot, he remained in the car, restlessly. The second site was on rough ground with great rock outcroppings and not a sign of a tree. The moment he saw it, FLlW's eyes lit up. "Stop" he cried and fairly leaped from the car. Moving with the grace and vigor of a youth, he roamed the hills and dales clearly enraptured by the austere crags. "This is *it; this* is New England. . . . No need to look further. This is where we shall build our project." When mention was made of the probable site preparation costs and the need of a good deal of landscaping, Wright stated, "We'll bring in trees. Mature, beautiful pines and dogwood and evergreens. We'll make it the showplace of the Berkshires."

Wegg concluded that Wright also did not help his cause when he loudly blamed the British for "suckering us into the war" and launched into a eulogy about the "wonderful Japanese people" while surrounded by high military officers—this, just a short time after the Japanese had almost decimated the American fleet at Pearl Harbor.

Cooperative Homesteads Community Project—Detroit, Michigan (Unbuilt, 1942).

The group that commissioned Wright for the Cooperative Homesteads Community Project was made up of professionals, teachers, and defense plant workers. These clients planned to help each other construct their homes, raise their own food, and possibly even raise crops as a partial source of income.

The plot plan Wright prepared for this rural site some 15 miles north of downtown Detroit could have been lifted directly off the Broadacre City model (Figure 8-5). Like its generic counterpart, the layout was based upon a grid of rectangular parcels and represents a good example of land planning. There is a single loop collector road servicing traffic from a dozen dead-end roads, each containing from three to six individual land units. While most lots computed to 1 acre in size, other parcels were platted as 1.5 acres, 2 acres, 3 acres, or 7.5 acres. Contour lines indicate that most of the site was relatively flat or gently rolling, except for the south end closest to East 13-Mile Road, where the topography is quite rugged and there is a stream and two ponds. This area is dedicated to wooded parklands to buffer community services such as a kindergarten with playground, a filling station, store, community center, and parking space. Masses of trees in the area where two entry roads cross the stream, labeled

"planted bank," support Wright's intent to preserve the natural environment. Windbreaks of trees also are proposed for several locations, although no shade trees are shown near the houses—possibly to assure root systems would not damage the proposed method of rammed-earth construction.

The plans that Wright devised for the efficient in-line, two-bedroom bermed houses he proposed for this project were perhaps the most ecologically sound design response of any he conceived during his ongoing search for the perfect low-cost residence; he estimated that each unit could be built for $4000. The benefits of rammed-earth construction over conventional construction include privacy; insulation from noise pollution; natural protection from fires, break-ins, and catastrophic storms; and lower heating/cooling costs—due to the thermal properties of soil, which remains at a fairly constant temperature year-round. And there is a significant reduction in the impact on the natural environment. Wright went even further. He made sure outward views would not be impeded, and access to breezes would not be compromised, by scaling the levee-like walls to end at the base of the window sills (Figure 8-6). He arranged the long cantilevered overhangs to protect the walls and berms from moisture. He proposed that sunken gardens surround the structures to serve as natural retention ponds for rainwater runoff. And he suggested that the earthen walls be planted with ground cover, so the root systems would minimize the potential for erosion.

Rammed-earth construction has been used for centuries in undeveloped countries around the globe, and was used successfully by such avant-garde designers as Bruce Goff during the early 1950s and Sim Van der Ryn during the 1980s. Wright's perception of this concept, however, did not address the "science" of rammed-earth construction. Anyone undertaking the design of this type of structure must have a thorough understanding of the mechanics of soil—that is, (1) which forms are appropriate for each soil type, (2) which soil types may be pneumatically rammed successfully, (3) what form of waterproofing should be used with each soil type, and (4) what type of drainage system would be most effective. This makes it difficult to understand why Wright essentially turned the entire project over to an apprentice: Aaron Green. Green stated he spent several months setting up the project and getting the first prototypical building started. "Wartime legislation made it necessary for us to obtain 'defense housing' status," he said, "in order to purchase . . . secondhand earth-handling and

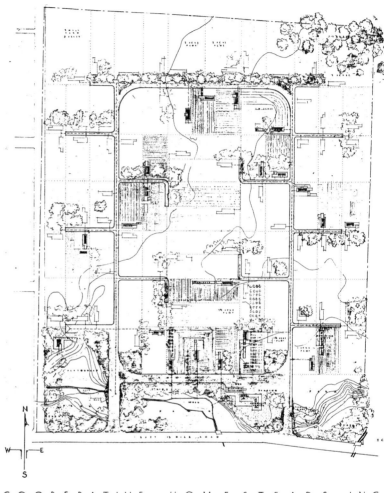

C O O P E R A T I V E   H O M E S T E A D S   I N C
DETROIT MICH
F R A N K   L L O Y D   W R I G H T   A R C H I T E C T

pneumatic-ramming equipment, and to experiment
with bitulithic additives and new techniques for expe-
diting the labor-intensive earth construction. The labor
demands of the war effort reduced the work force considerably, but we managed to accomplish enough construction to validate the techniques. When the Army
Air Corps snatched me away for training, the project
drainage system was still under construction. Without a
construction superintendent and without the anticipated workers, with the drainage system incomplete, the

project became a fatality of the war and literally washed
away."[466]

Wright never again undertook a rammed-earth
project, although he did recycle certain aspects of the
concept some eight years later for the Thomas E. Keys
residence in Rochester, Minnesota. Had at least one
rammed-earth prototype been completed, it might have
proven to be as successful as Wright's houses constructed of textile block or desert rubblestone—and far
less costly.

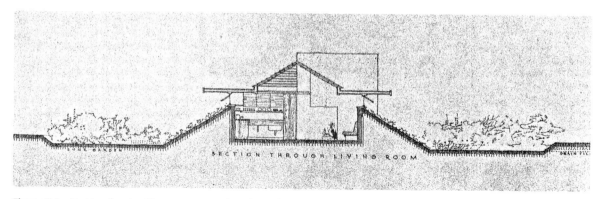

Figure 8-6   Section drawing illustrates rammed-earth residence proposed for 1942 Cooperative Homesteads Community Project. (© *2002 by The Frank Lloyd Wright Foundation, Scottsdale, Arizona.*)

Galesburg Country Homes, "The Acres," and "Parkwyn Village"—Galesburg, Michigan (1947)

The initial concept of creating a community of homes in a rural area, convenient to their workplace, was conceived by a group of five research chemists from the Upjohn Institute—a pharmaceutical company based in Kalamazoo, Michigan. Immediately following World War II, they formed a nonprofit corporation known as The Galesburg Country Homes Association and began searching for property. Fortunately, copies of all correspondence together with minute books of Association meetings and newspaper clippings survive intact due to the foresight of the initial secretary, Lillian Meyer (Mrs. Curtis). She coordinated all correspondence that dealt with planning the community as a whole and maintained the archival library. In 1991, these archives were in the possession of Christine Weisblat (Mrs. David), a one-time secretary for the Association and wife of the first president. This documentation provides valuable insight into the experience of working with Wright, as well as the organization, personal dedication, and behind-the-scenes work involved in developing a livable community with ecological soundness such as Wright envisioned.

During an extensive May 1991 interview conducted by the author, Weisblat reminisced about her involvement with the grassroots effort that culminated with this unique community of Wright-designed homes. She said: "A group of us spent every weekend for months scouring the countryside for 60 to a hundred acres of land on which to establish our small community. We started in 1943 or 1944, while the war was still on, so had to pool our gas rationing stamps, but we wanted to be ready to go as soon as the war was over and construction materials would become available. At that time, we had no thought of trying to obtain a big name architect. However, after we visited a weekend open house of model homes near Kalamazoo—each designed by a different well-known architect—Ann and Eric Brown suggested we try to get Frank Lloyd Wright to design our homes. And we all agreed." She went on to say they visited the land they eventually bought during the winter, but weren't very impressed—even though the 72 acres of rolling farm and forest land also had a spring-fed stream and a differential in elevation of 80 feet, assuring many attractive vistas. It was only after Curt Meyer returned on his own during early spring, she said, that the whole group returned, "fell in love with the beauty of the blooming dogwoods, redbuds, hawthorn, and the hillsides of wildflowers," and made the commitment "then and there" to purchase the acreage.

Based upon Eric Brown's telephone call to Wright, representatives of the five families first traveled to Taliesin in October 1946. Although postwar commissions at that time were gaining momentum, Weisblat said Wright seemed most eager to become personally involved with this group of professionals. He clearly was pleased when members of the group made favorable comparisons of the Taliesin landscape to their land and requested that roads within their community be narrow and winding as they were at Taliesin. He even agreed to prepare the land planning without charge—assumedly because they clearly had their act together and were ready to authorize him to plan the entire community layout, as well as their individual homes (for which he would receive his usual contractual fee of 10 percent).[467] The pathfinding group returned to Michigan better able to appreciate the portent of good land planning and what sensitive planning could add to an already beautiful parcel of land. As letters began to flow between Kalamazoo and Taliesin, members of the group completed work on the topographical map with two-foot contours they had been preparing during their spare time for a

period of three months. This layout carefully identified the spring, stream, tree masses, old farm features, apple orchards, pastureland, wetlands, and the principal scenic vistas. They also photographed the site from all angles, and additional photographs were annotated and keyed to the map index. Other detailed information identifying soils and frost pockets was assembled, along with microclimatic data.

Weisblat recalled Wright's visit to the site before the overall land planning was completed: "Mr. Wright insisted on walking over much of the land. He donned a pair of waders and walked right into our swampland. We

Figure 8-7 First land planning proposal (1947) for "The Acres" in Galesburg (Michigan) Country Homes development. (© *2002 by The Frank Lloyd Wright Foundation, Scottsdale, Arizona.*)

were quite concerned about a man in his eighties doing that, but he was like a young boy having the time of his life. We were fearful for his safety as well as his seeing what some of us believed was the worst part of our land, after the glowing descriptions we had presented to him. But in his most enthusiastic way, he insisted that this interesting feature was not a swamp at all, but an 'upland bog' such as he had played in as a youngster in Western Massachusetts."

Wright's first land planning proposal delineated 44 circular lots, each approximately 1 acre in size, with meandering narrow roads snaking around the edges of the circles (Figure 8-7). He explained the layout as follows: "Each and all private holdings the same size and outline but greatly varied in aspect and or accent of topography. Individual sites therefore have extreme individuality without impinging upon or even being in contact with other private holdings." In the common spaces between the lots, Wright suggested the owners create a system of parks, gardens, nature trails, and community recreation areas. The original plan bears the notation, "Green community planting requiring no upkeep," which the owners understood meant that these areas were to be left wild, with the most visual parcels and wedges planted with native trees and shrubs. The stream was to be dammed into three terraced ponds, much as was done to expand the former "water garden" at Taliesin. Provision also was made for a community garden and orchard along the edge of the floodplain of the stream that flowed through the property. An archival letter dated April 17, 1947, signed by Curtis E. Meyer documents that members of the Association responded with enthusiasm:

We are overwhelmed with the concept of your proposed development of our land—it is the stuff dreams are made of. . . . The idea of the triple pond of varying depths has captured us all. We wonder, however, if our stream can compensate for the enormous evaporation from so large a surface area. In Spring the flow is abundant and although in a dry summer the stream does not dry up since it is spring-fed, still it does shrink to about 12 inches in width and six inches in depth. What would you think of earthen dams with living willows and perhaps logs for a binder? We are particularly anxious that part of the stream where it enters our land and flows through the woods be retained and one of the ponds be deep enough for swimming and for maintaining

fish. . . . We approve heartily of the circular plots. While we do not feel that we have yet grasped all the subtleties which have been worked into this design, we do appreciate the advantages that have been taken of the contours and the inter-relationship of the houses with each other, the view and the immediate natural growths and we do not want to lose any of their worth. Still, I at least feel that with fewer sites, even greater fluidity can be realized and in a few cases better advantage taken of the trees. . . . In short we would be highly gratified if you should work out the same sort of plan as your present one, confining the projected fifteen sites of one acre each to the front area and developing the rest of the land as suggested in this letter.

By the time this letter was written, however, the original group had split into two factions. There was no animosity involved in this decision. It was just that some families simply felt they would prefer to live closer to downtown Kalamazoo, rather than in the more isolated rural environment. Included in this group were a dentist, an attorney, and two physicians who still made house calls. Members of this split-off group concurred with the concepts set forth by the Galesburg Association and wanted Wright to design their subdivision and house plans as well. Their Parkwyn Village Association was formed and a 47-acre site on the east shoreline of Lorenz Lake was located and purchased. Much of this acreage had been maintained as orchards and thus retained the character of a semirural area. Both communities continued to work together, more-or-less as a two-part cooperative group—even sharing the services of Eric Brown, as the attorney-of-record (Figure 8-8 a-b).

When the time came for Wright to design the individual affordable homes for residents in both communities, he resurrected the concept of textile block as the primary building material. These and subsequent textile block houses came to be known as "Usonian Automatics," based upon Wright's overall scheme for development of the community. Weisblat's description of the dedication, commitment, and sheer physical stamina invested by her entire family in this developmental process would be applicable to all the families involved, regardless of whether the location was under jurisdiction of The Acres or Parkwyn Village:

We all helped the men survey the land, drive stakes and markers, planted the community orchard, and

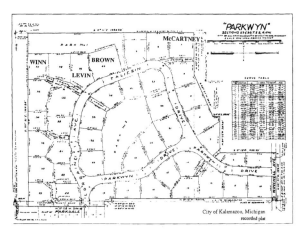

Figure 8-8 b Final layout for the "Parkwyn Village" portion of the two-part cooperative community. (© *2002 by The Frank Lloyd Wright Foundation, Scottsdale, Arizona.*)

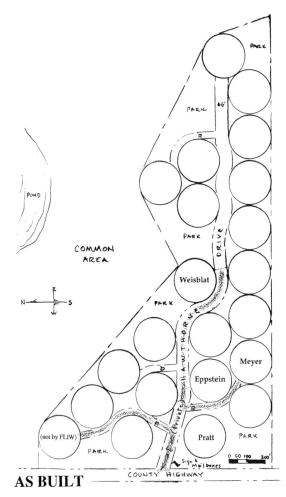

AS BUILT

Figure 8-8 a Final layout for "The Acres" portion of the Galesburg Country Homes community. (© *2002 by The Frank Lloyd Wright Foundation, Scottsdale, Arizona.*)

relocated small trees while we were waiting for our individual house plans to arrive. Our youngest son, then a pre-schooler, planted seeds he gathered from tulip poplar trees. Now, forty years later, that was the forest of trees you drove through at the lower end of the hill on the last curve. The real family activity, being a part of the house coming to life, was in the concrete block construction. The Association hired college students during their summer vacations in 1950 and 1951 for the three homes here at The

Acres, as well as the four at Parkwyn that used the Wright-designed blocks. They helped mix the concrete and we tried to get the texture and color that Mr. Wright specified. When our house was built in 1950, materials were still scarce because of wartime shortages and the postwar building boom. We never were able to obtain the type of Portland cement Mr. Wright wanted us to use. We waited a long time for what we thought was the shipping of the concrete forms in the many required shapes. . . . Finally, a package arrived from Taliesin but it was, to our chagrin, only the basic one-dimensional plans for the forms. The regular concrete block companies wouldn't even discuss the idea of making them for us. We had to locate a man who could draw up the full size patterns (shop drawings) for the many different forms. Next we needed to find a sheet metal person to fabricate them for us. We shared the cost for these and passed the forms on to the next family, along with what we had learned to do and not to do. We also received advice from the Levins, who were ahead of us in building their block home in Parkwyn.

We needed something like three dozen different block designs, some perforated and backed by glass for the gallery, and other forms for the corners (inside and outside are different), as well as other sizes for coping and special construction. Once the blocks were cast and stacked, it was awhile before they could be used and a project that involved the entire family was the curing process. This requires sprinkling water over each block every evening after work for one week and then once a week for four weeks. We spent many hours each evening and on weekends on the site, but it was a delightful experience and like a holiday to drive out to the country every day. At the time we were building, we were living in a second-floor apartment in Kalamazoo—with three young children. The outdoor activity was a blessing as well as fun—for the most part, that is.

Few of the blocks chipped but, just in case, we did make extra blocks than the more than two-thousand standard-sized ones needed. Some co-op members had blocks left over, and there was some exchange or trading as each house took shape. The blocks were actually laid by our carpenters, who had no real problems once they got used to following the 4 × 4 grid permanently scored in the concrete floor. Trained masons were only used for the floor and the fireplace. Carpenters built the movable furniture and all the built-ins. . . . All was done according to the details furnished by Mr. Wright. He had specified cypress, but it was hard to come by so the Association bought a carload of Honduran mahogany, which was shared by both groups.

Jack Howe was the apprentice assigned to all of us. He would visit for a few days at critical times and stay with whomever had a bedroom to put him up. Mr. Wright came to check our progress as the blocks were going up, and I remember him cautioning the workmen not to be too precise in laying the blocks, as we wanted to be able to see the "warp and the woof." He need not have worried, but the meaning of his textile system then really soaked in.

Wright's goal of designing 15 individual homes was never met. Nevertheless, the actualization of the Galesburg Country Homes communities was a landmark effort some 20 years ahead of its time.[468] And Weisblat's description of Wright's sensitive environmental design approach, together with their "sweat equity" involvement in the construction process, clearly elucidates the methodology for planned development Wright hoped to actualize as a means to replace the impersonal, hit-or-miss approach to decentralization.

Usonia II—Pleasantville, New York (1947).

The largest of Wright's Usonian communities is located some 30 miles north of New York City, near Pleasantville, on acreage originally assigned as a royal grant to the College of William and Mary. The beautiful forested environment of rocky glens, fast-running streams, and the remains of rock walls from earlier habitation is buffered on three sides by a pine-forest greenbelt established to protect the community watershed. In Wright's initial scheme, there were 55 circular lots of about 1 acre each, with 6 lots fronting on a centrally located minipark or playground. The triangular wedges between the circles were buffer areas, left in a natural state or planted with native trees and shrubs. Common sites were allocated to community vegetable gardens, a children's petting farm, playgrounds, swimming pool, community center, ball fields, and guest cottages. Winding roads that skirted and wove around the edge of the lots, or cut through common property, were narrow and intentionally designed to discourage fast driving or through traffic cutting across the community (Figure 8-9 a-b). As with the properties at The Acres and Parkwyn Village, the lots ultimately were formatted as polygons to conform to local ordinances.

David Henken, a young engineer, is credited with the development of this unique community. Inspired by Wright's much-published, alternative development concepts for Broadacre City, he began thinking about ways to acquire adequate land, engage Wright, and form a construction company to himself build the houses, community center, and other buildings.[469] After several years of talking with others and then making contact with Wright, the strategy decided upon was that he would become a Taliesin apprentice for two years in order to adjust his engineering skills to the informal style of domestic life represented by organic architecture. Following his apprenticeship, he and his wife Priscilla returned to New York to ascertain which of their friends were serious enough about the project to overcome the obstacles of wartime restrictions, high prices, material shortages, and the near-impossibility of securing financing for nontraditional houses.

The long history of failure for cooperative ventures discouraged many. But by 1944, enough people were involved to form the Rockdale Cooperative under the laws of the State of New York. Together, they located and purchased 97 acres. By the time Wright actually was commissioned, however, he was becoming inundated

AS PLANNED

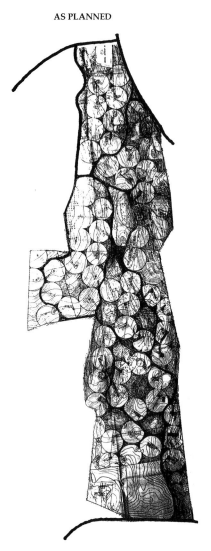

AS BUILT

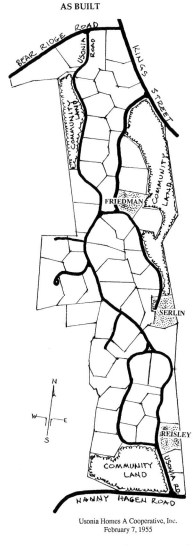

Usonia Homes A Cooperative, Inc.
February 7, 1955

Figure 8-9 a Wright's original layout for Usonia II (1947) in Pleasantville, New York, featured circular lots. (© *2002 by The Frank Lloyd Wright Foundation, Scottsdale, Arizona.*)

Figure 8-9 b Lots in the Usonia II layout were ultimately formatted as polygons to conform to local ordinances. (© *2002 by The Frank Lloyd Wright Foundation, Scottsdale, Arizona.*)

with postwar commissions, so the end agreement limited his participation to preparing the land development plan and designing five residences and the proposed community center. He also agreed to serve as a consultant to critique house plans designed by other architects "to assure that his principles of organic architecture

would be met, that the house design was suitable for the intended site, and that orientation accessed solar advantages and scenic views."[470]

It wasn't until March 1950 that a savings and loan association finally agreed to finance a group mortgage for the venture, based upon the soundness of cooperative ownership and strict architectural controls. The bankers felt this arrangement offered maximum protection against neighborhood deterioration. Ultimately, however, the decision was made for members to individually own their houses and lots while retaining community property, streets, and utilities as a cooperative venture. Other cooperative aspects included digging a well, constructing a pump house and storage tank, and installing water mains and fire hydrants. Five houses were built as a pilot project under the cooperative arrangement, followed by 10 more—with members pooling resources and holding 99-year leases, renewable for their heirs. Construction costs in these early days were contained by purchasing materials in wholesale lots. Some items, such as cypress and heating pipe, were purchased by the carload. When lumber was especially scarce, surplus army barracks were purchased and shipped in from a base in North Carolina, and members pitched in to remove nails or sort and stack the lumber. This was one of many ways members earned "sweat equity," as Wright always had envisioned for Broadacre City.

Wright designed three houses for Usonia II—for Sol Friedman, Roland Reisley, and Edward Serlin. He was closely involved with each design. Native stone was used for the fireplace of the Serlin House and was the primary building material for both Friedman and Reisley— a choice that retained the picturesque countenance of the countryside. Several architects became involved with the design of the 47 non-Wrightian homes eventually built within the community. Five of these residences were designed by former apprentice Kaneji Domato, who was both an architect and a landscape architect. Almost half of the rest were designed by David Henken and Aaron Resnick. With very few exceptions, these non-Wrightian residences basically adhere to Wright's Usonian grammar.

In an essay written for a catalog published to accompany a 1985 exhibition at the Hudson River Museum, Henken wrote of Usonia II:

> A community of remarkable stability has grown to maturity. . . . We have come to a wilderness, in the woods, and have created a world-famous community. . . . We have some beautiful buildings and some mediocrities . . . but all are held together by Wright's pervasive influence, all appearing to grow out of the earth, blending into the enhanced environment. . . . We have brought passive solar and

hot-water radiant heating, fine craftsmanship, and fine design into the New York metropolitan region. We have helped to raise the zoning standards merely by our existence. . . . We have served as a living classroom to many schools of planning, design, and architecture in the tri-state region. We have enriched and enhanced our greater community of Pleasantville and Westchester. . . . We have gone further than any similar group. We hope that others to come, learning from our history, will not be doomed to repeat our errors. This is how progress is truly made.[471]

THE USONIAN RESIDENCE

The definition of a lifestyle and an architecture designed "for simple living, in harmony with nature, at a cost people of average means can afford," put forth again and again within the many articles about Wright's Usonian architecture and Broadacre City published between 1932 and 1945, appealed to—and addressed real needs of—a large segment of the population at a time when the demand for housing was significant. Never before, or since, has this country experienced a building boom such as occurred during the mid-to-late 1940s—following, as it did, on the heels of the building dearth precipitated by the Depression, and the material shortages and civilian construction bans enforced during World War II. Moreover, hundreds of thousands of servicemen—backed by low-interest home loans made available through the Veterans Administration—were returning home ready, willing, and able to return to civilian life and buy into the American dream of home ownership. It was to this section of the buying public that Wright directed his contributions to two popular magazines during this time frame. The first was prepared for *Life* magazine in 1938 in anticipation of the end of the Great Depression; the second was prepared for *Ladies Home Journal* in 1945 in anticipation of the end of World War II.

"House for a Family of $5,000 Income," *Life* Magazine (1938)

Wright was one of eight distinguished architects commissioned to participate in this innovative collaboration between the trade periodical *Architectural Forum* and *Life* magazine, a sister family-oriented pictorial publication. The purpose of the undertaking was to herald the revivification of the depressive economy by encouraging typical renter families to build homes of their own. Four couples representative of different sections of the country were selected from those who not only wanted to build a home but "could afford to do so," meaning their annual income fell within the qualifying range of between $2000 and $10,000. Each couple was asked to describe the limitations of their present residence and detail their needs and desires for a new "dream" home. Two architects were assigned to each family, one to design a house in a "traditional" format and the other a "modern" structure. The design solutions were to be published in the September 26, 1938 issue of *Life* magazine.

Wright's assignment was the modern solution for the Albert R. Blackbourn family of Minneapolis, Minnesota. Royal Barry Wills of Boston was to design the traditional solution. The Blackbourns had two teenage children and an annual income of $5000. They already owned an urban lot next to their present home, and they had very specific ideas about the "dream" home they wanted to build there: "a Scotch peasant-type house with four bedrooms, two baths, a library-office for Mr. Blackbourn [who worked out of their present home], and a game room in the basement where the children could entertain their friends while father and mother entertain theirs in the living room." Considering all the years Wright had been promoting affordable organic housing and site-specific design, it would seem that he would have been prepared to invest considerable thought into this assignment. And yet, when the plans prepared by Wills and Wright are compared, it becomes apparent the differences are much more divergent than "traditional" versus "modern."

The Cape Cod saltbox Wills presented as the traditional solution had a steep roof, a time-honored treatment to prevent excessive snow buildup. The streetside portion of the house had one story; the rear had three full stories, including the walkout basement; and the primary living spaces on all three levels oriented toward the rear so each room could have large windows overlooking the lake and park. Wills is quoted in the *Life* article as having said that the shape and location of the Blackbourn's lot "practically dictates the plan of the house they hope to build."

The "Little Private Club" Wright presented as the modern solution, on the other hand, appears to have been designed for a flat urban site in Arizona, rather than for this site in Minnesota (Figure 8-10). His proposed flat roof and expanses of glass walls would be of questionable practicality for an area that often experiences an annual snowfall exceeding 100 inches, as well as the whole concept of a primary living space opening onto a large enclosed patio with a swimming pool. And because the square footage was much greater than the level area available before the steep drop off of the subject property, many truckloads of earth fill would have been required to level the site enough to accommodate this design format. Wright also proposed that trees and gardens be developed on all sides to screen views into and out from the property—including views of the lake and park amenities. In short, Wright's modern solution

Figure 8-10 Presentation perspective shows Wright's "Little Private Club," designed as a "modern solution" to the housing needs of 1930s families with limited financial resources. (© *2002 by The Frank Lloyd Wright Foundation, Scottsdale, Arizona.*)

ignored the desires and needs particularized by the Blackbourns, as it disregarded local climatic conditions, the natural dictates of the site, and aesthetic amenities. The *Life* article unassertively addressed these disparities through a parenthesized qualifying text: "Cost might make it necessary to substitute a sunken garden for the swimming pool." It does not seem surprising the Blackbourns subsequently chose to build the traditional solution.

Wright resurrected the *Life* plan for Bernard Schwartz of Two Rivers, Wisconsin in 1939 and again in 1956— for Edward Gordon of Aurora, Oregon (renamed Wilsonville in later years). Neither homeowner chose to build a swimming pool. The Schwartz House was constructed on a level suburban lot, and the glazed doors that opened onto the living-dining terrace were oriented toward the south-southeast to afford a better vista of a nearby river. From the Gordon's rural setting alongside the picturesque Williamette River, however, there were no views from the terrace or any of the primary living spaces—only from the second-floor bedrooms.[472]

"Opus 497, Glass House," *Ladies Home Journal* (June 1945)

In January 1944, the *Ladies Home Journal* originated a series of articles to feature "new house designs by the country's outstanding architects—houses that point the way to better, less expensive living after the war." The magazine prepared models for each design, complete with interior details showing furniture and accessories. These models were exhibited at the Massachusetts Institute of Technology and the Boston Museum of Fine Arts, and they were on display at The Museum of Modern Art in New York City when World War II officially ended on August 15, 1945.

The Usonian "Glass House" Wright designed for the series represents an orthogonalized wingspread horizontality such as he used for San Marcos in the Desert (Figure 8-11). By turning the living wing at a 60-degree angle to the bedroom wing, he was able to introduce a more expansive central workspace and a sizable interior planter to augment the indoor-outdoor character and all-encompassing garden imagery of the primary living space—labeled "Garden Room" on the plan. The ceilings for both wings were treated as a raised clerestory of operable windows with a continuous planter directly underneath, except in the area of the fireplace. There were skylights in the Garden Room ceiling, and the open space was girded on three sides with walls of glass— either fixed windows or French doors—affording sweeping views into the out-of-doors. It was to these aspects of Wright's plan that the *Journal* architecture editor Richard Pratt was referring in his editorial comments:

While sunlight and fresh air are free, few houses have ever taken full advantage of the health, comfort, and beauty they can provide. This house does . . . from the few outside doors there can be a

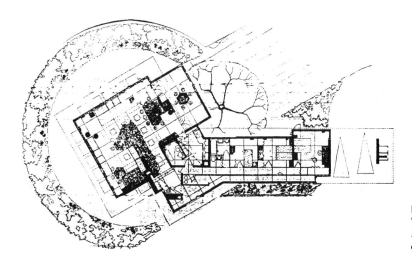

Figure 8-11 Wright's floor plan for "The Glass House." (© *2002 by The Frank Lloyd Wright Foundation, Scottsdale, Arizona.*)

full sweep of air . . . and there can be completely controlled ventilation through the movable sash of the clerestory that rises above the main roof. . . . These upper openings provide a beautiful source of light from above, through ceiling windows that throw shafts of sunshine on walls, floors, furniture and plants. These plants, growing in earth panels at floor level, not only help to decorate the room, excitingly and fragrantly, but form a flower-and-foliage partition between the sitting side of the room around the fireplace and the dining side, which opens upon a terrace for outdoor eating and entertaining.

It was toward this spacious open space that Wright choreographed the entry experience. Movement was directed from the carport past the brick wall of the bedroom wing toward the point of outdoor-indoor transition, sheltered under the broad overhang. Upon entering the modest foyer and entry hall, where the ceiling was not raised, there would be a momentary change in the perception of luminance before proceeding past the indoor planting bed and into the upward and outward expanse of the Garden Room, illuminated with natural light from all sides.[473] Thus, it was Wright's intent to create a sense of place within this modest home every bit as effective as he had created for his most expensive residences.

Since the Glass House was designed as an affordable model home for families of returning veterans, Wright proposed brick as the primary building material and arranged the layout for construction on the generic flat lot typical to Suburbia USA. The same reasoning determined the arrangement of operable windows and doors as well as the dimension of the eave overhangs, which were scaled to a generous depth—presumably in an attempt to protect the expanses of glass, regardless of orientation.

Ironically, although Wright proposed modified versions of this plan for several clients, the only one carried through to completion was a "luxury" version, built as a retirement home for wealthy industrialist Lowell Walter. It was under this ownership arrangement that the generic plan was featured in the September 1946 issue of *Architectural Forum*, published prior to modifications having been made or construction begun. The accompanying text read: "This masonry-type Usonian glass house

has concrete slab roofs with turned up eaves. No wood is used in the construction, exterior or interior. Partitions are of solid plaster, doors and sash are metal, floors usual precast tile. Gravity heat." This description did not apply to the Walter House as constructed, however. Walnut paneling was used extensively throughout and the interior space was modified and expanded, as it was featured in the January 1951 issue of *Architectural Forum* devoted entirely to the works of Frank Lloyd Wright.

Lowell Walter "Cedar Rock"—Quasqueton, Iowa (1946)

The site on which the Lowell Walters chose to build their home was a rugged limestone promontory on the left bank of a bend in the Wasipinicon River in rural northwest Iowa—anything but a "generic flat lot typical to Suburbia USA." During the authors' process of conducting the Walter House on-site analysis, it was noted that retaining walls had been installed to create a level platform around the house (Figure 8-12). The extent of the retaining walls raised questions regarding the original topography and the degree of site manipulation involved during the construction process. Insights gained through telephone interviews with Francis Reinhold, who grew up in the area with Mr. Walter and worked on the construction crew, and with John deKoven Hill, the apprentice assigned to work on the modification drawings and supervise construction, establish that procedures followed at this location again directly countermand many of Wright's most-quoted axioms of organic architecture.[474]

Reinhold described Cedar Rock as a natural feature that had served as a landmark for millennia and was within the confines of an Indian reservation for the Sauk and Fox tribes until 1891—by which time Wright already had completed a half-dozen designs on his own and was working with Adler and Sullivan. Reinhold recalled that many of the indigenous cedar trees that inspired the Cedar Rock designation already had been cleared from the site by the time he returned home from World War II. He also remembered Mr. Wright arriving on the site one day and ordering the removal of more trees to "develop a vista." He then described the extent to which the ecological structure of the site was altered to accommodate the generic layout. He said that "many cases of dynamite" were used to "blast out tons" of the natural geologic landmark—not only to provide a level base, but to accommodate the heating system, the septic field and tank, and other utilitarian accouterments of

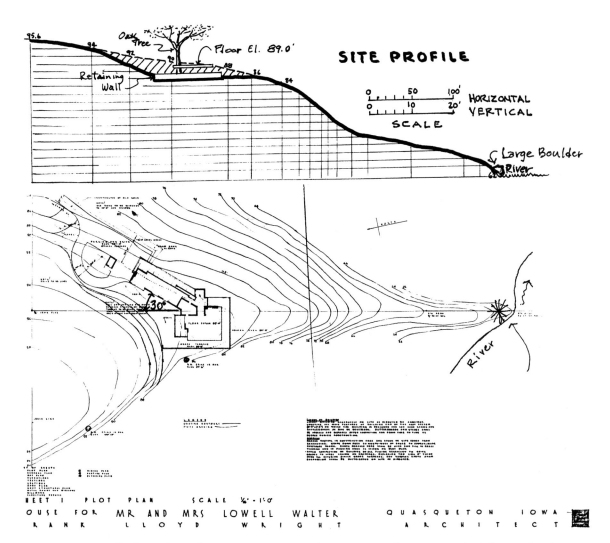

Figure 8-12 Site profile for "Cedar Rock" in Quasqueton, Iowa, where a Usonian Glass House was built for Lowell Walter. (*By Charles E. Aguar, based on personal analysis and plot-plan of record. © 2002 by The Frank Lloyd Wright Foundation, Scottsdale, Arizona. As delineated, © 2002 by Berdeana Aguar.*)

modern construction. He recalled "many, many wagon loads of black dirt" being hauled to the site so an expanse of lawn could be established. And he confirmed that the only remnant of the rock outcropping is located up the hillside near the outdoor cooking area.

Hill also remembered "lots of little cedar trees covering the hillside" during his first visit to the site with Wright, but said he was "not aware that rock was

removed or that much grading was needed." He did recall Wright sited the house on the topographic map and was proud of the way it came together. He also pointed out that "Mr. Walter had access to all the trucks and heavy construction machinery needed for site preparation." When asked why someone with a large budget would select a generic plan aimed at less expensive living, Hill said Walter "liked the substantial features of a brick home and concrete roof" shown in the magazine article and felt the plan would suit them with very little change. He said the all-walnut interior was selected because it "represented the type of quality that Mr. Walter was after." He elaborated: "I don't know of any other house by Mr. Wright where walnut has been used for all furniture, cabinets, and paneling. The solid black walnut used throughout the interior did not come from trees on the site, but was readily available from local farmers at a good price—in those days." With respect to the landscape treatment, Hill said: "Mr. Wright wanted the garden room to contain plants inside and the windows surrounded by flowers and other plants so it would appear within its own garden, and then left in a natural state beyond the retaining walls. That became the line between architecture and nature" (Figure 8-13).

Based upon these explanations, it does not appear that Wright made any effort to convince Mr. Walter the house could have been just as substantial, just as high in quality, less expensive, and more organically appropriate if built of the limestone quarried nearby, rather than brick. These explanations also do not explain why Wright would go to such effort to establish a formal lawn, or why the one flower he specified should be planted in front of the windows of the garden room— the Portalaca—was a garden annual indigenous not to Iowa, but to Brazil. There are other incongruous conditions that directly relate to the problem of forcing a generic plan onto a decidedly nongeneric site. The expansive glass walls in the Garden Room orient to the south and west, creating the need to use floor-to-ceiling draperies by early afternoon—despite the broad overhang and vine plantings introduced to screen the sun. Moreover, there is no exterior vantage point from which to view the river amenity, other than from the entry sidewalk (Figure 8-14). This, because the terrace is on the north side of the Garden Room facing the hillside, and the wraparound terrace shown on the plan was not implemented; this space instead was filled with foundation plants of junipers, flowers, and bulbs (Figure 8-15).

In the final analysis, it must be acknowledged that the plan, form, and character of the Walter House most assuredly were not determined by the "nature of the site." Nor did the plan develop "from within outward." Nor was the house constructed from "whatever material may be in hand." It also cannot be said that the structure

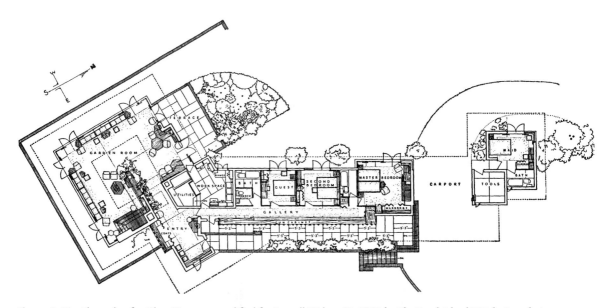

Figure 8-13   Floor plan for Glass House, as modified for Lowell Walter. (© *2002 by The Frank Lloyd Wright Foundation, Scottsdale, Arizona.*)

Figure 8-14 The entry approach to the Lowell Walter House is the only exterior vantage point from which to view the river amenity. (*Photograph by Charles E. Aguar. © 2002 by Berdeana Aguar.*)

was not "applied from without" or that the landscape of Cedar Rock was not "outraged" by its construction. At the same time, however, the Walter House actualized both the architectural grammar and the aesthetics put forth in the *Journal* article. The Garden Room literally glows with reflected light; the expanses of glass invite the eye to view the river below; and there is an ambiance and pervading sense-of-place in the best tradition of Wright's Usonian architecture. In other words, the Walter House presents the "illusion" of an organic architec-

Figure 8-15 Contained planting bed in front of Lowell Walter House facade facing river amenity. (*Photograph by Charles E. Aguar. © 2002 by Berdeana Aguar.*)

ture inspired by the nature of the site. And the clients were completely satisfied with the end result. As Wright concluded in the preface to the January 1951 *Architectural Forum* article: "To build this highly specialized fabric far away from manifest civilization cost us all more than considerable labor pains and cost Mr. Walter considerable money. He doesn't regret the money, nor do we regret the effort."

The procedures followed with the Walter House generally represent the process of change that evolved within the operation of the Fellowship during this time frame. As the economy improved and commissions became more forthcoming, the aging Wright of necessity began assigning more responsibility to the "senior" apprentices—that is, those charter apprentices who thrived within the unstructured format of the system and remained far beyond the time required to complete their education.[475] From within this group, some natural leaders emerged who progressively assumed more and more responsibility for the managerial aspects of operations and received a stipend for their services. During the 1989 interview, Wes Peters told the author that he began functioning as Wright's "outdoor" man—teaching construction techniques to apprentices, managing the farm, and supervising construction projects at Taliesin and Taliesin West. John "Jack" Howe began functioning as Wright's "indoor" man, teaching less senior apprentices how to draft while supervising the development of clients' working drawings and personally drafting many of the presentation drawings that bear Wright's name.[476] This circumstance becomes extremely relevant when one considers that in the precomputerization era of the 1930s through the 1950s, untold drafting hours were required for each Usonian structure. Even though this architecture appears simple in format, with millwork the average carpenter can construct easily on site, each house required a minimum half-dozen sheets of explicit drawings, as well as another sheet of standard details that served as the "key" to the entire Usonian system.

A procedure evolved whereby the majority of clients were invited to meet with Wright at Taliesin or Taliesin West, or at the Park Plaza Hotel in later years when Wright was involved with the years-long process of designing and building the Guggenheim Museum. Clients in most cases brought with them, or later provided, topographic survey maps (not uncommon to contain errors and omissions) and written explanations of

their housing needs, as well as photographs with written descriptions intended to document site conditions. When the clients arrived, Howe explained in *Frank Lloyd Wright Remembered*, "Mr. Wright would always closet himself . . . in his office because he liked to work with them in person. He didn't let us in on the conversations with clients. Never were apprentices asked to take care of clients."[477] After clients departed, Howe noted, Wright concentrated on creative concepts and sketching out his ideas, then turned the project over to him [Howe] for the drafting of working drawings, which included trying to interpret all Wright had promised the clients during their private meeting. While clients sometimes then made repeat visits to one or both Taliesins, or met Wright when circumstances brought him in proximity to their residence, questions that arose as to interpretation of the plans generally were handled by telephone, telegram, or letters—depending on the level of urgency in any-given situation. In essence, the Fellowship—although still classified as an educational facility—began performing as a professional architectural practice such as Wright directed at his Oak Park Studio, but staffed by the apprentices.

This economically feasible method of operations worked quite well for most clients, but the system was not without flaws. The analyses of four houses built early on within this reorganization process clearly illustrate the difference in the way problems were solved if Wright was professionally challenged or motivated to be personally involved and the problems that could, and often did, occur when he was not.

John C. Pew—Shorewood Hills, Wisconsin (1938)

Ruth and John Pew approached Wright in 1938 to see if he would possibly consider designing a modest home for them to build in a suburb of Madison, Wisconsin. Their lot was one of several being developed at that time along the north shore of Lake Mendota. The property was wooded and sloped gently away from the access road, but dropped off as it reached the shoreline. During a May 1992 interview, the Pews described how Wright came, looked at their lot, and "liked what he saw" but then informed them he never could fit even the small, low-budget house they had in mind on a 50-foot lot. "He insisted we must buy another 50 feet before he could proceed. Luckily, the owner to the east of our lot was about ready to build and he had enough land to let us have an additional 25 feet. We were in a bind to get the money to buy even that much more land, but he let us have it for a good price because the eroding ravine then would be entirely off his property and would be our problem alone." They went on to say that although Wright was disappointed they couldn't afford to buy more land, he so wanted to build on Lake Mendota, "something he had wanted to do since his boyhood," he agreed to continue.

Wright addressed the ravine as a challenge and found a way to site the house over it. The Pews explained: "Mr. Wright angled the house—what he called turn it on the reflex—to straddle the ravine and fit the house onto our narrow lot (Figure 8-16 a-c). This angle prevented us from seeing the neighboring houses from most rooms and proved to provide more beautiful views, better sunlight angles and sunset views than the neighboring houses set

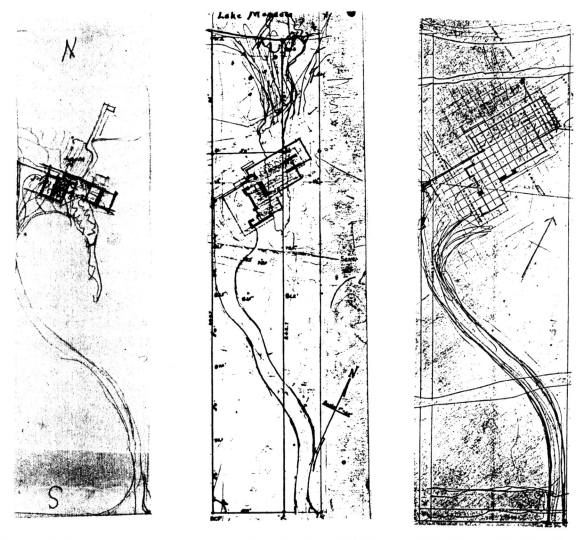

Figure 8-16 Evolutionary sketches of site layout for John C. Pew House (1938), Shorewood Hills, Wisconsin. (© *2002 by The Frank Lloyd Wright Foundation, Scottsdale, Arizona.*)

square with the street or shoreline. The house also was closer to the lake than other houses, which was fine with our family." That Wright was able to site the house so sensitively seems all the more remarkable when the Pews revealed that he did so without benefit of technical support: "The site plans with dotted contour lines and plants that sometimes are published with our house are strictly imaginary. Maybe some of the trees are located about right, but we never had a tree survey or topographic map with contours prepared for our property." The Pews then volunteered the information that Wright originally planned for two trees to grow through the living room

deck, instead of the one linden tree (Figure 8-17). It seems that a great deal of work had gone into saving and building around a basswood tree until members of the construction crew arrived one morning to find it cut down and neatly stacked for firewood.

It didn't surprise us to learn that it was done by the strongest, but not the smartest, member of the labor crew to "save us trouble." Earlier, he had gone through our entire lot and cut down trees carefully marked to be saved, thinking they were the ones to be removed. He had in fact assumed the right—we don't remember giving him permission—to camp on our lot so he could start work each morning before anyone else arrived. This crew member was so strong he could pull tree roots from utility trenches with his bare hands, while others were slowly chopping or digging them out. We had seen him drive spikes into boards with his bare hand. After the scolding he received because of the basswood tree incident, he removed his tent and left. Rumor was that he joined a carnival as a strong man.

The Pew House has been likened to an affordable version of Fallingwater. Certainly, the expansive water feature and the natural ravine topography of the two sites are comparable, even though the Pew's site is limited in size and the entry experience is straightforward and unimaginative. And although the primary building materials here are lapped wood siding and stone (originally specified as brick), rather than stone and concrete, the two structures share the architectural attributes of eyebrow corner overhangs, mitered corner windows, expanses of glass walls, and soaring balconies projecting over a ravine (Figure 8-18). But this modest 1200-square-foot Usonian does not in any way dominate nature. Rather, it establishes a true "union with nature," as corroborated by Cindy Edwards, who with her husband John purchased the house from the Pews when they moved to a retirement facility. She observed: "The interior wood walls and ceilings, the exposed sections of stone, and glass at just the right places to introduce the interplay of sun and shadow, the stone fireplace and stone floor in the kitchen—all work together to give the feeling that you are living *within* the natural environment. . . . From most seating positions, or from the beds, you feel like you are in a tree house. When seated in the arrangement Wright planned for each room, you see no other houses and have views of the lake, the trees, and

Figure 8-17   Photograph shows linden tree protruding through Pew deck. Wright originally planned to save two trees. (*Photograph by Charles E. Aguar. © 2002 by Berdeana Aguar.*)

Figure 8-18 View of the Pew House supports the claim that it establishes a true "union with nature." (*Photograph by Charles E. Aguar. © 2002 by Berdeana Aguar.*)

the sky—with a play of sun and shadow that establishes the whole house as a work of art. While standing or out on the balcony, it's as though you are on a boat; you don't see the ground, but you have an oak canopy overhead."[478]

Lloyd Lewis—Libertyville, Illinois (1939)

Few low-budget houses of this time frame were given more detailed study than the in-line, split-level Usonian that Wright designed for Lloyd Lewis, his friend of 20 years and editor of the *Chicago Daily News*. For this natural woodland setting on the bank of the Des Plaines River, Wright once again resorted to the raised basement approach—based on "A Typical Dwelling for Little Farms" designed for the Broadacre City Models, the plan originally proposed seven years earlier for the Willeys in Minnesota. In this case, however, the design format of raising the primary living spaces assumedly was motivated as much by the low-lying topography of the site and the sphere of influence inherent to any low-lying property situated in a hundred-year floodplain—that is, dampness, mold, and the potential for seepage and flooding—as it was to afford more expansive views of the peripheral environment of water amenity, marshes, and wildlife.

Four preliminary studies confirm the amount of attention given to siting the house and aligning the entrance approach route to better relate to the river, existing trees, proposed gardens for perennials and vegetables, and areas to be preserved as "wild" open space. Because of this attention, the architecture orients to the trajectory pattern of the sun throughout the year and coalesces with the site and river environment remarkably well. Although spring breakup has pushed ice floes from river to terrace, the current owners—who had resided in the house more than three decades at the time of the interview—never had seen the river rise higher than the second step above the terrace.

Wright's ground plan delineates planting beds in the garden area below the main balcony that echo the river and appear to flow from under the house (Figure 8-19). The concrete walkways that line these planting beds combine with the brick piers to establish a geometric rhythm comparable to some of the contained geometric gardens Wright used with his Prairie Houses. Here, they also contributed to the entry experience, which proceeds past the gardens along the 60-foot length of the loggia, before progressing up the twisting stairway to the upward and outward expanse of the second-floor living space and the expansive balcony (Figure 8-20). From these vantage points, the views of the river are comparable to standing at the rail of a houseboat.

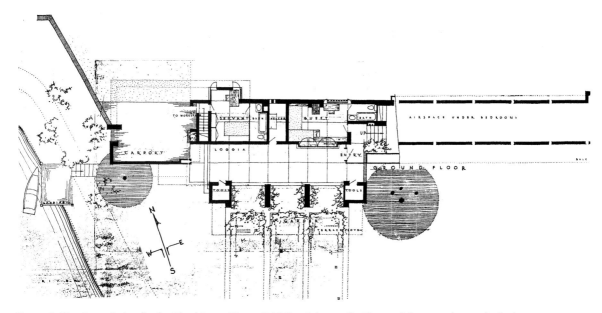

Figure 8-19   Ground plan for the Lloyd Lewis House (1939) in Libertyville, Illinois, delineates planting beds that appear to flow from under the house. (© *2002 by The Frank Lloyd Wright Foundation, Scottsdale, Arizona.*)

Leigh Stevens' "Auldbrass Plantation"— Yemassee, South Carolina (1939)

The design approach that Wright undertook for the complex of structures to be built upon the 4000-acre site of the former "Oldbrass" antebellum rice plantation—once the largest plantation in South Carolina—represents a complete about-face from his design approach for the Lewis House.[479] Here in this southern "low-country," equidistant from Charleston and Savannah, where the indigenous architecture raises the primary living spaces off the ground to access cooling breezes and cope with the climatic conditions of heat and humidity, Wright chose to place all structures at

Figure 8-20   Perspective sketch shows upward and outward expanse of Lewis House indoor-outdoor living spaces. (© *2002 by The Frank Lloyd Wright Foundation, Scottsdale, Arizona.*)

ground level on concrete mats. The only time-honored tradition evolved through the trial and error of settlement he chose to adopt was to separate the kitchen from the main house. By proposing to address climatic conditions in this nonhistorical fashion, he purposefully challenged himself to originate other ways to cope with these issues.

The portion of the acreage selected for development was approximately three-quarters of a mile south of the Cambahee River at the end of a canal, which led to the wharf from which rice and other produce formerly had been shipped to South Carolina's port city of Beaufort (Figure 8-21). Wright began by laying out a rambling complex of interconnecting one-story buildings in an all-inclusive spatial arrangement that devel-

oped a meaningful integration between his architecture and the sensuosity of the existing landscape. For the main house, he returned to the hexagon module used with the Hanna House and arranged the rooms to expose all sides as he had done at Wingspread and Taliesin West. The glass walls in the primary living spaces were oriented to face southeast and northwest, and roof clerestories were introduced to accentuate the play of sunlight and shadow and the glow of moonlight throughout the day and night. To create a fluid and organic relationship between indoors and outdoors, Wright related his architecture to the most character-defining attribute of the site: the massive Live Oak trees, draped with sinuous tendrils of Spanish moss. He battered the walls of native cypress at a 9-degree angle in

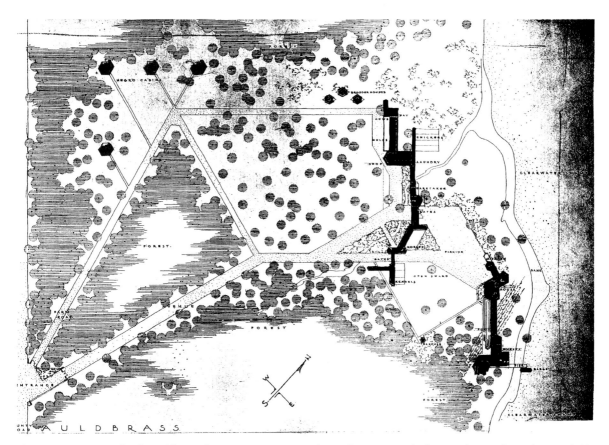

Figure 8-21 Master plan for Auldbrass Plantation, Yamassee, South Carolina (1939), which was only partially implemented. (© 2002 by The Frank Lloyd Wright Foundation, Scottsdale, Arizona.)

harmony with the sloping trunks of the trees (Figure 8-22). He fashioned a Live Oak tree branch motif into the fretted plywood inserts for the clerestory windows and the framework of the windowed walls.[480] And he designed downspouts that echo the graceful draping form of the Spanish moss and become works of art that come to life as rainwater runoff creates a myriad of kinetic patterns[481] (Figure 8-23). He also installed hinged trap doors at the base of the floor-to-ceiling windows, introduced hinging window panels under the eaves, and selectively placed copper roof ventilators to exhaust rising hot air to the outside. This treatment was intended to serve two purposes: (1) to create a convection and naturally air-condition the premises, and (2) to negate the problems of mildew and rotting associated with the low-country climatic conditions.

With this all-inclusive design methodology, Wright successfully met his challenge of creating an alternative organic architecture for the lowlands and cypress swamps of the coastal area.

By the time the authors first visited Auldbrass in 1981, the property was abandoned and open to trespass. During the course of having been used as a hunting camp for a number of years, much of the cypress paneling had

been carelessly patched and the main house had suffered the insult of jerrybuilt additions. Moreover, the hinged boards at the base of the slanted walls were extensively rotted or damaged by rodents. And all of Wright's specially designed furniture had been stripped away, as well as most of the artistic downspouts.

Sickened at seeing this one-of-a-kind, Wright-designed complex in such deplorable condition, the author began encouraging graduate students and fifth-year seniors enrolled in the University of Georgia School of Environmental Design to consider Auldbrass as subject matter for their final project. The thinking was that this process might be a method of interesting someone with means to protect and possibly restore this one-time gem. This prospect became even more relevant when it was discovered that the property was for sale, that the Charleston office of the National Trust for Historic Preservation was interested in its preservation, and that application was being made to list it on the National Register of Historic Places. But it was not until the summer of 1989 that Edward A. Browder, a native of Charleston, selected Auldbrass as his fifth-year Senior Project. During the process of conducting the detective work required to write his proposal, he learned that the property had been purchased by motion picture producer Joel Silver and

Figure 8-22 At Auldbrass Plantation, Wright battered walls of Native Cypress at a 9-degree angle to harmonize with sloping trunks of Live Oak trees. (*Photograph by Charles E. Aguar. © 2002 by Berdeana Aguar.*)

Figure 8-23 Wright designed downspouts at Auldbrass Plantation to echo the graceful draping forms of Spanish Moss. (*Photograph by Charles E. Aguar. © 2002 by Berdeana Aguar.*)

was being restored under supervision of Eric Lloyd Wright, grandson of the architect.[482] Within the restoration process, all of the unexecuted elements of the original design were actualized—including the formation of a lake in the area of the former cypress swamp. Auldbrass today represents one of the finest examples of restoration of any privately owned Wright property.

George D. Sturges—Brentwood Heights, California (1939)

This very modest, 900-square-foot, brick and weathered-wood residence is situated in a crowded suburban neighborhood of conventional houses on an excessively steep hillside site that personifies the type of "infill" lot Wright advised his clients to seek out—that is, "the type of lot no one else would want." Yet, here again, Wright successfully met the challenge of finding a way to site the house to "fit" with the topography, address climatic conditions, assure maximum privacy, and provide panoramic vistas across the city of Santa Monica and the Pacific Ocean (Figure 8-24).

To begin with, he arranged the plan so there were no windows on the northeasternmost wall and only one small window on the north wall (Figure 8-25). This treatment screened the primary living spaces from the entry driveway and public right-of-way and impeded the directional path of the Santa Ana winds. The incidence of the Santa Ana winds also determined the placement of the deflecting wall to the northwest of the door to the workspace, as well as the inset and placement of the main point of outdoor-indoor transition at the northwest corner of the house. This arrangement, in turn, created a diagonal viewpoint from the point of entry outward through the wall of floor-to-ceiling glass doors that open from the primary living-dining space onto the spacious wood deck—labeled "terrace" on the plans. Standing on this private deck, the panorama of the view could be likened to the experience of being on a yacht at sea.[483] Since the terrace is directly accessible to both bedrooms, as well, the visual and perceptive illusion is that the house is substantially larger than its minimal square footage would suggest.

Within the masterful simplicity of this compact plan, Wright heightened the illusion of soaring or accelerated motion—so popular in the streamlined architecture of the 1930s—through his symbolic, finely crafted all-wood interior, held together with cadmium-plated screws. To externalize the soaring illusionism, he worked with the slope—which dropped off to the south and southeast—by cantilevering the entire house over the brick-faced workshop and masonry mass of the chimney (Figure 8-26). Although this methodology can only be looked upon as an extremely expensive solution to the problems posed by a steep site, raising the structure entirely off the ground in this manner significantly minimized its impact on the site. Grading was required mainly to establish the steep driveway and level the automobile courtyard. Therefore, the excessive cut-and-fill so commonly required for sites such as this was avoided; the natural drainage was barely disrupted; and

Figure 8-26 With the Sturges residence, Wright met his goal of creating an indigenous architecture for Southern California, because this Wrightscape truly embodies its spirit-of-place like no other. (*Photograph by Charles E. Aguar. © 2002 by Berdeana Aguar.*)

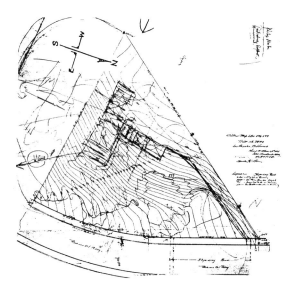

Figure 8-24 Wright's sketch over topographic survey for George D. Sturges House (1939) in Brentwood Height, California. (*© 2002 by The Frank Lloyd Wright Foundation, Scottsdale, Arizona.*)

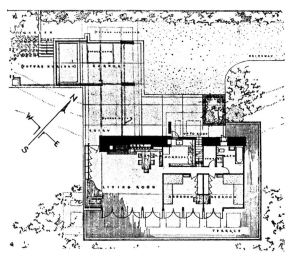

Figure 8-25 Floor plan for Sturges House reflects Wright's concerns with privacy and Santa Ana winds. (*© 2002 by The Frank Lloyd Wright Foundation, Scottsdale, Arizona.*)

the root systems of nearby vegetation were preserved. Moreover, the verticality of the sculptural clumps of eucalyptus trees provide counterpoint to the horizontality of the structure; the stark white bark contrasts with the dark green English ivy introduced to envelop the slope; and the aesthetic of the landscape synthetically merges with the simplistic lines of the architecture. All in all, the Sturges House embodies a remarkable spirit-of-place in the best tradition of an affordable Usonian.

Loran B. Pope—Falls Church, Virginia (1939)

The plans, siting, and orientation for the Loran B. Pope House were designed to conform to information derived from the topographic map furnished by the client (Figure 8-27a). On this basis, Wright proposed to site the house at the midpoint on a level area, so there would be a 77-foot setback from the public right-of-way and the walls of glass on either side of the primary living area faced due south and due north. This arrangement allowed maximum penetration of the low winter sun for solar gain and access to the prevailing southerly summer breezes, so excellent cross-ventilation could be achieved through natural convention by way of the French doors and the operable windows in the clerestory. It also placed the specimen Tulip-Poplar tree Pope specifically requested Wright should preserve in a location to shade both the west-facing facade of the bedroom wing and the south-facing facade of the living-dining wing. And it assured that an existing grove of mature evergreens would partially block the impact of prevailing winter winds, which originate from the northwest. Wright also designed a trellis and perforated shutters to filter the winter sun and privatize the bedrooms from the public street. And he proposed that a low wall and plantings parallel the driveway to introduce a geometric extension into the out-of-doors and that a privacy fence and berry hemicycle containment feature be added to create a sphere of privatization and a grass terraced outdoor living space.

The environmental benefits of this layout were never realized, however, because the mapping inaccu-

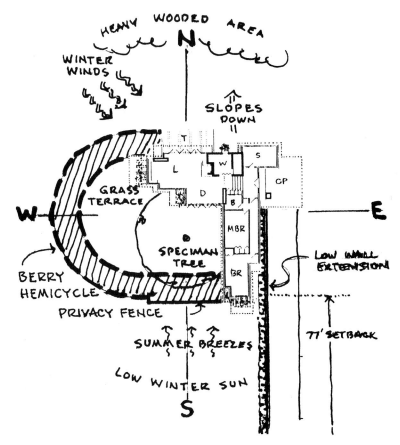

Figure 8-27 a Proposed siting and orientation of Loren Pope House (1939) in Falls Church, Virginia, based on topographic map. (*By Charles E. Aguar, based on personal analysis and plans of record. © 2002 The Frank Lloyd Wright Foundation, Scottsdale, Arizona. As delineated, © 2002 by Berdeana Aguar.*)

rately delineated the steepness of the terrain that in actuality sloped rapidly downward to the north—a circumstance not discovered until an apprentice arrived to stake out the house. Inasmuch as this assignment represented this apprentice's first on-site construction experience, other than working at the construction camp at Taliesin West during his brief two-year stint with The Fellowship, a senior apprentice was called in to assist with the re-siting; and he had to leave for another assignment prior to construction getting underway. It was during the period of watching several of their unsuccessful attempts to rotate the floor plan and accommodate the specimen tree during the re-staking process that Pope dubbed his house "Poplar Misconception."[484]

As sited and built, the Pope House was moved 50 feet south of the specimen tree, as well as 50 feet closer to the public street, and it was reoriented 135 degrees to the west so the walls of glass in the primary living area faced southeast and northwest (Figure 8-27 b). The

negative consequences of this relocation were: (1) the Tulip-Poplar tree only shaded the far end of the bedroom wing; (2) the setback line was a mere 27 feet from the street right-of-way; (3) the trellis and perforated shutters became nonfunctional; (4) the prevailing northwest winter winds funnelled directly onto the walls on one side of the living area; and (5) the solar penetration was compromised on the other side. The changed relationship between the house and the existing evergreen woods limited winter sun penetration even more. Moreover, the dense plantings selected and introduced by Pope to establish a natural privacy screen between the street and house compromised access to summer breezes and eventually blocked all access to solar gain. In addition, there were no geometric extensions into the out-of-doors; the driveway was shortened and reversed; and neither the grass terrace outdoor living space nor the hemicycle containment feature could be developed.

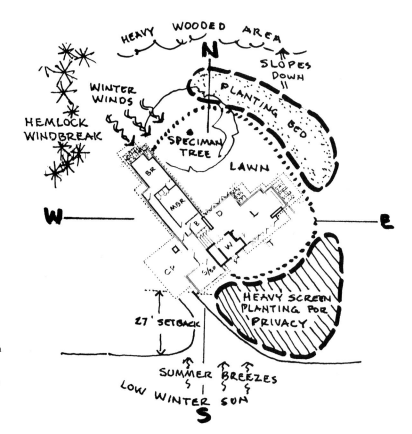

Figure 8-27 b Actual siting and orientation of Pope House, based on observed climatic conditions. (*By Charles E. Aguar, based on personal analysis and plans of record.* © 2002 *The Frank Lloyd Wright Foundation, Scottsdale, Arizona. As delineated,* © 2002 *by Berdeana Aguar.*)

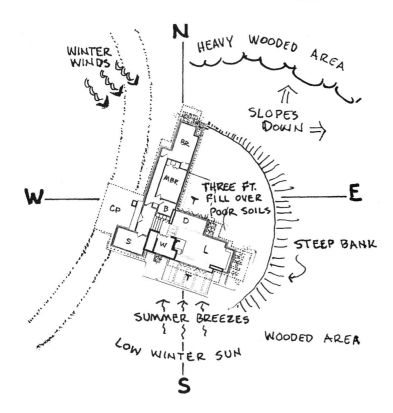

Figure 8-27 c The Pope House, as sited and oriented after being moved by National Trust, did not address actual climatic conditions. (*By Charles E. Aguar, based on personal analysis and plans of record. © 2002 by The Frank Lloyd Wright Foundation, Scottsdale, Arizona. As delineated, © 2002 by Berdeana Aguar.*)

Based upon this analysis, it is difficult to understand why Wright would write a letter to Pope stating: "This placing of the house is much better orientation, with sunlight and a less formal attitude—throughout. More our stuff, I believe." Assumedly, he was making reference to his developing preference for siting on the diagonal to maximize the infiltration of natural light throughout the day. At the same time, of course, he effectively disavowed responsibility for the cumulative negative aspects of the re-siting brought about by the inaccurate mapping and his decision to address the situation by adaptation, rather than site-specific design.

The Pope family only occupied this home until 1946. Because of the more extensive length of occupancy by the Robert Leighey family, the residence generally has been identified as the Pope-Leighey House since that date. In 1963, shortly after the widowed Mrs. Leighey offered the house to the National Trust for Historic Preservation—subject to her right to life tenancy—a planned extension of Interstate 66 threatened the property. When the National Trust then moved the structure to a site at Woodlawn Plantation in Mount Vernon, Virginia, where it would be restored as a museum, they sited it 70 degrees east of the siting at Falls Church (Figure 8-27c). This reorientation faced the walls of glass in the primary living area to the southwest and northeast and so changed and devitalized the former ambiance of sunlight filtering through the horizontal and vertical fretted boards that Marjorie Leighey is said to have expressed displeasure. Nor was consideration given to the impact that prevailing winter winds would have on visitors waiting under the carport to enter the front door. And no effort was made to try to either re-create the choreography of Wright's original entry experience or the approach as it was crafted at Falls Church, where there was a slight incline. At Woodlawn Plantation, cars were excluded from the road and all visitors were required to approach from above, looking down on the large flat roof and thereby forming an unfavorable first impression. But the most devastating consequence of the resiting occurred because the house was erected on 3 feet of unstable fill over an already unsuitable mix of silt, sand, and clay—resulting in 1-inch cracks in the concrete slab, broken heating pipes, large cracks in the board-and-batten walls, and a sagging ceiling. These conditions precipitated yet another move and an estimated $500,000 restoration—this, for a structure that originally cost $7000.

The saga of the Pope-Leighey House emphasizes the consequence of ignoring the environment when undertaking the restoration, reconstruction, or relocation of Wright's domestic architecture. Wright did not limit his design process to the footprint of the structure. Restoration cannot begin and end there.

From 1932 until Wright's death in 1959, a total of 650 projects emanated from the Fellowship, of which 217 (34 percent) were executed and 362 (56 percent) were not.[485] During this same time frame, a total of 330 apprentices spent varying lengths of time on the premises, some for just a few months or no more than a year. Many used the Fellowship as an educational stepping stone for careers in other art forms—interior design, set design, sculpturing, and painting. Kevin Lynch returned to formal study and became a respected professor of urban studies and planning at the Massachusetts Institute of Technology. At least 3 went on to specialize in landscape architecture: James Drought (1932–1934), Kaneji Domoto (1939), and John Paul (1949–1952). Approximately 80 former apprentices developed distinguished national and international architectural practices in their own right. And 17 at one time or another taught on the Fellowship faculty, while also working professionally as Taliesin Architects.[486]

Although the general perception seems to be that it was standard procedure for each apprentice to be closely involved with at least one commission on an ongoing basis throughout construction as part of their training, this was not the norm. Less than 10 percent, in all, actually assumed this responsibility. While it is true that apprentices—most frequently seniors, but not always—were assigned to at least stake out a majority of the residences, their ongoing involvement with actual construction varied from project to project. This, even though Wright's standard contract calculated 2 percent of the total 10-percent fee as an allocation for "architect's supervision." The contract also set forth a means

for apprentices to receive compensation for supervisory or clerk-of-the-works duties, as follows:

> The architect, where good general contractors are not available, undertakes to itemize mill work and material for the building, at cost—let contracts to subcontractors for piece work and eliminate the general contractor where possible by sending a qualified apprentice of the Taliesin Fellowship at the proper time to take charge, do the necessary shopping and hold the entire building operation together. The apprentice will check cost—layouts, bids, etc., refer proposed changes to the architect and endeavor to bring the work to successful completion. This apprentice is to be lodged and fed by the owner, his necessary traveling expenses paid by the owner who also pays the apprentice $30.00 per week for his services so long as he is required on the work.

Ruth and John Pew stated that Cary Caraway interpreted the blueprints for them and "did some work" on the steel cantilever supports for their house. They also recall his having supervised apprentice Herb Fritz during a portion of his on-the-job construction training—working with their local contractor and reporting directly to Wes Peters whenever problems arose. And they remember that "the boys" from Taliesin located and hauled in the huge rock slab for over their fireplace and made sure it was placed "just right." But neither recalled apprentices being otherwise involved with the construction process. The significance here is that their site is within an hour's drive of Taliesin.

In the case of newlyweds Gerte and Seamour Shavin (Chattanooga, Tennessee, 1950), Wright never mentioned the likelihood of an apprentice being made available to them during any of several trips they made to Taliesin. They said it wasn't until they were at Taliesin awaiting completion of their working drawings that apprentice Marvin Bachman approached them and offered to supervise the construction of their house for a small salary. It seems he was at that time planning to leave Taliesin. Based on the fact that Bachman also had completed two years in the architectural program at Carnegie Tech, the Shavins decided to take him up on his offer; and he doubled up with them in the home of Mr. Shavin's parents until shortly before their house was finished, when he was killed in an auto accident.[487] The

Shavins refer to Bachman's sensitive and caring involvement with the construction of their beautiful home as a "stroke of luck," because he insisted on details being properly executed.

Few of the other first families interviewed by the author had an apprentice spend more than a day or two, or make occasional visits. Sometimes, four different apprentices participated—one to stake out the structure and others to check on various stages of construction. Even then, apprentices might arrive only after much urging by the client, as verified through communications-of-record during construction of the William Palmer House (Ann Arbor, Michigan, 1950). Perhaps because in that post–World War II era the realms of familial responsibility were definitive as to "homemaker" and "provider," it most often was "the wife" who took over the task of maintaining these lines of communication.

The clients first asked for help on *September 2, 1950:* "We understand that someone from Taliesin comes to Michigan about once a month. We would appreciate being notified of the next visit." Three letters followed in quick succession. *September 6, 1950:* "We hope to see someone from Taliesin soon." *September 14, 1950:* "We still feel that it would be mighty desirous for one of your men to see the site before you make your winter move to Arizona." *September 24, 1950:* "We still feel that it [the visit of an apprentice mentioned in the last letter] would be advantageous to every one concerned."

Six months later, the clients sent two telegrams. *March 17, 1951:* "We plan to begin construction any day. Please get us off to a perfect start by sending us someone to help lay out house and answer questions." *March 24, 1951:* "Please have some one telephone me reverse Friday or Saturday. Urgent." Wright's response, telegraphed six days later, was extremely noncommittal and reflected the increase in the Fellowship work load. *March 31, 1951:* "Will send someone soon. Blueprints in mail."

During the month of April, the clients sent two letters, two weeks apart. *April 1, 1951:* "Your telegram which we received yesterday telling us that someone will soon be here to help us get started with the house was wonderful news—as we are really all set to go." *April 13, 1951:* "Sorry to have to ask for help in laying out the house—but we are aiming toward perfection. You have been wonderful—we thank you—and await hearing from you the date when we can expect someone." This

letter was reinforced with a telegram, for good measure. *April 13, 1951:* "When can we expect someone to lay out the house? Our hearty thanks for sticking by us."

Two weeks later, another approach was taken. *May 2, 1951:* "We heard today that your lecture at Lawrence Tech in Detroit has been moved ahead to May 14th. If by any chance you can come see us in Ann Arbor either before or after your speaking engagement we would be very happy to have you see the site at your convenience. . . . In any case, we are planning to hear you speak on the 14th. We are waiting to hear from you before we can go ahead with breaking ground." Again, Wright's response was relatively noncommittal. *May 6, 1951:* "Will try. Shall see you in Detroit at Laurence Institute."

Finally, 10 months after the initial request was made, the clients received the notification they were seeking—from Eugene Masselink, Wright's personal secretary. *June 19, 1951:* "Jack Howe plans to be in Ann Arbor toward the end of next week—if that is convenient for you." *June 22, 1951:* "Do come—tell Jack—would express our emphatic sentiments, and would be in your manner of letter writing . . . we are looking forward to having him here."

The clients expressed their appreciation on *August 14, 1951:* "Again let us say many thinks for sending Jack to us. He was so very helpful in getting us started, and we want you to know that any time you can send him our way again we would appreciate having him." Six weeks later, however, another rather urgent telegram was sent. *October 3, 1951:* "We have six brick masons on our job and things are moving at a fast clip. Can't you please send someone to help us avoid mistakes?" Wright's unhurried response to this plea was ambiguous, to say the least. *October 16, 1951:* "Dear William Palmers: We'll send someone along in the 'nick of time' before we go west. Faithfully, Frank Lloyd Wright."

Despite the frustrations the clients must have experienced during this protracted interchange, their respect for Wright never wavered. This same sentiment was expressed by each of the 37 first families interviewed by the author. All also felt he respected their needs and family lifestyles, was receptive to their participation in the design process, and maintained an express interest in the design and construction of their residence. This, even though he never personally visited the site. Wright only visited 3 of these properties prior to construction, and but 10 after construction began or was completed—a circumstance that did not seem to cause him or them undue concern. Mildred Rosenbaum (Mrs. Stanley) lightheartedly paraphrased Wright's rationale for not responding to repeated invitations to visit their well-known 1939 Usonian in Florence, Alabama: "I don't need to come. I see your house in my mind's eye and know exactly what it looks like."[488] Similar insight into Wright's thinking was provided by Mrs. Herman T. Mossberg (South Bend, Indiana, 1948): "Mr. Wright visited us only once, when he was giving a lecture at Notre Dame and we were still under construction. He never got beyond the living room and, when we invited him to see the rest of the house, he informed us, 'I saw it two years ago when I designed it.' "[489] She added, "He seemed to be pleased with how it was proceeding but said nothing else as he turned back to the door and left." These accounts bear testament to Wright's extraordinary charisma, his legendary stature, and his ability to foster an image of overall control with each commission.

As the demand for Wright's services increased during the waning years of the 1940s and the pace of construction continued to accelerate throughout the 1950s—when Wright's age ranged from 80 to 91 years—his level of oversight control diminished. Moreover, a great deal of his energy went into the completion of the Guggenheim Museum, a new Arizona State Capitol, new public buildings for Baghdad (Iraq), and the Marin County (California) government complex. Therefore, it was inevitable that a certain level of standardization began to evolve in the architecture of the Usonian residences that bore his name.

Analysis supports that the effect on the "whole design" was almost a replay of what occurred when Griffin left The Studio in 1905—but magnified many times over. Why? One obvious reason is the sheer volume of commissions involved. Another is that the clients were representative of Suburbia USA, so an increasing number of sites involved irregular topography—never one of Wright's strong points. Moreover, the locations represented the entire latitudinal spectrum. Wright learned how to design for the prairies of the Midwest through trial and error while apprenticing under Silsbee and Sullivan, by personally living there, and by working side-by-side with Griffin and Jensen. He learned how to design for the coastal and desert regions of the Southwest through the trial and error of personally living there and by working side-by-side with Lloyd. Now, however, many of the commissions were

originating in locations out of his bailiwick, and he was not sufficiently involved at the personal level to objectively judge the cause and effect of decisions being made via remote control. The reality of the situation is that Wright never did become conversant with either the technical or functional concerns of site development. And the weakest element of design for any structure not built on a level prairie lot was, and always had been, site planning. The scenario evolving during the mid-1900s only made this weakness more apparent—because he couldn't teach what he didn't know, just as he couldn't teach his intuitive acumen.[490] This reasoning again is supported through analysis.

Of the more than 150 topographic surveys and/or site plans analyzed for this research, none provide guidance or specificities as to how to accommodate elements shown on the plan—even for such basic components as driveways, autocourts, or terraces. There are very few reference factors—such as rock outcroppings, loose boulders, specimen trees, or best views—that would affect building location and orientation. Nor have any soils maps been located, or specific references addressing soils suitability or limitations. And although sections or elevation-sections provide insight into existing topography, only two or three plans even suggest proposed contour lines necessary for regrading. Most significantly, there is only one grading plan of record in the Frank Lloyd Wright Archives—prepared, or supervised by, Lloyd Wright for the Olive Hill property in Los Angeles.

Grading plans specify the amount of alteration that needs to be made to the natural landform to accommodate the structure and install the driveway and parking through grading and cut-and-fill. Grading plans also detail the degree of slope necessary to drain surface water away from structures—especially in areas involving doorways and steps. The delineation of contour lines, existing and proposed, is essential to avoid retaining walls whenever possible and control the final appearance of the land form as a whole.

There also is only one site analysis of record—prepared by Howe in 1939 for the Andrew F. H. Armstrong Usonian in Ogden Dunes, Indiana—and it is rather cursory, compared to most site analyses (see Appendix K). The Armstrong site analysis most probably was conducted because of the ecological sensitivity of the site of secondary sand dunes, and because of its location—one block from Lake Michigan and six miles to the east of the border for Indiana Dunes State Park.[491] The work map contains a perspective rendered in Wright's own hand and a rough sketch plan of the house—which apparently was designed to at least this stage prior to Howe's visit to the site (Figure 8-28). The notations on the map are far from complete and very generalized, but they would have been of at least some value to Wright and Howe when paired with photographs apparently taken during the survey process. There is a north point, but E(ast) and W(est) are reversed and incorrectly labeled. To the north of the building site, a curving road (today known as Cedar Trail) has been sketched in, together with the notations "goes down fast" and "steep sand cut." There are letters and notes scattered about, apparently keyed to photographs—such as "telephone pole at right in pic B and F;" "approx. region of large tree

in foreground of E;" and "dead pine in N somewhere near here." Neighborhood associations are noted, including the location of telephone poles, a mailbox, and two houses—one to the southwest "up steep hill . . . drive made of R.R. ties," the other to the north "up steep hill." A number of dimensions have been penciled in. And there are some arrows identifying viewpoints, as well as notes such as "best view of lake about ¼ mile away" and "view across rolling series of dunes."

The significance here is that this nondescript mapping seems to be the extent of site planning for the Armstrong commission. There is no site plan with the construction drawings. There is no topographic survey of record. And the set of original plans preserved by the

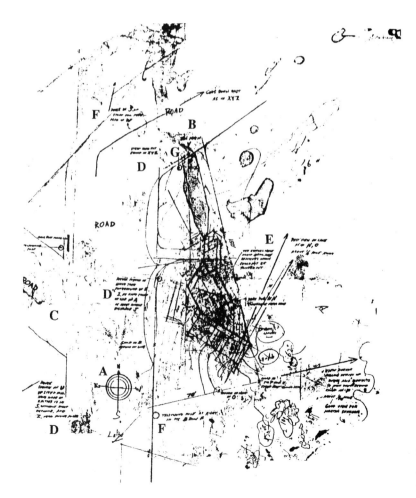

Figure 8-28   Site analysis of Andrew Armstrong site (1939) at Ogden Dunes, Indiana. (© *2002 by The Frank Lloyd Wright Foundation, Scottsdale, Arizona.*)

present owners only has a small location diagram in one corner to indicate how the house should be sited on the property.

The sometimes subtle, sometimes marked difficulties precipitated by site planning inadequacies such as these can perhaps best be understood by summarizing causes and effects associated with "Accommodating the Automobile," the "30/60° Triangle Syndrome," the "Solar Hemicycle," and "Articulation of the Landscape."

Accommodating the Automobile

The majority of Usonians were located in suburban areas that were relatively rural at the time of their construction. Therefore, the automobile could not be overlooked as an integral element of the extended environment of the house. The siting, circulation, entry experience, and even the overall layout of the architecture were significantly influenced by considerations for approaching the property by automobile, interactivity between the automobile and residence, and accommodation of the automobile itself. In essence, the automobile became a mobile object of environmental sculpture to be routed in the most direct path from the public right-of-way to the autocourt or parking area nearest the house entrance, and to the requisite carport—contained under the protracted roofline of the house.

The driveway entrance became the point of prefatory affirmation for many Usonians, by way of what has come to be known as a "Wrightian" identifying feature—a lamp, mailbox, gate, or other art form—such as Wright first designed with Jensen for the Booth Project. The driveway itself became part of the entry experience, since most Usonians were sited well back on the property—both to assure privacy and to provide an approach that had the appearance of being expansive. Inasmuch as driveways were laid out on a topographic map without benefit of actual site analysis, however, they took on a variety of forms—straight-line, curved, conventional loop, cul-de-sac, and angular grid—with preference given to the grid of the architecture, for the most part, rather than the lay of the land. Autocourts also tended to assume the conformation of the architectural grid, as can be discerned when viewed from the perspective of the ground plans (Figure 8-29). Some even exceeded in area the square footage allocated for use by the occupants. Since angular grids do not address the reality of turning radii and wheel movements, some of these driveway-autocourt conformations caused problems with maneu-

verability from the onset, as demonstrated with the Pew carport (Figure 8-30 a-b).

The Usonian entry experience was compromised by the fact that most—in the interest of economy—were designed with only one point of entry, accessed directly from the autocourt (50 percent) or the carport (30 percent). In many cases, only a few feet at best separate car door from front door; and everyone—family and visitor alike—must first squeeze past parked vehicles to access the residence. At the opposite extreme were the Usonians designed with unduly long walkways leading from the carport to the door, where the distance ranged from 72 feet for the Duey Wright House (Wausau, Wisconsin, 1956) to 130 feet for the John O. Carr House (Glenview, Illinois, 1950). The Herman T. Mossberg residence (South Bend, Indiana, 1946) is unusual in that it has a front entrance off the public street and a separate service entrance off the carport, screened from public view by a high brick wall extension. Few other Usonians have a service entrance.

The straight-line driveway frequently sited along one edge of Usonian properties was in all probability a carryover from the era of the prairie house—when garages converted from stables were accessed either directly from an alley or, where alleys were absent, straight down one side of the property. Or this treatment could have been seen as a means to retain a large portion of the property as one expansive unit of naturally picturesque open space. John and Ruth Pew suggested cost was a factor: "Although our plans show the driveway with curves, or a wiggle, it always has been straight along the west property line. Maybe this was done to keep it shorter and save money, even though it is steeper that way." According to subsequent owner Cindy Edwards, the steepness of the Pew driveway makes it difficult to negotiate when there is an accumulation or buildup of snow, ice, or sleet—a not-infrequent occurrence in Wisconsin. The Roland Reisleys (Pleasantville, New York, 1950) eventually installed electric coils under the surface of their similarly steep driveway, to negate the hazard created by accumulations of snow or ice.[492] Other original clients told the author they felt a need to change and regrade the straight-line driveway shown on their plans. Russell Kraus (Kirkwood, Missouri, 1951), an artist whose modular Usonian was sited by apprentice Ling Po, described his experience as follows: "Mr. Wright's original driveway from paved county road to the house (about 800–1000 feet) was a straight line with a steady even up-hill grade. It was PRACTICAL, both in maintenance and access. But we decided upon a more 'romantic' curving driveway through the woods that separate the house from the county road. The more romantic driveway, as we have found, is difficult to maintain and difficult to maneuver the up-grade curves in slippery winter weather. But it IS a beautiful drive through the woods at any time of the year. Taliesin apprentices who have visited all comment on the drive through the beautiful woods."[493] (It should be noted here that a curving approach would make a steep slope easier to negotiate than the straight approach, "if" the natural contours are taken into account.)

Gravel was the surface material most generally specified for Usonian driveways and autocourts, although Wright sometimes introduced other pervious

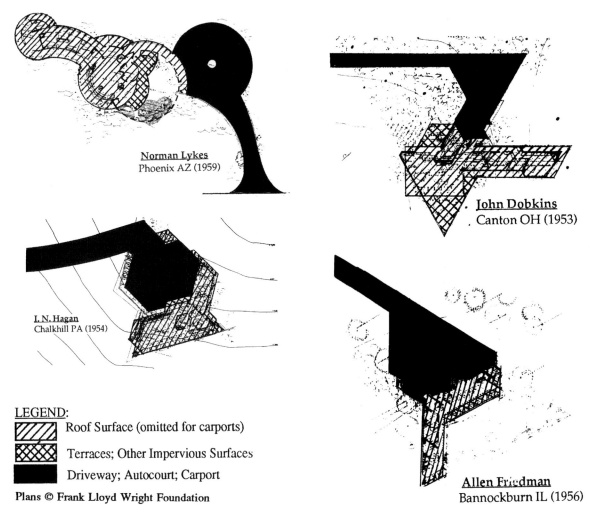

Norman Lykes
Phoenix AZ (1959)

John Dobkins
Canton OH (1953)

I. N. Hagan
Chalkhill PA (1954)

Allen Friedman
Bannockburn IL (1956)

LEGEND:

▨▨▨ Roof Surface (omitted for carports)

▨▨▨ Terraces; Other Impervious Surfaces

███ Driveway; Autocourt; Carport

Plans © Frank Lloyd Wright Foundation

Figure 8-29 Accommodating the automobile, as observed from the perspective of Usonian ground plans. (*By Charles E. Aguar, based on personal analysis and plans of record.* © 2002 by The Frank Lloyd Wright Foundation, Scottsdale, Arizona. *As delineated,* © 2000 by Berdeana Aguar.)

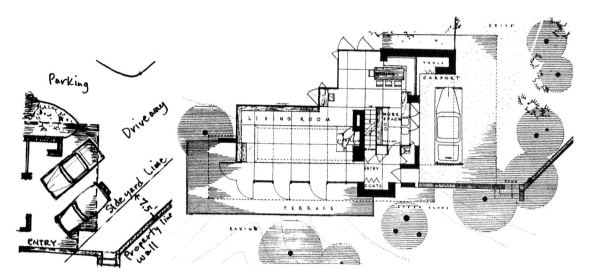

Figure 8-30 a–b   Theoretical, but physically impossible placement of automobile in Pew House carport. (*By Charles E. Aguar, based on personal analysis and plans of record. © 2002 by The Frank Lloyd Wright Foundation, Scottsdale, Arizona. As delineated, © 2002 by Berdeana Aguar.*)

surface material—such as crushed red rock or crushed red brick—to better harmonize with entry steps, terrace surfaces, and interior floors. In some cases, he even went so far as to select, redesign, and color-coordinate a certain style of low-slung roadster in Cherokee red, because he felt it made a "statement" when parked adjacent to his genus of architecture. Problems began to occur, however, as Usonian autocourts were paved with concrete, asphalt, or bricks. The introduction of any form of impervious substance negatively impacts the site environment by warming the microclimate through heat and glare. When paved areas are as expansive as Usonian driveways and autocourts tend to be, this condition is exacerbated.

Another situation aggravated by the introduction of impervious surfacing had to do with the expanse and design of the Usonian roofs—this, in addition to the legendary leakage problem that has been dotingly incorporated into Wrightian lore. Because the Usonian roofs are much larger in area than normal—to shelter the terrace and windows and emphasize the horizontality and aesthetic proportions of the architecture—and because Wright determined that gutters and downspouts compromised the architectural lines of his design, a copious amount of rainwater runoff is generated. As long as the autocourts were covered with gravel or other pervious

surfacing material, the runoff was absorbed with relative expediency. After the carports and forecourts were paved, however, owners oftentimes found the quantity and velocity of runoff unmanageable. Several first families told the author they were unable to use the front door during a rainstorm because of standing water. Some described heightened problems with erosion. Others spoke of wet basements and furnace rooms, cracked retaining walls and terrace surfaces. The solution in many cases required the creation of earthen swales or the installation of sump pumps and infrastructure such as French drains and catch basins.

All these problems support Wright's rationale for initially specifying pervious surfacing for the Usonian driveways and autocourts. But they also bring to light another fundamental problem that was only magnified by the rainwater runoff—that is, the inappropriate siting and grading for sites of varying topography. These circumstances assumed even more relevance when Wright's penchant for the 30/60° triangle is factored into the Usonian design formula.

The 30/60° Triangle Syndrome

In *The Natural House*, Wright wrote: "Proper orientation of the house . . . is the first condition of the lighting of that house. . . . Day lighting can be beautifully managed by the architect if he has a feeling for the course of the sun as it goes from east to west and at the inevitable angle to the south."[494] He then went on to identify the 30° adjustment as his orientation of preference. During this same 1950s time frame, an apprentice told the author: "The 30/60° triangle is Mr. Wright's favorite drawing instrument. He can design anything with a T-square, a 30/60° triangle, and a handful of colored pencils."[495] The reality of these observations became very relevant to this writing, because a generalization such as this can cause irreparable problems if that is the primary basis for siting and orientation.

More than half (59 percent) of the Usonians evaluated were sited with the entire structure or the bedroom wing, at least, angled exactly 30° from a north-south or east-west orientation. Of these, only two were positioned parallel to the contours. This translates into a preponderance of Usonians sited in direct contrariety to the natural lay of the land, in essence "defying" the very nature of the site. Although this divergent 30-degree siting introduced a third dimension that sometimes provided an expedient and logical means to extend and integrate the grid system of the architecture into the out-of-doors and unify indoor-outdoor space, it also significantly increased the extent to which the natural landform had to be manipulated. It is customary and advisable to prepare site-specific grading plans to address these issues, because once a structure has been disadvantageously sited and floor levels set, there is no economically feasible way to address the problems thoughtless siting precipitates. It is precisely because

these issues were not addressed at the drawing board that so many Usonian properties evidence an excessive reliance on retaining walls and other costly fabricated forms of site engineering and topographic manipulation.

One design feature Wright conceived to create a relatively uniform methodology for addressing the issue of irregular topography was the masonry-retaining base (Figure 8-31). His technique was to "level out" the first-floor elevation by projecting the structure out from the slope, supported by 10-to-30-foot-high retaining walls of concrete block, brick, or stone, then backfilled with many truckloads of rock or earth[496] (see Appendix L). The triangular living room terraces supported by Wright's masonry retaining bases often are described as having a "prow," like a ship. The intent was that these terraces serve as the line between architecture and nature, similar to the hemicircular garden feature. The parapet wall was to privatize and contain the terrace as an outdoor room, open to the sky. For this reason, very few provide direct access to the rear yard.

The projecting masonry-retained terrace today is looked upon as a "signature" design feature of Usonians built on sites with steeply sloping topography—regardless of building material, from moderate to upper scale. However, this technique frequently was employed merely to dramatize sites of moderate topography, as well. Of 31 Usonians sited on moderate slopes, 30 used this design methodology. All were beautiful residences, but beauty that came with a price tag—both economically and ecologically. The fact that many of these have been referenced as being "in harmony" with the site

Figure 8-31 Photograph of masonry retaining base Wright conceived to address problems of irregular topography. (*Photograph by Charles E. Aguar. © 2002 by Berdeana Aguar.*)

environment underscores the reality that "illusion" is an important factor of perception.

The most effective and logical introduction of the masonry-retaining base occurred when this technique was used to accentuate very rugged hillside topography and Wright was personally involved throughout the design process. Two Usonians that truly appear to "grow" out of the natural environment due to these factors were designed for Mrs. Clinton Walker and the Roland Reisleys.

Mrs. Clinton Walker—Carmel, California (1948–1952)

Few of Wright's site-specific designs have better captured his goal of achieving an organic "oneness" with the nature of the site than the efficient Usonian he conceived for Della Walker (Figure 8-32). His challenge was to design for her an affordable "vacation cottage" on a relatively constrained rocky promontory overlooking Monterey Bay—one of the most magnificent environments anywhere. The promontory offered panoramic views of the ocean, from horizon to horizon. At its base were massive rock formations carved out by the pounding surf, seaside vegetation, birds, sea otters, sea lions, and a vast expanse of beach at low tide. Wright was personally and emotionally involved with this house through the entire design-construction process, which spanned a period of several years because of the Korean War.

For this site above all others, the introduction of the masonry-retaining base shaped like the "prow of a ship" was most appropriate—particularly as the Carmel Stone terrace extends over the natural rock formations to the ocean level at high tide. Viewed from any angle, the terrace appears to grow out of the rock promontory, and the cantilevered turquoise metal roof appears to float over the spacious, hexagonal-shaped living space that extends towards the ocean—girded by an incredible 240-degree expanse of windows, facing every direction but southeast. Thus, from sunrise to sunset—whether inside the house or on the terrace sunbathing or relaxing—the aura of the ocean, the crashing surf, and saltwater spray are omnipresent. Each room benefitted from the constancy of the ocean breezes, as well, due to Wright's unique, key-shaped arrangement and orientation of the rooms, windows, and French doors (Figure 8-33). He also gave considerable thought to privatizing the public side of the property and to the proximity of the ocean to the primary living space. For these reasons, Wright placed no windows on the south-southwest walls of the most publicly compromised portion of the site. With equal consideration, he designed underside venting into the three-tiered, corbelled bands of glass in the primary living space to deflect the saltwater spray and lessen the impact of gusty winds.

The saltwater spray also dictated what would, or would not, survive in the way of plantings. Inasmuch as no definitive planting plan was provided, Walker con-

Figure 8-32 Masonry retaining base of terrace for Della Walker House (1948–1952) in Carmel, California. (*Photograph by Charles E. Aguar. © 2002 by Berdeana Aguar.*)

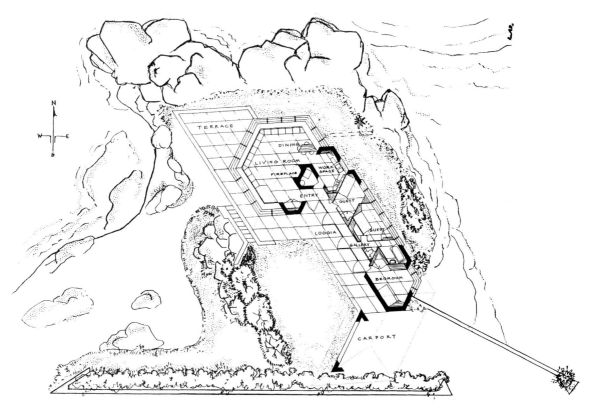

Figure 8-33 Conjectured site plan suggests character of Walker House prior to subsequent expansions. (*Site details by Charles E. Aguar, based on personal analysis and plans of record. © 2002 by The Frank Lloyd Wright Foundation, Scottsdale, Arizona. As delineated, © 2002 by Berdeana Aguar.*)

sulted with landscape architect Thomas Church. When Wright got word of this, it elicited an unusually emotional reaction: "Distressing news from several quarters. One of my former apprentices . . . says to Aaron Green 'someone has ruined Mr. Wright's house with landscaping.' Walter Olds, distressed, said 'Mrs. Walker hired a professional landscaper to undo all Mr. Wright had done for her.' If you did employ one it is the first time it has happened to me in a long lifetime of building. The first destructive insult. I don't believe it. . . . The professional Wurster side-kick is quoted as saying, 'I know Wright won't like what I've done,'—showing that assasination [sic] was his intent. . . . I hope what I hear is not true and love's labor not lost. I love the Cabin and had it in my heart as well as my head."[497]

Of course, Wright's allegation that no other client had consulted with a landscape architect was totally incorrect. Not only had Griffin, Jensen, and Lloyd Wright been consulted many times, Church himself had prepared planting plans for A. C. Mathews (Atherton, California, 1950) and was preparing revisions for Auldbrass Plantation at about the same time these letters were written, in 1952. In any event, Walker's chiding response must have set Wright at ease:

What a scolding!! And I don't deserve it. Some one is trying to make trouble. Nothing has been done to harm *our* house. . . . I asked Tommy Church, whom I have known since he was a child, to help me. . . . I planted myself about 2000 succulants or ice plants and brought rocks from the beach . . . to put in places where you said it should go. I went into the woods and got small pine trees which all died. It is going to be difficult to find anything that will stand the wind and salt spray. Planting young shrubs seems to be the answer but I can not wait for them to grow (wish I could). I did not want grass to care for and Tommy suggested . . . gravel like the terrace and I have put that in and like it. But if you do not, out it comes. No real change has been made and there is *no* reason for anyone's quoting Tommy as saying that you would not like it. His one idea has been to follow the little sketches in planting that you made.

The client's reference to conditions inherent to the oceanside environment is extremely relevant—not only to the selection of plantings, but to the architectural intrusion in and of itself. As at Fallingwater, the cost of maintenance at this sensitive site is ongoing. From the beach, it is obvious that many attempts have been made over the years to battle the dominance of the unyielding systems of nature. A stone wall has been added to contain the eroding bank, and many yards of concrete have been pumped onto the rock underpinnings (Figure 8-34). Yet, the house foundation evidences extensive erosion; a drain pipe once hidden in the rocks projects 5 feet into space; and large concrete chunks are being converted into sand by surf action. *All* attest to the expense and futility of attempting to battle "Mother Nature."

Roland Reisley—Pleasantville, New York (1950)

The Roland Reisley Usonian was the third and last residence Wright designed for his "Usonia II" community (Figure 8-35). Again, he was personally involved throughout the entire process—to the extent that he designed the fireplace grate on the kitchen counter during his final visit to the construction site. This was in June 1952, shortly after the Reisleys moved into their as-yet unfinished house. It was at this time also that he exhibited his uncanny ability to visually and mentally assess and evaluate existing conditions in any given situation. During a 1992 interview, the Reisleys told the author that Wright pulled into the driveway, exited his car, pointed his cane toward the chimney, and immediately ordered the height increased by two feet—to be proportionate with the peak of the roof and optimize the functionality of the fireplaces. The Reisleys believe they received "a lot of special attention and helpful advice from Mr. Wright." They said he visited the site three or four times during construction and also assigned senior apprentice Allen L. "Davey" Davison to supervise the construction.

It was Davison's responsibility to make sure that the house was carefully staked out to fit among the boulders

Figure 8-34 Oceanside view of Walker House shows extensive erosion of rocks that serve as its foundation. (*Photograph by Charles E. Aguar. © 2002 by Berdeana Aguar.*)

Figure 8-35 View toward original living room terrace for Roland Reisley House (1950) in Pleasantville, New York. (*Photograph by Charles E. Aguar. © 2002 by Berdeana Aguar.*)

and follow the natural contours of the rugged topography. The original house was in fact rotated counterclockwise by 13 degrees to avoid excessive blasting of the massive outcropping that has become so explicitly identified with this structure. This would be a logical and normal adjustment, and certainly within the scope of Wright's original design intent. And since the banks of French doors line the southeast, south, and southwest sides of the equilateral triangle grid of the primary living space, the rotation did not in any way compromise orientation for solar benefit (Figure 8-36). The soaring cantilevered roof that makes such a strong architectural statement works with these walls of glass to provide shade from the summer sun and to access maximum solar gain during the winter, after the leaves of the deciduous trees have fallen. The interior stone walls act as solar collectors and radiate warmth throughout the living area. And cross-ventilation is excellent.

The indoor-outdoor relationships at the Reisley House are extensive, particularly off the living area where the French doors open onto the terrace and the parapet of native stone rests on the massive stone boulder so carefully preserved during construction. The prow of the terrace parapet directs the eye into the nature of the seemingly undisturbed woodland where shagbark hickory, gray birch, dogwood, sumac, mountain laurel, bayberry, and bluestem grass reign supreme. There also is a dining terrace tucked behind the kitchen

that is protected by the deep overhang of the cantilevered roof.

A partially earth-sheltered bedroom-playroom-storage wing added in 1956 essentially doubled the original square footage of the Reisley House. The solid stone wall wrapping along the north wall of the addition extends the wing to the southeast of the living area, so all the above-ground-level windows face south. It is important to note, however, that more bulldozing occurred at this time than when the original house was built—a consequence of the 13-degree rotation never having been recorded in the Fellowship files. This oversight necessitated the introduction of more expansive retaining walls than anticipated, as well.

The Reisleys hired landscape architect A. E. Bye to help them address the radical site changes: "The angled stone steps to the upper lawn, the rock garden, ground covers, and native shrub plantings were all part of Ed Bye's design [Figure 8-37]. His planting plan called for species that are about 90-percent native. The hemlocks, mountain laurel, leucothae, dogwoods, and various junipers fit right into nature's scheme of things. And the beds of groundcovers extend the grid of the house plan into the outdoors." However, the Reisleys themselves must be given credit for their sensitivity in maintaining the integrity of this landscape. It is only because they never have allowed the plants to be trimmed or sheared with precise straight edges that the native landscape

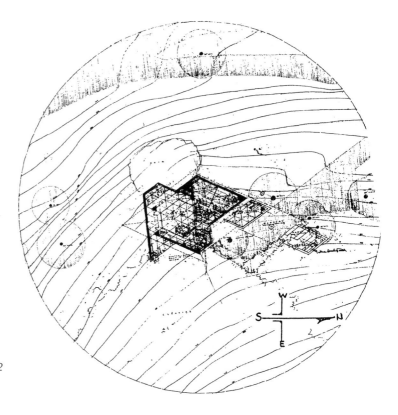

Figure 8-36 Layout for Reisley
House, as sketched on topographic
map, confirms orientation. (© 2002
*by The Frank Lloyd Wright
Foundation, Scottsdale, Arizona.*)

imagery prevails (Figure 8-38). In the end, it is this sensitivity that makes it almost impossible to determine where the architecture leaves off and nature begins, or vice-versa—the most important criteria for this best-of-the-best Wrightscape.

Despite the inadequacies of the site planning, there can be no doubt that Wright and his apprentices were able to successfully combine sensory experiences so that a substantial number of his Usonian residences evoke a consummate spirit-of-place, both inside and outside. Without exception, those original clients interviewed exhibited strong emotional ties to the environments in which they live, or had lived. This is a testament to the spatial methodization inherent to the Usonian "system," which was flexible enough to permit a great deal of variety in arrangement to reflect the personality of the owners. It also is a testament to the technological innovations and imaginative touches that were as humanly satisfying as they were economical. But the very essence of the

Usonian architecture is the interrelationship between the architecture and the natural environment—not only to vistas, intrinsic land forms, nearby water bodies, and existing site vegetation, but to local atmospheric conditions, and the angle of the sun and prevailing winds in particular.[498]

Of these natural environmental influences, orientation to the sun is the most seminal and precise. The orbital angle of the sun can be ascertained from published tables for any time of day at any time of year, based upon the latitude of the site. Wright was a master extraordinaire at utilizing this natural asset. Orientation to seasonal and prevailing winds or breezes is less precise, because air movement is influenced by such variables as the rotation of the earth, proximity to the sea, and the intermittent heating affects of the sun's radiation on the air itself. Air movement also can be impacted by variations in site-specific microclimates caused by dissimilar exposure to sun and wind, which may be as imperceptible as differences in the species of trees on the site and the resulting overhead cover—dense or

Figure 8-37 Hillside garden for Reisley House, with steps designed by landscape architect A. E. Bye. (*Photograph by Charles E. Aguar. © 2002 by Berdeana Aguar.*)

sparse, evergreen or deciduous, young or mature, sick or healthy. Prevailing or seasonal wind directions therefore vacillate from month-to-month and year-to-year, and can best be platted when based upon detailed records maintained by local airports or scientific stations—a resource that would have been available to Wright and the apprentices during the postwar years when most Usonians were designed.

The saga of the use and abuse of Wright's inspired design for a solar hemicycle best demonstrates the problems that occurred when homeowners and others involved with the construction process did not under-

Figure 8-38 Reisley House as seen from Usonia Road. The structure seems part of the natural rock and woods environment. (*Photograph by Charles E. Aguar. © 2002 by Berdeana Aguar.*)

stand the significance that siting and orientation had to do with his Usonian architecture.

The Solar Hemicycle

The prototype for the solar hemicycle was the second house Wright designed for Herbert and Katherine Jacobs in 1944 for a site in Middleton, Wisconsin (a suburb of Madison). During two interviews, two years apart—in March 1990 and August 1992—Jacobs graphically characterized Wright's preliminary visit to their site and his uncanny ability to assess intuitively and with fair accuracy where and how best to site the structure he would design to be built there:

> We had sold off all but three or four acres of our fifty-two acre farm outside Madison but were not yet sure where we would build. We had envisioned it would be on the highest point of our land—to the

north, where we had a distant view of Lake Mendota. But we were waiting for a decision from Mr. Wright. When he and Mrs. Wright arrived, it was a dramatic and romantic occasion as they walked, or marched, through a field of white clover with our family. Mr. Wright quickly dismissed our site of preference as being too close to a county highway. He explained, "You can't depend on the highway department except to widen and straighten roads and bring in more people and, besides, no one should build on top of their best view. You'll appreciate it more if you build near it, and walk to it whenever you want."

Mr. Wright always carried a cane—not that he needed it, except for the purpose of pointing and gesturing. He soon came to a spot where he waved his cane to and fro and said, "This is the place where the various prospects converge." We took this to

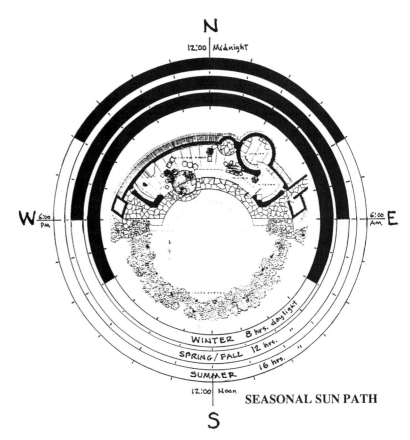

Figure 8-39 Declination chart for the second Wright house built for Herbert and Katherine Jacobs of Middleton, Wisconsin—the first "Solar Hemicycle" Usonian dwelling—shows four-season sun path and sunrise-sunset locations. *(By Charles E. Aguar, based on personal analysis and plans of record. © 2002 by The Frank Lloyd Wright Foundation, Scottsdale, Arizona. As delineated, © 2002 by Berdeana Aguar.)*

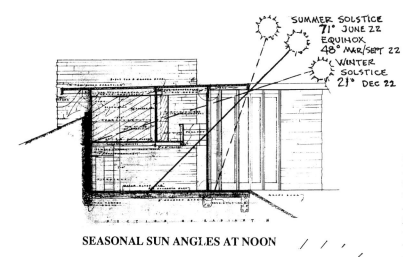

SEASONAL SUN ANGLES AT NOON

Figure 8-40 Section of the Jacobs II House showing overhang controls for summer solstice, spring/fall equinox, and winter solstice. (*By Charles E. Aguar, based on personal analysis and plans of record.* © 2002 by The Frank Lloyd Wright Foundation, Scottsdale, Arizona. As delineated, © 2002 by Berdeana Aguar.)

mean that we had an almost limitless vista: green farmland to the south, a nice view into the edge of the oak woods to the west, and a curve in the road to cut off the outlook to the east. It was as though our house, which we didn't yet know was to be the first solar hemicycle, would open up with a sweeping view of the whole out-of-doors. Our daughter Susan, then about five, was intrigued with Mr. Wright's cane-waving and whispered to me, "You know, Mother, it's like he's conducting music!"[499]

While it may have appeared to the Jacobs that Wright was walking randomly across the site, it must be presumed that he was "reading" the land by conducting a visual survey of the site anatomy—the hydrology, geology, topography, and natural vegetation—inherent to the site. He also was taking note of intrinsic land forms and mentally appraising local atmospheric conditions that would affect the siting and orientation of the future structure. In all these respects, Wright was functioning as a landscape architect—as he personally was qualified to do, every bit as much as he qualified to function as an architect.

Jacobs tried to convey the sense of anticipation Wright put forth in his letter inviting them to come see the plan he ultimately designed to build on their site. She said: "Mr. Wright wrote that he was about ready to make us 'the goat' again for what he called 'a fresh enterprise in architecture.' He warned us that if we didn't accept what he had designed, someone else would. He

called it a 'real first' that we would like a lot. He even penciled in a note that we should 'watch out' because 'it's *good!*'" Jacobs went on to say that the plan he exhibited when they arrived at Taliesin the following Sunday was incomprehensible to them until he patiently explained the functionality of this first "solar hemicycle" (Figure 8-39).

The semicircular residence Wright conceived for Jacobs II—as it has come to be known—oriented all the primary living spaces toward the south, used stone as the primary building material (inside and outside), and buried the northernmost facade in an earthen berm. His intent was that this Usonian would function as the sod houses did for the original settlers in the vast prairies of Midwest America—that is, the bermed construction would maintain the coolness of the earth during summer and retain heat during winter. The sunken garden nestled within and framed by the south-facing concave façade was designed to trap the winter sun by forming a ball of dead air, a technique Wright described as "streamlining in place."[500] Jacobs said Wright told her husband the air would be so still in the sunken garden he could light his pipe there in a strong wind. Wright also specifically proportioned the depth of the overhanging eave to admit maximum sun penetration during the winter solstice, so the heat-retentive stone walls would radiate warmth throughout the residence—even for the bedrooms on the mezzanine (Figure 8-40). During the spring and fall equinoxes, on the other hand, sun penetration reaches midway into the living area. And during the summer solstice, the overhang

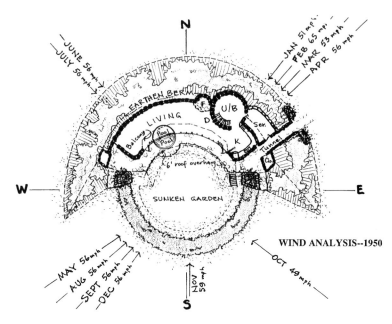

Figure 8-41 A wind analysis for 1950 for the Jacobs II House shows no "prevailing" wind pattern; it fluctuated wildly from month to month. (*By Charles E. Aguar, based on Weather Bureau data. © 2002 by Berdeana Aguar.*)

precisely blocks summer sun penetration while the glass doors access cooling prevailing breezes, which permeate throughout the house.

The natural airfoil created by Wright's layout functioned basically as he intended. The only flaw to the arrangement was the northeast-southwest orientation of the tunnel entrance through the berm. According to records maintained by the Weather Bureau, U.S. Department of Commerce, winds during the median year of 1950 vacillated widely in this section of Wisconsin—originating from due south in November, from the southwest in December, and from the northeast during January, February, and March (Figure 8-41). Inasmuch as winter wind velocities have been recorded as high as 65 miles per hour, the tunnel entrance has the potential to convert into a virtual wind tunnel.[501] Nonetheless, the solar hemicycle truly was an exceptional common sense design approach to the climatic stresses of Wisconsin, where temperature extremes are widely varying, from as low as −37° Fahrenheit in the winter to as high as +107° in the summer.

Following the design and construction of the Jacobs II solar hemicycle prototype, Wright and/or his apprentices drew plans for more than a dozen variations of single-story or two-story hemicycle or hemicircular residences. Ten of these homes were erected during the early-to-mid 1950s at varying latitudes across the United States: Andrew Cooke (Virginia Beach, Virginia); Kenneth Laurent (Rockford, Illinois); George Lewis (Tallahassee, Florida); Louis Marden (McLean, Virginia); Curtis Meyer (Galesburg, Michigan); Wilbur C. Pearce (Bradbury, California); John L. Rayward (New Canaan, Connecticut); Dudley Spencer (Wilmington, Delaware); Robert Winn (Kalamazoo, Michigan); and R. Lewellyn Wright (Bethesda, Maryland) (Figure 8-42).

It is important to note, however, that although all of these homes are generally identified as solar hemicycles, only four were oriented so that the glass façade faces south and can be correctly identified as such—for Cooke, Pearce, Spencer, and Wright. The others were incorrectly oriented for solar benefit and would be more appropriately identified as hemicircular, whether of concave or lozenge conformation. This brings into question whether the apprentices sent out to site these semicircular houses were thoroughly briefed on the importance of the due-south orientation. There can be a variance of up to 20 degrees east of south to obtain maximum solar benefit from the predictable arc of the sun, but no more than that. With the Lewis House in Florida, the orientation of the expanse of glass toward the northeast is inconse-

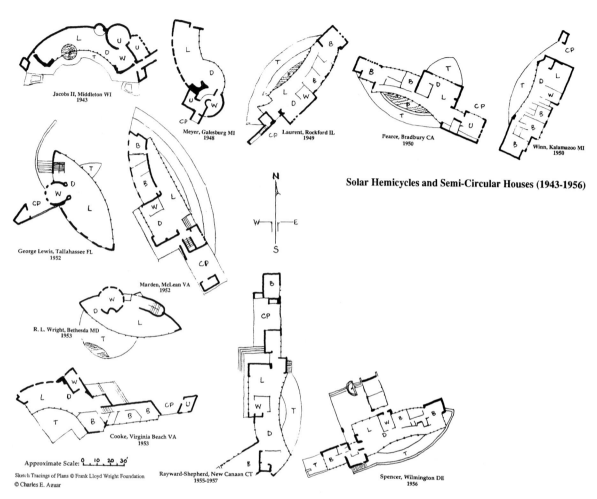

Figure 8-42 Variations in siting of true solar hemicycles, showing improperly oriented semicircular structures. (*By Charles E. Aguar, based on personal analysis and plans of record. © 2002 by The Frank Lloyd Wright Foundation, Scottsdale, Arizona. As delineated, © 2002 by Berdeana Aguar.*)

quential, since protection from the sun and access to prevailing breezes is preferential for any structure constructed below 35° latitude. But the two hemicycles built in Michigan and northern Illinois—locations where temperatures have been known to drop below 20° Fahrenheit—were oriented to face northwest, so the primary living spaces are fully exposed to the direct impact of winter winds and access absolutely no solar benefit.

Sometimes, of course, the client motivated the reorientation. Correspondence of record confirms that Lillian and Curtis Meyer requested that their house be

rotated to minimize the possibility of snow drifting into the carport, even though the consequence of this change—a rotation of some 90 degrees—was that the two-story glass façade faced northeast.[502] During a 1992 interview by telephone with Mrs. Luis Marden, it was learned that their two-story façade was faced northwest to provide a better view of the Potomac River and the Washington, D.C., monuments. She said they personally moved the layout stakes, and "the Frank Lloyd Wright organization had nothing to do with the actual siting of the house or any landscape that now exists."

The Articulation of the Landscape

The Fellowship contract placed plantings within the realm of Wright's architecture: "personal architectural services are available for ten percent of the cost of the completed building, which invariably includes the planting of the grounds." With the earliest Usonians of the late 1930s and mid-to-late 1940s, however, the planting of the grounds most often evolved over a period of time, long after Wright was out of the picture. John Pew, a professional forester-researcher, expressed the thinking of most owners of the early Usonians: "Mr. Wright never drew what you could call a landscape or planting plan. We wouldn't have had the funds to purchase plants needed to carry out a plan anyway." Ruth Pew added: "Mr. Wright liked wild grape and bittersweet and we grew these vines around the house for many years. Bittersweet makes colorful arrangements, which we dried and brought into the house also."

Based upon this insight, it must be assumed that the pattern for never really developing the Usonian landscape in a definitive sense evolved as a cost-effective measure. It is precisely because there was no direction other than suggestive delineations drafted directly onto plot plans, however, that so many of the early Usonian residences and autocourts are not shaded by trees such as would be recommended under normal circumstances. Even as construction budgets increased and the sophistication of the architecture reflected the increased prosperity of the times, however, the level of landscape design made available to clients remained relatively static. This reasoning is supported by notes written on the plot plan for Eric Brown (Kalamazoo, Michigan, 1950): "maple, oak, or birch," "sumach [sic] and dogwood," "pine," "horizontal juniper," "wildflowers and tall grass," and "mixed shrubs in groups of two or three—spirea, forsythia, etc."[503] John Howe's 1951 letter responding to Curtis Meyer is equally nonspecific: "use native flowering shrubs, such as are already on the property. The circle should contain cedars and junipers of varying heights grouped in groups of three or four, with dogwood in between."[504] Such generalities create problems for clients who then must choose from literally thousands of possible species, varieties, and hybrids—many of which might not be hardy in the plant zone where they were to be planted.

By the late 1950s, many Usonian homeowners sought and received landscape advice from nurseries and purchased specimen and exotic plants—such as Japanese Maple, Oriental Cherry, and Chinese Juniper—to develop their uncommon properties in a manner common to the more nondescript houses within the subdivision in which they were located. When these Usonians were sited on flat suburban lots devoid of vegetation and the intended native landscape materials were replaced with exotics, the distinctive lines of Wright's architecture often were seriously compromised. The notable exceptions were those where landscape architects were hired to develop customized planting plans—as for Della Walker and the Roland Reisleys—or where knowledgeable clients had a predilection for the landscape and directed or supervised professionals, or developed their own landscapes. This observation is supported by the construction and landscape articulation undertaken by Sara and Melvyn Maxwell Smith; the planting plan of record drafted by John Howe for Gertrude and Herman T. Mossberg; the siting and landscape development undertaken by Mary and William Palmer; the professional landscape designs prepared for subsequent owners of the John L. Rayward hemicycle and the Andrew Cook solar hemicycle; and by the individualistic landscape developed over time by Elizabeth and William B. Tracy.

Melvyn Maxwell Smith—Bloomfield Hills, Michigan (1946–1949)

When newlywed schoolteachers Sara and Melvyn Smith made their initial trip to Taliesin in 1941, their enthusiasm far exceeded their means—as was true of so many early followers of Wright's Usonian ideals. They met briefly with Wright at that time and told him they had no construction budget but were determined they one day would live in a house designed by Frank Lloyd Wright. Nonplussed, Wright told them to find a site and send him a topographic survey. He recommended that they locate property nobody else wanted, preferably with "some drop to it." Although their plans were put on hold after Smith was called for military service following Pearl Harbor, they continued to dream and kept themselves abreast of Wright's work.

Soon after the war was over, the Smiths found what they felt was an "ideal" site—far from the congestion of Detroit, but near the famed Cranbrook Educational Community (later identified as "upper scale" on real estate maps). The property was tangled with vines and native vegetation and had served as a dumping ground for old railroad crossties, but it most certainly qualified as a site no one else wanted. More important to them, the purchase price was within their budget and the site had amenities they were looking for, in that there were many large trees, it was on high ground, and it overlooked a marsh with a small pond (Figure 8-43).

To cut costs, Smith decided to serve as their contractor. He spent two years studying Wright's developmental plans and specifications. Then, during a visit to Taliesin in June 1947—shortly after receiving the working drawings—he made a design suggestion he felt would improve the clerestory windows, half expecting Wright would ignore his idea. Instead, Wright instructed Howe to immediately make the change, and then told Sara: "your husband would make a fine architect."

During a 1991 interview, Sara Smith told the author: "Mr. Wright visited our home, which he referred to as his 'little gem,' three or four times during the 1950s. We discussed the need for a future expansion when we could afford it. The addition and south terrace finally were erected in 1969, following drawings prepared by the Taliesin Architects." She also described how her husband personally cleared out underbrush, installed a lawn, and planted many junipers and other plants, but was dissatisfied with the overall image of the property, which they had named "Myhaven." She then elaborated on her husband's strong character and explained the development of their environmentally sensitive landscape:

Smithy was a remarkable man. A good synonym for him would be "perfection." He became very knowl-edgeable about the landscape, as well as the architecture. He thought that Mr. Wright was the best architect and Thomas Church was the best landscape architect. And after the war was over, he saw no reason we should not obtain the best from each. . . . During the late 1960s, or maybe the early '70s, he heard that Mr. Church would be visiting Cranbrook, so we contacted him and asked him to spend some time with us. He stayed overnight, got up early in the morning, and walked the grounds. He came indoors and drew up a landscape plan, using our dining room table as a drafting board. What a wonderful man he was!

Before he left, Smithy discussed his landscape ideas with him and mentioned having him design a lake to replace the marsh. Mr. Church told him "you have all the ideas; you don't really need me." Still, Smithy wanted him to design it. Smithy carefully carried out his plans for our landscape. Then several years later we had a flood, which extended beyond the marsh and destroyed the little pond. Railroad ties were floating all over the place. Smithy decided this was the time to bring in Mr. Church. But we waited too long. He had passed on. So Smithy personally directed the heavy equipment operators about how to build the lake he had in mind. That winter was especially cold, but he sat in the cab and told the man who engineered the work exactly where to throw every shovelful of dirt. Myhaven now fronts on Clover Leaf Lake, and we are located on one of

Figure 8-43   Melvin Maxwell Smith House (1946–1949) in Bloomfield Hills, Michigan, showing pond and environmentally sensitive landscape. (*Photograph by Charles E. Aguar. © 2002 by Berdeana Aguar.*)

Figure 8-44   M. M. Smith landscape, as developed over the years. (*Photograph by Charles E. Aguar. © 2002 by Berdeana Aguar.*)

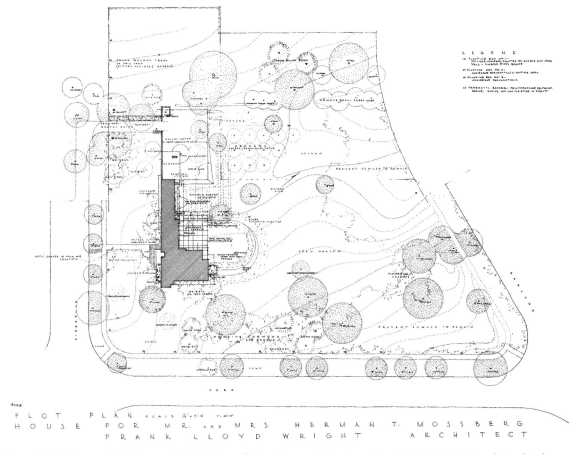

Figure 8-45   Planting plan delineated by John Howe for the Herman T. Mossberg House (1948–1951) in South Bend, Indiana, with actual landscaping envisioned and directed by Gertrude Mossberg. (*© 2002 by The Frank Lloyd Wright Foundation, Scottsdale, Arizona.*)

the three bays. So everything you see is the result of Smithy's persistency and determination. Myhaven is a beautiful expression of Soul, and it brings much joy to many people, including myself (Figure 8-44).

Herman T. Mossberg—South Bend, Indiana (1948–1951)

The planting plans prepared for Gertrude and Herman Mossberg are the most complete for any Usonian of this period in the Archives (Figure 8-45). When the author questioned Howe about the singularity of these plans, he gave all the credit to Gertrude Mossberg: "The plan is detailed due to the plant and landscape design expertise of Mrs. Mossberg. I drew the landscape plan to follow her specific wishes. She walked around with me to show what and where to place each plant. She was terrific." After reading this statement to Gertrude Mossberg— then 94 years of age—during our April 1992 interview, she smiled, chuckled, and said, "Jack has remained a good friend. You know, he lived with us for two months in our old house and obtained the estimates and drew the beautiful perspective drawings in color on our dining room table. We still have the original drawings upstairs."

During the course of the interview, Mrs. Mossberg pointed out that her husband "arranged for the street behind us to become a cul-de-sac" so they would have no traffic on the quiet side of their deep parklike property. She said the design and construction evolved into a two-year process because the "plaster trades were on strike" and that she and her husband visited both Taliesins to go over changes they wanted to make on the plans. "The main change was making the kitchen an outside room. Mr. Wright first had it where I couldn't see out and I told him I wanted to look out onto the garden when I cooked. He gave me even more than I asked for by adding French doors onto a large terrace at floor level, directly off both the kitchen and the dining area. The terrace had been planned to be on a different level, but the site was regraded to allow for this. It required installing an underground drainage system because much of the lot sloped downward."

Mrs. Mossberg's site plan was so explicit she arranged to leave unpaved one of the squares in the 5-foot, 6-inch grid pattern of brick surfacing on the terrace—as delineated on the ground floor plan enhanced by the author— for the specific purpose of providing space to plant a sycamore tree that would shade both the terrace and the south-facing walls of glass (Figure 8-46). She said that she thought the Sycamore would provide "a sculptural accent" to the hemicircular terrace that visually and effec-

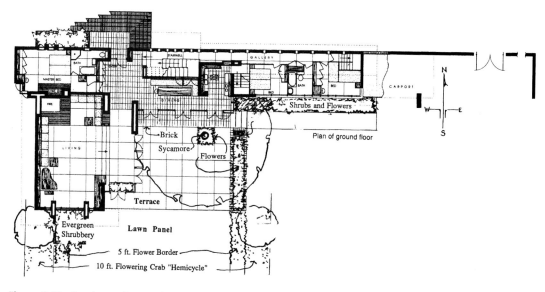

Figure 8-46   Landscape features for the Herman T. Mossberg residence. (*By Charles E. Aguar, based on personal analysis and floor plan S.302 in* The Frank Lloyd Wright Companion, *by W. A. Storrer, © 1993. Original plan © 2002 by The Frank Lloyd Wright Foundation, Scottsdale, Arizona. As delineated, © 2002 by Berdeana Aguar.*)

tively separates the formal lawn from the transitional meadow area and the outer edges of the property that are retained as a natural forest. She pointed out that the grass in the meadow is mowed less frequently and at a higher level to preserve the introduced ground cover and a colorful drift of wild flowers (Figure 8-47).

William Palmer—Ann Arbor, Michigan (1950)

The William Palmer House provides opportunity to study the articulation of the landscape, but it also reinforces the importance Wright placed upon orienting the Usonians for solar benefit and/or to better experience dramatic patterns of sun and shadow, than to access a scenic vista.

During the May 1991 meeting of the Frank Lloyd Wright Building Conservancy, Mary Palmer turned to the author and said: "You know, we asked Jack Howe to rotate our house 90 degrees from its intended position on the site so our triangular porch would be lowered and fewer steps would be needed to enter our garden. We didn't want to be stuck high in the air on a balcony without access to the lawn, woods, and garden." She was referring to their desire to lower the marked elevation of the prow for the masonry retaining base (Figure 8-48). Howe confirmed the reorientation during a subsequent telephone interview: "I recall the house was shifted on the site to meet the clients' request, but I don't remember how much or what affect it had on the intended orientation. If Mary Palmer said it was rotated ninety

degrees, it was rotated ninety degrees. She knows everything there is to be known about the house and is your most accurate source. It would only have been changed, however, with Mr. Wright's approval."[505]

Wright's agreement to make the change most probably came about in response to the reasoning the Palmers put forth based upon their very thoughtful study of local conditions:

> Ever since our visit to Taliesin when we first saw the general plan for our house we have been disturbed by the placing of the house on the site. . . . We have been experimenting with other possibilities than the one incorporated in the first plan. This experimentation has been carried out both on paper and on the site. We have finally arrived at a location which seems to us ideal. It retains all the beautiful features of the house plan itself and at the same time takes full advantage of the view to the north, which is one of the most attractive features of the site. To the north we overlook a forest of magnificent hardwood trees in the summer. In the winter when the views are deforested the view extends for two miles over the beautiful Huron Valley. We feel it would be a shame to sacrifice this natural advantage of the location by the alternative placing of the house. Several other major advantages would also follow. At least four large and beautiful trees would be saved—the two hickories that you proposed to remove from the driveway, and a marvelous spread-

Figure 8-47 1991 photograph shows developed landscape as seen from naturalistic portion of Mossberg homesite. (*Photograph by Charles E. Aguar. © 2002 by Berdeana Aguar.*)

Figure 8-48   1992 photograph of lowered prow and masonry retaining base terrace for William Palmer House in Ann Arbor, Michigan. (*Photograph by Charles E. Aguar. © 2002 by Berdeana Aguar.*)

ing apple tree and an elm that would have to be removed for the bedroom wing. Mr. Hough [sic] will remember our initial reaction to the length of the driveway. The new proposed location of the house would reduce materially this length. Finally our request for a study-guest room (it seems to us) might be more easily met with the changed location than with the old.[506]

When the Palmer house plan is laid out on the topographic map as Wright originally proposed and as the Palmers suggested, the advantages and disadvantages are quite graphic (Figure 8-49). Wright's proposed siting literally crossed the natural contours of the site. The corner bedroom and study would have been cut into the southern slope of the small hill—the highest elevation of the site—but the streetside appearance would have been of a house nestled snugly into its setting. As sited and built, the main body of the house "goes with the grain" of the contours, generally following a slight ridge that slopes gently downward. In this alignment, the study was cut into a slope of the hill and the depth of the rear yard was significantly increased. The most negative result of the resiting is that it created the need to install twelve steps between the carport and the level of the first-floor living space (Figure 8-50). Very few houses designed by Frank Lloyd Wright have this drastic a grade

change or require this many steps to access the main point of outdoor-indoor transition.

The primary advantage to the original siting was that the living-dining open space would be oriented to maximize direct solar gain during the winter, from sunrise to sunset. The disadvantages were: (A) corner bedroom within 25 feet of public street; (B) terrace level 5 feet above natural grade, limiting access to garden; (C) expanses of plate glass in primary living space exposed to prevailing southwesterly winter winds; and (D) long driveway. Moreover, the morning sun would not have been accessible to the bedroom wing at any time of year (Figure 8-51 a-b). The advantages of the reorientation were: (E) corner bedroom more than 50 feet from public street; (F) terrace just a few steps above natural grade, providing easy access to garden; (G) only one window exposed to prevailing southwesterly winter winds; (H) shorter driveway; and (I) panoramic view of the distant Huron Valley. The primary disadvantage, of course, was that there was no direct solar gain in the living-dining space. Because of the triangular shape of this space, however, some of the floor-to-ceiling windows face southeast, so the early morning sun angles could penetrate under the broad cantilever roof between 6:00 A.M. to 9:00 A.M. during the chilly days of spring and fall. Moreover, sunlight would begin to penetrate the bedroom wing as early as 7:30 A.M.

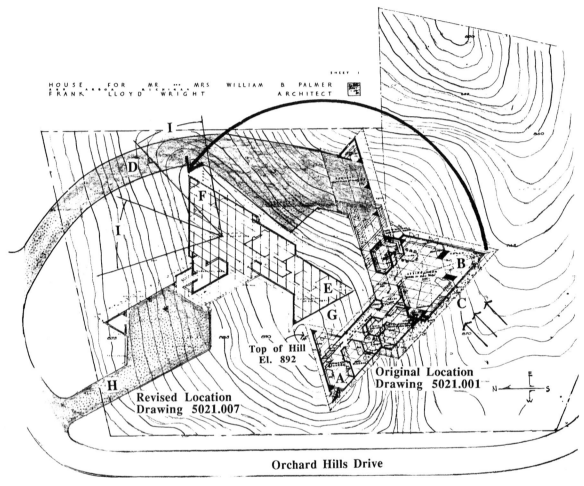

Figure 8-49 Wright's proposed siting for Palmer House, versus as-built siting with 90-degree rotation. (© *2002 by The Frank Lloyd Wright Foundation, Scottsdale, Arizona. As delineated,* © *2002 by Berdiana Aguar.*)

The Palmer House today represents an exceptional blending of indoor-outdoor connectedness as the naturalistic landscape of indigenous plantings and winding garden pathways have been thoughtfully developed by the Palmers over the years. Both Palmers were avid gardeners, and Mary Palmer said they also consulted with faculty and students of landscape architecture at Michigan State College. The result is a sensitive Wrightscape that imparts an unprecedented interrelationship between Wright's architecture and the nature of the site, even on a rainy day (Figure 8-52 a-b).

Andrew B. Cooke—Virginia Beach, Virginia (1953–1959)

Unlike most clients, the Cookes never traveled to either of the Taliesins, although Maude Cooke met with Wright one time in his suite at the Plaza Hotel in New York. It seems that working drawings were drafted for two separate houses—a brick solar hemicycle and a concrete-block Usonian Automatic. Inasmuch as actual construction did not get underway until 1959, however, and there was no communication during the interim, no one from

Figure 8-50 Rotation of Palmer House necessitated adding 12 entry steps. (*Photograph by Charles E. Aguar. © 2002 by Berdeana Aguar.*)

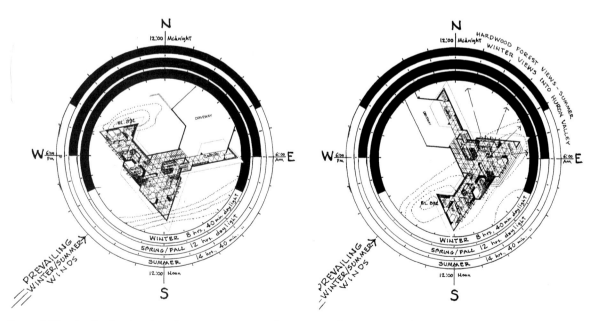

Figure 8-51 a–b Declination chart showing environmental impact on Palmer House with (a) Wright's planned siting and orientation, versus (b) Palmer's as-built siting and orientation. (*By Charles E. Aguar, based on personal analysis and plans of record. © 2002 by The Frank Lloyd Wright Foundation, Scottsdale, Arizona. As delineated, © 2002 by Berdeana Aguar.*)

Taliesin was involved with the implementation process. Therefore, exactly which house was built on the site was for a long time a mystery. The end result is the only solar hemicycle where brick was used as the primary building material.

Even though the Fellowship was not physically involved in the construction process, the house was correctly sited to face due south, as delineated by Howe, and was built with careful exactitude—following his carefully written instructions and well-crafted working drawings (Figure 8-53). The only obvious variance from the plans is the driveway—laid out with flowing curves to match the wheel radii of the automobile rather than with straight edges and angles, as delineated. The topography and most trees were left undisturbed to more effectively wed the architecture to the site—which slopes down to a large lake connecting to Chesapeake Bay. The streetside portion of the property is maintained as a natural forest, so the house cannot be seen from the public street. And as the entry experience proceeds through this landscape by way of the curving driveway, the first view of the house is the rather conservative façade of the rectangular bedroom-carport wing (Figure 8-54). It is not until a visitor passes through the point of

Figure 8-52 a–b Ambiance of naturalistic landscape surrounding Palmer House, as developed over the years. (*Photographs by Charles E. Aguar. © 2002 by Berdeana Aguar.*)

outdoor-indoor transition and enters the primary living space that the upward and outward expanse of the dramatic cathedral ceiling becomes manifest and the sweeping view of trees and water emerges through the curving wall of glass. The overall sense of place is of a rural waterfront location, rather than a suburban lot (Figure 8-55).

During a September 1994 interview with second owners Mr. And Mrs. Dan Duhl, they said they have "more privacy here on 1 acre than at our Woodstock, New York property with 18 acres." They went on to detail the extensive renovation they undertook with both grounds and house after they purchased the property in the late 1980s. Within this process, they hired landscape architect J. Barry Frankenfield to redesign the site and develop a multiple-level garden to accommodate a sizable spa and excercize room in an underground bunker (Figure 8-56). The result is one of the more innovative landscape redesigns for a Wright-designed property, in that it effectively meets the contemporary needs and lifestyle of new owners some 30 years after construction.

John L. Rayward—New Canaan, Connecticut (1957)

The Rayward House is one of several variations of Jacobs II often incorrectly identified as a solar hemicycle. Inasmuch as the glass façade faces east, this reference is a misnomer.

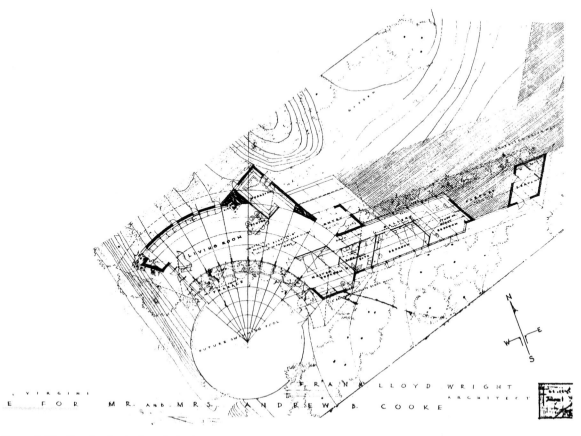

Figure 8-53 Site plan for Andrew B. Cooke property (1953–1959) in Virginia Beach, Virginia. (© 2002 by The Frank Lloyd Wright Foundation, Scottsdale, Arizona.)

Figure 8-54 First impression of Andrew B. Cooke property is rectangular bedroom wing. (*Photograph by Charles E. Aguar. © 2002 by Berdeana Aguar.*)

Even though the original structure was built of common concrete block and Philippine mahogany as a cost-saving measure, it is situated on a heavily wooded, 20-acre site in an upper-scale community of rural estates and has been substantially expanded upon in incremen-tal stages from the late 1950s through the 1980s. And the private botanical garden surrounding the structures connected by a covered esplanade is a place of peace and tranquility set apart from the mundane world (Figure 8-57). The harmonious "fit" of the cultivated and natural

Figure 8-55 Upon entering the Cooke House, a sweeping view of trees and water emerges through curving wall of glass. (*Photograph by Charles E. Aguar. © 2002 by Berdeana Aguar.*)

Figure 8-56 The landscape architect for the Cooke House designed a multiple-level garden and sizable underground spa and exercise space. (*Photograph by Charles E. Aguar. © 2002 by Berdeana Aguar.*)

Figure 8-57 The tastefully designed botanical garden at the John Hayward House (1957) in New Canaan, Connecticut, was designed by landscape architect Frank Lkamura. (*Photograph by Charles E. Aguar. © 2002 by Berdeana Aguar.*)

Figure 8-58   A rock-edged pool adds to the sensuosity of the singular environment of Tirranna, the John Hayward homesite in New Canaan, Connecticut. (*Photograph by Charles E. Aguar. © 2002 by Berdeana Aguar.*)

landscape was orchestrated by landscape architect Frank Lkamura. It is the coalescence of Lkamura's sensitive placement and intermix of indigenous plantings, his extensive use of rocks and boulders to relate the dam spillway and rocky-edged pond, and his layout of pathways and bridges leading to original sculptures, hidden nooks, and quiet sitting areas that create the sensuosity of this singular site environment (Figure 8-58).

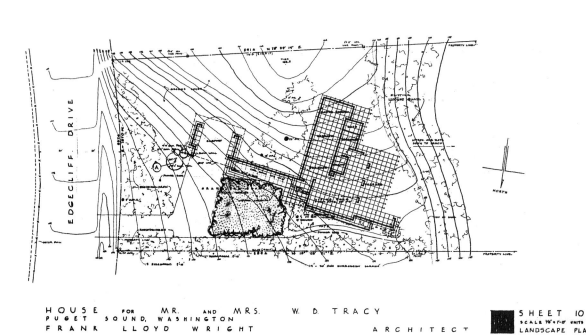

Figure 8-59   Topographic map layout shows the cross-grained siting of the William B. Tracy House (1955–1960s) in Normany Park, Washington. (*© 2002 by The Frank Lloyd Wright Foundation, Scottsdale, Arizona.*)

William B. Tracy—Normany Park, Washington (1955–1960s)

The layout for the compact Usonian "Automatic" designed for Elizabeth and William Tracy is very straightforward and fashioned on a 2-foot-square module. By definition, the structuring was designed for low-cost, do-it-yourself construction, and all the textile blocks interwoven with steel bars were formed on site as a cost-saving measure. Yet, the "standard" 100-foot by 150-foot lot is located in one of Seattle's upscale subdivisions atop a cliff that affords magnificent views of Puget Sound.

Wright's personal involvement with the Tracy House was limited to meeting with them when they visited Taliesin and Taliesin West, developing a conceptual sketch on a topographic map, making suggestions as drawings evolved, and signing his approval when the apprentice assigned to drafting the design completed the working drawings. The actual construction did not take place until after his death.

In this case, climatic conditions bore no relevance at all to the siting of the structure. There is no southern exposure. In fact, the glass façade of the primary living space faces due west to overlook the water feature. Nor was any consideration given to the natural topography. The main mass of the structure cuts across the contours, and the bedroom wing, detached carport, and storage walls burrow into the brow of the hill (Figure 8-59). Moreover, the living room terrace rests on fill added to the top of the cliff, which drops off steeply.

Nevertheless, the Tracy House exhibits an exceptional sense-of-place and indoor-outdoor connectedness (Figure 8-60). The precise placement of the custom glazed blocks dispenses ambient lighting throughout the house. A parapet of pierced textile block draws the viewer's eye from the inside outward past the terrace toward the magnificent views, as it also screens off a view of the nearby neighboring house and intercepts cold winter winds blowing down from Canada. And within the mature landscape environment of the 1990s, the structure appears to nestle naturally onto the site (Figure 8-61). This illusion directly relates to the talents of the Tracys, both of whom are avid gardeners. They planted ground cover to limit the need for constant maintenance required by a lawn.

Figure 8-60 A 1992 photograph of the Tracy House shows its sense-of-place and indoor-outdoor connectedness. (*Photograph by Charles E. Aguar. © 2002 by Berdeana Aguar.*)

Figure 8-61   The Tracy House appears to nestle into its site. (*Photograph by Charles E. Aguar. © 2002 by Berdeana Aguar.*)

They asked the staff at Taliesin Associates to design a pond-and-fountain water feature to be installed to the side of the detached carport to enhance the entry experience by introducing the sight and sound of trickling water (Figure 8-62). And they converted much of the former autocourt into an entrance garden planted with indigenous vegetation that perceptively links the house with the site environment and the series of carefully arranged steps that access the natural wooded portion of the property. Thus, the entry experience correlates with approaching and entering a natural woodland (Figure 8-63).

Figure 8-62   A small reflecting pool and fountain designed by Taliesin Associates enhances the entry experience at the Tracy House. (*Photograph by Charles E. Aguar. © 2002 by Berdeana Aguar.*)

Figure 8-63 The entry experience at the Tracy House creates the illusion of approaching and entering a natural woodland. (*Photograph by Charles E. Aguar. © 2002 by Berdeana Aguar.*)

This thoughtfully articulated landscape represents one of the most peaceful, well executed, and well maintained environments to be found anywhere. And every bit of it was crafted in the best Wrightscape tradition by the owners themselves—from forming the textile blocks to the selection and cultivation of the naturalistic plantings. Therefore, except for the fact that it was not sited in one of the Usonian communities, this very modest Usonian Automatic embodies every aspect of Wright's intent to ultimately create a lifestyle and an architecture "for simple living, in harmony with nature, at a cost people of average means can afford."

9 | Afterword

Frank Lloyd Wright died on April 9, 1959. He was 91 years of age. His death was mourned by people throughout the world. The ballad "So Long, Frank Lloyd Wright" was composed and recorded by folk singers Simon and Garfunkle to eulogize the event. And when Wright's works were catalogued, his legacy of creativity totaled an incredible 1150 designs. More than half of this total workload (650) emanated from The Taliesin Fellowship during the last 25 years of his life. Approximately 10 percent of these were nonclient projects, however—Broadacre City Models, Taliesin, or Taliesin West—and only 217 (34 percent) reached the stage of implementation. Perhaps the most remarkable aspect of this compilation is the fact that the major body of Wright's work was domestic architecture. There were relatively few "monuments" such as form the foundation upon which the careers of most eminent architects are based. While these monuments are all the more notable because of their singularity, it is Wright's "affordable" Usonian architecture that has been most lauded within the extensive writings compiled since his demise.

The influence of Wright's single-family homes upon modern America's domestic architectural form has been well documented and celebrated. Wright himself most probably would agree that the ardent quality of this recognition alone would meet his qualifications for "success," as he so perceptively worded it during a 1957 interview conducted by Alistair Cooke: "Who knows who is a success until long after the circumstances? Success is measured not in ordinary terms, but what will transpire 50 years later. So 50 years from now you will know whether or not I am a successful person."[507] Even so, Wright undoubtedly had opportunity to personally realize at least some perception of his success in this area the year before his death, in 1958, when Joseph E. Howland indirectly paid tribute to his indisputable impact upon America's domestic architecture within an independent evaluation of construction in America in the *House Beautiful Book of Gardens and Outdoor Living*—if only by way of the very omission of his name:

> At midpoint of the twentieth century Americans show, more than ever before, an intense, abiding interest in lessening the confinements of indoor living, going to immense effort and expense to bring to their daily lives those benefits of the outdoors that were once mainly within the reach of the well-to-do.
>
> With the growing desire to be closer to the land and its benefits, Americans build houses that seem to rise from the ground itself, that blend in form and material, that frequently eliminate lines of wall and foundation that traditionally have divided the house from the land. . . . The house may flow into the outdoors to gain space, both visual and actual. . . . The trend has been, not to create strong contrasts between garden and house, but to harmonize, to complement the natural with the man-made. Today the garden may be considered in new lights—as integral living space, as a room open to the sky, as part of the house. . . . Design of both house and garden tends more, now, to follow the contours of the site, and it has become almost a point of dedication for both the amateur gardener and the professional to make full use of existing trees and shrubs and of natural formations, rather than to make obvious nature's bending to man's projects. . . . The house may flow into the outdoors to gain space, both visual and actual. . . . The aggressive use of expanses of glass as stationary or sliding walls . . . have had widespread effect upon indoor-outdoor relationships. . . . Terrace and living room may achieve a oneness in a matter of seconds disallowing the senses to note when, exactly, one has ended and the other begun.[508]

Within the text of *Wrightscapes*, the authors have investigated Wright's possibly even greater influence upon the American domestic landscape, spaces for outdoor living, and the countenance of the urban-suburban landscape across America. With respect to Wright's domestic architecture, it was determined that he did not always adhere to nature's plan, and the end results were not as successful when designed to be built *against* the grain of the land as when designing *with* nature was the order. With his own Taliesin, it can be said that he did, in fact, articulate the landscape and surrounding environment as well as Thomas Jefferson had done a full century earlier—combining agricultural methodology and artistic principles to shape the land. However, he was not the astute gardener, experimenter of horticultural matters and site engineering as was Jefferson, who made lasting landscape contributions equal to his architecture. Wright's solutions to the outdoor areas immediately related to his buildings usually were architectonic and more frequently a very convincing "illusion" of being a part of nature, rather than true integration based on synthesizing the site's resources and arriving at architectural and landscape architectural solutions responsive to natural values. Had the two alter egos of Frank Lloyd Wright and Jens Jensen actually collaborated to teach architecture and landscape architecture as an entity, as Wright originally proposed—rather than operating separate schools in the same state, as they ultimately did—both professions perhaps would have been propelled into a new dimension.[509] The design dimensions evidenced throughout the first 40 years of Wright's career could have been perpetuated and aggrandized, and there would have been a true marriage of modern architecture and modern landscape architecture: the organic architecture so forcefully expressed in Wright's rhetoric.

Nevertheless, the authors also determined that the misrepresentation of Wright's landscapes—architectonic and illusionistic though they may be—is the single most missing link needed to consummate the total environmental ambiance of Wright's original intent within the restoration, rehabilitation, rebuilding, or adaptive reuse of his domestic architecture, irregardless of when it was designed. The good news is that the negative cosmetic features of nondescript landscapes, exotic landscapes, or unnaturalistically "stylized" Japanese landscapes—which Wright most assuredly did not support—can be reversed. Evergreen foundation plantings can be eliminated. Overgrown plantings can be pruned properly, or replaced. Broken walls and other outdoor construction can be repaired. And glassed-in porches again can be opened to the out-of-doors. Moreover, when homeowners themselves do not have the time or talents to personally redevelop their landscapes to be more in keeping with Wright's architecture, professional landscape architectural designs can be prepared and implemented, "if" the designer of choice is skilled in the art of naturalistic landscapes and the maintenance person is skilled in the art of pruning to retain the natural form. (See "Do's and Don'ts for Owners of Frank Lloyd Wright Designed Homes," Appendix N.) In other words, when every effort is made to understand and interpret Wright's holistic design philosophy *before* the process of restoring the landscape is initiated, the "nothing special" landscapes always can be developed into "something special" landscapes that enhance, and are in consort with, his "special" architecture.

Wright's Usonian community concepts had the potential to impact the American urban persona just as forcefully as his domestic architecture. His expertise with textile block and prefabricated units, combined with the time and thought he invested into his built and unbuilt community planning projects involving affordable housing, could have made a pronounced impact on new town development in America—and perhaps throughout the world. That this did not occur is directly attributable to the regrettable circumstance that Wright's demonstration Usonian communities never were implemented as full-scale prototypes. Because within Wright's plans for The Acres, Parkwyn Village, and Usonia II (Pleasantville, New York)—as well as his broader unbuilt concepts for Broadacre City—he was essentially pioneering the new discipline of environmental design, decades before the term was used by academia. By concerning himself with everything that influenced the lives and well-being of his clients; by planning to develop communities as neighborhood centers with parks, recreation facilities, gardens, orchards, and separation of pedestrian and mobile traffic; and by involving everyone in the planning, management, and construction processes of development; he effectively merged his skills as an architect, a planner, and an environmentalist with the skills he exhibited in so many other spheres of design. No one since Leonardo da Vinci has exhibited such brilliant versatility as a designer.

Perhaps if Jensen had supported Wright's efforts to be appointed architect-in-chief for the State Department's building program, or if Wright had been willing to adhere to the standards and policies of government planning and become involved or identified with the Federal Works Agency Division of Defense Housing or the Resettlement Administration's Greenbelt towns, a credible Broadacre City prototype might have become reality.[510] It seems this could have been a possibility since he had many friends and valuable connections within these agencies—including former apprentices James Drought, Philip L. Holliday, Joseph Kastler, Samuel Ratensky, Lewis Stevens, and Harry Hardley. Had Wright used these connections to sell his Broadacre City concepts, rather than ineffectively blowing his own horn, he perhaps then could have orchestrated a transformation of the American community—which interests, he professed, were "of greater value to the whole."

This brings us to the countenance of the urban-suburban landscape across America at the onset of the twenty-first century. Analysis supports that many more aspects of Wright's Broadacre City prophecy have been fulfilled than generally realized. Within Robert Fishman's comprehensive analysis of the suburbanization of postwar America, he observed that "the massive rebuilding that began in 1945 represents not the culmination of the 200-year history of suburbia, but rather its end. Indeed, this massive change is not suburbanization at all but the creation of a new kind of city, with principles that are directly opposed to the true suburb."[511] Fishman credits H. G. Wells along with Wright as the only two prophets to perceive the forces that would lead to these "edge cities" and supports their prophecies as constituting "a remarkable insight into the decentralizing tendencies of modern technology and society." He elaborates: "Something like the transformation that Wells and Wright foresaw has taken place in the United States, a transformation that is all the more remarkable in that it occurred without a clear recognition that it was happening. While diverse groups were engaged in what they believed was 'the new suburbanization' of America, they were in fact creating a new city. Wells and Wright were powerless to bring about the new city they foresaw. Nevertheless, the inherent forces in twentieth-century technology and society asserted themselves to form a new pattern of urban life."[512]

The central city of course did not disappear, as Wright believed it would. Nor did the central city evolve exactly as Wells believed—losing financial and industrial functions and becoming a gallery or "bazaar" of shops and entertainment centers. The new city form, or "technoburbs," that Fishman described are best expressed in the areas surrounding the high-tech industries that have located in places such as Silicon Valley in northern California, Route #128 in Massachusetts, or the Research Triangle in North Carolina. Such viable socioeconomic units that spread out along highway growth corridors with their campuslike office parks, shopping malls, and a full range of housing types more and more resemble Wright's vision for Broadacre City—but with design controls that attempt to avoid look-alike houses, rather than to seek harmony or any sense of organic appearance. Rarely are they laid out on a gridiron or other geometric basis; the street patterns relate more closely to Olmsted's Riverside.

Consider all the benefits of living and working in areas such as these. Open space in the form of common areas has been created by clustering houses in creative ways, relieved of the straight-jacketed rules of traditional zoning—much as Wright attempted to introduce as early as 1901 and continued to pursue into the 1950s, using variations of his Quadruple Block layout. Moreover, less time is spent traveling to and from work—as he predicted it could be—because houses, workplaces, shops, schools, and other services all are within a reasonable commuting distance.

Apart from these elite areas, many more elements of Wright's prophecy have come into being across the length and breadth of America. The Interstate Highway System and the many thousands of miles of tollways have created a transportation network convenient to most parts of the nation as he proposed, despite many shortcomings. In some areas of the country—such as on portions of the New Jersey Turnpike—separate truck lanes have been installed to better facilitate travel by way of the private automobile. Performing arts centers, once the exclusive province of the central city, more and more are being relocated to places like Wolf Trap Farm Park outside Washington and similar areas beyond dozens of other large American cities. Country western entertainment has even become decentralized from Nashville to the more rural environment of Branson, Missouri. First-run movie theaters have moved from downtowns to suburban and regional malls.[513] Convenience stores located at highway intersections, as well as street intersections within the central city, resemble the gasoline service stations Wright proposed to use as community centers. His roadside markets could be seen as the forerunner to the shopping center. And nature preserves, natural areas, and entire ecosystems are being conserved and defended—despite the perceived impression that the countryside has become one huge paved parking lot. Drained wetlands also are being restored, in keeping with Wright's concept that developed land should avoid sensitive areas and the best agricultural soils. Moreover, Americans increasingly are returning to part-time farming, or at least gardening for recreation, as a means of supplementing fresh produce brought in from long distances. Greenways to protect streams, bicycle routes, pathways, and greenbelts to avoid urban sprawl are positive open space projects of recent decades. And although forests sometimes are destroyed by development, urban tree planting programs have never been more popular—similar to the "tree banks" or municipal forests that Wright proposed should be developed to create a sustained yield and multiuse of forest resources.

In other words, the Broadacres vision of a decentralized city form that Wright first set forth more than 60 years ago has indeed come into being, and exactly as he said it would occur: "it should be everywhere, yet nowhere." Moreover, the Informational Age of computers, fax machines, and other telecommunication breakthroughs more and more create a basis for making the concept of working out of the home more practical— another of Wright's Broadacre concepts that was conceived decades in advance of the needed technology. It also is not inconceivable that within the foreseeable future we might see the actualization of Wright's helicopter taxis, flywheel hansom cabs, and atomic barges. More significantly, Wright's proposed all-powerful "county architect" could replace the scores of individuals representing a crazy-quilt pattern of overlapping jurisdictions that currently direct development. Only time will tell.

Many of the conclusions put forth in this writing most probably will be argued and challenged. This is as it should be for a project this all-encompassing. The evalu-

ation of the landscapes and environments of Frank Lloyd Wright has never before been attempted. The writing of *Wrightscapes* will have been worthwhile if it prevents any more destruction of the type that resulted from saving an endangered landmark, but relocating it with a siting and orientation foreign to its former occupants, such as happened with the Pope-Leighey Usonian in 1964 and the Stockman Prairie House in 1990. It will have been worthwhile if it creates an awareness for the importance of replacement planting to assure that a mature tree with an established root system will be in place to more readily fill the void created whenever a character-defining tree inevitably succumbs to natural forces. And it will have been worthwhile if it encourages restorationists—whether private owners, public or nonprofit organizations—to undertake the kind of in-depth research of Wright's proposed site environment and the rationale behind his siting and orientation as preceded the restoration of the structure.

NOTES

1. Donald L. Johnson. "Notes on Frank Lloyd Wright's Paternal Family," *Frank Lloyd Wright Newsletter* (Vol. 3, No. 2, 1980) p. 7.
2. Maginel Wright Barney. *The Valley of the God-Almighty Joneses* (Appleton-Century, New York, 1965).
3. Meryle Secrest. *Frank Lloyd Wright: A Biography* (Alfred A. Knopf, Inc., New York, 1992) p. 26.
4. Frank Lloyd Wright. *An Autobiography* Third edition (Horizon Press, New York, 1977) p. 38.
5. Ibid. 1977, pp. 26, 192.
6. Wright often interchanged the words "natural" and "organic."
7. Some of the more commonly planted flowers were the daisy, lily of the valley, crocus, larkspur, sweet william, foxglove, gladiola, sunflower, daylily, lupine, violet, and hollyhock.
8. Wright. 1977, p. 26.
9. Frank Lloyd Wright. "In the Cause of Architecture," *The Architectural Record* (March 1908).
10. Wright. 1977, pp. 77, 79.
11. Thomas S. Hines, Jr. "Frank Lloyd Wright—The Madison Years," *Wisconsin Magazine of History* (Winter 1967). pp. 109–119.
12. Walter Havighurst. "Land Sales in Chicago, 1856," *Land of the Long Horizons* (Coward-McCann, Inc., New York, 1960) p. 269.
13. The invention of the elevator by E. G. Otis in 1857 allowed building heights to 6 stories during the first rebuilding of Chicago.
14. Donald L. Miller. *City of the Century* (Simon & Schuster, New York, 1996) p. 304.
15. Bruce Brooks Pfeiffer. "The Japanese Print: An Interpretation" as reprinted in *Frank Lloyd Wright Collected Writings, 1894–1930* (Rizzoli/The Frank Lloyd Wright Foundation, Vol. 1, New York, 1992) p. 122.
16. Kevin Nute. *Frank Lloyd Wright and Japan* (Van Nostrand Reinhold, New York, 1993) p. 22.
17. Ibid. 1993, pp. 22–25. Also Chapter 1, footnote 70.
18. Ibid. 1993, pp. 22–25.
19. Bruce Brooks Pfeiffer. "Japanese Influences and Froebelian Training," *Frank Lloyd Wright: His Living Voice* (The Frank Lloyd Wright Foundation/The Press at California State University, Fresno, California, 1987) pp. 32–33.
20. Nute. 1993, p. 44.
21. Edward S. Morse. *Japanese Homes and Their Surroundings* (Charles E. Tuttle, 1972 reprint of 1904, 1886, 1885 versions) pp. 273–295.
22. Clay Lancaster. *The Japanese Influence in America* (Walton H. Rawls, New York, 1963) p. 7.
23. Grant Manson. Archival notes of record at Oak Park Public Library, Oak Park, Illinois.
24. Peter O. Muller. *Contemporary Suburban America* (Prentice-Hall, Inc., Englewood Cliffs, New Jersey, 1981) p. 33.
25. Excerpted from Olmsted's 1893 report to the Commission.
26. John Coleman Adams. "What A Great City Might Be—A Lesson From The White City," *The New England Magazine* (New Ser. 14, March 1896) pp. 3–13.
27. Donald Leslie Johnson. *The Architecture of Walter Burley Griffin* (The MacMillan Company of Australia Pty. Ltd., South Melbourne and North Sydney, Australia, 1977) p. 27.
28. Christopher D. Vernon. "Walter Burley Griffin, Landscape Architect," *The Midwest in American Architecture* (University of Illinois Press, Urbana, 1991) p. 218.
29. Excerpt from 4/25/1906 edition of *Illinois State Journal* (Lincoln Library in Springfield, Illinois. Located by librarian Robert Moore).
30. John L. Hancock. "Planners in the Changing American City, 1900–1940," *AIP Journal.* (1967) pp. 293–294.

31. William H. Wilson. *Introduction to Planning History in the United States.* (The Center for Urban Policy Research, Rutgers University, New Brunswick, New Jersey, 1983) p. 113.

32. The shopping arcade was demolished in 1926. Florence Hotel was still partially functional in the 1990s. The clock tower atop the administration building was a landmark on Chicago's South Side until this facility was destroyed by fire on December 1, 1998.

33. Miller. 1996, p. 224. (f. 224, p. 586. *A Visit to the States,* 395.)

34. H. Allen Brooks. *The Prairie School: Frank Lloyd Wright and His Midwest Contemporaries* (W. W. Norton & Company, New York, 1972) pp. 4, 16–17.

35. Jane Laura Addams was an American social reformer, pacifist, and women's rights advocate. Hull House became a model for many other settlement houses in the United States. Addams became president of the Women's International League for Peace and Freedom in 1919 and, together with Nicholas Murray Butler, received the Nobel Peace Price in 1931.

36. Grant Manson. Notes from 1940 interview with Marion Mahony Griffin (Oak Park Public Library, Oak Park, Illinois).

37. Robert E. Grese. *Jens Jensen: Maker of Natural Parks and Gardens* (Johns Hopkins Press, Baltimore, 1992) p. 25.

38. The University of Illinois was the second American institution to initiate a professional degree program in Landscape Architecture; Harvard University established the first program in 1901.

39. Grese. 1992, p. 23.

40. Leonard Simutis. "Frederick Law Olmsted, Sr.: A Reassessment," *AIP Journal.* (September 1972) p. 278, also f. 6, p. 284.

41. Bruce Brooks Pfeiffer. *Letters to Architects: Frank Lloyd Wright.* (California State University Press, 1984) pp. 51–52.

42. Wilhelm Miller. "The Prairie Style of Landscape Architecture," *Architectural Record.* (US, XL, December 1916).

43. Leonard K. Eaton. *Landscape Artist in America: The Life and Work of Jens Jensen* (University of Chicago Press, 1964) pp. 12–18, 34.

44. The file of correspondence supporting the Wright-Jensen friendship within the archives at the Getty Center in Los Angeles is quite extensive.

45. Jensen thought that all of his photographic records were destroyed in the fire. In mid-1970s, a suitcase full of historic photographs was discovered in an attic at The Clearing by Professor Darrel G. Morrison of UGA School of Environmental Design.

46. Eaton. 1964, p. 87.

47. Stephen Christy. "Jens Jensen," *American Landscape Architecture: Designers and Places* (Preservation Press, 1989) pp. 78–81.

48. Paul Kruty (Essay, Catalog, and Selected Bibliography by) and Mati Maldre (Photographs and Essay by). *Walter Burley Griffin in America* (University of Illinois Press, Chicago, 1996) pp. 15–16.

49. James Birrell. *Walter Burley Griffin.* (University of Queensland Press, Saint Lucia, Australia, 1964) p. 11.

50. Vernon. 1991, p. 12.

51. Birrell. 1964, p. 11.

52. Wright. 1977, p. 101. The family unit at that time consisted of Wright, his mother, and sisters Jennie and Maginel.

53. Miller. 1996, p. 277.

54. Wright. 1977, p. 91.

55. Ibid. 1977, p. 104. Wright described John Blair as "a Scotch landscape gardener with a true feeling for nature."

56. The verandas provided 900 square feet of outdoor living space, 65 percent more than living space on the first floor.

57. Restoration Committee of Frank Lloyd Wright Home and Studio Foundation. *The Plan for Restoration and Adaptive Use of the Frank Lloyd Wright Home and Studio.* (University of Chicago Press, Chicago, 1977, 1978) p. 19. Most published plans do not show door leading from dining room to rear veranda; original door verified during restoration process.

58. Morse. 1972, pp. 235, 241–243.

59. Ibid. 1972, pp. 241–243.

60. The vine most likely used during Wright's occupancy would have been Engelman Ivy (*Parthenocissus engelamarini*) or Boston Ivy (*Parthenocissus tricuspidata*). Both varieties are hardy in Chicago area and exhibit good foliage and splendid fall color.

61. This entry approach is entirely different from—and should not to be confused with—the contradictory effect created by the narrow (conventional width) concrete walkway and the dense mass of

the evergreen tree that was introduced into the disparate ornamental planting bed at the base of the southwest projection during the process of restoring Wright's Oak Park Home and Studio as a museum. See "Oak Park Home and Studio Remodeling" in Chapter 4.

62. The five entry steps have 6-inch risers, equalling 2.5 total feet of elevation from the ground.

63. Teiji Itoh. *The Elegant Japanese House: Traditional Sukiya Architecture* (Walker/Weatherhill, New York-Tokyo, Translated from Japanese version originally published in 1967 by Tankosha, Kyoto, under the title *Sukiya*, 1969) p. 110.

64. See William H. Winslow (1894), Frank Thomas (1901), Arthur Heurtley (1902), and Frederick C. Robie (1908). All had deep, overhanging eaves over the west-facing windows and elaborately protected main entrances except Winslow, where Wright designed a separate family entrance protected by the porte-cochere; the "beautiful elm" was intended to shade the west facade.

65. The McArthur House also appears appreciably lower than the Blossom House because the majority of the entry steps were installed on the interior between the ground-floor entry foyer and the first-floor entry hall.

66. "Water table" was Wright's term for the stylobate base, defined as "the top part or surface of a stereobate—a solid mass of masonry serving as a base for a wall or other structure; foundation." (*World Book Dictionary*, Volume 2, L–Z) p. 2052. Wright often used broad bands of wood to create the "appearance" of a stylobate as another means of accentuating the horizontality of his architecture.

67. Frank J. Scott. *The Art of Beautifying Suburban Home Grounds of Small Extent* (John B. Alden, 1886) pp. 34–37.

68. Palladian windows belong to "the school of Andrea Palladio (1508–1580), an Italian architect, or to his adaptation of ancient Roman architecture." (*World Book Dictionary*, Volume 2, L–Z, 1990) p. 1498.

69. Frank Lloyd Wright. *The Natural House* (1954) p. 51.

70. Norman T. Newton. *Design on the Land: The Development of Landscape Architecture* (The Belknap Press of Harvard University Press, Cambridge, Massachusetts, 1971) pp. xxiii-xxiv.

71. Pfeiffer. 1984, p. 51.

72. Wright. *Ausgefüührte Bauten und entwürfe Von Frank Lloyd Wright* (Ernst Wasmuth, Berlin, 1910) p. 24, Plate 1.

73. Scott. 1886, pp. 33–34.

74. Early plans depict the parterre as a reflecting pool surrounded by an informal perennial garden. If there ever was a reflecting pool, it was long-ago filled with dirt and planted with clipped evergreens.

75. Manson. 1958, p. 71.

76. Pfeiffer. 1992, pp. 31–32.

77. Jack Lesniak. *Hills-DeCaro House: Frank Lloyd Wright 1906*. (Wright Plus, 1999) p. 2, f. 11. The authors are indebted to John D. Tilton, who put us in touch with Oak Park historian Jack Lesniak. Tilton served as restoration architect for the Hills House (formerly Gray) after fire destroyed the entire upper floor in 1976.

78. Wright. 1977, p. 153.

79. Scott. 1870, pp. 51–52.

80. Lesniak. 1999, pp. 2–6. Lesniak notes that the redesign of the Gray House reflects what Wright was doing at the turn of the century. The "Japanese theme in his roof design" is like roofs of other houses he designed during this time frame.

81. William G. Purcell. "That Haunted House," *Northwest Architect* (Volume XVi, Number 6, 1952) pp. 16–17.

82. Telephone conversations with Sidney Oscar Hills (5/24/1999) and Nathan Grier Hills (6/8/1999).

83. Carla Lind. "Moore House I and Pergola," *Lost Wright: Frank Lloyd Wright's Vanished Masterpieces* (Simon & Schuster Editions, Archetype Press, Inc., 1996) p. 46.

84. Lesniak. 1999, section of historical family pictures.

85. Wright's wordage relates to the large perspective in the Wasmuth Portfolio.

86. In the vernacular of landscape architecture, the term "softscape" relates to earth sculpting and plant material, while the term "hardscape" relates to structural elements introduced onto the landscape such as walls, paving material, water features, paths, parking areas, and outdoor furniture.

87. Wright. 1977, p. 162.

88. Gwendolyn Wright. "Architectural Practice and Social Vision in Wright's Early Designs," *The Nature of Frank Lloyd Wright* (University of Chicago Press, Chicago and London, 1988) p. 100.

89. Ibid. 1988, p. 100.

90. Brooks. 1960, pp. 168–169.

91. Van Zanten. "Schooling the Prairie School: Wright's Early Style as a Communicable System," *The Nature of Frank Lloyd Wright* (University of Chicago Press, 1988) p. 79.

92. Janice Pregliasco. "The Life and Work of Marion Mahony Griffin," *The Prairie School: Design Vision for the Midwest* (The Art Institute of Chicago Museum Studies, Vol. 21, No. 2, 1995) p. 165.

93. Brooks. 1977, p. 221. Pertaining to Footnote No. 14, referencing Byrne's comment to Wilhelm Miller on July 3, 1915.

94. Ibid. 1977, pp. 73–74.

95. Kruty. 1996, p. 18.

96. Vernon. 1991, pp. 219–220. Vernon notes that Griffin already had established an independent practice in landscape architecture, having prepared the landscape plan for Eastern Illinois State Normal School, Charleston, Illinois, in 1900.

97. Presumably, these imaginary cosmetic plans were developed so they would compare favorably to those prepared while Griffin was supervising the plans originating from The Studio.

98. Dorathi Bock-Pierre, Ed. *Memoirs of an American Artist: Sculptor Richard W. Bock.* (C. C. Publishing Co., Los Angeles, California, 1989) p. 67. Bock and Wright would develop a lifelong friendship.

99. Bruce Brooks Pfeiffer, Ed. *Frank Lloyd Wright Collected Writings (1894–1930)* (Rizzoli/New York in association with The Frank Lloyd Wright Foundation, Vol. 1, 1992) pp. 55–57.

100. Ibid. 1992, pp. 55–57.

101. Ibid. Footnote 16, p. 7. *Chicago Architectural Annual.* (1902), unpaginated. The "glen" undoubtedly contributed to the name by which the Bradley House is known: Glenlloyd.

102. Christopher Vernon. "The Evolution of the Bradley Landscape," *Glenlloyd Historic Landscape Report.* (1990) p. 2. The authors are indebted to Professor Vernon and current owner Ronald L. Moline, AIA, for sharing the historic report, the circa-1900 site plan, and proposed landscape design.

103. Caption describing the "A Home in a Prairie Town" article that Wright prepared for *The Ladies Home Journal* (Feb. 1901).

104. Regrettably, there is scant evidence that Wright's landscape treatment, illustrated equally to the architecture in the *Journal* articles, ever was understood or even noticed. Builders and owners of Prairie Houses, then and now, have continued to "smother" houses with exotic foundation plantings, to misplace and misuse urns or other container plantings.

105. Excerpt from Wright's handwritten notes on what is believed to be his first sketch of the quadruple block plan.

106. Excerpt from Wright's text for "A Small House with Lots of Room in It" in the April 1901 issue of the *Journal*, p. 15.

107. Ibid. p. 15.

108. Brooks. 1977, p. 197.

109. Twombly. p. 57, footnote 24.

110. This is a technique still in popular use when it is thought necessary to "sell" a new concept, especially when the new methodology would result in two additional housing units as this scheme does.

111. Manson unpublished notes. Oak Park Public Library in Oak Park, Illinois.

112. Johnson. 1977, p. 41.

113. Johnson. 1977, pp. 34, 149.

114. Park Dixon Goist. "Patrick Geddes and the City," *AIP Journal.* January 1974.

115. In the *Frank Lloyd Wright Newsletter* (Vol. 3, No. 1, 1st Quarter, 1980). A copy of a January 1901 letter announces the short-lived copartnership of Wright and Tomlinson; the letter was discovered by Narisco Menocal in 1979–1980.

116. Manson. Notes from 1940 interview with Mahony (Oak Park Public Library, Oak Park, IL).

117. Birrell. 1964, pp. 38–39.

118. The Husser House overlooked Lake Michigan. Thomas, Huertly, Tomek, Coonley, and Robie all were built on typical level prairie lots, but were raised to afford views of a peripheral environment. The Gilmore House was built on a hill, but was elevated to place the primary living space above the height of other houses and so afford unobstructed views of Lake Mendota.

119. Pfeiffer. 1992, p. 35. Wright's first reference to this design element was made four years earlier, in 1896, in an article prepared for a lecture he gave to the University Guild of Evanston, Illinois. He was describing his concepts for a "home," as opposed to a house, and described the porch as "that curse of the American home."

120. With similar foresight, Wright introduced an overhanging eave at the first-floor level to extend across the kitchen and sitting porch so that these spaces would benefit from natural light year-

round, but would not have solar penetration—minimizing overheating while cooking. Windows on the east end of the breakfast-dining bay and the sitting porch were placed to access the low angle rays of the early morning sun.

121. Vernon. 1991, p. 224.

122. Johnson. 1977, p. 36.

123. This description applies to the privacy wall as it was constructed; the plans delineate a privacy wall of unknown height encompassing the entire property, which may have been financially prohibitive.

124. Little House planting plans were used for reference by the landscape architect retained by the State of Illinois when the famed Dana-Thomas house and site were undergoing restoration during the 1980s.

125. Jack Lesniak. *Arthur Heurtley House: Frank Lloyd Wright, 1902* (Wright Plus, 1998).

126. See "Nathan G. Moore—Oak Park, Illinois (1895)."

127. Wright did not begin experimenting with the cantilevered roof extension until after his first trip to Japan in 1905, for A. P. Johnson (Delavan, Wisconsin, 1905) and F. F. Tomek (Riverside, Illinois, 1905–1906)

128. There originally were three rows of pierced brick, but photographs taken by the author in mid-1970s support that the openings in the lowest row had been filled in by that date.

129. Jack H. Prost. "Perceiving a Masterpiece: The Heurtley House," *The Frank Lloyd Wright Newsletter*, p. 4. Prost is an associate professor of biological sciences at the University of Illinois; he was the fourth owner of the house.

130. Grant Carpenter Manson. *Frank Lloyd Wright to 1910: The First Golden Age* (Reinhold, New York, 1958) pp. 124, 126.

131. Much of the historical background for the W. E. Martin House was obtained during a telephone interview with granddaughter Carolyn Mann Brackett (12/19/1996), from her letters of 1/13/1997 and 2/22/1997, and from correspondence with Susan Winifred Martin Penner (another granddaughter). The authors also are indebted to Laura Talaske, current owner-occupant.

132. Excerpts from 2/7/1903 letter from Winifred Martin to her husband, provided by granddaughter Carolyn M. Brackett.

133. Excerpts from letters of January 13 and February 22, 1997.

134. Carolyn Brackett said that her family lived in the Martin home for three or four years. Moreover, her mother (Lois Martin Mann) and father purchased a home in an adjacent suburb, enabling Carolyn and her sisters—Susan Mann Penner and Donna Mann Duncan–to continue to visit their grandparents for many years.

135. Historic photographs were provided by Carolyn M. Brackett and current owner-occupant Mrs. Richard Talaske, or were excerpted from 1911 version of *Wasmuth Portfolio* and the Gilmore Lake collection on file at the Oak Park Public Library, Oak Park, Illinois.

136. The authors are indebted to Mr. and Mrs. Richard Talaske for lending their print of this plan as reference support material.

137. Vernon. 1991, Footnote 11, p. 228.

138. Ibid. 1991. In a footnote, Vernon notes this recognition appeared only in a manuscript draft of Miller's writing, not in published format. "Apparently, Griffin objected to the phrase 'while in the employ of other men,' as Miller marked the passage 'rejected.' "

139. Brackett remembers Boch also "was a friend of Grandfather's." She explained: "All the Wright owners were acquainted. Mr. Winslow in River Forest was visited often, along with the Avery Coonley's in Riverside. . . . FLW spent many Sundays with them (her grandparents) listening to the Opera on records. His children considered it as much their home as the Martins and often pulled up in their pony cart to raid the kitchen. . . . Bernice was the first born and of the same age as Frances Wright. They were in school together and good friends for many years. . . . Winifred was a loyal friend of Catherine Wright."

140. Letter from Laura Talaske to author, dated January 22, 1997.

141. Wright. *A Testament* (Horizon Press, New York, 1957).

142. The dropped sections at the midpoint of the parapet walls on either side of the terrace are additional places for viewing the garden amenity; as these modifications do not appear on working drawings, they must have been added during construction.

143. Murray S. Haines, son of S. J. Haines and a second-generation architect, was chairman of the Planning

Commission during the late 1950s when the author served as the first executive director of the Springfield-Sangamon County Planning Commission.

144. Donald P. Hallmark. "Frank Lloyd Wright's Dana-Thomas House: Its History, Acquisition, and Preservation," *Illinois Historical Journal* (Vol. 82, No. 2, Summer 1989) p. 8. Hallmark is administrator of Dana-Thomas House State Historic Site.

145. According to September 1997 correspondence from Hallmark, the screened doors were replaced with glazed French doors during the 1940s to allow enclosure during inclement weather and assure year-round usability.

146. Terry L. Patterson, AIA. *Frank Lloyd Wright and the Meaning of Materials* (Van Nostrand Reinhold, 1994) p. 95. Note: see this publication for more insight into Wright's attention to detail in this area.

147. James Johnson. *Historic Structures Report, Dana-Thomas House.* (Used with permission of Hasbrouck/Hunderman, Architects. 1985) Plantings identification were excerpted from the landscape analysis prepared by landscape architect James Johnson of Moss, Johnson, Sandoval Associates, Ltd.

148. Heinrich Engel. *The Japanese House: A Tradition for Contemporary Architecture.* (Charles E. Tuttle Co., 1964) p. 254.

149. The authors are indebted to long-time friends Nora and Byron Peters for furnishing news clippings over a period of 10 or more years detailing the progress of the Dana House restoration.

150. Hallmark. 1990, p. 14.

151. Bock-Pierre. 1989, pp. 78–80.

152. Secrest. 1992, p. 182.

153. Wright. 1977, p. 217.

154. Lancaster. 1963, pp. 140–142. Japan also was allotted additional exhibition space in 10 other locations. These included another grouping of Japanese buildings in the amusement area, near the north entrance to the midway, that included two replicated Japanese gateways, a bazaar, and a Japanese theater in which anglicized Kabuki theater was performed.

155. Kenzo Tange. *Katsura: Tradition and Creation in Japanese Architecture* (Yale University Press, New Haven, Connecticut, 1972) p. 8.

156. Julie Moir Messervy. *The Inward Garden: Creating a Place of Beauty and Meaning* (Little, Brown & Co., Boston, New York, 1995) p. 164.

157. Engel. 1964, pp. 268, 275.

158. The design form of the D. D. Martin pergola allies more with the definition for an "arcade." An arcade is "any covered passageway," whereas a pergola is "an arbor made of a trellis supported by posts, for training vines or other plants." Wright used the terms "pergola" and "arcade" interchangeably—regardless of function or manner of construction—as he interchanged the words "veranda," "terrace," and "porch."

159. Bruce Brooks Pfeiffer. *Letters to Clients: Frank Lloyd Wright* (California State University Press, Fresno, California, 1986) p. 11.

160. Ibid. 1986, p. 13.

161. Ibid. 1986, p. 9.

162. This preliminary site plan does not bear a date, but it clearly identifies Wright's thought process as to site layout and appears to be in Wright's hand, which would indicate that it was prepared prior to construction during 1904.

163. That Wright was sensitive to both aesthetic and environmental considerations of heating and ventilating the D. D. Martin house is supported by the manner in which he addressed these environmental considerations in the freestanding groups of brick piers, which he identified as "sun traps" in July 1904 correspondence and detailed in his Wasmuth text.

164. The Wasmuth plan omits the direct axial sight line established by Axis "E" that extends out into the unlabeled 12′ × 100′ panel and the grounds environment. It instead shows an offset rectangular "garden," shifted to the east so the axis aligns with the west edge of the garden.

165. Martha Neri's insightful comments were in response to a number of specific questions raised by the authors during August and November 1995. The authors also studied the plans-of-record on file at the University at Buffalo Archives, SUNY, provided on microfilm to the University of Georgia through interlibrary loan.

166. Engel. 1964, p. 262.

167. Pfeiffer. 1986, pp. 13–14.

168. Neri. Letter, dated August 29, 1991.

169. Excerpt from the 1905 "New Plan of Floral Arrangement" credited to Frank Lloyd Wright, Architect; Oak Park, Illinois.

170. Within plans-of-record on microfilm at the University at Buffalo Archives, SUNY, there is one

more planting plan signed by Walter Burley Griffin dated October 15, 1910. As this date coincides with the period when Wright was in Europe and Griffin was working on the W. E. Martin garden addition, it is presumed that Darwin Martin and Griffin reestablished some sort of working relationship to revise some planting details.

171. Brooks. 1972, p. 81.

172. The west window wall was set apart and privatized with deep piers, window mullions, and a large planter—in the manner of the library and dining room window walls of the Darwin Martin House.

173. It was Griffin's extensive personal involvement with the Ullman Project, coupled with the fact that it never reached the stage of execution, that bore upon Griffin's subsequent departure from The Studio following Wright's return from Japan in late May.

174. Wright. 1977, pp. 218–219.

175. Horiguchi Sutami. *Tradition of Japanese Gardens* (Second edition, East West Center Press, Tokyo, 1963) pp. 9–10.

176. Wright. 1977, pp. 218–219. Auther Charlie Aguar first saw Japan from a B-29 as a 19-year-old. His description of this viewpoint in his first uncensored (September, 1945) letter to me sounds surprisingly like Wright: "That's the most beautiful country I've ever flown over. . . . It was even prettier than California. . . . The coast lines were very rugged and with beautiful coral formations. . . . Every bit of the land is cultivated . . . not in squares like in the U.S. but in irregular curving patterns all over. They live everywhere—on all the mountain sides and everywhere. . . . Most of the farmland is flooded with water but you can only see it when the sun reflects a certain way because it all looks green. Everything really looked neat and clean—I guess I was surprised."

177. Teiji Itoh. *Space and Illusion in the Japanese Garden* (Weatherhill/Tankosha, New York, Tokyo, & Kyoto, 1973) p. 50.

178. Ibid. 1973, pp. 15–18.

179. Horiguchi. p. 16. Unfortunately, the large sheltered veranda-like balcony has been glazed, significantly compromising Wright's original intent as to indoor-outdoor connectedness.

180. Wright also would use rough-sawn, dark-stained, horizontal board-and-batten for Millard I, the Cheney garage, Mrs. Gale's Summer Cottage, and other cottages.

181. Wright. 1977, p. 219.

182. Pregliasco. pp. 167–169. While it is true this artwork was completed by Mahony, the concept was in all likelihood originally sketched out by Wright. The Japanese magnolia bloom seems inappropriate for a Wisconsin site, but its location in midair is a Japanese technique frequently used by Mahony to obtain a feeling of three dimensions. It should be noted that Wright's consideration of the site environment as detailed on the ground plan in the Wasmuth Portfolio proposes an unfortunate use of the slope and beach below in the form of a symmetrical pair of pathlike stairways leading from both sides of the rear terrace, then crossing over on a diagonal line to intersect midway down the steep slope before proceeding to a formalized pool to be built upon the rocky beach of Lake Michigan. Although there is no indication there ever was any attempt to execute an impractical design such as this—which would cause serious environmental impact on such an erosion-sensitive site—the layout is significant because it exhibits Wright's continued reliance upon geometric artificiality.

183. Morse. pp. 9, 50, 51.

184. Nute. 1993, pp. 59–60. Nute also likens the cruciform-like parti of the Hardy House to the Ho-o-den.

185. Kruty. 1996, p. 20. It seems that Griffin's parents and the Ullmans knew each other socially.

186. Brooks. 1972, p. 81.

187. Pfeiffer. 1992, p. 66. Also, Pierre-Bock. 1989, p. 89.

188. Brooks. 1972, pp. 81–82.

189. Observations made by Maya Moran during an interview conducted by the author on September 3, 1990.

190. Itoh. 1969, p. 158.

191. Maya Moran. *Down to Earth: An Insider's View of Frank Lloyd Wright's Tomek House.* (Southern Illinois University Press, 1995) p. 87.

192. Perhaps it was for this reason that Wright at some point erased the doorway and centered entryway from the original colored perspective, left the garden privacy wall in place, and sketched in a new walkway leading directly to an opening in the wall. Wright sometimes would change the archival drawings to reflect his retrospective thinking as to what should have been.

193. Moran. 1995, pp. 75, 83–84.

194. James Alexander Robinson. 1989. pp. 17–19. (The authors wish to thank William Majewski, a city planner and longtime friend, who introduced us to this manuscript.) Wright met Robinson when he appeared as guest speaker for the University of Illinois Architectural Club; he had been invited by Robinson in his capacity as club president. Robinson accepted the position with Wright, after declining the offer of a teaching position at the University of Texas Department of Architecture.

195. Walter L. Creese. *The Crowning of the American Landscape: Eight Great Spaces and Their Buildings.* (Princeton University Press, Princeton, New Jersey, 1985) p. 252.

196. Wright. See text for "A Fireproof House for $5,000" in the April 1907 issue of the *Ladies Home Journal.* The function of the flat roof as a "space expander" requires interpretation, as it was not referenced by Wright. By extending the overhang over the top of the bands of the casement windows, Wright caused the second-floor ceiling to appear to continue on outside the structure, creating a direct association with the out-of-doors and at the same time perceptively enlarging the modest size of the bedrooms.

197. The Lamp residence appears to be the precursor of several variations leading to the perfection of the Fireproof House. Its corner piers and other external massing, as well as signature diamond hearth and wraparound brick terrace, suggest Griffin was responsible for more than its "drafting" for which he is usually credited. In *Walter Burley Griffin in America*, Mati Maldee illustrates the Lamp House as one of two under "Griffin's Work in the Office of Frank Lloyd Wright" (University of Illinois Press, 1996). p. 160.

198. There is some speculation that the Gale House was designed as early as 1904 and not constructed until 1907–1908. Based on the cantilevered roofs and other environmental design aspects, however, it is more analogous to houses designed after Wright's 1904 trip to Japan.

199. While Wright did not install a water table with the Gale House, he emphasized the baseline of the house with a dark-hued wood facing that contrasted with the cream color of the stucco.

200. From transcripts of videotaped oral history conducted by author on September 6, 1990, and a telephone interview of April 7, 1999. In addition to designing and supervising the modernization and restoration of the Ingalls House for their personal use, Tilton served as restoration architect for the Hills-Decaro House in Oak Park, IL, and the Meyer May House in Grand Rapids, MI.

201. Excerpts from interview conducted by author in September 1990.

202. Ibid. This was the only error in judgement, and it is the same one being made by other Wright homeowners—that is, replacing the overgrown foundation Junipers with new evergreen shrubs, which ultimately will again hide the water table and violate Wright's strong committment to exposing the point where the structure meets the ground.

203. This initial conceptual drawing shows that two large structures on the northern and central portions of the property were on the site originally, both of which were razed before the Wright-designed complex could be built.

204. Messervy. 1995, p. 38.

205. Turek. 1991, p. 157.

206. Research conducted by Robert E. Grese during the 1990s confirms that Jensen worked on various landscape plans for the Coonley commission. Sources listed include the Jensen Collections, Morton Arboretum, Lisele, Illinois, and Art and Architecture Library, University of Michigan.

207. Eaton. 1964, p. 109. Also, Turerk. p. 145.

208. Historic letters-of-record between Jensen and Wright were sourced from the Frank Lloyd Wright Archives housed at the Getty Researh Institute for the History of Art and the Humanities in Los Angeles, California.

209. Eaton. 1964, p. 109.

210. Transcript from videotaped oral history interview conducted by the author on September 5, 1990. James W. Howlett (deceased December, 2000) was a photographer and advertising art specialist; Carolyn S. Howlett is a professor emeritus, Art Institute of Chicago.

211. Stephen Siek. "Frank Lloyd Wright's Westcott House in Springfield," in *Ohio History* (Vol. 87, No. 3, 1978) p. 289. Historical background in his article is based upon personal interviews with Mrs. John Westcott, daughter-in-law to Burton and Orpha Westcott, and with William Hicks, who worked as an electrician during construction under William Poole, the contractor.

212. Siek, 1978, pp. 288–289.

213. Ibid. 1978, p. 291.

214. Ibid. 1978, pp. 289, 292. There also was a clay tennis court that was dug up and replaced by a "Victory Garden" during World War I. According to family members, "At the rear of the house in the northwest corner was a 125-barrel cistern which collected the rain water trapped by four basic receptacles at each corner of the house, these being ultimately fed by Wright's carefully concealed downspouting in the roofing and wall structures. This water was in turn used for bathing, fed into Wright's large distinctive tubs by a third spigot . . . that tended to resemble a miniature waterfall when in use."

215. Excerpt from undated letter Seik received during his original research on the Westcott property.

216. The author wishes to thank friends June and Wayne Severance for sending the *Montana Standard* article in time for this reference to be included prior to publication.

217. All Chicago architects were familiar with building massive structures on the spongy soils close to Lake Michigan. They used The Chicago Foundation System developed by Frederick Baumann in 1873 for isolating piers to provide adequate bearing capacity.

218. Donald Hoffman. *Frank Lloyd Wright's Robie House* (Dover Publications, New York, 1984) p. 17, Footnote 21.

219. Ibid. 1984, p. 17.

220. Ibid. 1984, p. 57. Robie's son was remembering these experiences more than 50 years after moving from the house.

221. A large historic marker erected in the space of the built-in north wall planter nearest the sidewalk secretes what Wright had intended to be a discreet element of mystery within the entry experiences and also compromises a formerly excellent angle of "photo opportunity."

222. Grant Hildebrand. *The Wright Space: Pattern and Meaning in Frank Lloyd Wright Houses* (University of Washington Press, Seattle, 1991) p. 53.

223. John Ormsbee Simonds. *Earthscape: A Manual of Environmental Planning* (McGraw-Hill, New York, 1979) pp. 125–126.

224. For more detail on Wright's detailing of ventilation, see: Donald Hoffman. *Frank Lloyd Wright's Robie House.* pp. 32, 77, 78.

225. Engel. 1964, p. 258.

226. Jean Louis Guarino. "Robie House Restoration Planned," *The Quarterly Newsletter* of the Frank Lloyd Wright Building Conservancy (Vol. 6., Issue 2, Summer 1997) pp. 8–9. Hopefully, restoration planting will be included in this process, so replacement trees will be firmly established whenever in the future existing trees deteriorate and must be removed.

227. Pfeiffer. *Collected Writings,* (Vol. 5, 1995).

228. The porch on the west end of the house would benefit from prevailing breezes, but it has been enclosed.

229. It should be noted that there is absolutely no basis for the rumored suggestion put forth in some publications that Jens Jensen designed the landscape plans for the Isabel Roberts' property.

230. Van Bergen's comments made during a February 19, 1940 interview with Grant Manson. (Oak Park Public Library, Oak Park, Illinois).

231. Since no pre-1913 BRVICo correspondence seems to exist, much of the background for the Bitterroot River Valley projects cited herein was excerpted from Montana Historical Society (MHS) records and undated newspaper articles furnished in 1995 by then-director Lawrence C. Sommer. Of particular interest were writings by Donald Leslie Johnson in 1987 and 1990. Johnson was a history professor at The Flinders University of South Australia in Bedford Park when he conducted the first in-depth study of Bitter Root in preparation for writing his manuscript, *Frank Lloyd Wright versus America: The 1930s* (MIT Press, 1990).

232. It has added to the confusion of Wright's work in the Bitterroot Valley that archival numbers in the Frank Lloyd Wright job files have been assigned to "Como Orchard Summer Colony," "Bitter Root Town Project," and "Bitter Root Inn," but no archival number has been assigned for "Village of Bitter Root Plan," for which the Bitter Root Inn was designed. It is equally misleading that the project listed as "Como Orchard Summer Colony" is known locally and identified on USGS maps as "University Heights."

233. It was because of a chance observation by landscape architect Robinson Fisher that authors sought out the 1905 report on the preliminary plan prepared by Burnham. The resemblance to Boguio was immediately remarked upon by Fisher when he was shown the Como Orchard-University

Heights site plan and bird's-eye perspective. Fisher with his wife Barbara, who also is a landscape architect, visited Baguio in the early 1990s while in the Philippines consulting on developmental problems for the World Bank.

234. Wright had known Daniel Burnham since the mid-1890s. At that time, Burnham and real estate speculator Edward Carson Waller—a longtime patron of Wright—had offered to take care of Kitty and their children while paying all his expenses for six years' study in Paris and Rome. And Wright was guaranteed a position with Burnham's prestigious firm when he returned. Waller first commissioned Wright in 1895, to design the Edward C. Waller Apartments and the Francisco Terrace Apartments ("a solution of the low cost housing problem"). In 1905, he would commission Wright to remodel the lobby of the Rookery (a Burnham-designed 1886 skyscraper). He also sponsored several of Wright's unbuilt projects, including a residence (1893), two summer houses (1902–1902), the Wolf Lake Amusement Park (1895), and the Cheltenham Beach Amusement Center (1899).

235. Donald Leslie Johnson. 1987, pp. 19–20. Source: Nichols, "The Bitter Root." March 1910. p. 23.

236. Lawrence Summers (MHS) Source: October 1, 1909 article in the Stevensville (MN) *Northwest Tribune*, wherein it notes that promotional literature would not have been developed before mid-1909, at least, because the Big Ditch would not have been extended close enough to this area much before 1910.

237. Ibid. 1987, p. 22.

238. Burnham. Plan of Baguo, Luzon, Phillipine Islands. 1905. pp. 197, 201.

239. Ibid. 1905, pp. 197, 201.

240. Ibid. 1905, pp. 198–199.

241. Ibid. 1905, p. 199.

242. Manson notes, Oak Park Public Library, Oak Park, Illinois.

243. John Lloyd Wright. *My Father Who Is On Earth.* p. 40.

244. Bruce Brooks Pfeiffer. *Frank Lloyd Wright: His Living Voice.* (California State University Press/FLIW Foundation, 1987) pp. 145–146.

245. Ibid. 1987, pp. 103–104.

246. Ibid. 1987, pp. 149–150.

247. Newton. p. 59. For readers interested in details on the Villa Medici, see John and Ray Oldham: *Gardens in Time* (1980) pp. 144–152. For 12 weeks during summer quarter 1981, the author taught classes in landscape design to senior students of architecture and 4th or 5th-year senior students of landscape architecture under the auspices of the UGA Studies Abroad Program, based in Cortona, Italy. The class toured and studied the Villa Medici (still privately owned and occupied), the Baroque gardens of Isola Bella on Lake Maggiore, Villa Garzoni at Collodi, Villa Lante at Bognaia, and several villas around Rome—including the remarkable water gardens of the Villa d'Este at Tivoli. Compared to these and others, the Villa Medici seemed very small and conservative. We did not become experts on the Italian villa but were guided and taught by local Italian artisans, leading designers, architects, and landscape architects. Three trips to Fiesole included one guided by the late Pietro Porcinai, a renowned landscape architect whose studio-villa adjoined the Villa Medici and elicited comparable views of Florence.

248. Wright. 1977, p. 218.

249. Pfeiffer. 1984, pp. 145–146.

250. Ibid. 1984, pp. 148–152.

251. Chicago newspaper reporters learned that Wright was advertising his former home for rental property, which ended Wright's thinly veiled subterfuge and perhaps precipitated his move to Taliesin sooner than intended.

252. A stairway provided access to the loft that later would be finished as an apartment for additional rental revenue.

253. The committee from which the Foundation emanated began negotiating for the purchase even earlier, when the site was announced for sale in 1972.

254. There is no site inventory and analysis of record in existence. This conjectural study incorporates many of the elements that would have had to be given consideration.

255. H. W. S. Cleveland was Chicago's earliest resident landscape architect, moving his office to the city in 1869. His partner was William M. R. French, a civil engineer and garden designer who founded and was the first director of the Art Institute of Chicago.

256. The authors are indebted to architectural historian Susan Solway for bringing to our attention Booth's park development interests and his official capacity with the Glencoe Park District. Dr. Solway and

her husband have owned and restored two Wright-designed buildings: the Lute F. Kissam residence in Ravine Bluffs, where they lived from 1978 to 1986, and the Edmund F. Brigham residence in Glencoe, where they have lived since 1986.

257. Jens Jensen. "Report of the Landscape Architect," Part 6 of the 1904 *Report of the Special Park Commission*, compiled by Dwight Perkins (City of Chicago, Hartman Company Printers and Binding, 1905) p. 80.

258. Ibid. 1905, pp. 65–67. Also, Figure 19, p. 66. A considerable portion of the open space proposed in the 1904 plan still exists as protected open space. The famed Cook County Forest Preserve championed by Jensen includes the Skokie Lagoons, with the portion converted to the Chicago Botanical Gardens only 1.5 miles to the southwest of the Booth property. The Lake Shore Country Club designed by Jensen in 1929 is immediately to the north, and the Glencoe Golf Club is 1 mile to the west; both properties are in the area of proposed open space preservation.

259. Anthony Alofsin. *Frank Lloyd Wright—The Lost Years, 1910–1922* (University of Chicago Press, Chicago, Illinois, 1993) p. 308.

260. The most important reasons for a site inventory and analysis are to locate the optimum site for the footprint of the main building and to lay out the main access road—not a minor consideration with this site. There would need to be topographic and soils studies, a tree survey, and a strong awareness of climatic factors that affect natural lighting, aesthetics, and living comfort—that is, prevailing summer and winter winds, natural vegetation, most advantageous sight lines, the arc of the sun, and the direction of the sunrise and sunset (both at the beginning of summer or winter and at the vernal or autumnal equinox).

261. Excerpt from October 18, 1912 letter from Jensen to Wright, written on his letterhead with a Steinway Hall address. (The Getty Research Institute, repository for the Frank Lloyd Wright Foundation—hereinafter referenced as "GRI/FLIW").

262. The exhibit sponsored by The Museum of Modern Art in 1994 attributed the "landscape plan" for the Sherman Booth property as if Jens Jensen was a draftsman. Moreover, Jensen's name is omitted from the text of the 344-page book-sized catalogue *Frank Lloyd Wright Architect*, edited by Terence Riley with Peter Reed, except as a parenthetic reference, which they explain is used to denote a "delineator." Furthermore, Bruce Brooks Pfeiffer's text in *Frank Lloyd Wright Monograph, 1907–1913*, Volume 3 includes a greatly reduced, generally illegible drawing identified as "Plot Plan" for the Sherman Booth Project, but does not assign credit and makes no mention of Jensen's signature or of his overall design of the property as both an estate and a park.

263. None of these processes could have been accomplished by Wright without having years of experience, such as Jensen possessed. To acquire this type of professional expertise in modern-day America requires completion of five years' study for a bachelor's degree and working several years as an intern. All this is required before anyone qualifies to even apply for the opportunity to take—and pass—a two-day examination to meet the requirements for being licensed by the state.

264. These gateways—one labeled "park ornament" in Wright's hand—are featured in *Frank Lloyd Wright Monograph, 1907–1913*, Vol. 3, edited and photographed by Yukio Futagawa with text by Bruce Brooks Pfeiffer (A.D.A. EDITA Tokyo, 1984) Plate 353, p. 180.

265. Eaton. 1964, p. 39.

266. Grese. 1992, p. 79.

267. Ibid. 1992, p. 82.

268. Eaton. 1964, p. 40.

269. Grese Caption under photographic insert; unpaged.

270. Alofsin. 1993, p. 308.

271. Brooks E. Wigginton, Landscape Architect. *Japanese Gardens*. (Marietta College, 1963) p. 13.

272. Peter Harper with Chris Madsen and Jeremy Light. *The Natural Garden Book: A Holistic Approach to Gardening* (Simon & Schuster, Inc., New York/London/Toronto/Sydney/Tokyo/Singapore, 1994) p. 54.

273. Wright. 1977, p. 191.

274. Ibid. 1977, pp. 159.

275. Anne Whiston Spirn. "Frank Lloyd Wright: Architect of Landscape," *Frank Lloyd Wright: Designs for an American Landscape, 1922–1932*. (Canadian Centre for Architecture, Montreal/Henry N. Adams, Inc., New York, 1996) p. 162, footnote 22.

276. Wright. 1977, pp. 192–195.

277. Wright oriented most of his houses to have no "dark side." It would not be until more than 50 years later in *The Natural House* (1954, p. 154) that Wright would explain his reasoning: "Ordinarily, the house should be set 30–60° to the south." In actuality, 20–30° east of south is most ideal in the latitude where most of Wright's houses were built.

278. Wright. 1977, p. 195.

279. Teiji Itoh. 1969, pp. 98, 110. On page 70, Itoh explains that sukiya architecture evolved from the original sukiya teahouse where the tea masters applied the principle of *sakui*, which was always controlled by "the important concepts of *wabi* and *sabi*. These terms, though difficult to define in any precise way, may be taken to mean something like 'rustic simplicity' and . . . 'patina of age.' In a word, creative originality was to be expressed within the limits of the rustically simple and the attractively antique."

280. Ibid. 1969, pp. 80, 95, 98.

281. The later addition of double-door vestibule entries for both the studio and living quarters would suggest that Wright did not plan as thoughtfully for maximum protection of points of outdoor-indoor transition from exposure to winter winds.

282. Donald Elmer and Fuller Moore, researchers. "Passive Cooling: Designing Natural Solutions to Summer Cooling Loads," *Research & Design: The Quarterly of the AIA Research Corporation*, (Vol. 11, No 3, Fall 1979) pp. 5–9. Research has shown that "when a body of water is placed in a hot and relatively dry space, the water evaporates into the air and increases humidity. In the process it turns sensible heat into latent heat, literally lowering the temperature of the air at a rate equivalent to 1,000 BTUs for every pound of water added to the air."

283. Many of these same techniques were used by Thomas Jefferson in his design for Monticello (circa 1805). Moreover, if any of the transom windows in the original belvedere above the Taliesin living room and kitchen were opened, the convection that would have been created would have provided additional cooling by drawing in shaded air from the breezeway through ceiling vents installed for that purpose.

284. Itoh. 1969. p. 83. By "technique," Itoh is referring to the basic, non-load-bearing method of sukiya construction.

285. John Ormsbee Simonds. *Landscape Architecture: A Manual of Site Planning and Design* (McGraw-Hill, Inc., New York City, 1983) p. 238. Simonds describes this visionary design concept as follows: "Each structure, aside from its primary function as a building, has many secondary functions in relation to the assemblage. The buildings as units are arranged to shape and define exterior volumes in the best way possible . . . to develop closed or semi-enclosed spaces that best express and accommodate their function, that best reveal the structural form, facade, or other features of the surrounding structures, and that best relate the group as a whole to the total extensional landscape."

286. The pond in 1912 was small and very oriental in its free form and intimate relationship with the creek, so that it more closely captured the essence of the Japanese water garden than the constructed pond seen today.

287. The Italian-like garden tillage did not prove feasible for this space, due to erosion, and trees were reintroduced into this area over time, although the underground cisterns remained in place.

288. Excerpt from 10/18/1912 letter from Jensen to Wright, written on his letterhead with a Steinway Hall address. (GRI/FLIW).

289. Jean D. France, an adjunct professor of art at the University of Rochester in New York, discovered the correspondence between Wright and Jensen and the nursery while going through the collection of Ellwanger and Barry/Mount Hope Nurseries housed at the University of Rochester. The authors are indebted to Dixie Legler with the Frank Lloyd Wright Foundation who enclosed a copy of an "in house" newsletter containing this information with her correspondence dated June 26, 1997.

290. David H. Engel. *Japanese Gardens for Today* (Charles E. Tuttle Company, Rutland, Vermont/Tokyo, Japan, 1959) p. 21.

291. Teiji Itoh. *The Japanese Garden: An Approach to Nature* (Yale University Press, New Haven/London, 1972) pp. 181–183.

292. Lorraine E. Kuck. *The Art of Japanese Gardens* (The John Day Company, New York, 1940) p. 191.

293. Itoh. 1973, p. 84. The space where the water basin once was has been filled in with soil and is being used as a planter.

294. Ibid. 1973, p. 83. The plaster cast of *A Flower in the Crannied Wall* was placed at different loca-

tions over time, including atop a pier at the entry gateway.

295. Alfred B. Yeomans, ed. *City Residential Land Development: Studies in Planning* (University of Chicago Press, Chicago, Illinois, 1916) p. 1.

296. Ibid. 1916, pp. 1–2.

297. Ibid. 1916, p. 111.

298. Pfeiffer. 1987, p. 145.

299. Overlays of street and open-space systems were prepared to help interpret the complexity of Wright's design.

300. Wright. 1977, p. 202.

301. Simonds. 1983, pp. 251–252.

302. Wright. 1977, pp. 202, 203.

303. There is no reason to assume that Wright had authority to make recommendations for the entire block; this was likely speculation on his part. However, by providing for competing uses in this way, Wright anticipated the technique of future shopping centers.

304. The winter garden restaurant, club room, and tavern were the only spaces enclosed during inclement weather.

305. Wright. 1977, p. 208.

306. Twombly. 1979, p. 121.

307. Paul Kruty. *Frank Lloyd Wright and Midway Gardens* (University of Illinois Press, Urbana and Chicago, 1998), pp. 52–59.

308. Wright. 1977, p. 209.

309. Robinson. 1989, pp. 22–23. Also, Yeomans. p. 23. The Griffins proposed that Robinson set up a joint practice with them in Australia while they concentrated on design details for Griffin's award-winning design for the new capital city of Canberra.

310. Carla Lind. *Lost Wright.* Architectural historian Susan Solway states that the station was in use until the 1950s when the electric commuter service was discontinued; the easement space has been converted into a bike trail.

311. As pointed out by Terry L. Patterson in *Frank Lloyd Wright and the Meaning of Materials* (Van Nostrand Reinhold, New York, 1994, p. 92), the Allen House represents Wright's last use of brick for a period of 16 years.

312. Wright used the same technique of uniform placement of narrow brick masses in the F. C. Bogk house, built that same year in Milwaukee, Wisconsin, and in similar structures he designed while in Japan.

313. Teiji Itoh. 1969, p. 80. This measurement has been the Japanese module for all elements of interior and exterior structural and spatial arrangement since the seventeenth century.

314. Messervy. 1995, p. 164.

315. As the garden house provides a diagonal counterbalance to the dominance of the architecture, originally left open as outdoor living space and roofed to introduce a sense of human scale into the openness of the courtyard, it allies with the semidetached garden pavilions Wright designed for Winslow, Fricke, and Glasner.

316. Henry J. Allen. Historical correspondence. (GRI/FLIW).

317. Howard W. Ellington/Allen-Lambe House Foundation. Excerpts from August 1997 correspondence.

318. Allen historical correspondence. (GRI/FLIW) According to Ellington, Don Schuler was a young architect originally from Wichita who functioned as Wright's initial field rep on the Allen House. Allen misspelled his name in this correspondence.

319. Alofsin. 1993. Chronology, p. 310.

320. Ibid. Note: The underlinings of "Allen" are as delineated by the correspondent (Ellington).

321. Ellington. Excerpts from communications of April 30, 1998 and November 12, 2001.

322. Allen. FLIW Archives, Getty Center, Los Angeles, California.

323. Ellington. August 1997 and April 1980 correspondence.

324. The Allen-Lambe House Foundation is named after the original owners and in memory of Claude and Polly Lambe whose foundation, the Claude R. Lambe Charitable Foundation, provided a grant for the purchase of the house and a substantial contribution toward restoration costs. (1997 Newsletter) Excerpted from History/Mission Statement.

325. Antonin Raymond. 1973, p. 46.

326. There was an earlier California project credited to Wright for the George C. Stewart house in Montecito, designed between 1906 and 1909, built by 1911; but there is no record of his having visited the site. Other of Wright's children also had lived and worked in southern California. David had traveled there with Lloyd in 1911, and John was working for San Diego architect Harrison Albright and sharing a house with Lloyd at the time Wright asked him to work on Midway Gardens in 1913.

Segrest wrote that Wright's daughter also had written to tell him he ought to come west to take advantage of the development boom of that period.

327. Wright. 1977, p. 263. Wright further observed: "the Italo-Spanish buildings of the early missionaries' own 'back-home' had just happened to be more in keeping with California" because "this Southern type of building had already given shelter from a sun that could blister the indiscreet in Spain or Mexico just as it was now able to do in Southern California."

328. Ibid. 1977, pp. 262–264.

329. Raymond. 1973, p. 53.

330. Wright. 1977, p. 249.

331. Grolier Electronic Publishing, Inc. The climate of Los Angeles is Mediterranean. Annual precipitation averages 12 inches. Temperatures range from a July mean maximum of 73°F. to a January mean maximum of 56°F.

332. Pfeiffer. 1992, "A Philosophy of Fine Art." p. 43.

333. The late Calvin C. Straub was a noted professor of architecture who served on the faculty at the University of Southern California and the University of Arizona. These quotations were excerpted from the "preliminary edition" of an unpublished manuscript sent to the author for review in 1983 (pp. 16, 32) and are used with the consent of Straub's daughter, Christin Straub.

334. Ibid. p. 67.

335. Ibid. p. 34.

336. Kathryn Smith. *Frank Lloyd Wright, Hollyhock House and Olive Hill.* (Rizzoli, New York, 1992) p. 217, Chapter 5, footnote 4: 'Eminence to Be Made Rare Beauty Spot,' *Los Angeles Examiner.* July 6, 1919."

337. Ibid. p. 217. July 6, 1919 article in *Los Angeles Examiner.*

338. Gayther L. Plummer, emeritus climatologist for the State of Georgia. Observations made on March 3, 1998 were based upon personal knowledge and as referenced from *The Weather Book,* by Jack Williams (Vintaga, *USA Today,* April 1992).

339. Gebhard and Von Breton. 1971. pp. 19–23. Lloyd by this time was a professional designer in his own right. He began working on architectural drawings under his father's direction at the age of nine and had completed two years of architectural training at the University of Wisconsin before joining his father in Italy to work on the drawings for the Wasmuth Portfolio (1909–1910). Lloyd's understanding of organic form was further developed and articulated by his self-study of developed landscapes and his work as a landscape draftsman-designer—first for Olmsted and Olmsted in Boston and California and then in his own partnership with Paul Thiene and/or under the direction of architects Irving Gill or William J. Dodd. Lloyd also had been socially interactive with Barnsdall since 1917 when he was introduced to the Aline Barnsdall circle and married the actress Elaine Hyman (stage name of Kira Markham), so the client most probably would have felt more comfortable with Lloyd as Wright's liaison than anyone else he could have chosen for this task.

340. An October 16, 1917 letter to Wright's client Mr. S. M. B. Hunt in Oshkosh, Wisconsin—found in the Frank Lloyd Wright Home and Studio Archives and furnished to the authors by Meg Klinkow—verifies that Lloyd was working with his father as a landscape designer at this point in time.

341. The inappropriate "promenade" labeling for these steps on the plan seems to be a carryover from prior to site selection.

342. This retaining wall serves the same function as the one demarcating the boundary of the Hillside Garden at Taliesin, but is some three times higher and more noticeable and/or intrusive within the context of the entry experience.

343. Historic ground and aerial photographs document that the pine grove with eucalyptus border was installed as designed. Gebhard and Von Breton (1971, p. 23) correlate this design layout to the landscape design Lloyd originated earlier in his partnership with Paul Thiene. Both Lloyd and Paul Thiene worked for Olmsted and Olmsted in 1911 and set up a partnership in landscape design for approximately one year, before going their separate ways.

344. Wright. 1977, p. 262.

345. Smith. 1992, pp. 83 and 218, footnotes 22, 23. The date on the plan for the pine-eucalyptus grove was 1/27/1920. Groundbreaking for the house was April 28, 1920.

346. The man-made lake was not a presence in Wright's original sketch on the 1919 topographic layout.

347. Charles E. Aguar. "City Planning Lecture Notes," School of Environmental Design, University of Georgia. (Unpublished, 1975–1980).

348. Smith. 1992, p. 165. (f. 6, p. 221.)

349. Wright. 1977, p. 258.

350. Johnson. p. 56.

351. Gebhard and Von Breton. 1971, p. 34.

352. Wright's earliest communication that he was considering such a move was through his October 5, 1922 letter to Lloyd. (Frank Lloyd Wright Foundation).

353. G. Gordon Whitnall, "Regional Planning Progress in the Los Angeles District," *The American City Magazine*, (29, December 1923) pp. 578–579.

354. At the same time a business address was maintained at the Hollywood location; however, Wright—true to form—also continued to travel back and forth to, and work from, Taliesin. As he explained: "I have never had an 'office' in the conventional manner. . . . There was never organization in the sense that the usual architect's office knows organization. Nor any great need of it so long as I stood actually at the center of the effort. Where I am, there my office is: my office is me." Wright. 1977. p. 260.

355. Kohler, Wisconsin was a model industrial town laid out by Werner Hegermann and Elbert Peets. Kingsport Tennessee was another model industrial town, designed by John Nolen. Palos Verdes Estates was a satellite of Los Angles, designed by the Olmsted Brothers—under whom Lloyd Wright apprenticed. The perhaps more well known planned communities that would develop in ensuing years were Venice, Florida (1926), Chicopee, Georgia (1927), and Radburn, New Jersey (1928).

356. It should be noted that Kevin Lynch—a former Wright apprentice who became a professor of urban studies and planning at MIT—used this first rough diagram of the Barnsdall Beverly Hills Project site layout in his book *Site Planning* Third edition, (MIT Press, Cambridge, Massachusetts, 1984) p. 140, f. 41) to illustrate how Wright organized building and site as one entity. Note: sketch is incorrectly identified as Coonley House.

357. This was an extension of parapet for the staircase leading from the entrance court to the terrace bay viewing platform built into wall of ravine.

358. Smith. 1992, p. 169. (p. 222, f. 24. "Will Build in Beverly Hills." *Holly Leaves* (Vol. 12, No. 20, May 18, 1923: 28).

359. Wright. 1977, p. 276.

360. Wright. 1977, p. 275. Also, De Long. 1996. p. 17. (1923 statistic).

361. Ibid. 1977, pp. 257, 265.

362. Ibid. 1977, p. 268.

363. Ibid. 1977, p. 268.

364. *Webster's New Students Dictionary.* (American Book Company, 1969) p. 46.

365. Wright. 1977, p. 273.

366. Simonds. 1983, p. 88.

367. Ortho Books. "Harnessing the wind," *Weather-Wise Gardening.* (Chevron Chemical Company, 1974) p. 43.

368. Wright. 1977, p. 275. It should be noted that the cultivation of a manicured lawn—such as existed when the author visited La Miniatura in 1992—detracts from the illusion of Wright's intent of a house being "lost" in, or enveloped by, nature.

369. Historic preservation officials for the city during the time of our search (1992–1995) were unable to locate evidence that Ms. Deusner worked with Wright, although they found records of work she did with other architects.

370. Gebhard and Von Breton. 1971, p. 27. Lloyd recalled that his father "was trying very hard to get started on the West Coast, and he had all kinds of projects going out here, but somehow he could not get the people to play ball with him. He spent considerable time with the Chandlers and General Sherman trying to interest them in his architectural schemes—they were very amused and entertained by F. L. W., but were unreceptive."

371. Frank Lloyd Wright. Excerpt from "In the Cause of Architecture," *The Architectural Record* (March 1908) p. 94.

372. Robert L. Sweeney. *Wright in Hollywood: Visions of a New Architecture* (MIT Press, 1994) p. 67.

373. This sunken garden was converted into a swimming pool by architect Eric Lloyd Wright (Lloyd's son) during the restoration-remodeling of the 1980s after the property had been purchased by Joel Silver.

374. The awnings on the east end had no function other than to counter-balance the functional awnings directly opposite.

375. Sweeney. 1994, pp. 67–68. "On June 7 [1935] the owners of three lots directly above the Storer house filed suit, charging that the Druffels [5th owners of the property] had allowed eucalyptus trees growing on their property and on the boundary line between the properties to grow to such a height that views and light were obstructed and

that the plaintiffs' property consequently had depreciated in value." The trees were topped off then and at other times in future years.

376. It is important to note he would not have been allowed to site and/or build the Freeman House as he did on this particular piece of property, had he been presented with this same challenge even a few years later. The Los Angeles County Regional Planning Commission had been created the previous year and, although scant attention had been given to setting standards for subdivision of land and zoning for height, building coverage, setbacks and the like by 1923, Los Angeles was among the first cities to adopt such provisional regulations after the United States Supreme Court established the constitutionality of comprehensive zoning in 1926. Los Angeles was one of the earliest cities to engage in a civic improvement program, in 1907, but this addressed city beautification rather than comprehensive planning. New York City's pioneer action on zoning in 1916 received a great deal of publicity and was studied by the larger cities. A Standard City Planning Enabling Act drafted by the Department of Commerce in 1928 is the model law. By 1931, some 800 cities (including Los Angeles) had adopted zoning regulations.

377. The similar depth of the eave overhang on the east side of the living cube was a decision of symmetry, rather than functionality.

378. Debra Pickrel. "Key Preservation Initiatives Passed at Los Angeles Board Retreat," *Bulletin, The Quarterly Newsletter of the Frank Lloyd Wright Building Conservancy.* (Vol. 7, Issue 2. Spring 1998) p. 8.

379. Sweeney. 1994, p. 95. (f. 67, p. 249.)

380. Wright. 1977, p. 276.

381. Gallion, Arthur B., FAIA and Simon Eisner, AIP. *The Urban Pattern: City Planning and Design.* (Third Edition. D. Van Nostrand Company, New York, 1975) p. 149. Real estate foreclosures jumped from 68,100 in 1926 to 248,700 in 1932.

382. The addition proposed to be built upon the hill crown never progressed past the drawing board.

383. Wright. 1977, pp. 194–195.

384. This Chinese artifact appears to be the same vessel that marked the entry to Hillside Home School and was photographed by the authors when they visited the Fellowship and toured Taliesin in 1948.

385. During an interview at Taliesin on August 10, 1989, William Wesley "Wes" Peters talked about Wright's predilection for change: "You mentioned the changes you've seen in Taliesin over the past forty years. If we could return in another forty years, we might not recognize all the original structures, for it is the nature of organic architecture to grow and not remain static. Until the day he died, Mr. Wright was making revisions and modifications to Taliesin. It was part of his youthful zest and excitement, even as he lived past his ninety-first year, that he was deriving great satisfaction from altering and improving upon his own work."

386. Letter from Wright to Aust dated December 7, 1926. (GRI/FLIW).

387. Sweeney. 1994, p. 143. (f. 40, P. 254. "Wright to Lloyd, April 19, 1928. ELW.")

388. Ibid. 1994, p. 143 (f. 41, p. 254.) Wright to Chandler. April 10, 1928). Also, De Long. 1996. p. 102. (f. 227, p. 132.)

389. Sweeney. 1994, pp. 143–144. Also, DeLong. 1996. p. 104.

390. Wright. 1932, pp. 331, 333.

391. A west-southwest exposure of large expanses of glass should be avoided at any latitude, because there is no manageable method for controlling excessive sun penetration and glare late in the day.

392. Wright. 1932, p. 320. Also Sweeney. 1994. p. 144, f. 44. Re letter from Chandler to Wright dated September 25, 1928.

393. Secrest. 1992, p. 345.

394. Mary Jane Hamilton, Anne E. Biebel, John G. Holzheuter. "Frank Lloyd Wright's Madison Networks," *Frank Lloyd Wright and Madison: Eight Decades of Artistic and Social Interaction* (Board of Regents, University of Wisconsin System, 1990) p. 5, f. 25.

395. Ibid. 1990, p. 3, f. 26.

396. Sweeney. 1994, p. 183, f. 5.

397. Secrest. 1992, p. 349. Also, letters from Frank Lloyd Wright Archives.

398. Ibid. 1992, p. 349. Also, letters from Frank Lloyd Wright Archives.

399. Wright. 1977, p. 332. "Ocatilla" was suggested by Olgivanna and inspired by the scarlet bloom of a cactus that grows in the Salt River Valley; the bloom is spelled with an "o" at the end, rather than as labeled on all Wright's original drawings.

400. Wright. 1977, pp. 332–333.

401. Ibid. 1977, p. 335.

402. Ibid. 1977, p. 335. The interconnecting wall had the additional purpose "to keep out varmints."

403. The camp fire analogy could relate equally as well to Jensen's signature campsite "council rings," as explained within the text for the Sherman Booth property (1912).

404. The "cess pool" that also was located in this arroyo (labeled "wash") seems an illogical placement, since flooding during a torrential rain would precipitate problems.

405. Letter from Wright to Aust, dated March 5, 1929. (GRI/FLIW).

406. Johnson. 1990, pp. 21–23. Also, Sweeney (1994. pp. 145–146) and DeLong (1996. p. 111).

407. Gebhard and Von Breton. 1971, pp. 37, 72. (ff 22, 23, 24).

408. Wright. 1977, p. 337.

409. Ibid. 1977, p. 337.

410. Excerpt from Wright to Aust, dated March 5, 1929. (GRI/FLIW).

411. Letter from Wright to the president of the university and Aust, dated December 16, 1929. (GRI/FLIW).

412. Raymond Jontowne Wahl. *An Analysis of "Westhope," The Richard Lloyd Jones House by Frank Lloyd Wright* (Department of Art, Graduate School, University of Tulsa, 1967.) p. 12. The authors are indebted to Tulsa residents and longtime friends John and Merle Schwendimann for their library research, which led us to the Wahl thesis.

413. Letter from Jones to Wright, dated November 26, 1928. (GRI/FLIW).

414. Letter from Wright to Jones, dated November 18, 1929. (GRI/FLIW).

415. Sweeney. 1994, p. 187, f. 9.

416. Letter from Jones to Wright, dated November 12, 1929. Letter from Wright to Jones, dated November 18, 1929. (GRI/FLIW).

417. The vegetation to be introduced was in the form of vines growing across the interior wall or ground covers, flowerage, shrubbery, and shade trees in generously arranged planting beds.

418. Wahl. 1967, p. 24.

419. The north, east, and west-facing bays were designed as two-story elements.

420. Through the years, LeCorbusier would apply variations of *Lavilla Radieuse* to many cities of the world, starting with the redevelopment of central Paris in 1925. Twenty-five years later, this layout would become the prototype for American urban renewal and public housing. In 1951, in collaboration with Matthew Nowicki, LeCorbusier had opportunity to apply his planning concepts to a totally new city in India, known as Chandigarh.

421. St. Marks Tower would materialize immediately after the end of World War II with construction of the innovative tap-root, cantilever-floor design of the Johnson Wax Research Tower and again in 1952 with the Price Company Tower in Bartlesville, Oklahoma.

422. Wright's American System-Built Houses were designed to be constructed from component parts—some precut and some prefabricated—delivered on the job site. This was another instance where Wright was fulfilling a need decades before most developers and the buying public would realize the financial benefit of this "prefabricated" construction methodology, which would become a mainstay of the building industry in years to come.

423. Frank Lloyd Wright. "America Tomorrow," *American Architect.* (May 1932 issue) p. 16.

424. Frank Lloyd Wright Foundation. *The Industrial Revolution Runs Away* (Horizon Press, New York, 1969) Footnote, p. 23. Note: Reprint and facsimile of *Disappearing City*, 1932 publication.

425. Frank Lloyd Wright. *The Natural House* (Horizon Press, New York, 1954).

426. The initial concepts of MacKaye's "highwayless towns" and "townless highways" inspired the first "bypass" to access the TVA planned garden city of Norris, Tennessee (1936) and formed the basis for the interstate highway system. Mumford's best-known books from this period are *Sticks and Stones* (1924), *Brown Decades* (1931), *Culture of Cities* (1938).

427. Patrick J. Meehan, AIA, Editor. "Aaron G. Green," *Frank Lloyd Wright Remembered.* (The Preservation Press, National Trust for Historic Preservation, 1991) p. 157. Wright's respect for Mumford developed over a number of years, from the 1920s.

428. William H. Wilson. "Moles and Skylarks," *Introduction to Planning History in the United States* (4th printing, The Center for Urban Policy Research, Rutgers University, New Brunswick, New Jersey, 1987) p. 88. "The national conferences on city planning were [since 1909] drawing together planners, social and settlement-house workers, housers,

architects, and sympathetic professionals in other fields for searching discussions of the urban crisis. . . . Planning commissions were the spawn of the same quest for efficiency and order. . . . Planning literature mushroomed. The *Survey* magazine, *American City*, and other periodicals carried news of planners' activities and aspirations. Published plans such as *The Plan of Chicago* (1909) were a well-established means of disseminating planning ideas. A wealth of 'how-to' books complemented the plans. They conceded greater social sophistication to European, especially German, cities with their careful land-use controls [zoning], their reservation of grounds for public purposes, and their restrictions on urban land speculation."

429. Excerpt from Jensen's letter to Wright, dated January 3, 1929.

430. Kassler, Elizabeth Bauer (former apprentice). *The Taliesin Fellowship: A Directory of Members* (Privately published, 1981).

431. Frank Lloyd Wright. Quoted in *Frank Lloyd Wright Quarterly* (Fall 1992).

432. Edgar Tafel. *Apprentice to Genius: Years With Frank Lloyd Wright* (McGraw Hill, New York, 1979) p. 156.

433. Mary Commings, byline. "Dream Remembered: Wright House in Wrong Era," (The Southampton Press. Southampton, New York. May 17, 1991). The authors are indebted to Bill Swain for forwarding a copy of this article to us. Swain was at that time a principal in the Pittsburgh firm of GWSM, Landscape Architects, but has since retired.

434. A model of this plan was constructed as "A Typical Dwelling for Little Farms" for the Broadacre City Models.

435. Between 1932 and 1936, nonsponsored or unfunded projects—including work at Taliesin and the Broadacre City models and drawings—made up 59 percent of the work of The Fellowship. Of the 54 designs prepared, only 7 were executed; these included nonarchitectural projects such as graphic designs and exhibits.

436. Wright's original concept for the "motel" was designed in 1928 for the San Marcos Water Gardens Project (unbuilt).

437. *House Beautiful Magazine* (November, 1955 Issue). This entire issue was devoted to Wright's career, and there were 18 articles in all. The two articles most important in reference to this study were "The Character of the Site is the Beginning of Architecture" and "Wright as a Landscape Architect." Although neither article carried a by-line, it must be assumed that former apprentice John deKoven Hill—who left The Fellowship in 1953 after 16 years to assume the position of architectural editor—had a great deal to do with article content. Wright edited and/or approved the context of the articles, as well.

438. Vincent J. Scully. *Frank Lloyd Wright* (Georgia Brazilter, Inc., New York, 1960) p. 26. Scully likened Fallingwater "not only previous European work in general but specifically with the Lowell House, Los Angeles, built in 1929–1930 by Richard Neutra, Viennese architect of the International Style who had studied with Wright in the twenties."

439. Secrest. 1992, p. 424. It should be noted that Bill Swain, a principal of the Pittsburgh firm of GWSM Landscape Architects, served for many years as the consulting landscape architect for the immediate environs surrounding Fallingwater.

440. Edward J. Kaufmann, Jr., *Fallingwater, A Frank Lloyd Wright Country House* (Abbeville Press, New York, 1986) p. 50.

441. Simonds. 1983, p. 21.

442. While Wright often referenced Jacobs I as the prototype Usonian, in the 1943 version of *An Autobiography*—some 30 years after construction of the Millard II House—Wright titled one chapter "La Miniatura, First-Born Usonian of California." No explanation was set out in the text, however. William A. Storrer in *The Frank Lloyd Wright Companian* disagrees with most historians and states that Wright at age 86 declared that the first five Usonian System houses were the four textile structures in California, as was the Jones house in Tulsa, but no source was provided. For the purpose of this book, the Usonian residence will be identified as those of horizontal appearance—whether designed from a grid using the rectangle, square, circle, hexagon, parallelogram, equilateral, or other triangular form—and with wood panels and/or limited sections of brick or stone inside and outside, or as the later do-it-yourself versions constructed of custom design concrete blocks formed on site.

443. Herbert and Katherine Jacobs. *Building With Frank Lloyd Wright.* (Chronicle Books, San Francisco, 1978).

444. Frederick Gutheim. "The Turning Point in Mr. Wright's Career," *AIA Journal.* (June 1980) pp. 48–49.

445. Paul R. and Jean S. Hanna. *Frank Lloyd Wright's Hanna House: The Clients' Report.* (Southern Illinois University Press, 1981) p. 18.

446. The Hannas did not purchase the property, but arranged for a long-term lease.

447. Hanna. 1981, Appendix Two. p. 141.

448. Telephone interview on February 9, 1995. Kaneji Domoto grew up in the atmosphere of his father's large plant nursery in Oakland, California, but he arrived at Taliesin in 1939 with formal training in both architecture and landscape architecture. Edgar Tofel remembers that young "Kan" Domoto had considerable landscape design and horticultural skills and he "would get furious with Mr. Wright having plants in wrongly oriented places."

449. Robert King Reitherman. *AIA Journal,* (June 1980) p. 43.

450. Martin Ell Well. "Hanna Honeycomb House Restoration Outlined: But Stanford Lacks Funds For It," *Journal of the Taliesin Fellows.* (Issue 7; Summer 1992) pp. 5–7. Note: As can be seen in the panoramic photograph of the property taken by the author in 1992, the earthquake damage is not visible from the exterior and the grounds have been well maintained by the University, except for the shearing of the shrubs lining the brick walls that define the contour of the driveway. To more accurately reflect Wright's well-established intent with respect to the landscape, all exterior plantings should be allowed to cascade naturally—whether the structure represents the era of the Prairie House or the Usonian residence.

451. Eaton. 1964, pp. 221–222.

452. When visited by the author and other students during a University of Illinois field trip during the late 1940s, the Johnson Research Tower was under construction. The alternating round and square floors were still exposed, prior to the installation of the tubular glass. This was the most dramatic architectural form any of us had ever seen in America, although several of us who were WWII veterans made comparisons to the Japanese pagodas we had seen in Japan or during time spent on the islands of the South Pacific.

453. Wright. "Wingspread," *Frank Lloyd Wright Monograph: 1937–1941.* (A.D.A. EDITA Tokyo Co., Ltd, 1986) p. 4.

454. This technique was described during separate interviews with former apprentices Comelia Brierly and Wes Peters. Stan White, a legendary professor of landscape architecture at the University of Illinois during the 1930s and 1940s, used a similar technique in the classroom—by taking a handful of coins from his pocket and throwing them onto the drafting paper. Professor White was very pleased with one assignment prepared by the author, which only appeared so naturalistic because each tree was placed to hide spatters of grease—the result of living in a 15-foot trailer and drafting on a pull-down table next to the two-burner hot plate where the coauthor was preparing dinner.

455. Ibid. p. 479.

456. Observation made by Peters during August 10, 1989 interview by the author.

457. Comelia Brierly interview conducted by the author at Taliesin West.

458. The Land Planning and Housing Division of TVA was headed by Earle S. Draper, a landscape architect and town planner. This was the first time a landscape architect would direct a collaborative team of specialists to both plan and supervise the building of towns, roads, parks, and schools. His staff also relocated or removed towns, roads, and cemeteries in the path of reservoir flooding and originated the policy of lake shoreline protection.

459. The parenthesized dates denote the year of completion and occupancy of the residences.

460. Five more new communities were scheduled for development but, as the program was not explicitly authorized by statute nor reviewed by Congress, opponents embroiled the program in legal entanglements before construction began at the fourth site in New Jersey, and the project fell by the wayside. Shortly after World War II, the greenbelt towns were sold. Since that time, parts of the protective greenbelts for all three communities have been sold and subdivided so that each is surrounded by conventional development and sprawl. The demonstration nevertheless was a success insofar as learning what could be done, as opposed to what *not* to do, when the opportunity is presented to meet broad social and economic objectives, including the provision of needed housing

461. Braswell and Frank Lloyd Wright. *Architecture and Modern Life.* (Harper & Brothers, New York, 1937) pp. 62, 66–67.

462. Wright's efforts in this regard are supported by correspondence of record. Wright asked Jensen to write a letter of endorsement. When he refused, stating that he did not believe Wright's selection would be "good public policy," there was an exchange of angry letters and the two old friends never saw each other again.

463. As distasteful as these requirements might have appeared to Wright, adherence to such minimum standards might have saved exorbitant costs later incurred by other Usonian homeowners who were forced to replace entire roofs and add steel reinforcement such as became necessary for Jacobs, Rosenbaum, Goetsch-Winkler, et al.

464. This project is referenced as Usonia I, based upon the 1939 "List of Projects."

465. Talbot Wegg. "FLIW versus the USA," *AIA Journal* (February, 1970) pp. 49–52. The Agency hired leading architectural firms to design these defense housing projects, including Gropius, Breuer, Eliel and Eero Saarinen, Neutra, Wurster, Stubbins, Raymond, Louis Kahn, Stone, Stein, and Gruzen.

466. Aaron G. Green. "Organic Architecture: The Principles of Frank Lloyd Wright," *Frank Lloyd Wright: In the Realm of Ideas,* edited by Bruce Brooks Pfeiffer and Gerald Nordland (Southern Illinois University Press, Carbondale, 1988) p. 139.

467. Because only eight houses were designed in all, Wright eventually did charge the Association a fee for the land planning.

468. Parkwyn Village was taken into the City of Kalamazoo; the community was resubdivided to satisfy local regulations; and Wright's circular lots were converted to more conventional polygon shapes. Since then, all of the lots have been built upon— some with conventional houses, and some featuring organic details more compatible with Wright's Usonians. The neighborhood association remains active. The remaining circular lots never have been actively marketed. The five families maintain a rural, nonagricultural lifestyle and function as a cooperative community, as they continue to share expenses for maintaining common open spaces

and a trail system, road maintenance, snow removal, and managing the forested areas.

469. Priscilla Henken. "A 'Broad-Acre' Project," *Town and Country Planning.* (June 1954) This historic background was supplemented by the author's 1992 video interview with Roland Reisley, one of the original Usonia II homeowners.

470. Ibid. The community center and two of the houses of his design never were built.

471. David Henken. "Usonia Homes: A Summing Up," *Realization of Usonia: Frank Lloyd Wright in Westchester* (Published to accompany an exhibition at The Hudson River Museum February 3 through April 7, 1985) p. 15.

472. Wright originally agreed to accept the Gordon commission only because former apprentice Burton Goodrich maintained an architectural practice in nearby Portland and could supervise construction. When actual construction was delayed until 1964 (five years after Wright's death), Taliesin Associated Architects sited the structure without ever visiting the site, and the Gordons then called on Goodrich to resite it. During an August 17, 1992, telephone conversation with the author (calling from Mrs. Gordon's house), Goodrich was unable to recall any details of site planning, except to say he knew he "moved the house to be within a short walk to the river." The Gordon farmland has been subdivided and occupied as a large planned development. Within this process, this beautiful structure became so isolated from the original environment that it could only be accessed through an apartment parking lot. The house was slated for demolition in 2001 until the FLIW Building Conservancy arranged to have it moved to the Oregon Garden, where it will be restored.

473. The main point of outdoor-indoor transition is separated from the service entry by a brick wall that parallels the bedroom wing and splits the sidewalk leading from the carport, which might lead to some confusion.

474. The interviews were conducted during October, 1999. Francis Reinhold still supervised the grounds as an employee of the state agency that manages the property as a museum during the 1990s. John deKoven Hill was a 10-year senior member of The Taliesin Fellowship when he was assigned to the Walter House.

475. Between 1929 and 1938, there were only 10 executed commissions, or approximately one a year. In 1938 there were 4 executed commissions and in 1939 there were 11. From the end of the war in 1945 through 1949, there were 43 executed commissions.

476. Background for this chapter may vary from other published accounts of the Fellowship, as it is based upon the author's personal interviews with Wesley Peters and Cornelia Brierly, as well as telephone conversations with John Howe, Edgar Tofel, and John Hill.

477. Meehan. 1991, p. 133

478. Excerpt from May 1992 interview with the authors.

479. Wright is said to have chosen the whimsical spelling of "Auldbrass" to identify with the Scotch ancestry of his client.

480. This detail in the fretwork also has been identified as a feathers-and-arrow design relating to the Native Americans who originally occupied this region. One cost-saving measure Wright originally employed was to use canvas behind the fretwork, apparently unaware of how cold some winters can be in this region of South Carolina; the canvas soon was replaced with glass.

481. Wright's original drawings were for the downspouts to be fashioned from artistically patterned copper, but he then designed the wooden version that were executed, due to the high cost of materials and difficulty in finding artisans at this late stage of the Great Depression. When Joel Silver purchased and restored the property in the 1980s, he used the copper.

482. The 1939 Master Plan for Auldbrass Plantation was only partially implemented, including a rambling dirt road system. By the time Joel Silver acquired the property, a number of buildings had burned to the ground and all of the original cypress furniture had been sold at auction, some as late as 1981. During the restoration process, a road-walkway system was installed similar to that shown on the Master Plan and surfaced with crushed red brick. All the furniture has been reconstructed based upon the original plans. All elements of Eric Lloyd Wright's restoration process were supervised by former apprentice Bennett Straham.

483. Dramatic panoramic views also can be accessed from the roof terrace, reached by exterior stairs near the front door.

484. The term "Poplar Misconception" was used by Pope when making speeches or writing articles about this residence that he and his family loved and enjoyed, even though they only resided there for five years.

485. Ten percent of the total workload were nonclient projects, such as for Taliesin and Taliesin West.

486. Elizabeth Kassler. *The Taliesin Fellowship: A Directory of Members* 1932–1982.

487. Excerpts from videotaped interview with Gerte and Seamore Shavin conducted in November 1989 during the open house celebrating the restoration of Auldbrass, outside Yamassee, South Carolina.

488. 1991 interview.

489. 1992 interview.

490. The realization that Wright did not teach site planning, per se, became apparent through interviews with several former senior apprentices. Answers to questions pertaining to landscape treatment never once referenced site analysis, site planning, or other complexities of site engineering. In the eyes of most, anything relative to the landscape was associated with the aesthetic cultivation of the site—more specifically, to the use of plantings for cosmetic purposes.

491. Consideration of ecological matters generally were ignored in 1939. However, this particular dunes area is known as the birthplace of the "science" of ecology and was set aside for protection as a state park in 1925, based upon scientific investigation conducted by Professor Henry Cowles of the Botany Department at the University of Chicago since 1896. Jens Jensen was a close friend of Cowles and often accompanied him on field studies; it may have been because of this association that Wright instigated this site analysis. The Ogden Dunes community today is an inholding parcel surrounded by the Indiana Dunes National Lakeshore, authorized by Congress in 1966; as formally established in 1972, the boundaries protect the Lake Michigan beach and shoreline, as well as the dunes on all sides of the the Ogden Dunes community.

492. September 1992 interview.

493. Excerpt from August 1992 correspondence with the author.

494. Wright. 1954, pp. 33 and 154.

495. This comment was made to the author in conversation during one of his visits to Taliesin at Spring Green, when Wright was still alive.

496. Most landscape architects would look at this methodology as an easy, but nonecological, response to a need to change the natural order of the site. In the design studio of landscape architects, every effort is made to disturb the natural land form as little as possible, to balance cut and fill, and avoid damming storm water flow or other unnatural changes to the ecological system.

497. Excerpts from March 21, 1952 letter from Wright to Walker. Aaron Green was the apprentice assigned to the Walker House. Wright's mention of "Wurster" is in reference to noted architect William H. Wurster, former dean of architecture at the University of California—Berkeley.

498. In parts of New York State, for instance, a southwesterly orientation provides the sunniest and most comfortable exposure because of prevalent morning mists.

499. 1992 interview.

500. This was a principle of physics that Wright had used successfully 50 years earlier when he built the Lake Mendota Municipal Boathouse, but had never used with a residence.

501. Source: local climatological data from the U.S. Department of Commerce. Such detailed records were not at this time available to Frank Lloyd Wright, although many of his activities—like those of his farm family forebears—were controlled by the seasons which were dependent upon such phenomena as the arc of the sun and the course of the winds.

502. Letter from Curtis Meyer (May 23, 1948) excerpt: "Since our prevailing winds are from the southwest and west as we pointed out in our Association letter of February 1947, the carport is incorrectly oriented. This will entail a considerable change in the orientation of the whole house."

503. An interesting aside must be introduced here— that is, Anne Brown told the author that neither she nor her husband were aware that a site plan had been prepared for their property until it was published in *Monograph #7*.

504. Excerpt from letter to Curtis Meyer from John Howe, dated March 20, 1951.

505. Excerpt from telephone interview conducted by author on August 27, 1991.

506. Excerpts from letter written by Mary S. Palmer, dated September 24, 1950.

507. Pfeiffer. *Frank Lloyd Wright: The Crowning Decade* (California State University Press, Fresno, 1989) p. 48.

508. Joseph E. Howland. *The House Beautiful Book of Gardens and Outdoor Living* (Doubleday & Company, Inc., 1958) pp. 6–7.

509. By the early 1970s, architect Patrick Horsbrugh had established a graduate program in environic studies at the University of Notre Dame and organized the Environic Foundation International. Environics expanded upon the concept of omnitecture to encourage leadership in understanding, controlling, and managing natural resources in addition to the design skills of architecture, landscape architecture, and city planning.

510. Eaton. 1964, pp. 221–222. Jensen told Wright he admired his architectural talents enormously, but he did not believe his selection would be good public policy; he therefore refused to write a letter of support. Following an exchange of angry letters, the two longtime friends never spoke to each other again.

511. Robert Fishman. *Bourgeois Utopias: The Rise and Fall of Suburbia* (Basic Books, Inc., New York, 1987) p. 183.

512. Ibid. 1987, pp. 187–189.

513. Frank Lloyd Wright was decades ahead of the nation by attracting people from nearby towns for an evening of films or concerts at Taliesin, along with dance and music performances.

APPENDIX A

Frank Lloyd Wright Buildings and Sites Visited and Evaluated by Charles E. Aguar

Storrer ID#	Specific Identification	Dates Visited	Person Interviewed	Date
0	Unity Chapel, Spring Green WI	1975, 1976, 1989, 1992		
1	Hillside Home School, Spring Green WI	1948, 1996		
2, 3, 4	FLIW Home & Studio, Oak Park IL	1947, 1976, 1989, 1990, 1996	Carla Lind	8/29/1990
5, 6, 7, 8	Winter Bungalows, Ocean Springs MS	1993		
11–13	Warren McArthur Res., Chicago IL	1990	Ruth Michael, owner L. McPharlin, daughter	9/4/1990 3/1/1990
14, 133	George Blossom Res., Chicago IL	1990	Alice Shaddle, owner	9/4/1990
16	Thomas H. Gale Res., Oak Park IL	1947, 1976, 1990, 1992		
17	R. P. Parker Res., Oak Park IL	1947, 1976, 1990, 1992		
20	Walter M. Gale Res., Oak Park IL	1947, 1976, 1990, 1992		
23	Francis Wooley Res., Oak Park IL	1990, 1992		
24, 25	W. H. Winslow Res./Stable, River Forest IL	1947, 1990, 1992		
33	Chauncey Williams Res., River Forest IL	1947, 1990, 1992		
34, 35	Nathan G. Moore Res., Oak Park IL	1947, 1976, 1990, 1992		
36	H. P. Young Res., Oak Park IL	1990, 1992		
37	Romeo & Juliet Windmill, Spring Green WI	1948, 1952, 1959, 1975, 1976, 1980, 1989, 1990, 1992, 1996		
42	Harry C. Goodrich Res., Oak Park IL	1992		
43	George Furbeck Res., Oak Park IL	1990, 1992		

44	Rollin Furbeck Res., Oak Park IL	1990, 1992		
45	George W. Smith Res., Oak Park IL	1976, 1990, 1992		
51	Edward R. Hills Res., Oak Park IL	1976, 1990, 1992		
52	B. Harley Bradley Res., Kankakee IL	1962, 1992	Ron Meline, owner	1//6/1993
			Chris Vernon, LA	4/29/1991
54	Ward Willits Res., Highland Park IL	1990, 1992	Sybie Robinson, owner	8/30/1990
55	Warren Hickox Res., Kankakee IL	1962, 1992		
58, 60	Wm. G. Fricke Res., Oak Park IL	1989, 1990, 1992	Wm. & Jan Dring, owners	9/3/1990
61	Wm. E. Martin Res., Oak Park IL	1989, 1990, 1992, 1996	Jan Dring, former res.	9/6/1990
			C. M. Brackett,	
			Martin granddaughter	2/22/1997
			Laura Talaske, owner	1/22/1997
67	F. W. Thomas Res., Oak Park IL	1947, 1976, 1989, 1990, 1992	Karen Brammen, owner	9/4/1990
68	E. Arthur Davenport Res., River Forest IL	1990, 1992	Jeanette Fields, owner	9/4/1990
70, 71, 72	Francis W. Little Res., Peoria IL	1992	Ms. Swardenski, owner	5/3/1992
72	Susan L. Dana Res., Springfield IL	1930s, 1950s, 1990	J. Johnson, LA	1/22/1993
74	Arthur Heurtley Res., Oak Park IL	1947, 1976, 1989, 1990, 1992	Jack Prost, owner	9/17/1990
96	Unity Temple, Oak Park IL	1947, 1976, 1989, 1990, 1992		
98	Thomas H. Gale Res., Oak Park IL	1990, 1992	Meg Klinkow, owner	8/31/1990
99	Burton J. Westcott Res., Springfield OH	1987, 1991	Burt Sparer, former res.	9/6/1991
104	Edwin H. Cheney Res., Oak Park IL	1989, 1990, 1992, 1996	Dale Smirl, owner	8/30/1990
			Jim Stobie, craftsman	9/6/1990
106	Harvey P. Sutton Res., McCook NB	1992	M&M J. Cannum, owners	8/6/1992
108	Mary M. W. Adams Res., Highland Park IL	1990		
109	W. A. Glasner Res., Glencoe IL	1990, 1992		
110	Chas. A. Brown Res., Evanston IL	1990		
111	Rookery Bldg. Remodeling, Chicago IL	1960s, 1990		
115	Thomas P. Hardy Res., Racine WI	1989		
117	P. A. Beachy Res., Oak Park IL	1990, 1992	John Tilton, Restore Arch.	8/6/1990
119	River Forest Tennis Club, River Forest IL	1990		
120	P. D. Hoyt Res., Geneva IL	1992		
121	A. W. Gridley Res., Batavia IL	1992		
125	Kersey C. DeRhodes Res., South Bend IN	1992	Tom Miller, owner	5/6/1991
126	G. M. Mallard, Highland Park IL	1990	Juan Montenegro, owner	4/23/1995
127	F. C. Robie, Chicago IL	1947, 1989		

128	Ferdinand F. Tomek Res., Riverside IL	1947, 1976, 1989, 1990, 1992	Maya Moran, owner	9/3/1990
129	Col. G. Fabyan remodel., Geneva IL	1992	Darlene Larson, owner	5/6/1991
134	A. T. Porter "Tanyderi," Spring Green WI	1959, 1976, 1989, 1990	Susan Lockhart, staff	3/1/1990
135	Avery Coonley, Riverside IL	1959, 1990, 1992, 1996	Nicketas Sablas, owner	4/30/1992
137	Coonley Coach House, Riverside IL	1959, 1990, 1992, 1996	M/M Jim Howlett, owners	9/5/1990
138	Stephen M.B. Hunt Res., LaGrange IL	1990	M/M Ed Marcisz, owners	9/3/1990
139	G. C. Stockman Res., Mason City IA	1989	David Christiansen	5/11/1991
146	E. A. Gilmore, Madison WI	1992	Dr. Annette Beyer-Mears	5/10/1991
148	Meyer May Res., Grand Rapids MI	1991	Carla Lind	8/29/1990
150	Isabel Roberts Res., River Forest IL	1947, 1990, 1992, 1996	Bill Pollak, owner	8/27/1990
151	Frank J. Baker Res., Wilmette IL	1947, 1990	Walter Sobel, owner	8/30/1990
155, 156	City Nat'l Bank/Hotel, Mason City IA	1989		
158, 159	Wm. H. Copeland Res., Oak Park IL	1990		
161	J. Kibben Ingalls Res., River Forest IL	1990, 1992	John & Betty Tilton, owners	9/6/1990
165	E. P. Irving Res., Decatur IL	1957	David Bell, LA	3/18/1993
166	J. H. Amberg Res., Grand Rapids MI	1991	Tom Logan, owner	5/6/1991
168	O. B. Balch Res., Oak Park IL	1990, 1992		
174	Avery Coonley Playhouse, Riverside IL	1959, 1992	Ted Smith, owner	4/30/1992
176	Wm. B. Greene Res., Aurora IL	1992		
179	Henry S. Adams Res., Oak Park IL	1990, 1992	M/M Blumenthal, owners	8/28/1990
183	A. D. German Warehouse, Richland Ctr. IL	1959, 1976, 1989		
184	E. D. Brigham Res., Glencoe IL	1990, 1992	Susan Solway, owner	8/30/1990
185	Sherman M. Booth Bridge, Glencoe IL	1990, 1992		
187	Sherman M. Booth Res., Glencoe IL	1990, 1992		
188	Charles R. Perry Res., Glencoe IL	1990, 1992		
189	Hollis R. Root Res., Glencoe IL	1990, 1992		
190	Wm. F. Kier Res., Glencoe IL	1990, 1992		
191	Wm. F. Ross Res., Glencoe IL	1990, 1992		
192	Lute F. Kissam Res., Glencoe IL	1990, 1992		
193	Emil Bach Res., Chicago IL	1990		
197	Ernest Vosburgh Res., Grand Beach MI	1990, 1992		
198	Joseph J. Bagley Res., Grand Beach MI	1990, 1992		

199	W. S. Carr Res., Grand Beach MI	1990, 1992		
201	Arthur L. Richards Duples, Milwaukee WI	1976		
203.2	A. L. Richards properties, Wilmette IL	1990	Mary Sample, owner	8/30/1990
203.4	A. L. Richards 2-story, Monona IA	1992		
214	Millard II "La Miniatura" Pasadena CA	1992	Stephanie DeWolf, pres. Bob Sweeney, author	10/7/1992 10/7/1992
215	John Storer Res., Hollywood CA	1992	Joel Silver, owner Eric Wright, Pres. Arch.	4/23/1995 4/23/1995
218, 219	FLIW Taliesin III, Spring Green WI	1948, 1952, 1959, 1975, 1976, 1980, 1989, 1992, 1996	Wesley Peters	8/10/1989
221, 222	McArthur Biltmore Hotel, Phoenix AZ	1990		
227	Westhope, Tulsa OK	1992		
228	FLIW Taliesin Fellowship, Spring Green WI	1948, 1952, 1959, 1975, 1976, 1980, 1989, 1992, 1996	Wesley Peters	8/9/1989
229	M. E. Wiley Res., Minneapolis MN	1992		
230	Kaufmann Fallingwater, Mill Run PA	1989	Thomas Schmidt, Dir. Lynda Waggoner, Curator Bill Swain, LA	4/23/1995 8/1/1989 8/1/1989
234	Herbert Jacobs I, Madison WI	1992	Katherine Jacobs, client James Dennis, owner	3/1/1990 4/29/1992
235	Paul H. Hanna, Stanford CA	1990	Jonathan Ryan, Res. Arch. Kanaji Domoto, LA	8/19/1992 2/9/1995
237, 238	S. C. Johnson Bldg-Tower, Racine WI	1952, 1959, 1976, 1989		
239	H. Johnson "Wingspread," Wind Point WI	1989		
240	Ben Rebhuhn Res., Great Neck Est. NY	1992	John Horn, owner	10/16/1992
241, 245	FLIW Taliesin West, Scottsdale AZ	1991, 1992,	Wes Peters Cornelia Brierley	8/10/1989 3/1/1990
248	Suntop Homes, Ardmore PA	1992	Edmond Anzalone, owner	10/17/92
251–258	Florida Southern College, Lakeland FL	1985, 1990		
260	Andrew Armstrong Res., Ogden Dunes IN	1990	John/Pat Peterson, owners	9/1/1990
261–164	C. L. Stevens Auldbrass, Yamassee SC	1981, 1982, 1987, 1989, 1995	Joel Silvers, owner Eric Wright, Restore Arch.	4/23/1995 4/23/1995
265	Lloyd Lewis Res., Libertyville IL	1992	M/M Bruce Haines, owners	4/1/1992
267	Stanley Rosenbaum Res., Florence AL	1991	Mildren Rosenbaum, client	4/21/1991

268	Loren Pope Res., Alexandria VA	1992	Loren Pope, client	12/23/1994
269	Goetsch-Winckler Res., Okomos MI	1991	Mildren Rosenbaum, client	4/21/1991
270	Joseph Euchtman Res., Baltimore MD	1992		
272	George Sturges Res., Brentwood Hts. CA	1992		
273	John C. Pew Res., Shorewood Hills WI	1992	John & Ruth Pew, clients	4/24/1992
274	George Affleck Res., Bloomfield Hills MI	1991		
278	James Christie Res., Bernardsville NJ	1992	Mike McNalley, owner	10/12/1992
282	Stuart Richardson Res., Glen Ridge NJ	1992	M/M Saladina, own. parents	10/13/92
283	Jacobs II Solar Hemicycle, Middleton WI	1992	Katherine Jacobs, client	3/1/1990 9/23/1992
284, 285	Lowell Walter Res., Quasqueton IA	1989	John deKoven Hill, Arch. Francis Reinhold Joanne Arms, mgr.	9/27/1993 9/28/1993 5/10/1991
287	M. M. Smith Myhaven, Bloomfield Hills MI	1991	Mrs. M.M. Smith, client	5/3/1991
289	Dr. Alvin Mill Res., Charles City IA	1989		
291	Unitarian Church, Shorewood Hills MI	1952, 1968, 1992		
292	Dr. A. H. Bulbulian Res., Rochester MN	1992		
294	David Weisblat Res., Galesburg MI	1991	Christine Weisblat, client	5/5/1991
295	Eric Pratt Res., Galesburg MI	1991	Sam B. Lovall, owner Arlene Moran, owner	5/9/1991 4/23/1995
296	Samuel Eppstein Res., Galesburg MI	1991	James Hemenway, owner	5/9/1991
297	Curtis Meyer Res., Galesburg MI	1991	Dr. Rbt. Adrienne, owner	5/9/1991
298	Robert Levin Res., Kalamazoo MI	1991	Dr. Richard Williams, owner	5/9/1991
299	Dr. Ward McCartney Res., Kalamazoo MI	1991	Dr. Ward McCartney, client	5/6/1991
300	Eric Brown Res., Kalamazoo MI	1991	Eric/Anne Brown, clients	5/6/1991
301	Robert Winn Res., Kalamazoo MI	1991		
302	Herman Mossberg Res., South Bend IN	1992	Gertrude Mossberg, client	4/22/1991
306	Ms. Clinton Walker, Carmel CA	1992		
309	Maynard Buehler Res., Orinda CA	1992	M/M Buehler, clients	8/25/1993
310	V. C. Morris Gift Shop, San Francisco CA	1948, 1957, 1992		
312	Erling Brauner Res., Okemos MI	1991	Ms. E. Brauner, client	5/3/1991
313	James Edwards Res., Okemos MI	1991		
314	Henry Neils Res., Minneapolis MN	1959, 1992	Ed Reid, LA	1959, 1989

316	Sol Friedman Res., Pleasantville NY	1992	M/M M. Osheowitz, owners	4/24/92
317	Edward Serlin Res., Pleasantville NY	1992	Doris Abramson, owner	10/14/1992
318	Roland Reisley Res., Pleasantville NY	1992	M/M R. Reisley, clients	10/14/1992
319	Kenneth Laurent Res., Rockford IL	1992	K. Laurent, client	5/1/1992
321	Thomas Keys Res., Rochester IL	1992		
322	David Wright Res., Phoenix AZ	1992		
325	J. A. Sweeton Res., Cherry Hill NJ	1992	Albert H. Clark, owner	10/19/1992
326	Raymond Carlson Res., Phoenix AZ	1990, 1992	Christian Peterson, owner	3/1/1990
328	Donald Schaberg Res., Okemos MI	1991	Mary Lou Schaberg, client	5/3/1991
330	Robert Berger Res., San Anselmo CA	1992	Gloria Berger, client	8/21/1992
332	Wm. Palmer Res., Ann Arbor MI	1991	Mary Palmer, client (telephone follow-up)	5/5/1991 5/18/1994
334	Robert Muirhead Res., Plato Center IL	1992	Chas. Muirhead, grandson	5/2/1992
339	Seamour Shavin Res., Chattanooga TN	1983, 1994, 1995	M/M Shavin, clients	11/5/1989 7/16/1995
340	Russell Kraus Res., Kirkwood MO	1955, 1992	Russell Kraus, client	5/6/1992
341	Charles Glore Res., Lake Forest IL	1990, 1992	M/M Larry Smith, owners	9/6/1990
342	Patrick Kinney Res., Lancaster WI	1990	M/M P. Kinney, clients	4/27/1992
344	Benjamin Adelman Res., Phoenix AZ	1990	Dr. Bertram Karpf, owner	3/1/1990
345	E. & C. Austin Res., Greenville SC	1990, 1992	M/M Roy Palmer, owners	10/8/1990
349	Arthur Pieper Res., Paradise Valley AZ	1992		
350	Ray Brandes Res., Issaquah WA	1992		
351	Quintin Blair Res., Cody WY	1992	M/M Q. Blair, clients	8/9/1992
355	Price Company Tower, Bartlesville OK	1992		
356	Anderton Court Shope, Beverly Hills CA	1980		
358	R. Llewellyn Wright (son), Bethesda MD	1992	Elizabeth Wright, client	10/22/1992
359	George Lewis Res., Tallahassee FL	1992	M/M Geo. Lewis, clients	9/29/1992
360	Andrew Cooke Res., Virginia Beach VA	1994	M/M Dan Duhl, owners	9/18/1994
361	Jorgine Boomer Res., Phoenix AZ	1990	Ms. Chas. Kinter, owner	3/1/1990
364	Lewis H. Goddard Res., Plymouth MI	1991		
366	Abraham Wilson Res., Millstone NJ	1992	Laurence Tarantino, owner	10/12/92
367	Riverview Terrace Restraurant, S.P. WI	1976, 1989		
373	Beth Sholom Synagogue, Elkins Park PA	1992		

375	John E. Christian, W. Lafayette IN	1992	John Christian, client	5/9/1991
378	H. Price, Sr., Paradise Valley AZ	1992		
379	Cedric Boulter Res., Cincinnati OH	1992	David Gosling, owner	4/17/1992
380	Hoffman Auto Showroom, New York NY	1984		
383	J. L. Rayward "Tirranna," New Canaan CT	1992	Ms. T. Stanley, owner	10/15/92
385	Randall Fawcett Res., Los Banos CA	1992	M/M R. Fawcett, clients	8/29/1992
386	Gerald Tonkens Res., Amberley Village OH	1992	Beverly Tonkens, client	4/17/1992
388	Dr. Dorothy Turkel Res., Detroit MI	1991		
389	William Tracy Res., Normany Park WA	1992	M/M Wm. Tracy, clients	8/15/1992
392	Theodore Pappas Res., St. Louis MO	1992	M/M Ted Pappas, clients	5/6/1992
399	Greek Orthodox Church, Wanwatosa WI	1978		
400	Guggenheim Museum, New York NY	1958, 1984, 1988		
401	Wyoming Valley Grammar School, WI	1989, 1992, 1996		
403	Allen Friedman Res., Bannockburn IL	1990	M/M Sam Fraerman, owners	8/29/90
406	Eugene Van Tamelon Res., Madison WI	1956, 1992	Ms. E. Van Tamelen, client	5/9/1991
			Ralph Hatfield, owner	4/28/1992
412.1	Walter Rudin Res., Madison WI	1992		
412.2	James McBean Res., Rochester MN	1992		
414	Lindholm Service Station, Cloquet MN	1960s, 1989		
415–417	Marin Cty. Civic Center, San Raphael CA	1968, 1992		
419	C. E. Gordon Res., Wilsonville OR	1992	Ms. C. E. Gordon, client	8/17/1992
422	Sterling Kinney Res., Amarillo TX	1992	Sterling Kinney, client	8/13/1992
427	Dr. Paul Olfelt Res., St. Louis Park MN	1992	M/M Paul Olfelt, clients	5/23/1992
428	Dr. George Ablin, Bakersfield CA	1992	M/M G. Ablin, clients	8/30/1992
431	Polgram Congregational Church, Redding CA	1992		
432	Gammage Memorial Aud., Tempe AZ	1990		
433	Norman Lykes Res., Phoenix AZ	1992		

APPENDIX B

Chronicle of Wright's Community Planning and Urban Designs

During Frank Lloyd Wright's 71-year career, there were 41 commissions where a number of land uses were coordinated into the design whole and should be considered community planning or urban design in scale.

Only 8 of these designs reached the stage of execution:

Taliesin Housing-Farm-Hillside Home School
    Complex (1911–1959)
Midway Gardens (1913)
Imperial Hotel (1916)
Ocatilla Camp (1928)
Usonia Homes, Pleasantville NY (1947)
Parkwyn Village (1947)

Four reached the stage of partial completion:

Como Orchards Summer Colony (1908)
Florida Southern College Campus Plan (1938)
Sun Top Homes (1938)
Galesburg Country Homes (1947)

The remaining 29 designs never progressed past the project stage:

Wolf Lake Amusement Park (1895)
Cheltenham Beach Resort (1899)
Quadruple Block Plan (1900)
Roberts Quadruple Block Plan (1903)

Bitter Root Town Plan (1909)
Plan for Bitter Root Village (1909)
City Club Land Development Competition
    (1913)
Monolith Homes and Subdivision (1919)
Wenatchee, Washington Town Plan (1919)
Tahoe Summer Colony (1922)
Doheney Ranch Resort (1923)
Skyscraper Regulations (1926)
San Marcos in the Desert (1928)
St. Marks Tower (1929)
Broadacre City Master Plan (1934)
Usonia I Master Plan (1939)
Circle Pines Resort (1941)
Cloverleaf Housing (1941)
Cooperative Homesteads (1942)
Pittsburgh Civic Center (1947)
Huntington Hartford Resort (1947)
Pittsburgh Point Park/Twin Bridges (1948)
Floating Gardens Resort (1952)
Paradise on Wheels (1952)
Mile High Illinois Building (1956)
Fiberthin Village (1956)
Bimson Housing (1957)
Baghdad University (1957)
Greater Plan for Baghdad (1957)

APPENDIX C

Plant Materials Identified for Ward W. Willets, Highland Park, Illinois (1901)

Walter Burley Griffin, Landscape Architect

Botanical Name	Common Name	Notes	Hardiness Zone
Trees			
Betula papyrifera	Paper or Canoe Birch	Native ornamental	2
Crataegus mollis	Downy Hawthorne	Native, horizontal branching habit	4
C. oxyacantha	English Hawthorne	Densely round habit	4
Elaeagnus authustifolius	Russian Olive	Distorted branching, silver leaf	2
Juniperus communis	Common Juniper	Native, variety of shapes	2
Laburnum xwateri	Waterer Laburnum	Small, fine-textured tree	5
Sorbus americana	American Mountain Ash	Small native tree, red fruit	2
Shrubs			
Cornus alba	Red or Tatarian Dogwood	Red stemmed shrub; hardy	2
C. paniculata	Gray or Panicled Dogwood	Native, attracts birds	4
Euonymus atropurpurea	Eastern Wahoo	Native shrub or small tree	4
Lonicera bella	Belle Honeysuckle	Hardy hybrid	4
L. tatarica	Tatarian Honeysuckle	Tall, broad spreading	3
Rhamnus cathartica	Common Buckthorn	Vigorous tree-shrub	2
Sassibucus canadensis	American Elder	Native woodland border	3
Syringa vulgaris	Common Lilac	Hardy shrub or small tree	3
Viburnum plicatum	Japanese Snowball	Horizontal branching habit	4
Flowers			
Altheae rosea	Hollyhock	Popular Wrightian flower	3
Coreopsis lanceolata	Lance Coreopsis	Daisylike prairie native	3
Delphinium hybrids	Larkspur var.	Especially tall English strain	3
Digitalis purpurea	Foxglove	Popular European biennial	4
Eupatorrium coelestinum	Hardy Ageratum	Native, eastern U.S.	
Helianthus	Sunflower var.	Native, edible seed	3–4
Iris Kaempperl	Japanese Iris	Beardless var., many colors	4
Ligustrum vulgare	Common Privet	Naturalized, rapid growth	4
Paeonia	Peony hybrids	Long-lived perennial	3–4

Botanical Name	Common Name	Notes	Hardiness Zone
Flowers (Cont.)			
Papaver orientale	Oriental Poppy	Popular plant, range of colors	2–3
Rosa xalba	Cottage Rose	Late-blooming hybrid	4
Rudbeckia hirta	Black-eyed Susan	Native annual or perennial	4
R. lanciniata	Cutleaf Coneflower	Native perennial, moist woods	3
Ground covers			
Achillea millfolium	Yarrow or Milfoil	Naturalized groundcover	2

SOURCE: Grounds plan © Frank Lloyd Wright Foundation. (Due to the overlapping of names and plant symbols, the above list is believed to comprise 80 to 90 percent of the recommended plant materials. The freehand notes of botanical names were written by Walter Burley Griffin; Common names and Hardiness Zones were added by author. Existing trees include red and white oak. A medium-size Ginko tree located to the west of the house in 1992 and not shown on Griffin's drawing is believed by the owners to have been specified by Wright.

APPENDIX D

Plant Materials Identified for Francis W. Little, Peoria, Illinois (1903)

Walter Burley Griffin, Landscape Architect

Botanical Name	Common Name	Notes	Hardiness Zone
Trees			
Ailanthus glandulosa	Tree of Heaven	Weed tree, not desirable as ornamental	4
Cercis canadensis	Eastern Redbud	Native, purplish-pink flower	4
Cornus alba 'Sibirica'	Siberian Dogwood	Outstanding ornamental	2
Cornus florida	Flowering Dogwood	Native, one of best ornamentals	4
Crataegus cocciniodes x Mollis	Downey Hawthorn	Native, horizontal branches	5
Crataegus tometosa (sic)	Hawthorn	Native, horizontal branches	5
Fagus grandifolia	American Birch	Native, excellent shade tree	3
Juglans nigra (?)	Eastern Black Walnut	Native, not good ornamental	4
Juniperus virginiana	Red Cedar	Native, hardy tall accent	2
Juniperus chinensis	Chinese Juniper	Pyramidal accent; Messy in garden or lawn	4
Magnolia stellata	Star Magnolia	Fragrant bloom before leafing	5
Magnolia x soulangiana	Saucer Magnolia	Protect from late frost	5
Platanus occidentalis	American Plane Tree	Native, good shade tree	4
Platanus orientalis	European Plane Tree	Good shade for city conditions	6
Ulmus americana	American Elm	Native, shade tree, disease prone	2
Shrubs			
Aralia spinosa	Devil's Walking-stick	Native, course tree / shrub	5
Amelanchier canadensis	Juneberry	Native, good foliage and bloom	4
Clethra alnifolia	Summersweet	Native, fragrant white blooms	3
Corylopsis grandiflora	Winter-hazel	Late frosts can kill blossoms	5
Hibiscus syriacus	Shrub Rose of Sharon Althea	Late flowers in harmony with hollyhocks	5–6
Hydranga arborescens	Smooth Hydrangea	Native, masses of white blooms	4
Ligustrum vulgare	Common Privet	Thrives under neglect but can become invasive	4
Ligustrum (illegible)	Privet		
Lonicera morrowii	Morrow Honeysuckle	Dense shrub from Japan	3

Notes and Hardiness Zones were added by author.

Botanical Name	Common Name	Notes	Hardiness Zone
Shrubs (Cont.)			
Philadelphus coronairus	Sweet Mock Orange	Old garden favorite	4
Ribes alpinum	Alpine Current	Limited value hedge	2
Rosa blanda	Meadow Rose	Native, very hardy	2
Rosa rugosa	Rugosa Rose	Orange autumn foliage	2
Syringa x persica	Persian Lilac	Hybrid w/profuse flowers	5
Syringa vulgaris	Common Lilac	Hardy shrub-small tree	3
Viburnum prunifolium	Black Haw	Native, small tree Horizontal branching	3
Viburnum tomontosum (plicatum)	Japanese Snowball	Durable, horizontal branching	4
Flowers			
Altheae rosea	Hollyhock	Old garden favorite	3
Boltonia latisquama	Violet Boltonia	Native, perennial	3
Delphinium (illegible)			
Helianthus annus	Common Sunflower	Native, edible seed	4
Helianthus orgyalia	Prairie Sunflower	Native	4
Helianthus tuberous	Jerusalem Artichoke	Native, edible root	4
Hibiscus moschentos	Rose Mallow	Strong perennial, large flowers	5
Lobelia cardinalis	Cardinal Flower	Native, moist soil, shade	2
Lupinus polyphyllus	Washington Lupine	Native, well-drained soil	3
Paconia	peony hybrids	Long-lived perennial	3–4
Phlox (illegible)			
Phlox panicutata	Garden Phlox	Native, hundreds of varieties	4
Phlox subulata	Grand Pink	Long-blooming ground cover	3
Rudbeckia hirta	Black-eyed Susan	Native annual or biannual	4
Spiraea (illegible)			
Thalictrum (illegible)			
Ground covers			
Rosa wichuraiana	Memorial Rose	Excellent on slopes	5
Vinca minor	Periwinkle, Myrtle	Easily reproduced	4
Vines			
Ampelopsis (Parthenocissus) tricuspidata	Boston Ivy	60' clinging vine, scarlet in fall	4
Clematis x jackmanii	Jackman Clematis	12' hybrid vine, 5" flowers	5
Clematis paniculata	Sweet Autumn Clematis	Fragrant autumn blooming	5
Clematis virginiana	Virgin's Bower	Native, naturalistic planting	4
Lonicera japonica 'Halliana'	Hall's Honeysuckle	A nuisance weed when it becomes invasive	4
Lonicera semperviens	Trumpet Honeysuckle	Native, twining vine	3

SOURCE: Grounds Plan of Plantings Groups I, II, III © Frank Lloyd Wright Foundation. This detailed planting plan at various scales showing botanical names only was prepared by Walter Burley Griffin. No existing trees on site are noted. Notes and Hardiness Zones were added by author. Due to blurring of original lettering, the above plant composite approximates 75 percent of the harbaceous materials and 80 to 90 percent of the trees and shrubs recommended.

APPENDIX E

Indigenous (Native) Plants Identified in Report of the Special Park Commission (1904)

Jens Jensen, Landscape Architect

Moist Bottom Lands	Higher Levels	Forest Floor	Evergreens (Conifers)
Soft Maple	Oak	Violets	Red Cedar
Willow	Hard Maple	Dogtooth Violets	White Pine
Swamp Oak	Hickory	Hepaticas	Scrub Pine
Ash	Butternut	Trillium	Common Juniper
Elm	Walnut	Phloxes	Creeping Juniper
Cottonwood	Mulberry	Anemones	
Linden	Ironwood	Spring Beauty	
Hackberry	Hop Hornbean	Asters	
Red Maple	Juneberry	Goldenrod	
Alder	White Ash		
Hawthorn	American Bud Cherry		
Elder	While Red Cherry		
Ninebark	Choke Cherry		
Blackhaw	Crabapple		
Wild Grape Vine	Plum		
Roses	Arrow-Wood		
	Witch-Hazel		
	Hazel		
	Sumac (h)		
	Honeysuckle		

APPENDIX F

Plantings Identified for Sherman M. Booth, Jr.—Glencoe IL (1911–12, Unbuilt)

Jens Jensen, Landscape Architect

Botanical Name	Common Name	Notes	Hardiness Zone
Trees, Accent or Special Purpose			
Amelanchier canadensis	Juneberry	Native	4
Betula alba	White Birch	Native	4
Gladitsia trescanthos	Common Honeylocust	Native	4
Prunus americana	American Plum	Native	3
Prunus pennsylvania	Pin Cherry	Native	2
Prunus serotina	Black Cherry	Native	3
Pyrus communis	Common Pear		4
Sorbis americana	Mountain Ash	Native	2
Trees, Evergreen			
Pinus strobus	Eastern White Pine	Native	3
Thuja occidentalis	Northern White Cedar	Native	2
Shrubs, Deciduous			
Cornus alba	Red or Tatarian Dogwood	Red stemmed shrub, hardy	2
Hamamelis virginiana	Witch-hazel	Native	4
Physocarpus opulifolius	Eastern Ninebark	Native	2
Rhus typhina	Staghorn Sumac	Native	3
Symphoricarpos exbiculatus	Indian Currant	Native	2
Symphoricarpos albus laevigatus	Snowberry	Native	3
Vaccinium angustifolium	Highbush Blueberry	Native	3
Vaccinium corymbosum	Lowbush Blueberry	Native	2
Viburnum acerifolium	Mapleleaf Viburnum	Native	3
Viburnum dentatum	Arrowwood	Native	2
Viburnum lantanodes (alnifolium)	Hobblebush	Native	3
Viburnum opulus	European Cranberry		3

Botanical Name	Common Name	Notes	Hardiness Zone
Shrubs, Evergreen			
Juniperus communis	Common Juniper	Native	2
Juniperus virginiana	Eastern Red Cedar	Native	2

SOURCE: Planting Plan, Grounds of Sherman M. Booth, © Frank Lloyd Wright Foundation.

This plan was signed by Jens Jensen. Freehand notes of botanical names are in his handwriting; Common names and Hardiness Zones were added by author.

Notes: Plant on bridge and all buildings: *Vitis labrusa* (Fox Grape), *Ampilopsis Engelmini* (Engelman Ivy). Around spring plant ferns, *Clematis virginiana* (Virgin's Bower) and Trillium. On ledge of pool group common and creeping Juniper, ferns, Trillium, Euonymous and *Clamatis virginia*. Edge of swimming pool covered with limestone slabs or St. Peters sandstone.

APPENDIX G

Plantings Identified at Taliesin— Spring Green, Wisconsin (1912–)

Sweet Flag (*Acorus calamus*), Carpet Bugle (*Ajuga varety*), Water plantain (*Alisima sp.*), Aloe (*Aloe sp.*), Hollyhock (*Althea rosea*), Anemone (*Anemone appenina*), Pasque-flower (*Anemone patens var. nuttalliona*), Snapdragon (*Antirrbinum glutinosum*), Golden Columbine (*Aquilegia chrysantha*), Emerald Fern (*Asparagus specengeri*), Aster (*Aster bigelovii*), Snow-in-summer (*Cerastium tomentosum*), Chrysanthemums (*Chrysanthemum sp.*), Clematis (*Clematis heroclerefolia*), Autumn Crocus (*Colchicum automnale*), Lily-of-the-Valley (*Convallaria majalis*), Dahlia (*Dahlia sp.*), Tall Larkspur (*Delphinum elatum*), Sweet William (*Dranthus barbatus*), Foxglove (*Digitalis purpurea*), Giant Snowdrop (*Galanthus elvesii*), Double Perennial Sunflower (*Helianthus sp.*), Christmas Rose (*Helleborus niger*), Day Lily (*Hermerocallis flava*), Poppy (*Hydrocleys nymphoides*), Morning Glory (*Ipomaea purpurea*), Crested Iris (*Iris cristata*), Japanese Iris (*Iris orientalis*), Turk's-cap Lily (*Liliu superbosa*), Tiger Lily (*Lilium tigrinum*), Cardinal Flower (*Lobilia cardinalis*), Purple Loosestrife (*Lythrum solicoria*), Partridge Berry (*Mitchella repens*), Bee Balm (*Monarda didyma*), Gall Evening Primose (*Clenothera sp.*), Peony (*Paeonia sp.*), Annual Poppy (*Papaver sp.*), Phlox (*Phlox carolina*), Bachelor's-button (*Ranunculus speciousus*), Giant Rhubarb (*Rheum palmatum*), Large Cone-Flower (*Rudbeckia maxima*), Bloodroot (*Sanguineria canadensis*), Trillium (*Trillium sp.*), Nasturtium (*Tropaelum majus*), Tulips (*Tulip sp.*), Common Lilac (*Syringa vulgaris*) was one of the few nonnative plant materials used at Taliesin; it originated in southeastern Europe, possibly before the 1700s, but is now naturalized to North America. Native ferns were dug out of the woods for shade spots. And the low, native Creeping Juniper (*Juniper horizontalis*) was popular with Wright for use in hot, dry situations. Wild grapes, such as Fox Grape (*Vitis labarusea*) or Riverbank Grape (*Vitis riparia*), were used to make wine but were also used on a beautiful painted steel scaffold-like trellis designed to stand out from the wall and add dimension to the south-facing studio wing and provide counterbalance to the Oak Trees in the Tea Garden after the loss of the remaining trees appropriating the hillside garden during the third fire.

APPENDIX H

Wright's Text for City Club of Chicago Land Development Competition (1913)

City Residential Land Development: Studies in Planning

(Publications of the City Club of Chicago. The University of Chicago Press. Chicago, Illinois. 1916)
Edited by Alfred B. Yeomans, Landscape Architect. pp. 96–102.

*"Fool! The Ideal is within thyself. Thy condition is but the stuff
thou shalt use to shape that same ideal out of."—Carlyle.*

Accepting the characteristic aggregation of business buildings, flats, apartments, and formal and informal dwellings for well-to-do and poor natural now to every semi-urban section about Chicago, this design introduces only minor modifications in harmony with the nature of this aggregation.

The proposed site locates the given tract upon the prairie within eight miles of the city's center, and so makes it an integral feature of Chicago. The established gridiron of Chicago's streets therefore has been held as the basis of this subdivision. The desired improvements have been effected by occasional widening or narrowing of streets, shifts in the relation of walks to curbs, the provision of an outer border or parkway planted with shrubbery to withdraw the residences somewhat from the noisy, dusty city streets (shelters in which to await cars are features of this parkway at street crossings), the arrangement of a small decorative park system planned to diversify the section in the simplest and most generally effective manner possible, and, finally, the creation of a new system of resubdivision of the already established blocks of the gridiron.

Grouped with the small park system are recreation features such as groves, open playgrounds, tennis courts, pools, music pavilion, athletic fields, and sheltered walks. The groups are so planned that adults and young people are attracted to the less quiet portion of the park near the public buildings, the children and more quietly inclined adults to the small park in the opposite direction.

The inevitable drift of the population toward the business center of the city is recognized in the grouping of the business buildings, more formal dwellings, and apartment buildings, large and small, on the streets next to the railway going to the city's center. A branch bank, post office, temple of worship and secular clubhouses, branch library and exhibition galleries, cinematograph and branch of civic theater are also grouped with the business buildings; but all these are grouped as features of the small park system. To the rear of the theater and also located on the street railway to town is the central heating plant and garbage reduction plant with smokestacks made into sightly towers. Here also there is a public garage and near the center of this side of the block a public produce market is designed in the form of a large open court, the court paved and screened from the park by a simple pergola.

These various buildings are all utilized as 'background' buildings and so are continuously banked against the noisy city thoroughfare, and the upper stores are carried overhead across intervening streets to give further protection from dust and noise, and to provide, in a picturesque way, economically roofed space for the combination business and dwelling establishments that cling naturally to the main arteries of traffic.

By thus drawing to one side all the buildings of this nature into the location they would naturally prefer, the greater mass of the subdivision is left quiet and clean for residence purposes. No attempt is made to change the nature of these things as they naturally come. The commercial buildings, however, are arranged with a system of interior courts which care for all the necessities that are unsightly. Space is thus provided, quietly and in order, adapted to all commercial requirements, with great economy of expenditure necessary for exterior effect, and without the exposure of unsightly conditions. The market has been treated as a desirable picturesque feature of the whole arrangement. The bank and post office are located where they will be passed morning and evening to and from the city as are the various shops. There is but one temple for worship, but there are sectarian clubrooms opening on courts at the sides and rear and in connection with it.

The library has top-lighted galleries for loan collections and a cinematograph hall. With this library are grouped separately a boys' club, branch of Y.M.C.A., and apartments for men. The school buildings, kindergarten, teachers' departments, and Y.W.C.A. building are grouped on the opposite side of the quarter-section on the axis of the children's recreation grounds. A shallow boating and swimming pool and a zoölogical loan collection from, say, Lincoln Park are features of the park system on this side. All building groups have internal green courts for privacy as well as their relation to public playground, greensward, and shrubbery. The space between this park portion of the quarter-section and the outside city street to the south is devoted to an inexpensive type of detached dwelling, with closed interior courts. Facing the outside city street are modest, grouped cottages for working men and women.

The division of the small park systems into two groups draws the children going and coming from school, kindergarten, and playground in the direction opposite to the business quarter. The remainder, the larger proportion of the quarter-section, has been left intact as a residence park, developed according to the principle of the 'quadruple block plan.' This remaining area has been kept as large and unbroken as possible, as

it is from the sale of this property that the profit would come that would make the park system possible.

In this real body of the subdivision an entirely new arrangement of the resubdivision of property is shown, dispensing with alleys, and wherein the simple expedient of an established building line protects every individual householder from every other one and insures maximum community benefits for all. At the same time it is possible to put as many houses in all necessary variety upon the ground (several schemes of arrangement are shown), and still maintain these benefits, as is possible now under the wasteful, absurd, and demoralizing practice which universally obtains, wherein the unsightly conditions of city life are all exposed to the street, and either a dirty alley is open to the sides of the blocks or useless rear courts are left with all outhouses abutting upon them, rendering the prospect of the entire neighborhood unsightly to every one and making impossible any real privacy for any one. Under the present system of subdivision, all attempts at beautifying the premises may prove futile, as any man turned loose upon his own lot may render himself obnoxious to his neighbors.

The "quadruple block plan" will prove immune from the possibilities of such abuse. Each householder is automatically protected from every other householder. He is the only individual upon the entire side of his block. His utilities are grouped to the rear with his neighbors' utilities, and his yard, front or rear, is privately his own. His windows all look upon open vistas and upon no one's unsightly necessities. His building is in unconscious but necessary grouping with three of his neighbors', looking out upon harmonious groups of other neighbors, no two of which would present to him the same elevation even were they all cast in one mould. A succession of buildings of any given length by this arrangement presents the aspect of well-grouped buildings in a park, of greater picturesque variety than is possible where facade follows facade.

Architectural features of the various buildings in the general public group recognize and emphasize in an interesting way the street vistas, and nowhere is symmetry obvious or monotonous. The aim has been to make all vistas equally picturesque and attractive and the whole quietly harmonious.

The virtue of this plan lies in the principle of subdivision underlying its features—the practical, economic, and artistic creation of an intelligent system of subdivision, insuring greater privacy together with all the advantages of co-operation realized in central heating, shorter sewers, well-ordered recreation areas, the abolition of all alleys, fewer and shorter cement walks and driveways, and airiness of arrangement in general with attractive open vistas everywhere. Always there is the maximum of buildings upon a given ground area, dignity and privacy for all.

There is an idea in this plan of subdivision which I believe to be valuable to the city and immediately available wherever several blocks remain without substantial improvement, because it may be put into practice without concession to the cupidity of the average real estate man, since he gets as many lots to sell under this system as he does in the one now in use. Moreover, the quadruple arrangement insures to the purchaser greater freedom and privacy with no decrease of any privileges he now enjoys. It is as valuable for low cost cottages as for luxurious dwellings.

Artistically this principle is susceptible of infinite variety of treatment without sacrificing the economic advantages which the householder gains through commercial repetition and to which he is entitled. The individual unit may vary harmoniously and effectively with its neighbors, without showing as under present conditions veritable monotony in the attempt to be different.

In skilled hands these various treatments could rise to great beauty, but, even if neglected, the nature of the plan would discipline the average impulse of the ordinary builder in a manner to insure more harmonious results.

Other rhythms in grouping than those suggested here are easily imagined, so that all the charm of variety found in the Gothic colleges of Oxford could easily find its way into the various workings of the underlying scheme.

Much has been written, said, and done recently in relation to civic planning all over the world. For the most part, what has happened with us in this connection is what has happened to us in individual building: we are obsessed by the old world thing in the old world way with the result that, in this grim workshop, our finer possibilities are usually handed over to fashion and sham. Confusing art with manners and aristocracy, we ape the academic Gaston or steal from 'My Lord' his admirable traditions when our own problems need, not fashioning from *without*, but development from *within*."

FRANK LLOYD WRIGHT

APPENDIX I

Plantings Identified for Stephen M. B. Hunt II, Oshkosh WI (1917)

Frank Lloyd Wright, Jr., Landscape Architect

Letter Sent to Client on October 16, 1917 (Originated from Chicago, Illinois Office)

I have forwarded to you plans and specifications for the planting of your grounds and am sending this letter of explanation.

I should like to make a particular point of the value of proper soil preparation. As you will note, I have given special instructions as to its preparation, and for this reason,—That without food of the proper sort, no matter how good the plants may be or how well planted, good or rapid results can never be obtained. You no doubt are anxious to have your place made beautiful in as short a time as possible, and the few extra dollars that will be required to put your soil in proper condition will be well worth the added expense.

I have also given in my plant lists the sizes of trees and shrubs that would most quickly give the planting an appearance of maturity. Naturally, the stock sizes listed are large. If you are not anxious, however, for an immediate effect, so called, it will be possible to cut out the cost of plants by reducing sizes. However, I would advise that the trees, at least, be of the size specified, and if any reductions or eliminations are to be made in the plant list that the perennials be the last things set. Then again, it is hardly worth the cutting of a few dollars from the total cost, particularly as plants require time to mature. I should say that the total cost of this work, including labor and materials, should not run over $400.00

The trellises are of the lightest construction possible, yet conform to the lines and style of the house. The gravel walks will prove satisfactory as garden paths. The rock steps will give you variation and the needed soft-

ening incidental touch. You can expend as much effort as you desire in selecting and adjusting these slabs of rock and, by planting of the interstices with rock cress and other rock plants, you will find your labor repaid with the charm of the incident and the enrichment of the garden.

The terraces, if carried out so that their lines are true and parallel with the house, will increase the interest in and support the house properly. You will note that I have set the screen, or rather the trellis, some feet from the property line and have planted in back of it a mass of trees—in fact, apparently overplanted. However, this is not the case, and is done for a purpose,—to force the growth and to give you a solid screen, cutting off the view of your neighbors' barns and giving to the garden some privacy, as well as forming a background for the same. The trees are grouped so as to settle the house into its site and properly support it with masses of green.

The perennial garden is a color scheme in blues and whites in spring, later turning to reds, oranges, and purples in the fall. The flowers are confined to only borders, as you will note, concentrating the color effect. However, I have intersperced [sic] amid the jungle planting asters and other perennials to increase the interest of the mass and act as a ground cover.

The little vegetable garden is somewhat separated from the garden as a whole by the terraces which make it appear as a sunken garden—an adjunct of the garden proper. In this way we utilize the whole space and make the truck garden a part of the decorative scheme, as vegetables are sometimes equal to any of the other herbs in their decorative effectiveness.

In regard to the labor for carrying out this scheme: Would suggest that the most intelligent gardner [sic] that can be found be given the work on day-labor basis, as it is rather difficult to contract such work and get good results. A man should be found capable of doing the work for something like $3.00 a day.

You will note that plant lists have been prepared and bound separately so that you may send them to various nurseries to get bids upon them. Nursery stock can be obtained from a distance, and if you desire I will place your order with several nurseries with whom I am acquainted, and may be able to get your material with a reduction in cost and of a better grade than you might be able to find in your district.

No doubt various questions will come up in carrying out this work. I shall, of course, be only too glad to answer any questions and furnish a solution to any problem that may arise in the carrying out of the plans.

YOURS MOST SINCERELY,
FRANK LLOYD WRIGHT, JR.

STEPHEN M. B. HUNT II, OSHKOSH, WISCONSIN (1917)
Frank Lloyd Wright, Jr., Landscape Architect

Botanical Name	Quantity	Botanical Name	Quantity
Juniperus aurea	5	*Celastrus paniculata*	2
Pinus strobus (dwarf)	2	Grape vines: Concord	4
Pinus sylvestris	1	Niagra	3
Acer saccharum	1	Moore's early	3
Ailanthus clandulosa	14	*Sedium aizon*	10
Tilia americana	5	Peonies: Deep pink	2
Craetaegus crus galli	1	White	2
Mountain ash	3	*Anchusa italica*	10
Cornus alba	20	Aster	20
Berberis vulgaris (atro.)	10	*Aster tartaricus*	10
Robinia	10	*Campanula carpatica*	50
Rhustyphinia	130	*Campanula alba*	50
Rhus glabra	10	*Digitalis purpuria*	100
Samabucus canadensis	30	*Heuchera sanguinea*	100
Symphiocarpis racemoses	50	*Phlox panniculata*	20
Symphiocarpis racemoses vulgaris	50	*Tritoma pfitzeria*	10
Blackberries	20		
Ampelopis quinqufolia	10	***For Pots and Vases***	
Ampelopis veitchi	10	Nasturtiums and aristolochia	
Veitis cordifolia	10		

SOURCE: Found in Archives at Oak Park Home and Studio Research Center by Meg Klinkow (February, 1992).

APPENDIX J

Plantings Identified for Barnsdall Hollyhock House, Olive Hill; Los Angeles CA (1920s)

Frank Lloyd Wright, Jr., Landscape Architect

Botanical Name	Common Name	Notes
Pinus radiata	Monterey Pine	Native. Use largely limited to seaside plantings
Eucalyptus globulus	Blue Gum Eucalyptus	Australia. Too coarse for many landscape plantings. Valued for windbreaks
Acacia decurrens mollis	Black Acacia	Australia. Fine textured tree w/ small yellow flowers
Nerium oleander	Oleander	Mediterranean native withstands hot, dry situations
?	Boxleaf Asaras	
Asplenium bulbiferum	Mother Fern	Australia. Shade/moisture loving. Mostly used inside
Caladium bicolor	Fancyleafed Caladium	Exotic leaves. Native to South America.
Cistus villosus	Sage Rockrose	Mediterranean plant. Drought/fire resistant.
?	Sky Flower	
Fuchsia hybrids	Hybrid Fuchsia	Colorful flowers native to Central and South America
Hedera helix	English Ivy	Clinging evergreen vine. Native to Europe.
Hibiscus rosa-sinensis	Chinese Hibiscus	Large flowers of many colors. Native to China.
Populus nigra	Lombardy Poplar	Native. Short-lived. Fast-growing temporary screen.
? May be Asplenium (aloe)	Australean Fern	
Schinus molle	California Peppertree	Thrives in poor soils. Drops litter on well-kept lawns. Native to Peru.
? (Several hundred species & varieties)	Lily	Native of Europe and Orient
Syringa (more than 500 varieties)	Lilac	Native of Europe and Orient
Vinca minor	Periwinkle (Myrtle)	Evergreen ground cover. Native to Europe, W. Asia
Verbena tenera	Sand Verbenae	Lilac flowers. Native to South America.

SOURCE: Planting Materials identified from Survey of May 10, 1927.

APPENDIX K

Usonians Built with Masonry Retaining Base Terrace (1941–1959)

Carlton David Wall—Plymouth, Michigan (1941)
Lowell Walter—Quasqueton, Iowa (1945)
Arnold Friedman—Pecos, New Mexico (1945)
Douglas Grant—Cedar Rapids, Iowa (1946)
Dr. A. H. Bulbulian—Rochester, Minnesota (1947)
David Weisblat—Galesburg, Michigan (1948)
Samuel Eppslein—Galesburg, Michigan (1948)
Mrs. Clinton Walker—Carmel, California (1948)
Sol Friedman—Pleasantville, New York (1948)
James Edwards—Okemos, Michigan (1949)
Kenneth Laurent—Rockford, Illinois (1949)
Roland Reisley—Pleasantville, New York (1950)
William Pearce—Bradbury, California (1950)
Richard Davis—Marion, Indiana (1950)
Robert Berger—San Anselmo, California (1950)
Russell Kraus—Kirkwood, Missouri (1951)
Gabrielle and Charlcey Austin—Greenville, South Carolina (1951)
R. W. Lindholm—Cloquet, Minnesota (1952)

Luis Marden—McClean, Virginia (1952)
Robert L. Wright—Bethesda, Maryland (1953)
John Dobkins—Canton, Ohio (1953)
Willard Keland—Spring Green, Wisconsin (1953)
Ellis Feiman—Canton, Ohio (1954)
I. N. Hagan—Chalkhill, Pennsylvania (1954)
Harold Price—Paradise Valley, Arizona (1954)
Louis Fredrick—Barrington Hills, Illinois (1954)
Gerald Tonkens—Amberley Village, Ohio (1954)
Robert Sunday—Marshalltown, Iowa (1955)
John L. Rayward—New Canaan, Connecticut (1955)
Frank Iber—Stevens Point, Wisconsin (1957)
Sterling Kinney—Amarillo, Texas (1957)
Joseph Mollica—Bayside, Wisconsin (1958)
Paul Olfelt—St. Louis Park, Minnesota (1958)
George Ablin—Bakersfield, California (1958)
Donald Stromquist—Bountiful, Utah (1958)
Norman Lykes—Phoenix, Arizona (1959)

APPENDIX L

Site Analysis and Site Plan Prepared by C. E. Aguar for the Coauthors' Personal Residence in Athens, Georgia

This *Site Inventory and Analysis* was prepared by the author preparatory to designing his family's personal residence and is presented to illustrate the vast amount of information that is available to a designer who takes the time to study the natural and built environment, in order to obtain a sense-of-place *prior* to designing and siting the structure. This is a normal subdivided lot, ¾ of an acre in size, but with better than normal site conditions—such as a north-sloping riverfront setting with many mature deciduous trees, native vegetation, birds, and other wildlife. The land is situated between river rapids with shoals to the north, other residences to the east and west, and the University of Georgia golf course on the opposite side of the main access road to the south. Viewpoints and vistas were as important as topography in establishing the optimum center point of the house. The arc of the sun and points of sunrise and sunset suggested that the house could be oriented somewhat east of south, with the final determination made by a close inspection and evaluation of size and types of trees that needed to be removed to fit the footprint of the structure to be designed in consort with the site analysis.

The *Site Plan* that evolved orients the south façade 33 degrees east of south. Only a few smaller trees had to be removed. The American Holly trees were transplanted closer to the front of the property. The drawing contains a cross section of the slope, looking southwest toward the house, which was placed on pressure-treated wood piers to retain the maximum natural vegetation and not disturb the root systems for the two native American Beech trees between which the house was sited. This construction methodology also protected the masses of 10-to-12-foot-high native Mountain Laurel that lined the northern slope; no other house in the area was able to preserve this natural attribute. A house section shows the angle of the sun in summer and winter, as well as the fall equinox, to determine the depth of penetration of sun rays through the solarium-kitchen after deciduous trees have shed their leaves.

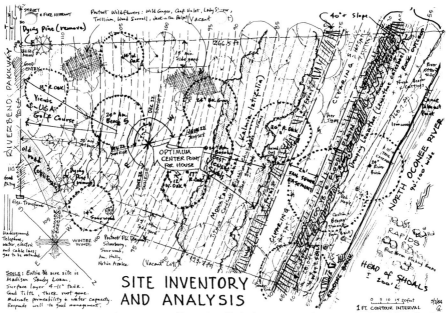

SITE INVENTORY AND ANALYSIS

The Riverscape at Kalmia Shoals... a section of the North Oconee River Greenway System. Athens, Georgia.

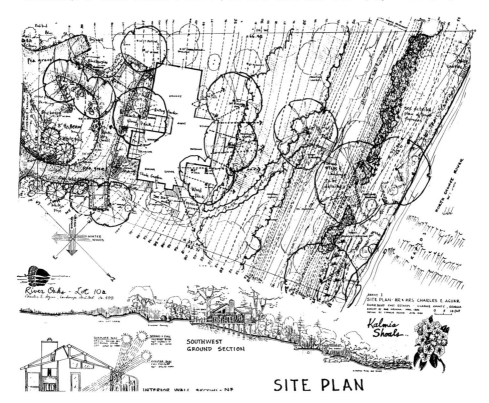

SITE PLAN

APPENDIX M

Landscape Do's and Don'ts for Owners of Frank Lloyd Wright–Designed Homes

Do — keep in mind that your home is unlike any other in your neighborhood—perhaps in the world, for that matter.

Don't — try to make your yard and garden look like others or try to landscape "the way the neighbors expect."

Do — build your landscape design on shapes, textures and forms.

Don't — plant shrubbery mainly for colors or for the short-term flowering effect.

Do — realize that most of the early Wasmuth drawings and Marion Mahony's Japanese-like prints—beautiful as may be—are artistic and stylistic creations and often were entirely out-of-scale with reality.

Don't — depend on these beautiful prints for developing your landscape, despite what you may have read. Japanese magnolias will not survive in the shorelines of Lake Michigan.

Do — plant trailing vines or cascading plantings in the urns and planters to present the form and texture Wright intended.

Don't — plant upright plant forms or only geraniums in urns and planters, since they do not present the form and texture Wright intended.

Do — expose the foundation of the home to emphasize where it meets the ground, even if you don't live in a prairie house with a "water table."

Don't — install foundation planting to make the house appear to "float in space," a Victorian age practice held in disdain by Mr. Wright.

Do — maximize the use of native or indigenous vegetation as such trees and shrubs will require less care, less watering, and will always appropriately complement the organic architecture designed by Wright.

Don't — plant evergreen foundation plants or fussy exotics such as Japanese maples, variegated varieties, and showy flowering shrubs except in an intimate space and on the nonpublic side of your house.

Do — use perennials for color and cutting as floral arrangement, as shown in historic drawings or photographs of Wright-designed residences.

Don't — plant flowers as edging or in the usual sense of garden displays of public gardens and parks.

Do — plant in ways that will follow and complement, rather than compete with, the architectural form of your Wright-designed residence.

Don't — expect all landscape architects or other garden designers to have the interest and skills required to create a complementary planting plan for a Wright-designed residence.

Do — expect that design and restoration costs may be higher for sites of Wright-designed homes, due to the current shortage of skilled designers trained to interpret Wright's organic architecture

Don't — count on saving money with a landscape designer who is learning at your expense, any more than you would with someone inadequately trained to repair art glass, restore furniture, or fix a leaky roof.

Do	give as much attention and responsibility to the setting and maintenance of exterior spaces of your distinctive home as you do the furnishings and upkeep of the interior.	Don't	bother to try to save overgrown evergreens and other plants that have grown out-of bounds, or been sheared into unnatural shapes for 40 or 50 years.
Do	learn the basics of retaining the natural form of plants. Invest in the purchase of a copy of *Guide to Proper Pruning,* an inexpensive book that can be found in any garden shop or bookstore.	Don't	invest in expensive plant materials unless you install an irrigation system or love gardening - and have the time required to really work at it.
Do	remember the cardinal rule of landscape design and maintenance to preserve an organic landscape: THOU SHALT NOT SHEAR THY SHRUBS!	Don't	employ a yard maintenance person who only knows how to shear plantings. Insist that whomever you hire knows how to prune naturally and not form your shrubs into domes or other unnatural forms.

PERMISSIONS AND COPYRIGHTS

FRANK LLOYD WRIGHT ARCHIVAL NUMBERS

The following table provides Frank Lloyd Wright archive numbers for drawings and photographs appearing in indicated figures in this book. Drawings are copyright © 2002 The Frank Lloyd Wright Foundation in Scottsdale, AZ, and photographs* are courtesy The Frank Lloyd Wright Archives, Scottsdale, AZ.

Fig. #	FLW ID	Fig. #	FLW ID	Fig. #	FLW ID
1-2	9003.01	3-57	0604.0193	5-3	1705.055
2-14a	9503.002	3-59	0402.005	5-4	1705.052
2-16*	9503.002	3-60	0607.004	5-6	2104.005
2-21	0527.001	3-66a	0803.02	5-8	2009.001
2-24	9510.017	3-66b	0803.021	5-11	2009.001
3-2	0004.003	3-66c	0803.018	5-12	2009.015
	0002.002	3-68	0803.105	5-13a	2302.020
3-3	007.009	3-73,a-b	0712.038	5-13b	2302.021
3-4	007.009	3-73c	0712.039	5-13c	2302.022
3-5	0014.008	3-78	0901.002	5-14	2302.0006
3-6	0019.008	3-82	0918.019	5-16	2304.021
3-7a	008.002	3-84	0918.018	5-17	2402.001
3-7b	008.003	4-1	1127.003	5-19	2401.09
3-8	0309.001	4-4	1118.001	5-20b*	2401.004
3-9a	0309.006	4-7	1118.014	5-21	2402.003
3-9b	0309.003	4-11b	2501.134	6-1b	1403.023
3-11a	0019.005	4-12b	1403.0003	6-4	2701.001
3-11,b-c	0019.004	4-14b	1103.020	6-5	2704.103
3-13	0106.16	4-15a	1104.001	6-6	2702.004
3-14	0106.16	4-15b	1104.003	6-7*	2701.037
3-19	0208.018	4-16	1403.013	6-8a,b	2902.002
3-20	0009.18	4-18a*	1403.044	6-12	2902.004
	0009.19	4-18b*	1104.0003	6-13*	2901.0021
3-25	921.001	4-19*	1104.0011	7-1	3401.007
3-27	921.001	4-20*	1104.0010	7-3,a-b	3401.024
3-32	0401.012	4-22a	1508.02	7-4a	3402.001
3-34, a-b	401.0053	4-26	1401.102	7-5	3407.013
3-43	0405.028	4-27	1401.103	7-8	3702.005
3-46a	0405.011	4-29	1401.179	7-9	3702.01
3-47	0411.0063	4-32	1701.014	7-11	3701.005
3-48	0411.007	4-34	1701.016	7-12	3701.012
3-51	0506.021	5-1	1705.061	7-16	3703.033
3-55	0711.012	5-2	1705.052	7-17	3703.014

Fig. #	FLW ID	Fig. #	FLW ID	Fig. #	FLW ID
7-18a	3703.002	8-12	4505.009	8-33	5122.001
7-19*	3803.0671	8-13	4505.007	8-36	5115.002
7-20	3803.168	8-14a	1403.044	8-39	4812.017
8-1	3906.001	8-16a	4012.005	8-40	4812.017
8-2	3903.003	8-16b	4012.024	8-45	4914.018
8-3	3912.002	8-19	4008.019	8-49	5021.001
8-5	4201.004	8-20	4008.009		5021.007
8-6	4201.026	8-21	4015.056	8-51a,b	5021.001
8-7	4828.001	8-24	3405.024	8-53	5214.001
8-9,a-b	4720.002	8-25	3905.029	8-59	5512.012
8-10	3806.001	8-28	3901.002		
8-11	4510.001	8-30,a-b	4012.09		

SELECTED BIBLIOGRAPHY

Birrell, James. *Walter Burley Griffin* (University of Queensland Press, Saint Lucia, Australia, 1964).

Brooks, H. Allen. *The Prairie School: Frank Lloyd Wright and His Midwest Contemporaries* (W.W. Norton & Co., New York, 1972).

Christy, Stephen. *American Landscape Architecture: Designers and Places* (The Preservation Press, 1989).

Creese, Walter L. *The Crowning of the American Landscape: Eight Great Spaces and Their Buildings* (Princeton University Press, Princeton, New Jersey, 1985).

Eaton, Leonard K. *Landscape Artist in America: The Life and Work of Jens Jensen* (University of Chicago Press, 1964).

Engel, David H. *Japanese Gardens for Today* (Charles E. Tuttle Co., 1959).

Engel, Heinrich. *The Japanese House: A Tradition for Contemporary Architecture* (C. E. Tuttle Co., 1964).

Gebhard, David and Harriette Van Breton. *Lloyd Wright, Architect* (University of California-Los Angeles, 1971).

Goodman, William L. *Principles and Practice of Urban Planning* (The Municipal Management Series, 1968).

Grese, Robert E. *Jens Jensen: Maker of Natural Parks and Gardens* (Johns Hopkins University Press, Baltimore, 1992).

Hallmark, Donald P. "Frank Lloyd Wright's Dana-Thomas House: Its History, Acquisition, and Preservation," *Illinois Historical Journal* (Vol. 82, No. 2, Summer 1989).

Hancock, John L. "Planners in the Changing American City, 1900–1940," *AIP Journal* (1967).

Hanna, Paul R. and Jean S. *Frank Lloyd Wright's Hanna House: The Clients' Report* (Southern Illinois University Press, 1981).

Havighurst, Walter. "Land Sales in Chicago, 1856," *Land of the Long Horizons* (Coward-McCann, Inc., New York, 1960).

Heinrich, Engel. *The Japanese House: A Tradition for Contemporary Architecture* (Charles E. Tuttle Co., 1964).

Hines, Thomas S., Jr. "Frank Lloyd Wright—The Madison Years," *The Wisconsin Magazine of History* (No. 50, Winter 1967).

Hoffman, Donald. *Frank Lloyd Wright's Robie House* (Dover Publications, New York, 1984).

Howland, Joseph E. *The House Beautiful Book of Gardens and Outdoor Living* (Doubleday & Company, Inc., 1958).

Itoh, Teiji. *The Japanese Garden: An Approach to Nature* (Yale University Press, New Haven/London, 1972).

———. *Space and Illusion in the Japanese Garden* (Weatherhill/Tankosha, New York, Tokyo, & Kyoto, 1973).

———. *The Elegant Japanese House: Traditional Sukiya Architecture* (Walker/Weatherhill, New York-Tokyo).

Jacobs, Herbert and Katherine. *Building with Frank Lloyd Wright* (Chronicle Books, San Francisco, 1978).

Johnson, Donald Leslie. *The Architecture of Walter Burley Griffin* (The MacMillan Company of Australia Pty. Ltd., 1977).

———. "Notes on Frank Lloyd Wright's Paternal Family," *Frank Lloyd Wright Newsletter* (2nd Quarter, 1980).

Kaufmann, Edward J., Jr. *Fallingwater: A Frank Lloyd Wright Country House* (Abbeville Press, New York, 1986).

Kruty, Paul. *Walter Burley Griffin in America* (University of Illinois Press, 1996).

———. *Frank Lloyd Wright and Midway Gardens* (University of Illinois Press, 1998).

Kuck, Lorraine E. *The Art of Japanese Gardens* (The John Day Co., New York, 1940).

Lancaster, Clay. *The Japanese Influence in America* (Walton H. Rawls, New York, 1963).

Lesniak, Jack. *Arthur Heurtley House: Frank Lloyd Wright* (Oak Park, Illinois, 1902; Wright Plus, 1998).

———. *Hills-DeCaro House: Frank Lloyd Wright.* (Oak Park, Illinois, 1906; Wright Plus, 1999).

Lind, Carla. "Moore House I and Pergola," *Lost Wright: Frank Lloyd Wright's Vanished Masterpieces* (Simon & Schuster, 1996).

Manson, Grant Carpenter. *Frank Lloyd Wright to 1910: The First Golden Age* (Reinhold, New York, 1958).

———. Archival notes of record at Oak Park Public Library; Oak Park, Illinois.

Meehan, Patrick J. *Frank Lloyd Wright Remembered* (The Preservation Press, National Trust for Historic Preservation, 1991).

Miller, Donald L. *City of the Century.* (Simon & Schuster, New York, 1996).

Miller, Wilhelm. "The Prairie Spirit in Landscape Gardening," *Circular 184* (Illinois Agricultural Experiment Station, 1915).

———. "The Prairie Style of Landscape Architecture" *Architectural Record* (December, 1916).

Moran, Maya. *Down to Earth: An Insider's View of Frank Lloyd Wright's Tomek House* (Southern Illinois University Press, 1995).

Morse, Edward S. *Japanese Homes and Their Surroundings.* (Charles E. Tuttle, 1972 reprint of 1904, 1886, 1885 versions)

Muller, Peter O. *Contemporary Suburban America.* (Prentice-Hall, Inc., Englewood Cliffs, New Jersey, 1981).

Newton, Norman T. *Design on the Land: The Development of Landscape Architecture* (Belknap Press of Harvard University Press, Cambridge, Massachusetts, 1971).

Nute, Kevin. *Frank Lloyd Wright and Japan* (Van Nostrand Reinhold, New York, 1993).

Patterson, Terry L. *Frank Lloyd Wright and the Meaning of Materials* (Van Nostrand Reinhold, 1994).

Pfeiffer, Bruce Brooks. *Letters to Architects: Frank Lloyd Wright* (California State University Press, Fresno, 1984).

———. *Letters to Clients: Frank Lloyd Wright* (California State University Press, Fresno, 1986).

———. "Japanese Influences and Froebelian Training," *Frank Lloyd Wright: His Living Voice* (Frank Lloyd Wright Foundation. The Press at California State University, Fresno, 1987).

———. *Frank Lloyd Wright: His Living Voice.* (The Press at California State University/FLIW Foundation, 1987).

———. *Frank Lloyd Wright: In the Realm of Ideas.* Gerald Nordland, co-editor (Southern Illinois University Press, 1988).

———. "The Japanese Print: An Interpretation" as reprinted in *Frank Lloyd Wright Collected Writings, 1894–1930* (Rizzoli in New York/The Frank Lloyd Wright Foundation, Vol. 1, 1992).

———. *Frank Lloyd Wright Collected Writings* (1894–1930). (Rizzoli/New York/FLIW Foundation. Vol. 1. 1992)

Pregliasco, Janice. "The Life and Work of Marion Mahony Griffin," *The Prairie School: Design Vision for the Midwest* (The Art Institute of Chicago Museum Studies, Vol. 21, No. 2, 1995).

Scott, Frank J. *The Art of Beautifying Suburban Home Grounds of Small Extent.* (John B. Aolden, Publisher, 1886).

Scully, Vincent J. *Frank Lloyd Wright* (Georgia Brazilter, Inc., New York, 1960).

Secrest, Meryle. *Frank Lloyd Wright: A Biography* (Alfred A. Knopf, Inc., New York, 1992).

Siek, Stephen. "Frank Lloyd Wright's Westcott House in Springfield," *Ohio History* (Vol. 87, No. 3. 1978).

Smith, Kathryn. *Frank Lloyd Wright, Hollyhock House and Olive Hill* (Rizzoli, New York, 1992).

Spirn, Anne Whiston. "Frank Lloyd Wright: Architect of Landscape," *Frank Lloyd Wright: Designs for an American Landscape, 1922–1932* (Canadian Centre for Architecture, Montreal. Henry N. Adams, Inc., New York, 1996).

Sutami, Horiguchi. *Tradition of Japanese Gardens* (Second ed., East West Center Press, Tokyo, 1963).

Talbot, Wegg. "FLIW Versus the USA," *AIA Journal* (February, 1970).

Tofel, Edgar. *Apprentice to Genius: Years with Frank Lloyd Wright* (McGraw Hill, New York, 1979).

Van Zanten. *The Nature of Frank Lloyd Wright.* (The University of Chicago Press, 1988).

Vernon, Christopher. "The Evolution of the Bradley Landscape," *Glen Historic Landscape Report* (1990).

———. "Walter Burley Griffin, Landscape Architect," *Midwest in American Architecture.* (University of Illinois Press, 1991).

Wilson, William H. *Introduction to Planning History in the United States.* (Center for Urban Policy Research, Rutgers University, New Brunswick, New Jersey, 1983).

Wright, Frank Lloyd. "In The Cause of Architecture," *The Architectural Record,* (March 1908).

———. *Ausgeführte Bauten und entwü Von Frank Lloyd Wright* (Ernst Wasmuth, Berlin, 1910).

———. and Braswell. *Architecture and Modern Life* (Harper & Brothers, New York, 1937)

———. *The Natural House* (1954).

———. *An Autobiography* (Horizon Press, New York. 3rd Edition. 1977)

Wright, Gwendolyn. "Architectural Practice and Social Vision in Wright's Early Designs," *The Nature of Frank Lloyd Wright* (The University of Chicago Press, Chicago and London, 1988).

Yeomans, Alfred B. *City Residential Land Development: Studies in Planning* (University of Chicago Press, Chicago, 1916).

INDEX

ABOUT THE AUTHORS

The coauthors of *Wrightscapes* came to this project uniquely prepared for the task at hand. One possessed the well-founded savvy of an experienced landscape architect and city planner who had collaborated with architects over a long period of time; the other has extensive writing expertise. They also shared more than a half-century of avocational interest in the subject matter and spent the better part of the last decade conducting travel-field investigations and supportive research, evaluating and interpreting findings, and developing the *Wrightscapes* manuscript.

Charles E. Aguar (deceased) distinguished himself in three areas of his professional life, as an educator, a landscape architect, and a city planner. He was Professor Emeritus of Landscape Architecture at the University of Georgia, a charter member of the American Institute of Certified Planners, and a member of the Society for American City and Regional Planning History. He was very active in historical and cultural initiatives across the country, earning awards and grants from the American Planning Association, the National Endowment for the Arts, and many other organizations.

Berdeana Aguar collaborated with her husband on the writing of many of his works during the five decades of their marriage and began working full-time on *Wrightscapes* in 1994. She is a scriptwriter for commercial videos and documentary films, with clients that include The Nature Conservancy, the University of Georgia School of Environmental Design, Mitsubishi, the American Arbitration Association, WSB-TV, and PBS.